Oven heat	Minutes per pound	Temperature on roast thermometer
Ham (precooked)	To heat and glaze, bake about 30 minutes.	400°		
Chicken (stuffed)	Without stuffing, reduce time 5 minutes per pound.	325°	30-35	180°
Duck and Goose (domestic)		325°	25-30	175°
Turkey	Under 8 pounds, 3-4 hours; 8-12 pounds, 4-5 hours; 12-16 pounds, 5-6 hours; over 16 pounds, up to 7 hours.	325°		180°

Substitutions

Arrowroot. 1 tablespoon = 2 tablespoons flour (as thickening).

Baking powder (tartrate or phosphate). 1 teaspoon = ⅔ teaspoon double-action type or ¼ teaspoon baking soda plus ½ teaspoon cream of tartar.

Chocolate. 1 ounce (1 square) = 3 tablespoons cocoa plus 1 teaspoon to 1 tablespoon shortening (less for Dutch cocoa).

Cornstarch. 1 tablespoon = 2 tablespoons flour (as thickening).

Flour
> **Pastry flour.** 1 cup = 1 cup all-purpose or bread flour less 2 tablespoons.
> **Potato flour.** 1 tablespoon = 2 tablespoons flour (as thickening).

Milk
> **Fresh, whole.** 1 cup = ½ cup evaporated milk plus ½ cup water or ½ cup condensed milk plus ½ cup water (reduce the sugar in the recipe) or ¼ cup powdered whole milk plus 1 cup water or ¼ cup powdered skim milk plus 2 tablespoons butter and 1 cup water.
> **Fresh, skim.** 1 cup = ¼ cup powdered skim milk plus 1 cup water.
> **Sour.** 1 cup = 1 cup lukewarm fresh milk (less 1 tablespoon) plus 1 tablespoon vinegar. Let stand 5 minutes.

THE
Fannie Farmer
COOKBOOK

THE
Fannie Farmer
COOKBOOK

Revised by

WILMA LORD PERKINS

Drawings by Alison Mason Kingsbury

Eleventh Edition

Little, Brown and Company · Boston · Toronto

LIBRARY OF CONGRESS CATALOG CARD NO. 65-25022

*Published simultaneously in Canada by Little, Brown
& Company (Canada) Limited*

PRINTED IN THE UNITED STATES OF AMERICA

Preface

What can one say in presenting a new edition of Fannie Farmer that has not been said over and over again? Chiefly that in making any changes Aunt Fannie's own words have been the inspiration. "Could it be better?" was a regular phrase of hers, a phrase which sometimes caused at least temporary dismay to her devoted teachers and helpers but to which they always responded with skill and pride. So it has been with this revision. I have tried to make the presentation of each recipe as clear and helpful as possible and to take account of the many new products and techniques which make the cook's task easier. But chiefly my aim is to maintain the high standards which have characterized the book since its first edition in 1896.

New recipes have been added with caution, since many are passing fads and my purpose is to keep the cookbook the clear and dependable basic it has always been. With such a book at hand it is easy to branch out and try some of the many exotic recipes which appear from time to time.

May I express once more my deep gratitude to the many friends who have helped me create this revision? Some have sent in valuable suggestions, others have worked steadily with me, and the aid of both groups has been beyond calculation. Most of all, I would like to thank my daughter-in-law, Nancy Tucker Perkins, Mrs. S. Stanley Kent, Mrs. Mary Rackliffe, and also Alison Mason Kingsbury, whose excellent illustrations have added so much to the book.

To all friends of Fannie Farmer, old and new, my warmest greetings.

WILMA LORD PERKINS

Harvard, Massachusetts

Preface to the First Edition

"But for life the universe were nothing; and all that has life requires nourishment."

With the progress of knowledge the needs of the human body have not been forgotten. During the last decade much time has been given by scientists to the study of foods and their dietetic value, and it is a subject which rightfully should demand much consideration from all. I certainly feel that the time is not far distant when a knowledge of the principles of diet will be an essential part of one's education. Then mankind will eat to live, will be able to do better mental and physical work, and disease will be less frequent.

At the earnest solicitation of educators, pupils, and friends, I have been urged to prepare this book, and I trust it may be a help to many who need its aid. It is my wish that it may not only be looked upon as a compilation of tried and tested recipes, but that it may awaken an interest through its condensed scientific knowledge which will lead to deeper thought and broader study of what to eat.

F. M. F.

Contents

THE
Fannie Farmer
COOKBOOK

A Few Helpful Objects

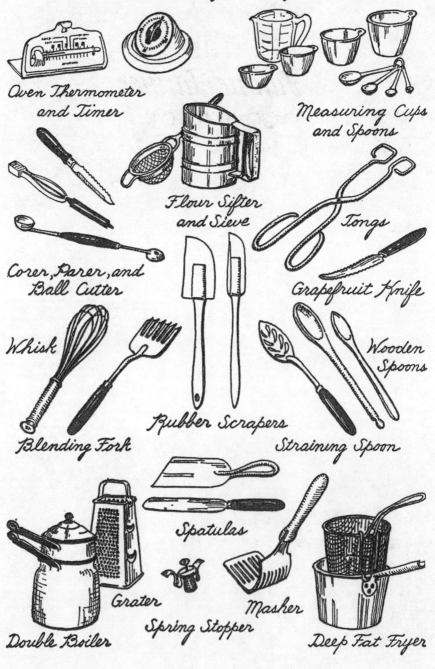

Oven Thermometer and Timer

Measuring Cups and Spoons

Flour Sifter and Sieve

Tongs

Corer, Parer, and Ball Cutter

Grapefruit Knife

Whisk

Wooden Spoons

Rubber Scrapers

Blending Fork

Straining Spoon

Spatulas

Double Boiler

Grater

Spring Stopper

Masher

Deep Fat Fryer

Success with Recipes

Good cooking is an art which is easily acquired. There are only **a** few basic processes, and once they are mastered, even elaborate dishes seem simple to produce. A recipe is not as precise as a chemical formula, since ingredients vary slightly, as do cooking utensils and stoves. But a little difference is sometimes refreshing, and so it will not matter if there is a slight change in the finished product. For example, a sauce or a pudding may be thicker or thinner without being a failure. Don't apologize! Just present it differently — the softer pudding in dessert glasses instead of on a serving dish as you had planned.

Read a recipe all the way through before you start. Check on the necessary ingredients and equipment. If any of the directions are not clear to you, read the general information at the beginning of the section or the basic material in this chapter.

Measuring

Level measurements are the rule in modern recipes. Use standard measuring cups and spoons. To save washing an extra cup, measure dry ingredients first, put them on wax paper, then use the same cup for liquids or fats.

Dry ingredients. Fill the cup or spoon and level the top with a straight-edged knife. Do not shake or pack down (except brown sugar). If sugar, baking soda, baking powder or dry mustard are lumpy, stir or sift them before measuring.

Cooking oils, syrups, honey or molasses. Scrape out the measure with a rubber spatula to get the full amount.

Solid fats. Have them at room temperature, not icy hard. Pack firmly into the measure and level off with a knife. Measuring cups with sloping sides are easy to scrape out. Butter and margarine in ¼-pound sticks are a convenience. One stick equals ½ cup (8 tablespoons).

Mixing

The recipe will suggest the method to be used to blend the ingredients.

To stir. Hold the spoon upright and move it in wider and wider circles until all is blended.

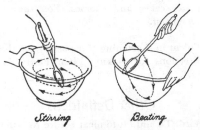

Stirring   *Beating*

To beat. The purpose of beating is to make a mixture light by enclosing air. Briskly turn the ingredients over and over, using a large mixing spoon or a wire whisk. Once the mixture is light, be careful not to overbeat, especially with an electric mixer. Otherwise the air bubbles break down and the mixture does not rise as it should.

3

To cut and fold. When a mixture has been beaten until light, other ingredients must be added very gently so that the air will not be lost. Add new ingredients little by little and blend in by two motions with a mixing spoon — cut down with the edge of the mixing spoon, then move the bowl of the spoon along the bottom and up to the surface again in order to turn the mixture very gently. Continue only until the ingredients are evenly blended.

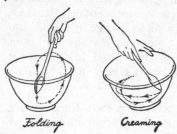

Folding　　　*Creaming*

To cream. Put the butter or other shortening in a bowl and let stand at room temperature until soft but not melted. Beat with an electric beater or rub against the side of the bowl with the back of a wooden spoon or a blending fork until smooth and fluffy. Gradually beat or rub in sugar or flour according to the recipe. The more thorough the creaming, the finer will be the grain of butter cakes and cookies. *You cannot overcream.*

To cut in shortening (for pastry), see the directions for making Plain Pastry (p. 407).

Other Definitions

Bard. To add fat to meat before roasting to keep it from drying out. Lay strips of fat salt pork, bacon or other fat on top of the meat. See also Lard (below).

Baste. Moisten by spooning a liquid over a roast or other food as it cooks.

Blanch. Dip in and out of boiling water to loosen the skins of fruit or nuts or to prepare food for freezing.

Dredge. Coat with flour or sugar.

Dust. Sprinkle lightly with flour or sugar.

Glaze. Cover with a thin coating of jelly, meat juices or caramel.

Lard. Have the butcher thread strips of fat salt pork through very lean meat. See also Bard (above).

Marinate. Cover with a liquid (usually wine or a highly seasoned sauce) and let stand to season or become tender. See Marinades (pp. 99–100).

Parboil. Partially cook (usually in boiling water) in preparation for further cooking.

Reduce. Cook a liquid until some has been carried off as steam.

Scallop. Bake in a sauce with crumbs on top. Often with grated cheese as well.

Score. Make a series of shallow cuts on the surface of a food.

Sear. Cook at high temperature over direct heat or in the oven until the surface is browned.

Cooking Methods

The various methods of cooking sound more complicated than they really are. All are variations of two basic methods — cooking by dry heat and cooking by moist heat.

Baking and Roasting

Preheat the oven unless your oven heats so rapidly that preheating is not necessary. Do not crowd the oven — free circulation of air is essential for even baking. Directions for roasting meats are on p. 152, for baking bread p. 323, for baking cookies p. 433, and for baking cakes p. 459. Have the oven control checked occasionally by the utility company.

250°	Very slow
300°	Slow
325°	Moderately slow
350°	Moderate
375°	Moderately hot
400°	Hot
450–500°	Very hot

Braising

Cook, tightly covered, in a small quantity of liquid at a low temperature, either in the oven or over direct heat. Braising is an excellent method for cooking less tender cuts of meat.

Broiling (Grilling)

Preheat the broiler or prepare the charcoal fire. Grease the broiling rack and arrange the food on it. Unless the recipe suggests a special method, cook the food briefly on one side, turn and cook about half the total time required, then turn again to complete the cooking. Thin pieces of fish need not be turned at all; cook until they flake when tested with a fork.

Barbecuing

Broil, basting every few minutes with a savory sauce (p. 100). Usually, extra sauce is served with the food. See also p. 153.

Pan-Broiling

Cook in a shallow, heavy pan over direct heat. Unless the food to be cooked is very lean, such as minute steaks and liver, you will not need to grease the pan — a sprinkling of salt in the pan is enough to keep the food from sticking. Otherwise, grease the pan very lightly.

Pan-Frying (Sautéing)

Heat cooking oil or fat in a frying pan large enough to hold the food in a single layer. If necessary, use two pans. The amount of fat varies from a thin coating to approximately 1 inch of fat for such foods as Southern Fried Chicken, but is never deep enough to cover the food completely. When the fat is hot but not smoking, put in the food and cook until it is nicely browned and tender. Adjust the heat as necessary to cook without burning.

French (Deep-Fat) Frying

This quick method of cooking is excellent and, contrary to old-fashioned ideas, is as healthful as any other, if the fat is kept at the proper temperature. An electric frying kettle with controlled heat is the best equipment, but any straight-sided heavy pan at least 5 inches deep will do. Unless you are using an electric fryer, put a frying thermometer in the kettle so that you will be certain to have the correct temperature.

Croquette Sauce. Make Cream Sauce (p. 90) but increase the butter and flour to 4 tablespoons each. This very thick sauce is combined with cooked chicken, meat or fish to make croquettes. See Chicken Croquettes (p. 227), Meat Croquettes (p. 202) and Lobster Croquettes (p. 144) for directions, then vary to suit yourself.

To egg and crumb. Beat an egg just enough to blend evenly. Add 2 tablespoons water or oil (for attractive browning). Put bread or cracker crumbs (p. 7) on a piece of wax paper. Coat the prepared food thoroughly with crumbs, then dip in the egg mixture, carefully covering the entire surface. Roll in crumbs once more. Set on a piece of wax paper. If convenient, prepare ½ hour before frying and chill so that the coating will be less likely to slip off during frying.

To dip in fritter batter, see directions for Fruit Fritters (p. 429).

Fats for frying. Vegetable oils or fats do not smoke and break down as easily as lard and may be stored for reuse without spoiling. If you have used fat for fritters or potatoes, pour it back into its container through a strainer lined with a double thickness of cheesecloth. Discard the scraps. If you have cooked onions, fish or other foods with a strong flavor, cut a potato in ¼-inch slices, add to the fat, and set over low heat until the fat stops bubbling and the potato slices are brown, then strain as above. Store in a cold place.

To heat fat. Put enough oil or fat in the kettle to cover the food to be cooked, but keep it at least 3 inches below the top of the kettle. Put the thermometer in place if you are not using an automatic fryer with controlled heat. Heat to the required temperature and regulate the heat to keep the temperature even during frying. Do not overheat the fat or the food will brown on the outside — or even burn — before it is cooked in the center. Instructions as to temperature are given in individual recipes. As a general guide, use the following:

370°: Doughnuts, fritters, fish fillets, breaded chops, oysters and other uncooked foods.

380°: Potatoes, onion rings and other watery foods.

390°: Croquettes and other precooked foods.

To fry. If you are using a frying basket, dip it in and out of the fat before you put the food into it so that the food will not stick.

Fry only a small quantity at a time; otherwise the fat will become too cool to cook the surface quickly and the fat will soak into the food. Cook the length of time required by the recipe.

To drain. Lift the cooked food from the fat and put on crumpled paper towels to absorb any excess fat. Keep warm until all the food is fried.

Poaching

Cook in liquid kept just below the boiling point. Except for poached eggs, the liquid is not deep enough to cover the food completely and is often used to make a sauce.

Steaming

Cook on a rack over boiling water or in a double boiler over boiling water. Do not have the water deep enough to touch the bottom of the upper pan. Consult the index for steamed puddings and fruit cakes.

Stewing

Cook in a liquid deep enough to cover. Use the liquid to make sauce or gravy. See the various recipes for stews, fricassees and ragouts.

Pressure-Cooking

Cook in steam under pressure in a special pan. Follow the instructions which come with the pan. Excellent for dishes which would otherwise require long cooking and for vegetables, which can be cooked this way in very little water so that soluble vitamins are not lost.

Preparing Ingredients

Many basic ingredients are prepared the same way for use in different recipes. Instead of repeating the directions with each recipe, reference is made to the information which follows.

Crumbs

Packaged crumbs are a convenience—plain or seasoned, ready to use in stuffing or meat loaf.

Dry bread crumbs. Use bread which is several days old. Dry it thoroughly in a very slow oven (250°) until it is crisp but not brown. Put through a food chopper or a blender or put in a paper bag and crush with a rolling pin. Sift. Store in a closed jar, ready to use for topping scalloped dishes, for coating croquettes, or as required in other recipes.

Soft bread crumbs. Crumble the soft part (no crusts) of day-old bread with your fingers until it is in even bits. Soft crumbs are used for stuffings, fondues and puddings.

Cracker crumbs, potato chips, corn flakes. Roll like dry bread crumbs. Potato chips, corn flakes and wheat germ make delicious topping, buttered or not.

Buttered crumbs. Melt 1 tablespoon butter for each ½ cup crumbs. Add the crumbs and stir lightly with a fork until the crumbs are well coated.

Eggs

Strictly fresh eggs are best for poaching, boiling, frying, and for dishes in which whites and yolks are separated. Dried eggs are seldom an economy but may be a convenience for camping trips. For the equivalent of 1 fresh egg, mix 2 tablespoons egg powder with 2½ tablespoons water.

To test eggs for freshness. Place in deep cold water. A fresh egg sinks to the bottom.

To store eggs. Place in the refrigerator.

To measure eggs. Recipes in this book are based on 2-ounce eggs, usually described as "large." In many recipes it is unimportant if a little more or a little less egg is used. For example, if you wish to make half a cake recipe that calls for 3 eggs, use 2 eggs with no fear of trouble.

$$4 \text{ to } 6 \text{ egg whites} = \frac{1}{2} \text{ cup}$$
$$6 \text{ or } 7 \text{ egg yolks} = \frac{1}{2} \text{ cup}$$
$$1 \text{ egg white} = 1\frac{1}{2} \text{ tablespoons}$$
$$1 \text{ egg yolk} = 1 \text{ tablespoon}$$
$$1 \text{ egg} = 2\frac{1}{2} \text{ tablespoons}$$

To separate eggs. Eggs separate most easily if they are very cold. Tap the center of the egg against the sharp edge of a bowl or pan to crack it slightly. Hold it over a bowl and lift off the top half, letting some of the egg white flow into the bowl but keeping the yolk in the shell. Pour from one half of the shell to the other until all the egg white has flowed out and only the egg yolk remains in the shell.

To beat egg whites. Use a wire whisk, a rotary beater or an electric beater. Use a deep bowl (not plastic) with a rounded bottom and sides that flare only slightly. Have it large enough for the increased volume after beating.

Separate the whites from the yolks. If even a tiny particle of yolk drops into the bowl with the whites, remove it carefully with a piece of eggshell. Otherwise the whites will not beat well. Add a few grains of salt. If the eggs are very cold, let the whites stand for a few minutes before beating.

Beat until "stiff but not dry" if the egg whites are to be used to make a mixture light and fluffy. If the whites are over-beaten, some of the elasticity of the albumen is broken down. When at the

proper stage, egg whites stand in soft peaks when you lift out the beater, but the tops droop over a bit and the surface still looks somewhat moist.

Beat until "stiff and dry" for meringues and meringue-type cookies. When you lift out the beater, the peaks stand up straight and the surface looks dry.

To beat egg yolks. Beat with a rotary beater until the yolks are thick and lemon-colored.

To add beaten whites to a mixture. If there is sugar in the recipe, beat some of it (1 tablespoon for each egg white) into the beaten whites. This keeps the egg whites fluffy until you are ready to add them. Cut and fold (p. 4) only long enough to blend. Do not beat the mixture after folding in the whites.

To add yolks to a hot mixture. Beat the yolks and add a little of the hot mixture, stirring thoroughly, then add this to the rest of the hot mixture and continue stirring until it thickens. Be careful not to overcook.

Leftover egg whites. Use in:

  Angel Food Cake (p. 475) or other
    white cakes (pp. 463, 464)
  Chocolate Meringue Cookies (p. 450)
  Divinity Fudge (p. 499)
  Frostings (p. 492)
  Meringues (p. 449)

Leftover egg yolks. Use in:

  Butterscotch Parfait (p. 393)
  Cream soups (stir in just before serv-
    ing)
  Custards (pp. 362–364)
  French Vanilla Ice Cream (p. 385)
  Gold Cake (p. 462) and Golden
    Layer Cake (p. 463)
  Mayonnaise (p. 289)
  Orange Cookies (p. 435)
  Orange Portsmouth (p. 492) and But-
    ter Frostings (p. 493)
  Sauces (pp. 89–99 and pp. 398–405)
  Scrambled Eggs (p. 104)
  Soup garnishes such as Egg Balls (p.
    59) or Royal Custard (p. 58)

Fats and Shortenings

Vegetable and animal fats add both food value and flavor to many dishes. As "shortening," fat is used to make a flour mixture tender and flaky ("short") by separating the flour into thin layers between layers of fat.

Butter

Butter has a special place in fine cooking. The best cooks prefer not to economize on butter in recipes where its incomparable flavor is important, such as hard sauce, butter cakes and butter cookies.

To cream butter. See p. 4.

To wash butter. For special recipes such as Puff Paste (p. 409), washing butter is recommended by perfectionists because it makes the butter more pliable. Put the butter in a large bowl of ice water and squeeze it gently between your fingers until it feels smooth and waxy. Shape it in a flat cake and pat it briskly to remove all extra water.

To clarify butter. Melt butter in a small pan over low heat. When it is melted, carefully pour off the clear butter; then discard any sediment or milk in the pan.

Butter pats. Cut neat squares from a bar of butter. To add a bit of decoration, dip a fork in hot water and draw it diagonally across each square. Or put a tiny sprig of parsley on each square.

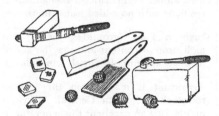

Butter balls. Scald and chill a pair of wooden butter paddles. Measure the butter by teaspoonfuls to have the balls the same size. Roll lightly between the paddles to shape into balls or cylinders. Place on a chilled plate and store in the refrigerator or drop into a bowl of ice water.

Butter curls. Beginning at the far side of a pound block of butter, draw a butter curler lightly and quickly towards you, making a thin shaving of butter which curls into a cylinder. Dip the curler into hot water each time.

Margarine

Margarine is enriched to have the same nutritional value as butter and may be substituted for it.

Cooking Oils

Olive oil is used principally in salad dressings. Combined with an equal amount of butter, it is excellent for sautéing.

Other cooking oils (corn, peanut, soy, cottonseed, etc.) are used for frying and sautéing and in salad dressings. There are special recipes which call for oil as the shortening, such as Chiffon Cakes (p. 474) and Stirred Pastry (p. 409).

Other Fats

In substituting lard or a vegetable fat for butter in a recipe, use ⅛ less, since butter is not solid fat but contains some liquid. Add salt to taste.

Lard. Pastry made with lard is especially flaky. Store old-fashioned lard in the refrigerator. Some lard may be stored on the pantry shelf — read the label.

Vegetable shortenings. Use as an ingredient and for sautéing and deep-fat frying.

Bacon fat. Strain into a jar, cover, and store in the refrigerator. Use within 3 or 4 days for pan-frying potatoes, eggs, lamb patties, liver, etc.

Salt pork. Recommended in special recipes, such as fish chowder, for its excellent flavor.

Chicken fat. Try out (below). Excellent for gingerbread, cookies and steamed puddings. In substituting for butter, use ⅔ as much and increase the liquid slightly.

Fats from roasts are used chiefly in making gravy to serve with the roast or as the basis for second-day dishes.

Suet is excellent for Oven-Fried Potatoes (p. 266) and is the traditional shortening for pastry in England. Render (below). Store in the refrigerator.

To render (try out) fats. Cut solid uncooked fat in small pieces or put through a food chopper. Melt in a double boiler over hot but not boiling water, or in a shallow pan in a 250° oven, or in a heavy pan over very low heat. Pour off the melted fat. If bits of meat or gristle still cling to the fat, add boiling water and let stand until cool. Lift off the cake of fat and scrape the under side with a knife. Store in the refrigerator.

Wheat Flours

Store in a cool dry place in a tightly closed container. Buy in small amounts, especially if you use unbleached flour, which has an attractive creamy color and excellent flavor. Freshly ground whole wheat flour has the highest food value and is sometimes to be found in a small local mill.

Flours vary in starch content or thickening property. Experienced cooks reserve a fraction of the amount of flour called for in a recipe for cake or cookies and add it at the last if the "feel" of the batter requires it. In substituting all-purpose or bread flour for pastry or cake flour, reduce the amount by 2 tablespoons per cup.

All-purpose flour is made of a mixture of hard and soft wheats. It is satisfactory for most recipes except the most delicate cakes and pastries. Granulated all-purpose flour is excellent for thickening sauces and gravies, since it cooks smoothly with no danger of lumping.

Bread flour is made of hard wheat, rich in gluten. Gluten makes a mixture elastic so that it can expand successfully.

Pastry flour is more delicate than bread or all-purpose flour. It is perfect for pastry and fine cakes.

Cake flour makes a very fine-textured cake but it may be somewhat dry.

Whole wheat (graham) flour contains the bran and germ of the wheat. It is rich in protein and other food values and has a pleasant nutty flavor.

Other Flours and Meals

Buckwheat is usually mixed with wheat flour. Its distinctive flavor makes it popular for pancakes.

Potato flour is especially successful as a thickening. It cooks quickly and smoothly in a liquid and leaves no "raw" taste. Use ⅓ the amount of flour called for in the recipe.

Rye flour is usually mixed with wheat flour, since it makes a heavy bread if used alone. Pumpernickel is made from rye flour with no added wheat flour.

Soybean flour (ground soybeans) has high protein content and may be added in small amounts to enrich white flours.

Arrowroot is made from the ground rootstock of certain Central American plants. It is an excellent thickener and is clear and almost tasteless.

Cornstarch is refined starch made from corn. As a thickening agent, it cooks smoothly and is particularly useful for clear sauces, gravies and puddings.

Corn meal may be yellow or white. "Water-ground" meal (usually white) retains much of the skin and germ and should be refrigerated.

Oatmeal (rolled oats or quick oatmeal) is used as a cereal or as an ingredient in breads and cookies.

Milk

Use milk generously, since it has an important role in good nutrition.

To scald milk. Heat, preferably in a double boiler, until a row of tiny bubbles appears around the edge.

Homogenized milk is whole milk which has been mechanically treated so that the globules of cream will not separate from the rest of the milk.

Skim milk is high in protein and calcium because the cream has been replaced by milk. Do not substitute for whole milk in a recipe unless directed.

Buttermilk is excellent in many recipes such as pancakes, doughnuts and spice cake.

Sour milk provides the acid which combines with baking soda to produce leavening action in some biscuits, pancakes and other dishes. To make sweet milk sour, stir in lemon juice or vinegar (1 tablespoon to 1 cup) and let stand a few minutes.

Condensed milk is sweetened, so use less sugar when substituting it for regular milk. Follow package directions.

Evaporated milk is not sweetened. Whip it as a low-calorie substitute for whipped cream. Chill thoroughly before whipping. It has a different flavor and is best used when a dish has highly flavored ingredients such as coffee, lemon or spices.

Dry milk solids or powdered milk. Follow instructions on the package for mixing with water. If you are substituting powdered milk for liquid milk in a recipe, mix the dry milk with the dry ingredients and use water as the liquid.

Yogurt is prepared from milk partly evaporated and fermented. Since it is thick, it is an excellent lower-calorie substitute for sour cream.

Cream

Dairy cream is available as light, all-purpose (medium) or heavy, according to the amount of butter fat it contains.

To whip cream (light cream will not whip successfully without adding a commercial whipping aid). Chill the cream, the bowl and the beater. The bowl should be large enough so that the beater will not knock against the sides but small enough so that the cream will be at least 1½ inches deep. A straight-sided bowl is best. As the cream begins to thicken, whip slowly, especially if you are using an electric beater, so that you can stop before the cream begins to turn to butter. If the cream is very heavy, add a little milk as you beat.

To freeze cream. Heavy cream freezes successfully. Whip it and pack in a covered container. Defrost in the refrigerator to use whipped. Defrost at room temperature and stir to use in liquid form.

Sour cream (commercial) is treated to provide an even product of good flavor. To make sweet dairy cream sour, add lemon juice or mild vinegar (1 tablespoon to a cup) and let stand a few minutes. As an ingredient, add sour cream slowly so that the acid in it will not cause the mixture to curdle.

Powdered cream is a useful item for the emergency shelf.

Chocolate and Cocoa

Cooking chocolate is usually sold already divided into 1-ounce blocks, so it is simple to measure the required amount. Unless otherwise indicated in the recipe, use unsweetened baking chocolate. Some recipes call for semisweet or sweetened chocolate, or sweetened and flavored chocolate, or for chocolate bits. Dipping chocolate is especially prepared for dipping candies.

To melt chocolate. Melt slowly over hot water in a small double boiler or in a small bowl set in hot water. One or two ounces may be melted on aluminum foil or wax paper set in a warm (not hot) place on the stove.

Cocoa usually has most of the fat removed. Dutch-process cocoa is richer in fat than the regular type.

To use cocoa in place of chocolate. For each ounce of chocolate use 3 tablespoons cocoa. To make the mixture as rich as if made with chocolate, add 1 tablespoon shortening.

Leavening Agents

A flour mixture would bake in a heavy flat mass without a leavening agent to lighten it by distributing through it carbon dioxide gas, air or steam, all of which expand in the hot oven during baking. Yeast, baking powder and baking soda develop carbon dioxide gas. Beaten eggs enclose air in the mixture, and liquid turns to steam during the baking.

Compressed yeast is sold in cakes and dry (granular) yeast in packages or envelopes. Compressed yeast is more perishable because of higher moisture content and must be kept refrigerated. Dry yeast will keep without refrigeration for weeks, but must be stored in a cool dry place.

Baking powder is of several types, each plainly marked on the package. Use interchangeably in recipes in this book unless otherwise indicated. "Double action" baking powder is so called because expansion of the gas does not begin until heat is present. It is therefore useful when the baking is to be done a considerable time after mixing.

Baking soda (bicarbonate of soda) reacts with an acid (such as sour milk) to release carbon dioxide gas which makes a batter or dough rise. The usual amount is ½ teaspoon soda to each cup of molasses, buttermilk, sour milk or sour cream.

Cream of tartar may be combined with baking soda to make baking powder. To substitute for 1 teaspoon baking powder, use ¼ teaspoon baking soda and ½ teaspoon cream of tartar.

Eggs, when beaten, enclose air in tiny cells. See p. 3 for details.

Gelatine

Plain unflavored gelatine is sold in small packages of 4 envelopes, each containing 1 tablespoon. However, it is both economical and convenient to buy gelatine in a 1-pound package. A recipe sometimes requires more or less than 1 tablespoon. Gelatine keeps almost indefinitely in a tightly covered box.

One tablespoon of gelatine stiffens 1 pint of liquid, as a general rule. However, a jelly requires more (see recipes) if fruit or an acid is added or if it is molded in a large mold. Measure gelatine with care, remembering that it is better to use too little than too much. Stiff, rubbery jelly is unappetizing, but you can serve soft jelly in dessert glasses if it is not firm enough to hold its shape.

Mold jelly in large or small molds or chill in dessert glasses or a bowl ready for the table. Dip molds in cold water before filling and shake out the loose drops of water. Brush molds for salad with olive or other cooking oil. A ring mold makes a most attractive jelly with the center filled with a sauce or other accompaniment. A 1-quart ring mold is very practical — whether the amount prepared fills it completely or not. If more than enough is prepared, chill the extra amount in cups or small timbale molds.

Set filled molds in the refrigerator. Allow 2 hours for plain jellies to stiffen and as much as 4 hours for jellies containing fruit or vegetables. If jelly is very stiff, set in a warm room to soften slightly before serving.

To unmold jelly, dip the mold in warm water almost deep enough to cover it. Let stand 30 seconds and lift out. Loosen around the edges with a thin sharp knife, invert on the serving dish, and tap the mold. If the jelly does not drop out easily, cover the outside of the mold with a cloth wrung out of hot water; let stand for 2 minutes and try again. Ease the jelly out so that it will not break apart.

Serve jelly plain or garnished appropriately. (See suggestions with individual recipes.) One pint yields 3 or 4 servings.

Nuts

Nuts are high in food value and also add delicious flavor to many foods. Consult the index for recipes for cakes, cookies, candies, desserts and hors d'oeuvres which feature some special nut.

Salted Nuts (p. 507). Glacéed Nuts (p. 508).

To crack nuts (1 pound in the shell yields about ½ pound of nut meats):

Soft-shell nuts (almonds, peanuts and lichee nuts). Crack with the fingers and remove the kernels.

Hard-shell nuts (filberts, walnuts, pecans, butternuts and Brazil nuts). Crack with a nutcracker. To shell butternuts easily, pour boiling water over them, let stand 15 minutes and drain. Cover Brazil nuts with boiling water, boil 3 minutes, drain and cool before shelling.

To blanch nuts:

Almonds and pistachios. Shell and cover with boiling water. Let stand 2 minutes. Drain, put in cold water, rub off the skins with the fingers and spread on a paper towel to dry.

Chestnuts. Cut a ½-inch crisscross gash on the flat side of each nut with a sharp vegetable knife. Cover with boiling water and bring slowly to the boiling point. Take out the nuts one by one and remove the shell and inner skin with a sharp pointed knife.

Filberts. Shell, cover with boiling water, let stand 6 minutes and drain. Remove the skins with a sharp pointed knife.

To chop nuts. To chop a few, cut on a board with a long straight knife; to chop a larger amount, chop in a bowl or in a special nut chopper, not a meat grinder, which makes nuts pasty. To chop nuts very fine, whirl in a blender — not too long or they will become pasty.

Coconut

A fresh coconut should sound full of liquid when you shake it. Grated coconut is sold dry or moist, also toasted. Moist coconut tastes more like fresh coconut.

To grate fresh coconut. Pierce the "eyes" with a screwdriver and let the milk drain off into a bowl or jar. Set the coconut in a 400° oven for 20 minutes. Tap all over with a hammer to loosen the shell. Split with a heavy knife or crack with a mallet or hammer. Pry out the white meat with a strong sharp knife. Pare off the dark skin. Grate the white meat on a rotary grater or in a blender. *A medium-sized coconut yields 3 to 4 cups of grated coconut.*

To toast grated or shredded coconut (fresh or canned). Spread in a shallow pan. Set in a 350° oven until delicately brown (about 20 minutes).

To tint coconut. Put a few drops of food coloring in a jar. Add a few drops of water. Put in shredded coconut and shake until evenly tinted.

Sugar

Granulated sugar is called for in most recipes.

Fine or superfine sugar is used in some recipes and to sprinkle over fruit.

Confectioners' sugar is used for uncooked frostings and for some sauces.

Loaf sugar is pressed in cubes or dominoes. One pound contains 100 dominoes or 110 half-inch cubes.

Brown sugar contains some molasses. It is packaged according to color, light or dark. Recipes specify the type, since they differ in flavor. To prevent caking, store in the refrigerator. If it lumps, set it in the oven until it softens enough to crumble or whirl in an electric blender. Granulated brown sugar never cakes because much of the moisture has been removed. Do not substitute it for other kinds of brown sugar in a recipe and expect the same result. Pack brown sugar firmly when you measure it.

Maple sugar has a distinctive flavor. Use it in special recipes (see index), as a confection or, crushed, on breakfast cereal or pancakes.

To sprinkle or dust with sugar. Sift sugar out of a shaker-top container. To sugar fresh hot doughnuts or lady fingers, put a few in a paper bag with ½ cup sugar and shake gently until they are lightly coated. Repeat until all are sugared, adding more sugar as you need it.

To caramelize sugar. Rub a heavy frying pan lightly with butter. Put in the sugar (not more than ½ cup at a time) and set the pan over moderate heat. (If you have a stove with controlled heat burners, the heat will be reduced before the sugar caramelizes.) Stir constantly until the sugar melts. Add more sugar by half-cupfuls and stir as before until you have as much clear brown syrup as you need.

Caramel Syrup. Caramelize 1 cup sugar and add ½ cup boiling water very slowly so that the mixture will not boil over. Simmer 10 minutes.

Caramel for coloring gravies. Caramelize sugar and continue cooking it until it is almost black. Then add boiling water very slowly and simmer until all the sugar dissolves. Store in a covered jar and use as needed to color gravy. No sweet flavor remains.

Brittle for flavoring. Caramelize sugar and pour it into a slightly buttered pan. Cool, roll with a rolling pin, and sift.

Nut Brittle or Praline Powder. Add a few grains of salt and an equal amount of chopped blanched almonds or pecans to caramelized sugar. Proceed as for Brittle.

Syrups

Molasses is the product remaining after granulated sugar has been removed from sugar cane. It may be light or dark. Natural molasses has excellent flavor. Store molasses in a tightly closed jar in a cool place.

Corn syrups. Use light or dark corn syrup in sauces, frostings and other recipes. Corn syrup helps prevent sugaring or crystallization. Golden syrup is a delicious light syrup imported from England.

Honey varies in flavor according to the different flowers the bees have fed on. Strained honey is sometimes mixed with glucose syrup. Either serve honey in the comb (the comb is edible) or else heat it in a double boiler until the liquid separates so that you can strain it off.

Maple syrup is boiled-down maple sap. If you buy syrup by the gallon, keep it refrigerated or heat it to the boiling point, pour into sterilized pint jars, and seal. Otherwise it will sugar or ferment unless used promptly.

Chopping Fruits and Vegetables

Prepare for chopping by washing, peeling, removing pits, tough stems and wilted or discolored parts.

In a glass. Discard heavy stems and bruised leaves of mint, watercress, parsley or other herbs. Wash. Dry thoroughly

on a towel. Put in a glass and snip with scissors until finely cut.

On a board. Place on a chopping board, preferably fairly large so that you can work without spilling. Hold a long, flexible French-type knife by the handle

and blade. Chop straight up and down. For a small amount (nuts or parsley, for example) pivot the blade on its tip.

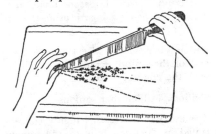

To mince or dice onions, beets, potatoes, etc. Cut off a slice. Cut the flat surface in squares, as deep as required. Slice off with a long sharp knife.

To cut dates, marshmallows or other sticky foods. Cut with scissors or with a sharp knife, dipped frequently in cold water.

To cut in julienne strips. Cut in pieces about the size and shape of kitchen matches.

Seasonings

Seasonings add sparkle and zest to your cooking. Many foreign recipes owe much of their special quality to unusual seasonings. Season with discretion, to enhance the flavor of a dish, not overwhelm it. No recipe can do more than suggest the right amount, since seasonings and individual tastes vary.

To keep seasonings at their best, store them in tightly closed containers.

Salt. Table salt is mixed with another ingredient to keep it from caking. Common salt has no added ingredient and so is stronger. Iodized salt should be used in the many parts of the country where the soil is low in iodine and foods grown there lack this important element for good nutrition. Rock salt, freshly ground in a tiny wooden mill, has perfect flavor. Seasoned salts have other seasonings blended with them, such as powdered garlic, onion and herbs.

Pepper. Black pepper is made from the whole berry, white pepper from the inner kernel. For sparkling flavor, grind whole peppercorns in a pepper mill instead of using ground pepper. Cayenne pepper is red pepper. It is very strong. Use it sparingly.

Paprika. The dried and ground shell of large red peppers. The best quality is Spanish or Hungarian or a blend of the two.

Never use pepper in a dish seasoned with paprika. The pepper overwhelms the paprika flavor.

Chili peppers. Tiny red peppers with very pungent flavor, used in meat stews.

Pimiento. Sweet red peppers preserved in oil. Use whole, stuffed (see index) or cut small in salads and sauces.

Pimiento purée. Press canned pimientos through a sieve.

Monosodium glutamate. A powder which is not actually a seasoning but which is used to emphasize flavor. It is packaged under various trade names. It has been used for many years in Oriental cooking.

Meat concentrates and bouillon cubes. Use to intensify color and to add flavor to sauces, soups, stews, gravy, hash, meat loaf, casseroles, etc.

Mustard. Dry mustard is made of mustard seeds ground fine. **Prepared mustard** is dry mustard mixed with vinegar or water. **French (Dijon)** and **Louisiana** mustards are mild-flavored prepared mustards sometimes seasoned with added herbs. **English mustard** is very sharp. Herb mustard is flavored with herbs.

Sugar, as a condiment. Use very sparingly in sauces and gravies. It helps brown meats. See also Caramel (p. 14).

Vinegar. Be cautious in using vinegar. Old-fashioned cider vinegar is usually mild, but other vinegars may be very sharp.

> **Mint Vinegar.** Pick young mint leaves before blossoms appear. Pack in a pint jar; fill it with wine vinegar; close and let stand at least 2 weeks. Strain through cheesecloth. Bottle.
>
> **Herb Vinegar.** In place of mint, use a combination of herbs, such as tarragon and rosemary, thyme and marjoram, or chervil and basil.
>
> **Tarragon Vinegar.** Crush 2 cups fresh tarragon leaves, add 1 pint wine vinegar, 2 cloves, 1 clove garlic cut in half. Cover, let stand 24 hours, and take out the garlic; then cover and let stand 2 weeks. Strain and bottle.

Wine Vinegar. Let opened red or white wine stand in a warm dark place for several months. If you add "mother" from cider vinegar, the vinegar will be ready to use in 4 or 5 weeks.

Garlic adds particularly appetizing seasoning to many dishes. A garlic bulb is composed of several smaller bulbs, called cloves, beads or buds. Put a split clove in the French dressing bottle or rub the salad bowl with a cut clove. For convenience use **garlic powder** (garlic cloves, dried and ground) or **garlic salt**. To make garlic salt, split a clove of garlic and crush it with 1 teaspoon salt in a garlic press or on a board, using the tip of a knife.

Onion juice. Cut a slice from the root end of the onion; scrape out the juice with the edge of a teaspoon.

Shallots. Milder than onions.

Tomato paste. Use this highly concentrated product not only to add tomato flavor but, in smaller amounts, to add color to soups and other dishes, especially ones made with lobster.

Lemon juice. One medium-sized lemon yields 3 tablespoons juice and 1 tablespoon grated rind. However, some lemons have thick skins and are so pulpy that they yield much less juice.

Grated orange and lemon peel. Wash the fruit, wipe dry, and grate without peeling. Do not grate beyond the color margin. Clean the grater with the point of a knife.

Whole Spices

Whole spices keep their pungency longer than ground spices.

Grate nutmeg in a special grater. Grind whole **peppercorns** in a pepper mill. Put pieces of **stick cinnamon** or **dried gingerroot** into the dish to be flavored and remove them before serving. Put a few **cassia buds** in each jar of grape juice to add a pleasant flavor.

To flavor with a spice bag, put whole spices (according to the recipe) in a small cloth bag, tie firmly and cook with the dish to be flavored, removing the bag before serving. Pickling spices are mixed whole spices in a suitable combination for pickling.

Ground Spices

Buy ground spices (such as allspice, cinnamon, cloves, ginger, mace and nutmeg) in the smallest packages available because spices begin to lose their strength after grinding. You may find you need to use more as you get to the bottom of the box.

Use spices in cakes, cookies and desserts according to the recipes. Mace is particularly good in pound cake or cherry pie and adds a pleasant flavor to fish. Use nutmeg with chicken, mushrooms, spinach and stewed or baked fruits. Saffron is used principally for its brilliant yellow color and is distinctive in bouillabaisse. Imported saffron is very expensive but domestic saffron is almost as good. Buy it at a drugstore.

Pepper is a spice by definition but is listed with the basic seasonings (p. 15) for convenience.

Curry is a blend of turmeric, garlic, pepper, ginger and other strong spices. See index for special dishes but try a little in stuffed eggs, soups, sauces and salad dressing.

Seeds

For cookies, breads and coffee cakes. Benne, caraway, cardamon, poppy seed and sesame seed.

For pickles, sauces and stews. Caraway, coriander, dill, mustard, celery, onion and fennel seeds. Add in small amounts.

For fish, fish salads and sauces. Pickled capers and nasturtium seeds.

For cottage and cream cheese. Caraway seeds.

For vegetables. Mustard seed for beets, cabbage and sauerkraut; anise seeds for buttered carrots; dill for green beans and potatoes.

Herbs

Fresh herbs (free of woody stems and wilted leaves) may be used as sprigs or chopped fine. Dried herbs are at least three times as strong as fresh herbs, so measure accordingly. To bring out the flavor of dried herbs, soak them in lemon juice or wine before adding them to a dish.

Herbs take up little space in the garden, and it is pleasant to have them to store for future use or for gifts to friends.

To store herbs in the freezer, select perfect young sprigs. Dip quickly in and out of boiling water. Pat dry on paper towels. Put small amounts in cellophane bags or envelopes, seal, label, and store in the freezer.

To store herbs in the refrigerator, wash perfect sprigs, gently shake dry, and put in a jar. Close tightly. Store in the refrigerator. Parsley and watercress stay fresh and crisp for days this way.

To dry herbs. Use only the young tender leaves that appear before the plant flowers. Then there will be a second growth as tender as the first. Pick the leaves in the morning after the dew has

A Few Aromatic Herbs

Garlic

Nasturtium Seeds

Chives

Basil

Sage

Borage

Burnet

Sweet Bay Leaf

Rosemary

Peppermint and Apple Mint

Thyme

Marjoram, related to Oregano

Celery Leaves

Caraway Seeds

Dill, related to Caraway, Anise, Cummin, and Fennel

disappeared. Pick from the stems and spread in shallow pans. Dry in a 150° oven until they crumble between the fingers (1 to 2 hours). Discard any stiff stems that remain. Pack in airtight jars and label.

To prepare herb seeds. Gather the entire stalk when the seed pods are just ready to burst. Spread in a thin layer on a cloth stretched over a wooden rack. Dry in the sun, bringing in at night and turning daily until thoroughly dried. Fennel leaves and seeds are both used, so keep the flower stalks picked off early in the season while you are gathering the young leaves and then let the flower heads develop so that you can gather the seeds.

Cooking with Herbs

Used imaginatively, herbs can add a refreshing new flavor to a familiar dish. It is important not to add too much: herbs should not overwhelm the taste of the basic ingredients. Experiment on your own in addition to following some of the suggestions below. Add a few tender sprigs to a green salad or flavor a salad dressing with a pinch of dried herbs. If you are seasoning a stew with herbs, add them for only the last hour of cooking so that the stew will be delicately seasoned.

Aux fines herbes means that a dish is flavored with a mixture of finely chopped fresh herbs, usually including both parsley and chives. Vary the amount of each to suit your taste. Some successful combinations are:

Parsley, chives, watercress and tarragon
Parsley, chives and chervil
Parsley, chives and basil
Parsley, burnet and thyme

Herb bouquet or bouquet garni. Tie in a small cheesecloth bag ½ carrot cut lengthwise, 1 leek, a few sprigs of parsley, 1 sprig of celery top, a bit of thyme,

2 cloves and ¼ bay leaf. Cook in a stew or soup. Remove before serving. Vary the combination as you like, adding other herbs, such as marjoram, and omitting the leek.

Herb butter (for sandwiches, to spread on Italian bread, or to serve in pats with hamburgers or fish fillets). Soften butter and cream into it finely chopped chives or watercress or a combination of several fresh herbs. Taste and add a few drops of lemon juice if needed.

Herb vinegars (p. 16).

Some Familiar Herbs and Their Uses

Basil has a clovelike flavor. It is good with eggs, fish, cheese, meat loaf, meat pie, stews and chowders. It is especially good with venison and duck and with tomatoes, tomato soup and spaghetti sauces.

Bay leaf, one of the most popular, adds zest to meat pie, stews, soups (especially pea soup) and tomato juice.

Borage and burnet are cucumber-like in flavor. Add tiny leaves to iced tea, lemonade, claret cup and other punches. The leaves are somewhat rough but the flavor is excellent in a salad.

Chervil is similar to parsley but more delicate in flavor. Add young sprigs to a green salad. Chop to use as a garnish on soup, to add zest to cream or tomato sauce or to cottage or cream cheese.

Chives belong to the onion family. Snip fine with scissors and add to cottage or cream cheese or to egg or fish dishes or to any dish which needs a delicate onion flavor. Delicious on new potatoes, peas or carrots.

Dill is especially good with lamb, either roast or stewed. Also good in fish sauces and in cheese dishes. Add a few sprigs to a green salad. Dill Pickles (p. 520).

Fennel is widely used in Italian cookery. It is similar to celery. It is good raw as a relish, or cooked.

Marjoram is similar to thyme and is used to flavor pork or lamb, meat loaf, hash, meat pie and stews. Also good, chopped, on peas, carrots and spinach and in salads.

Mint is the classic seasoning for any lamb dish. Chopped, it is a perfect addition to new peas and tiny boiled potatoes. Add sprigs to iced tea and lemonade. Mint Sauce (p. 98). Mint Jelly (p. 512). Mint Vinegar (p. 16).

Orégano (wild marjoram) is the most familiar herb in Italian cookery. Add it to spaghetti sauce, tomato sauce and minestrone. A "must" on pizza. Good in a green salad.

Parsley is the perfect garnish for eggs, meat, fish or salad. Chopped fine, add it to cottage or cream cheese and sprinkle it on soup and creamed or boiled potatoes.

Rosemary is delicately aromatic and goes well with chicken, fish, lamb, pork, hash and meat pie. Add a few sprigs to a green salad. It is also a pleasant addition to a fruit punch.

Sage is most familiar in stuffings (p. 80), but is also excellent in sausage or pork dishes and is a tasty addition to cheese spreads.

Savory is similar to sage but more delicate. Use it in omelets and salads and on green beans.

Tarragon is very pungent. Use it with restraint with eggs, chicken and veal. Add young sprigs to salad. Tarragon Vinegar (p. 16).

Thyme is perhaps the most popular herb in French cookery. Add it to fish, chowder, oyster or clam bisque, meat loaf, hash, meat pie and stews. Especially good with chicken and turkey and in salads and cheese spreads.

Wine in Cooking

Wine in cookery adds an elusive flavor which makes many a dish memorable. Use it with discretion so that the wine emphasizes and improves the flavor of the other ingredients but does not dominate them. Certain recipes list wine as an ingredient, but it is simple to experiment with wine in others. Inexpensive wines are useful in cooking, but the better the wine, the better the flavor of the finished dish. Save any leftover wine to use in cooking.

Sherry. Add to soups and sauces. Particularly delicious with seafood and chicken dishes and in many desserts. See special recipes such as Oysters in Sherry Cream (p. 146) and English Trifle (p. 363).

White wines. Add to fish or chicken dishes.

Red wines. Marinate meats in wine to improve both texture and flavor. Use the marinade in making gravy or sauce. Add red wine to meat stews.

Dessert wines improve hot or cold fruit compotes and season sweet sauces pleasantly. Marsala is the traditional flavoring for Zabaglione (p. 364).

Brandy adds fine flavor to many dishes. To flame, warm a small amount of brandy, pour it over the food and light it with a match. Spoon over the food until the flame dies down.

Rum is delicious over any fruit cup, especially one which includes pineapple. Use rum as the flavoring in any chocolate dessert.

Vodka flames very successfully (see directions for flaming brandy, above).

Wine-Seasoned Dishes

Beef Bourguignonne (p. 164)
Braised Duck à l'Orange (p. 229)
Chicken Contadine (p. 217)
Chicken à la King (p. 224)
Creamed Shrimp with Curaçao (p. 150)

Kidney Stew (p. 206)
Lobster Newburg (p. 143)
Oysters in Sherry Cream (p. 146)
Poached Fillets of Fish (p. 120)
Scallopini of Veal (p. 195)
Scallops Newburg (p. 148)
Shrimp Newburg (p. 150)

Wine-Flavored Desserts

Cherries Jubilee (p. 352)
English Trifle (p. 363)
French Chocolate Mousse (p. 365)
Fresh Fruit Cup (p. 345)
Pudding Sauces (pp. 398–405)
Rum Cake (p. 483)
Strawberries Flambé (p. 360)
Wine Jelly (p. 378)
Zabaglione (p. 364)

Planning Meals

Most normal diets contain all the calories necessary — often too many — and a little attention will make sure the elements are included which are needed to maintain the highest standards of health. It is not necessary to concentrate so heavily on food values that you destroy your interest in planning meals with imagination. Do not be too quick to follow food fads. Read government bulletins for well-balanced information and depend on your doctor to advise you in case of specific vitamin deficiency.

As a general rule, provide the following for each person each day, then add other foods as you like.

Milk for high-quality protein, plenty of calcium and several important vitamins. Some may be provided by cheese, ice creams, soups and puddings.

Fats and oils are valuable for their vitamin and mineral content. Both animal and vegetable fats and oils are important.

Cereals (preferably whole-grain or enriched) as breakfast foods or in puddings and breads.

Fruits. Citrus and others, fresh or dried.

Vegetables are rich in vitamins and minerals. Tomatoes, parsley and peppers are high in vitamin C. Include raw vegetables and salad greens.

Meat, fish and poultry are the best sources of "complete" protein and the B vitamins.

Eggs for many important food values.

Menu Making

Menu planning is much more appealing than it was in our grandmothers' day. The range of recipes — many of them exotic foreign ones — is so wide that meals need never be routine. Our markets offer a much greater variety, especially of fruits and vegetables, throughout the year.

For many women—and men as well—cooking has become as much a means of self-expression as any of the arts. Countless "convenience foods" free us of some of the duller tasks so that we have time to concoct a culinary work of art with enthusiasm.

22

Most housewives who are bored with planning meals are those who have a limited cooking repertory and who are conservative about trying anything new. No cookbook can provide the spark of genius, but it can serve as a source of inspiration and information. An excellent first step away from old habits is to look for variations to use with familiar dishes — a new sauce or garnish, new shapes and seasonings for breads, or a variation on a well-known salad theme.

For the Beginner

Plan ahead to assure yourself of relaxation and confidence at the important moment of putting things together just before serving time. Write out the menu. Read the recipes you will follow and check to be sure the staples you will need are on hand. Then make out the complete shopping list.

Concentrate on one or two dishes at first. Do not hesitate to complete the meal with prepared foods, canned or frozen, until you have acquired a familiar repertory.

Thoughtful timing is important. Allow for interruptions and remember that suggested timing for meats is based on having the meat at room temperature when you start. Avoid more than one last-minute task.

Be ready for at least one emergency meal by keeping on hand a supply of canned foods and/or frozen foods sufficient for a complete menu. Even if you do not have a freezer, keep a few packages of frozen foods in the storage compartment of your refrigerator.

How much to prepare. *Serves 4* or *Serves 6* indicates the number of average-sized servings. But appetites vary according to many factors — the weather or the way a dish is presented, whether at a meal of many courses or just one or two. A pudding or ice cream served in dessert glasses "goes farther" than one served from a bowl.

Breakfast

Start the day with a sturdy breakfast to provide plenty of energy-building foods for the day's activities. In most families, the pattern is standardized — fruit or fruit juice; cereal and/or eggs, perhaps with bacon; a beverage and toast, doughnuts, or a hot bread such as popovers or blueberry muffins.

On a leisurely Sunday morning, serve waffles with sausage patties, French toast or pancakes with maple syrup, chicken hash, sautéed tomatoes with strips of bacon, fish cakes, finnan haddie, kedgeree, or, in the old New England fashion, warm apple pie.

Lunch or Supper

Often a sandwich with a bowl of soup or a beverage will be sufficient. For a pleasant contrast, serve crisp carrot sticks or celery. Even in summer, one hot thing is refreshing — soup or beverage or toast or a hot bread. Top off, if you like, with fresh whole fruit or a fruit cup with simple cookies. For other ideas, see the list of casserole dishes (p. 24). Some suggestions are:

Eggs. See pp. 101–108 and the index, especially omelets, custards, timbales and soufflés.

Meats. Cooked meat sliced and served cold or reheated in gravy, sausages, hamburg patties in various ways, hash, liver and bacon.

Chicken and turkey in various ways, especially in dishes using cooked chicken or turkey (pp. 223–228).

Soups and chowders. Minestrone,

oyster, lobster, or scallop stew, fish chowder, Queen Victoria soup or any cream soup with toasted cheese sandwiches.

Fish. Broiled fillets, broiled scrod, codfish balls, finnan haddie.

Cheese. Welsh rabbit, Swiss fondue, cheese soufflé, and other cheese dishes (pp. 110–116).

Waffles or pancakes with sausages or bacon.

Dinner

As the principal meal of the day, dinner deserves careful planning, but long, elaborate meals are outmoded except for state occasions. Decide on the main course first, so that you can choose the other courses to supplement it wisely.

The first course (omit it altogether if you like) may be fruit or tomato juice, a fruit or seafood cocktail or a simple soup. For suggestions on serving hors d'oeuvres as a first course, see p. 43.

The main course is usually a satisfyingly hearty one. With it serve one or two vegetables and a simple salad or fresh relishes such as celery or carrot sticks. Many families serve either potatoes or bread, not both at the same meal. Vary with spoon breads, baked hominy or rice, pasta dishes and gnocchi.

Salad may be served with the main course, as a separate course following the main course or — in the West Coast fashion — as the first course. Dinner salads should be simple, especially if they are served with the main course. A mixed green salad is always right, or a salad of grapefruit or avocado pear with lettuce and watercress.

Dessert possibilities are many. If the main course is very rich and hearty, serve fruit or a simple fruit dessert, or let the salad course be the final one, served, if you like, with cheese or cheese wafers.

If the main course is on the lighter side, such desserts as pastries, cakes, tortes and puddings may be served. For ways to serve ice cream, see pp. 383 and 396.

Coffee in small cups (demitasse) is the proper finale to dinner, but many enjoy coffee throughout the meal. If you have omitted the dessert course, you may like to serve candy or salted nuts — or both — with the coffee.

Appetizing Ways to Use Leftovers

If there is only a little meat or vegetable to use, chop it, season well, heat in a sauce, and serve in a Rice, Green Rice, or Noodle Ring (pp. 294, 295, 302).

Breads. Toast (p. 343). Croûtons (p. 58), Crumbs (p. 7). Bread Puddings (p. 367). Stuffings (p. 80).

Cake. Special suggestions (p. 457). Substitute for lady fingers in Quick Charlotte Russe (p. 380) and other recipes.

Cheese. Special recipes (pp. 51ff.). Sandwiches (p. 340). Canapés (pp. 48–50). Top casseroles or soups with grated cheese.

Chicken and turkey. Special recipes (p. 223). See also suggestions for Meats (p. 200).

Egg yolks and whites (p. 8).

Fish. Special recipes (pp. 128ff.). Canapés (p. 49). Salads (pp. 278–280).

Meats. Special recipes (p. 200). Stuffed Peppers (p. 255); Stuffed Tomatoes (p. 259); Stuffed Zucchini (p. 261). Sandwiches (p. 339). Cocktail Pastries (pp. 50–51). Fashion Park Salad (p. 273).

Vegetables. Vegetable Soups (pp. 61–62). American Minestrone (p. 62). Stuffed Peppers (p. 255); Stuffed Tomatoes (p. 259); Stuffed Zucchini (p. 261).

Casserole Dishes

In addition to the suggestions listed below and in the index, prepare any braised, creamed or scalloped dish or stew or fricassee. Keep it hot in a covered casserole and serve directly from the casserole.

Baked Rice with Cheese (p. 295)
Beef and Corn Casserole (p. 172)
Casserole of Meat (p. 202)
Cheese and Olive Casserole (p. 114)
Cottage Pie (p. 202)
Deviled Crabs (p. 138)
Eggs Florentine (p. 104)
Epicurean Finnan Haddie (p. 133)
Fish Soufflé (p. 130)
Jo Mazzotti (p. 184)
Lamb à la Breck (p. 203)
Macaroni and Cheese (p. 300)
Moussaka (p. 179)
Savoy Scallops (p. 149)
Scalloped Fish or Ham (p. 128)
Scalloped Lobster (p. 143)
Shapleigh Cheese (p. 114)
Spanish Rice (p. 296)

Dinner Parties

Even for company dinners, it is no longer customary — or even desirable — to serve a succession of rich courses, each elaborately decorated. Most hostesses nowadays do their own cooking and serving and have learned to plan company meals so that there is no last-minute rush. Nobody enjoys a party given by a harried hostess! Include only dishes you have practiced on for your family until you are sure of your skill with them. You do not need to have a new idea each time — many successful hostesses are famous for only a few especially good dishes and are proud of them.

To simplify service, many hostesses omit an appetizer or first course at table and, in its place, serve plenty of tidbits with cocktails or fruit juice, or pass cups of clear, hot broth in the living room beforehand.

In planning a dinner party, follow the standard pattern for dinner (p. 24), adding an extra course if you like — a shrimp cocktail before the soup or a delicate fish course after it.

Dinner party soups may be attractively garnished consommé or chicken broth or an elegant Cream of Almond (p. 63), Lobster Bisque (p. 78) or Shrimp Bisque (p. 77).

The main course is traditionally a fine roast of beef or lamb, turkey or guinea hen or herbed roast chicken, but unless you are following a strict old-fashioned pattern, you will serve whatever you like, such as broiled chops, steak, veal cutlets, baked ham, even corned beef hash or finnan haddie. Whatever you serve, present it with a flair!

Vegetables to serve with the main course may be prepared in advance. A few suggestions are Potatoes Hashed in Cream (p. 262), Cheese Potatoes (p. 263), Gnocchi (p. 240), Tomatoes stuffed in various ways (p. 254), Vegetable Casserole (p. 233), Huntington Cabbage (p. 240), Purée of Peas (p. 254), and Spinach Soufflé (p. 256).

Relishes and jellies, especially if homemade, add an attractive touch.

Desserts may be festive for a special occasion. A few popular ones are Baked Alaska (p. 397), Gâteau Riche (p. 397), Crème Brulée (p. 363), Chocolate Cream Squares (p. 365), Meringue Glacé (p. 449), and the various coupes (p. 395) and other desserts based on ice cream. Fruit desserts are definitely in vogue and are most refreshing after a rich dinner.

Buffet Parties

Choose foods that are easy to serve and easy to eat, especially if the guests must balance a plate and a cup at the same time. It is better to have dishes that do not need cutting with a knife. Breads may be buttered in advance — hot rolls or fruit or nut breads, for example. Keep hot foods as warm as possible, preferably on an electric hot plate or in a chafing dish. Otherwise, serve hot foods in heated dishes and replenish frequently. For suggestions, see the list of casserole dishes (p. 24) and the recipes for hearty salads (p. 278).

Smörgåsbord

The Swedish version of a hearty buffet meal always includes fish, cheeses and seasoned cold vegetables. To be correct in the Swedish fashion, begin with hot boiled potatoes and herring, a surprisingly good combination. Serve with tiny glasses of aquavit or schnapps.

Provide at least two kinds of bread — crisp Swedish Knäckebrod (packaged) and dark sour rye; also pats of unsalted butter and a variety of cheese. Beer is the usual beverage.

Arrange on a table as many different items as convenient. Suggestions follow, but visit a delicatessen for other ideas.

Sardines in oil or tomato sauce.
Herring, smoked or pickled.
Lobster meat in chunks.
Shrimp.
Pickled eel.
Finnan haddie.
Smoked salmon.
Tuna chunks.
Sliced cold roast beef, veal, turkey or ham.
Swedish Meat Balls (p. 170).
Stuffed Egg Salad (p. 279) on tomato slices.
Mixed vegetable salads.
Chopped pickled beets and chopped apple, covered with whipped cream seasoned with horseradish.
Radishes.
Cucumbers, sliced thin and covered with mild vinegar.

Chafing Dish Entertaining

Your guests will enjoy watching you prepare a succulent dish at the table. Use an electric saucepan if you like. All the preliminaries, even to measuring the ingredients, should be done in advance, so that preparation may seem miraculously simple.

Some successful main dishes are:

Beef Fondue (p. 161)
Beef Stroganoff (p. 164)
Buttered Lobster (p. 142)
Chop Suey (p. 171)
Corn Fritters (p. 245)
Hamburg Patties (p. 169)
Kidney Stew (p. 206)
Liver Venetian Style (p. 206)
Lobster Newburg (p. 143)
Lobster Stew (p. 78)
Omelets (pp. 105–107)
Oyster Stew (p. 79)
Oysters in Sherry Cream (p. 146)
Pancakes (pp. 304–306)
Scallop Stew (p. 79)
Scrambled Eggs (p. 104)
Swiss Fondue (p. 113)
Welsh Rabbit (p. 114)

Some excellent desserts are:

Sautéed Bananas (p. 350)
Bananas au Rhum (p. 350)
Cherries Jubilee (p. 352)
Crêpes Suzette (p. 306)
Hot Fruit Compote (p. 346)
Soufflé au Rhum (p. 373)
Stewed Pears (p. 356)
Strawberries Flambé (p. 360)

Luncheon Parties

The menu should be light. Omit the first course if you like, or serve a clear consommé, a delicate cream soup, a fruit cocktail or other appetizer; then an interesting but not too hearty main dish such as Crêpes Nicholas (p. 306), Curried Shrimp (p. 150), Cheese Soufflé (p. 115), Chicken Almond Suprême (p. 225), Huntington Scalloped Fish (p. 129) or Fashion Park Salad (p. 273). Afterwards either fruit or a light but delicious dessert such as a fruit sherbet, Coffee Soufflé (p. 372), Angel Pie (p. 422) or Pears with Zabaglione (p. 357).

Bridge luncheons are often one-course affairs. A suitable menu might be Crab Bisque (p. 78) with salad and hot biscuits, or Fruit Salad (p. 276) with toasted cheese sandwiches.

Sunday lunch ("brunch") is a combination of breakfast and lunch served at table or buffet-style. Serve hearty breakfast dishes such as Chicken Hash (p. 226), Waffles (p. 307) or Pancakes (p. 304) with sausages, bacon or ham. Complete the menu with fruit or fruit juices, plenty of coffee, and a hot bread such as Blueberry Muffins (p. 313), Popovers (p. 314) or Corn Bread (p. 314).

Large Teas and Receptions

Set a large table in the dining room or living room with plenty of space for tea or coffee service at one end and an ice or punch at the other. Along the sides, arrange plates of small sandwiches or canapés and small cakes. Do not crowd the table or the plates. Replenish the plates from time to time so that the table will always look attractive.

Cocktail parties. Hors d'Oeuvres (pp. 43ff.). Appetizers (pp. 46ff.).

Wedding receptions. Serve sandwiches and small cakes or cookies with coffee and champagne or punch. Let the wedding cake be the chief decoration of the table and do not cut it until all the guests have arrived.

Wedding breakfasts or luncheons. Toast the bride and groom in champagne, Sauterne Cup (p. 40), Champagne Punch (p. 40) or a fruit punch (p. 37). Serve any canapés or hors d'oeuvres.

For a luncheon served at tables, the first course may be something very light, such as clear Chicken Broth (p. 72) or a Fruit Cocktail (p. 36). For a buffet luncheon, omit this course.

For the main course, Creamed Lobster (p. 143), Chicken à la King (p. 224), Chicken Tetrazzini (p. 225), Chicken (p. 278) or Lobster Salad (p. 280), Chicken Mousse with Mushroom Sauce (p. 222), Fish Mousse with Lobster Sauce (p. 129). Relishes, hot rolls and coffee with this course.

For dessert, the wedding cake alone or with ice cream.

Quantity Cooking

In a family-size kitchen, preparing food for a large number means very careful planning.

Main course. Casserole dishes (p. 24) simplify serving and avoid last-minute activity. See also Chicken Almond Suprême (p. 225), individual Chicken or Meat Pies (pp. 219, 201), Smothered Chicken (p. 216), Scalloped Scallops (p. 149), Spaghetti (p. 298), Jo Mazzotti (p. 184), Spanish Rice (p. 296). Some old stand-bys are Meat Loaf (pp. 172, 188, 198, 201), Baked Beans (p. 237) or Baked Ham (p. 185).

If you serve a roast, carve it ahead of time and keep the pieces warm.

Some of the best vegetables are Potatoes Hashed in Cream (p. 267), Candied Sweet Potatoes (p. 269), Vegetable Casserole (p. 233), and any frozen vegetables. Serve individual molded salads, tossed salad in your largest bowl, or a variety of crisp relishes. Hot buttered rolls, coffee (Coffee for Fifty, p. 33), and an assortment of pickles and jellies complete the main course.

Dessert. Ice cream must be taken out at just the right moment, so consider other desserts as well:

Baked Lemon Pudding (p. 367)
Coconut Macaroon Pie (p. 418)
Denver Chocolate Pudding (p. 365)

English Trifle (p. 363)
Fruit Cup (p. 345)
Fruit Tarts (p. 424)
Fudge Pie (p. 487)
Gingerbread (p. 466)
Tortes (p. 485)
Washington Pie (p. 483)

Buying to serve 100. The amounts suggested are approximate.

Coffee, 2½ pounds.
Tea, ½ pound.
Cream. For coffee, 6 pints. For whipped cream to accompany desserts, 2 quarts.
Butter (to cut in squares), 2 pounds.
Ice cream, 3 gallons.
Meat loaf, 18 pounds.
Roast pork, 36 pounds.
Roast beef or veal, 40 pounds.
Roast chicken or turkey, 60 pounds.
Baked ham, 30 pounds.
Potatoes, 35 pounds.
Salad dressing, 2 quarts.
Peas. Frozen, 10 packages (40-ounce size). Canned, 3 #10 cans.
Apples for applesauce, 2 pecks.
Canned applesauce, 3 #10 cans.

Children's Parties

Ice cream and cake are a "must." The cake should be a simple one, but the decoration may be as elaborate as you like (p. 490).

For very young children, serve sliced chicken, scrambled eggs or thin broiled meat patties. Peas and baked potatoes are invariably popular. For a very simple party, serve a variety of sandwiches (peanut butter, chopped chicken, jelly) with tomato juice, milk or a cream soup.

For older children, serve any plain dish easy to cut or serve.

Beef and Corn Casserole (p. 172)
Hamburg Patties (p. 169)
Lamb Chops (boned) (p. 176)

Pea Soup (p. 67) with assorted sandwiches
Pizza (p. 336)
Roast Chicken (p. 211)
Spaghetti and Meat Balls (p. 170)
Swiss Steak (p. 163)

Picnics and Barbecues

Keep special picnic equipment packed in a basket. A wire broiler and long-handled forks and tongs are essential for broiling over a fire. A gallon jug for fresh water is useful. A bag of charcoal for the fire avoids the necessity of finding wood at the picnic site. A basket with an ice compartment is excellent for cream, milk, butter, salads and relishes.

Cooking out of doors is increasingly popular. The food tastes superb and work is simplified. Out-of-door appetites are apt to be huge, so plan on at least ½ pound of boned meat or 1 pound with the bone for each person.

Sandwiches will be at their best if you wrap them tightly, freeze, and carry them without defrosting. Make them without lettuce — you can add lettuce when you are ready to serve them, if you like, or serve crisp carrot or celery sticks instead.

Hot foods are always welcome. Heat thoroughly and pack in vacuum jars or in heavy casseroles wrapped in a thick layer of newspapers, or reheat them over the fire, rubbing the underside of the pan with soap so that it will be easier to clean after using. Some good hot foods for picnics are vegetable soup or minestrone, Boston baked beans, chicken fricassee, creamed or buttered vegetables, goulash, pot roast, smothered chicken and spaghetti.

Salads and other cold foods. Green salad (the dressing carried separately in a jar, ready to add), chicken salad, mixed vegetable salad, potato salad, baked ham, sliced roast meat, meat loaf, savory cottage cheese, whole peeled tomatoes, carrot curls, celery, olives, pickles.

Grilled foods. General directions for barbecuing are on p. 153.

There are many suggestions in the chapters on meat, fish and poultry. Among the best are steaks, broilers (split in half), and lamb chops (marinated in French dressing). Fish, hamburg or chopped lamb patties, sausages and frankfurters are easier to turn in a greased folding grill or a well-salted pan. As a variation, sandwich two thin hamburg patties with a slice of tomato or dill pickle or with a bit of cheese, relish or chopped onion. Press firmly around the edges. Split frankfurters and stuff with relish or a slice of cheese or wrap in bacon. Shish Kebabs (p. 177).

Brush vegetables with salad oil seasoned with salt and pepper. Good vegetables for broiling are halved tomatoes, sliced eggplant and potatoes, and wedges of zucchini and carrot. Fresh or canned pineapple wedges, halved peaches and apricots and quartered apples are tasty as relishes with broiled meats and are delicious as dessert. Sprinkle with sugar or not as you prefer. Brown evenly on both sides and serve hot.

Rotisserie cooking is excellent for a large piece of meat — a boned roast of lamb or beef or an unsliced strip of Canadian bacon. Marinate at least 2 hours and baste frequently with the marinade (pp. 99–100) during the cooking.

Foil cooking is successful for many foods. Wrap in aluminum foil and cook on the grill. Potatoes take about 1 hour, corn 15 minutes, frozen vegetables (with a dab of butter and a sprinkling of salt) about 30 minutes. Dip small whole fish in salad oil, sprinkle with salt and pepper, and roll in corn meal. Sprinkle fish fillets and sliced fish with salt and pepper and dot with butter. Cook about 10 minutes on each side. Serve wrapped in the foil.

Wine with Meals

Wine adds a festive, but not necessarily extravagant, touch to a meal. There are excellent moderately priced wines, both imported and domestic. The best American wines are not imitations of European ones but have a character of their own.

Eastern wines are generally made from native grapes, such as Delaware and Catawba. The best California wines are made from European-type grapes in the valleys near San Francisco Bay, and are labeled with the name of the valley (Napa, Sonoma, Livermore, Santa Clara, Santa Cruz, etc.) and with the variety of the grape used (Semillon, Cabernet, Pinot Noir, Pinot Blanc, Riesling, etc.) to show that they are "varietal," i.e., not made of an indiscriminate blend of grape juices.

The vintage year is not important for American wines, since the climate is almost uniform in the wine-producing areas.

Buy wine following the advice of a dependable dealer or the recommendation of a wine expert as indicated on the label. A bottle contains 28 ounces, which is a modest amount for 4 persons, if you are serving wine throughout a meal — 2 or 3 small glassfuls each.

Store wine in a cool dry place. Place bottles of unfortified wines on their sides so that the cork will stay damp. If the cork dries out, air gets into the bottle and the flavor of the wine begins to change. Fortified wines (sherry, Madeira and port) keep well upright, since the added alcohol helps to preserve the flavor. Move bottles gently so that any sediment in the bottom is undisturbed.

Serve red wines at cool room temperatures (about 65°). Chill white or rosé wines in the refrigerator several hours before serving. Chill champagne in an ice bucket so that it is icy cold.

Remove the cork very carefully so that bits of cork will not drop into the bottle.

Serve in simple uncolored glasses, half to three-quarters full. Chill the glasses for champagne.

It is not necessary to follow a strict pattern in serving wine. Try various types and serve what you enjoy. In general, delicate white wines (such as sauterne or Rhine wine) or rosé wines seem to go best with chicken and fish, while the stronger-flavored red wines (such as Burgundy or claret) maintain their character with sturdier foods like beef, pork, game, and cheese.

To serve throughout a meal, select a wine that is not too sweet (called "dry" or "sec"). Serve a sweet wine with dessert or between meals. Before a meal, serve dry sherry or chilled vermouth with a thin twist of lemon peel. Sherry and Madeira go well with clear soup. Port is excellent at the close of a hearty meal, with cheese, walnuts or fruit. Serve champagne for any festive occasion, at a reception, throughout a meal or with dessert.

Beverages

Selecting the appropriate beverage is important. Coffee goes with every meal and almost every occasion. Tea is welcome at afternoon functions, and many people like it at meals, especially breakfast. Cocoa and chocolate with whipped cream are popular with the young. Cold drinks are especially good for summer meals and functions. Fruit punches — with or without liquor — are party refreshment.

Cocoa and Chocolate

Dutch-type cocoa retains more of the fat than other cocoas, and so has a richer flavor.

Hot Cocoa

Mix in a saucepan
  1½ tablespoons cocoa
  2 tablespoons sugar
  Few grains salt
Add
  ½ cup boiling water
Boil 3 minutes. Add
  4 cups milk
Heat slowly to just below the boiling point. Beat well with an egg beater or wire whisk. Flavor with
  Few drops vanilla
Makes 6 cups.

Mexican Chocolate. Add 2 teaspoons instant coffee. Flavor with vanilla or cinnamon to taste.

Hot Chocolate

Put in a saucepan
  4 cups milk
  2 ounces sweet chocolate or 1½ ounces unsweetened chocolate and ¼ cup sugar
  Few grains salt

Heat until the chocolate melts. Beat until smooth and foamy. Add
  1 teaspoon vanilla
Serve with
  Whipped cream
Makes 6 cups.

Iced Chocolate. Chill. Pour over crushed ice, stir well, and sweeten to taste. Serve with whipped cream.

French Chocolate

Put in a saucepan
  2 ounces unsweetened chocolate
  ½ cup cold water
Stir over low heat until the chocolate melts. Add
  ¾ cup sugar
  Few grains salt
Cook until thick (about 10 minutes). Cool. Fold in
  ½ cup heavy cream, whipped
When ready to serve, heat
  1 quart milk
Pour hot milk into each cup, and top with a spoonful of the chocolate cream.
Serves 6.

Coffee

Try different blends to learn which type you like best. Change once in a while, too. French-type and espresso coffees are mixed with chicory, and have a distinctive sharp flavor. Inexpensive coffee is not always an economy, since you may need to use more of it to make coffee as strong as you like.

Buy ground coffee or, for the finest flavor, buy coffee in the bean and grind it as needed, according to the coffee maker you are using.

Instant coffee is convenient, not only for making a single cup of coffee in a hurry but in milk shakes and as a flavoring.

Store coffee in a can or a glass jar with a tight lid. Store it in the refrigerator, upside down, to retain the pungent flavor.

Hot Coffee

Buy the grind recommended for the type of coffee maker you are using. Two level tablespoons of coffee for each cup is the standard amount to use, but experiment — you may prefer stronger or weaker coffee, or you may need to vary the amount according to the quality of the coffee.

Use a coffee maker the right size for the amount you are making. Keep it scrupulously clean. Wash it with baking soda or, if you wash it with soap, be extra careful to rinse it thoroughly so that there will be no trace of soap to spoil the fine coffee flavor.

If the water in your area has a definite taste due to minerals in it, you may prefer to use bottled spring water (not carbonated, of course).

Automatic electric coffee makers simplify coffee making and keep the coffee at the correct temperature. Follow the manufacturer's directions.

Drip or Filtered Coffee. Measure the coffee into the proper section. Set the pot in hot water or on an asbestos mat over low heat. Add fresh boiling water. For the finest flavor, add the water a little at a time, so that it will drip through slowly.

Percolator Coffee. Measure the coffee into the strainer section. Measure either cold or boiling water into the pot. Set over moderate heat or turn on the current. Bring to the boiling point, reduce the heat and percolate gently until the coffee looks dark enough (about 10 minutes).

Boiled Coffee

Old-timers think that boiled coffee, made with an egg, has the finest flavor of all. Make it strong and boil it long enough (or it will be cloudy) but not too long (or it will be bitter).

Heat the coffeepot (or a saucepan with a tight cover) by rinsing with boiling water. Mix in the pot
   1 egg, slightly beaten
   1 eggshell, crushed
   ½ cup cold water
   ½ cup coffee (regular grind)
   Few grains salt
Add
   6 cups freshly boiling water
Stir thoroughly. Stuff the spout of the pot with soft paper to prevent escape of fragrant aroma.

Set the pot over moderate heat, bring slowly to the boiling point, and simmer 3 minutes. To aid clearing, add
   ½ cup cold water

Set the coffeepot in a pan of hot water and place over very low heat to steep and keep hot without boiling.

Pour carefully into cups without straining (it will be crystal-clear, since the egg and the coffee grounds stay in the bottom of the pot).

Coffee for Fifty

In a clean cotton bag or cloth, large enough to allow for expansion, put
  1 pound coffee (regular grind)
Tie loosely. Place in a big kettle. Add
  8 quarts cold water
Let stand several hours or overnight. Bring to the boiling point three times, removing from the heat for a few minutes each time the boiling point is reached, so that the coffee will steep slowly, which improves the flavor.

Picnic Coffee

For each cup of water, measure 2 level tablespoons coffee (regular grind) into a cotton bag or cloth and tie loosely to allow for expansion. Add the water, bring to the boiling point three times, removing from the fire for a few minutes each time the boiling point is reached.

Café au Lait

Especially for breakfast, as in France, served with croissants or sweet buns.

Serve strong hot coffee with hot milk. Pour the milk and the coffee into the cup simultaneously — a pot in each hand.

After-Dinner Coffee (Café Noir)

For a pleasant change of flavor, sprinkle a few cardamon seeds in each cup before you pour the coffee.

Serve strong coffee (3 tablespoons to each cup of water) in demitasse cups.

Espresso Coffee. Use espresso-type coffee. Put a thin twist of lemon peel in each cup.

Vienna Coffee. Serve with whipped cream.

Irish Coffee

Put in a tall glass 1 jigger of Irish whiskey. Add 1 teaspoon sugar. Fill the glass with strong hot coffee. Stir well and top with a spoonful of whipped cream.

Café Brûlot

In New Orleans, café brûlot is made in a special silver bowl kept hot over an alcohol flame.

In a chafing dish or brûlot bowl, mix
  ½ stick cinnamon
  6 whole cloves
  1 curl orange peel
  1 curl lemon peel
  6 lumps sugar
  6 ounces brandy or 2 ounces rum and
    4 ounces brandy
Heat and set afire with a lighted match. Stir with a ladle. Add slowly
  3 cups strong hot coffee
Stir. Ladle into demitasse cups. *Serves 6.*

Iced Coffee

Strain very strong hot coffee over ice in glasses or in a pitcher. Or use 1 teaspoon instant coffee for each cup of cold water, shake thoroughly, and pour over crushed ice.

Serve with cream and fine sugar. Or serve clear and unsweetened as a particularly refreshing drink on a warm summer day.

Iced Coffee with Ice Cream. Serve in tall glasses, with a small scoop of vanilla ice cream in each glass.

Tea

Keep a variety of teas on hand. Orange pekoe and English breakfast are the most popular blends to serve with a meal. Delicate oolong, smoky souchong and the spicy blends are appropriate for afternoon tea.

One-fourth pound of tea will make 50 or more cups, according to the strength you like. With loose tea you can use as little or as much as you need at a time. Tea bags are convenient but comparatively expensive — 48 bags equal about ¼ pound. Store tea in a tightly covered tin away from spices or other aromatic foods.

Hot Tea

Warm a china or earthenware pot (metal changes the flavor of the tea) by rinsing it with boiling water.

Measure the tea into the pot — ½ to 1 teaspoon per cup according to the quality of the tea and the strength you like. Pour in just enough boiling water so that the tea leaves float freely. Cover and let stand 3 minutes (longer steeping develops a bitter taste). Strain, and dilute with boiling water.

To make tea with tea bags. Pour fresh boiling water over tea bags in a heated pot or cup. Cover, let steep 3 minutes, and remove the tea bags.

To serve with tea. Serve cube sugar or rock candy, cream or milk (English tea lovers insist on milk), and thin slices of lemon. For a spicy flavor, stick each lemon slice with two or three cloves.

Serve delicate China tea or smoky souchong tea clear, with nothing to detract from the distinctive bouquet.

An Austrian fashion is to serve tea with sugar and rum.

Tea for Fifty

Bring 1½ quarts water to the boiling point. Add ¼ pound tea, stir, cover, and let stand 4 minutes. Strain into a warmed pot. Dilute with fresh boiling water as you serve it.

Iced Tea

Pour strong hot tea over cracked ice or ice cubes in glasses or a large pitcher. Add more ice, if needed. Garnish with sprigs of mint and slices of lemon or orange. Serve with fine sugar. Do not use confectioners' sugar, because it makes the tea cloudy.

Cold-Water Iced Tea. *An easy way to make very clear sparkling tea.* Put 1 teaspoon tea for each cup of water in a large pitcher. Add cold water. Cover. Let stand in the refrigerator 12 hours. Strain.

Madeleine's Iced Tea. *Somewhat cloudy but delicious.* Allow 1 teaspoon sugar and 1 sprig mint for each glass to be made. Measure into a large pitcher and add strong hot tea. Stir to dissolve the sugar. Dilute with ice cubes to make the required amount. Add lemon juice to taste and strain.

Milk Drinks

Chocolate Milk Shake

If the ingredients have been thoroughly chilled in the refrigerator, you will not need ice.

For each milk shake, beat together with an egg beater, or put in a shaker and shake thoroughly
  2 tablespoons finely crushed ice
  ⅔ cup milk
  2½ tablespoons Chocolate Syrup (below)
Strain into a glass. A few gratings of nutmeg or a few grains of cinnamon may be sprinkled on top.

Chocolate Syrup
(for Milk Shakes)

Bring to a boil in a saucepan
  2 cups water
Stir in
  2 cups sugar
  ⅛ teaspoon salt
  6 ounces unsweetened chocolate or 1 cup cocoa
Cook and stir over moderate heat until smooth. Cool.
Add
  1 teaspoon vanilla
Store in a covered jar. *Makes about 3 cups.*

Molasses or Maple Milk Shake

Blend or shake together
  1 glass milk, ice cold
  2 tablespoons molasses or maple syrup

Chocolate Ice Cream Soda

Cream makes a superlative soda.

For each soda, put in a tall glass
  3 tablespoons Chocolate Syrup (above)
  1 tablespoon heavy cream
Mix well. Add
  Small scoop chocolate, mint or vanilla ice cream
  Soda water to fill the glass
Stir thoroughly.

Eggnog

See also Holiday Eggnog (p. 39).

Beat until evenly mixed
  1 egg
  2 teaspoons sugar
  Few grains salt
Stir in slowly
  ½ teaspoon vanilla or 1 tablespoon sherry, rum, whiskey or brandy
  ⅔ cup cold milk
Strain into a tall glass. Sprinkle over the top
  Grated nutmeg

Fruit Drinks and Cocktail Juices

Fresh or canned fruit juices are refreshing additions to the menu. Serve them at breakfast, as a between-meal pick-me-up, as the first course at luncheon or dinner, as an after-school treat or as a party drink. Blend several juices for an interesting flavor — see suggestions under Fruit Punch (p. 37) and Three-Fruit Cocktail (p. 36). If the juice is not tart enough, add lemon juice. Sweeten drinks with Sugar Syrup (see top of next page), since dry sugar may settle in the bottom of the glass.

Sugar Syrup

For sweetening drinks.

Put in a saucepan
  2 cups water
  2 cups sugar
Boil 5 minutes. Chill. Store in a covered jar.

Rhubarb Juice

Excellent to prepare in quantity. Can it to have ready for refreshing summer drinks.

Cut in small pieces
  1½ pounds rhubarb
Add
  1 quart water
Cook until the fruit is soft. Squeeze through a double thickness of cheesecloth. Add
  1 cup sugar
Stir and heat to the boiling point. *Makes about 3 pints.*

Lemonade

Frozen concentrated lemonade is easy to use but may be too sweet for your taste. Improve it by adding fresh lemon juice.

For each serving, mix
  2 tablespoons lemon juice
  2 tablespoons sugar or ¼ cup Sugar Syrup (above)
Stir thoroughly to dissolve the sugar. Add
  1 cup ice water or water and crushed ice or ice cubes
Stir well. Decorate with
  Maraschino cherries or sprigs of fresh mint

To frost glasses. Set the glasses on a tray and put them in the freezer compartment until they are covered with frost. Dip the rims in sugar. Return to the compartment to refrost, if necessary.

Pineapple Lemonade. Add ½ cup unsweetened pineapple juice.

Limeade. Instead of lemon juice, use 4 tablespoons lime juice. Garnish with a thin slice of lime.

Orangeade

For each tall glass, prepare ¾ cup orange juice or dilute ¼ cup frozen concentrated juice with ½ cup water. Sweeten if necessary with Sugar Syrup (above), or add lemon juice to make more tart. Fill glasses half full of crushed ice. Pour in the orange juice and stir well.

Apricot Nectar

Add lemon juice to taste to canned apricot juice. Pour over crushed ice.

Grape Juice Fizz

Mix
  1 quart ginger ale
  1 pint grape juice, frozen or bottled
Pour into glasses half filled with finely crushed ice. *Serves 8.*

Grapefruit Fizz. Use grapefruit juice in place of grape juice.

Fruit Juice Cocktail

Garnish orange or pineapple juice with a sprig of mint. Or pour fruit juice over a spoonful of sherbet. Apricot nectar with orange sherbet and cranberry juice with lemon sherbet are two delicious combinations.

Three-Fruit Cocktail

For each tall glassful, mix
  ¼ cup grapefruit juice
  2 tablespoons orange juice
  1 tablespoon lemon juice
  3 tablespoons Sugar Syrup (above), or to taste
  Few grains salt
  ½ cup soda water
  Crushed ice
Pour into glasses and garnish each with
  A sprig of mint

Clam Juice Cocktail

Season canned clam juice with salt, celery salt, and a few drops of Tabasco sauce and lemon juice. Chill or pour over crushed ice.

Tomato Juice Cocktail

Season plain tomato juice, canned or homemade (p. 531), to taste with lemon juice, sugar, and a few drops of onion juice. If it needs more flavor, add a stalk of celery, a bit of bay leaf or basil. Let stand an hour, chill, and strain.

Tomato and Clam Juice Cocktail. Combine tomato juice and clam juice, using two-thirds clam juice and one-third tomato or half of each.

Sauerkraut Juice Cocktail

Season sauerkraut juice with lemon juice. Serve very cold.

Punches and Other Party Drinks

Coffee Punch

Put in a large bowl
  1½ pints ice cream (vanilla or chocolate), frozen hard
Pour over the ice cream
  4 cups hot coffee
Beat lightly with a wire whisk until the ice cream is partially melted. Pour into punch glasses and sprinkle with
  Grated nutmeg
Serves 8.

Fruit Punch

Blend fresh, canned or frozen fruit juices. Sweeten to taste, if necessary, with Sugar Syrup (p. 36) and sharpen with lemon juice. Pineapple juice is particularly delicious combined with orange juice, grape juice or lime juice. Chill thoroughly. When ready to serve, dilute with water, soda water or ginger ale, and pour over ice cubes or a block of ice in a punch bowl.

Garnish with lemon or orange slices, bits of pineapple, strawberries or raspberries or mint leaves.

Vodka Fruit Punch. Add 80-proof vodka to any fruit punch combination. Vodka has no flavor of its own. Use about 1 cup vodka for each 4 cups of fruit juice.

Sherbet Punch. Pour cold fruit juice over sherbet in a punch bowl or individual punch cups. Stir to blend and chill, but serve before the sherbet is entirely melted. Some good combinations are grape juice with lemon sherbet; orange juice, pineapple juice or ginger ale with lemon or lime sherbet. *One quart of juice with 1 pint of sherbet makes 8 to 10 servings.*

Fruit Punch for Fifty

Boil together 5 minutes
  1 cup water
  2 cups sugar
Add
  1 cup strong hot tea
  2 cups Fruit Syrup (below)
  1 cup lemon juice
  2 cups orange juice
  2 cups unsweetened pineapple juice
Let stand 30 minutes. Add
  4 quarts ice water
  1 cup maraschino cherries
  1 quart soda water
Pour over ice in a punch bowl.

Fruit Syrup (for Fruit Punch). Cook a cup of strawberry, raspberry or loganberry jam with a cup of water about 10 minutes, stirring well. Strain.

Tea Punch

Mix
  1 cup sugar
  1 cup strong hot tea
When the sugar is dissolved, add
  ⅓ cup lemon juice
  ¾ cup orange juice
Just before serving add
  1 pint ginger ale
  1 pint soda water
Pour over ice in a punch bowl. Garnish
with
  Few slices orange
Serves 12.

Harvard Punch

*To make raspberry syrup, see Fruit Syrup
(p. 37).*

Mix
  3 cups orange juice
  1 cup lemon juice
  1 cup pineapple juice
  1 cup raspberry syrup, homemade or
    canned
  1½ cups strong hot tea
Boil 5 minutes
  1 cup water
  1¼ cups sugar
Add to the fruit juices and tea. Chill.
Just before serving add
  1 quart soda water
Pour over ice in a punch bowl. *Serves 30.*

Mint Tulip

Discard the stems and injured leaves of
  1 bunch fresh mint
Cover the perfect leaves with
  1½ cups sugar
  ½ cup water
  1 cup lemon juice
Let stand 30 minutes. Pour over ice in a
large pitcher. Add
  3 pints ginger ale
Serves 10.

Mulled Cider

*Serve in mugs with hot doughnuts for a
winter party.*

Mix in a saucepan
  1 quart cider
  2 whole allspice
  2 whole cloves
  1 stick cinnamon (3 inches long)
Boil 5 minutes. Add
  ⅜ cup brown sugar
Boil 5 minutes longer. *Serves 6.*

Cranberry Punch

Mix
  1 quart cranberry juice, canned or
    homemade (below)
  Sugar Syrup (p. 36) to taste
  2 cups water
  1 cup orange juice
  Juice ½ lemon
Chill. Just before serving, add
  1 quart ginger ale or soda water
Serves 20.

To prepare cranberry juice. Cook 1
pound cranberries in 4 cups water until
soft. Crush. Drain through cheesecloth to
make crystal-clear.

Hot Spiced Cranberry Punch

Serve in mugs or punch glasses.

Heat slowly until the sugar dissolves
  1 quart cider or grape juice
  1 quart cranberry juice (to prepare,
    see above)
  6 cloves
  1 stick cinnamon (3 inches long)
  4 whole allspice
  ½ cup brown sugar
Taste, and add more sugar if needed.
Serves 12.

Rhubarb Punch

Heat to the boiling point, stirring well
  1½ quarts Rhubarb Juice (p. 36)
  ½ cup sugar
Cool. Add
  ⅓ cup orange juice
  4 tablespoons lemon juice
  Few grains salt
Chill. Just before serving add

1 quart soda water or ginger ale
Pour over ice in a large pitcher or
punch bowl. *Serves 12.*

Holiday Eggnog

*Make at least a week before serving so
that it will mellow.*

Beat until stiff
    12 egg whites
Beat in
    ½ cup sugar
Beat until very light
    12 egg yolks
    1 cup sugar
    ¼ teaspoon salt
Combine the egg mixtures and stir until
thoroughly blended. Add
    1 quart heavy cream, beaten stiff
    1 quart milk
    1 quart Bourbon whiskey
Beat well. Add
    1 cup rum
Pour into a gallon jug (put the extra in
a quart jar). Store in a cool place. Shake
or stir thoroughly before serving. Ladle
from a big punch bowl into small cups
and sprinkle with
    Nutmeg
Serves 30.

Rum Swizzle

*Almond-flavored falernum gives a swizzle
its special character.*

Mix in a big pitcher or a punch bowl
    3 parts light rum
    1 part falernum
    1 part lime juice
    Dash of bitters
Add
    1 or 2 squeezed halves of lime
Add plenty of ice cubes. Mix hard with
a swizzle stick, or stir with a spoon. A
swizzle is still delicious as the ice melts
and dilutes it.

Rum Punch

Mix
    1½ cups lemon juice
    1½ cups grapefruit juice
    5 cups orange juice
    6 cups unsweetened pineapple juice
    8 cups water
    1 cup Sugar Syrup (p. 36)
    1 bottle Jamaica (dark) rum
    2 bottles West Indies (light) rum
Let stand at least 1 hour to blend. Pour
over ice in a punch bowl. *Makes about
75 glasses.*

Hot Jamaica Punch

Simmer ½ hour
    1 gallon cider
    Few sticks cinnamon
    ½ teaspoon whole mace
    ½ teaspoon whole allspice
Add
    1 cup Jamaica (dark) rum
    1 cup brandy
Serve hot. *Makes about 40 glasses.*

Regent Punch

Mix
    1 quart rye whiskey
    1 quart rum
    1 quart strong tea
    Juice 6 lemons
    Juice 6 oranges
    1 pound sugar
When ready to serve, pour over ice in a
punch bowl. Add
    1 quart champagne
    1 quart soda water
Makes about 40 glasses.

Fish House Punch

Put in a punch bowl
    1½ cups sugar
    7 cups water or tea
Stir until the sugar dissolves. Add
    3 cups lemon juice
    1 bottle Jamaica (dark) rum
    1 bottle light rum
    1 bottle Cognac
    ½ cup peach brandy
Let stand at least 2 or 3 hours, stirring
occasionally. When ready to serve, pour
over a block of ice in a punch bowl and
stir gently until the punch is chilled.
Makes about 40 glasses.

Club Punch

Mix
 1 quart Burgundy
 1 cup rum
 ⅓ cup brandy
 ⅓ cup Benedictine
 1 quart soda water
 3 sliced oranges
 ½ cup crushed pineapple
 Juice 2 lemons
 1 cup strong hot tea
 Sugar Syrup (p. 36), to taste
Pour over ice in a punch bowl. *Makes about 25 glasses.*

Champagne Punch

For a more economical punch, add soda water and more tea. Sweeten to taste wth Sugar Syrup (p. 36).

Mix
 1 cup brandy
 ½ cup rum
 ½ cup Cointreau
 2 cups strong tea
When ready to serve, pour over ice in a punch bowl. Add
 1 gallon champagne
Stir with a ladle. *Makes about 50 glasses.*

Dover Rum Punch

Mix
 1 quart dark rum
 1 quart ginger ale
 1 quart soda water
 ¼ cup Cointreau
 1 cup lemon juice
 2 ounces brandy
 1 cup Sugar Syrup (p. 36)
Pour over ice in a punch bowl. *Makes about 25 glasses.*

Champagne and Sauterne Punch

A perfect wedding punch. If you like, put three well-pricked fresh peaches in the bowl; then add the ice.

Put a block of ice in a punch bowl. Mix
 1 bottle sauterne (a fifth)
 1 teaspoon Angostura bitters
Pour over the ice. Add

 2 bottles dry champagne (fifths)
Makes about 25 punch glasses.

Claret Cup

To garnish, add ¼ cup diced pineapple and ¼ cup halved fresh strawberries.

Mix and stir well
 1 quart claret
 ⅓ cup sugar
 ½ orange, sliced
 ½ lemon, sliced
Cover. Chill 1 hour. Add
 1 quart soda water
Pour over ice in a large pitcher or punch bowl. *Serves 12.*

Claret Punch. Add 1 cup orange juice, 1 cup lemon juice, 2 cups Sugar Syrup (p. 36) and 1 quart water. *Serves 25.*

Sauterne Cup

Ripe strawberries are a perfect garnish.

Mix
 ¼ cup brandy
 ¼ cup Curaçao
 Rind ½ orange
 Rind ½ lemon
 ¼ cup sugar
Cover and let stand 2 hours. Add
 1 quart sauterne
Strain and chill. Just before serving, remove the rind. Add
 1 quart soda water or champagne, chilled
Garnish with
 Mint leaves
 Few slices orange
Serves 12.

Whiskey Cup

Mix
 2 quarts whiskey
 1½ cups sugar
 Juice 3 lemons
 2 oranges, sliced thin
Stir until the sugar dissolves. Add
 ¼ bottle grenadine
 2 quarts soda water
Pour over ice in a punch bowl. *Serves 25.*

Cocktails

Chill both the ingredients and the mixing glass or shaker to keep the ice from melting so fast that it dilutes the cocktails as they are being chilled. Prepare one round of cocktails at a time.

Cocktail recipes are countless and varied. Those which follow are a few of the standard ones, but liquor stores will give you pamphlets full of others.

To serve cocktails very cold, chill the glasses or keep them filled with crushed ice until you are ready to pour the drinks.

A jigger holds 1½ ounces.

To shake. Measure the ingredients into the shaker. Add cracked ice. Put on the cover and shake hard until thoroughly chilled.

To stir. Measure the ingredients into a tall pitcher or glass. Add ice cubes. Stir with a long-handled spoon until thoroughly chilled.

Alexander Cocktail

Shake together
   1 jigger gin or brandy
   1½ tablespoons crème de cacao
   1½ tablespoons heavy cream
   Cracked ice

Bloody Mary

Shake together
   1 jigger tomato juice
   ½ jigger vodka
   1 tablespoon lemon juice (or less)
   Dash of Worcestershire
   Salt and pepper to taste
   Cracked ice
Strain into a cocktail glass.

Champagne Cocktail

Put a small lump of sugar in a champagne glass. Add a dash of Angostura bitters. Fill the glass with iced champagne. Add a twist of lemon peel.

Old-Fashioned Cocktail

Add fruit, if you like — a cherry, a slice of lemon or orange, or a pineapple stick.

Put in an old-fashioned glass
   1 lump sugar
   2 dashes of Angostura bitters
   1 tablespoon boiling water
Stir until the sugar melts. Add
   2 ice cubes, cracked
   1 jigger rye or Bourbon
Stir and add a dash of
   Soda water

Daiquiri Cocktail

Shake together
   1 jigger white rum
   Juice of ½ lemon or 1 small lime
   1 teaspoon sugar
   Finely shaved ice
Strain into a cocktail glass.

Frozen Daiquiri. Mix in an electric blender 1 minute or until the consistency of sherbet. Pour, without straining, into a chilled champagne glass or sherbet glass.

Manhattan Cocktail

Stir together until well chilled
   1 jigger whiskey
   ½ jigger sweet vermouth (or part dry vermouth)
   ½ teaspoon maraschino cherry juice (from the cherry jar)
   1 or 2 ice cubes
Strain into a cocktail glass. Add
   Maraschino cherry

Martini Cocktail

A Gibson is a very dry martini with a cocktail onion in it.

Measure into a cocktail pitcher gin (or vodka) and dry vermouth in any proportion from 3 parts gin or vodka to 1 of vermouth (the old standard) to 5 to 1 for a very dry martini. Add ice cubes and stir until well chilled. Strain into cocktail glasses. Add a twist of lemon peel, a pitted olive or a cocktail onion.

Whiskey Sour

Instead of lemon juice and sugar, you can use a tablespoon each of frozen lemonade concentrate and water.

Shake together
  1 jigger whiskey
  Juice of ½ lemon
  1 teaspoon sugar
  Cracked ice
Strain into an old-fashioned glass. Garnish with a maraschino cherry.

Long Drinks

Tom Collins

Put 2 or 3 ice cubes in a tall glass. Add 1 teaspoon fine sugar dissolved in the juice of ½ lemon. Add 2 ounces gin (1 large jigger). Fill the glass with soda water. Stir well.

Rum Collins. Use rum in place of gin.
Whiskey Collins. Use whiskey (any type) in place of gin.
Brandy Collins. Use brandy in place of gin.

Highball

Put a jigger of whiskey in a highball glass. Add 1 or 2 ice cubes. Fill the glass with plain or soda water.

Gin Fizz

Shake together
  1 jigger gin or sloe gin
  Juice of ½ lemon
  1 teaspoon sugar
  Cracked ice
Strain into a highball glass. Fill with soda water.

Gin Rickey

Put in a tall glass
  2 or 3 ice cubes
  1 jigger gin
  Juice of ½ lime

Fill the glass with
  Soda water
Stir.

Gin and Tonic

Refreshing on a summer afternoon.

Put in a tall glass
  2 or 3 ice cubes
  1 jigger gin
  1 slice of lime or lemon
Fill the glass with
  Quinine water

Mint Julep

Allow 2 ounces Bourbon or rye whiskey for each julep.

Set tall thin glasses or silver julep cups on saucers or a tray so that you will not have to touch them and disturb the frost as it forms. Set in the refrigerator or freezer compartment.

When ready to serve, put in each glass a sprig of mint, a lump of sugar and a teaspoon of whiskey. Crush with a spoon. Fill to the brim with finely shaved ice. Tamp down hard. Pour in part of the whiskey and stir gently with a long-handled spoon. Add more ice, tamp down, add whiskey, and continue until the glass is full of ice, packed hard.

Garnish with a generous bouquet of mint.

Hors d'Oeuvres

Serving interesting appetizers as the first course for dinner or luncheon has become increasingly popular, which means that the hostess who is also the cook may prepare this part of the meal well in advance. It may take the place of the soup course, or—for a more elaborate meal—soup can be served after the hors d'oeuvres.

Hors d'Oeuvres as the First Course

Served at the table, hors d'oeuvres may be more elaborate than appetizers passed with cocktails in the living room. It is sometimes pleasant to serve the cocktails or sherry at the table.

In addition to the recipes in this chapter, see the recipes for fruit juice cocktails and others in the chapter on Beverages; fruit cocktails and other ways to present fruit as the appetizing start of a meal—for example, Guatemala Orange Cup (p. 355) and Watermelon Cocktail (p. 361) in the chapter on Fruits; and highly seasoned shellfish dishes, such as Oysters Casino (p. 145), Oysters in Sherry Cream (p. 146) and Deviled Crabs (p. 138), which can be served in hot ramekins or scallop shells. Browse through the section on Appetizers for other ideas— Guacamole (p. 53), Caviar (p. 54), Smoked Salmon (p. 55) and Liver Pâté (p. 56) are all popular.

Hors d'Oeuvres Platter

Also an idea as the main course at lunch. A special hors d'oeuvre dish is divided into sections, but any large platter or large round plate will do.

Make an attractive arrangement with a variety of hors d'oeuvres and garnish with sprigs of watercress or parsley. Include at least one hearty hors d'oeuvre, one salad, vegetable or fruit, and one highly seasoned relish.

Eggs. Eggs à la Mimosa (p. 102) or hard-cooked eggs, sliced, and sprinkled with finely cut parsley, chives or watercress.

Fish. Anchovies, herring, smoked salmon, sardines (with wedges of lemon or thin slices of onion), shrimp with mayonnaise, canned or cooked salmon with Tartare Sauce (p. 97) and cucumber dice, tiny cream puff or pastry shells filled with lobster, shrimp or crab salad.

Fruits. Avocado or melon in thin strips. Prosciutto and Melon (p. 45).

Relishes. Celery, green or ripe olives, pickled onions, radishes, finely cut Pickled Beets (p. 238).

Marinated vegetables. Cover with French dressing cooked or canned artichoke hearts or bottoms, fresh okra, whole string beans, asparagus tips or mushrooms. Sprinkle with minced onion and parsley. Uncooked vegetables are delicious this way, too—carrot slivers, cauliflowerets, sliced cucumbers and sliced mushrooms.

Vegetable salads. Russian Salad, Allerton Salad or other mixed vegetable salads (p. 274). Also sliced tomatoes sprinkled with chopped chives, parsley or watercress.

Antipasto

*The Italian version of hors d'oeuvres.
As a convenience, have on hand prepared antipasto, which is marketed in
jars, ready to chill and serve.*

Arrange on individual plates a small
serving of each type of appetizer listed
below. Garnish with Italian olives. Serve
with crisp bread sticks.

> A vegetable, such as Green Beans
> Fiesole (p. 44), Celery Remou-
> lade (p. 44) or Artichokes Vinai-
> grette (p. 274).
> Prosciutto, sliced cold chicken or
> veal, sardines, anchovies, chunks
> of lobster or tuna or Stuffed Egg
> Salad (p. 279). See also Prosciutto
> and Melon (p. 45).
> Tomato chunks or sliced cucumber
> in French dressing or Russian
> Salad (p. 274).

Plateau Prunier

*The pattern is from a famous restaurant;
vary it as you like.*

On each plate put 2 or 3 scallop shells
or deep oyster shells. Fill each shell with
a different hors d'oeuvre such as shrimp,
crab or lobster in mayonnaise, Oyster
Cocktail (p. 45, Seafood Cocktail) and
Russian Salad (p. 274). On each plate
put a tiny roll, split, buttered, and filled
with smoked salmon.

Avocados (Alligator Pears)

*Hearty enough for the main luncheon
dish when filled with chicken or seafood
salad.*

Prepare half an avocado for each person.
Cut in half lengthwise. Remove the seed
but do not pare.

Fill with highly seasoned Tomato Cocktail Sauce (p. 45). Or sprinkle with lemon
juice and a few grains of salt and fill with

Chicken (p. 278) or Lobster Salad (p. 280)
or with seasoned cooked or canned
shrimp or crab meat.

Green Beans Fiesole

*Also excellent as an unusual relish, or in
place of salad.*

Wash and snip off the ends from
> 1 pound tender young green beans
Add
> ½ cup water
Cook until just tender (not more than
10 minutes). Drain, reserving the cooking water. To ⅓ cup of the water add
> ⅓ cup cider vinegar or wine vinegar
> ⅓ cup salad oil
> 1 teaspoon salt
> 1 onion, sliced thin
> 1 clove garlic, split
> ¼ teaspoon orégano
Pour over the beans. Cover and chill at
least 6 hours.

Celery Root Remoulade

*May be one of the items for a buffet or
smörgåsbord.*

Cut celery root or celeriac in julienne
strips. Cover with boiling water and
cook 1 minute. Drain, cover with French
dressing, and refrigerate at least 6 hours.
Drain and moisten with mayonnaise
highly seasoned with prepared mustard
and chopped parsley. Add (for 2 cups) 1
tablespoon capers and 1 sour pickle,
chopped fine.

Tomato Hors d'Oeuvres

Peel small ripe tomatoes.

I. Scoop out the centers. Chill and stuff
with caviar, any mixed vegetable salad,
or Chicken, Lobster, Tuna or Crab Meat
Salad (pp. 278–280). Serve on lettuce.

II. Cut in half. Top with a spoonful of
cottage cheese. Serve on lettuce with
Russian dressing (p. 290).

Tomatoes High Wick

A perfect beginning for a summer dinner.

Put through a grinder
  7 large ripe tomatoes
  1 small white onion
  1½ teaspoons salt
Season to taste with
  Freshly ground pepper
Put in a freezing tray. Chill until icy.
Mix
  5 tablespoons mayonnaise
  1 tablespoon finely cut parsley
  1 teaspoon curry powder
Stir the tomatoes well and spoon into bowls. Top with the mayonnaise mixture. *Serves 4.*

Prosciutto and Melon

Peel and seed cantaloupe or honeydew melon. Cut in thin slices. Arrange on individual plates alternately with thin slices of prosciutto ham.

Seafood Coquilles

Delicious as the main course at luncheon.

Mix creamed diced lobster, shrimp, crab meat and sautéed sliced mushrooms. Season to taste with Worcestershire, sherry or brandy.
Spoon into scallop shells or individual baking dishes. Sprinkle with a thick layer of grated Parmesan cheese. Put a square of butter (about 1 tablespoon) on each. Stick a toothpick through the butter to hold it in place until it melts.

Brown in the broiler. Remove the toothpicks. Serve piping hot with small brown bread sandwiches.

Seafood Cocktail

(oysters, clams or cooked or canned crab meat, lobster, shrimp or scallops)
If you like, combine two or more such as crab, lobster and shrimp.

Use about ⅓ cup of seafood for each serving. Mix with Cocktail Sauce or Sauce Remoulade (below) or serve the sauce separately. Put on lettuce or watercress in chilled dessert glasses.

Cocktail Sauce

To use as a dip, mix with mayonnaise or cream cheese.

Mix and let stand at least 2 hours
  ½ cup tomato catsup
  3 tablespoons cider vinegar or lemon juice
  10 drops Tabasco
  Salt and pepper to taste

To vary, add 1 teaspoon each of chopped parsley, chopped chives and horseradish and season with prepared mustard and Worcestershire to taste. Or add finely chopped celery or parsley.

Sauce Remoulade

Perfect with shrimp or lobster. The mustard should be mild.

Mix
  1 cup mayonnaise
  1 teaspoon lemon juice
  3 tablespoons chopped chives
  3 tablespoons chopped parsley
  Dijon or Louisiana mustard to taste
Let stand at least 2 hours to blend.

Oysters or Clams
on the Half Shell

Open the oysters (p. 144) or clams (p. 135), or have it done at the market if it can be done shortly before serving time. Leave each oyster or clam in the deep half of the shell. Put 4 or 6 on each plate. To keep them appetizingly cold, set them on a layer of finely crushed ice.

Serve with Cocktail Sauce (below), wedges of lemon, grated horseradish, Tabasco or Worcestershire. The cocktail sauce may be in tiny dishes in the middle of each plate.

For a cocktail party, put the oysters or clams on a large platter on a bed of crushed ice.

Appetizers

Cocktails before dinner need only the simplest accompaniments but they should be perfect of their kind. Olives, salted nuts, popcorn or potato chips are good with drinks. Unless the nuts are freshly toasted (p. 507), heat them in the oven (350°) long enough to make them crisp. Homemade wafers and pastries (pp. 50–51) are a special treat.

Cocktail party fare may be as hearty as for a buffet supper, but it is usually "finger food." Have at least one hot dish such as Swedish Meat Balls (p. 170) and a conversation piece such as Party Cheese Ball (p. 51) or Quiche Lorraine (p. 115). A Cocktail Bowl (p. 53) is a refreshing contrast to heartier foods.

Pecan Surprises

Put perfect pecan halves together in pairs with a filling of anchovy paste, pâté de foie gras, Mock Pâté de Foie Gras (p. 56) or other canapé spread.

Curried Peanuts

Spread salted peanuts in a shallow pan. Sprinkle with curry powder and dot with butter. Heat in a 350° oven, stirring several times.

Cocktail Grapes

Slit Malaga or Tokay grapes without cutting all the way through. Remove the seeds. Stuff with cream cheese blended with Roquefort and highly seasoned with onion juice, salt and Worcestershire. Smooth the filling along the cut. Chill.

Cocktail Olives

All sorts of olives are good with drinks. Especially delicious are pitted ripe olives, stuffed with toasted almonds or filberts or with bits of anchovy.

Garlic Olives

Pour out part of the juice from a pint jar of stuffed olives. Add to the jar the juice of 2 limes and a cut clove of garlic. Close the jar. Let stand 24 hours.

Crackers and Wafers

Packaged crackers vary endlessly in shape, size and seasoning. Some are tasty enough to serve as interesting accompaniments to beverages or salads. Others are simple and so are good with dips and spreads (pp. 47ff.) or with cheese as a satisfying epilogue to a meal.

Store crackers in tightly closed packages or tins. If they lose their crispness, heat them in a moderate (350°) oven for a few minutes before you serve them.

Toasted Crackers. Spread simple crackers lightly with butter. Sprinkle with grated cheese or not, as you like. Place on a cooky sheet and brown delicately in the broiler or in a 350° oven.

Souffléed Crackers. *Only old-fashioned unsalted crackers (usually called "common crackers") will puff up successfully.* Cover with ice water, soak 8 minutes and drain. Place on a cooky sheet and dot with butter. Bake at 500° until puffed (10 minutes). Reduce the heat to 375° and bake until the crackers are browned (about 45 minutes).

Corn Crisps

Wonderful with drinks, soups or salads.

Set the oven at 425°. Butter 2 cooky sheets or use heavy unbuttered pans or lay pieces of foil on pans. Mix
   ½ cup corn meal (white or yellow)
   1 teaspoon salt

Stir in
   ¾ cup boiling water
   2 tablespoons butter
Arrange by teaspoonfuls on the cooky sheets, no more than 10 to each sheet, to leave plenty of room for spreading. Sprinkle with
   Celery seed or poppyseed
Bake until delicately brown (about 8 minutes). Let stand a moment to stiffen slightly, then remove carefully with a wide spatula. Repeat until all the batter is baked. *Makes 48 2-inch wafers.*

Cocktail Dips

Many savory mixtures are adaptable as dips. See the recipes which follow for dips and spreads and also cocktail sauces (p. 45) and sandwich fillings (p. 338). Thin, if necessary, with mayonnaise or sour cream. Prepared spreads are convenient, but may need more seasoning.

Put the dip in a bowl. Have ready a plate of crisp packaged wafers or crackers, potato chips, Melba toast, pretzel sticks, small squares of hot toast or homemade Corn Crisps (above). Each person dips his own.

Sour Cream Dip

Mix
   ½ pint thick sour cream
   1 package dried onion soup mix or a
      small jar of red caviar or 1 cup
      drained canned minced clams
Stir well, cover, and chill at least 2 hours.

Deviled Ham Dip

Mash together
   1 small can deviled ham
   2 hard-cooked eggs, chopped
Thin with
   Mayonnaise, yogurt or sour cream
Season more highly, if you like, with
   Curry or Worcestershire

Mushroom Dip

Also good as a filling for Rolled Sandwiches (p. 338), toasted before serving.

Melt
   2 tablespoons butter
Add
   ½ pound mushrooms, chopped fine
Cook 5 minutes. Sprinkle with
   1 teaspoon flour
Stir and add
   ½ cup heavy cream
Cook until thick. Season with
   Salt, pepper and nutmeg
Serve hot with toast or crackers. Best of all, serve in a chafing dish or electric saucepan.

Canapés

A canapé is a tiny open sandwich spread with a savory mixture. The base may be a crisp cracker or a small piece of bread toasted on one side. The bread may be cut in squares, rounds, triangles or crescents.

Spread the base generously with Savory Butter (below) or one of the spreads on pp. 48–49. Spread toast canapés on the untoasted side well to the edge.

Garnish, if at all, very simply with a shake of paprika, a leaf of parsley or watercress, a slice of stuffed olive, or a bit of chopped cooked egg white or crumbled egg yolk. Press the garnish lightly into the spread so that it will not fall off.

Savory Butter

Cream butter until it is soft and fluffy. Season with anchovy or sardine paste or other fish or meat pastes, minced shrimp or lobster, sieved pimiento, caviar, chutney, chopped pickle, grated horseradish, finely cut watercress or parsley. Season to taste with French dressing, prepared mustard, a few drops of onion juice or lemon juice or other seasonings.

Roquefort Butter

Cream butter. Blend in crumbs of Roquefort and a few drops of onion juice.

Bleu Cheese Butter

Put in a small heavy bowl
    ½ pound bleu cheese
    ¼ pound soft butter
Blend with a fork. Add
    ¼ cup port
Set in a pan of hot water and beat until smooth and creamy. Add
    2 tablespoons chopped parsley
    Few drops onion juice
Cover the bowl and chill several hours to blend the flavors. Take from the refrigerator long enough ahead of time to serve at room temperature, not icy cold.

Cream Cheese Butter

Mash cream cheese. Add cream or melted butter until soft enough to spread. Season highly to taste with grated onion, chopped chives, chopped stuffed or ripe olives or chopped parsley.

Anchovy Spread

Mash
    1 small package cream cheese (3 oz.)
Add
    2 teaspoons capers
    ½ teaspoon grated onion
    1 teaspoon anchovy paste
    Few drops Worcestershire
Mix well. Stir in
    Heavy cream or mayonnaise
until thin enough to spread.

To use as a dip, thin with more cream.

Avocado and Bacon Spread

Mash avocado with a silver fork (to prevent discoloring). Mix with crumbled crisply cooked bacon. Season with lemon juice, salt and pepper to taste.

Ripe Olive Spread I

Put dabs on canapé bases spread with cream cheese.

Put in a jar
    1 small tin chopped ripe olives
    2 drops olive oil
    1 clove garlic
Close the jar. Refrigerate at least 1 day.

Ripe Olive Spread II

Moisten chopped ripe olives with mayonnaise or mix with cream cheese and mayonnaise. Season highly with Worcestershire, chopped parsley and paprika.

Liver Sausage Spread

Mash liver sausage. Moisten with melted butter and season with port or brandy.

Chicken Liver Spread

Sauté livers in butter 5 minutes. Mash with a fork and add crumbled cooked bacon, chopped hard-cooked egg or chopped cooked or canned mushrooms. Season highly with minced onion, salt and pepper. Add mayonnaise until thin enough to spread.

Chicken Liver Balls. Keep the mixture firm enough to shape in small balls. Roll in chopped pickled beets and serve on cocktail picks.

Lobster, Shrimp or Tuna Spread

Chop the fish fine. For 1 cupful, hard-cook 4 eggs. Mash the yolks and add to the fish. Moisten with melted butter and a little cream, sweet or sour. Season with salt, cayenne, mustard and a few drops of beef extract.

Hot Canapés

Prepare toasted canapé bases (p. 48). Spread the untoasted side with any of the mixtures suggested below or invent your own savory spread. Put on a cooky sheet.

Just before serving, broil or bake at 400° until thoroughly heated or until the bacon crisps or the cheese melts. Serve immediately on a warm plate.

Spreads for Hot Canapés

Bacon Spread. Mince uncooked bacon and mix with chopped ripe olives or with grated cheese seasoned with mustard and paprika.

Bacon and Cheese Spread. Grind together equal amounts of bacon and sharp Cheddar cheese. Season to taste with onion salt, pepper and Worcestershire. Especially good spread on split common crackers (small size). Bake about 15 minutes at 350°, then brown lightly under the broiler.

Cheese Spread. Slice sharp Cheddar cheese and cut slightly smaller than the canapés. Sprinkle with paprika.

Parmesan Cheese Spread. Moisten grated Parmesan cheese with heavy cream and season to taste.

Onion Spread. Mix chopped onion with mayonnaise. Top or not with grated cheese before baking.

Mushroom Spread. Use Mushroom Dip (p. 47) with a square of bacon on top.

Peanut Butter Spread. Spread the canapé base with peanut butter and sprinkle with bits of uncooked bacon before baking.

Finnan Haddie Canapés

Piping hot, these are excellent with drinks.

Melt
   3 tablespoons butter
Add
   2 teaspoons finely chopped onion
   2 mushroom caps, chopped fine
Cook 5 minutes. Sprinkle with
   2 tablespoons flour
Stir in
   ⅔ cup thin cream
Bring to a boil. Add
   2 tablespoons grated cheese
   2 egg yolks, slightly beaten
   1 cup cooked shredded finnan haddie
     (p. 133)
Season to taste with
   Cayenne
Pile on
   Circular pieces of hot toast
Sprinkle with
   Grated cheese
   Buttered bread crumbs
Just before serving, bake at 375° until brown. *Makes 24 or more.*

Hot Seafood Canapés

Spread canapé bases with any of the following and bake or broil.

Minced clams (fresh or canned), mixed with mayonnaise and seasoned with curry.

Chopped crabmeat, lobster, shrimp or tuna, creamed or mixed with mayonnaise. Season highly. Before baking sprinkle with grated cheese.

Deviled Ham Canapés

Prepare toasted canapé bases (p. 48). Spread with deviled ham. Add onion soup mix to mayonnaise (1 teaspoon or more for ¼ cup mayonnaise). Spread over the ham.

Just before serving, heat in a 450° oven or in the broiler until delicately brown.

Cocktail Pastries

Plain Pastry (p. 407) makes delicious accompaniments for drinks. The possibilities are many. Here are a few suggestions.

Savory Rounds

Roll out Plain Pastry (p. 407). Sprinkle with grated cheese and paprika, or spread lightly with anchovy paste or finely chopped ham or ham spread mixed with melted butter. Cover with a sheet of wax paper and roll lightly to press the cheese or the spread into the pastry. Remove the paper. Cut in fancy shapes. Bake at 450° until pale brown.

Cocktail Bouchées

Make very small Tart Shells (p. 424), Cream Puff Shells (p. 428) or Swedish Timbales (p. 430). Fill with finely cut Lobster (p. 280) or Chicken Salad (p. 278) or any spread.

Cocktail Pinwheels

Roll Plain Pastry (p. 407) into an oblong ⅛ inch thick. Spread with prepared mixture. Roll up firmly, beginning with the long side. Cut in pieces ⅓ inch thick. Bake at 425° about 15 minutes and serve hot.

Anchovy Tuna Filling. Mix 1 can tuna (not drained) with 3 chopped anchovies, 1 tablespoon lemon juice, 2 tablespoons tomato paste and ¼ teaspoon Tabasco.

Bleu Cheese Filling. Mix bleu cheese and cream cheese and moisten with cream.

Mushroom Filling. Sauté finely chopped mushrooms in butter. Season to taste.

Deviled Ham Filling. Add finely chopped pickle if liked.

Benne Pastries

If brown sesame seed is not available, put white sesame in a small heavy skillet and cook and stir over low heat until it browns a little.

Prepare
  Half the recipe for Plain Pastry (p. 407)
Mix into it
  ½ cup sesame seed
  Few drops Worcestershire
Roll ¼ inch thick. Cut out with a tiny biscuit cutter. Bake at 400° until lightly browned (about 8 minutes).

Cocktail Turnovers

Fill tiny turnovers (p. 426) with a bit of sharp cheese or any savory mixture such as the spreads on pp. 48–49. Serve hot.

Rissolettes

Roll Plain Pastry (p. 407) or Puff Paste (p. 409) ¼ inch thick. Shape with a small round cutter dipped in flour. Place in the center of half the pieces 1 teaspoon highly seasoned filling of chopped meat, sausage, fish or cheese. Wet the edges, cover with the remaining pieces, press and prick well. Bake at 450° until pale brown (about 6 minutes).

Caviar Rissolettes. Fill with caviar seasoned with lemon juice.

Piroshki. *Traditionally made of Puff Paste.* Fill with a mixture of ham, chives, onion, parsley and hard-cooked egg (all chopped), moistened with sour cream and seasoned with salt and cayenne. Another good filling is sautéed mushrooms, green onions and hard-cooked egg (all chopped). Serve hot with sour cream.

Cheese Appetizers and Wafers

One of the most popular accompaniments for drinks is an assortment of cheese on a large plate, served with crisp crackers.

Cocktail Cheese Balls

Mash cream cheese. Add any of the seasonings suggested below and shape in ¾-inch balls. Dust with paprika or roll in finely cut dried beef, chopped nuts or crushed potato chips. Serve on cocktail picks.

Walnuts, chopped fine, and brandy to taste.
Onions or chives, chopped fine, and prepared mustard or horseradish to taste.
Chopped ham or shrimp.

Cheese Roll

Serve with cocktails, coffee or salad.

Put through the grinder
    ¼ pound American cheese
    ½ cup unblanched almonds
    Sliver of garlic
Add and blend well
    1 3-ounce package pimiento cream cheese
    1 3-ounce package cream cheese
Pat into a roll. Sprinkle a thick layer of paprika on wax paper. Coat the cheese roll with paprika and roll tightly in the paper. Store in the refrigerator. Serve with crisp crackers.

Party Cheese Ball

    1 cup chopped pecans or parsley
Set aside half. Add the rest to
    1 pound Roquefort
    2 pounds cream cheese
    1 3-ounce package processed sharp Cheddar
    1 onion, minced fine
    1 teaspoon Worcestershire
    Salt to taste
Blend well and shape in a ball. Roll in the reserved parsley or pecans. Chill. Place on a large plate and surround with crisp crackers. *For a large cocktail party.*

Liptauer Cheese

Serve with beer, cocktails or salad.
Cream together
    2 3-ounce packages cream cheese
    ¼ cup butter
Add
    1 teaspoon capers
    1 teaspoon paprika
    2 anchovies, chopped fine
    1 shallot or 1 slice onion, minced
    ½ teaspoon caraway seed
    ½ teaspoon salt

Mix thoroughly and press into a small mold or form in a roll and wrap in wax paper. Let stand several hours in the refrigerator to blend the flavors.

Stuffed Edam Cheese

Scoop out the center of an Edam cheese. Measure, and add an equal amount of Roquefort. Grind together in the food chopper. Add about half as much butter as cheese. Blend well and season with Worcestershire or brandy. Pile on a plate or spoon into the cheese shell.

Sherried Cheese

Serve with cocktails, with salad, or, in the English fashion, as the savory last course at dinner.

Put through the food chopper
    ½ pound Cheddar cheese
Add
    3 tablespoons sherry
    2 tablespoons butter, creamed
    1 teaspoon prepared mustard
    ½ teaspoon salt
    Few grains cayenne

Cheese Wafers

It is not necessary to bake all the wafers at once. Bake as many as you need, wrap the rest of the pastry tightly, and store it in the refrigerator to use another day. Freshen leftover wafers by heating a few minutes in a 350° oven.

Put in a bowl and let stand to soften
    1 6-ounce roll blended sharp cheese
    ½ cup butter
Cream together. Blend in
    1 cup pastry flour
    ¼ teaspoon salt
Pat into a firm ball, cover, and chill at least 1 hour. Roll, half at a time, about ⅛ inch thick. Cut out with a small cooky cutter and place on an unbuttered cooky sheet or on sheets of aluminum foil on a cooky sheet. In warm weather, chill ½ hour or longer before baking.

Bake at 400° until delicately brown (about 5 minutes). Serve warm or not with drinks or salad. *Makes 60 or more wafers.*

Cheese Shortbreads. *Surprisingly good sprinkled very delicately with confec-* tioners' sugar while they are hot. Roll ½ inch thick. Cut with a 1-inch biscuit cutter. Bake at 400°.

Savory Cheese Squares. Season more highly with cayenne, Worcestershire and garlic salt. Pat into an oblong ½ inch thick. Cut in 1-inch squares with a knife or pastry wheel and bake.

Cheese Straws

Prepare Plain Pastry (p. 407) and roll into an oblong ¼ inch thick. Sprinkle lightly with grated Parmesan cheese or mixed Parmesan and Edam. Sprinkle with salt and a few grains of cayenne.

Fold double, press the edges firmly together, fold again, and roll out as before. Again sprinkle with cheese, fold and roll. Repeat twice more so that you will have four layers of cheese and pastry.

Cut in strips ¼ inch by 5 inches. Bake 8 minutes at 450°.

Cheese Pastries

Prepare Plain Pastry (p. 407). Roll ¼ inch thick. Cut with a small cooky cutter or in oblongs or diamonds. Sprinkle with grated cheese and pat the cheese in lightly. Bake at 400° until the cheese melts and browns (about 10 minutes). Serve hot.

Cheese Puffs

Put in a small saucepan
    ½ cup boiling water
    2 tablespoons butter
When the butter melts, add
    ¼ cup flour
    ¼ cup grated cheese
    ⅛ teaspoon salt
    Few grains paprika
Stir and cook 3 minutes. Add
    1 egg
Beat with a wooden spoon until stiff. Arrange by half-teaspoonfuls on a buttered cooky sheet. Bake 15 minutes at 375°. Reduce the heat to 350° and bake until the puffs are dry (10 to 15 minutes). *Makes 30 1-inch puffs.*

Cheese Brambles

Tasty with soups, salads and drinks.

Make Cream Cheese Turnovers (p. 427), adding to the pastry a dash of cayenne and a few drops of Worcestershire. Instead of jelly or jam, put a ½-inch piece of sharp cheese on each. Chill until ready to bake. Bake at 450° until brown (about 10 minutes). Serve hot.

Vegetable Appetizers

Many raw vegetables are delicious as appetizers. They must be top quality — fresh and crisp. Some of the best are carrots, cauliflower, celery, tiny whole tomatoes, and turnips. Cut the vegetables in small, attractive pieces or slices and chill. Some cooked vegetables are excellent, too, especially cooked or canned artichoke hearts and asparagus tips. Drain and marinate in French dressing.

Cocktail Bowl

An attractive way to serve a variety of appetizers.

Season mayonnaise highly with curry or Worcestershire. Thin with a little cream, sweet or sour. Put in a small bowl in the center of a large round plate. Around the bowl arrange a variety of raw and cooked vegetables. Also neat pieces of lobster meat and whole shrimp, if you like.

Cocktail Artichoke Leaves

Cook an artichoke (p. 234). Cool. Pull off the leaves and spread them, hollow side up, on a large plate or platter. (Save the base to add to a salad.) On the fleshy end of each leaf, put a shrimp and a bit of avocado. Top with a dab of mayonnaise delicately seasoned with curry.

Guacamole

If you make this good spread long ahead of serving time, put a thin layer of mayonnaise over it to be sure it will not darken. Stir in the mayonnaise before you serve the guacamole.

Mash avocado with a silver fork. Season highly with onion juice or onion salt, lemon juice, salt and pepper. Beat in mayonnaise, tomato pulp or tomato catsup until the consistency of whipped cream. To season more highly, add chili powder.

Pile in a bowl and serve with corn wafers or Corn Crisps (p. 47).

Stuffed Celery

Wash and dry pieces of celery from the heart. Leave on a bit of the foliage as decoration. If the pieces are large, cut in 1½-inch lengths after filling. Fill the grooves with:

Caviar sprinkled with a few drops of onion juice.

Cream cheese highly seasoned with French dressing, tomato catsup and Worcestershire sauce.

Cream cheese blended with Roquefort crumbs and softened with mayonnaise or sour cream.

Prepared cheese spread.

Chopped raw mushrooms seasoned with Worcestershire and garlic salt.

Celery Rounds

Wash and dry two perfect stalks of celery. Fill with any cream cheese filling and press together. Wrap tightly in wax paper and chill. Cut in ½-inch slices and place on rounds of buttered brown bread.

Eggplant Caviar

Bake at 350° until soft
  1 eggplant
Peel, chop fine, and set aside. Put in a pan
  ½ cup minced onion
  ¼ cup olive oil
Cook together slowly until the onion is soft. Add the eggplant. Add
  4 tablespoons tomato paste
Cook and stir until thick (about 15 minutes). Add
  1 tablespoon lemon juice
Season with
  Salt, pepper and garlic salt
Cool. Mound on a serving dish.

Pickled Mushrooms

For cocktails or as a relish with cold chicken or beef.

Mix and boil 10 minutes
  ⅔ cup mild cider vinegar or wine vinegar
  6 peppercorns
  1 slice onion
  1 sprig parsley
  1 bay leaf
  3 celery leaves or 1 teaspoon celery salt

Wash
  ½ pound mushrooms
Cut the stems even with the caps. (Use the stems for soup, a sauce, or Duxelles, p. 249.) Peel if the skin is discolored. Slice very large mushrooms. Leave small ones whole. Cover with
  2 cups boiling water
  2 teaspoons salt
Simmer 5 minutes and drain. Pour the vinegar mixture over the mushrooms. Cool. Add
  ¼ cup olive oil
Put in a tightly covered jar. Shake well. Refrigerate at least 1 day, and drain before serving.

Cocktail Mushrooms

Serve Broiled Mushrooms (p. 250) or French-Fried Mushrooms (p. 250) on cocktail picks. Have them piping hot, replenishing them from time to time.

Stuffed Cocktail Mushrooms. Fill perfect mushroom caps (raw or sautéed in butter) with highly seasoned cream cheese or chopped ham mixed with mayonnaise.

Mushrooms à la Grecque

Peel perfect mushrooms. Leave small ones whole. Cut large ones in half. Cover with French dressing. Tuck in 2 bay leaves for each cup of mushrooms. Cover and chill 12 hours or more. Drain (saving the dressing to use on a salad). Serve the mushrooms on cocktail picks or add to a salad.

Fish and Meat Appetizers

Black Caviar

The best imported caviar is one of the great luxuries. Put it in a bowl set in a bed of crushed ice. The classic accompaniments are thin fingers of dry, unbuttered toast, lemon wedges, finely chopped hard-cooked egg white, crumbled hard-cooked egg yolk and finely minced onion.

Red Caviar

Spread on crackers or canapés on a layer of cream cheese or put it in a bowl, ready to dip out.

Caviar Ring

Serve with wafers for a cocktail party or as a first course at dinner.

Rinse a ring mold with cold water. Sprinkle black or red caviar in it. Fill with highly seasoned Tomato Aspic (p. 281). Chill until firm. Turn out on a serving dish. Fill the center with mayonnaise or chopped hard-cooked egg mixed with mayonnaise.

Bacon-Wrapped Oysters

Cooked chicken livers, cooked cocktail sausages, stuffed olives and pickled onions are good this way too.

Wrap oysters in half-slices of bacon. Fasten with toothpicks. Grill in the broiler or bake at 425° until the bacon is crisp. Replace the toothpicks with fresh ones or with croquette sticks.

Smoked Salmon

Smoked salmon is marketed in tins or by the pound. The best is pale pink, fine-grained and not too salty. Serve with lemon wedges, capers, black pepper (freshly ground in a pepper mill) and thin slices of pumpernickel or dark rye bread spread with unsalted butter.

Ham, Dried Beef or Salmon Rolls

Cut thin slices of ham, dried beef or smoked salmon in neat pieces. Spread with cream cheese highly seasoned with prepared mustard or horseradish. Roll up tightly and fasten with a cocktail pick.

Horns of Plenty. Shape in cornucopias. Fill as above or with caviar seasoned with lemon juice or with finely chopped cucumber mixed with mayonnaise.

Cocktail Bacon

Cook strips of lean bacon, keeping them as flat as possible. Drain well. Just before serving, sprinkle with grated Parmesan cheese and set in the broiler long enough to melt the cheese slightly. The strips should be crisp enough to take in the fingers.

Beef Tartare

This raw beef is also delicious made into sandwiches for lunch.

Remove all the fat from high-grade lean raw beef (top round or sirloin). Put twice through the grinder so that it will be very fine. Season to taste with onion juice, salt, pepper and A–1 sauce or Worcestershire. Shape in a loaf.

Serve with squares of toast or sliced and buttered party rye.

Cocktail Sausages or Meat Balls

Pan-fry or broil small sausages or tiny balls of sausage meat or hamburger. Keep hot in a chafing dish or electric saucepan or put on picks and stick in a bright red apple. Swedish Meat Balls (p. 170) are popular, too, with drinks.

Cocktail Croquettes

Make tiny (1-inch) Chicken (p. 228) or Lobster (p. 144) Croquettes. Serve very hot on picks.

Cocktail Fish Balls

Make 1-inch Codfish Balls (p. 132). Serve hot with Cocktail Sauce (p. 45).

Cocktail Puffs

Fill tiny Cream Puffs or Eclair Shells (p. 428) with chopped cooked shrimp mixed with mayonnaise, or with Chicken, Lobster, Shrimp or Crab Meat Salad (pp. 278–280), or with cream cheese blended with Roquefort and beaten with a little heavy cream. See also Cheese Puffs (p. 52).

Liver Pâté

Serve with cocktails, as a first course, or as one item at a buffet supper.

Have ready
    ¼ pound bacon, sliced thin
Line a 1-pint mold with some of the bacon and set it in the refrigerator. Cut the rest in small pieces and cook 5 minutes with
    1 tablespoon chopped shallots or 1 teaspoon grated onion
    1 tablespoon chopped parsley
Add
    ½ pound sliced calves' liver cut in 2-inch pieces
Stir and cook until brown (5 minutes). Set aside until cool. Meanwhile let stand in a bowl
    1 cup bread crumbs
    1 cup milk or consommé
When the liver is cool, put it through a very fine sieve or chop in an electric blender. Stir in
    1 egg yolk
Drain the liquid from the crumbs and set aside. Add the crumbs to the liver mixture. Season to taste with
    Salt, pepper, allspice, marjoram and thyme
Add enough of the liquid to make a thick paste that will drop from a spoon. Pack into the mold. Cover. Set in a pan of hot water. Bake 2 hours at 300°. Cool. Turn out onto a serving dish. Garnish with
    Watercress
    Quartered tomatoes dipped in French dressing

Mock Foie Gras

Remove the skin from
    ½ pound liver sausage
Mash the sausage with a fork. Add
    1 3-ounce package cream cheese
    1 tablespoon melted butter
    1 tablespoon Worcestershire
    Salt and paprika to taste

Blend well. Serve with crackers or thin dry toast, at the table or with cocktails.

As a variation, add ½ cup sliced mushrooms sautéed in butter or season with port or with curry powder.

Chicken Liver Pâté Suprême

A delicacy to serve with drinks or with salad at a summer luncheon.

Put in a pan
    2 tablespoons butter
    2 onions, chopped fine
Cook slowly until the onion is soft. Add
    ½ pound chicken livers
Cook ten minutes. Put in a bowl. Mash with a fork or in a blender. Add to the pan juices
    2 tablespoons dry sherry
Stir and scrape to get all the good brown bits and add to the liver. Cool.
Cream
    ½ cup butter
Stir in the liver. Season with
    Salt, and more sherry if needed
Pack into a small bowl or crock and serve with Melba toast or crackers.

Pâté Maison

An excellent and attractive way to use bits of leftover cooked meat.

Cut the meat in small pieces, add a few slices of raw carrot, and put through the meat grinder, using the finest knife. Season to taste with salt, pepper, melted butter and brandy or sherry. Pack in a small crock or bowl to serve with cocktails, or shape in a loaf to serve at luncheon or supper.

To vary, add a few finely chopped mushrooms or almonds.

Improve canned pâtés (liver, chicken or ham) by combining any two and seasoning as above.

Soups and Chowders

Soup is not served as a first course as regularly as it used to be, but it has come into its own as a main course and as a party beverage. It is often at its best the second day, so do not hesitate to make more than you need for one meal.

Soup as the first course. Allow about ½ cup for each serving. A clear light soup is the best choice if the rest of the meal is hearty. A rich cream soup can supplement a simple main course. For a company dinner, service may be simplified by passing cups of soup in the living room, either in place of cocktails or after them.

Chilled soup is delightfully refreshing in summer. Vichyssoise (p. 68), Madrilène (p. 69), Consommé (p. 71) and Gazpacho (p. 62) are the most popular, but there are many other possibilities. Experiment with chilling leftover soup to serve another day. A thickened soup becomes thicker as it cools; if it is too thick, add consommé or thin cream, season to taste, and chill.

Soup as the main course. Allow plenty of soup for second servings — a cup or more per person. Serve in generous bowls with crusty French or Italian bread and a crisp and colorful salad. The hearty soups listed below are popular as main-course soups, but a lighter soup can be supplemented by sandwiches or crackers and cheese.

Chicken Gumbo (p. 74)
Clam Chowder (p. 77)
Corn Chowder (p. 65)
Fish Chowder (p. 75)
Lobster Stew (p. 78)

Minestrone (p. 62)
Mulligatawny Soup (p. 74)
Oxtail Soup (p. 72)
Oyster Stew (p. 79)
Parsnip Stew (p. 67)
Philadelphia Pepper Pot (p. 74)
Queen Victoria Soup (p. 74)
Scallop Stew (p. 79)
Scotch Broth (p. 72)
Split Pea Soup (p. 67)

Soup as a party beverage. A clear hot broth or bouillon is often a welcome substitute for coffee as a party beverage. Pour it from a handsome pot or coffee urn. Good accompaniments are cheese wafers or individual pizzas or crackers with a variety of cheeses. Olives, celery and salted nuts too, if you like.

The best soups to serve this way are Chicken Broth (p. 72), Consommé (p. 71), Mushroom Bouillon (p. 66), Madrilène (p. 69) or Clam Broth (p. 76). If you use canned broth, improve the seasoning by adding sherry or a trace of curry.

Soup accompaniments. Many packaged wafers and crackers are good with soup. They should be crisp; heat them in the oven to be sure. For a special touch, see the recipes for homemade crisps and wafers (pp. 47, 52). Another idea is to serve chilled Vegetable Relishes (p. 83).

Soup Garnishes

Simple Garnishes

Paprika (for cream soups).
Grated cheese.
Parsley, chives or dill, cut fine.
Slivers of cooked ham or chicken (for cream soups).
Lemon or lime slices (for consommé or chicken broth).
Avocado slices (for consommé, chicken broth, green pea or tomato soup).
Heavy cream beaten slightly (for tomato soup or clam broth).
Sour cream.

Croûtons

Croûtons are the favorite soup garnish for many gourmets. They are usually made in ¼-inch cubes but may be larger or smaller. You may like to make a few extra for a Croûton Omelet (p. 106).

Sautéed Croûtons. Cut the crusts from slices of day-old bread and cut the bread in even cubes. Sauté in a little butter, turning to brown on all sides. Drain on a paper towel.

Baked Croûtons. Spread sliced bread lightly with butter, cut it in cubes, spread on a cooky sheet, and bake at 350° until brown.

Cheese Croûtons

Put on a cooky sheet
    4 slices firm bread (1 or 2 days old)
Toast on one side under the broiler.
Blend
    1 egg yolk
    2 tablespoons butter
    ¼ cup grated Parmesan cheese
Turn the slices over and spread with the cheese mixture. Cut in squares. Bake at 350° until golden-brown.

Pimiento Cream

Force drained canned pimiento through a sieve to make 2 tablespoons purée. Add to ½ cup heavy cream, whipped. Salt to taste.

Royal Custard

Beat slightly
    1 egg
    3 egg yolks
Add
    ½ cup consommé or milk
    ⅛ teaspoon salt
    Few grains nutmeg
    Few grains cayenne
Pour into a buttered custard cup. Put in a pan of hot water and bake at 350° until firm. Cool. Remove from the cup and slice thin. Cut the slices in diamonds or fancy shapes. Serve in consommé or chicken broth.

Chicken Custard

Rub through a sieve (or whirl in a blender with the broth)
    ¼ cup chopped cooked chicken (white meat)
Add
    ¼ cup chicken broth
Stir in
    1 egg, slightly beaten
Season to taste with
    Salt, pepper and celery salt
    Nutmeg or anchovy paste
Bake like Royal Custard (above). Cut in small cubes. Serve in chicken, pea or tomato soup.

Crêpes

Mix
    ½ cup flour
    1 egg, slightly beaten
    ½ cup milk or chicken broth
    Pinch of salt
Make thin pancakes (p. 304) and cut into fine strips. Put a spoonful in each cup of soup. Serve in any clear soup.

Choux Puffs

Almost the same as Cream Puff batter (p. 428). Save a little when you make cream puffs; it freezes well, and ¼ cupful makes about 20 tiny puffs.

Heat to the boiling point
  2 tablespoons milk
  1 teaspoon butter
Add
  ¼ cup flour
  Few grains salt
Stir hard until the mixture forms a ball. Remove from the heat. Add
  1 egg (medium size)
Beat until well mixed. Cool.

Heat fat in a frying kettle to 370°. Drop bits of the pâte from the tip of a teaspoon into the fat. Fry until brown, turning once. Drain on a paper towel.

Put 2 or 3 in each serving of any clear soup. *Makes about 50.*

Parmesan Puffs. Add 2 tablespoons grated Parmesan cheese to the mixture.

Egg Balls

Rub through a sieve
  1 hard-cooked egg yolk
Add
  1 hard-cooked egg white, chopped fine
  ⅛ teaspoon salt
  Few grains cayenne
  ½ teaspoon melted butter
Moisten with
  Raw egg yolk, slightly beaten
Use enough raw egg yolk so that you can shape the mixture. Make marble-sized balls. Poach in boiling water or stock, or roll in flour and sauté in butter. Add a few to each serving of any clear soup.

Butter Dumplings

Cream
  2 tablespoons butter
Beat in
  2 eggs
  ¼ teaspoon salt
  6 tablespoons flour
Drop from a teaspoon into simmering soup and cook 5 minutes. Serve one or two in each bowlful of clear soup.

Canned and Frozen Soups

Many are delicious heated and served just as they come from the can. Others are improved by being diluted with milk, thin cream or consommé instead of water. See also Condensed Soups as Sauces (p. 99).

Season critically to vary the flavor. For example, add nutmeg to chicken soup or mushroom soup, curry to chicken soup with rice, orégano to tomato soup, chili powder to black bean soup and thyme to clam chowder. Heat tomato soup with a bay leaf. Season mock turtle soup with lemon juice, sherry or Madeira. Add chopped clams to frozen potato soup to make clam chowder in a hurry. Add chopped cooked or canned corn to tomato soup.

Garnish as suggested on p. 58.

Combine two soups for a change. Some successful combinations are:

  Chicken with rice and cream of tomato
  Cream of celery and clam chowder
  Cream of celery and cream of tomato
  Cream of chicken and cream of mushroom or celery
  Cream of pea and cream of tomato
  Cream of pea and green turtle
  Scotch broth and consommé
  Tomato bouillon and clam broth

Cheese and Celery Soup

Cook together 5 minutes
  1 tablespoon butter
  1 or 2 tablespoons chopped onion
Add
  1 can condensed celery soup
  Milk (an equal amount)
  1 small package pimiento cream cheese
Cook and stir until the cheese melts.
Serves 4 to 6.

Pea Soup Louise

An elegant but easy dinner party soup.

Simmer together for ½ hour
  1 can condensed cream of pea soup
  ½ cup water
  1 chicken bouillon cube
  ⅛ teaspoon mace
  ¼ teaspoon dried tarragon
When ready to serve, add
  ½ cup cream
  ½ cup dry white wine or champagne
Heat. Garnish with
  Sprigs of fresh mint or tarragon
Serves 4.

Vienna Pea Soup

A satisfying lunch or supper dish.

Put in a pan
  1 tablespoon butter
  1 Vienna sausage or frankfurter, sliced
  1 small onion, diced
Cook slowly 10 minutes. Add
  1 can condensed split pea soup
  Milk (an equal amount)
Heat thoroughly. *Serves 2 or 3.*

Boula

Combine, adding water according to the
directions on the cans
  1 can pea soup
  1 can green turtle soup
Bring to the boiling point. Season to
taste with
  Salt and pepper
  Sherry
Fill individual pottery bowls arranged
on a cooky sheet. Whip

  ½ cup heavy cream
  Few grains salt
Put a spoonful on each bowl. Set under
the broiler a moment to brown the
cream. Serve immediately. *Serves 4 to 6.*

Boula with Cheese. Sprinkle the whipped
cream with grated Parmesan cheese before browning.

Chilled Shrimp Bisque

Mix
  1 can condensed cream of mushroom
    soup
  2 cups milk
  1 small can shrimp, cut small
Season to taste. Add (if you like)
  Sherry
Chill. Top each serving with
  Chopped chives
Serves 4 to 6.

Quick Crab or Shrimp Bisque

Mix
  1 can condensed pea soup
  ½ can condensed tomato soup
  2 cups milk or Chicken Stock (p. 72)
    or canned chicken broth
  ½ to 1 cup flaked crab meat or shrimp
    broken in pieces
Heat. Season to taste with
  Rum, sherry or Worcestershire
Serves 4.

To vary, use a whole can of tomato soup
and 1 cup cream in place of the milk or
stock.

Curry Soup

An easy but unusual dinner party soup.

Chop
  1 tart apple
  1 small onion
Add to
  4 cups consommé
Simmer 20 minutes. Strain. Add
  1 cup cream
  Salt, pepper and curry powder to taste
Serve hot or chilled. *Serves 6.*

Vegetable Soups

Thick vegetable soups are welcome winter fare, either for lunch with crisp, hot crackers and cheese or as a first course at dinner.

Cream soups are popular, too, and may be thickened or not as you choose. As a first course, a more delicate soup is usually preferred, but as the main dish, a thicker soup may be your choice.

To bind (thicken) cream soups, melt 1 tablespoon butter for each 2 cups soup, and stir in 1 tablespoon flour or 1 teaspoon potato flour. Cook slowly until smooth, stirring constantly (about 5 minutes). Add a little of the hot soup, stir well and pour into the rest of the soup. Reheat, stirring constantly. Potato flour is excellent for this as it cooks quickly and smoothly.

Vegetable Soup

Add other vegetables as convenient — shredded cabbage, tomatoes, green beans or corn. For a heartier dish, serve grated cheese to sprinkle on the soup or add noodles.

Put in a deep pan
  4 tablespoons butter
  ½ cup diced carrot
  ½ cup diced turnip
  ½ cup diced celery
  ½ onion, sliced thin
Cook 10 minutes, stirring constantly. Add
  ½ cup diced potatoes
Cover. Cook 2 minutes. Add
  1 quart water, consommé, Brown Stock
    (p. 70) or Chicken Stock (p. 72)
Cook slowly 1 hour or until the vegetables are tender. Add more water, if needed, to make 1 quart. Season with
  Salt and pepper
Add
  1 tablespoon butter
  1 tablespoon chopped parsley
Serves 6 to 8.

Pressure-cooked. Sauté the vegetables 5 minutes in the pressure saucepan. Add 2 cups water and cook at 15 pounds pressure for 3 minutes. Let the pressure drop normally. Add 1 cup stock or water and bouillon cubes or meat concentrate to taste. Add salt and pepper and parsley.

Petite Marmite. This hearty soup should be as thick as a chowder. Make Vegetable Soup, using stock. Omit the potatoes. Add plenty of other vegetables, such as shredded cabbage and green beans. Spoon into generous bowls and sprinkle with freshly grated cheese. Serve with thick slices of crusty French bread.

Cream of Vegetable Soup I

For any leftover vegetables (see next page for cauliflower or spinach) or a combination of several; see also such recipes (below) as Cream of Celery and Cream of Corn Soup. Chopped parsley, chives or hard-cooked egg, or crisp croûtons, add color and zest.

Put in a double boiler
  ½ cup cooked vegetables, mashed or
    chopped
  1½ cups milk
  1 slice onion
Heat 20 minutes. Rub through a sieve or whirl in a blender. Reheat. If desired, add
  1 or 2 bouillon cubes
Bind (above) if you like a smoother, thicker soup. If the soup is thicker than you like, thin it with a little more milk. Season to taste with
  Salt and pepper
  Paprika or any herb seasoning
Serves 2 or 3.

Cream of Cauliflower Soup. Use cooked cauliflower. Keep out a few tiny flowerets to add whole. Use part Chicken Stock (p. 72) and part milk.

Cream of Spinach Soup. Use well-drained cooked spinach. Use Chicken Stock (p. 72) in place of half the milk or add a chicken bouillon cube. Add a trace of nutmeg.

Cream of Vegetable Soup II

Make Cream Sauce (p. 90), reducing the amount of butter and flour to 1 tablespoon each. Add any puréed cooked vegetable, such as peas, carrots or broccoli. Season to taste.

Minestrone

A treasure from the Italian cuisine. A satisfying main dish served with a green salad and crusty French or Italian bread.

Put in a large pan
  1 cup dried white beans
  1 quart water
Bring to the boiling point and boil 2 minutes. Cover, remove from the heat, and let stand 1 hour to soften the beans. Simmer until the beans are tender. Do not drain.

Put in a soup kettle
  2-inch cube salt pork, diced
  1 onion, chopped fine
  1 tablespoon minced parsley
  ½ clove garlic (or more)
Cook and stir 10 minutes. Stir in
  1 can tomato paste
  2 cups boiling water or consommé
Simmer 15 minutes. Add
  1 cup coarsely chopped cabbage
Cook 10 minutes longer. Add the beans with their cooking water and stir gently to blend. Bring to the boiling point. Add
  1 cup elbow macaroni
Cook until it is just tender (7 to 10 minutes). Season to taste with
  Salt and pepper
Add more water or stock if needed to make about 1½ quarts. The soup should be very thick. Heat. Sprinkle each serving generously with
  Grated Romano or Parmesan cheese
Serves 6 to 8 generously.

To vary, use almost any combination of vegetables, such as tomatoes, celery, carrots, onions, turnips, cabbage, peas, green peppers, potatoes, zucchini, summer squash and leeks. Add a little finely chopped ham to each serving, if you like.

American Minestrone

Use any of the vegetables suggested for Minestrone (above).

Put in a large kettle
  2 tablespoons olive oil or butter
Add
  1½ cups thinly sliced vegetables
Sauté slowly 15 minutes. Add
  1 quart boiling water or water and consommé
  1 sprig parsley
  ½ bay leaf
  Bit of thyme
  Salt and pepper to taste
  ½ cup elbow macaroni or spaghetti
Boil 5 minutes, then reduce the heat and simmer 30 minutes. Sprinkle each serving generously with
  Grated Parmesan or Romano cheese
Serves 3 or 4.

To make with frozen vegetables. Use 1 cup sliced celery, 1 chopped onion, and 1 package of frozen mixed vegetables. Increase the water to 6 cups and add 4 bouillon cubes.

Gazpacho

A refreshing Spanish soup which needs no cooking. Pleasant as the first course for a summer dinner or as the main dish for lunch.

Crush together
  1 clove garlic, split

½ teaspoon salt
Add
  2 tablespoons olive oil
  5 ripe tomatoes, cut in pieces
  1 chopped onion
  ¼ teaspoon pepper
  ¼ teaspoon paprika
  1½ tablespoons vinegar
  1½ cups cold water or bouillon
Let stand 1 hour.

Put the mixture through a food mill or crush it through a coarse strainer. Taste, and add more salt if necessary. Stir in
  ¼ cup dry bread crumbs
Divide in 4 soup bowls or 6 bouillon cups. Put an ice cube in each. Pass (to sprinkle on the soup)
  Croûtons
  Chopped cucumber
  Chopped green pepper
Serves 4 to 6.

Cream of Almond Soup

A delicate dinner party soup to serve either hot or chilled.

Chop very fine in a nut chopper or an electric blender
  ⅓ cup blanched almonds
  3 bitter almonds (if available)
As you chop, add slowly
  2 tablespoons cold water
Add to
  2 cups Chicken Stock (p. 72) or canned chicken broth
  1 slice onion
  1 stalk celery, cut fine
Simmer 30 minutes. Rub through a sieve. Add more stock or water if needed to make 2 cups.

When ready to serve, heat
  2 cups milk or milk and cream
Stir it into the hot soup. Do not boil. Season to taste with
  Salt, pepper and mace
Sprinkle each serving lightly with
  Nutmeg
Serves 8.

Cream of Artichoke Soup

A party soup with an unusual flavor.

Bring to a boil
  4 cups water
Add and cook until soft
  6 Jerusalem artichokes, peeled
Rub through a sieve, without draining. Pare and cut in cubes
  2 cucumbers
Sauté in
  Butter
Melt
  2 tablespoons butter
Stir in
  2 tablespoons flour
  1 teaspoon salt
  Few grains of cayenne
  Few gratings of nutmeg
Add the hot sieved artichoke and cooking water slowly, and cook 1 minute. When ready to serve, reheat and stir in
  1 cup scalded cream
  2 tablespoons sauterne
  1 egg, slightly beaten
Add the cucumbers to the soup. *Serves 8.*

Cream of Asparagus Soup

Cook
  1 bunch asparagus (1 pound) or 1 package frozen asparagus
Drain, reserving the cooking water. Cut off the tips to add later. To the asparagus water, add the stalks and
  1 thin slice onion
  1½ cups Chicken Stock (p. 72) or water
Boil 5 minutes, and rub through a sieve or purée in an electric blender. Melt
  2 tablespoons butter
Blend in
  2 tablespoons flour
Add the strained soup. Cook and stir 5 minutes. Measure. Add
  Scalded milk or cream to make 3 cups in all
  Salt and pepper to taste
Put the asparagus tips in the soup plates and pour the soup over them. *Serves 6.*

Baked Bean Soup

The traditional garnishes for this soup are slices of hard-cooked egg and lemon.

Put in a deep pan
    1 cup baked beans
    1 slice onion
    1 stalk celery
    2 cups water
Simmer 30 minutes. Add
    ¾ cup stewed or canned tomatoes
Rub through a sieve or put through a food mill. Add
    Water, consommé or Brown Stock (p. 70) to make 3 cups
Reheat and season to taste with
    Chili sauce
    Salt and pepper
Serves 4.

Black Bean Soup

If you use canned black bean soup, season it critically and garnish as below.

Put in a large kettle
    2 cups dried black beans
    2 quarts cold water
Bring to the boiling point, simmer 10 minutes, cover and set aside 1 hour. Add
    1 small onion, sliced
    2 stalks celery, chopped, or ¼ teaspoon celery salt
    1 hambone (optional) or bits of left-over ham
Simmer until the beans are soft (3 to 4 hours). Add water if needed, to make about 1½ quarts. Remove the bone. Rub the soup through a very fine sieve or whirl in an electric blender. Add
    2 teaspoons salt
    ½ teaspoon pepper
    ¼ teaspoon dry mustard
    Few grains cayenne
    Sherry to taste, if liked
Heat. Garnish with
    2 hard-cooked eggs, sliced thin
    1 lemon, sliced thin
Serves 8 generously.

Guatemala Style. In place of egg and lemon, garnish with bits of alligator pear.

Borscht

Use homemade Brown Stock (p. 70) if convenient.

Put in a kettle
    1 quart consommé or beef broth
    2 cups raw beets, peeled and chopped or shredded
    1 onion, chopped fine
    1 to 2 cups cabbage, shredded
Simmer, tightly covered, until the vegetables are very tender. Add
    1 tablespoon lemon juice or vinegar
Add enough water to make 1½ quarts. Taste, and season further, if necessary. Serve hot or chilled.

Just before serving, stir in
    ½ cup sour cream
or put a spoonful in each bowl. *Makes 4 to 6 big bowlfuls.*

Quick Borscht. Sieve canned beets (or use prepared baby food) and season to taste with onion juice, lemon juice and a trace of sugar. Dilute as you like with consommé. Serve as above.

Cream of Celery Soup

Cook together until the vegetables are soft
    1 cup chopped celery, stalks and leaves
    1 slice onion (or more)
    2 cups chicken broth or water
Rub through a sieve, without draining, or whirl in an electric blender. Add
    1½ cups milk or light cream
    Salt and pepper to taste
Heat slowly. Bind (p. 61) if you prefer a thicker, smoother soup. *Serves 4 to 6.*

Cheese Soup

At its best, made the day before serving and reheated.

Melt in a large saucepan
    1 tablespoon butter
Add
    1 tablespoon chopped onion
Cook slowly until the onion is yellow. Stir in
    1 tablespoon flour

Add slowly, stirring constantly
  1 cup Brown Stock (p. 70) or canned
    consommé
  2 cups milk
Bring to the boiling point. Strain. Add
  ¾ cup grated Cheddar cheese
Stir until the cheese melts. Serve sprinkled with paprika, bits of canned pimiento or croûtons. *Serves 4 to 6.*

To vary, add 2 tablespoons each of chopped cooked carrot and chopped cooked celery. Sprinkle with chopped parsley.

Cream of Chestnut Soup

Bring to the boiling point
  1 quart Chicken Stock (p. 72) or
    canned chicken broth
Add and simmer until soft
  1 cup shelled chestnuts (p. 13)
Rub through a sieve or whirl in an electric blender. Add
  1½ cups cream or milk, heated
  ½ teaspoon salt
  ⅛ teaspoon paprika
Serves 8.

Cream of Corn Soup

Put in a saucepan or double boiler top
  1 cup cooked or canned (cream-style)
    corn
  1 cup boiling water
  1 cup milk
  1 small slice onion (or season with
    onion salt)
Heat slowly. Bind (p. 61) with
  1 tablespoon butter
  1 tablespoon flour
Season to taste with
  Salt and pepper
Serves 4 to 6.

Curried Cream of Corn Soup. Season delicately with curry powder.

In a blender. Omit the flour. Whirl the other ingredients in the blender, heat and season.

Corn Chowder

Use 3 tablespoons butter in place of salt pork, if it is more convenient.

Dice and put in a deep pan
  1½-inch cube salt pork
Cook slowly until the fat is melted and the pork bits are crisp and brown. Add
  1 small onion, sliced
Cook slowly 5 minutes, stirring often. Add
  4 potatoes, cubed or sliced
  2 cups water
Cook until the potatoes are tender. Add
  2 cups cream-style corn
  4 cups milk
Heat. Add
  3 tablespoons butter
  Salt and pepper to taste
Serves 6 to 8 generously.

Cream of Cucumber Soup

An unusual dinner party soup.

Peel, slice and seed
  3 large cucumbers
Cook 10 minutes in
  2 tablespoons butter
Stir in
  3 tablespoons flour
Add gradually
  3 cups Chicken Stock (p. 72) or canned
    chicken broth
Scald together
  1 cup milk
  1 slice onion
  Few grains mace or nutmeg
Combine the mixtures. Rub through a sieve or whirl in an electric blender. Just before serving, reheat to the boiling point. Stir in
  ½ cup cream
  2 egg yolks, slightly beaten
Season to taste with
  Salt and pepper
Serves 8.

Chilled Cucumber Soup. Omit the egg yolks. Chill before adding the cream. Season with a few drops of Angostura bitters.

Mushroom Bouillon

You may like to add ½ teaspoon caraway seeds and a tiny sprig of marjoram.

Simmer together 1 hour
    ½ pound mushrooms, chopped
    4 cups consommé or water
    ½ teaspoon grated onion
    Salt to taste
Let stand several hours or overnight. Strain. Serve hot or chilled. *Serves 6.*

To vary, put a spoonful of chopped or finely cut raw mushrooms in each cup, add a teaspoon of sherry, and fill with hot or cold soup.

Cream of Mushroom Soup

Put ½ teaspoon sherry in each serving, if you like.

Melt in a deep pan
    3 tablespoons butter
Add
    1 tablespoon chopped onion
    ¼ pound mushrooms, chopped fine, or stems from ½ pound mushrooms, chopped fine
Cook slowly 15 minutes. Stir in
    1 tablespoon flour
Add slowly
    2 cups Chicken Stock (p. 72), canned chicken broth, or water
Bring to the boiling point. Cook slowly 20 minutes on an asbestos mat or in a double boiler. Strain if you like, but the soup is delicious with bits of mushroom and onion in it. Season to taste with
    Salt and pepper
    Lemon juice or grated nutmeg
Just before serving add
    ½ cup cream or milk
Heat but do not boil. *Serves 4 to 6.*

For a richer soup, prepare the mushrooms with stock as above, then add ½ cup boiling water and 2 tablespoons quick-cooking tapioca. Cook until the tapioca is clear. Season. Just before serving, heat and stir in 1 cup heavy cream and 2 egg yolks, slightly beaten. *Serves 8.*

In a blender. Whirl chopped mushrooms and cream or milk in an electric blender, add more milk, heat and season. Add a bouillon cube, if you like.

French Onion Soup

To develop the finest flavor, let this soup mellow for a day.

Melt in a large pan
    1 tablespoon butter
Add and cook slowly until soft
    ¾ cup sliced onions (or more)
Add
    ½ teaspoon sugar
    1 tablespoon flour
Stir and cook 1 minute. Add
    4 cups water or consommé
Season to taste with
    Salt and pepper
Simmer at least 30 minutes. Add more water, if needed, to make 4 cups.

When ready to serve, toast
    4 thick slices French bread or rounds cut from sliced bread
Put a slice in each bowl. Pour the soup over the toast, and sprinkle with
    Grated Italian cheese
Set the bowls in a 400° oven to melt and brown the cheese. Pass extra cheese to sprinkle over the soup. *Serves 4.*

Parker House Onion Soup. Use large mild onions and Chicken Stock (p. 72) or canned chicken broth. Just before serving, add a tablespoon of heavy cream for each bowlful.

Cream of Onion Soup

Cook together for 10 minutes, stirring constantly
    2 large mild onions, sliced thin
    ¼ cup butter
Add
    4 cups Chicken Stock (p. 72) or canned chicken broth
Cook slowly 30 minutes. Strain or not, as you prefer. Add
    1 cup milk or light cream
Heat. Just before serving, add

1 tablespoon chopped green pepper
   or ¼ cup grated cheese
Season to taste. *Serves 6 to 8.*

Parsnip Stew

An old-fashioned lunch for a winter day.

Put in a kettle
   1-inch cube salt pork, diced
Fry slowly until the fat melts and the
scraps are crisp. Add
   2 medium-sized parsnips, pared and
     diced
   2 medium-sized potatoes, pared and
     diced
   1 cup water
Cook until the vegetables are tender.
Add
   2 cups milk
Bind (p. 61) with
   1 tablespoon butter
   1 tablespoon flour
Heat. Season to taste with
   Salt and pepper
Serves 4 to 6.

Cream of Pea Soup

*If the peas are very young and tender,
cook a few pods with them.*

Cook together for 5 minutes
   2 tablespoons butter
   1 tablespoon chopped onion
Add
   2 cups fresh or frozen peas
   ½ teaspoon salt
   1 teaspoon sugar
   2 cups water
Cook until the peas are soft (about 20
minutes). Put through a sieve or whirl
in an electric blender. Add
   1 cup milk or light cream
Heat slowly. Season to taste with
   Garlic salt or mace
   Pepper
Sprinkle with
   Chopped parsley
Serves 6.

Quick Pea Soup. Use cooked or canned
peas the same way, but cooking will not
be necessary after the onion is cooked.

Potage Longchamps. Reheat with a few
sprigs of fresh mint. Remove the mint
before serving.

Potage St. Germain. Cook with the peas
2 leaves of lettuce and 1 small carrot,
sliced thin. Use Chicken Stock (p. 72)
in place of water and use cream rather
than milk. Sprinkle with croûtons.

Split Pea Soup

*Read the directions on the package of
split peas to see if previous soaking is
required. See the variations on p. 68; also
Vienna Pea Soup (p. 60).*

Bring to the boil in a large kettle
   1 quart water
Add
   1 pound dried split peas
Cover, remove from the heat, and let
stand 1 hour. Add
   2-inch cube fat salt pork or a hambone
   1 onion (or more), sliced
For extra savor, add
   ½ cup chopped celery
   ¼ cup chopped parsley
   Pinch of herbs such as thyme or rose-
     mary
   1 bay leaf
Simmer until the peas are soft (1 or 2
hours).

Remove the salt pork or the hambone.
Rub the soup through a sieve or crush
the peas with a blending fork. Dilute to
the thickness you like with
   Milk
Heat. Season to taste with
   Salt and pepper
As an attractive garnish, put on each
cup
   A few crisp croûtons
   A few cooked fresh green peas
*As a thick soup, serves 4 or 5. Diluted
further, it can serve 8 to 10 as a first
course.*

Jules's Split Pea Soup. After rubbing the soup through a sieve, add cooked carrot slivers and sliced frankfurters or Vienna sausage. Serve with rye bread as a hearty supper dish.

Lentil or Lima Bean Soup. Use dried lentils or lima beans instead of split peas. (Dried lentils will cook tender in a shorter time.) You may wish to use butter rather than salt pork or a hambone, increase the onion, or use tomato juice as part of the liquid. In Lentil Soup, add lemon juice to taste.

Potato Soup

For each bowl of soup, pare and dice 1 medium-sized potato. Add a slice of onion (or more) and cover with boiling water. Add salt. Cover tightly and cook slowly until the potatoes are very soft (about 15 minutes).

Crush the potatoes with a fork without draining them. Add hot milk to make the soup as thin as you like it. Season to taste with salt, pepper, celery salt and cayenne. If you like, sprinkle with chopped parsley or chives.

With mashed potato. *A good way to use up a leftover.* Scald 2 cups milk with a slice of onion. Add 1 cup mashed potato and mix with a whisk or a blending fork. Season to taste.

Leek and Potato Soup

Put in a pan
    1 bunch leeks, sliced very fine
    3 stalks celery, sliced very fine
    3 tablespoons butter
Cook 10 minutes, stirring constantly. Add
    1 cup water
Cover. Cook 10 minutes. Add
    2½ cups potatoes, diced
    Water to cover
Cover and cook 10 minutes longer. Add
    3 cups milk
Simmer until the potatoes are tender.

Season to taste with
    Salt, pepper and cayenne
Strain, or serve for lunch as a chowder. *Serves 6.*

Vichyssoise

Purists demand unsalted butter for this soup. For perfectly blended flavor, prepare Vichyssoise the day before serving it. If you have some left over, eke it out with more top milk or chicken stock and season to taste.

Melt (preferably in an enamelware or glass saucepan)
    4 tablespoons butter
Add
    4 leeks (white part only), cut fine
    1 onion, chopped
Cook very slowly until the vegetables are tender but not brown. Add
    4 cups Chicken Stock (p. 72) or canned
        chicken broth
    2 sprigs parsley
    2 small stalks celery
    2 potatoes, sliced thin
    Salt and pepper to taste
    Few grains nutmeg or curry powder
    Few drops Worcestershire
Cook until the potatoes are tender. Put through a very fine sieve or mix in an electric blender. Add more stock if necessary to make 2 cups.

Just before serving, stir in
    1 cup heavy cream
Serve hot, or chill in the refrigerator and serve icy cold. Sprinkle with
    Finely chopped chives, dill or parsley
Serves 8.

Carrot Vichyssoise. Use only 2 leeks and add 3 carrots, cut small.

Tomato Soup

Use Garden Special (p. 532), Savory Tomato Juice (p. 531) or canned tomatoes as a basis for soup. Dilute with water or stock and add seasonings, such as a bit of bay leaf, a sprig of thyme and a few whole cloves. Simmer ½ hour. Strain or not, as you prefer.

Tomato Soup Portugaise. Put in each dish a tablespoon of cooked rice and a bit of tomato, peeled and sautéed in butter.

Tomato Bouillon. Combine tomato juice with an equal amount of Chicken Stock (p. 72) or bouillon. Season with a little lemon juice, salt and a few grains of sugar. If you like a sharper flavor, heat with a bit of bay leaf or basil, chopped onion, one or two cloves, a few celery seeds, and peppercorns. Strain, and heat or chill.

Float on each cupful a little chopped parsley or chives or a thin slice of lemon or orange, or add a spoonful of salted whipped cream or sour cream.

Thick Tomato Soup. For 1 pint of soup, cook 2 tablespoons butter until brown, add 2 tablespoons flour, and cook 5 minutes. Stir into the soup. Bring to the boiling point and strain.

Cream of Tomato Soup. *See also Tomato Bisque (below).* Add ½ cup cream or milk to Thick Tomato Soup. Serve with crisp croûtons and a sprinkling of chopped chives.

Tomato Madrilène

If you make this soup with plain tomato juice, add extra seasoning.

Put in a saucepan
   ½ cup cold water
   1 tablespoon gelatine
Let stand 5 minutes. Add
   1 cup Tomato Bouillon (above) or tomato juice cocktail
Stir over moderate heat until the gelatine dissolves. Add
   1 cup Tomato Bouillon (above) or tomato juice cocktail
Chill until slightly firm. Break up with a fork and pile in bouillon cups. Top with chopped chives or dill or a bit of caviar. *Serves 4.*

Creole Soup

As a garnish, cut strips of cooked macaroni to make tiny rings.

Melt in a saucepan
   2 tablespoons bacon fat
Add
   1 tablespoon chopped green pepper
   1 tablespoon chopped onion
Cook 5 minutes. Stir in
   2 tablespoons flour
Add
   1 cup tomatoes
   3 cups canned consommé or Brown Stock (p. 70)
Simmer 15 minutes. Strain. Season highly with
   Salt, pepper, cayenne
Add enough water to make 4 cups. Just before serving, heat and add
   1 tablespoon grated horseradish
   ½ teaspoon vinegar
(If you use bottled horseradish, omit the vinegar.) *Serves 8.*

Tomato Bisque

This excellent old-fashioned version of Cream of Tomato Soup was called a bisque because it resembles lobster or crab bisque in color.

Cut in pieces and put in a pan
   2 cups tomatoes (drain canned tomatoes if used)
Add
   2 teaspoons sugar
Cook 15 minutes. Rub through a sieve. Heat
   4 cups milk or light cream
   ½ cup dry bread crumbs
   ½ onion, stuck with 6 cloves
   Sprig of parsley
   Bit of bay leaf
Remove the seasoning and rub the thickened milk through a sieve. When ready to serve, combine the mixtures and heat just to the boiling point. Season with
   Salt and pepper
Stir in, bit by bit
   ⅓ cup butter (or less)
Serves 6 to 8.

Cream of Watercress Soup

Simmer together for 10 minutes
  2 bunches watercress, cut fine
  4 cups Chicken Stock (p. 72) or canned
    chicken broth
Strain to remove bits of stem and leaves.
Melt
  ¼ cup butter
Stir in

  2 tablespoons flour
Cook slowly 5 minutes. Add a little of
the hot soup and stir until smooth. Add
to the rest of the soup and bring to the
boiling point, stirring constantly. Add
  1 cup cream (not icy cold)
  Salt and pepper to taste
Color delicately with
  Green vegetable coloring
Serves 6 to 8.

Meat Soups

Brown Stock (Bouillon)

*The basis for many good soups and
sauces. As a clear broth, serve as a first
course or a beverage. Many good cooks
take pride in having homemade stock on
hand, and make it either from soup meat
ordered for the purpose or from bones
or bits of leftover cooked meat such as
chops or roast beef, lamb, veal or fowl.
Do not use bones from pork or mutton,
and do not use burned pieces, smoked
or corned meats or lamb surrounded by
fat. When you order meat, ask the
butcher to give you any bones and trimmings and use them for stock.*

*If it is not convenient to use marrow
bones, brown the meat in 3 tablespoons
of shortening instead of the marrow.*

Scrape the marrow from
  1 to 2 pounds cracked marrow bones
Remove the lean meat from
  6 pounds beef shin or other soup meat
Cut in 1-inch cubes. Melt the marrow
(or fat if used) in a large kettle and
brown half the meat cubes in it. Add the
remaining meat, the bones and
  3 quarts cold water
Cover and bring slowly to the boiling
point. Skim off the scum. Add
  8 peppercorns
  6 cloves
  ½ bay leaf
  3 sprigs of thyme or pinch of dried
    thyme

  1 sprig of marjoram or pinch of dried
    marjoram
  2 sprigs of parsley
  ¼ cup diced carrot
  ¼ cup diced turnip
  ¼ cup diced onion
  ¼ cup diced celery
  1 tablespoon salt

Simmer 3 hours or more or cook in a
pressure saucepan about 1 hour. Skim
occasionally. Strain. Cool quickly. *Makes
about 2½ quarts.*

To store. Cover and refrigerate. Do not
remove the cake of fat which forms on
the stock when it is cold. This excludes
air and aids in preserving the stock until it is used.

To remove fat. If the stock is cold, run
a knife around the edge of the bowl and
carefully lift off the fat. To remove the
small quantity of fat which remains,
pass a cloth wrung out of hot water
around the edge and over the top of the
stock.

To remove the fat before the stock has
cooled, spoon out as much as possible
and remove the rest by passing crumpled
paper towels over the surface, or drop a
few ice cubes into the stock and take them
out when the fat has collected on them.

To clear stock. Remove the fat and put
the stock to be cleared in a pan. Taste.

If further seasoning is needed, add it at this point, not after clearing. For each quart add 1 egg white, beaten slightly with a fork and mixed with 2 teaspoons cold water. Add the eggshell broken in small pieces. Bring to the boiling point, stirring constantly, and boil 2 minutes. Let stand 20 minutes over very low heat. Strain through a fine strainer lined with a double thickness of cheesecloth.

White (Veal) Stock

A savory old-fashioned basis for cream soups and many sauces. It may be used in any recipe calling for chicken stock. See also Chicken Stock (p. 72).

Cut in small pieces
    4-pound knuckle of veal or 3-pound knuckle and 1 pound lean beef
Put in a kettle. Add
    3 quarts cold water
    1 tablespoon salt
    10 peppercorns
    1 onion
    2 stalks celery
    Blade of mace
    1 carrot, sliced
    ½ bay leaf
    2 sprigs of thyme **or** pinch of dried thyme
    2 cloves
Bring slowly to the boiling point, skimming frequently. Reduce the heat, cover, and simmer 4 or 5 hours. Pour through a strainer lined with a double thickness of cheesecloth. Further clearing should not be necessary. *Makes about 2 quarts.*

Consommé

True consommé owes its distinctive flavor to the combination of beef, veal and chicken. It is seldom made at home these days because it is expensive and time-consuming to prepare. Canned consommé or consommé made from cubes or flakes is quite acceptable if you make it somewhat stronger than the directions on the can or package suggest.

Also, combine consommé and chicken broth or stock to make a tastier soup.

Heat consommé. Season to taste with lemon juice, sherry, celery salt or onion salt.

Garnish each serving with a leaf of parsley, a thin slice of lemon, cooked macaroni cut in ¼-inch rings, a few strands of cooked and drained fine noodles or a special garnish like Royal Custard (p. 58) or Parmesan Puffs (p. 59).

Consommé with Cream. Add a little top milk or cream. Season well with Maggi's seasoning or sherry or sprinkle with chopped chives.

Consommé with Avocado. Put 2 or 3 cubes of avocado in each bouillon cup. Pour hot consommé over them and serve immediately.

Consommé with Herbs. Simmer consommé ½ hour with a sprig or two of thyme, marjoram, parsley or chervil, or a bay leaf or a blade or two of chives. Strain and reheat.

Consommé Julienne. Add, for 1 quart, 2 tablespoons each of cooked peas and string beans and ¼ cup each of cooked carrots and turnips or leeks cut in matchlike strips.

Consommé mit Ei. *A European recipe hearty enough for lunch in itself.* Have eggs at room temperature. Heat consommé to the boiling point and pour into heated bowls. Break an egg into each bowl. Cover immediately so that the eggs will be slightly poached. Each person stirs the egg into his bowl of soup.

Consommé Princess. Add cooked green peas and diced cooked chicken.

Iced Consommé. Season hot consommé to taste with lemon juice or sherry. Chill. Pour into bouillon cups and garnish with a sprig of parsley or a thin slice of lemon.

Jellied Consommé. Chill consommé in a shallow dish until firm, or chill undiluted canned consommé in its can. Break up lightly with a fork and serve in chilled soup cups. Garnish with parsley or chives or top with thin slices of lemon or lime.

Consommé à la Barigoule. Add to the consommé diced cooked chicken and thin slices of stuffed olives and raw mushrooms.

Consommé du Barry. Put in each cup a bit of cooked cauliflower, a teaspoon of hot cooked rice and a sprinkling of shredded toasted almonds.

Scotch Broth

Use rice in place of barley, if you prefer, adding it ½ hour before the soup is to be served.

Discard the fat and cut the lean meat in 1-inch cubes from
   3 pounds lamb or mutton (bony cuts such as neck, flank or breast)
Put the meat and bones in a deep kettle. Cover with
   Cold water
Bring quickly to the boiling point. Add
   ½ cup barley
(Soak old-fashioned barley 12 hours and drain.) Simmer 1½ hours or until the meat is tender. Remove the bones. Cool the soup and skim off the fat.

Put in a pan
   2 tablespoons butter

¼ cup each of finely cut carrot, celery, turnip and onion
Cook 5 minutes. Add to the soup. Season with
   Salt and pepper to taste
Cook until the vegetables are soft. (Add more water if the soup is too thick.) Just before serving, add
   Chopped parsley
Serves 8 or more.

Oxtail Soup

A tablespoon of Madeira enhances the flavor of this good soup.

Have the butcher cut in 2-inch lengths
   1½ pounds oxtail
Sprinkle with
   Flour
   Salt and pepper
Melt in a deep kettle
   3 tablespoons fat
Add the oxtail. Cook 10 minutes, turning to brown on all sides. Add
   2 quarts Brown Stock (p. 70), consommé or water
Simmer until the meat falls away from the bones (2 or 3 hours). Remove the bones. Add
   ½ cup diced carrot
   ½ cup diced turnip
   ½ cup diced onion
   ½ cup diced celery
Simmer until the vegetables are soft. Add
   1 teaspoon lemon juice
   1 teaspoon Worcestershire
Add enough water to make about 1½ quarts. Heat. *Serves 8.*

Chicken Soups

Chicken Stock, Broth or Bouillon

Homemade chicken stock is particularly delicious. Save the broth when you poach chicken (p. 216) for salads, adding seasoning such as celery tops to improve the flavor. For superior flavor and darker color, brown the pieces of chicken first in fat.

Use the leftover cooked chicken meat in any way you like, such as in creamed chicken dishes or in salads or sandwiches.

Clean and wipe
 4-pound fowl (cut as for fricassee)
Put all except the breast in a deep kettle. Add
 6 cups cold water
 1 carrot, sliced
 2 stalks celery (with leaves)
 1 onion, sliced
 ½ bay leaf
 6 peppercorns
 1 teaspoon salt
Heat slowly to the boiling point and add the breast. Cover and cook slowly until the breast meat is tender. Cool. Remove the fat. Bring to the boiling point, strain and season. *Makes 1 quart.*

Pressure-cooked. Use all the bones and bits of meat from broilers, roast chicken or fricassee, scraping the plates and the platter. Put into the pressure cooker. Add a slice each of onion and carrot and a few celery tops. You may like to add more onion and, for a spicier flavor, a bay leaf, 2 whole cloves, 6 peppercorns and ½ teaspoon whole allspice.

Add any leftover broth or gravy. If necessary, add enough water to make at least 2 cups of liquid. Adjust the cover, bring up to pressure, then cook 20 to 30 minutes. Let the pressure drop normally.

Strain the broth and add salt to taste. If there is enough fat to show on the surface, cool the broth until you can spoon off most of the fat.

Chicken Soup

Season homemade or canned chicken stock to taste. If convenient, add 1 tablespoon chopped cooked chicken to each 2 cups of soup. For color and flavor, add finely diced pimiento or green pepper, or minced parsley.

Vary by adding cream or a little boiled rice. Or add 2 tablespoons uncooked rice or tapioca to the soup and cook about 15 minutes.

In a blender. Put chicken stock or broth in an electric blender, with a few bits of leftover cooked chicken and well-browned chicken skin. Blend until perfectly smooth. Add more broth, cream or milk until as thin as you like it. Season carefully. Serve hot or chilled.

Vary the flavor by blending with the chicken 1 tablespoon blanched almonds, ¼ cup sautéed chopped mushrooms or ½ cup cooked peas.

Greek Lemon Soup

The classic Greek recipe uses broth made from lamb bones and scraps of meat. It has a distinctive and delicious flavor.

Heat to the boiling point
 6 cups chicken broth
Add
 ⅓ cup uncooked rice
Simmer 30 minutes or until the rice is tender.

Beat until frothy
 2 egg yolks
 Juice of 1 lemon
Add 1 cup of the broth gradually, then pour it back into the rest of the soup, stirring constantly with a wire whisk. Reheat to just below the boiling point and serve immediately. *Serves 6.*

Cream of Chicken Soup

Heat chicken stock (canned or homemade). For each pint of stock, heat ½ cup of cream or evaporated milk. Add it slowly to the soup. Season to taste with salt and a trace of nutmeg.

Sprinkle each serving with chopped parsley or a shake of paprika.

Potage à la Reine. Add a few slivers of cooked white meat of chicken to each serving.

Cream of Chicken with Rice. Heat the stock to the boiling point. Before adding the cream, add ¼ cup cooked rice for each pint of stock.

Chicken Gumbo Soup

*For a heartier soup, add canned corn or
cooked rice or both. See also Chicken
Gumbo (p. 221).*

Put in a saucepan
  ¼ cup butter
  1 onion, finely chopped
Cook and stir 5 minutes. Add
  1 quart Chicken Stock (p. 72) or
    canned chicken broth
  ½ green pepper, chopped fine
  1 cup cooked or canned okra
  2 teaspoons salt
  ¼ teaspoon pepper
  1 to 2 cups canned tomatoes
Bring to the boiling point and simmer
40 minutes. If you like, add diced cooked
chicken. *Serves 6 to 8.*

Queen Victoria Soup

*A modern adaptation of a rich and
famous English recipe. Hearty enough
for the main dish at lunch or supper.*

Put in a deep pan
  1 tablespoon butter
  1 teaspoon finely chopped onion
Cook slowly until the onion is yellow.
Add
  ½ cup finely cut mushrooms
  1 cup diced celery
Cook 10 minutes. Add
  4 cups Chicken Stock (p. 72) or canned
    chicken broth
  1 tablespoon quick tapioca
  ½ cup diced cooked chicken
  ½ cup diced cooked ham
  Sage, nutmeg and onion salt to taste
Cook 20 minutes. Add
  2 hard-cooked eggs, chopped fine
  1 or 2 cups cream
Heat. Serve in large bowls. Garnish with
  Chopped parsley
Serves 7 or 8.

To simplify. Use a can of mushroom
soup in place of the fresh mushrooms
and cream, and canned luncheon meat
in place of ham. Not the same, but very
good and a thought for the emergency
shelf.

Mulligatawny Soup

Serve fluffy rice to spoon into the soup.

Put in a deep pan
  ¼ cup butter or other fat
  ¼ cup diced onion
  ¼ cup diced carrot
  ¼ cup diced celery
  1 pepper, chopped fine
  1 apple, sliced
  1 cup diced raw chicken
Cook slowly until brown. Stir in
  ⅛ cup flour
Add
  1 teaspoon curry powder
  ½ teaspoon nutmeg or mace
  2 cloves
  1 sprig parsley
  Salt and pepper
  1 cup tomatoes, canned or chopped
  5 cups canned chicken broth or
    Chicken Stock (p. 72)
Simmer 1 hour. Strain, reserving the
liquid. Pick out the bits of chicken and
set aside. Rub the vegetables through a
sieve. Add the puréed vegetables and
the chicken to the soup. Heat, and season
to taste. *Serves 6 to 8.*

Philadelphia Pepper Pot

Serve as the main dish for supper.

Put in a deep pan
  3 tablespoons butter
  ¼ cup chopped onion
  ¼ cup chopped celery
  ½ cup chopped green pepper
  1½ cups potato cubes
Cook slowly 15 minutes. Stir in
  3 tablespoons flour
Stir and cook 5 minutes. Add
  5 cups Chicken Stock (p. 72) or canned
    chicken broth
  ½ pound cooked honeycomb tripe
    (p. 209), cut in ½-inch squares
  ½ teaspoon freshly ground pepper
  2 teaspoons salt
Cover. Cook slowly 1 hour.
Just before serving, reheat. Stir in
  ½ cup heavy cream (not icy cold)
  1 tablespoon butter
Serves 6 to 8 as a main dish.

Fish and Shellfish Soups and Chowders

Old-Fashioned Fish Chowder

Fish stock made with bones improves the flavor of the chowder. There was a time when New Englanders always put into the chowder common or Boston crackers soaked in milk. Nowadays the crackers are usually omitted.

Have the butcher skin a
    4-pound cod or haddock
and remove the fish from the backbone. Break the head, tail and bone in pieces and put in a deep kettle. Add
    2 cups cold water
Simmer slowly 10 minutes. Drain and save the liquid.

Put in a small frying pan
    1½-inch cube fat salt pork, diced
Cook slowly 5 minutes. Add
    1 onion, sliced thin
Cook until the onion is soft (about 5 minutes). Strain the fat into a deep pan and set the scraps aside. Add to the fat
    4 cups thinly sliced potatoes
    2 cups boiling water
Cook 5 minutes. Add the fish, cut in 2-inch pieces, and the liquid drained from the bones. Cover and simmer 10 minutes. Add the scraps of onion and pork. Add
    4 cups scalded milk or cream
    1 tablespoon salt
    ⅛ teaspoon pepper
    3 tablespoons butter
Heat but do not boil. *Serves 8 generously.*

Fish Chowder

A simplified version of the classic recipe above. Chowder is improved if you make it one day and serve it the next.

Put in a saucepan
    1 pound fillet of haddock
    1 cup water

Cook slowly until the fish flakes when tried with a fork. Remove the fish and separate it into flakes. Add to the cooking water
    2 cups potatoes cut in ½-inch cubes
Cook until tender but still firm.

Meanwhile, put in a frying pan
    1-inch cube salt pork, diced very small
Fry slowly until the fat melts. Add
    1 small onion, diced
Cook slowly until the onion is soft and lightly browned. Add to the potatoes. Add the fish.

Pour into the pan in which the pork and onion were cooked
    2 cups milk or milk and cream
Heat and stir to get all the flavor. Add to the chowder. Heat but do not boil. Add
    Salt, pepper and butter to taste
If you used cream as part of the liquid for the chowder, you will not need butter. *Serves 4.*

For a delicious garnish, fry an extra panful of pork scraps (without onion), drain on a paper towel, and pass to sprinkle over the chowder.

To vary, cook the fish in clam juice instead of water, or add minced clams or oysters to the finished chowder.

Connecticut Fish Chowder

Follow either recipe for Fish Chowder (above), but instead of milk, add tomato juice.

Season to taste. If you prefer a slightly thickened chowder, stir in ⅔ cup cracker crumbs just before serving.

Bouillabaisse

This famous French dish is ideal for a supper party main course. Use several kinds of fish such as flounder, red mullet, whiting, sole, haddock, perch or whitefish.

Put in a big kettle
  ½ cup olive oil
  1 carrot, chopped
  2 onions, chopped
  2 leeks, cut small
  1 clove garlic, crushed
Cook slowly until golden-brown. Add
  3 pounds boned fish, cut in 3-inch squares
  2 large tomatoes, cut in pieces, or 1 cup canned tomatoes
  1 bay leaf
  2 cups Fish Stock (p. 120), clam juice or water
Simmer 20 minutes. Add
  ½ cup shrimp, crab or lobster meat, cooked or canned
  1 dozen oysters, clams or mussels (in the shell)
  ½ cup pimientos, cut small
  Few grains saffron
Simmer until the shells open (about 5 minutes). Season to taste with
  Salt and pepper
Add
  Juice of 1 lemon
  1 cup dry white wine
Put in a soup tureen or a large bowl
  8 slices French bread, toasted
Pour the bouillabaisse over the bread. Sprinkle with
  1 tablespoon chopped parsley
Serves 8.

Clam Broth

Season homemade or canned clam broth to taste. Serve hot or chilled. Garnish each cup with chopped parsley or a dab of salted whipped cream or Pimiento Cream (p. 58).

To prepare broth. Wash clams in the shell, scrubbing them with a brush and changing the water several times. Put in a kettle and add ½ cup water for each quart of clams. Cover tightly and steam until the shells open wide (about 30 minutes). Let stand 15 minutes so that the sediment will settle. Strain carefully. Chop the cooked clams fine, season, and use as a canapé spread.

Clam and Tomato Broth. Combine clam broth and tomato bouillon or tomato juice. Season with celery salt. Serve hot or chilled.

Clam and Chicken Consommé. Combine 1 cup clam broth and 3 cups chicken stock or consommé. Season to taste. Heat. Just before serving, stir in ½ cup cream.

Clam and Chicken Frappé. Mix 1⅔ cups clam broth and 2½ cups chicken stock or bouillon. Season highly. Freeze to a mush in an ice-cube tray. Stir with a fork.

Serve in bouillon cups or small glass bowls as the first course at a summer luncheon or dinner. Garnish each serving with a dab of salted whipped cream.

Manhattan Clam Bisque. For each cup of broth, brown 1 tablespoon butter, stir in 1 tablespoon flour, and brown well. Add the broth slowly and simmer 20 minutes. Add ¼ cup cream.

Clam and Tomato Bisque

Heat together (but do not boil)
  1 cup Clam Broth (above)
  1 cup Tomato Soup, homemade (p. 68) or canned
  1 cup milk or cream
For added flavor, heat with the soup
  Few grains mace or nutmeg
  1 stalk celery
  1 sprig parsley
  Bit of bay leaf
  Slice of onion
Strain, reheat, and season to taste. *Serves 4 to 6.*

Cream of Clam Soup

Heat
  1 cup minced fresh or canned clams
Add to
  2 cups scalded milk or light cream
Season to taste. Top each serving with
  Salted whipped cream
  Paprika
  Sprig of parsley
Serves 3 or 4.

Manhattan Clam Chowder

The New York version always has to-matoes in it.

Put in a deep saucepan
  1½-inch cube fat salt pork, diced
Cook slowly until the fat melts. Add
  1 onion, sliced thin
Cook and stir 5 minutes. Add
  1 cup cubed potatoes
  1 teaspoon salt
  2 cups boiling water
Boil 10 minutes. Add
  2 cups stewed or canned tomatoes
Cook until the potatoes are soft (5 to
10 minutes). Add
  1 pint fresh or canned clams, chopped
    fine
  ¼ teaspoon dried thyme
  Salt and pepper to taste
Simmer 3 minutes. *Serves 4.*

To vary, cook with the onion ½ cup
chopped celery, ½ teaspoon caraway
seeds and a bit of bay leaf.

New England Clam Chowder

*Old-fashioned cooks discarded the pork
scraps, but they add a savory touch to
the chowder.*

Put in a deep pan
  1½-inch cube salt pork, diced fine
Cook slowly until the fat melts and the
scraps are crisp and brown. Remove the
pork scraps and set aside so they will be
crisp when they are added. Add to the
fat
  1 onion, chopped fine
Cook slowly until the onion is golden.
Put into the pan in layers
  3 cups cubed potatoes
  1 quart shucked chowder clams
Sprinkle each layer with
  Flour, salt and pepper
Add
  2½ cups boiling water
Simmer until the potatoes are tender
(about 20 minutes). Add
  4 cups hot milk
  4 tablespoons butter
  Salt and pepper to taste

Sprinkle pork scraps on each bowl of
chowder. *Serves 8 generously.*

Quick Clam Chowder

Put in a deep pan
  1-inch cube fat salt pork, cut small
Cook slowly until fat melts and the pork
scraps are crisp and brown. Remove the
bits of pork and set aside. Put in the
pan
  1 slice onion
  1 cup cubed potatoes
  2 cups boiling water
Simmer 20 minutes.
When ready to serve, add
  1 pint chopped clams, fresh or canned
Cook 2 minutes and add
  2 cups hot milk
  3 tablespoons butter
  Salt and pepper to taste
Sprinkle some of the pork scraps over
each bowlful. *Serves 4.*

Shrimp Bisque

*See also Shrimp Bisque (p. 60) made
with canned mushroom soup.*

Put in a deep pan
  3 tablespoons butter
  2 tablespoons chopped celery
  ¼ cup chopped mushrooms
  2 slices each of onion and carrot
  Bit of bay leaf
  Sprig of marjoram
  Few grains of mace or nutmeg
  ½ teaspoon peppercorns
  ½ teaspoon salt
Cook slowly 5 minutes. Add
  1 tablespoon lemon juice
  2 cups Chicken Stock (p. 72) or canned
    chicken broth
Simmer 15 minutes and strain. Add
  1 cup cooked or canned shrimp, cut
    small
Cook 5 minutes.
Just before serving, add
  1 cup heavy cream or milk (not icy
    cold)
  Dry sherry or white wine to taste, if
    desired
Serves 6 to 8.

Lobster or Crab Bisque

Put in a pan
    2 tablespoons butter
    1 teaspoon chopped onion
    Sprig of parsley
Cook slowly until the onion is yellow.
Add
    1½ cups finely chopped lobster or
    crab meat (fresh-cooked, canned or
    frozen)
Cook and stir 5 minutes. Stir in
    2 tablespoons flour
    1 tablespoon tomato paste (for color,
    but omit it if you wish)
Add
    2 cups Chicken Stock (p. 72) or canned
    chicken broth
Simmer 20 minutes. Remove the parsley.
Add
    2 cups thin cream or milk (not icy
    cold)
Heat but do not boil. Season with
    Salt and cayenne
Serves 6.

Lobster Bisque de Luxe

*The classic version — more complicated
than the preceding one and a superb
creation. Order the lobster split at the
market if you can cook it promptly.*

Put in a deep kettle
    2 cups Brown Stock (p. 70), canned
    consommé or water
    ¼ cup rice
Cook until the rice is very soft. Do not
drain.
In another pan, put
    2 tablespoons butter or olive oil
    1 carrot, sliced
    1 onion, sliced
Cook slowly 5 minutes. Add
    Bit of bay leaf
    Sprig of thyme or ½ teaspoon dried
    thyme
    1½-pound fresh lobster or 2 smaller
    ones, killed and split (p. 141,
    Broiled Live Lobsters)
Cover and cook until the lobster shells
are red. Add
    1 teaspoon salt

    ¼ teaspoon pepper
    1 cup dry white wine or ½ cup sherry
Cook slowly 15 minutes. Add
    2 cups Chicken Stock (p. 72) or
    canned chicken broth
Remove the lobster and strain the broth.
Take the lobster meat out of the shells
and set aside. Break up the shells and
scrape out of them as much of the bits
of meat as possible. Set aside.

Put the shells and the strained hot broth
in a pan, cover and simmer 1 hour (or
cook 10 minutes in a pressure pan).
Strain and add to the rice. Add the lob-
ster meat, cut small, and
    2 cups Chicken Stock (p. 72) or
    canned chicken broth
Put in a small pan
    1 tablespoon butter or olive oil
    1 tablespoon tomato paste
    Lobster liver (and coral, if any)
Stir over low heat until smooth. Add
slowly to the soup.
Just before serving, heat the soup and
add
    1 cup cream (not icy cold)
Season. Sprinkle with
    Croûtons or chopped parsley
Serves 8 to 10.

Lobster Stew

*The perfect lobster stew or chowder
should "age" at least 5 hours, so prepare it well ahead of serving time.*

Melt in a deep pan
    3 tablespoons butter
Add
    1 cup cooked or frozen lobster meat,
    cut in ¾-inch cubes
Cook and stir 5 minutes. Add very slowly,
stirring constantly
    1 quart milk (use part cream, if con-
    venient)
Heat slowly but do not boil. Season to
taste with
    Salt and paprika or cayenne
Serves 4.

To simplify. Scald the milk, add the
lobster meat, cover, and let stand 2 days

in the refrigerator to develop flavor. Heat and season.

Marblehead Lobster Stew. Boil 2 small lobsters (p. 141), remove the meat (p. 141), and cook in butter as above. Break up the shells and cook 10 minutes with 1 cup clam broth. Strain and add the broth to the stew.

Amsterdam Oyster Soup

Put in a saucepan
   1 pint shelled oysters, chopped
   1 cup water
Simmer 20 minutes. Strain. Add enough water to make 1 pint. Melt
   1 tablespoon butter
Cook until brown. Add
   1 tablespoon flour
Stir until brown. Add the oyster liquor gradually, stirring constantly. Simmer ½ hour. Season with
   Salt, paprika and celery salt
Just before serving, add
   ½ cup cream (not chilled)
Serves 4.

Oyster Stew

Put in a saucepan
   2 tablespoons butter
   ¼ teaspoon Worcestershire
   ½ teaspoon celery salt
Cook slowly 5 minutes. Add
   ½ pint shelled oysters (or more, if you like)
Heat gently until the oyster edges start to curl. Add
   2 cups hot milk or milk and cream

   1 tablespoon butter
Season with
   Salt and pepper
Pour into bowls and garnish with
   Paprika, chopped parsley, chopped chives or chopped green onion
Serves 2.

Oyster Stew with Celery. Melt 1 tablespoon butter, add ½ cup celery, cut fine, and cook slowly until tender. Add to the stew. Season delicately with sherry.

Mildred's Oyster Stew

Simple but delicious.

Heat in a double boiler
   2 cups milk or milk and cream
Add
   1 pint shelled oysters
Heat until the oysters curl. Add
   Salt and pepper to taste
   1 teaspoon butter (or more)
Serves 2.

Scallop Stew

Melt
   1 tablespoon butter
Add
   1 pint scallops, cleaned (p. 148) and (if large) cut in two
Cook 5 minutes. Add
   2 cups milk or milk and cream
   Salt and pepper to taste
Cook slowly 15 minutes. Add
   1 tablespoon butter
Serves 3 or 4.

Stuffings

Stuffing recipes serve as general guides. Vary them as you like. As a rule, prepare a cup of stuffing for each pound the bird weighs (allow 2 to 4 tablespoons of stuffing for each squab or Rock Cornish game hen) and 1 to 2 cups for a 4-pound fish or roast prepared with a pocket for stuffing. (Stuffed Roast Lamb, p. 175. Stuffed Roast Veal, p. 193. Baked Stuffed Fish, p. 119.)

Stuffing expands as it cooks, so do not pack it too firmly. If you have any left over, bake it separately in a greased pan. Serve leftover dressing cold with sliced meat, or spread it in a buttered pan, cover with sliced mushrooms, sprinkle with salt and pepper, dot with butter, and bake about 15 minutes at 400°.

Prepare crumbs for stuffing as directed on p. 7 or buy packaged crumbs, plain or seasoned. For very dry stuffing, which some people prefer, use homemade (p. 58) or packaged croûtons.

Bread Stuffing

This light and crumbly stuffing is delicate and buttery and so does not overwhelm the flavor of a young roast chicken. If your family prefers a more savory dressing, try any of the variations below.

Mix lightly with a fork
  4 cups dry bread crumbs
  ½ cup melted butter
  ½ teaspoon salt
  ⅛ teaspoon pepper
  1 tablespoon minced onion
Makes 4 cups.

Savory Bread Stuffing. Season with sage, poultry seasoning or celery seed, or increase the onion to as much as ¾ cup. In a highly seasoned dressing, try using bacon or sausage drippings or chicken fat in place of butter.

Stuffing Variations

Start with packaged crumbs or stuffing, or prepare Bread Stuffing (above). Add chopped chives, green pepper or pimiento, or leftovers such as chopped cooked meat or vegetables.

Apricot Stuffing. Omit the onion. Add 1 cup cooked apricots, cut in strips. Moisten with some of the water in which the apricots were cooked. Add ½ cup chopped celery.

Corn Bread Stuffing. Use dry corn bread for a third to a half of the crumbs. *Especially good for turkey.*

Corn Stuffing. Add to Corn Bread Stuffing 1 cup whole kernel corn.

Cranberry Stuffing. Chop 1 cup raw cranberries. Cook 5 minutes in the fat, stir in ¼ cup sugar, and add to the dressing.

Fruit Stuffing. Cut in small pieces drained fruit such as pineapple, mixed fruit cocktail, apricots, peaches, prunes or oranges. Add to plain stuffing and season to taste. For a richer stuffing, add chopped pecans, peanuts or other nuts.

Giblet Stuffing. Simmer the giblets in water until tender. Drain, reserving the broth, and chop. Add to the stuffing. Moisten with a little of the broth.

Herb Stuffing. Add thyme, sweet basil, summer savory or marjoram (1 tablespoon fresh or 1 teaspoon dried). Cut fresh herbs fine with scissors.

Mushroom Stuffing. For each cup of crumbs, add ½ cup chopped mushrooms, cooked 5 minutes in butter. If you like, add nutmeg to taste, or chopped parsley or chives.

Onion Stuffing. Parboil 6 onions 10 minutes. Drain, chop fine. Add to dressing with 1 egg slightly beaten.

Oyster Stuffing. Wash 1 pint oysters and remove the tough muscles. Add whole if small, chopped if large. Moisten with ¼ cup oyster liquid and lemon juice to taste. Season with salt, pepper and mace.

Parsley Stuffing. Add ¼ to ½ cup finely cut parsley. Cooked parsley is more delicate in flavor than uncooked, so put in plenty.

New England Stuffing

Lighter than Bread Stuffing.

Toast slowly until dry
    12 slices bread
Crumble into coarse crumbs and moisten with
    Stock or water
Add
    2-inch cube fat salt pork, finely chopped, or ⅛ pound sausage meat
    1 egg, well beaten
    Salt and pepper
    Sage or poultry seasoning
For chicken or turkey. Makes 3 cups.

To vary. Follow any of the suggestions for varying Bread Stuffing (above). Or replace some of the bread with mashed potato or cooked rice.

Apple Stuffing

Put in a saucepan
    4 tablespoons bacon fat
    2 cups diced tart apples (unpeeled)
    2 teaspoons sugar
Cook 5 minutes. Add
    ½ cup dry bread crumbs
    Salt, nutmeg and cinnamon to taste
For duck or pork. Makes about 2 cups.

Savory Apple Stuffing. Cook ½ cup each of chopped celery, onion and parsley in the fat for 2 minutes before adding the apple. Omit the nutmeg and cinnamon and season with salt and pepper.

Celery Stuffing

Put in a saucepan
    2 tablespoons butter
    ½ cup chopped celery
    2 tablespoons minced onion
    2 tablespoons chopped parsley
Cook 3 minutes. Add
    2 cups fine dry bread crumbs
    ¼ teaspoon savory seasoning
    ¼ teaspoon celery seed
    ½ teaspoon salt
    Few grains pepper
For chicken, duck or fish. Makes 3 cups.

Chestnut Stuffing

Put through ricer or food mill
    3 cups canned or cooked chestnuts
Add
    ¼ cup cream
    ¼ cup butter
    Salt and pepper
Mix
    ¼ cup melted butter
    1 cup cracker crumbs
Combine mixtures. *For chicken or turkey. Makes 4 cups.*

To vary, season more highly with thyme and marjoram, and add brandy to taste. See also Sausage and Chestnut Stuffing (p. 82).

Mint Stuffing

Put in a saucepan
  3 tablespoons butter
  1½ tablespoons chopped onion
  3 tablespoons chopped celery
Cook 2 minutes. Add
  ¾ teaspoon salt
  ⅛ teaspoon pepper
  ½ cup fresh mint leaves, finely cut
Cook until the liquid evaporates. Mix
  3 tablespoons melted butter
  3 cups fine dry bread crumbs
Stir into the first mixture. *For chicken, lamb or fish. Makes 3 cups.*

Watercress Stuffing. In place of mint use 1½ cups finely cut watercress.

Orange Stuffing

Toast lightly
  3 cups bread cubes (¼ inch)
Add
  ½ cup hot water or orange juice
Let stand 15 minutes. Add
  2 teaspoons grated orange rind
  ⅔ cup orange sections, freed from membrane
  2 cups finely cut celery
  ¼ cup melted butter
  1 egg, slightly beaten
  ½ teaspoon salt
  ⅛ teaspoon pepper
For duck. Makes 4 to 5 cups.

Prune and Apple Stuffing

Pour boiling water over
  ½ pound dried prunes
  2 tablespoons seeded raisins
Let stand 5 minutes. Drain. Remove the pits and cut the prunes in pieces. Add
  2 tablespoons cracker crumbs
  ⅛ teaspoon salt
  ¼ teaspoon sugar
  1 egg yolk, beaten
  1 large apple, peeled, cored, and sliced
For duck and pork. Makes 2 cups.

Wild Rice and Mushroom Stuffing

Steam until soft
  1 cup wild rice (or use 2 cups canned cooked wild rice)
Cook together for 5 minutes
  2 tablespoons butter or cooking oil
  ¼ pound chopped mushrooms
  ¼ cup chopped onion
Add to the rice. Season to taste with
  Salt, pepper and nutmeg
Makes about 3 cups. Enough for 4- or 5-pound chicken or 8 or more squab or Rock Cornish game hens.

Sausage Stuffing

Cook and stir until brown
  1 pound pork sausage meat
Add
  12 cups dry bread cubes (¼ inch)
  2 tablespoons minced onion
  Salt to taste
  1 teaspoon pepper
  2 tablespoons minced parsley
Makes 12 cups. Enough for 12- to 14-pound turkey.

Sausage and Sweet Potato Dressing. Use 6 instead of 12 cups bread cubes and add 5 cups mashed sweet potatoes and 1 cup finely cut celery (with the tops).

Sausage and Chestnut Stuffing

Boil and shell (p. 13)
  4 dozen Italian chestnuts
Mash half of them. Put in a pan
  2 tablespoons butter
  1 small onion, finely chopped
Cook 3 minutes. Add
  ½ pound sausage meat
Cook and stir 5 minutes. Add the mashed chestnuts. Mix well. Season with
  2 teaspoons salt
  ¼ teaspoon pepper
  ⅛ teaspoon powdered thyme
  2 teaspoons finely chopped parsley
Mix in the whole chestnuts and
  1 cup fresh bread crumbs
For chicken or turkey. Makes 4 cups.

Garnishes and Quick Relishes

Over-elaborate decorations are out of style. As with seasonings, garnishes should enhance, not overwhelm, the dish with which they are used. Special garnishes and relishes are described throughout the book, for example under Consommé (p. 71), Roast Lamb (p. 174) and Buttered Spinach (p. 255), and in the introductory material for Fish (p. 117) and Salads (p. 270). Often the best garnish of all is no more than a few sprigs of parsley, mint or watercress or a sprinkling of paprika.

Horseradish (p. 527) is a traditional accompaniment for cold meats and for hot roast beef and corned beef.

Mustard is also good with cold meats. Moisten dry mustard with water or vinegar or use a seasoned mustard.

Lemons or limes, in thin slices, lengthwise sections or fan-shaped pieces.

Truffles (marketed in small tins or jars) add epicurean elegance to a molded salad or other cold entree.

Fresh Vegetable Relishes

Crisp raw vegetables are welcome relishes with lunch or dinner, especially when no salad is served. They are popular, too, with pre-dinner drinks and as snacks for children. Prepare and put in ice water to crisp. Drain just before serving.

Carrots, cut in matchlike sticks or in curls (p. 270).

Cauliflower, separated into flowerets.

Celeriac (celery root), sliced and seasoned with salt and vinegar.

Celery, hearts or sticks (p. 270).

Cucumber, cut in sticks 4 inches long and as thick as a pencil.

Radishes (p. 270).

Relish Bowl. Fill a shallow bowl with crushed ice. Stick crisped celery stalks, carrot and cucumber sticks into the ice, upright.

Fried Parsley

Wash perfect sprigs and pat dry on a paper towel. In a small deep pan, heat vegetable oil or fat to 390°. The fat should be deep enough to cover the parsley completely. Add the parsley, a few sprigs at a time, and fry 1 minute. Remove with tongs and drain on a paper towel. Serve immediately on fish, broiled chops or steak.

Fruit Relishes

A fruit relish adds flavor and color to enhance what might otherwise be too bland a dish. Fruits go especially well with pork, veal and poultry. Many other recipes are in the fruit section (p. 345) — applesauce and cinnamon apples to serve with pork, sautéed bananas and hot fruit compotes, which are excellent with turkey

Simple Garnishes

Carrot Sticks and Curls

Watercress

Radish Slices and Roses

Parsley

Hard-Boiled Eggs

Lemon Shapes

Cucumber

Tomatoes

Pepper Rings

Mushrooms and Truffles

Croûtons, Nuts, and Cheese Balls

Pickles and Olives

and goose. Improvise a fruit relish, hot or cold, by using canned fruit, drained and seasoned with cinnamon, brandy or rum.

Fruit Kabobs

A good barbecue relish.

String on skewers pineapple cubes, spiced apricot or peach halves and cooked and pitted prunes. Brush with butter and broil 5 minutes. *Serve hot with chicken or lamb chops.*

Fried Apple Rings

Core tart apples. Pare only if the skins are very tough. Cut in ½-inch slices. Sauté in butter or in bacon or sausage fat until just barely tender. Turn once with a broad spatula. When the apples are nearly tender, sprinkle lightly with brown sugar or grated cheese. Cover, and cook until the sugar or cheese melts. *Serve with sausage, ham or pork.*

Spiced Crabapples

Put in a saucepan
 1 cup sugar
 2 cups boiling water
 24 whole cloves
 6 allspice berries
 2-inch stick of cinnamon
 Few grains salt
Add
 1 pound crabapples (washed)
Simmer gently until the apples are tender. Skim out the fruit and pour a little of the juice over it. If it is to be stored overnight, cover with the juice and drain off most of it when you serve the fruit. *For ham or pork.*

Spiced **Cranberries or Carrots.** Add raw cranberries or tiny new carrots to the syrup in place of crabapples.

Spiced **Apricots or Peaches.** Pour the syrup over cooked or canned pitted apricots or peach halves. Do not cook, but let stand until the syrup is cold.

Cranberry Sauce

Put in a saucepan
 1 pound cranberries (washed)
 1½ cups sugar
 2 cups boiling water
Cook 10 minutes. Watch to prevent boiling over. Skim off the white froth. Cool. *Serves 6.*

Baked Cranberries

Put in a baking dish
 1 pound cranberries (washed)
Sprinkle with
 1½ cups sugar
Cover. Bake 1 hour at 350°. *Serves 6.*

Cranberry Jelly

Put in a saucepan
 1 pound cranberries (washed)
 2 cups boiling water
Boil 20 minutes. Rub through a sieve and cook 3 minutes. Add
 2 cups sugar
 Few grains salt
Cook 2 minutes. Pour into a mold or bowl. Chill. *Serves 8.*

Spiced **Cranberry Jelly.** Cook the cranberries with a 2-inch piece of stick cinnamon, 24 whole cloves and 6 allspice berries.

Cranberry Jelly with Celery. When the jelly begins to thicken, fold in 1½ cups celery, cut crosswise in ⅛-inch slices.

Sparkling Cranberry Mold

Wash and drain
Make a slit partway through each berry. Add
 3 cups perfect cranberries
 3 cups sugar
 1 cup cold water
Bring very slowly to the boiling point, stirring gently. Boil 1 minute. Remove from the heat. Stir in
 ½ bottle liquid pectin
Skim off the foam. Pour into a mold. *For chicken, turkey or pork.*

Cranberry and Orange Relish

Wash
2 cups cranberries
Cut in pieces and remove the seeds from
1 small orange
Put the fruit through a food chopper.
Add
¾ cup sugar
Mix thoroughly. Let stand 30 minutes or
more. *Serves 6 to 8.*

Cranberry Catsup

*A quickly made relish to serve with pork,
veal, chicken or turkey.*

Put in a saucepan
1 pound cranberries
½ cup mild vinegar
⅔ cup water
Boil until the berries are soft (about 5
minutes). Put through a food mill. Add
1 cup brown sugar
½ teaspoon each of clove, ginger and
paprika
1 teaspoon cinnamon
½ teaspoon salt
¼ teaspoon pepper
Simmer 3 minutes. Add
2 tablespoons butter
Serve at room temperature. *Makes 1 pint.*

Orange Slices

Slice a whole orange. Remove the seeds.
Dot the slices with currant or mint jelly.
Arrange on the platter around *roast
lamb, duck, veal or chicken.*

Broiled Orange Slices. Dot the slices with
butter and sprinkle lightly with brown
sugar and a trace of curry powder. Broil
until the sugar melts.

Baked Oranges

Cover small seedless oranges with cold
water. Bring to the boiling point, simmer
½ hour and drain. Cut a slice off the top
of each orange and put in a teaspoon of
sugar. Bake in the pan with *roast turkey
or duck.*

Broiled Peaches or Apricots

Also delicious as dessert.

Put fresh or canned peach or apricot
halves in a shallow pan, cut side up. Dot
with butter and sprinkle with brown
sugar. Broil until the sugar melts. *For
turkey or duck.*

Broiled Peaches with Blueberries. Put a
spoonful of blueberries in each half, dot
with butter and sprinkle with sugar.
Broil slowly.

Broiled Brandied Peaches. Put ½ teaspoon brandy in each peach half.

Glazed Pineapple

Drain canned pineapple slices. Put in a
single layer in a shallow baking pan.
Place over very slow heat or in a 250°
oven. Cook until the pineapple is almost
transparent (2 to 3 hours). Garnish each
slice with a candied cherry. *For ham.*

Sautéed Pineapple

Drain canned sliced pineapple. Dry on a
paper towel. Sauté in butter until delicately browned. *For lamb chops or ham.*

Bacon-Wrapped Prunes

Cook prunes until plump and tender
but not soft. Drain and remove the pits.
Wrap in half-slices of bacon. String on
skewers, put in a shallow pan, and bake
at 450° until the bacon is crisp. Remove
from the skewers and serve on the platter
around *turkey, ham or pork.*

Chutney Prunes. Stuff with chutney before wrapping in bacon.

Deviled Raisins

Stem large raisins and sauté in salad oil
until plump. Drain on a paper towel.
Sprinkle with salt and paprika or with
a few drops of rum. *For chicken or veal.*

Deviled Almonds

Mix
  1 tablespoon chutney
  2 tablespoons chopped pickles
  1 tablespoon Worcestershire
  ¼ teaspoon salt

Few grains cayenne
Sprinkle over
  ⅔ cup sautéed blanched and shredded
    almonds (p. 13)
Heat. *For fish or chicken.*

Pickles and Relishes

Beginning on p. 519 there are many recipes for pickles and relishes to be made in quantity and stored to use throughout the year. Drain pickles thoroughly and chill.

Beet Relish

If you use bottled horseradish, drain it well.

Mix well
  1 cup chopped cooked or canned beets
  3 tablespoons grated horseradish root
  2 tablespoons lemon juice
  2 teaspoons fine sugar
  1 teaspoon salt
See also Pickled Beets (pp. 238, 521).
Makes 1 cup.

Celery Relish

Mix
  1½ cups chopped celery, including
    small tender leaves
  4 teaspoons fine sugar
  1 teaspoon salt
  ½ teaspoon mustard
  ¼ cup vinegar
Cover and let stand in a cold place 1½ hours. Drain before serving. *Serves 6.*

Quick Chili Sauce

Combine
  2 cups canned tomatoes
  1 onion, chopped
  ½ teaspoon salt
  Few grains cayenne
  ⅛ teaspoon each of ground cloves and
    ground cinnamon

  ⅛ cup sugar (or more)
  ½ cup mild vinegar
Simmer 1 hour. Add
  2 tablespoons chopped green pepper
Simmer ½ hour. *Makes about 1½ cups.*

Quick Mustard Relish

Mix
  2 cups shredded cabbage
  1 pimiento, chopped fine
  ½ large green pepper, chopped fine
  ⅓ cup chopped onion
  1 cup vinegar
  1½ cups water
  2 tablespoons salt
Let stand several hours.

Mix
  ¼ cup sugar
  3 tablespoons flour
  2 teaspoons mustard
  ¼ teaspoon turmeric
  ¼ teaspoon celery salt
  ½ teaspoon salt
Add slowly, stirring constantly
  ½ cup cold water
  ½ cup vinegar
Stir and cook over hot water or low heat until thick. Cover and cook 10 minutes. Bring the vegetables to the boiling point and drain off the liquid. Add them to the dressing and simmer 5 minutes. Serve cold. *Makes about 3 cups.*

Philadelphia Relish

Mix
    2 cups finely shredded cabbage
    2 green peppers, finely chopped
    1 teaspoon celery seed
    ¼ teaspoon mustard seed
    ½ teaspoon salt
    2 tablespoons brown sugar
    ¼ cup vinegar
Let stand at least an hour before serving.
Makes 2½ cups.

Summer Relish

Chop and mix
    1 cored apple
    1 onion
    3 tomatoes
    3 stalks celery
Add
    1 tablespoon finely chopped mint
        leaves
    ½ cup raisins
    2 tablespoons vinegar
    ¼ teaspoon cardamon seeds
    1 clove garlic, crushed
    1 teaspoon salt
    1 fresh chili, seeded and chopped, or
        ½ teaspoon cayenne
Heat to the boiling point. Serve either
hot or cold. *Makes 2 cups.*

Sherbets and Frappés as Relishes

Tart sherbets and frappés are refreshing accompaniments for the
main course, especially for holiday dinners. Simple fruit sherbets,
such as lemon or lime, are suitable as well as the special ices for
which recipes follow.

To serve, stir or beat slightly and put small scoops in chilled
sherbet glasses.

Cranberry Frappé

*A frappé should be slightly icy, not
smooth.*

Cook together 8 minutes
    1 quart cranberries
    2 cups water
Put through a sieve. Add
    2 cups sugar
    Juice of 2 lemons
Cool. Pour the mixture into a refrigerator tray and freeze without stirring until
firm. *For chicken or turkey.*

Currant Ice

Boil together 5 minutes
    2 cups water
    ¾ cup sugar
Add
    1 cup currant juice
Cool. Freeze like Cranberry Frappé
(above). *For roast lamb, chicken or
turkey.*

Tomato Frappé

Combine
    1¾ cups tomatoes, cut small
    3 apples, cored, pared and chopped
    2 cups water
    1 cup sugar
    3 tablespoons lemon juice
    Piece gingerroot or ¼ teaspoon ginger
Cook 35 minutes. Rub through a sieve
and freeze to a mush. Makes 1 quart. *For
roast lamb, ham or turkey.*

Sauces for Fish, Meat and Vegetables

Many gourmet dishes owe their special appeal to a perfectly made sauce, subtly seasoned. Simply cooked meat or fish can become superb company fare when served with one of the classic sauces or with an interesting variation.

Sauces to serve with spaghetti (p. 298).

Thickening sauces. A thickened sauce should be satin-smooth. If necessary, put it through a strainer. Flour is the most commonly used thickener. The new easy-blending type is excellent for sauce making. Blend the flour smoothly with the melted fat over very low heat before adding the liquid. Frequent stirring keeps the sauce velvety as it cooks.

The mixture of fat and flour is called a roux. White roux is made without browning, brown roux by browning the fat and flour before adding the liquid, as in a brown gravy.

Potato flour and cornstarch are particularly successful as the thickening for a clear sauce. To substitute for flour, use 1 teaspoon potato flour or cornstarch for each tablespoon of flour in any sauce recipe.

Seasoning sauces. A recipe can only give the approximate amount of seasoning needed. Avoid over-seasoning, especially with herbs.

Maître d'Hôtel Butter

Also called Parsley Butter.

Cream
    ½ cup butter
Beat in
    ½ teaspoon salt
    ⅛ teaspoon pepper
    2 tablespoons finely chopped parsley

Beat in, drop by drop
    1 tablespoon lemon juice
For steak, chops or broiled fish. Makes about ½ cup.

Herb Butter. Add 1 teaspoon dried thyme or marjoram and 1 teaspoon dried basil. Or add fresh herbs, chopped fine. Add ¼ teaspoon garlic salt. *Spread on broiled lamb chops.*

Parsley Butter Pats. Put Maître d'Hôtel Butter on a piece of wax paper. Shape into a cylinder about 1 inch thick. Wrap and chill. When ready to serve, slice and place a pat on each serving of *steak, lamb chops or broiled fish.*

Black Butter

Beurre Noir in French cuisine. Instead of using all butter, you may use the fat remaining in the pan after frying fish or meat and add enough butter to make about ⅓ cup.

Put in a small pan
    ⅓ cup butter
Stir over low heat until melted and dark brown. Add
    1 teaspoon lemon juice or mild vinegar
    Salt and pepper
For fish or meat.

Tart Black Butter. Add 1 tablespoon vinegar and 1 tablespoon Worcestershire.

Almond Black Butter. When the butter begins to brown, stir in ⅓ cup blanched almonds, cut in pieces.

Lemon Butter

Cream butter until very light and fluffy. Season with a few drops of lemon juice. *For canapés and sandwiches as well as for fish.*

Savory Butter (p. 48).

Cream Sauce (White Sauce)

Every cook should learn to make a perfect cream sauce. It is the basis for many dishes, such as soufflés and cream soups, as well as for such recipes as creamed chicken or tuna fish and scalloped dishes. As a convenience, keep a jar in the refrigerator ready for hurry-up meals. A blending fork helps keep the sauce smooth as it cooks.

Melt in a double boiler top or a small heavy pan
    2 tablespoons butter
Stir in
    2 tablespoons flour
Blend well over low heat. Stir in slowly
    1 cup milk or part milk and part cream
Stirring constantly, bring slowly to the boiling point and cook 2 minutes. Season to taste with
    Salt and pepper
Makes 1 cup.

To season more highly, add paprika, meat extract, onion juice, onion salt or herbs, or mix ¼ teaspoon dry mustard with the flour.

For a richer sauce, beat 1 egg yolk slightly and stir it into the sauce just before serving.

Brown Almond Sauce. Add to the melted butter ¼ cup (or more) chopped blanched almonds. Cook and stir until delicately brown.

Curry Cream Sauce. Add to the flour 1 teaspoon curry powder and ¼ teaspoon ground ginger. Season highly to taste with onion juice and paprika.

Lobster Sauce. Add 1 teaspoon meat extract and ½ cup diced cooked or canned lobster meat. Add the lobster coral if

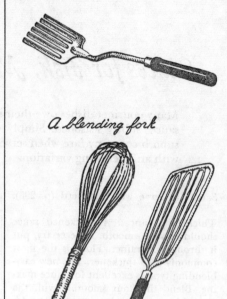

A blending fork

Two types of wire whisk

you are using fresh lobster. See also Lobster Velouté Sauce (p. 92).

Mock Hollandaise. Just before serving, stir in 2 egg yolks, 6 tablespoons butter (a tablespoon at a time) and 1 tablespoon lemon juice.

Onion Sauce. Add to the butter 3 tablespoons chopped onion and cook 3 minutes. For a richer sauce, stir in 1 egg yolk, slightly beaten, just before serving.

Parsley Cream Sauce. Add 1 to 4 tablespoons chopped parsley.

Truffle Sauce. Add 1 tablespoon chopped canned truffles and 1 tablespoon Madeira.

Hot Tartare Sauce

Mix
    ½ cup Cream Sauce (above)
    ⅓ cup mayonnaise
    ½ shallot, finely chopped, or
        1 teaspoon finely chopped onion

½ teaspoon vinegar or tarragon
vinegar
½ tablespoon each of finely chopped
pickles, olives and parsley
1 tablespoon capers

Set over low heat. Stir constantly until thoroughly heated, but do not bring to the boiling point. *For fish or ham. Makes about 1 cup.*

Cheese Sauce

Make Cream Sauce and add to it ¼ to ¾ cup mild or sharp cheese, grated or cut in small cubes. Heat in a double boiler or over very low heat until the cheese melts. *For eggs, toast and vegetables.*

Sauce Mornay. This French sauce is usually made with a combination of two kinds of cheese such as Parmesan and Swiss. One-fourth cup will be enough for this delicate sauce. Just before serving, stir in an egg yolk, slightly beaten, and 2 tablespoons butter, bit by bit. Taste, and add more salt, if necessary.

Jiffy Cheese Sauce

This sauce keeps well in the refrigerator. Convenient for hurry-up meals such as cheese toast or sliced cooked eggs in cheese sauce.

Heat in double boiler or in a saucepan over very low heat
1 small can evaporated milk (1 cup)
Add
½ cup mild or sharp cheese, cut small
Stir until the sauce is smooth. Season to taste with
Salt, paprika, dry mustard, curry powder or bits of pimiento
If the sauce is too thick, add
A little milk or cream
Makes about 1½ cups.

Béchamel Sauce

A tasty cream sauce made with part stock and part milk. Use it with any of the variations suggested on p. 90.

Cook together 20 minutes
1½ cups Chicken Stock (p. 72)

1 slice onion
1 slice carrot
Bit of bay leaf
Sprig of parsley
6 peppercorns

Strain. There should be 1 cupful.
Melt
¼ cup butter
Add and blend well
¼ cup flour
Add gradually, stirring constantly, the strained chicken stock and
1 cup milk or milk and cream
Cook and stir until thick. Season with
Salt and pepper
Makes 2 cups.

Yellow Béchamel Sauce. Just before serving, add 1 egg yolk, slightly beaten and mixed with a small quantity of the hot sauce.

Drawn Butter

Melt
2 tablespoons butter
Add
2 tablespoons flour
½ teaspoon salt
⅛ teaspoon pepper
Stir until smooth. Stir in slowly
1 cup hot water or Fish Stock (p. 120)
Boil 5 minutes. Add
1 teaspoon lemon juice
2 tablespoons butter, bit by bit
For fish. Makes 1 cup.

For a richer sauce, stir in a slightly beaten egg yolk just before serving.

To vary, season with anchovy paste or add a tablespoon of drained capers.

Egg Sauce. Add 2 hard-cooked eggs, sliced ¼ inch thick.

Shrimp Sauce. Add ½ cup cooked or canned shrimps, cut in pieces.

Normandy Sauce. Just before serving, pour slowly over 2 well-beaten egg yolks. Season to taste with more lemon juice or with grated cheese and Madeira. Madeira is traditional, but sherry is good, too.

Berçy Sauce

Melt
   1 tablespoon butter
Add
   1 tablespoon finely chopped shallot or
     1 teaspoon finely chopped onion
Cook 5 minutes. Add
   2 tablespoons flour
Blend well. Add gradually, stirring constantly
   1 cup Chicken Stock (p. 72) or canned
     chicken broth
Simmer 15 minutes and strain. Add
   2 tablespoons butter
Season to taste with
   Salt and pepper
For chicken or fish. Makes 1 cup.

Lemon Sauce

Heat in a small, deep pan
   1 cup Chicken Stock (p. 72) or broth
   1 tablespoon butter
Mix until smooth
   2 tablespoons cornstarch
   ¼ cup cold water
Stir slowly into the heated stock. Cook 5 minutes, stirring constantly.

Beat together until frothy
   2 egg yolks
   Juice and grated rind of 1 lemon
Stir in a little of the hot mixture, then pour slowly back into the pan. Heat but do not boil. Season to taste. *For cauliflower, spinach, zucchini or other vegetables. Makes 1½ cups.*

Velouté Sauce

Many famous sauces are actually Velouté Sauce with special seasoning added. Strong chicken stock makes all the difference. All these sauces are delicious over steamed or pan-broiled fish fillets.

Melt
   2 tablespoons butter
Add
   3 tablespoons flour
   ¼ teaspoon salt
   Few grains pepper
Blend well. Add slowly, stirring constantly

   1 cup Chicken Stock (p. 72) or canned
     chicken broth
Bring to the boiling point and boil 2 minutes. Add
   ⅓ cup cream
Makes about 1 cup.

For a simpler sauce, use 2 tablespoons flour and omit the cream.

As a variation, use only ½ cup chicken stock and add ½ cup white wine.

Suprême Sauce (Poulette Sauce). Just before serving, stir in 1 or 2 egg yolks, slightly beaten. Season to taste with a few grains of nutmeg and a dash of lemon juice.

Allemande Sauce. Add 3 tablespoons grated Parmesan to Suprême Sauce.

Lobster Velouté Sauce. Cover lobster shells with water. Cover and simmer 1 hour or cook 20 minutes in a pressure cooker. Strain off the liquid and boil until it is reduced to 1 cupful. Use this stock as the liquid for Velouté Sauce. Season with salt, paprika and lemon juice. Just before serving, add ½ cup diced cooked lobster. For a richer sauce, stir in 2 egg yolks, slightly beaten, and remove the sauce from the heat.

Olive and Almond Sauce. Just before serving, add ¼ cup shredded toasted almonds, 1 teaspoon beef extract, 8 olives, pitted and quartered, and ½ tablespoon lemon juice.

Russian Sauce. Before adding the cream, add ½ teaspoon finely chopped chives, ½ teaspoon prepared mustard, and 1 teaspoon grated horseradish. Cook 2 minutes. Strain, add the cream and 1 teaspoon lemon juice. Reheat.

Soubise Sauce. Cook 2 cups sliced onions 5 minutes in boiling water to cover. Drain. Cover with boiling water and cook until soft. Drain, rub through a sieve, and add to the sauce. Season.

Mushroom Velouté. Add ¼ cup sliced mushroom caps to Velouté or Suprême Sauce. Cook 5 minutes. Season.

Brown Sauce

See also Brown Gravy (p. 156).

Melt
  2 tablespoons butter or bacon fat
Add
  ½ slice onion (if desired)
Cook slowly until the fat is well browned
but not black. Add
  2 tablespoons flour or 2 teaspoons
    potato flour
  ½ teaspoon salt
  ⅛ teaspoon pepper
  Few grains sugar
Add gradually
  1 cup Brown Stock (p. 70), con-
    sommé or water
Bring to the boiling point. Boil 2 minutes. Strain or remove the bit of onion.
Cook 15 minutes in a double boiler or
over very low heat. Serve over cooked
sliced meats. *Makes about 1 cup.*

For a thinner sauce, add more boiling
water or stock and stir thoroughly. Taste,
and correct the seasoning.

For a stronger onion flavor, mince the
onion and leave it in the sauce, or add a
few drops of onion juice.

Anchovy Sauce. Season with anchovy
essence or paste. *For fish.*

Bordelaise Sauce. Cook with the onion
1 shallot, chopped fine, 2 slices of carrot,
a sprig of parsley, a bit of bay leaf and a
whole clove. Season highly with Worcestershire, catsup or sherry.

Brown Curry Sauce. Season highly with
curry powder and dry mustard.

Chestnut Sauce. Add ½ cup boiled
French chestnuts, chopped or broken in
pieces.

Currant Jelly Sauce. Omit the onion.
Melt ¼ glass currant jelly in the sauce.
Season with 2 tablespoons sherry or port.

Sauce Espagnole. Cook in the bacon fat
1 tablespoon each of chopped ham, celery
and carrot. Add with the stock ⅓ cup

stewed tomatoes. Cook 5 minutes. Strain
or not.

Olive Sauce. Add 1 or 2 tablespoons
chopped ripe or stuffed olives.

Sauce Piquante. Add 1 tablespoon vinegar, ½ small shallot, finely chopped, 1
tablespoon capers, 1 tablespoon chopped
pickle and a few grains cayenne.

Brown Russian Sauce. Stir in ¼ cup
tomato catsup and ½ cup sour cream.

Marchand de Vin Sauce

Melt
  ¼ cup butter
Stir in
  6 scallions, minced, or ½ cup minced
    onion
Cook 5 minutes. Add
  ¾ cup red wine
Simmer 20 minutes. Add
  1 cup Brown Gravy (p. 156) or Brown
    Sauce (above)
  2 tablespoons lemon juice
Just before serving, heat and stir in bit
by bit
  2 tablespoons butter
*For steak or roast beef. Makes about 2
cups.*

Bread Sauce

*The English serve bread sauce—almost as
thick as mayonnaise—and thin dish gravy
with fowl or game.*

Heat in a double boiler
  2 cups milk
Add
  ⅓ cup fine stale bread crumbs
  1 onion stuck with 6 cloves
Cook slowly 30 minutes. Remove the
onion. Stir in
  1 teaspoon salt
  Few grains cayenne
  2 tablespoons butter
Put in a frying pan
  1 tablespoon butter
  ½ cup coarse dry bread crumbs
Stir over moderate heat until brown. Put
the sauce in a serving bowl and sprinkle
with the crumbs. *Makes about 2 cups.*

Mushroom Sauce

Another good mushroom sauce is gravy thick with sliced sautéed mushrooms. See also Mushroom Velouté (p. 92) and Tomato and Mushroom Sauce (p. 95).

Melt
  3 tablespoons butter
Add
  ½ pound mushrooms, sliced
Cook 5 minutes. Stir in
  3 tablespoons flour
  Few drops onion juice
Cook 5 minutes over low heat. Add gradually, stirring constantly
  1 cup cream
Season with
  1 teaspoon beef extract
  Salt and paprika
Makes 1½ to 2 cups.

Roberts Sauce

Melt in a small saucepan
  1 tablespoon butter
Add
  3 shallots, finely chopped, or 2 tablespoons chopped mild onion
  1 teaspoon flour
Cook 5 minutes. Add
  1 tablespoon vinegar
  ½ cup Chicken Stock (p. 72) or canned chicken broth
  2 chopped pickles
  ½ tablespoon chopped capers
  1 teaspoon chopped olives
  ½ teaspoon prepared mustard
  ½ teaspoon salt
  Few grains cayenne
Cook 10 minutes, stirring constantly. *For fish. Makes about 1 cup.*

Oyster Sauce

Put in a pan
  1 pint shelled oysters
Cook slowly until the oysters are plump (about 5 minutes). Remove the oysters. Measure the liquid in the pan and add to it
  Milk, water, Chicken Stock (p. 72) or canned chicken broth (enough to make 1¾ cups)

Melt
  ¼ cup butter
Blend in
  ¼ cup flour
Stir well and add the oyster liquid gradually, stirring constantly. Boil 2 minutes. Add the oysters. Season with
  Salt and pepper
For fish. Makes about 2 cups.

Russian Oyster Sauce

Put in a pan
  1 cup chopped shelled oysters
Cook 5 minutes. Strain, and measure the liquid in the pan. Add
  Chicken Stock (p. 72) or canned chicken broth (to make 1 cup)
Melt
  3 tablespoons butter
Blend in
  ¼ cup flour
Stir in slowly
  ½ cup cream
Add the oyster liquid. Bring to the boiling point. Add the oysters. Stir in
  2 egg yolks, slightly beaten
  ½ tablespoon vinegar
  1 tablespoon lemon juice
  2 tablespoons capers
  1 tablespoon grated horseradish
  Salt and pepper to taste
For fish. Makes about 2 cups.

Tomato Sauce

The number of tomato sauces is endless — from the simplest made of tomato paste diluted to the desired thickness with water to the delicious variations which require many ingredients and long, slow cooking. See pp. 298–299 for sauces to serve with spaghetti and other pastes.

Melt until brown
  2 tablespoons butter
Stir in
  2 tablespoons flour
Add slowly
  1 cup tomato juice or tomato cocktail or strained cooked or canned tomatoes
Cook and stir over low heat until thick.

Season to taste with
  Salt and pepper
  Onion salt
  Orégano or nutmeg
Makes about 1 cup.

Tomato and Mushroom Sauce. Add 1 cup sliced mushrooms, canned or sautéed in butter.

Mexican Tomato Sauce

Cook together 5 minutes
  1 onion, chopped fine
  2 tablespoons butter
Add
  1 red pepper, chopped fine
  1 green pepper, chopped fine
  1 clove garlic, minced
  2 tomatoes, peeled and cut in pieces
Cook 15 minutes. Season with
  1 teaspoon Worcestershire
  ¼ teaspoon celery salt
  Salt
Makes about 1 cup.

Sauce Finiste

Cook until well browned
  3 tablespoons butter
Stir in
  ½ teaspoon mustard
  Few grains cayenne
  1 teaspoon lemon juice
  1½ teaspoons Worcestershire
  ¾ cup stewed and strained tomatoes
For steak, hamburg or fish. Makes about 1 cup.

Hollandaise

This queen of sauces is superb with artichokes, asparagus, broccoli, green beans, fish, steak, veal or broiled chicken, or in special dishes such as Eggs Benedict. Mock Hollandaise (p. 90).

Put in a small heavy saucepan or double boiler top
  3 egg yolks
Beat with a wooden spoon or wire whisk until smooth but not fluffy. Add
  2 tablespoons lemon juice or mild
    vinegar

½ cup butter or margarine, melted
2 tablespoons hot water
¼ teaspoon salt
Few grains cayenne
Set over very low heat or over hot water and beat until the sauce begins to thicken (about 5 minutes). The sauce will be thicker as it cools. *Makes about 1 cup.*

Sauce Trianon. Season with sherry.

Béarnaise Sauce. Add 1 teaspoon finely chopped parsley and 1 teaspoon chopped fresh tarragon or ½ tablespoon tarragon vinegar. Or make Hollandaise with tarragon vinegar and add 1 teaspoon finely chopped parsley.

Cucumber Hollandaise. Pare cucumber. Chop and squeeze in a piece of cheesecloth to drain thoroughly. Add ¼ to ½ cup to the Hollandaise. Add a few grains of cayenne.

Sauce Mousseline. Fold in ¼ cup heavy cream, whipped.

Sauce Henriette. Add 1 tablespoon each of tomato paste and chopped parsley.

Sauce Figaro. Season Sauce Henriette to taste with sherry or Worcestershire.

Victor Hugo Sauce. Stir 1 teaspoon meat extract into the butter. To the finished sauce add 1 tablespoon grated horseradish and a few drops of onion juice.

Blender Hollandaise

Incredibly easy and quick — made in less than a minute.

Melt
  ½ cup butter or margarine
Put in an electric blender
  3 egg yolks (at room temperature)
  2 tablespoons lemon juice
  ¼ teaspoon salt
  Few grains cayenne
Blend at low speed for a few seconds, just long enough to mix smoothly.

Pour in the hot butter slowly. Blend a few seconds longer, until the sauce is smooth. *Makes about 1 cup.*

Edie's Hollandaise

Less rich than classic Hollandaise.

Beat until thick and set aside
    2 egg yolks
Heat in a double boiler top
    ¾ cup water
    2 tablespoons lemon juice
    ¼ teaspoon salt
Stir together until smooth
    2 tablespoons cornstarch
    ¼ cup water
Add to the first mixture and stir to mix
well. Pour slowly over the egg yolks,
stirring constantly. Pour back into the
double boiler top and set over hot water.
Add
    2 tablespoons butter
Cook and stir until thick. *Makes about
1 cup.*

Hot Mayonnaise

Put in a small heavy pan or double
boiler top.
    2 egg yolks
Beat slightly. Stir in slowly
    2 tablespoons olive oil
Stir in, a little at a time
    1 tablespoon vinegar
    ¼ cup hot water
Stir and cook over very low heat or over
hot water until thickened. Season with
    Salt and a few grains cayenne
Add
    1 teaspoon finely chopped parsley
*For fish or vegetables. Makes about ½
cup.*

Aioli

*A famous French sauce of the mayon-
naise type with a strong garlic flavor.*

Have ready
    1 cup olive oil
Peel and split
    8 cloves garlic
Mash in a garlic press or as described on
p. 16. Mix with
    1 egg yolk
    ¼ teaspoon salt
    Few grains pepper

Stir in, drop by drop, 3 tablespoons of
the olive oil and
    Juice of 1 lemon
Stir in the rest of the oil, a little at a
time. *For bland-flavored fish such as sole,
flounder or halibut. Makes about 1 cup.*

Guaymas Sauce

Just before serving, mix
    ⅓ cup tomato juice, canned or home-
        made
    1 cup mayonnaise
    2 tablespoons olives, cut in slivers
For fish. Makes about 1½ cups.

Littleton Sauce

Mix in a heavy pan or double boiler top
    1 teaspoon flour
    1 teaspoon dry mustard
Stir in
    1 tablespoon butter
    1 tablespoon vinegar
    ½ cup boiling water
    3 egg yolks, well beaten
Cook over boiling water or very low
heat until thickened, stirring constantly.
Season with
    ¼ teaspoon salt
    Few grains pepper
    Few grains cayenne
Just before serving, stir in
    1 tablespoon currant jelly
For fish. Makes about 1 cup.

Horseradish Sauce

Mix
    ½ cup cracker or bread crumbs
    ½ cup grated horseradish
    1½ cups milk or milk and cream
Let stand 2 hours. Cook 20 minutes over
hot water or very low heat. Add
    3 tablespoons butter
    ½ teaspoon salt
    ⅛ teaspoon pepper
*For ham, roast beef or pot roast. Makes
about 2 cups.*

Horseradish Cream

Beat until stiff
    ½ cup heavy cream

Stir in
  ½ teaspoon salt
  Few grains cayenne
  2 to 4 tablespoons grated horseradish
  4 teaspoons vinegar
For beef. Makes about ¾ cup.

Epicurean Sauce. Omit the vinegar. Add ½ teaspoon prepared mustard and 3 tablespoons mayonnaise.

Mustard Sauce

See also prepared mustard (p. 16).

Mix
  2 tablespoons dry mustard
  1 teaspoon flour
  ¼ teaspoon salt
  ¼ cup evaporated milk or cream
Put in a heavy pan or double boiler top
  ¾ cup evaporated milk or cream
  ¼ cup sugar
Heat. Stir in the mustard mixture. Add
  1 egg yolk beaten until thick
Cook and stir until thick. Stir in
  ½ cup vinegar, heated
For fish, beef, ham or spinach. Makes 1½ to 2 cups.

Colony Mustard Sauce

Melt
  2 tablespoons butter
Add
  1 teaspoon mustard
  1 teaspoon Worcestershire
  2 tablespoons Escoffier sauce
Stir until smooth. Just before serving, add
  2 tablespoons (or more) heavy cream
Serve hot with *broiled steak, hamburger or lamb chops. Makes about ½ cup.*

Sweet and Sour Sauce

Traditionally, sliced tongue is heated in this sauce; for added flavor, use the water in which the tongue was cooked. Delicious, too, with hot or cold ham.

Simmer together
  4 cups water
  ⅓ cup mild vinegar

  2 small onions, sliced thin
  ½ cup raisins
  1 lemon, sliced paper-thin
  ½ cup brown sugar
  1 teaspoon allspice
  Cayenne, salt, ginger
  2 bay leaves
Simmer until the lemon and onions are tender. Add
  1 cup fine gingersnap crumbs
Stir until smooth and slightly thickened. *Makes about 1 quart.*

Tartare Sauce

Mix well
  ¾ cup mayonnaise
  ½ shallot, chopped fine, or
    1 teaspoon chopped onion
  1 teaspoon capers
  1 teaspoon finely chopped pickles
  1 teaspoon chopped olives
  1 teaspoon chopped parsley
  1 tablespoon tarragon vinegar
For fish and shellfish, especially fried shrimps, clams or scallops. Makes about 1 cup.

Vinaigrette Sauce

Mix well
  1 teaspoon salt
  Few grains pepper
  ¼ teaspoon paprika
  1 tablespoon tarragon vinegar
  2 tablespoons cider vinegar
  6 tablespoons olive oil
  1 tablespoon chopped green pepper
  1 tablespoon chopped cucumber pickle
  1 teaspoon finely chopped parsley
  1 teaspoon finely chopped chives
Change the proportions or add other herbs, if you like. *For fish. Makes about 1½ cups.*

Rochester Sauce

Blend together 1 cup chili sauce, ½ cup sherry and ½ cup brown sugar. *For ham or tongue.*

Mint Sauce

Heat together
 ½ cup mild vinegar
 ¼ cup sugar
Pour over
 ½ cup chopped mint leaves (no stems)
Let stand 1 hour or more. If you like a sweeter sauce, add more sugar. *For lamb. Makes about ½ cup.*

Currant Mint Sauce

Separate a glass of currant jelly into small pieces with a fork. Do not beat. Sprinkle with 1 tablespoon grated orange rind and stick in a few perfect sprigs of mint. *For lamb.*

Cucumber Sauce

Pare cucumbers. Grate or chop, and drain thoroughly. Season to taste with salt, pepper and vinegar. *For fish, especially for cold fish or fish mousse.*

Cucumber Cream

Pare and chop
 1 cucumber
Drain thoroughly. Add
 ¼ teaspoon salt
 Few grains pepper
Chill. Fold in
 ½ cup sour cream, or sweet cream beaten stiff and seasoned with 2 tablespoons vinegar
Taste, and add more seasoning if necessary. *For fish. Makes about ¾ cup.*

Raisin Sauce

Mix
 ½ cup brown sugar
 ½ tablespoon mustard
 ½ tablespoon flour
Add
 ¼ cup seedless raisins
 ¼ cup vinegar
 1¾ cups water
Cook slowly to a syrup. *For ham or tongue. Makes about 1½ cups.*

Spicy Raisin Sauce

Cook together 5 minutes
 1 cup sugar
 ½ cup water
Add
 1 cup seedless raisins
 2 tablespoons butter
 3 tablespoons vinegar
 ½ tablespoon Worcestershire
 ½ teaspoon salt
 ¼ teaspoon cloves
 Few grains each of mace and pepper
 1 glass tart fruit jelly
Cook until the jelly melts. *For ham or tongue. Makes 1 to 1½ cups.*

Currant Chili Sauce

Mix 1 cup chili sauce with a 6-ounce glass of currant jelly. Season with 4 tablespoons prepared horseradish. *For ham or tongue.*

Green Herb Sauce

Whatever herbs your garden offers will make a delicious sauce. Select perfect leaves and discard the stems.

Chop lettuce, celery, and plenty of fresh herbs until very fine. You should have about 1 cupful. Stir in olive oil (¼ cup or more according to the greens used) drop by drop until the sauce is as thick as mayonnaise. Season with salt and vinegar. *For broiled or steamed fish, cold salmon or cold sliced lamb.*

Orange Sauce

Mix
 6 tablespoons currant jelly
 3 tablespoons sugar
 Grated rind 2 oranges
Beat 5 minutes. Add
 2 tablespoons port wine
 2 tablespoons orange juice
 2 tablespoons lemon juice
 ¼ teaspoon salt
 Few grains cayenne
Stir until well blended. For duck or lamb. Makes about 1½ cups.

Spiced Fruit Sauce

Simmer 15 minutes
  ¾ cup claret
Add
  1 cup grape jelly
  ⅛ teaspoon cinnamon
  ⅛ teaspoon nutmeg
  Salt and pepper
Slice in thin strips
  Peel of 1 orange (removing the white membrane)
Add to the sauce, with
  Slices of orange, seeded
For ham, tongue or duck. Makes about 1½ cups.

Condensed Soups as Sauces

Condensed canned or frozen soups make tasty sauces to serve over fish, meat, vegetables, rice, toasted sandwiches, toast or crackers. They are also useful as the basis for casseroles. Heat the undiluted soup slowly and thin it with a little milk or consommé if it is too thick.

Season to taste. Here are a few suggestions, but experiment with others.

Celery Sauce. Add a bouillon cube to condensed cream of celery soup. Heat and season to taste.

Mushroom Sauce. Heat condensed cream of mushroom soup. Add sliced sautéed mushrooms, if convenient. Add a trace of freshly ground nutmeg.

Onion Sauce. Heat condensed onion soup. Taste. If too salty, add a trace of sugar and a little cream.

Shrimp or Lobster Sauce. Heat canned or frozen shrimp or lobster bisque. Thin slightly with cream and season with sherry.

Tomato Sauce. Heat condensed cream of tomato soup. Add 2 tablespoons butter, For a more savory sauce, add a pinch of orégano or a shake of garlic salt.

Tomato Cheese Sauce. Add 1 cup grated cheese to Tomato Sauce (above) and stir until the cheese melts.

Marinades and Barbecue Sauces

Meats, fish and vegetables may be soaked before cooking in a marinade, a savory blend of seasonings, oil, and an acid such as lemon juice, tomato juice or wine. The simplest is French dressing (below). The marinade is also used to baste the meat during cooking. The basic combinations below can easily be varied.

French Dressing Marinade

You may prefer to use the basic recipe for French Dressing (p. 287) or one of the variations following it.

Mix
  1 cup French dressing, preferably made with wine vinegar
  1 clove garlic, crushed
  1 teaspoon chopped parsley
  ⅛ teaspoon each of dried tarragon and thyme
For chicken, lamb, veal, fish or vegetables.

Wine Marinade

For chicken or duck, add ½ cup orange or pineapple juice.

Mix
  1 cup wine (white for poultry and veal, red for other meats)
  1 cup olive oil
  2 or 3 cloves garlic, split
  2 teaspoons dried herbs, such as rosemary, thyme and marjoram
  ¼ cup chopped parsley
  ½ teaspoon freshly ground pepper
For meat and poultry.

Barbecue Sauce

Mix in a saucepan
   1 teaspoon salt
   1 teaspoon chili powder
   1 teaspoon celery seed
   ¼ cup (or less) brown sugar
   ¼ cup vinegar
   ¼ cup Worcestershire
   1 cup tomato catsup
   2 cups water
   Few drops Tabasco
Simmer half an hour. *For meats.*

To vary. Cook 1 grated onion and 1 minced clove of garlic 5 minutes in butter and add to the sauce.

Herbed Barbecue Sauce

Mix in a saucepan
   1 cup dry white wine
   ¼ cup olive oil
   2 tablespoons butter
   1 medium onion, minced
   1 crushed clove of garlic
   1 teaspoon salt
   ¼ teaspoon paprika
   2 teaspoons fresh rosemary, minced
   1 teaspoon parsley, minced
Simmer ½ hour. *For chicken or turkey.*

Smoky Barbecue Sauce

Mix in a small saucepan
   3 tablespoons Worcestershire
   1 tablespoon meat glaze such as B–V
   ½ cup catsup
   2 tablespoons butter
   3 tablespoons shortening
   1 tablespoon sugar
   1 tablespoon vinegar
   2 teaspoons liquid smoke
   1 medium onion, grated
   1 teaspoon salt
   Few drops Tabasco
Heat to the boiling point. *For beef or lamb.*

Chicken Barbecue Sauce

Mix
   1 egg, well beaten
   ½ cup cooking oil
   1 cup cider vinegar
   2 tablespoons salt
   1½ teaspoons poultry seasoning
   ¼ teaspoon pepper
If you like, use other seasonings in place of poultry seasoning, such as finely chopped onion and chopped parsley, with a shake of celery salt and a pinch of tarragon or thyme. Ginger is good, too. *Enough for 6 half broilers.*

Eggs

In New England brown eggs are more popular than white ones but in some other parts of the country white ones are considered superior. Actually, the color of the shell is no indication of the flavor of the egg.

Eggs one or two days old are best for poaching, boiling and frying, since the yolks are certain to keep their perfect shape.

For general information about eggs, see p. 7.

There are countless ways to vary egg recipes; the suggestions in this chapter can be a starting point for your own inventions.

Hard-Cooked or Soft-Cooked (Boiled) Eggs

Not actually boiled, because the water should be kept below the boiling point.

To start in boiling water. Have ready a pan of boiling water deep enough to cover the eggs. Have the eggs at room temperature; eggs icy cold from the refrigerator may crack when they touch the water. Slip each one carefully from a tablespoon into the pan. Reduce the heat so that the water just simmers.

Cook 3 to 5 minutes for soft-cooked eggs, 5 to 10 for medium, and 15 to 20 for hard-cooked. If the eggs are very small or very large, modify the time slightly.

To start in cold water. Put the eggs in a pan with enough water to cover them. Bring slowly to the boiling point. For very soft eggs, take from the water immediately. Cover and simmer 2 minutes for soft-cooked eggs, 3 to 5 for medium, and 12 to 15 for hard.

To prepare hard-cooked eggs for stuffing and to use in other recipes. Crack the cooked eggs and plunge immediately into cold water. This helps prevent the yolk from darkening.

Eggs with Cheese Sauce. Cook 10 minutes so that the white is firm but the center still creamy. Shell carefully and cover with hot Cheese Sauce (p. 91).

Coddled Eggs

Let eggs stand at room temperature long enough to lose chill. Put into a heavy pan filled with boiling water. Cover very closely and turn off the heat. Let stand 4 to 8 minutes, according to individual preference.

Stuffed Eggs

Stuffed egg halves, put together in pairs, are good picnic or lunchbox fare. See further variations p. 102; also Stuffed Egg Salad (p. 279).

Shell hard-cooked eggs and cut in half. Mash the yolks and moisten with melted butter or mayonnaise. Season to taste with salt and pepper. To season more highly, add lemon juice or vinegar, mustard, cayenne or other seasoning. Fill the whites with the seasoned yolks and smooth the top neatly. Garnish if you like with paprika or a tiny leaf of parsley.

Anchovy Eggs. Omit the mustard. Add anchovy paste to taste.

Bacon Stuffed Eggs. Add crumbled crisp bacon to the yolks.

Chicken, Ham or Veal Stuffed Eggs. Add chopped cooked chicken, ham or veal to the mashed yolks. Season to taste.

Deviled Eggs. Season highly. If you like, add 1 teaspoon grated cheese or minced pickles or olives for each egg.

Eggs en Casserole. Arrange in a baking dish. Cover with Cheese (p. 91), Tomato (p. 94) or Mushroom Sauce (p. 94), or undiluted canned tomato, or cream of chicken, celery or mushroom soup. Sprinkle with grated cheese or buttered crumbs. Bake at 350° until brown.

Eggs à la Mimosa

An attractive cold dish for a summer luncheon.

Cut hard-cooked eggs in half lengthwise. Remove the yolks and fill the whites with chopped cooked or canned lobster, crab meat, tuna or ham. Cover with mayonnaise and sprinkle with egg yolk, crumbled evenly with a fork.

Creamed Eggs

A useful basic recipe which helps with the problem of leftovers. Add chopped cooked ham, veal, chicken, lobster or shrimp, boned and mashed sardines, finely cut pimientos, cooked peas or asparagus tips.

Cut in slices, quarters or eighths, or chop fine
    4 hard-cooked eggs
Prepare
    1½ cups Cream Sauce (p. 90)
Add the eggs. Season to taste. Serve over
    Toast, waffles, pancakes, or hot buttered cooked rice
Dust with paprika or decorate with a sprig of parsley or a few buttered crumbs. *Serves four.*

To vary, use undiluted canned tomato soup or cream of chicken or mushroom soup in place of Cream Sauce. See also Scalloped Ham (p. 188).

Curried Eggs. Season highly with curry powder or use Curry Sauce (p. 90). Add ½ cup cooked rice to the sauce.

Goldenrod Eggs. Chop the whites of the cooked eggs. Add to the sauce and pour it over the toast. Crumble the yolks over the top.

Scotch Woodcock. Chop the eggs fine. Season the sauce with anchovy paste.

Poached Eggs

Perfect poached eggs have firm whites and creamy soft yolks. Use an egg poacher, if you like.

Fill a heavy frying pan two-thirds full of boiling salted water. Break each egg separately into a saucer and slip carefully into the water. Cover the pan and turn off the heat. Let stand 5 minutes. Test by pressing the yolk lightly with the back of the fork. If you like eggs firmer, turn on the heat again and cook slowly a minute or two more. Take out of the water very carefully with a skimmer.

To serve, place on buttered toast or sautéed rounds of bread.

To vary, spoon over the eggs sautéed mushrooms or any mushroom or tomato sauce, or put on the toast a sautéed chicken liver or a thin slice of ham, or spread the toast with mashed liver sausage or foie gras.

Poached Eggs on Tomatoes. For each egg, sauté a thick slice of tomato in olive oil seasoned with salt and pepper and a pinch of basil or orégano. Cook a sliver of garlic with the tomato, if you like. Put a poached egg on each slice.

Poached Eggs au Gratin. Set the oven at 350°. Butter a shallow baking dish. Put poached eggs in it. Sprinkle with grated Parmesan cheese. Cover with Tomato (p. 94), Cream (p. 90) or Yellow Béchamel

Sauce (p. 91). Sprinkle with more cheese. Bake until browned.

Eggs Benedict. Split and toast English muffins. Put on each piece a thin round of ham, sautéed 5 minutes in butter. Put a poached egg on each. Cover with Hollandaise (p. 95), thinned with cream.

French Poached Eggs

Eggs poached this way look very attractive.

Bring about 3 pints of water to a full boil in a deep saucepan. Add 1 tablespoon vinegar and ½ tablespoon salt. Break an egg into a saucer. Stir the boiling water vigorously around and around the edge of the pan with a wooden spoon held almost upright.

As soon as a well forms in the middle of the water, stop stirring and slip the egg into the center of the well. Lower the heat and cook until the white is set. Take out with a skimmer. Repeat until the desired number of eggs is prepared.

Serve in any of the ways suggested under Poached Eggs.

Eggs Chasseur

Poached eggs in a wonderful sauce.

Cook and stir 3 minutes
    1 tablespoon butter
    1 shallot, chopped fine, or 1 teaspoon chopped onion
Add
    3 mushrooms, chopped
Cook 5 minutes. Add
    ¼ cup chicken stock or bouillon
    1 tablespoon sherry
    ⅛ teaspoon salt
    Pepper and cayenne to taste
Bring to the boiling point. Simmer 10 minutes. Pour into a shallow baking dish.

Poach about 5 minutes
    4 eggs
Put the eggs in the sauce in the baking dish. Sprinkle over them
    2 tablespoons cream

    1 tablespoon grated Parmesan cheese
Bake at 400° until the cheese melts. *Serves 4.*

Shirred Eggs

These "oeufs sur le plat" are traditionally cooked and served in shallow individual baking dishes ("shirrers") just large enough for one or two eggs.

Set the oven at 400°. Put ½ teaspoon butter in each dish and heat until the butter melts. Break one or two eggs into each dish. Sprinkle with salt and add a teaspoon of cream or melted butter. Bake until the white is just barely firm (4 or 5 minutes).

For a heartier luncheon dish, put in each dish any of the following and heat 5 minutes before adding the eggs.

    Mushrooms, sliced or chopped and sautéed in butter.
    Cooked vegetables, such as asparagus tips, peas, spinach, sliced carrots or tiny whole ones.
    Bits of cooked ham, fish or seafood.

Shirred Eggs with Crumbs. Butter the shirrers. Cover the bottoms and sides with fine cracker crumbs. Slip in the eggs. Cover with buttered crumbs. Bake as above.

Eggs Shirred in Cream. For each egg, mix 1½ tablespoons heavy cream with 2 tablespoons fine bread crumbs and ¼ teaspoon salt. Put half in the shirrer, slip in the egg, cover with the rest of the mixture and bake.

Shirred Eggs with Sausages. Cut 6 small pork sausages in ½-inch pieces. Cook 10 minutes in 1 teaspoon butter. Add 1 cup Tomato Sauce (p. 94) or canned tomato soup and divide in 6 egg shirrers. Break 1 or 2 eggs into each and bake.

Eggs Mornay. Make Mornay Sauce (p. 91); there will be enough for 6 eggs. When the eggs are ready to bake, cover with the sauce and sprinkle with grated cheese. Bake as above.

Eggs Florentine

Set the oven at 350°. Butter individual casseroles. Put in each a tablespoon of chopped cooked spinach, seasoned with salt and butter. Sprinkle with grated Parmesan cheese. Break an egg into each casserole and cover with 1 tablespoon cream. Sprinkle with more cheese. Bake until the eggs are set (about 8 minutes).

Scrambled Eggs

Soft, creamy scrambled eggs, served piping hot with a slice or two of boiled ham or crisp bacon, can be an epicurean dish. Cook slowly and be sure not to let the eggs brown at all. An easy but slow way is to scramble eggs in a double boiler, stirring occasionally.

Mix
    5 eggs, slightly beaten
    ½ teaspoon salt
    ⅛ teaspoon pepper
    ½ cup milk or cream
Heat an omelet pan. Melt in it
    2 tablespoons butter
Add the eggs. Cook over low heat until creamy, constantly stirring and scraping from the bottom and sides of the pan. Serve them the moment they are firm enough; if you leave them in the pan they will go on cooking and be dry instead of creamy. *Serves 4.*

To vary, use sour cream, or when nearly done, stir in 1 cup cottage cheese, or 1 small package cream cheese, crumbled.

Scrambled Eggs with Mushrooms. Sauté 1 cup sliced mushrooms in butter, sprinkle lightly with flour, add a few drops onion juice, salt and cayenne, and cook 8 minutes. Add the eggs and milk and cook.

Scrambled Eggs Country Style. Melt the butter and break the eggs into the pan without beating them. Add the milk or cream and salt and pepper. Cook over very low heat, stirring with a fork.

Scrambled Eggs New York Style. Cook 1 cup match-shaped pieces of ham (1 thin slice) with 2 tablespoons chopped onion and 1½ tablespoons butter. After 5 minutes, add 5 mushroom caps, peeled and sliced, and cook 5 minutes longer. Serve as a border around the eggs.

Piperade Basque. A piquant lunch or supper dish. Make a sauce as for Spanish Omelet (p. 107), using 3 onions and 2 peppers. Add 4 eggs and cook as above.

Scrambled Eggs Creole

Put in a skillet
    2 tablespoons butter
    1 slice onion, diced
Cook 5 minutes. Add
    1 cup tomatoes
    1 teaspoon sugar
    Salt and pepper
Cook 5 minutes. Add
    5 eggs, beaten slightly
    ¼ cup grated cheese (if desired)
Stir and cook until creamy. *Serves 4.*

Eggs à la Caracas

Cut fine, with scissors
    2 ounces dried beef
Add
    1 cup tomatoes, canned or fresh, cut small
    ¼ cup grated cheese
    Few drops onion juice
    Few grains cinnamon and cayenne
Melt in an omelet pan
    2 tablespoons butter
Add the mixture and heat 3 minutes. Pour into the pan
    3 eggs, well beaten
Stir and cook over direct heat until creamy. *Serves 4.*

Fried Eggs

For ham and eggs, see p. 187.

Heat a heavy frying pan. Put in 1 tablespoon butter or bacon fat. Heat until the fat sizzles but doesn't smoke. Break an egg into a saucer. Slip it into the pan, reduce the heat and cook slowly until the white is firm. Cook one or more at a time. Add a little more fat as needed, using just enough to keep the eggs from sticking.

Cook the eggs without turning ("sunny side up") or turn and cook the other side. Or, if you wish to cook the tops a little, spoon the fat over the eggs during cooking; or, after the eggs are in the pan, add 1 teaspoon hot water, cover closely, turn off the heat, and let stand until as firm as you like; or slide the fried eggs under the broiler when they are almost finished.

Buttered Eggs à la Roberts. Fry 6 eggs in butter on one side only. Arrange on a hot platter. Pour around Roberts Sauce (p. 94).

Buttered Eggs with Tomatoes. Serve eggs fried in butter on tomato slices seasoned and sautéed in butter.

Eggs au Beurre Noir. In the same pan, brown quickly 2 tablespoons butter, add 1 tablespoon vinegar, and pour over the eggs.

Egg with a Hat

Plenty of butter makes this dish perfect.

Cut a round out of a slice of bread with a 2½-inch cooky cutter. Melt 2 tablespoons butter in a heavy frying pan. Put in both pieces of bread. Cook over moderate heat until they begin to brown.

Break an egg into the hole and sprinkle it with salt and pepper. Continue cooking until the bread is brown, turn and brown the other side. Add butter as needed to keep the bread from sticking. Serve with the cut-out piece on top.

Eggs à la Suisse

Melt in a small omelet pan
    1 tablespoon butter
Add
    ½ cup cream
Slip in, one at a time
    4 eggs
Sprinkle with
    Salt, pepper and cayenne
Cook slowly until the whites are nearly firm. Sprinkle with
    2 tablespoons grated cheese
Continue cooking until the whites are firm. Serve on
    Buttered toast
Pour the cream from the pan over the eggs. If you like, season the cream with
    Sherry to taste.
Serves 4.

Eggs in White Wine. Use dry white wine in place of cream.

Eggs in Tomato Sauce. Use Tomato Sauce (p. 94) in place of cream. Season to taste with minced thyme, basil or parsley, or a combination of herbs. Heat a piece of garlic in the sauce, if desired.

French Omelet

Never make an omelet with more than 4 eggs. Make several small ones instead. Select an omelet pan carefully. It is not necessary to keep a pan just for omelets, but the pan should be a heavy one (cast aluminum is excellent because it heats evenly). Keep the surface of the pan very smooth.

a French omelet pan is curved

Beat slightly, just enough to blend the yolks and whites

    4 eggs

Add

    ¼ cup water
    ½ teaspoon salt
    ⅛ teaspoon pepper

Melt in a hot omelet pan

    2 tablespoons butter

When the butter begins to sizzle tip the pan to make sure it spreads over the surface. Add the eggs and reduce the heat slightly. As the omelet cooks, lift it with a spatula, letting the uncooked part run under, until the whole is creamy. Increase the heat to brown very slightly underneath. A perfect omelet is creamy inside, or what the French call *baveuse*. Turn onto a hot platter and fold double. *Serves 2 or 3.*

To vary, sauté in the butter 1 teaspoon minced parsley or 2 tablespoons minced green or red peppers.

Croûton Omelet. Add to the eggs ¼ cup croûtons (p. 58).

Cheese Omelet. Add to the eggs ¼ cup grated cheese and cook as above. Gruyère is especially good.

Sweet Omelet. Omit the pepper. Add 1½ tablespoons very fine sugar and ½ teaspoon vanilla. Before folding, spread with jam, tart jelly or marmalade. Sprinkle with sugar. As a fancy touch, score with a hot skewer. Serve as dessert.

Omelet aux Fines Herbes. Add to the egg mixture ½ teaspoon each of finely cut parsley, watercress, chives, and tarragon or chervil. Use any of these alone, or any combination, to make a savory omelet.

Omelet Soubise. Turn the omelet out onto a hot ovenproof platter. Pour Onion (p. 90) or Soubise Sauce (p. 92) over the omelet. Sprinkle with 2 tablespoons Parmesan cheese. Bake at 425° until the cheese melts. For Omelet Boulestin, use Mushroom Sauce (p. 94).

Omelet Paysanne. Cut ¼ pound bacon into small squares. Fry until crisp and brown. Drain off the fat and in it fry 1 cup ¼-inch potato cubes until delicately brown. Drain and mix with the bacon. Fold half into the omelet and put the rest around the edge.

Chicken Noodle Omelet. *An emergency supper dish.* Use 5 eggs. Mix with 1 can concentrated chicken noodle soup. Cook as above.

Filled Omelet

An excellent way to present leftovers.

Make a French Omelet (above), but before folding it, spread with 2 tablespoons heavy sweet or sour cream, grated cheese, crumbled cooked bacon or chopped cooked sausage. Or fill with any of the following, heated so that the omelet will not be cooled.

    Chicken or turkey, cooked, chopped, and creamed or seasoned.
    Chicken livers, cooked and minced.
    Fish, cooked and flaked or creamed.
    Ham, cooked and ground fine, or ham spread.
    Kidney, cooked and minced.
    Lobster, shrimp, tuna or crab meat, cooked or canned, cut small and creamed or heated in butter.
    Mushrooms, creamed or sautéed.
    Tomato, fresh or canned, cut small and seasoned to taste.
    Cooked vegetables, cut small and heated in butter. Asparagus tips, peas and chopped spinach are especially good.

Lobster Omelet

Cook together 5 minutes

    1 teaspoon butter
    1 small onion peeled and sliced thin

Add

    1 stalk celery, diced
    ⅛ teaspoon sugar
    2 tablespoons Chicken Stock (p. 72) or canned chicken broth
    1 teaspoon soy sauce
    ⅓ cup diced cooked lobster

Turn the mixture into a heated and buttered omelet pan. Add

2 eggs, slightly beaten

Spread evenly and cook until the eggs are set. Turn and fold. *Serves 2.*

Omelet Savoyarde

A savory French peasant dish.

Wash and boil until soft

2 potatoes

Cool, pare, cut in ½-inch cubes, and set aside.

Melt in a small frying pan

1 tablespoon butter

Add the potato cubes and

¾ teaspoon onion juice

¼ teaspoon salt

Few grains pepper

Cook until the potatoes are slightly browned.

Cut in thin slices crosswise

½ cup leeks (white part)

Cook in boiling water until soft. Drain and set aside.

Melt in an omelet pan

2 tablespoons butter

Mix

5 eggs, slightly beaten

⅔ cup cream

½ teaspoon salt

⅛ teaspoon pepper

Pour into the pan. Cook 5 minutes, pricking and picking up with a fork. Add the potatoes, leeks and

1 tablespoon chopped parsley

Continue cooking until creamy. Add

3 tablespoons grated cheese

Increase the heat to brown the omelet quickly underneath. Fold and turn out on a hot serving dish. Garnish with

A sprig of parsley

Serves 6.

Spanish Omelet

Sliced mushrooms and a few capers may be added to the sauce for extra zest.

Put in a saucepan

3 tablespoons butter or bacon fat

1 tablespoon finely chopped onion

1 tablespoon finely chopped red or green pepper

Cook until the onion is yellow. Add

1¼ cups tomatoes, cut in quarters

Cook until thick. Season to taste.

Make a French Omelet (p. 105), using

4 eggs

Pour the sauce around it. *Serves 2 or 3.*

Puffy Omelet

Milk is sometimes used in place of hot water, but hot water makes a more tender omelet.

Put in a bowl

4 egg yolks

Beat until thick and lemon-colored. Add

¼ cup hot water

½ teaspoon salt

Few grains pepper

Beat until stiff

4 egg whites

Cut and fold the whites into the yolks, until the mixture is well blended.

Heat an omelet pan with a metal or heatproof handle. Butter the sides and bottom. Spoon the omelet mixture into the pan and spread it evenly. Cook slowly, occasionally turning the pan to brown the omelet evenly. When well puffed and delicately browned underneath, put the pan in a 375° oven to finish cooking the top. If you like, sprinkle with

Grated cheese

The omelet is cooked if it is firm to the touch when pressed with a finger. If it clings like beaten egg white, the omelet needs to be cooked longer.

Fold and turn onto a hot platter. *Serves 4.*

Vary in any of the ways suggested for French Omelet (p. 105).

Almond Omelet with Caramel Sauce. *A dessert omelet.* Prepare 1 cup Caramel Sauce (p. 398) and add ¼ cup to the beaten yolks. Add ½ teaspoon vanilla and fold in the beaten whites. Sprinkle the buttered omelet pan with ½ cup shredded almonds before pouring in the omelet mixture. Cook as above. Pour the rest of the sauce around the omelet.

Frittata

This Italian dish makes good use of bits of leftover cooked vegetables such as asparagus tips, peas, green beans, chopped spinach, zucchini or artichoke bottoms.

Put in an 8 or 9 inch frying pan
  1 tablespoon olive oil
  ½ clove garlic (on a toothpick)
  1 tablespoon minced onion
Cook slowly until the onion is yellow. Remove the garlic. Mix
  4 eggs, slightly beaten
  1 cup cooked vegetable
  ⅓ cup grated crumbs, soaked in ¼ cup tomato juice, milk, consommé or water
Reheat the frying pan containing the onion and add to it
  1 tablespoon olive oil
Pour in the egg mixture. Cover and cook slowly until the frittata shrinks from the side of the pan. Prick the center if it puffs up. Set in the broiler to brown the top. Cut in wedges like a pie. *Serves 4.*

Luncheon Custard

Mix
  4 eggs, slightly beaten
  1 cup milk
  ½ teaspoon salt
  ⅛ teaspoon pepper
  Few grains cayenne
  Few drops onion juice
Fill buttered timbale molds or small custard cups. Set in a pan of hot water. Bake at 350° until firm (about 25 minutes). Unmold and serve with
  Tomato (p. 94) or Mushroom Sauce (p. 94)
Serves 4.

Custard Ring. Bake in a ring mold. Turn out onto a serving dish. Fill the center with buttered peas or creamed mushrooms.

Cheese Custard. Add ½ cup grated cheese and 2 tablespoons melted butter to the custard mixture.

Egg and Pimiento Timbales. Line the buttered custard cups or timbale molds with whole canned pimientos.

Eggs Foo Yung

Put in a bowl
  3 eggs
Beat well and add
  ½ cup diced shrimp, crab meat or lobster
  1 cup drained bean sprouts, fresh or canned
  3 green onions, sliced thin
  Salt and pepper to taste
Heat in a heavy frying pan
  1 tablespoon peanut oil
Cook the egg mixture by tablespoonfuls in the hot fat. Add more fat as needed. Brown on both sides. Keep hot until all are cooked. Serve with
  Chinese Gravy (below) or soy sauce
Serves 3.

To vary. There are many excellent ways to vary this famous Chinese dish. Use chicken, ham or lean meat in place of shellfish, finely cut celery in place of bean sprouts, or slivered onions (¼ cup) in place of green onions. Add ½ cup sliced water chestnuts or mushrooms, if you like.

Chinese Gravy. Mix 1 cup chicken broth, 1 teaspoon sugar, 1 teaspoon soy sauce, ¼ teaspoon MSG, and 1 tablespoon cornstarch mixed with a little water. Cook and stir over low heat until thick. Add salt and pepper to taste.

Herb Soufflé

For other soufflés, see the index.

Melt
  2 tablespoons butter
Stir in
  2 tablespoons flour
Add slowly
  2 cups milk or milk and cream
Stir and cook 5 minutes. Beat
  4 egg yolks

until thick and lemon-colored. Stir into
the sauce. Remove from the heat. Add

1 teaspoon salt
Few grains cayenne
1 tablespoon grated onion
1 teaspoon each of chopped fresh
     herbs (basil, tarragon and parsley)

Cool slightly. Beat

4 egg whites

until stiff. Stir 1 tablespoon beaten
white thoroughly into the soufflé mixture. Fold in the rest. Turn into an unbuttered straight-sided dish and set in a
pan of hot water. Bake at 350° until as
firm as liked (45 to 60 minutes). Serve
from the baking dish. *Serves 4 to 6.*

Cheese and Cheese Dishes

Cheese goes well with almost every course and is also ideal for between-meal snacks. There are many recipes featuring cheese in other chapters as well as this one: consult the index for suggestions. Some of the most popular are Macaroni and Cheese (p. 300), Cheese Soufflé (p. 115), Toasted Cheese Sandwiches (p. 341), Cheese Soup (p. 64), Pizza (p. 336), and Cheese Cake (p. 422).

Cheeses

Shops specializing in cheese offer many others as well.

Fresh cheeses: Cottage, ricotta, cream.

Soft cheeses: Brie, Camembert, Liederkranz, Limburger, mozzarella, Pont l'Évêque, Poona.

Semi-hard cheeses: American (also hard), Bel Paese, blue (bleu), Cheddar (also hard), Gorgonzola, Gouda, Gruyère, Jack, Munster, Port du Salut, provolone, Roquefort, Scandinavian (also hard), Stilton, Swiss.

Hard cheeses: American, Cheddar, Cheshire, Edam, Parmesan, pineapple, Romano, Scandinavian.

Store cheese, tightly wrapped, in a cool, dry place. Store cottage and cream cheeses in the refrigerator and use within a few days.

Grate cheese just before buying or buy freshly grated cheese in small quantities. The best cheeses for grating are dry and hard — Cheddar, Gruyère, pineapple, Parmesan or Romano. One pound of cheese yields 4 to 5 cups, grated.

Cook cheese at low temperature. Cooking too fast or too long makes cheese tough or stringy. Cheddar cheese, often called "American" or "store" cheese, is the standard cooking cheese. It may be mild or sharp in flavor. Process cheeses melt to creamy smoothness in sauces but are often somewhat bland in flavor. Other good cheeses for cooking are the Italian types such as mozzarella and provolone. Some recipes call for special cheeses — cottage, ricotta, cream, Swiss or Roquefort.

Serve cheese at room temperature, not icy cold. Put Camembert, Brie, Pont l'Évêque and similar cheeses in a slightly warm place (on a radiator or near the stove), so that the soft center will be almost liquid when the cheese is served.

Cheese spreads are marketed, ready to use. Or prepare your own (p. 49).

Cheese for Dessert

As a last course, cheese adds a gourmet touch to a meal. Crusty French bread, toasted or not, goes superbly with it, also unsalted crackers, preferably lightly buttered and toasted. Fine pears or apples are delicious with cheese, especially with provolone.

Cream cheese is excellent with jam or Bar-le-Duc. For a handsome effect, mold the cheese in a cone, cover with whipped cream or sour cream, and spoon the jam or jelly around it. See also Coeur à la Crème (p. 111) and Petit Suisse (p. 112).

Edam or Gouda. Cut a slice off the top and serve from the shell with a cheese scoop.

Cheese with pie should be a Cheddar type, cut in small wedges or cubes.

Cheese with Salads

Cheese is a natural complement to many salads. It provides a pleasantly contrasting flavor, especially for crisp greens and fresh fruit, and adds protein to make a light salad appropriate as a main dish. Assorted cheeses and crackers, Cheese Straws (p. 52), or Cheese Soufflé (p. 115) are often passed with a salad which is served as a separate course.

Cream Cheese Balls

A garnish for any simple salad.

Mash cream cheese. Moisten with cream or salad dressing. Season to taste with salt and paprika. Shape into balls about 1 inch in diameter.

Cheese and Nut Balls. Roll in finely chopped nut meats.

Ginger Cheese Balls. Add 2 teaspoons finely chopped Canton ginger (for 1 small package). Moisten with ginger syrup.

Roquefort Cheese Balls. Blend in crumbs of Roquefort cheese. Season with a few drops of onion juice.

Chive Cheese Balls. Roll in finely cut chives. Or use chive cream cheese.

Stuffed Figs or Prunes

Put one or two on each serving of a simple green salad or a fruit salad.

Mash cream or cottage cheese, moisten with heavy cream, and season highly with salt and cayenne. If desired, add a few chopped seedless raisins or blanched almonds. Wash and dry figs or pit cooked prunes. Stuff with the cheese mixture.

Fried Cheese Balls

Also for green salads.

Mix
  1 cup grated mild cheese
  2 teaspoons flour
  ¼ teaspoon salt
  Few grains cayenne
Add
  2 egg whites, beaten stiff
Shape in small balls and roll in
  Fine cracker meal
Fry in deep fat heated to 375°. Drain on paper towels. *Makes 24.*

Cottage Cheese

Widely popular as the mainstay of a luncheon plate. Serve with a green salad, a vegetable salad, a fruit salad (jellied or not), or with fresh fruit, celery or radishes or a combination of these. Garnish as you like with sprigs of watercress, a dash of paprika or bits of pimiento.

Savory Cottage Cheese. Moisten cottage cheese with melted butter and a little sweet or sour cream. Season to taste with salt and, if you like, finely cut chives, parsley, or herbs such as basil, chervil or orégano.

Spring Salad. *To carry on a picnic, pack in individual paper cartons. It need not be icy cold to be refreshing, nor does it need to be served on lettuce.* Add to cottage cheese finely cut olives, celery, radishes and raw carrot. Moisten with mayonnaise and season to taste.

Coeur à la Crème

An easy but festive dessert. To present it in the classic French fashion, mold it in a special heart-shaped basket.

Put through a coarse sieve
  ¼ pound cottage cheese
Add and beat together until smooth
  ¼ pound cream cheese
  ½ cup sweet or sour cream
  ½ teaspoon confectioners' sugar
Pack in a mold lined with damp cheesecloth. Chill 2 hours. Turn out onto a plate and serve with cream and sugar or with strawberry jam.

Petit Suisse

Imported petit suisse is very perishable and so is rarely available, but it is simple to prepare a delicious substitute.

Mash a package of cream cheese with a fork and add ½ teaspoon granulated sugar. Stir in heavy cream, a little at a time, until the cheese is softened but still firm enough to shape into a cylinder about 1½ inches across. Roll in wax paper. Chill, turn out onto a plate, and serve like Coeur à la Crème.

Cheese Alexandra

A tasty last course at dinner or, with salad and hot biscuits, the main course for a party luncheon.

Cream together
    ½ cup butter
    ¼ pound Roquefort, crumbled
Mix in
    1 teaspoon salt
    ½ teaspoon paprika
    1 teaspoon minced chives
    2 tablespoons sherry
Pack in a small mold or ice-cube tray and freeze.

Cheese Pimientos

A colorful and delicious luncheon dish.

Drain canned pimientos thoroughly. Cut mild cheese in slices ⅓ inch thick and sprinkle with salt and cayenne. Put a slice of cheese in each pimiento and sprinkle with flour. Sauté in butter until the cheese melts.

Cheese Toast

Use a tasty Cheddar or a combination of cheeses. Season more highly, if you like, with Worcestershire or curry.

Melt in a saucepan
    2 tablespoons butter
Stir in
    1 tablespoon flour
    ¼ teaspoon salt
    Few grains pepper

Add slowly
    1 cup milk
Cook and stir until thick. Add
    ¾ cup grated cheese
Cook until the cheese melts. Add
    2 egg yolks, slightly beaten
Cook and stir until thick. Fold in
    2 egg whites, beaten stiff
Stir just enough to blend. Pour over
    6 slices toast
Garnish as you like with
    A shake of paprika, a bit of crisp bacon, a sprig of parsley or watercress, or a few slices of stuffed olive
Serves 3.

English Monkey

A simple luncheon or supper dish. Also delicious as a hot cocktail dip.

Mix in a double boiler
    1 cup crumbled bread (not too fresh)
    1 cup milk
    1 cup sharp or mild cheese, cut small
Cook until the cheese is melted, stirring occasionally. (It can be left several hours or a short time, whichever is convenient.)
Season to taste with
    Salt, pepper and prepared mustard
Pour over
    Crisp buttered crackers or toast
Serves 4.

Rum Tum Tiddy

Especially good for the teen-age crowd.

Mix
    1 can condensed tomato soup
    ½ pound sharp cheese, cut in small pieces
Cook and stir over low heat or in a double boiler until the cheese melts. Season to taste with
    Salt, pepper and mustard
Serve hot on
    Crackers or toast
Serves 4.

For a heartier dish, add 1 cup cooked rice or 1 can drained whole kernel corn.

Chilaly

Melt in a double boiler top
    1 tablespoon butter
Add
    2 tablespoons chopped green pepper
    1 tablespoon chopped onion
Cook slowly 3 minutes. Add
    ½ cup drained canned tomatoes
Cook 5 minutes. Add
    ¾ pound soft mild cheese, cut in small
        pieces
    ½ teaspoon salt
    Few grains cayenne
Cook slowly over hot water until the
cheese melts. Stir in
    2 tablespoons milk
    1 egg, slightly beaten
Serve on
    Toast or crackers
Serves 4 to 6.

Hot Cheese Savory

*Rich hot cheese to serve at lunch with
a generous green salad, or in the English
fashion as the savory last course at dinner.*

Mix
    2 eggs, slightly beaten
    ⅔ cup heavy cream
    ½ cup Swiss cheese, cut small
    ½ cup grated Parmesan cheese
    Salt and pepper
    Cayenne
    Nutmeg
Spoon into a small casserole or into 6
small ramekins. Bake 15 minutes at 450°.

Swiss Fondue

*A conversation piece served in a chafing
dish or a heavy casserole with thick
cubes of crusty French bread to dip (on
forks) directly into the fondue. If you
prefer, ladle the fondue into well-heated
individual pottery bowls.*

Use either a chafing dish or a heavy casserole on an asbestos mat over very low
heat. Rub the dish with

    A clove of garlic, split
Pour in
    ¾ cup dry white wine
Heat just until it bubbles. Add
    1 pound well-aged Swiss cheese, diced
        or grated
Cook and stir with a wooden spoon un-
til just melted and smooth. Season to taste
with
    Salt, nutmeg and pepper
Thin, if necessary, with more wine.
For the authentic Swiss touch, flavor,
just before serving, with
    Kirsch
Serves 4.

If the fondue is not smooth, add ¼ teaspoon cornstarch to 3 tablespoons Kirsch
and stir it into the fondue.

Fondue Celestine

*An adaptable recipe. You will think of
other fillings to use — chopped hard-
cooked eggs, crab meat, tuna or ham.*

Mix
    1 pound cooked or canned lobster
        meat, chopped
    1 cup finely cut celery
    2 tablespoons chopped onion
    ½ cup mayonnaise
    1 tablespoon prepared mustard
    ½ teaspoon paprika
Remove the crusts from
    16 thin slices of bread
Make into sandwiches, using the prepared filling. Cut in quarters. Butter a
baking dish and put in layers of the
sandwiches, alternating with layers of
    Sliced or grated cheese (about ¾
        pound in all)
Mix
    1 egg, slightly beaten
    2 cups scalded milk
    Salt and pepper
Pour over the sandwiches. Let stand at
least 30 minutes. Set the baking dish in
a pan of hot water. Bake at 325° until
firm (about ½ hour). *Serves 8.*

American Fondue

Firmer than a Swiss fondue and easier to make. It can wait, too.

Scald in a saucepan
   1 cup milk
Stir in
   ¼ cup soft bread crumbs
   ¼ pound mild cheese, cut small
      (1 cup)
   1 tablespoon butter
   ½ teaspoon salt
Cook over low heat until smooth, stirring with a fork. Remove from the heat. Stir in
   2 or 3 egg yolks, beaten thick
Cut and fold in
   2 or 3 egg whites, beaten stiff
Pour into a buttered 1-quart casserole. Bake 20 minutes at 350°. *Serves 4.*

For a firmer fondue, bake 30 minutes.

Quick Fondue

Put in a saucepan or double boiler top
   1 can evaporated milk
   ½ pound sharp cheese, cut small
Cook and stir over low heat until the cheese melts. Remove from the heat. Stir in
   ¼ teaspoon dry mustard or prepared
      mustard to taste
   1 egg, slightly beaten
   Salt and pepper to taste
Mix thoroughly. Serve hot on crackers or toast. *Serves 4.*

Welsh Rabbit

The secret of perfection is the quality of the cheese — an honest Cheddar or Cheshire type, either mild or sharp as you prefer.

Put in a double boiler or chafing dish or in a pan over low heat
   ½ pound cheese, cut small
   1 tablespoon butter
   ¼ teaspoon salt
   ½ teaspoon dry mustard
   Few grains cayenne or 1 teaspoon
      paprika

Cook slowly until the cheese melts, stirring occasionally. Add
   ½ cup cream or milk
   1 egg, slightly beaten
Stir constantly until thick (a wooden spoon is best). Taste, and add more seasoning if you like, such as a few drops of Worcestershire. Pour over toast, saltines or broiled tomato slices. *Serves 4.*

With ale or beer. Instead of cream or milk, use ale or beer.

To vary, spoon the rabbit over any of these:

   Slices of cooked chicken or turkey
      breast on buttered toast. Top with
      a strip of bacon and set under the
      broiler until the bacon crisps.
   Slices of tomato on toast.
   Broccoli, cauliflower or asparagus
      (cooked) on toast or on sliced
      ham.
   Sliced hard-cooked eggs or poached
      eggs on toast.
   Toast spread with deviled ham.
   Bits of cooked lobster, shrimp, crab
      meat or tuna on rice or toast.

Cheese and Olive Casserole

To vary, use cooked chicken or tuna in place of the olives or with them.

Butter
   5 slices bread
Cut off the crusts in thin strips. Cut the centers into 1-inch squares. Mix the squares with
   1 cup grated cheese
   3 eggs, slightly beaten
   2 cups scalded milk
   ½ cup sliced stuffed olives
Season to taste and pour into a casserole. Sauté the bread strips in butter until golden-brown and put over the top. Bake at 300° until firm (40 to 60 minutes). *Serves 4 to 6.*

Cheese Shapleigh

Spread with butter
   4 slices dry bread about ⅓ inch thick

Cut each slice in 8 strips. Put a layer in a buttered baking dish. Arrange the rest of the strips upright around the sides. Mix and pour into the dish

2 eggs, slightly beaten
1 cup thin cream
1 teaspoon salt
½ teaspoon dry mustard
¼ teaspoon paprika
Few grains cayenne
½ pound mild cheese, cut small

Bake 30 minutes at 350°. *Serves 4.*

Quiche Lorraine

An elegant luncheon or supper dish, or — in bite-sized pieces — perfect with drinks. Serve warm, but not piping hot.

Set the oven at 450°.

Cook until crisp
¼ pound bacon

Crumble and set aside. In about 1 tablespoon of the fat, cook slowly until golden
½ cup finely chopped onion

Line a 9-inch pie pan or flan ring with
Plain Pastry (p. 407)

Bake 5 minutes. Remove from the oven. Sprinkle into the pie shell the bacon, the onion, and
½ pound Swiss or Gruyère cheese, cut small

Mix
3 eggs, slightly beaten
2 cups cream or milk
½ teaspoon salt
Cayenne and nutmeg

Strain into the pie shell. Bake 10 minutes, then reduce the heat to 325° and bake until firm (about 20 minutes).

Cut in wedges. *Serves 6.*

With Ham. Substitute ¼ pound diced ham for the bacon. Cook the onion in 1 tablespoon butter.

Quiche Tarts. Make in tiny tart shells. For 24 (1½-inch size), you will need only 2 slices of bacon, 3 tablespoons chopped onion, 1 egg and ⅓ cup cream. For cocktail tidbits, add, if you like, a few drops of Worcestershire.

Cheese Soufflé

Rush a soufflé to the table the minute it is done, especially if it is baked the French way — crusty outside but soft and creamy within. Vary the cheese sometimes by using a combination of Camembert and grated Parmesan or Swiss and bleu cheeses.

Melt over low heat
¼ cup butter

Blend in
¼ cup flour

Add gradually
1 cup milk

Stir until thick and smooth. Add
½ teaspoon salt
Few grains cayenne
½ to 1 cup grated cheese

Stir until smooth and remove from the heat. Add
4 egg yolks, beaten until light

Cool.

Just before baking beat until stiff
4 egg whites (5 for a very fluffy soufflé)

Stir a tablespoon of the white into the yolk mixture. Fold in the rest. Spoon into an unbuttered 1½-quart straight-sided baking dish. Set in a pan of hot water and bake (below). *Serves 4.*

For a firm soufflé, bake 30 to 45 minutes at 325°.

For a creamy soufflé (French fashion), bake 25 minutes at 375°.

For a heartier soufflé, add diced ham and sautéed mushrooms, or diced turkey or chicken, or diced ham with whole kernel corn.

Tomato Soufflé. Use tomato juice instead of milk. Season with orégano if you like.

Seafood Soufflé. Mix cooked or canned lobster or shrimp with sautéed mushrooms and enough mayonnaise to moisten. Put a layer in the baking dish before spooning in the soufflé mixture.

Cheese Soufflé with Tapioca

An easy version with a fluffy texture. Vary it in any of the ways suggested for the standard Cheese Soufflé (p. 115).

Mix in a saucepan
  3 tablespoons quick tapioca
  1 teaspoon salt
  1 cup milk
Cook and stir until the mixture boils. Add
  1 cup grated cheese
Stir until the cheese melts. Beat until stiff and set aside
  3 egg whites
Without washing the beater, beat
  3 egg yolks
Stir into the tapioca mixture. Fold in the egg whites. Spoon into an unbuttered 1½-quart straight-sided baking dish. Set in a pan of hot water and bake 20 to 25 minutes at 375°. *Serves 4.*

Cheese Croquettes

Delectable for lunch or supper with chicken, ham or creamed mushrooms.

Melt over low heat
  3 tablespoons butter
Stir in
  ¼ cup flour
  ⅔ cup milk
Stir until thick and smooth. Add
  2 egg yolks, unbeaten
Mix well. Add
  ½ cup Swiss or Gruyère cheese, cut small
Stir over the heat until the cheese melts. Remove from the heat. Fold in
  1 cup mild cheese, cut in small cubes
Season with
  Salt, pepper and cayenne
Spread in a shallow pan, 8 by 8 inches, and cool. Turn out onto a board, cut in small squares or strips. Roll in
  Crumbs
Fry (p. 5). *Serves 6.*

Fish

Gourmet cookery includes many superb recipes for fish, often very simple ones. The fish must be of high quality. Some fish do not freeze successfully but become dry and lose their finest flavor. Ocean or freshwater fish at the height of the season is a delight. Patronize a dealer who specializes in fresh fish, if you can.

Fish may be cooked successfully at either a very high temperature for a short period or at a low temperature for a longer period. By either method, cook until the fish flakes when tested with a fork but is still slightly moist. Do not overcook, or the flesh will be dry and will lose its delicate flavor.

How much to buy. If the fish is whole, or in pieces which include the bones, allow ¾ pound for each generous serving. Steaks or fillets provide 2 or 3 servings to the pound.

Store fresh fish (well wrapped in wax paper or foil) in the coldest part of the refrigerator but not in the freezer. Use promptly. Store frozen fish in the freezer or ice-cube compartment. Cook frozen fillets either frozen or thawed, but a large piece of frozen fish should be thawed before cooking so that it will cook evenly throughout. Do not refreeze frozen fish after it has thawed.

Sauces for Fish

Most fish requires only wedges of lemon or the simplest thin sharp sauce, such as Sauce Finiste, Cucumber Sauce, Vinaigrette, or the classic Beurre Noir (Black Butter) made of the juices in the pan.

Lean fish is often served with a rich sauce, although the juice in the pan, plus chopped parsley and more butter, if needed, serves very well. Look through the chapter on Sauces (pp. 88–98) for ideas, such as the various cream sauces, Hot Tartare Sauce, Oyster Sauce, Shrimp Sauce, Tomato Sauce, the Hollandaise family and the strongly garlic-flavored Aioli.

Garnishes for Fish

Sprigs of parsley or watercress are attractive with any fish. See pages 83 and 84 for various ways to cut lemons prettily. Chopped toasted almonds add a pleasant crunchiness.

Preparing Fish for Cooking

Fish bought in markets is usually ready to cook. Have the head and tail removed or not according to the way the fish is to be cooked. Keep the head and tail to make a savory Fish Stock (p. 120) as the basis for soup or a sauce.

To scale and clean fish. Place the fish on a piece of paper and hold it firmly with a clean cloth. Scrape off the scales with a fish scaler or a straight sharp knife. Work from the tail toward the head and slant the knife slightly toward you to keep the scales from flying. Make a gash on the under side of the fish with scissors or a sharp knife. Remove the entrails and any clotted blood

117

which clings to the backbone. Wipe inside and out with a paper towel or a damp cloth.

To skin fish. Remove the fins along the back with a sharp knife. Cut off a narrow strip of skin the entire length of the back. Loosen the skin on one side from the bony part of the gills. If the flesh is very firm, the skin will peel off easily. If it is soft, work slowly and carefully, pushing the flesh away from the skin with the back of the knife to keep it from tearing. Turn the fish and skin the other side.

To bone fish. Clean and skin. Beginning at the tail, run a long sharp knife under the flesh close to the backbone. Follow the bone (making as clean a cut as possible) its entire length to remove half the flesh. Turn the fish and cut the flesh from the other side. Pick out any small bones that remain.

Broiled Fish

Small whole fish such as smelts or brook trout, or split and cleaned bluefish, mackerel, pompano or scrod, or fillets or steaks from larger fish.

Preheat the broiler 10 minutes.

Rinse the fish in cold water and pat dry on a paper towel. Dip small whole fish in olive oil.

Put the fish on the broiler rack (split fish with the skin side down). Sprinkle with salt and pepper. Brush dry-meated fish with oil or butter. Sprinkle lightly with flour or buttered crumbs.

Set the rack 4 inches from the heat if the fish is about 2 inches thick, closer for thinner pieces. Cook until the fish flakes when tried with a fork (15 minutes or more). Unless the fish is very thick, it will not need to be turned to brown the skin.

Move the fish carefully to a hot platter, using two pancake turners or broad spatulas so that it will not break apart.

French-Fried Fish

Small whole fish or fillets.

Pat the fish dry with paper towels. Sprinkle with salt, dip in flour, slightly beaten egg, then in fine cracker crumbs. Fry (p. 5) in fat heated to 370°.

Pan-Fried Fish

Small whole fish, fillets or slices of larger fish — all may be pan-fried quickly and easily. Sliced haddock is particularly good done this way.

Wipe the fish dry with a paper towel. For 1 pound of fish, put ½ cup flour, fine cracker crumbs, cracker meal or corn meal on wax paper and mix with it 1 teaspoon salt (no salt if you use bacon fat or other salty fat for the frying). Roll each piece of fish in the flour.

In a shallow frying pan heat 4 tablespoons fat, which may be any vegetable shortening, butter, half butter and half olive oil, bacon fat or fat salt pork (cut small and heated until enough melts to keep the fish from sticking).

Put the fish in the pan, one layer deep, and cook slowly until brown on one side. Turn carefully with a broad spatula or pancake turner and brown on the other side. Test with a fork. When the fish flakes, it is cooked enough — about 10 minutes for a piece ½ inch thick.

Quick-Baked Fish

As good as broiled fish — and no broiler to wash! See also Baked Fish Fillets (p. 120).

Have ready
    1 pound fish fillets ¾ inch thick or
      small whole fish
Let stand at room temperature 15 minutes so that the fish will not be icy cold. Set the oven at 500°.

Mix
    ½ cup milk
    2 teaspoons salt
Dip the fish in it, then in plenty of

Dry bread crumbs

to make a thick coating. Put in an oiled baking pan or on an ovenproof platter. Sprinkle with

1 tablespoon salad oil or melted butter

Bake, uncovered, until the fish flakes when tested with a fork (about 10 minutes).

Serve with

Cucumber Sauce (p. 98), Olive Sauce p. (93), or Sauce Finiste (p. 95)

Serves 3.

Baked Fish with Welsh Rabbit. *Especially good for halibut fillets.* Pour hot Welsh Rabbit (p. 114) over the baked fish. *Serves 3.*

Baked Stuffed Fish

Whole bass, bluefish, cod, haddock or other fish weighing 3 to 5 pounds.

Stuff cleaned fish not more than two-thirds full with Bread (p. 80), Mushroom (p. 81), Celery (p. 81) or Oyster Stuffing (p. 81). Oyster Stuffing is especially good with cod. Close the opening with skewers or toothpicks laced together with string.

Put the fish on an oiled ovenproof platter or in a shallow baking pan. Cut 3 or 4 gashes through the skin on each side to keep the fish in shape during baking. For more zest, add a sprinkling of finely chopped herbs (fresh or dried) such as basil, dill, chives, parsley, tarragon or thyme. Sprinkle lean fish with cream, French dressing, or melted butter in an equal amount of hot water, and baste with the same mixture every 10 minutes during baking.

Bake at 400° until the fish flakes when tried with a fork (30 to 45 minutes). Place on a heated platter.

To serve, make a deep cut along the backbone, then cut in pieces at right angles to the backbone. Serve with Cream Sauce (p. 90), Mock Hollandaise (p. 90) or Drawn Butter Sauce (p. 91).

Steamed Fish

Dry-meated fish, especially salmon.

If you are steaming a whole fish or a large piece, wrap it in a piece of cheesecloth so that it will be less likely to break apart when you move it to a platter.

Unless the fish is to be served whole, cut it in pieces so that it will be sure to cook evenly. Sprinkle it with salt and put it on the rack in a steamer. Put boiling water in the lower part. Cover closely and steam until the fish flakes when tested with a fork (10 or 15 minutes to the pound). If the fish is thick, turn once during steaming. To serve, see Poached Fish (below). See also Molded Salmon (p. 285).

Oven-Steamed Fish. Set the fish on a rack in a roasting pan. Pour hot water into the pan, but do not have it deep enough to touch the fish. Add more as needed. Cover and steam in a 350° oven.

Poached Fish

Any fish except very oily ones like mackerel. To poach fish fillets, p. 120.

Cooking fish in a shallow liquid kept below the boiling point preserves its fine flavor better than the old-fashioned method of boiling.

Poach a large piece of fish in salted water or Court Bouillon (below). Wrap the fish in cheesecloth so that you can lift it out after cooking without breaking it.

Set the fish on a rack in a large kettle, add water or Court Bouillon to a depth of 2 inches. Cover closely and simmer until the fish flakes when tried with a fork (8 to 12 minutes to the pound according to the thickness of the fish).

Lift the fish out carefully so that it will not pull away from the bones. Place on a heated platter. If the stock is to be used in making sauce or soup, strain it.

Garnish and serve with Cream Sauce (p. 90), Brown Almond Sauce (p. 90), Egg Sauce (p. 91) or Bercy Sauce (p. 92).

Court Bouillon

For poaching fish.

Melt
  1 tablespoon butter
Add
  1 sprig parsley
  1 tablespoon each of finely cut carrot,
    onion and celery
Cook 3 minutes. Add
  3 peppercorns
  1 whole clove
  Bit of bay leaf
  1 teaspoon salt
  1 tablespoon vinegar
  1 quart water
Bring to the boiling point. Simmer 15
minutes.

Court Bouillon with Wine. Omit the
vinegar and add 2 cups dry red or white
wine.

Fish Stock. Cover fish bones and scraps
with Court Bouillon. Simmer 30 minutes
and strain. Use as the liquid in making
a sauce to serve with the fish or in fish
or vegetable soup.

Poached Fish Fillets

*So simple, yet the basis for many gourmet
recipes. Easy to vary, too, by adding
herbs, a bit of onion or other seasoning.
Poach in the oven if more convenient,
approximately 15 minutes at 400°. See
also Fillets of Sole Baked in Cream (p.
121).*

Fill a frying pan 1 inch deep with milk
or white wine or half dry vermouth and
half water. Heat to just below the boiling point. Add 1 pound fish fillets, sprinkled with salt. Reduce the heat and cook
gently until the fish flakes when tried
with a fork.

Lift out the fish and serve it with a sauce
made of the juices in the pan. *Serves 3.*

Sauce for Poached Fish Fillets. Melt 2
tablespoons butter, add 2 tablespoons
flour and stir until smooth. Add 1 cup

pan juices, adding cold water if necessary. Cook and stir 5 minutes. Season to
taste, adding salt, pepper and a teaspoon
of lemon juice. Just before serving, add
2 tablespoons butter, bit by bit.

Fish Fillets Poached in Tomato Sauce.
Use tomato sauce as the liquid. Sprinkle
with parsley.

Fish Fillets Suprême. Heat 1 can frozen
oyster stew or shrimp bisque. Add 1 cup
sliced mushrooms (fresh or canned). Add
1 pound fish fillets and cook as above.
Just before serving, add lemon juice to
taste. Serve with fluffy steamed rice.

Baked Fish Fillets

Cod, flounder, haddock, halibut or scrod.

Put fillets on an oiled or buttered
ovenproof platter. Sprinkle with salt,
pepper and lemon juice. Dot with butter
or cover with buttered crumbs. Bake at
400° until the fish flakes when tried with
a fork (12 to 30 minutes, according to
the thickness of the fish).

Fish Fillets Vermouth. Instead of lemon
juice, sprinkle generously with dry vermouth. Especially delicious for fillets of
flounder or halibut.

Stuffed Fish Fillets. Put fillets or slices
of fish on oiled baking dish. Sprinkle
with salt. Cover each with stuffing and
put another fillet or slice on top. Brush
with oil or melted butter and bake.

Oyster or Shrimp Stuffed Fillets. Put
fillets together with a layer of oysters
or shrimp. Brush the top with a slightly
beaten egg, then cover with buttered
cracker crumbs. Bake 50 minutes at 350°.
Serve with Hollandaise (p. 95).

Fish Fillets à la Preston. Put fillets together with Mushroom Stuffing (p. 81).
Put on an ovenproof platter. Pour light
cream over the fish (about ⅔ cup for
each pound of fish). Bake 25 minutes at
375°. Sprinkle with buttered crumbs.
Bake until brown.

Fish Fillets Métropole

Put in a baking dish in a single layer
  2 pounds fish fillets
Cover with
  Normandy Sauce (p. 91)
Bake at 400° until the fish flakes when
tried with a fork (about 15 minutes).

Beat until stiff
  ½ cup heavy cream
Add to the cream
  1½ tablespoons pimiento, rubbed
    through a sieve
  ½ tablespoon chopped chives
  ¼ teaspoon salt
Spread over the fish. Sprinkle with
  ½ cup buttered coarse bread crumbs
Bake until delicately brown. Serve with
  Hollandaise (p. 95)
Serves 6.

Stuffed Turbans of Fish

*Flounder or sole. "Sole" is usually
flounder in the United States, but English sole is sometimes available in metropolitan markets. If you do not have
muffin rings, use large cupcake tins.*

Trim into neat pieces
  8 fish fillets
Coil inside 8 buttered muffin rings placed
in a buttered pan.

Put in a pan
  ¾ cup chopped mushroom stems
  Few drops onion juice
  3 tablespoons butter
Cook 1 minute. Stir in
  ¼ cup flour
Add gradually, stirring constantly
  ½ cup cream
Stir until the mixture boils. Add
  Chopped soft part of 12 oysters or
    ½ cup crab meat
Season to taste with
  Salt, pepper, cayenne and mace
Fill the muffin rings with the mixture.
Cover with foil. Bake 20 minutes at
375°. Remove the foil. Sprinkle with
  Buttered bread crumbs
Bake until the crumbs are brown. Slip
from the rings to a hot platter. *Serves 8.*

Sole Meunière

*A traditional method for sole, but ex-
cellent for fillets or slices of other fish as
well.*

Dip the fillets lightly in salted flour.
Melt butter in a heavy frying pan. Put
in the fillets in a single layer and cook
until delicately brown. Squeeze a little
lemon juice into the liquid in the pan
and pour it over the fish. *One pound
serves 3.*

For a very rich and delicate flavor, have
the butter deep enough to cover the fish.
Remove the cooked fish to a warm platter. For each ½ cup of juice in the pan,
stir in 2 tablespoons flour, ½ cup chicken
stock, a few drops of lemon juice and 1
tablespoon chopped parsley. Blend well
and pour over the fish.

Fillets of Sole Amandine. Sprinkle with
sliced almonds sautéed in butter.

Fillets of Sole Baked in Cream

Dip the fillets in salted flour. Arrange
them in a baking dish and cover with
cream. Bake 15 minutes at 450°.

Remove the fish to a heated platter.
Season the pan juices delicately with
anchovy paste or beef extract and pour
over the fish. Or season with salt and
pepper only, and after you have poured
the sauce over the fish, sprinkle with
finely cut salted almonds or halved seedless white grapes. *One pound serves 3.*

Fillets of Sole Berçy. In place of cream,
sprinkle the fillets with dry white wine,
dry vermouth, or lemon juice mixed
with an equal amount of water. Serve
with Berçy Sauce (p. 92) made with the
liquid in the baking pan.

Fillets of Sole Véronique. Sprinkle seeded
or seedless white grapes over Fillets of
Sole Berçy (above) and reheat before
serving.

Sole Marguéry

The classic recipe calls for Fish Stock (p. 120) made with the lobster shell and the bones and scraps left after the fish is filleted. Other garnishes are good too — shrimp or tiny scallops with mussels, sliced mushroom caps, or a combination of any of these. All cooked in advance, of course.

Set the oven at 350°.

Place in a single layer in a buttered baking dish
    8 fillets of sole or flounder
Sprinkle with
    Salt and paprika
    ½ cup dry white wine
Cover closely with foil. Cook 15 minutes. Pour off the liquid from the baking pan and add to it.
    Fish Stock (p. 120), chicken broth or water to make 1½ cups
Keep the fillets warm.

Melt
    3 tablespoons butter
Stir in
    3 tablespoons flour
Add the liquid slowly. Bring slowly to the boiling point, stirring constantly. Season to taste with
    Salt and pepper
Arrange the fillets on an ovenproof platter. Strain the sauce over them. Garnish with
    ½ pound cooked sliced lobster meat
    18 littleneck clams
Sprinkle with
    ¼ cup grated Parmesan cheese
Bake until thoroughly heated. *Serves 6 to 8.*

Fillets of Sole St. Mâlo. In place of lobster meat and clams, garnish with ½ pint oysters. Parboil the oysters (p. 144), drain off the liquid, and add it to the stock made of the fish trimmings and bones. If you prefer, use water or chicken or clam broth in place of stock.

Sole Normande. In place of lobster and clams, garnish with ½ pound cooked or canned shrimp. Add to the sauce ½

pound mushrooms, sliced and sautéed in butter.

Fillets en Papillote

If parchment paper is not available, use aluminum foil. The effect will not be as festive as the prettily browned paper, but the fish will be just as tasty.

For each serving, put a neat piece of flounder fillet on a thin slice of cooked ham trimmed slightly larger than the fillet. Put on a piece of parchment paper. Dot with butter and sprinkle with salt, pepper, thyme and chopped parsley. Wrap like a package, folding the edges to keep in the juice. Put in a shallow pan. Brush the paper with melted butter. Bake 15 minutes at 400°.

Serve without removing the paper so that each person opens his own. Serve with melted butter seasoned with lemon juice.

To vary, put in each package 2 or 3 cooked or canned mushroom caps or tiny onions.

Bluefish Breslin

Cook other fish this way, too.

Set the oven at 400°.

Place in a well-buttered baking pan
    Bluefish, about 4 pounds, split and boned
Bake 20 minutes.

Mix
    ¼ cup butter, creamed
    2 egg yolks
    2 tablespoons finely chopped onion
    2 tablespoons chopped pickle
    2 tablespoons chopped parsley
    2 tablespoons capers
    2 tablespoons lemon juice
    1 tablespoon vinegar
    ½ teaspoon salt
    ¼ teaspoon paprika
Spread over the fish. Continue baking until the fish flakes when tried with a fork (about 30 minutes). *Serves 6 to 8.*

Bluefish Italienne

Set the oven at 375°.

Place on a well-buttered baking pan or ovenproof platter
  Bluefish, about 4 pounds, split and
    boned
Sprinkle over the fish
  Salt and pepper
  3 tablespoons dry white wine
  3 tablespoons mushroom liquid
    (below)
  ½ onion, chopped fine
  8 mushroom caps, chopped
Add enough water for basting. Bake 45 minutes, basting every 10 minutes.

Serve with
  Brown Sauce (p. 93), made with
    stock or water
Serves 6 to 8.

To prepare mushroom liquid. Chop the mushroom stems, barely cover them with water, and simmer 20 minutes. Strain. If you are using canned mushrooms, use the liquid in the can.

Halibut Poulette

Prepare
  Béchamel Sauce (p. 91)
  2 hard-cooked eggs
Clean and cut in 8 fillets
  1½ pounds halibut
Melt
  ¼ cup butter
Add
  ¼ teaspoon salt
  ⅛ teaspoon pepper
  2 teaspoons lemon juice
  Few drops onion juice
Set over low heat or over hot water to keep the butter melted. Take up each fillet on a fork, dip in the butter, roll and fasten with a toothpick. Put in a shallow pan and sprinkle with
  Flour
Bake 12 minutes at 400°.

Take out the toothpicks. Put the fish on a platter and pour the sauce around it. Garnish with the egg yolks rubbed

through a sieve, the whites cut in strips, and
  1 lemon, cut in fan-shaped pieces
  Parsley
Serves 4.

Halibut Creole

Set the oven at 400°.

Place on a buttered ovenproof platter or baking pan
  1½ pounds halibut in one slice
Sprinkle with
  Salt and pepper
Put over the fish
  5 thick slices peeled tomato
  ½ green pepper, chopped
  2 teaspoons chopped onion
Bake 25 minutes. Baste 3 times during baking with the pan juices and with
  ⅓ cup melted butter
Serves 4.

Hollenden Halibut

Cut in very thin slices
  ⅛ pound fat salt pork
Put 6 slices on an ovenproof platter or a shallow baking dish. Put on the pork
  1 small onion, sliced thin
  Bit of bay leaf
  2 pounds halibut in one piece
Cream together
  3 tablespoons butter
  3 tablespoons flour
Spread on the fish. Cover with the rest of the pork, cut in narrow strips, and
  ½ cup buttered crumbs
Cover with foil and bake 55 minutes at 350°. Remove the foil and bake 15 minutes longer to brown the crumbs. Garnish with
  Sliced lemon
Sprinkle with
  Chopped parsley
  Paprika
Serve with
  Cream Sauce (p. 90), made with the
    fat in the pan instead of butter.
Serves 6.

Halibut à la Suisse

Set the oven at 375°.

Place in a buttered baking pan
  2 pounds halibut, in one piece or cut
  in slices
Sprinkle with
  Salt and pepper
Dot with
  ½ cup butter
Bake a whole piece 15 minutes, slices 10
minutes, basting twice with the juices
in the pan. Cover with
  ¼ pound mushrooms, cut in pieces
  1 cup cream
Bake another 15 minutes for a whole
piece, 10 minutes for slices. Stir into the
pan juices
  1 teaspoon beef extract
Bake 10 minutes longer, basting twice.
Serves 6.

Halibut Swedish Style

Set the oven at 375°.

Remove the skin from
  1½-pound slice halibut
Put in a shallow casserole. Sprinkle with
  Salt and pepper
Brush with
  Melted butter
Mix and spread over the fish
  1 cup drained canned tomatoes
  ½ teaspoon fine sugar
Cover with
  1 onion, sliced thin
Bake 20 minutes. Pour over the top
  ½ cup heavy cream
Bake 10 minutes longer. *Serves 4.*

Halibut Timbales

Grind very fine
  1 pound halibut
Rub through a sieve. Add
  1 egg yolk
  1 teaspoon salt
  ¼ teaspoon pepper
  Few grains cayenne
  ¾ teaspoon cornstarch
Add gradually

⅔ cup milk
⅓ cup heavy cream, beaten stiff
Fill buttered timbale molds or a ring
mold. Set in a pan of hot water. Bake
and serve like Fish Mousse. *Serves 4.*

Halibut Timbales Farci. Line small
molds with the above mixture or with
Fish Mousse (below), reserving about a
quarter of the mixture for the top. Fill
with Creamed Lobster (p. 143), Shrimp
(p. 150) or Crab Meat (p. 139), and cover
with mousse. Set in a pan of hot water
and bake as above. Serve with Lobster
Sauce (p. 90) or Béchamel Sauce (p. 91).
Before filling the molds, sprinkle, if desired, with lobster coral rubbed through
a sieve.

Fish Mousse

*Also called Norwegian Fish Pudding.
Halibut or flounder makes a very delicate mousse. Salmon Mousse is excellent,
too, served with Normandy Sauce (p.
91) or Cucumber Hollandaise (p. 95).
To make the mousse even smoother,
prepare in an electric blender, starting
with one-third of the cream and one-
third of the fish, cut in small pieces.*

Put through a food chopper, using a
fine knife
  1 pound halibut or other delicate fish
Put in a bowl set in a pan of ice water.
Stir in very slowly
  3 egg whites
beating with a wire whisk to keep the
mixture very smooth. Stir in very slowly
  1 cup heavy cream or evaporated milk
  1 teaspoon salt
  ½ teaspoon pepper
Season to taste with
  Cayenne, nutmeg or celery salt
  Few drops of onion juice
Let stand 1 hour. Stir well. Butter or
oil a 1½-quart mold or a set of small
timbale molds. Pour in the mixture. Set
in a pan of hot water 1 inch deep. Cover
with foil.

Bake at 350° until firm or cook on top
of the stove over low heat so that the

water barely simmers. Do not overcook. Turn out onto a serving dish. Pour over the mousse

Lobster (p. 90), Shrimp (p. 91) or Mushroom Sauce (p. 94)

If you like, season the sauce with Sherry

Serves 4 to 6.

Jean's Fish Mousse. Not quite so delicate but simpler. Heat the cream and add 1 cup dry bread crumbs and the chopped fish. Season. Beat the egg whites stiff and fold into the fish mixture. Bake and serve as above.

Swedish Fish Balls. Shape the mixture in ovals with a buttered tablespoon. Slip from the spoon into boiling water. Cook 8 minutes. Cover with Normandy Sauce (p. 91) and sprinkle with chopped parsley.

Mackerel

Broil or pan-fry fillets (p. 118). Broil (p. 118) split whole fish or bake (p. 119) with or without stuffing.

Mackerel Baked in Milk. Split the fish, clean, and remove the head and tail. Put in a buttered baking pan. Sprinkle with salt and pepper, dot with butter (1 tablespoon to a medium-sized fish), and pour ⅔ cup milk over the fish. Bake 25 minutes at 400°.

Pompano

A delicious fish native to South Atlantic and Gulf waters.

Split. Broil or bake whole, or remove the bones and broil, sauté or poach the fillets. Cucumber Hollandaise (p. 95) and Brown Almond Sauce (p. 90) are excellent with pompano.

Royal Poinciana Pompano

Split and clean
1 pompano (about 2 pounds)
Put in a buttered baking dish.

Beat together
2 eggs
½ cup heavy cream
Add
2 cups shrimp, chopped fine
½ teaspoon salt
½ cup chopped mushrooms
¼ cup sherry
Spread over the fish. Pour around the fish
½ cup heavy cream
Bake 45 minutes at 350°. Garnish with
Sliced cucumber
Sliced lemon
Serves 4 or 5.

Steamed Salmon

Steam the salmon (p. 119).

Serve hot with Egg Sauce (p. 91) or Hollandaise (p. 95). Serve cold with Mayonnaise (p. 289), Cucumber Hollandaise (p. 95), Ravigote Mayonnaise (p. 290), or Cucumber Sauce (p. 98). See also Molded Salmon (p. 285).

A salad of cooked peas, Lima beans, and carrots (cut small), mixed with mayonnaise, is an excellent accompaniment for cold salmon.

Broiled Scrod

Scrod is young cod or haddock split down the back and with most of the backbone removed. Creamed or hashed brown potatoes are traditional with scrod.

Sprinkle with melted butter, fine crumbs, and salt and pepper. Broil (p. 118) skin side down until it flakes (about 10 minutes). *A small scrod (½ to ¾ pound) serves 1 or 2.*

Shad

Shad is at its best in the spring. Buy it with the roe if you can. A 3-pound shad serves 6.

Have the fish cleaned and split. Remove the roe to prepare separately (p. 126). To broil shad (p. 118); to bake (p. 126).

Boneless Shad

This old-fashioned method dissolves the shad's tiny bones. The flavor is excellent and the fish stays moist.

Leave on the head and tail. Remove the roe to cook (below) and serve with the shad. Stuff the shad with
    Savory Bread Dressing (p. 80)
Rub with
    Olive oil
Place on a piece of foil. Lay over the fish
    4 strips bacon
Fold the foil around the fish and close tightly by folding the edges together. Place on a pan and bake 6 hours at 225°.

Baked or Planked Shad

Remove the roe. Put the fish in a shallow baking dish or on a buttered plank, skin side down. Sprinkle with salt and pepper. Brush with melted butter.

Bake 25 minutes at 400° or broil about 15 minutes. Spread with butter, garnish with parsley and lemon, and serve on the plank with Roe Sauce (below).

Baked Shad with Creamed Roe. Spread Creamed Shad Roe (below) over the thin part of baked shad. Cover with ½ cup buttered crumbs and return to the oven to brown the crumbs.

Shad Roe

Fresh roe is usually served with the shad, either baked with it or creamed (below) or made into Roe Sauce. However, it is delicious served as a separate dish. Canned roe is very satisfactory and may be used in place of parboiled fresh roe. Roe from 1 shad gives 2 servings.

To parboil roe. Cover fresh roe with boiling water, add 1 tablespoon salt and 1 tablespoon vinegar or lemon juice, and simmer 15 minutes (2 minutes for small, young roe). Drain, cover with cold water, and let stand 5 minutes. Drain.

Broiled Shad Roe. Arrange the parboiled roe in a lightly buttered shallow pan. Broil quickly until golden-brown, turning once and sprinkling several times with melted butter. Properly cooked roe is firm but not dry or hard.

Creamed Shad Roe. Melt 3 tablespoons butter. Add 1 teaspoon chopped shallot or mild onion and cook 5 minutes. Mash the parboiled roe and stir it in. Sprinkle with 1½ tablespoons flour. Cook slowly 5 minutes. Season highly with salt, pepper and lemon juice.

Sautéed Shad Roe. Cut parboiled roe in pieces. Melt 3 tablespoons butter, add the roe, and cook 10 minutes. Serve plain or with broiled bacon. Or make a sauce by adding to the fat in the pan 1 tablespoon butter, ½ cup chopped celery, a few drops onion juice, a few drops lemon juice, salt and pepper. Serve with the roe.

Roe Sauce

Put in a small shallow baking dish
    ½ shad roe
Sprinkle with
    Salt, pepper, cayenne and nutmeg
Dot with
    2 tablespoons butter
Add
    2 tablespoons sherry
    2 tablespoons white wine
Cover with foil. Bake 30 minutes at 350°. Pick out the membranes.

Melt until brown
    3 tablespoons butter
Stir in
    ¼ cup flour
Cook until brown. Pour on gradually
    1 cup Chicken Stock (p. 72) or canned chicken broth
Bring to the boiling point, stirring constantly. Add
    ¼ teaspoon beef extract
    Salt to taste
Stir in the roe. Serve with Planked or Baked Shad (p. 126).

Sautéed Smelts

Split and clean smelts, allowing 1 or 2 per person. Cut 5 diagonal gashes on each side. Sprinkle with salt, pepper and lemon juice. Cover and let stand 10 minutes. Roll in flour. Sauté in butter or olive oil.

Smelts à la Meunière. Pour the juices from the pan over the cooked smelts. (If you like a bit more sauce, add a little butter to the pan juices and stir in a teaspoon of anchovy paste and a few drops of lemon juice.) Sprinkle with chopped parsley. Serve with lemon.

Smelts Amandine. Sprinkle the cooked fish with sliced almonds sautéed in olive oil.

Smelts au Beurre Noir. Put the cooked fish on a hot platter. Add enough butter to the pan juices to make about ⅓ cup. Stir until dark brown. Add 1 teaspoon lemon juice, salt and pepper. Pour over the fish. Sprinkle with chopped parsley.

Fried Smelts

Split and clean smelts, allowing 1 or 2 per person. Sprinkle with salt and pepper. Dip in crumbs, then in slightly beaten egg, and then in crumbs again. Fry 3 to 5 minutes in deep fat heated to 370°. As soon as the smelts are put into the fat, reduce the heat so that they will not brown too much before being cooked.

Serve with Tartare Sauce (p. 97).

Red Snapper Florida

Put in a buttered baking dish
   1½ pounds red snapper fillets
Sprinkle over them
   1 teaspoon salt
   ⅛ teaspoon pepper
   1½ teaspoons grated orange rind
   1 teaspoon grated grapefruit rind
   Few grains nutmeg
Cover with foil. Bake 15 minutes at 400°. *Serves 4 to 6.*

Broiled Swordfish

Thick slices broil more successfully than thin ones. They are still juicy and succulent after thorough cooking. The best are cut from the center of the fish, 2 inches thick. Two pounds serves 6.

Place on a buttered shallow pan. Sprinkle with salt, pepper and flour. Dot generously with butter. Cook in a broiler, 3 inches from the heat, until the fish flakes (20 minutes or longer).

Brook Trout Meunière

Clean and wipe the trout. Sprinkle with salt and pepper. Dip in flour. Sauté in butter until delicately brown. Squeeze a little lemon juice into the pan juices and pour over the fish. Sprinkle with chopped parsley. *One pound serves 3.*

Fried Whitebait

The perfect first course for a formal dinner, but rarely to be found except in a few de luxe metropolitan markets.

Wash the whitebait thoroughly. Dry carefully in a clean cloth. Shake to remove moisture. Sprinkle with salt and pepper, roll in flour, and shake lightly in a sieve to remove extra flour.

Sauté in butter or fry in deep fat heated to 370°, using a frying basket with very fine mesh. Whitebait are so tiny that they cook in 1 to 3 minutes. *One pound serves 6 to 8.*

As a first course, serve with thin sandwiches of brown bread and sweet butter.

As a luncheon dish, combine with Fried Shrimp (p. 144), or see Fried Oysters and Whitebait (p. 140).

Baked or Planked Whitefish

Split and bone the fish. Put skin side down on a buttered plank or baking dish. Sprinkle with salt and pepper. Dot with butter. Bake 25 minutes at 400° without turning. Or broil, if you prefer, about 15 minutes.

Fried Frogs' Legs

As sweet and tender as young chicken. Allow ½ pound per person.

Sprinkle frogs' legs with salt, pepper and lemon juice. Dip in crumbs, egg, and again in crumbs. Chill 1 hour.

Sauté in butter until brown, or fry 3 minutes in deep fat heated to 375°.

Frogs' Legs Newburg

Serve on thin toast or in patty shells.

Cut in ¼-inch strips
  ½ pound mushroom caps
Sauté 3 minutes in
  1 tablespoon butter
Steam (p. 119) until tender
  2 pounds frogs' legs
Add
  ¼ pound crab meat
  2 tablespoons melted butter
  ½ cup sherry
Cover and let stand 30 minutes.

Cook 5 minutes. Pour off about half the liquid in the pan. Add the mushrooms.

Scald in a double boiler.
  1½ cups cream
Mix and stir into the cream
  1 tablespoon cornstarch
  1 tablespoon cold water
Cook 20 minutes, stirring constantly until thick. Stir in
  1 egg yolk, slightly beaten
Add to the first mixture. Reheat, and season to taste. *Serves 6.*

Terrapin

Fresh terrapin is rarely available. Its preparation is so complicated that it is best to learn by watching someone do it. Canned terrapin is sold in some specialty shops. Heat it in a rich cream sauce. Add chopped sautéed mushrooms, if you like, and season with sherry or serve sherry with the terrapin.

Recipes Using Cooked or Canned Fish

Many of the following recipes may be used for either cooked or canned fish, such as tuna or salmon. Serve any of the creamed dishes over toast or with rice or noodles. Or fill a casserole, individual baking dishes or scallop shells, cover with buttered crumbs, and heat in a 350° oven until the crumbs are brown.

Creamed Fish

Flake cooked fish, removing the bones and bits of skin, or use canned tuna or salmon. Add to Cream Sauce (p. 90), using 1 cup of sauce for each ½ to 1 cup of fish. Heat in a double boiler. Season highly to taste.

Serve on toast or in a border of cooked rice or mashed potato. Sprinkle with paprika and/or chopped parsley.

To vary:

  Make a richer sauce by stirring in an egg yolk just before serving.
  Add a few sautéed mushrooms.
  Use part fish stock or chicken stock in making the sauce.
  Add crumbled hard-cooked egg yolks and season with anchovy essence.
  Mix the fish with concentrated mushroom soup in place of Cream

Sauce, diluting it to the right consistency with cream or water.

Kedgeree

A famous English breakfast dish, also delicious hot or cold for luncheon or supper.

Mix in a double boiler
  2 cups cooked rice
  4 chopped hard-cooked eggs
  3 tablespoons chopped parsley
  2 cups flaked cooked fish
  ½ cup cream
  Salt, pepper and curry, if liked
Heat thoroughly. *Serves 6.*

Fish Hash

Mix equal parts of cold flaked fish (especially halibut) and cold boiled potatoes chopped fine. Season with salt and pepper. Try out (p. 9) fat salt pork and remove the scraps, leaving enough fat in the pan to moisten the fish and potatoes. Put in the fish and potatoes and stir until heated. Cook until well browned underneath, fold, and turn like an omelet.

Scalloped Fish

Use the recipe for Scalloped Ham (p. 188) and vary it as you like. Or put creamed fish in a buttered casserole, ramekins or scallop shells. Cover with buttered cracker crumbs (½ cup to 2 cups of the scallop). Bake at 375° until brown.

Other toppings to use are crushed potato chips, corn flakes, or grated cheese mixed with crumbs.

Scalloped Fish with Cheese Meringue. Beat 2 egg whites until stiff and fold in ¼ cup grated cheese. Spread over the filled casserole or ramekins. Sprinkle with grated cheese. Bake at 450° until browned.

Huntington Scalloped Fish

A leftover dish with a flair — so good that you will often cook a fillet of fish especially for it.

Melt
  3 tablespoons butter
Add
  1 green pepper, cut fine
Cook until the pepper is soft. Stir in
  2 tablespoons flour
Blend until smooth. Add
  1½ cups cream or part milk
Cook and stir until thick and smooth. Add
  1 cup flaked cooked haddock or
    halibut
  ½ cup soft bread crumbs
  Salt, pepper and sherry to taste
Put in a baking dish. Cover with
  ½ cup buttered crumbs
Bake at 375° until brown (about 30 minutes). *Serves 4.*

To vary. Add ½ to 1 cup sautéed sliced mushrooms.

Fish Mousse

See also page 124.

Prepare
  2 cups finely chopped cooked fish
Season with
  Salt to taste
  Few grains cayenne
  1½ teaspoons lemon juice
Fold in gently
  ⅓ cup cream, whipped
  3 egg whites, beaten stiff
Spoon into a buttered 1-quart mold or into individual molds. Set in a pan of hot water 1 inch deep. Cover with foil.

Bake at 350° until firm (about 20 minutes) or cook slowly over moderate heat.

Take out of the molds. Cover with
  Béchamel (p. 91) or Lobster Sauce (p. 90)
Garnish with
  Parsley
Serves 6.

Fish Newburg

Many recipes call for sherry alone, but brandy adds a delicious flavor. See also the special recipes for Lobster Newburg (p. 143), Frogs' Legs Newburg (p. 128), Oyster Crabs Newburg (p. 140) and Seafood Newburg (p. 143).

Melt
  1 tablespoon butter
Stir in
  1 teaspoon flour
Add slowly
  1 cup thin cream
Cook and stir over low heat until thickened. Add
  2 cups cooked flaked halibut or sole
Keep warm in a double boiler or over very low heat. Just before serving, stir in
  2 egg yolks, slightly beaten
  2 tablespoons sherry, or 1 tablespoon each of sherry and brandy
Season to taste. *Serves 4.*

In place of fish you may use crab meat, shrimp, lobster or scallops.

Fish Soufflé

Prepare by removing bits of bone and skin and separating into flakes
  2 cups cooked or canned salmon, tuna or other fish
Add
  ¼ teaspoon salt
  ⅛ teaspoon paprika
  2 teaspoons lemon juice
Cook together 5 minutes
  ½ cup dry bread crumbs
  ½ cup milk
Add the fish and
  3 egg yolks, beaten thick
Fold in
  3 egg whites, beaten stiff
Spoon into a buttered baking dish. Set in a pan of hot water and bake at 350° until firm (about 30 minutes).

Serve with
  Hollandaise (p. 95) or Sauce Espagnole (p. 93)
Serves 6.

Salmon or Tuna Loaf

Vary this recipe according to the amount of salmon on hand. One cup of salmon may be combined with a cup of crumbs and a cup of hot milk.

Mix
  2 cups flaked cooked or canned salmon or tuna
  ½ cup fine bread crumbs
  ¼ cup butter
  2 eggs, slightly beaten
  1 tablespoon chopped parsley
  Salt, pepper and Worcestershire to taste
  Chopped onion, green pepper or celery, if you like
Put in a buttered baking dish. Set in a pan of hot water 1 inch deep. Bake at 350° until firm (about 30 minutes).

Serve hot with
  Mustard Sauce (p. 97)
or cold with
  Cucumber Sauce (p. 98)
Serves 6.

Salmon or Tuna Cheese Loaf

Mix
  2 cups flaked cooked or canned salmon or tuna
  1½ cups grated cheese
  1 egg, well beaten
  3 tablespoons milk
  1 tablespoon melted butter
  ½ teaspoon salt
  Few grains pepper
  Cracker or bread crumbs to make a stiff mixture
Pack into a loaf pan. Cover the top with
  Buttered crumbs
Bake at 375° until golden brown. *Serves 6.*

Spiced Salmon

For a summer supper with a mixed vegetable salad and pumpernickel.

Prepare (rinse canned salmon with hot water to remove the oil, and free fresh salmon of bones and skin)

2 cups canned or cooked salmon

Mix in a small pan

1 cup mild vinegar
1 teaspoon whole cloves
½ teaspoon allspice berries
8 peppercorns
¼ teaspoon salt

Bring to the boiling point. Pour over the fish. Cover and let stand 2 hours. Drain and separate into flakes. *Serves 4.*

Tuna

The most expensive is light-colored and in large chunks. Use it in salads or in scalloped dishes in which appearance is of importance. Sliced or grated tuna, light or dark, is less expensive. Use it in any recipe in which the tuna is to be cut in small pieces.

See the index for tuna recipes in other chapters. Use tuna in any of the following recipes, or substitute tuna for cooked chicken in any of the recipes listed under Recipes Using Cooked Chicken (p. 223).

Creamed Fish (p. 128)
Fish Sandwich Fillings (p. 340)
Fish Souffle (p. 130)
Kedgeree (p. 129)
Savory Meat or Chicken Roll (p. 202)
Scalloped Fish (p. 129)

Tuna Noodle Casserole

Use condensed cream of mushroom soup, if you like, instead of cheese sauce and mushrooms.

Butter a 1-quart casserole. Put in it

1 7-ounce can tuna, drained
2 cups cooked noodles
3 hard-cooked eggs, sliced
2 cups Cheese Sauce (p. 91)
½ cup sliced mushrooms
Salt, pepper and celery salt
Few drops onion juice

Mix gently. Cover with

Buttered crumbs

Bake at 375° until the sauce bubbles and the crumbs are brown (about 20 minutes). *Serves 4.*

Tuna Pie

Bake extra pastry to serve with seconds.

Combine

2 7-ounce cans tuna, drained and flaked
2 cups Cream Sauce (p. 90)
1 teaspoon Worcestershire
1 tablespoon sherry, if you like
1 tablespoon chopped parsley
Salt, pepper and celery salt to taste

Pour into a buttered 2-quart casserole or individual pottery bowls. Roll out

Plain Pastry (p. 407)

Shape it to fit the top of the casserole or bowls. Put on the crust and slit or prick it. Bake at 425° until brown (about 25 minutes). *Serves 6.*

Tuna Rice

Melt in a large saucepan

3 tablespoons butter

Add

¼ cup chopped onion
¼ cup chopped celery

Cook slowly until tender. Stir in gently

1 7-ounce can tuna, drained and flaked
2 cups cooked rice
¼ cup chopped parsley
Salt and paprika to taste

Heat thoroughly, stirring lightly to keep from sticking. *Serves 4.*

Creamed Sardines

For lunch or as an evening snack.

Drain

1 small tin sardines

Remove the backbones and mash the fish. Melt

¼ cup butter

Add

¼ cup bread crumbs
1 cup cream

Heat thoroughly. Stir in the sardines and

2 hard-cooked eggs, chopped fine

Season to taste with

Salt and paprika

Serve on

Toast

Serves 2 or 3.

Grilled Sardines

Drain canned sardines. Cook in an omelet pan until heated, turning frequently. Serve on small oblongs of dry toast with Maître d'Hôtel (p. 89) or Lemon Butter (p. 90).

Grilled Sardines with Anchovy Sauce. Serve with sauce made of 1½ tablespoons sardine oil (from the can), 2 tablespoons flour, and 1 cup Brown Stock (p. 70) or canned consommé. Season to taste with anchovy sauce or paste.

Recipes Using Dried Fish

Codfish Balls

Although these are usually made with dried salt codfish, you may use shredded cooked codfish, mashing it with the cooked potato.

Freshen, following directions on the package
  ½ pound salt codfish
Wash, pare and cube potatoes to make
  2½ cups potato cubes
Put the fish and potatoes in a pan. Add boiling water to cover, and cook until the potatoes are nearly soft. Drain thoroughly and shake over the heat until completely dry. Mash well. Add
  ½ tablespoon butter
  1 egg, well beaten
  ⅛ teaspoon pepper
Taste, and add salt, if necessary. Beat with a fork until smooth and light (about 2 minutes). Fry or sauté. *Serves 6.*

To fry. Heat fat to 375°. Take up the fish ball mixture by spoonfuls and fry 1 minute. Fry six at a time. Drain on paper towels.

To sauté. Shape in flat patties and brown in butter.

Codfish Hash. Dice a 2-inch cube of fat salt pork. Heat it in a frying pan until the fat melts. Remove the crisp bits of pork to use as a garnish on the hash. Pour off some of the fat, leaving enough to grease the pan well. Spread the codfish mixture in the pan and cook slowly until well browned underneath. Fold like an omelet. *Serves 6.*

Creamed Codfish

Following directions on the package, freshen
  ½ pound salt codfish
Add to
  1½ cups Cream Sauce (p. 90) or cream
Heat. Just before serving, stir in
  1 egg, well beaten
Garnish with
  Sliced hard-cooked egg, or with a sprinkling of crisp fried pork scraps or bacon
Serve with baked potatoes. *Serves 4.*

Spanish Codfish

Following directions on the package, freshen
  ½ pound salt codfish
Separate into small pieces. Slice
  4 cold boiled potatoes
Put alternate layers of fish and potatoes in a buttered casserole. Sprinkle with
  3 canned pimientos, cut in strips
  Salt and pepper
Pour over the top
  1 cup Tomato Sauce, homemade (p. 94) or canned
Cover with
  ½ cup buttered crumbs
Bake at 350° until the crumbs are brown. *Serves 6.*

Cod Cheeks and Tongues

If salted, soak overnight in water to cover. Drain, cover with fresh water, simmer 5 minutes and drain.

Sauté in butter until delicately brown (about 10 minutes). Pour over the browned butter, seasoned with lemon juice. Sprinkle with chopped parsley. *One pound serves 4.*

Scalloped Cod Cheeks or Tongues. Place in a baking dish. Pour over 1 cup Cream Sauce (p. 90) seasoned with lemon juice. Spread with buttered crumbs. Bake at 350° until the crumbs are brown.

Finnan Haddie

Finnan haddie is haddock, dried, smoked and salted.

Poached Finnan Haddie. Cover with milk and cook (covered) over moderate heat 25 minutes. Drain, dot with butter and sprinkle with pepper.

Broiled Finnan Haddie. Broil until brown on both sides. Put in a pan, cover with hot water and let stand 10 minutes. Drain, spread with butter and sprinkle with pepper.

Finnan Haddie Rabbit

Put in a double boiler top
  ½ pound Cheddar cheese, cut small
  1 cup heavy cream or evaporated milk
  ½ pound finnan haddie, flaked
Cook over hot water until well blended. Stir in
  1 egg, slightly beaten
Serve on
  Toast
Serves 6.

Finnan Haddie Delmonico

Put in a skillet
  1 pound finnan haddie, in strips
Cover with cold water, place over low heat and bring to the boiling point. Reduce the heat and simmer 25 minutes.

Drain and rinse thoroughly. Separate into flakes. Add
  ½ cup heavy cream
  4 hard-cooked eggs, sliced thin
  1 tablespoon butter
  Cayenne to taste
Reheat. Sprinkle with
  Finely chopped parsley
Serves 4.

Epicurean Finnan Haddie

Prepared in advance, this is an ideal supper party dish. Have it ready for the final heating and browning.

Put in a shallow baking dish
  1 pound finnan haddie
Cover with
  Milk
Let stand 1 hour. Bake 30 minutes at 350°. Separate into flakes. (There should be about 2 cups.)

Put in a pan
  ¼ cup butter
  1 tablespoon finely chopped green
    pepper
  ½ tablespoon finely chopped shallot
    or mild onion
  ½ tablespoon finely chopped red
    pepper
Cook 5 minutes. Add
  ¼ cup flour
  1 teaspoon salt
  ½ teaspoon paprika
  Few grains cayenne
Stir until well blended. Add gradually, stirring constantly
  1 cup milk
  1 cup cream
Bring to the boiling point. Add the finnan haddie and spoon into a buttered baking dish. Cover with
  Buttered crumbs
Bake at 350° until the crumbs are brown. *Serves 6.*

To vary. Add ¼ pound mushrooms, sliced and sautéed in butter. Instead of the peppers, add 1 pimiento, cut in small pieces.

Savory Finnan Haddie

Put in a shallow pan
   ½ pound finnan haddie
Cover with
   Milk
Let stand 1 hour. Cook until tender, drain, and separate into flakes.

Cook until tender and drain
   1½ cups small potato balls or cubes
Cut in tiny cubes
   ⅛ pound fat salt pork
Cook slowly until brown and crisp. Set the scraps aside. Put 2 tablespoons of the fat in a pan. Add
   2 tablespoons flour
Stir until well blended. Add slowly
   1 cup milk

Bring to the boiling point, stirring constantly. Add the finnan haddie, pork scraps and potatoes. Stir in
   2 eggs, slightly beaten
Reheat slightly, stirring constantly. *Serves 4.*

Kippered Herring

A typical English breakfast dish — good for brunch, too.

Arrange herring on an ovenproof platter. Sprinkle with pepper, brush over with lemon juice and melted butter, and cover with the liquid from the can. Heat in a 350° oven. Garnish with parsley and slices of lemon.

Shellfish

With new shipping methods, shellfish is available from coast to coast. Recipes using delicious fresh lobster, clams and oysters are superb additions to your cooking repertoire.

Abalone

A large mollusk, native to California waters and not available elsewhere. Buy it sliced, by the pound. One pound serves 2 or 3.

Pan-Fried Abalone. Pound slices thoroughly with a wooden mallet. Pat dry with a paper towel. Sprinkle with salt and pepper. Egg and crumb (p. 6), using cracker crumbs. Brown quickly in olive oil or butter, allowing about 1 minute on each side. Do not cook longer, as overcooking toughens abalone.

Clams

Buy clams in the shell by the dozen or by the quart or peck. See that the shells are tightly closed. This shows that the clams are alive and therefore fresh. If they are to be served raw, order them opened at the market, or open them with a special heavy knife clam opener. For Clam Chowder (p. 77), buy shelled clams by the pint or in cans.

There are three principal varieties in American markets: soft-shelled, hard-shelled, and the delicious razor clams which come from the Pacific. Soft-shelled New England clams are oval-shaped. Hard-shelled are round and come in three types: littlenecks (small), cherrystones (medium), and quahogs or chowder clams (large).

Clam Chowder (p. 77); Clams on the Half Shell (p. 45).

Seashore Clambake

Have at least 1 quart of clams for each person, preferably soft or long-necked variety. Live lobsters, too, and corn on the cob in its husks, if you are planning a hearty bake.

Dig a pit in the sand about 1 foot deep. Put a layer of stones in it. Build a wood fire on the stones and burn until it dies down and the stones are white-hot (about 1 hour). Meanwhile, scrub the clams well in sea water, kill the lobsters (p. 141, Broiled Live Lobster), and dip the corn in sea water. Rake off the ashes and spread a thin layer of rockweed on the stones. Put a piece of chicken wire over the rockweed and pile the clams, lobsters and corn on it. Cover with more rockweed and a piece of canvas to keep in the steam. Work quickly so that the rocks will not cool. Steam about 1 hour.

Baked or Broiled Clams

A delicious first course at dinner.

Remove the top shell from hard-shelled clams (medium size). Sprinkle with fine bread crumbs and a bit of melted butter. Bake about 10 minutes at 400° or broil 5 to 8 minutes. Serve very hot.

As a variation, top each clam with a ½-inch square of bacon instead of butter.

Clams Casino. Follow recipe for Oysters Casino (p. 145).

Shellfish

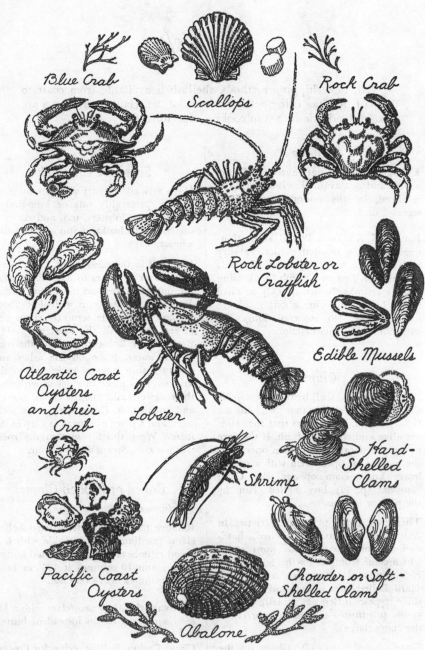

Blue Crab

Scallops

Rock Crab

Rock Lobster or Crayfish

Edible Mussels

Atlantic Coast Oysters and their Crab

Lobster

Hard-Shelled Clams

Pacific Coast Oysters

Shrimp

Chowder or Soft-Shelled Clams

Abalone

Steamed Clams

Soft-shelled clams are best for steaming. Allow 1 quart of clams per serving.

Scrub the shells thoroughly with a brush, changing the water until there is no trace of sand. Put in a deep kettle. Add 2 tablespoons water for each quart of clams. Cover closely and cook over low heat until the shells open a little (about 15 minutes). Do not overcook.

Remove with a perforated spoon to large soup plates. Serve with individual dishes of melted butter. If you like, add a few drops of lemon juice or vinegar to the butter. If a small quantity of boiling water is put into the dishes, the melted butter will float on top and remain hot much longer.

Strain the broth left in the kettle into small glasses and serve with the clams. Lift each clam from the shell by the black neck. Dip in the clam broth, then into the butter, and eat all but the neck.

Fricassee of Clams

Delicious as a first course for a party dinner or as an evening snack after bridge or the theater.

Put in a saucepan
   2 tablespoons butter
   1 pint chopped clams, fresh or canned
   2 tablespoons flour
Stir in gradually
   ½ cup cream
Stir and cook 1 minute. Add
   Salt and cayenne to taste
Stir in
   1 egg yolk, slightly beaten
Season to taste with
   Sherry or Madeira
Serve on
   Toast or in Patty Shells (p. 410)
Serves 4.

Stuffed Clams Union League

Put in a kettle
   ¼ cup butter

   ½ teaspoon finely chopped shallot or onion
Cook 5 minutes. Add
   18 small clams (in the shell)
   ½ cup dry white wine or water
Cover and cook until the shells open. Remove the clams from the shells and chop. Cook the liquid in the kettle down to ⅓ cup.

In a saucepan, melt
   2 tablespoons butter
Blend in
   2 tablespoons flour
Stir in the clam liquid, little by little. Add the clams and
   ¼ cup cream
Season with salt and pepper. Spoon into the shells. Sprinkle with
   Chopped parsley
Put on each
   Diced bacon or buttered crumbs mixed with grated cheese
Bake at 400° until the bacon is crisp or the crumbs are brown. *Serves 3 (or 6 as a first course).*

Clam Fritters

To serve as hors d'oeuvres with cocktails, measure with an after-dinner coffee spoon.

Drain
   1 cup chopped clams, fresh or canned
Measure the juice and add to it
   Milk to make ½ cup liquid
In a mixing bowl, beat
   1 egg
Add the clam juice and milk.

Sift together
   ⅔ cup flour
   1 teaspoon baking powder
   ½ teaspoon salt
   Pepper
Add to the liquids and blend well. Add the clams. Sauté by spoonfuls in bacon fat, or fry 3 to 5 minutes in deep fat heated to 375°. *Makes 12 large fritters or 30 cocktail size.*

Fried Clams

Allow about 6 soft-shelled clams for each serving.

Scrub the clams thoroughly with a brush. Using a special heavy knife, remove the clams from the shells. Pick out any bits of shell and sand and the black portion (the neck). Dip in seasoned flour or in Fritter Batter (p. 429), using no sugar. Fry in deep fat heated to 375°. Drain on paper towels. Serve with Tartare Sauce (p. 97).

Crabs and Crab Meat

Allow 1 or 2 crabs per serving, according to size. Buy them alive and active to be sure they are fresh. Or buy frozen crabs, ready to cook.

Soft-shelled crabs may be ordered cleaned at market. Otherwise, kill by sticking a small sharp knife into the body between the eyes, then lift and fold back the tapering points on each side of the back shell and remove the spongy substance under them. Turn the crab on its back, and with a pointed knife remove the small piece of the shell which ends in a point; this is called the apron. Soft-shelled crabs are eaten shell and all.

Hard-shelled crabs are cooked like boiled lobsters (p. 141) for 25 minutes. The edible crab meat is in the top of the back and in the claws. Discard the spongy fiber. Crack the claws with a nutcracker.

Crab meat may be bought fresh, by the pound, or in cans. Use fresh crab meat as soon after purchasing as possible. Remove the stiff tendons from canned crab meat.

Sautéed Crabs à la Meunière

Sprinkle soft-shelled crabs with salt, pepper and lemon juice. Sauté in butter 5 minutes on each side. Pour the pan juices over the crabs. Sprinkle with finely chopped parsley.

Sautéed Crabs Amandine. Instead of parsley, sprinkle with sliced almonds, sautéed in butter until delicately browned.

Fried Soft-Shelled Crabs

Sprinkle crabs with salt and pepper, dip in flour, then in slightly beaten egg, and then in crumbs. Fry (p. 5) in deep fat (375°) until brown, about 5 minutes. The crabs will rise to the top of the fat, and should be turned once while frying. Drain and serve with Tartare Sauce (p. 97).

Deviled Crabs

Season mayonnaise highly with lemon juice, dill, orégano and prepared mustard (or Worcestershire and grated onion). Stir in crab meat. Taste and add salt if necessary.

Fill ramekins or scallop shells. Cover with buttered crumbs or a tomato slice cut ½ inch thick and topped with a dab of mayonnaise.

Bake at 400° until well heated (about 15 minutes). Serve hot or cold.

Ipswich Deviled Crabs

Combine in a saucepan
    ¼ teaspoon dry mustard
    Salt, cayenne
    1 teaspoon Worcestershire or A–1 sauce
    ½ cup hot water
    ½ cup soft bread crumbs
    1 tablespoon cream
    1 tablespoon butter
Simmer 5 minutes. Stir in
    1 cup crab meat
    ¼ cup chopped stuffed olives
Fill ramekins or scallop shells. Cover with
    Buttered crumbs
Bake at 350° until brown. *Serves 6.*

Creamed Crab Meat

Blend together over low heat
    2 tablespoons butter
    2 tablespoons flour

Add slowly
 1 cup milk or part cream
Cook and stir over low heat until smooth and thickened. Season with
 ¼ teaspoon salt
 Pepper
Add
 ½ pound crab meat
Keep hot (a double boiler is the easy way) until served. Serve on
 Toast or in Patty Shells (p. 410)
Serves 4.

Crab Meat Urzini. Add ½ cup sliced mushrooms and cook 10 minutes over hot water. If you like, add 1 canned pimiento, cut in strips, and ½ cup grated Parmesan cheese.

Crab Meat Newburg. Season more highly with tomato paste and/or sherry. Add bits of pimiento. See also Seafood Newburg (p. 143) and the classic recipe for Lobster Newburg (p. 143).

Crab Meat au Gratin. Put in a shallow baking dish or in ramekins. Cover with ⅓ cup buttered crumbs (mixed, if you like, with ¼ cup grated cheese). Bake at 350° until the crumbs are a delicate brown.

Crab Meat à la King. Add ½ tablespoon finely chopped red and green pepper and ½ cup sliced mushrooms. Season to taste with sherry.

Crab Meat de Luxe. Season with a dash of Worcestershire. Use only ½ cup crab meat, and add ½ cup each of sliced mushrooms and blanched, shredded or whole almonds, and 1 hard-cooked egg, chopped.

Crab Meat Divan

Put a layer of well-seasoned and well-drained chopped cooked spinach in a shallow baking dish. Spread over it 1 cup of cooked or canned crab meat. Over the top pour 1 cup hot Cheese Sauce (p. 91). Bake at 350° until well heated and lightly browned. *Serves 4.*

Crab Meat Terrapin Style

Put in a pan
 2 tablespoons butter
 ½ small onion, sliced thin
Cook until the onion is yellow, remove it, and stir into the butter
 1 cup crab meat
 2 tablespoons sherry
Cook 3 minutes. Stir in
 ⅓ cup heavy cream
 2 egg yolks
Season with
 Salt and cayenne
Serves 2 to 4.

Crab Meat Indienne

Put in a pan
 2 tablespoons butter
 1 teaspoon onion, chopped fine
Cook 3 minutes.
Mix
 3 tablespoons flour
 2 teaspoons curry powder
Stir into the onion mixture. Add
 1 cup chicken broth or Chicken Stock (p. 72)
Bring to the boiling point. Add
 1 cup crab meat
Season to taste. *Serves 4.*

Crab Meat Casserole

Also good made with cooked halibut or flounder.
Mix
 1 cup cream
 1 cup mayonnaise (commercial, not homemade)
 1 tablespoon chopped parsley
 1 tablespoon minced onion
 ½ teaspoon each of salt and pepper
Add
 3½ cups crab meat (1 large and 1 medium-sized can)
 6 hard-cooked eggs, sliced
Put into a casserole. Top with
 1 cup buttered croûtons (p. 58) or buttered crumbs (p. 7)
Bake ½ hour at 350°. *Serves 8.*

To season more highly, add a dash of sherry or grated cheese to taste.

Crab Meat Mornay

As a first course, bake in eight or more small ramekin dishes.

Blend in a saucepan over low heat
   ¼ cup butter
   3 tablespoons flour
   2½ tablespoons cornstarch
Add gradually
   1 cup chicken broth or Chicken Stock
      (p. 72)
Cook 3 minutes, stirring constantly. Add
   1 cup milk
Blend and bring to a boil. Stir in
   2 egg yolks, slightly beaten
   ¾ teaspoon salt
   1 pound crab meat, cooked or canned
Spoon into a buttered 1½-quart casserole. Sprinkle with
   ½ cup grated cheese
Cook under the broiler until the cheese melts and browns. *Serves 6.*

Crab Cakes

Put in a saucepan
   2 tablespoons butter
   2 tablespoons minced onion
Cook until the onion is yellow. Remove from the heat. Add
   1 cup soft bread crumbs
   1 pound crab meat, cooked or canned
   1 egg, well beaten
   1 teaspoon dry mustard
   Salt and paprika to taste
If the mixture seems dry, moisten with
   Milk
Shape in flat cakes. Sprinkle with
   Flour
Brown quickly in
   Butter
Reduce the heat and cook slowly 5 minutes longer. *Serves 4.*

Crab Meat Tempura

A Japanese specialty. The piquant sauce should be served in tiny individual bowls into which the pieces of crab are dipped.

Prepare
   1 pound cooked or canned crab meat
Keep the large chunks whole and reserve to use later. Flake the small pieces of

crab meat and mix with
   1 egg, well beaten
   ¼ cup cracker crumbs
Shape in 1-inch balls. Chill.

Make a batter by mixing
   1 egg, slightly beaten
   ½ cup water
   ½ cup flour
Heat to 370°
   2 cups peanut oil
Dip the crab meat chunks and the balls into the batter and cook them in the hot oil until brown. Drain on a paper towel. Serve with sauce (below). *Serves 4.*

To make the sauce, mix
   ½ cup hot bouillon
   2 tablespoons soy sauce
   1 teaspoon sugar
   1 teaspoon prepared horseradish
   ½ teaspoon monosodium glutamate

Oyster Crabs

Oyster crabs are sold by the pound at specialty shops in a few large cities. They live in the oyster shell and are very small. They are eaten whole, shells and all. One pound serves 8 as the fish course at a formal dinner.

Fried Oyster Crabs. Wash and drain. Roll in flour and shake in a sieve to remove excess flour. Sauté 5 minutes in unsalted butter or fry in a basket in deep fat heated to 390°. Garnish with parsley and slices of lemon.

Serve with tiny boiled potato balls and sliced tomatoes with French dressing and chopped parsley. Or serve with cucumber sandwiches made with brown bread.

Fried Oyster Crabs and Whitebait. Mix fried oyster crabs and whitebait (p. 127) as a de luxe luncheon dish. *One half pound of each will serve 4.*

Oyster Crabs Newburg

Mix
   1 cup mushroom caps, broken in pieces
   1 cup oyster crabs
   ⅓ cup sherry
Cover and let stand 1 hour.

Melt in a saucepan
   ¼ cup butter
Add the first mixture and cook 8 minutes. Stir in
   1 tablespoon flour
Cook 2 minutes. Season with
   Salt, cayenne and nutmeg to taste
Add
   ¾ cup heavy cream
Just before serving, heat and stir in
   2 egg yolks, slightly beaten
   1 tablespoon brandy
Serves 4.

Lobsters

Allow 1 small lobster per person or, if the lobsters are larger, about 1 pound in the shell per person. Buy lobsters alive or already boiled at the market. Buy cooked lobster meat fresh, canned or frozen.

Boiled Lobsters

Fill a large kettle three-quarters full of water. Bring it to a rapid boil. Add 2 tablespoons salt for each quart of water or use sea water.

Put in the live lobsters, one at a time, grasping just behind the claws. Let the water boil again after putting in each lobster. Lower the heat, cover the kettle and simmer 15 minutes for small lobsters (¾ to 1 pound), 20 minutes for medium-sized (1½ to 2 pounds), and 40 for very large ones.

Cool in the broth, or, if the lobster is to be served hot, lift from the broth and drain.

To shell a cooked lobster and remove the meat. Place the lobster on its back. Twist off the claws. Separate the tail from the body. Break off the flippers. Stick a fork into the base of the tail meat and push the meat out in one piece. Remove and discard the black line which runs its entire length. Crack the body shell. Lobster meat lies in the four pockets where the small claws are attached.

The green part is tomally or liver, the coral is roe, and both are edible. Discard other portions.

Break open the large claws with a hammer or nutcracker, and remove the meat. Use the small claws for garnishing.

To serve boiled lobster. Split the lobster and serve hot with melted butter or cold with mayonnaise. If desired, remove the meat from the shell, arrange attractively on a platter and garnish with small claws.

Coral Butter. Put lobster coral through a fine sieve. Work it into ½ cup creamed butter. Use to color and season lobster soups and sauces or as a canapé spread.

Lobster Tails

Allow 1 or 2 per person.

Cover with boiling salted water. Bring to the boiling point and simmer 5 minutes. Serve with melted butter and lemon wedges, or use the meat in any of the recipes calling for cooked lobster meat.

Broiled Lobster Tails. Cook and drain. Cut lengthwise along each side of the membrane and remove it. Bend the tail backward to crack the shell. Put in a shallow baking pan, shell side down. Spread lightly with butter and sprinkle with a few crumbs. Broil about 5 minutes. Serve with melted butter and lemon wedges.

Broiled Live Lobster

Allow 1 small or ½ large lobster per person.

Kill by inserting a sharp knife between the body and shell at the tail to sever the spinal cord. Put the lobster on its back and make a deep, sharp cut through the entire length of the body and tail with a heavy sharp-pointed knife or lobster shears. Spread open and remove the black line and the stomach. Crack the claw shells with a mallet.

Place in the broiler, shell side down. Sprinkle with olive oil or melted butter. Broil slowly about 20 minutes or until the flesh is lightly browned.

Serve with melted butter.

Live Lobster en Brochette

Allow 1 small or ½ large lobster per person.

Kill and split the lobster (see Broiled Live Lobster). Remove the meat from the tail and large claws, cut it in pieces, and arrange on skewers, alternating the pieces with small slices of bacon. Fry in deep fat heated to 375°. Drain.

Cook the green lobster liver with 1 tablespoon butter 3 minutes, season highly with mustard and cayenne, and serve with the lobster.

Lobster à l'Américaine

A de luxe dish for a special occasion.

Kill and split (see Broiled Live Lobster, p. 141)
   1½-pound live lobster
Cut in pieces. Remove the liver and coral and set aside.

In a large frying pan heat
   1 tablespoon salad oil
   1 tablespoon butter
   ½ bay leaf
   Pinch of thyme
Put the pieces of lobster into the pan. Sprinkle with
   1 tablespoon chopped onion or shallot
   Few grains cayenne
Cover and cook 5 minutes.

Mix
   2 tablespoons tomato paste
   2 tablespoons sherry or ¼ cup dry white wine
Add to the lobster. Cover and cook over low heat until the lobster is tender and the shells are red (10 to 15 minutes). Take out the pieces of lobster and remove the meat. Strain the liquid. Put back in the pan. Add the liver and the coral. Cook and stir until thick. Add
   Sherry or white wine to taste
Add the lobster. *Serves 2.*

Lobster Flambé. Just before serving, pour ¼ cup warmed brandy or Pernod over the lobster. Light with a match and stir until the flame dies down.

Lobster Thermidor

Boil and split
   4 small or 2 large lobsters
Remove the meat and cut it in neat pieces.

Cook together 5 minutes
   2 tablespoons butter
   ½ pound mushrooms, sliced
Melt
   ¼ cup butter
Add the lobster and cook 5 minutes. Sprinkle over the lobster
   2 tablespoons flour
Stir until smooth. Add gradually
   1 pint heavy cream or milk and cream or evaporated milk
Stir well. Heat slowly until smooth. Add the mushrooms. Season to taste with
   Salt and paprika or cayenne
   Sherry
Spoon into the lobster shells. Set in a baking pan. Sprinkle with
   ¼ cup grated Parmesan cheese
Bake at 450° until browned or brown in the broiler. *Serves 4.*

Buttered Lobster

This simple dish is also delicious heated with grated Cheddar cheese and a sprinkling of rum.

Cut cooked, canned or frozen lobster meat in pieces. Sauté slowly in melted butter until well heated. Sprinkle with salt, pepper, and lemon juice.

Fried Lobster

Sprinkle large chunks of cooked, canned or frozen lobster meat with salt, pepper and lemon juice. Dip in crumbs, egg, and again in crumbs. Fry (p. 5) in deep fat, heated to 385°. Drain. Serve with Tartare Sauce (p. 97).

Creamed Lobster

Many people call this Lobster Newburg, but see the classic recipe, below. Add, if you like, chopped parsley, strips of canned pimiento, or sliced sautéed mushrooms.

Cook 3 minutes over moderate heat
   1 cup cooked lobster, cut small
   3 tablespoons butter
Sprinkle with
   2 tablespoons flour
Stir well. Add
   1 cup thin cream
Cook slowly and stir until well heated and thickened. Season to taste with
   Salt, nutmeg and cayenne
   Lemon juice
   Tomato catsup or tomato paste (if you like)
Serve on toast, in Patty Shells (p. 410) or with fluffy boiled rice. *Serves 3 or 4.*

Deviled Lobster. Add mustard to taste. Season highly.

Curried Lobster. Season with curry instead of catsup or tomato paste.

Baked Stuffed Lobster. Put the creamed lobster in the lobster shell, which has been brushed with olive oil to help keep its bright color. Sprinkle with fresh bread crumbs mixed with grated cheese. Bake at 375° until the crumbs are brown.

Scalloped Lobster. See Lobster Pie in the next column.

Lobster Newburg

The classic version, very rich and delicious. For a modified version, make Creamed Lobster (above) and season it with sherry and brandy.

Cook together 3 minutes
   2 cups cooked lobster meat, sliced
   ¼ cup melted butter
Add
   1 tablespoon sherry
   1 tablespoon brandy
Cook 1 minute and add
   1 cup cream
   Salt, cayenne, nutmeg
   3 egg yolks, slightly beaten

Stir over low heat until slightly thickened.

Serve on toast or with triangles of Puff Paste (p. 409). *Serves 4 or 5.*

Lobster Pie (Scalloped Lobster). Prepare Creamed Lobster or Lobster Newburg. Put in a baking dish or in individual dishes. Cover with a generous layer of buttered crumbs (p. 7) mixed with grated cheese. Bake at 375° until the crumbs are brown.

Seafood Newburg

Follow the recipe for Lobster Newburg or Creamed Lobster, using other shellfish separately or in combinations such as scallops (cut in half unless they are tiny) and shrimp, lobster and scallops or crab meat, lobster and scallops.

Lobster Mousse

Follow the recipe for Fish Mousse (p. 124), using 1½ cups lobster meat and ¼ pound flounder fillet, both ground fine in the food chopper or blender. Season with sherry.

Serve with Normandy Sauce (p. 91) or Hollandaise (p. 95).

Lobster Timbales

Luncheon party fare.

Cook together 5 minutes
   1 cup chopped cooked lobster meat
   1 tablespoon butter
Stir in
   1 tablespoon flour
   1 teaspoon salt
   ⅛ teaspoon paprika
   Few drops onion juice
   2 egg yolks
   ⅓ cup milk
Fold in
   ⅓ cup cream, beaten stiff
   1 egg white, beaten stiff

Turn into buttered custard cups. Set in pan of hot water. Bake at 350° until firm (35 to 45 minutes). Unmold and serve with Lobster Sauce (p. 90). *Serves 6.*

Lobster Croquettes

To vary seasonings, omit the mustard and add a few gratings of nutmeg and 1 teaspoon parsley, chopped fine.

Mix
   2 cups cooked chopped lobster meat
   ½ teaspoon salt
   ¼ teaspoon dry mustard
   Few grains cayenne
   1 teaspoon lemon juice
   1 cup Croquette Sauce (p. 5)
Chill. Shape, crumb, and fry (p. 6)) in deep fat heated to 375°. *Makes 12 or more.*

Lobster Cutlets. Add 1 egg yolk to the mixture. Shape in flat ovals and fry or sauté in butter.

Mussels

Allow 6 to 12 mussels per person. The shells should be tightly closed. Let stand 20 minutes in cold water with 1 table-spoon dry mustard. Scrub thoroughly under running water until all bits of sand are removed. Some specialty shops sell imported canned mussels.

Steamed Mussels. Put prepared mussels in a deep kettle. Add 2 tablespoons water for each dozen mussels. Cover and steam until the shells open (5 to 10 minutes).

Serve with melted butter seasoned with garlic and chopped parsley, or with Poulette Sauce (p. 92) made with the broth from the kettle.

Moules Marinière

Simmer together
   1 cup dry white wine
   6 shallots, finely chopped, or 3 table-
      spoons finely chopped onion
   1 tablespoon chopped parsley
   ½ bay leaf
   Few grains cayenne
When the sauce is reduced to about ½ cup, strain into a large kettle. Add
   4 dozen mussels, prepared (above)
Cover tightly. Heat 5 to 10 minutes, or until the shells open, shaking the pan

from time to time. Remove the mussels carefully to deep soup plates and keep hot. To the sauce in the kettle, add
   2 tablespoons butter
   Salt, if needed
Pour carefully over the mussels, leaving any sediment in the bottom of the pan. Sprinkle with
   Chopped parsley
Serves 6.

To vary, add fresh herbs, garlic, celery, or 1 or 2 slices of carrot.

Oysters

Fresh oysters in the shell are marketed by the dozen, or, if shelled, by the pint, quart or gallon. Be sure the shells are tightly closed, and that shelled oysters are plump and shiny and fresh-smelling. Oysters are in season all year on the Pacific Coast and from September through April on the Atlantic and Gulf coasts. Shelled oysters are a convenience; do not wash them but look them over and pick out bits of shell.

Oysters on the Half Shell, p. 45; Sea-food Cocktail, p. 45; Oyster Stew, p. 79.

Long cooking toughens oysters. Prepare them just before serving to develop the best flavor.

To open oysters. Insert the tip of a strong knife between the halves of the shell, just back of the muscle. Cut through the muscle. Lift off the shallow shell. Loosen the oyster from the shell with the point of the knife. Save the oyster liquid. Remove any bits of shell.

A special oyster knife has a thin, round tip

To parboil oysters. Put shelled oysters in a saucepan, adding any liquid drained from them. Heat and cook only until the oysters are plump and the edges begin to curl. Drain and add water, if necessary, to make up the amount of oyster liquid called for in the recipe. Strain the liquid through cheesecloth or a very fine sieve.

Oysters Casino

Allow 6 to 8 oysters per serving.

Open carefully to keep the juice. Remove the flat shell, leaving the oysters in the deeper half. Sprinkle each with a few drops of lemon juice and a bit of finely minced green pepper. Season with salt and pepper and put a ½-inch square of bacon on each. Arrange in a shallow pan on a bed of rock salt (salt holds the heat well).

Bake at 450°, or under the broiler until the bacon is crisp.

Roasted Oysters

Scrub oysters in the shell thoroughly with a brush. Put in a shallow baking pan, with the deep side of the shells down. Bake at 450° until the shells part. Open, sprinkle with salt and pepper, and serve in the deep halves of the shells.

Oysters Rockefeller

If you have an electric blender, use it to blend the butter and the greens. There are many versions of this dish, so vary it to suit yourself, such as by adding a few drops of Pernod, which has the flavor of licorice.

Chop fine
   3 green onions, stalks and tips
   ¼ cup chopped celery
   1 teaspoon minced chervil
   1 teaspoon minced tarragon leaves
   3 sprigs parsley
   ½ cup young spinach leaves
Add
   2 tablespoons soft bread crumbs
Season to taste with

   Salt and pepper
   Few drops Tabasco, Worcestershire
      and anchovy paste
Pound in a mortar until smooth. Blend well with
   1 cup butter, creamed
Force through a sieve. Put a bed of damp rock salt (which holds the heat well) in a large pan. Arrange on the salt
   2 dozen large oysters on the half shell
Put a tablespoon of the butter mixture on each. Bake at 450° until thoroughly heated (about 10 minutes). *Serves 6.*

Broiled or Sautéed Oysters

Drain and pat dry on a paper towel
   1 pint shelled oysters
Mix
   ⅔ cup cracker crumbs
   ½ teaspoon salt
   ⅛ teaspoon pepper
Dip oysters in
   ¼ cup melted butter
then in crumb mixture. Broil on a greased broiling rack 2 inches from the heat, or sauté in
   2 tablespoons butter
Turn once while cooking.

Serve on toast with Maître d'Hôtel Butter (p. 89) or sprinkle with sherry. *Serves 4.*

Fancy Roast

The traditional New England name for a very simple dish.

Cook 1 pint oysters with their liquid in a chafing dish or frying pan until the oysters are plump and the edges begin to curl. Shake the pan to keep the oysters from sticking. Season with salt, pepper and 2 tablespoons butter.

Serve on small pieces of toast. Garnish with parsley. *Serves 4.*

Oysters à la Thorndike. Add a slight grating of nutmeg and ¼ cup thin cream. Add 2 egg yolks, slightly beaten. Cook and stir until slightly thickened.

Pigs in Blankets

Serve for lunch or supper or with drinks.

Drain shelled oysters and pat dry on a paper towel. Wrap in thin strips of bacon and fasten with toothpicks. Arrange on a rack in a shallow pan. Bake at 425° until the bacon is crisp and brown. Turn once to cook evenly. Drain on a paper towel.

Fried Oysters

Allow 6 to 8 oysters per serving.

Drain and pat dry on a paper towel. For about 1 pint of oysters, make a batter by beating 2 eggs slightly and stirring in 2 tablespoons milk, 1 teaspoon salt and ⅛ teaspoon pepper. Dip oysters in the batter, then in fine dry bread crumbs or cornmeal.

Sauté in butter in a single layer or fry (p. 5) in deep fat heated to 375°. Drain on a paper towel.

Serve with Tartare Sauce (p. 97) or Philadelphia Relish (p. 88).

Oven-Fried Oysters. Arrange in a shallow baking pan in a single layer. Sprinkle with olive oil. Bake at 400° until nicely browned (about 15 minutes).

Oysters in Sherry Cream

Put in a shallow baking dish
    ½ pint shelled oysters
Sprinkle with
    Salt and pepper
Cover with
    ½ cup coarse bread crumbs
    1 tablespoon sherry
    ½ cup cream
Cook 2 minutes under the broiler, or just long enough to heat the cream and curl the edges of the oysters.

Serves 3 or 4 as a first course or 2 as a luncheon dish.

Panned Oysters

Arrange small oblong pieces of toast in a shallow baking pan. Put an oyster on each piece. Sprinkle with salt and pepper. Bake at 400° until the oysters are plump. Serve with Lemon Butter (¼ cup creamed butter with 1 tablespoon lemon juice beaten in drop by drop).

Oysters Algonquin. Instead of toast, put the oysters on sautéed mushroom caps, smooth side down. For a richer dish, serve with Béchamel Sauce (p. 91).

Oyster Fricassee

Parboil (p. 4)
    1 pint shelled oysters
Drain off the liquid and add to it
    Milk or cream (enough to make 1 cup)
Melt over low heat
    2 tablespoons butter
Add
    2 tablespoons flour
Stir until smooth. Add the liquid gradually and stir until thickened. Season with
    ¼ teaspoon salt
    Few grains cayenne
    1 teaspoon chopped parsley
Add the oysters and
    1 egg, slightly beaten
Cook and stir 1 minute. Serve on
    Toast, in timbale cases or in Patty Shells (p. 410)
Serves 4.

Savory Oysters. Brown the butter in making the sauce. Season with 1½ teaspoons lemon juice, 1½ teaspoons vinegar, ½ teaspoon beef extract, and 1 teaspoon Worcestershire, or with anchovy paste to taste.

Oysters Duxelles. *See also the recipe for Duxelles (p. 249).* Cook 2 tablespoons chopped mushrooms (or more) 5 minutes in the butter before stirring in the flour.

Scalloped Oysters

For a pleasantly subtle flavor, sprinkle each layer with a few gratings of nutmeg.

Drain, reserving the liquid
    1 pint shelled oysters

Mix
   ½ cup bread crumbs
   1 cup cracker crumbs
   ½ cup melted butter
Put a thin layer in a shallow buttered baking dish. Cover with half the oysters. Sprinkle with
   Salt and pepper
Add
   2 tablespoons oyster liquid or clam juice
   1 tablespoon milk or cream
Repeat. Cover the top with the rest of the crumbs. Bake 30 minutes at 450°. *Serves 4.*

Deviled Oysters

Chop
   1 pint shelled oysters
Cook together 3 minutes
   3 shallots, chopped fine
   1 tablespoon butter
Add
   2 tablespoons flour
Stir until well blended. Add
   ½ cup milk
   ¼ cup cream
Bring to the boiling point, stirring to keep smooth. Add the chopped oysters. Season with
   ½ teaspoon salt
   ⅛ teaspoon nutmeg
   Few grains cayenne
   ½ teaspoon prepared mustard
   ½ tablespoon Worcestershire sauce
   3 chopped mushroom caps
   ½ teaspoon chopped parsley
Simmer 12 minutes. Stir in
   1 egg yolk
Put the mixture in the deep halves of the oyster shells or in scallop shells. Cover with
   Buttered crumbs
Bake 15 minutes at 400°. *Serves 6 as a first course, 3 or 4 as a luncheon or supper dish.*

Oysters Louisiane

Parboil (p. 4)
   1 quart shelled oysters

Reserve the liquid and add
   Water to make 1½ cups
Cook together 5 minutes
   3 tablespoons butter
   2 tablespoons chopped red pepper
   ½ tablespoon chopped shallot
Stir in
   ¼ cup flour
Add the oyster liquid gradually, stirring constantly. Bring to the boiling point and season with
   ½ teaspoon salt
   ⅛ teaspoon paprika
   Few grains cayenne
Put the oysters in large buttered scallop shells or in individual baking dishes. Cover with the sauce and sprinkle with
   ½ cup grated Parmesan cheese
Bake at 400° until thoroughly heated. *Serves 6 to 8.*

Oysters Cape Cod

Drain, reserving the liquid
   ½ pint shelled oysters
Sift together
   1½ cups flour
   3 teaspoons baking powder
   ½ teaspoon salt
Cut in
   1 tablespoon butter
Add the oysters and the oyster liquid, adding enough water if necessary to make about ⅓ cup. Spread in a buttered shallow pan. Over the top, arrange
   8 pork sausages
Bake 30 minutes at 450°, turning the sausages once to brown. *Serves 4.*

Oyster Pie

Especially good served with sliced ham, hot or cold.

Line a shallow pie plate with pastry. Put in only two layers of shelled oysters. If you have more than two layers, the middle ones will be underdone. Sprinkle with salt and pepper. Dot with butter, cover with pastry, and prick well.

Bake at 400° until brown (about 20 minutes).

Scallops

Small bay or cape scallops are more delicate than large deep-sea scallops. One pint (1 pound) sautéed or fried serves 3, scalloped or in a sauce serves 6. Scallop Stew (p. 79).

To clean scallops. Dip quickly in cold water. Remove any bits of shell or sand. Pat dry on paper towels.

To parboil scallops. Barely cover with boiling water. Cook 5 minutes and drain.

Sautéed Scallops

Clean (above). Brush with melted butter and roll in salted flour. Sauté in butter about 5 minutes.

Arrange on a serving dish. Pour the butter from the pan over them. Sprinkle with lemon juice and finely chopped parsley. *One pound serves 3.*

Fried Scallops

Clean (above). Season with salt and pepper. Dip in slightly beaten egg, then in crumbs. Let stand 20 minutes to dry the coating. Fry (p. 6) 2 minutes in deep fat heated to 375°, or pan-fry not more than 5 minutes in melted butter.

Fried Scallops Huntington

Clean (above)
    1 quart scallops
Add
    Juice 1 lemon
    1 tablespoon olive oil
    1 teaspoon finely chopped parsley
    1 teaspoon salt
    ½ teaspoon pepper
Cover and let stand 30 minutes. Drain. Mix
    3 tablespoons chopped cooked ham
    ¼ cup soft bread crumbs
    2 tablespoons grated Parmesan cheese
    1 teaspoon finely cut chives
Egg and crumb the scallops (p. 6), using the prepared crumb mixture. Fry (p. 6) at 385°. Serve with

Tartare Sauce (p. 97)
Serves 6.

Deviled Scallops

Parboil (p. 4)
    1 pint scallops
Drain, reserving the liquid. Chop the scallops.

Cream together
    3 tablespoons butter
    ¼ teaspoon prepared mustard
    ½ teaspoon salt
    Few grains cayenne
Add ⅛ cup of the reserved liquid and the scallops. Let stand ½ hour. Put in a baking dish or in scallop shells. Cover with
    ⅓ cup buttered cracker crumbs
Bake 20 minutes at 375°. *Serves 3.*

Scallops Newburg

If desired, add ½ cup shrimps or ½ pound sliced sautéed mushrooms — or both. For a simple version, follow the recipe for Creamed Lobster (p. 143), using scallops instead of lobster, and season with sherry and brandy.

Clean (above) and cut in halves
    1 pint scallops
Cook 3 minutes with
    2 tablespoons butter
Add
    1 teaspoon lemon juice
Cook 1 minute and set aside.
Blend in a saucepan, over low heat
    1 tablespoon butter
    1 teaspoon flour
    ½ cup cream
Stir constantly and bring to the boiling point. Add
    2 egg yolks, slightly beaten
    2 tablespoons sherry
Add the scallops. Reduce the heat and stir well. If the mixture curdles from overcooking, add a little milk and stir until smooth again. Season to taste with
    Salt and cayenne
Serves 4.

Savoy Scallops

Parboil (p. 4), and cut into quarters
  1 quart scallops
Reserve the scallop liquid and add
  Water to make 1⅓ cups
Melt over low heat
  3 tablespoons butter
Stir in
  3 tablespoons flour
Blend well. Add the liquid slowly, stirring constantly. Bring to the boiling point and lower the heat. Stir in, a little at a time
  ½ cup mayonnaise
Add the scallops and
  ½ teaspoon dried thyme
Keep hot in a double boiler, or over very low heat so that the mixture does not boil. *Serves 6.*

Scalloped Scallops

Clean (p. 148) and cut in pieces if large
  1 pint scallops
Melt in a saucepan
  3 tablespoons butter
Add the scallops. Cook and stir 5 minutes. Stir in
  3 tablespoons flour
Blend well. Add, a little at a time
  1 cup cream
  ¾ cup milk
Cook and stir until slightly thick. Season to taste with
  Salt and pepper
Put in a buttered casserole. Cover with
  ½ cup buttered crumbs
Bake at 400° until the crumbs are brown (about 10 minutes). *Serves 4 to 6.*

Savory Scalloped Scallops. Cut fine 1 small onion and 1 green pepper. Cook in the butter until the onion is yellow. Add 1 cup sliced mushrooms. Cook 5 minutes. Add the scallops and continue as above.

Coquilles St. Jacques. Add ½ cup sautéed sliced mushrooms. Season to taste with sherry or brandy. Divide in ramekins or scallop shells. Sprinkle with crumbs as above and with grated Parmesan cheese. Bake as above.

Shrimp

Buy fresh shrimp in the shell, raw, cooked or frozen, or buy peeled shrimp cooked, canned or frozen. To serve 4, buy 1 pound in the shell or ½ pound cooked and peeled.

To prepare shrimp for cooking. Wash shrimp (cover frozen shrimp with cold water and let stand 15 minutes). Peel off the shells with your fingers. Take out the black line. The most convenient tool is a beer can opener because it has a firm but somewhat dull point. Or use the point of a knife or a toothpick or a special shrimp cleaner.

To cook shrimp. Put 1 cup boiling water in a pan. Add ½ teaspoon salt. To season more highly, add a sprig of parsley, a slice of onion, a tiny piece of bay leaf, a clove and 1 teaspoon vinegar or ¼ cup lemon juice. Add the shrimp, cover closely, and simmer until tender (5 to 12 minutes). Cool the shrimp in the cooking water. Drain.

Fried Shrimp

Shell and clean raw shrimp (above). Sprinkle with lemon juice, rum or brandy. Let stand 15 minutes. Dip in Fritter Batter (p. 429), made without sugar, or egg and crumb (p. 6). Fry (p. 6) 1 minute in deep fat heated to 370°. Drain on a paper towel. Serve with mayonnaise seasoned with horseradish, capers, or catsup with grated onion and lemon juice.

Sautéed Shrimp

Sauté canned or cooked shrimp lightly in butter. Pour the butter over the shrimp. Sprinkle with finely chopped parsley.

To serve Sautéed Shrimp with drinks. Serve on toothpicks. Dip in Mustard Sauce (p. 97) or melted butter, highly seasoned with lemon or lime juice and pepper. Or serve with mayonnaise seasoned as for Fried Shrimp (above).

Shrimp Newburg

For a simpler version, prepare Creamed Shrimp (below) and season with sherry and brandy.

Cook together 3 minutes
    2 cups cooked or canned shrimp
    2 tablespoons butter
Add
    1 teaspoon lemon juice
Cook 1 minute and set aside.

Melt in a saucepan over low heat
    1 tablespoon butter
Add
    1 teaspoon flour
Mix well. Add gradually, stirring constantly
    ½ cup cream
Cook until thickened. Remove from the heat. Stir in
    2 egg yolks, slightly beaten
    1 tablespoon sherry
    1 tablespoon brandy
Add the shrimp. Season with
    Salt and pepper to taste
Reheat but do not boil. *Serves 4.*

Creamed Shrimp

Heat 1 pint canned or cooked shrimp in Cream Sauce (p. 90) or in heavy cream lightly salted. Serve with boiled rice. *Serves 4.*

Creamed Shrimp with Curaçao. Add ¼ teaspoon celery salt, few gratings nutmeg and ½ teaspoon Curaçao.

Creamed Shrimp with Dill. Add 1 teaspoon finely cut dill.

Curried Shrimp. Heat in Curry Cream Sauce (p. 90) or Brown Curry Sauce (p. 93) seasoned with 3 tablespoons tomato catsup.

Shrimp Louisiana

Cook together 5 minutes
    2 tablespoons butter
    1 teaspoon chopped onion

Add
    ⅔ cup cooked or canned shrimp
      (1 small can), broken in pieces
    ⅔ cup hot boiled rice
    ⅔ cup heavy cream
Heat well. Add
    ½ teaspoon salt
    ¼ teaspoon celery salt
    Few grains cayenne
    3 tablespoons tomato catsup, if
      desired
Serves 4.

Shrimp Wiggle

Vary by adding lemon juice to taste, a tablespoon or two of chopped ripe olives, or toasted chopped almonds.

Melt over low heat
    2 tablespoons butter
Stir in
    2 tablespoons flour
Blend well. Add gradually
    1 cup milk or milk and cream
Cook and stir until smooth. Add
    Salt and pepper to taste
    ½ to 1 cup cooked or canned shrimp
    ½ cup cooked peas
Keep hot over boiling water or over very low heat. Pour over toast or crackers. *Serves 4.*

For a richer sauce, stir in an egg yolk before serving.

Shrimp Jambalaya

For variety, add 12 parboiled oysters (p. 144). Use this recipe also with cooked ham, chicken, sausage or tongue in place of shrimp. For a less highly seasoned dish, omit the chili powder.

Cook until the fat melts
    3 slices bacon, diced
Add
    3 tablespoons chopped onion
    2 tablespoons chopped celery
    2 tablespoons chopped parsley
    3 tablespoons chopped green pepper
Cook and stir until the onion is yellow.
Add

1 tablespoon flour
Stir until the flour is slightly brown. Add
   4 cups tomatoes, cooked or canned
   1 teaspoon salt
   Few grains cayenne
   1 teaspoon chili powder
Cook until thick. Add
   3 cups cooked rice
   2 cups cooked shrimp, broken in
      pieces
Stir well. Heat. Taste and add more seasonings, if needed. *Serves 8.*

Georgia Shrimp Mull

Use canned shrimp if more convenient.

Clean, cook, and peel (p. 149)
   2 pounds raw shrimp
Cook slowly
   1 can tomatoes (about 2½ cups)
until the liquid is almost evaporated.
Put in a saucepan
   ¼ cup bacon fat
   1 large onion, chopped
Cook until the onion is soft. Stir in
   ¼ cup flour
Add the tomatoes. Add
   1½ cups finely cut celery
   1 large or 2 small green peppers,
      cut fine
Cook until the vegetables are tender.
Add
   Salt to taste
   1 tablespoon Worcestershire

Add the shrimp. Cook slowly 20 minutes. Put in a baking dish. Prepare
   Baking Powder Biscuit dough (p. 311)
Cut out small biscuits and put over the
shrimp, close together. Put the rest of
the biscuits on a cooky sheet.

Bake at 450° about 15 minutes. Use the
extra biscuits for the second serving.
Serves 6.

Shrimp Polonaise

*Sometimes called Shrimp de Jonghe,
this is a superb dish to serve at lunch
or supper or in smaller portions as a first
course at dinner. It can be prepared in
advance — even the day before — ready
to bake when needed.*

Use ¾ pound canned shrimp, or clean,
cook, and peel (p. 149)
   1½ pounds fresh raw shrimp
Cream together
   ½ cup butter
   1 clove garlic, crushed
Stir in
   ½ cup bread crumbs
   ¼ cup finely cut parsley
   ¼ cup dry sherry
Taste, and add more seasoning if you
like — salt, a drop or two of Worcestershire, a shake of mace or nutmeg. Spread
the shrimp in a shallow baking dish.
Dot with the butter mixture. Bake 25
minutes at 400°. *Serves 4 or 5.*

Meats and Meat Cookery

In most families, meat is the favorite main dish for the principal meal of the day. It is more expensive than other protein foods, so it is especially important to select it wisely and cook it to perfection.

Shopping for meat. Deal regularly with a reliable butcher and depend upon his advice as to the best cuts available. It is difficult to judge the quality of pre-wrapped meat, especially hamburg, and your butcher will prepare it for you with just the proportion of fat you want. If you have a freezer or a freezer compartment, you can often take advantage of a special value even though you may not use it immediately.

Appetites vary with the individual, the type of meal, and even with the season, but as a general rule, 1 pound of meat free of bones gives 3 or 4 servings; with the bone left in, count on 2 servings. It is possible to increase the number of servings if the meat is prepared with a sauce or combined with vegetables or other foods in a casserole or stew.

Boned meat is easier to carve than meat with the bone in. The flavor is just as fine, contrary to the old belief, but of course an unboned roast looks handsome on the platter. If you order a roast boned, ask the butcher to give you the bones and the scraps to use for stock or soup.

Tender and less tender cuts have the same food value. Use the tender, expensive cuts for roasting and broiling and the less tender ones for stews and for dishes using chopped meat.

Storing meat before cooking. Remove the wrapping paper. Put the meat on a plate and cover loosely with wax paper. Store in the refrigerator. Use chopped meat within a day or two. A roast keeps fresh longer — four or five days. If you plan to keep meat longer than this before cooking, wrap it in freezer paper or self-sealing wax paper and set it in the freezing compartment or in the ice tray section.

Cooking chilled and frozen meats. Meat cooks more evenly if it is at room temperature when you start, so take it out of the refrigerator long enough before cooking to remove the chill — at least 1 hour.

Frozen roasts should be thawed completely before cooking begins — otherwise they will cook unevenly, with the center scarcely warmed through when the outside is thoroughly done.

Frozen steaks and chops may be thawed or not, as convenient. If you start cooking while the meat is still solidly frozen, allow at least 10 minutes longer than the cooking time in the recipe, and test by making a cut into the meat to be sure it is done to your taste before you serve it.

Roasting

Roasting is the easiest method of cooking meat. With the low-temperature method, a roast requires little or no attention. Times given for roasting are only approximate, because roasts of the same weight differ in shape and in the amount of fat. A chunky roast takes longer than a thin one. A lean roast takes longer than a fat one. However, it is simple, as serving time approaches, to adjust the oven temperature up or down to speed or slow the roasting. A roast continues to cook somewhat after it is out of the oven.

Preheat the oven at the temperature suggested in the recipe — 325° for most meats, 350° for pork.

Use a shallow roasting pan without a cover. Set a rack in the pan so that the roast will not stick. Put the roast on the rack fat side up. If the meat is very lean, put a piece of suet, bacon or salt pork on top and hold it in place with a toothpick.

A roast thermometer makes for carefree roasting. Make an incision with a skewer into the center of the roast, push in the thermometer, and make sure it does not rest against a bone. When the meat is done the dial will show the proper temperature.

Do not sprinkle with flour or salt. Do not baste, unless the recipe requires it. Add no water at any time. As the fat melts, it will moisten the meat.

Roast the required time. For a crisp brown surface, increase the heat to 400° for the last 15 minutes. Plan to have the roast ready at least 20 minutes before time to start carving. The meat will slice much more easily. Place it on a carving board or heated platter and cover it with aluminum foil to keep warm while you make the gravy.

Barbecuing

Meat cooked out of doors over a charcoal or wood fire has a wonderful flavor. A simple portable grill is a practical piece of equipment for the backyard or patio. A more elaborate one with an electrically operated rotating spit will make it possible to cook such tasty fare as Barbecued Leg of Lamb (p. 175). Any meat that can be broiled or pan-fried may be cooked on the grill. For delicious flavor, baste with a barbecue sauce (p. 100) during the cooking. Skewer cooking is successful for beef or lamb (see Shaslik, p. 177) but not for veal or pork; they need slow cooking.

Broiling

Take the broiler pan and rack out of the oven. Preheat the oven 10 minutes. Grease the broiling rack lightly by rubbing it with a piece of fat from the meat or with other fat. Arrange the meat on the rack and set it in place about two inches from the heat.

Cook half the required time on one side, then turn and complete cooking on the other side. Season with salt and pepper. Dot with bits of butter or spoon over the meat a small amount of the juices from the pan.

On a charcoal grill, fish, hamburg or chopped lamb patties, sausages and frankfurters are easier to turn in a greased folding grill or a well-salted pan.

Rotisserie cooking is excellent for a large piece of meat — a boned roast of lamb or beef or an unsliced strip of Canadian bacon. Marinate at least 2 hours and baste frequently with the marinade (pp. 99–100) during cooking.

Pan-Broiling

A heavy frying pan cooks meat more evenly and with less danger of burning than a thin one. If you must use a thin pan, set it on an asbestos mat.

If the meat is very lean, such as calves' liver or veal cutlets, grease the pan very lightly, just enough to keep the meat from sticking. When you pan-broil lamb or pork chops or ham, rub the pan with fat from the edge of the meat. For other meats, merely sprinkle the pan generously with salt.

Put the meat in the pan and cook on one side until brown. Turn and brown on the other side. Reduce the heat and cook the required time. If any fat accumulates in the pan, pour it off, so that the meat will cook by dry heat.

Serve the meat on a heated platter or plates. Season with salt and pepper. If you like, add just enough water or wine to the pan juices to loosen the tasty brown glaze, stir well, and pour over the meat. Vary by seasoning the pan juices with vinegar, lemon juice, mustard, Worcestershire or other table sauce.

Sour cream stirred into the pan juices makes a delicious sauce which can be varied by adding finely cut parsley.

Stewing, Pot-Roasting and Braising

Cooking by moist heat softens the fibers of less tender cuts of meat. Browning the meat in fat before adding the liquid gives the gravy rich color and flavor. See the index for special recipes, including all the delicious variations of ragouts and fricassees made with wine or tomato juice as the liquid, and with a whole range of interesting additions such as mushrooms, herbs, curry or saffron.

Beef

The favorite American meat is undoubtedly beef, whether the traditional Sunday roast, a savory stew or one of the innumerable hamburger variations.

Shopping for beef. Top-grade beef is dull red, firm and fine-grained. It should have a good coating of fat and should be well marbled — that is, showing threadlike lines of fat throughout the lean. The fat should be white or creamy. Yellow fat means that the animal was range-fed and therefore the flesh will be less tender. Suet (the fat around the loin) should be dry and crumbly.

Beef is graded as *prime* (rarely available in retail stores), *choice, good* and *commercial* or *utility*. *Good* beef needs long, slow cooking. *Commercial* or *utility* is usually disappointing.

Roast Beef
(rib, sirloin, rump, eye of the round)

Allow ½ to 1 pound per person if the bone is left in. A boned roast yields 3 or 4 servings to the pound. But appetites vary! Select a compact, chunky piece which will roast evenly. To cook well, a boned roast should weigh at least 3 pounds, an unboned one 4. A smaller roast is likely to be too dry to be appetizing. If a roast is very lean (such as the eye of the round), put a piece of suet on it so that it will melt and baste the meat while it is roasting.

General directions for roasting (p. 152). Put the meat on a rack in a shallow roasting pan without a cover. No rack is needed for an unboned rib roast —

the bones will keep the meat out of the pan juices.

For accuracy, use a meat thermometer (p. 153), which will register 140° for rare meat, 160° for medium, and 180° for well-done.

Roast at 325°, without basting. An unboned roast will take 18 to 35 minutes per pound but not more than 3 hours for even a very large roast. Add 10 minutes per pound for boneless roasts. Times are approximate, since the quality of meats varies and chunky roasts take longer than flat ones.

Carving Roast Beef

Place the roast on a heated platter, fat side up. If a rib roast does not stand firmly, place it on its side and cut slices off the top. With a pointed, thin-bladed, sharp knife, cut a sirloin or rib roast in thin slices, then cut the slices from the

ribs. If there is a section of tenderloin, remove it from under the bone and cut it in thin slices across the grain. Carve a

rump roast in thin slices with the grain of the meat; by so doing, some of the less tender meat will be served with that which is more tender. If you cut across the grain of the meat, the more tender portion is sliced by itself, as is the less tender portion.

Pan Gravy

Unthickened pan gravy is the choice of many epicures.

Spoon off most of the fat in the pan. Add ¼ cup boiling water to the pan. Stir and scrape with a blending fork or wooden spoon to loosen the brown glaze. Cook over low heat until well blended. Add water to dilute as much as you like. Taste and season.

Brown Gravy

Perfect gravy is rare, which is sad because it is not difficult to make. Avoid using too much fat, or the gravy will be greasy. Before adding any liquid, cook the flour thoroughly with the fat so that the gravy will be a rich brown. A blending fork will keep the gravy smooth and scrape all the savory glaze from the pan.

After taking out the roast, pour all the juices from the pan into a cup or a narrow jar so that the fat will rise quickly. Spoon off the fat.

Set the roasting pan on the stove over low heat. Put in it 4 tablespoons of the fat. Cook and stir to loosen the brown bits in the pan. Add (to help browning)
   ¼ teaspoon sugar
Cook and stir until brown. Add
   ¼ cup flour
Stir until rich, dark brown. Add slowly, stirring constantly
   1½ cups cool liquid (pan juices plus water or consommé)
Bring to the boiling point. Lower the heat and simmer 5 minutes. Add more liquid for a thinner gravy. Season with
   Salt and pepper

For clear gravy, thicken with cornstarch instead of flour, using only 1 tablespoon.

Brown Gravy with Onion. Before adding the flour, add 1 tablespoon chopped onion or 1 teaspoon dried onion flakes. Cook and stir until brown.

Yorkshire Pudding

Perfect with roast beef, especially with pan gravy to spoon over it. Traditionally, potatoes were served as well, but nowadays most families serve one or the other.

Unless the roast has plenty of fat on it, put extra suet in the roasting pan so that there will be enough for the pudding.

Take the roast from the oven about half an hour before it is completely done. Internal heat will continue cooking the meat.

Raise the oven heat to 450°. Beat together until well blended
   2 eggs
   1 cup milk
Stir in
   1 cup all-purpose or bread flour
   ¼ teaspoon salt
Beat until evenly blended but do not overbeat. Pour some of the fat from the roasting pan into a pan 9 by 9 inches (or in 8 or 9 cupcake tins). Pour in the pudding batter, ½ inch deep.

Bake until puffed and brown (about 30 minutes). Cut in squares and serve one with each slice of beef.

Thickening Gravy

For Roasts

Remove meat
Pour off drippings

Let fat rise
Spoon it off

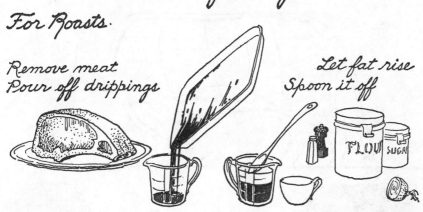

Put measured fat back into pan on stove, stir, scrape
Add sugar and flour, stirring each in until brown
Add cool liquid, stirring until thick, then season

For Stews

Mix measured flour and
cold water or milk into
a smooth paste

Pour, stirring,
into stew
Cook until
thick

Choice Cuts of Beef

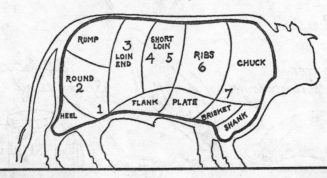

Sirloin Tip [1]
for Pot or Oven
Roast

Center Cut Round [2]
for Braising

Porterhouse and T-Bone Steaks [4] [5]
all for Broiling

Sirloin [3]
Minute Steaks

Filets
Mignons

Short Ribs

Rib and [6]
Rolled Rib
Oven Roasts

Shoulder Arm [7]
or Cross Rib
Pot Roast

Roast Tenderloin (Fillet)

Company fare, expensive but delicious, quick to cook and easy to serve.

A whole tenderloin weighs 4 to 6 pounds. It is solid meat and yields 3 or 4 servings to the pound. It is lean meat, so have it larded at the market or add fat by dotting with butter or by laying ¼-inch strips of fat salt pork or bacon over it.

Preheat the oven to 450°. Put the meat on a rack in an open roasting pan. Reduce the heat to 350° and roast 35 to 50 minutes or until fork-tender (140° on a roast thermometer).

Cut and remove any strings around the roast. Slice as many pieces as needed for the first serving and arrange them on the platter with the uncut piece at the end. Garnish with mounds of cooked vegetables, such as mushrooms, cauliflower, peas, glazed carrots or slivered green beans. Serve with Mushroom (p. 94), Figaro (p. 95) or Horseradish Sauce (p. 96).

Chateaubriand of Beef

Another way to prepare this dinner-party cut of beef (see Roast Tenderloin, above).

Order a whole tenderloin of beef and have it tied firmly. Sauté it 10 minutes in olive oil or butter, turning it to brown well on all sides. Cover closely, reduce the heat and cook 15 minutes longer. If you prefer the meat less rare, cook it another 15 minutes.

Cut in thin slices and arrange overlapping on a hot platter. Pour Espagnole (p. 93) or Mushroom Sauce (p. 94) over the meat. *Serves 8 to 12.*

Barbecued Eye of Round

Select a roast weighing about 3½ pounds. Cut shallow gashes in the meat and tuck in slivers of onion. Sprinkle with thyme. Place on a spit and cook 1½ hours, basting frequently with a barbecue sauce (p. 100). Slice very thin. *About 10 servings.*

Oven-roasted. Roast at 350°. Baste frequently with the sauce and turn the meat over during roasting so that it will be thoroughly seasoned.

Pot Roast of Beef
(chuck, shoulder, rump, round)

The piece should weigh 4 or 5 pounds (a smaller piece is apt to dry out too much). Have it trimmed, rolled, and tied firmly to make a compact piece that will cook evenly. The pan for pot-roasting should be a deep, heavy one with a tight cover.

Mix
   2 tablespoons flour
   2 teaspoons salt
   ¼ teaspoon pepper
   ½ teaspoon sugar (to help browning)
Pat into the surface of a
   4 or 5 pound piece of beef (see above)
Heat a deep, heavy pan over high heat, greasing it lightly if the beef is very lean. Put in the meat. Brown it thoroughly on all sides. Cook with it
   1 or 2 slices of onion (or add a
      package of onion soup mix later,
      with the liquid)
When the meat is a dark, rich brown (this may take 30 minutes or longer), put a low rack under it so that it will not stick to the pan. Add
   ½ cup water or tomato juice
Cover, lower the heat, and cook very slowly until the meat is fork-tender (3 to 4 hours). Add a little liquid from time to time as it cooks away, but never have more than 1 inch of liquid.

Put the meat on a heated platter to keep warm while you make the gravy (p. 156). Pour the liquid into a jar and cool it 10 minutes. You can then take off the fat easily, leaving plenty of clear juice. Add consommé or water to make enough gravy for second servings or for the next day. *Serves 10 to 12.*

To carve and serve. Cut pot roast in thin

slices with a very sharp knife. Serve it with mashed or boiled potatoes and plenty of gravy. Horseradish Sauce (p. 96) is excellent with it.

For another meal, reheat the gravy, add thin slices of the meat, and serve on a platter edged with sautéed mushrooms or other vegetables; or heat the vegetables in the gravy with the meat.

Pressure-Cooked Pot Roast. After browning, put the meat on a rack in a pressure pan. Add only enough water or tomato juice to cover the rack. Cover and bring the pressure to 15 pounds. Cook 45 minutes. Let the pressure drop, remove the meat, and make the gravy.

Herbed Pot Roast. Add with the liquid ½ cup chopped celery, a few sprigs parsley and thyme, or ½ teaspoon dried thyme. Experiment with other herbs, too (pp. 17–20).

Pot Roast with Vegetables. After cooking the pot roast 2 hours, add small whole peeled potatoes, tiny onions and small carrots. Or add canned potatoes and onions when the pot roast is almost done.

Beef à la Mode

This famous dish is a glorified pot roast.

Put in a deep glass or pottery bowl
    4-pound piece of rump or round (larded at market)
Add
    1 tablespoon salt
    ½ teaspoon pepper
    1 tablespoon mixed pickling spices
    3 onions, sliced
    3 carrots, sliced
    3 sprigs parsley
    2 bay leaves
    1½ cups red wine
Cover and let stand 12 to 24 hours.

Remove the meat and pat dry with a paper towel. Strain the liquid. Proceed as for Pot Roast (above), using the liquid.

When the meat is tender, remove it from the pan. Pour the liquid into a bowl and skim off as much of the fat as possible. Put the meat and the liquid back into the pan and cook very slowly 20 minutes longer, spooning the gravy over the meat. Taste, and add
    Salt (if necessary)
Do not thicken the gravy — it should be thin and dark.

Serve with
    Tiny whole carrots and onions
cooked separately but added to the dish long enough to heat thoroughly. *Serves 10 to 12.*

Onion Mushroom Roast

Chuck is not tender enough to roast by dry heat, like a rib roast, but is delicious prepared this way. Remove as much fat as possible.

Set the oven at 275°. Put a large piece of foil on a baking pan. Place on it
    5-pound piece of chuck beef
Mix and spread over the meat
    1 package onion soup mix
    1 can condensed mushroom soup
Fold the foil loosely, leaving room around the meat, but fasten it snugly. Roast 4 to 5 hours. *Serves 8.*

Sauerbraten

Pot roast European style. Even better reheated.

Put in a deep glass or pottery bowl
    4 to 6 pound piece of beef (eye of the round is the best cut)
Sprinkle with
    1½ tablespoons salt
    10 peppercorns
Pour over the meat
    1 cup mild vinegar or red wine
    Boiling water (to cover)
Add
    1 sliced onion
    2 bay leaves
    2 tablespoons mixed spices
    2 tablespoons sugar

Cover. Let stand at least 2 days, turning twice a day with 2 wooden spoons.

Take the meat out of the liquid. Brown and cook like Pot Roast (p. 159), using 2 cups of the strained liquid. Add more liquid as the meat cooks.

Mix
    1 tablespoon flour or 5 gingersnaps, rolled fine
    ½ cup sour cream
Stir into the liquid to thicken. Serve with Potato Dumplings (below). *Serves 8 to 10.*

Potato Dumplings

Especially to serve with Sauerbraten but good with other stews as well.

Boil, peel, and mash
    2 pounds potatoes
Add
    ½ cup flour
    1 egg
    Salt, pepper and nutmeg to taste
Have ready a deep pan of boiling salted water. Drop a tablespoon of the batter into the water. If it breaks apart as it cooks, add a little flour and test again.

Flatten a tablespoon of the mixture on your hand. Put 4 or 5 croûtons, homemade (p. 58) or packaged, on the dumpling. Roll into a ball. Repeat until the mixture is used. Drop into the boiling water, lower the heat and cook, uncovered, about 6 minutes. Remove with a slotted spoon. Serve plain or roll in buttered crumbs (p. 7).

Broiled Steak

Use sirloin, porterhouse, T-bone, club, tenderloin or rib. Allow ⅓ to ¾ pound per person. Have steaks cut 1 to 2 inches thick.

Broiling and pan-broiling, p. 153.

Take the steaks out of the refrigerator at least ½ hour before broiling them. Cook (half the time on each side) 15 to 40 minutes, according to the thickness of the steak and the way you like it. If the

meat browns very rapidly, move the rack farther from the heat.

When the steak is done, put it on a heated platter and sprinkle with salt and pepper. Serve immediately. For sauces to serve with steak, see next page.

Cut steak free from bone

Then slice in strips

To carve. Make cuts close to the bone to free all the meat. Cut a thick steak in narrow strips, slanting from top to bottom. Serve two or three strips at a time.

Beef Fondue

Tender steak is essential. Special individual casseroles and burners are available if you wish. Spear the meat with long-handled forks or toothpicks.

For each person allow ⅓ to ½ pound meat cut in 1-inch cubes. Prepare one or more steak sauces (p. 162) or serve with butter, salt and pepper.

In an electric saucepan or chafing dish on the dining table, heat cooking oil or butter (preferably unsalted) about 1½ inches deep until it begins to bubble (390°). To reduce spattering, put in a slice of raw potato. Each person spears a cube of meat, cooks it, dips it in sauce or butter, and eats it while it is hot. Repeat until all are done.

Sauces to Serve with Steak

A perfect steak needs no sauce, but you may like to dot it with butter for extra goodness or add one of these sauces.

Platter Sauce. Put 2 tablespoons butter on a hot platter and add 1 teaspoon dry mustard, a few drops Worcestershire or A–1 sauce, salt and paprika. Put the broiled steak on the platter and slice it. Stir the beef juices with the seasonings and pour a spoonful over the steak as you serve it.

Other steak sauces

Béarnaise (p. 95)
Black Butter (p. 89)
Bordelaise (p. 93)
Henriette Sauce (p. 95), half spread under the steak and half on top
Hollandaise (p. 95) to which add a few drops of onion juice and ½ tablespoon chopped parsley
Marchand de Vin Sauce (p. 93)
Mushroom Sauce (p. 94)
Mustard Sauce (p. 97)
Sauce Trianon (p. 95)
Tomato and Mushroom Sauce (p. 95)
Velouté (p. 92), flavored with catsup
Victor Hugo Sauce (p. 95)

Steak Suprême

A superb but easy company dish.

Order a sirloin or porterhouse steak 3 or 4 inches thick. One hour before cooking, sprinkle it with Bourbon or crushed garlic. Broil until brown (about 10 minutes on each side). Put in a shallow roasting pan and roast at 300° about 1 hour.

Pan-Broiled Steak
(Delmonico, club, rib, minute)

Have steaks cut ½ to 1 inch thick, minute steaks not more than ½ inch thick. Pan-broil (p. 153), adding a bit of fat if necessary to keep the meat from sticking, 2 or 3 minutes on each side for rare or medium steak. Spread lightly with butter if you like. Sprinkle with salt and pepper. Chopped parsley, too, if you wish.

Tournedos (Filet Mignon)

Expensive, delicious, easy — especially succulent served with Béarnaise Sauce (p. 95) in the classic French style.

Order slices cut ¾ to 1½ inches thick. Allow 1 slice per serving. If the meat is to be served plain or with a simple sauce, wrap each slice into a neat round, wrap a slice of bacon around the edge, and fasten firmly with a toothpick.

Sauté in butter 10 to 15 minutes or until cooked to your taste. The meat is so tender that it does not need long cooking. Serve with any of the sauces suggested for steak (above).

Broiled Tenderloin with Stuffed Mushroom Caps. Make Espagnole Sauce (p. 93), using stock or consommé. Prepare a large Stuffed Mushroom (p. 250) for each serving, using some of the sauce to moisten the stuffing mixture. Broil the meat 10 minutes and put in a baking dish. Put a mushroom on each piece and bake at 425° until the crumbs are brown. Put on a serving dish, surround with sauce, and garnish with strips of red and green pepper.

Tournedos Rossini. For each serving, sauté a large mushroom cap in butter until brown and tender. Put a dab of foie gras or foie gras mousse (canned) on each. Place the broiled tournedos on rounds of toast cooked in butter. Sprinkle with salt and pepper, and top with the stuffed mushrooms. Surround, if you like, with Béarnaise Sauce (p. 95) or Bordelaise Sauce (p. 93).

Pepper Steak (Steak au Poivre)

Some markets sell pepper steaks ready to broil.

Sprinkle each side of a thick steak with coarsely ground or crushed peppercorns (1 tablespoon for each pound of steak, but use less if you like). Press the pepper firmly into the steak, using the heel of your hand. Let stand ½ hour before broiling. Pan-broil (p. 153) until as well done as you like it. Put on a hot platter and sprinkle with salt. For added flavor, stir a little Bourbon into the pan juices and pour over the steak.

Planked Steak

An impressive company dish which combines the meat and vegetables in a handsome picture.

Planks for oven use are 1 inch thick, of oak, hickory or pine. To season, soak overnight in cold water; brush thoroughly with oil; warm 1 hour in a 250° oven. After each use, scrape it thoroughly but do not wash it. Wipe with a paper towel. Wrap in wax paper and store in a cool, dry place.

Broil or pan-broil a tender steak 1¾ inches thick for 5 minutes on each side or until nicely browned. Butter or oil a seasoned plank (see above). Arrange, close to the edge, a border of Duchess Potatoes (p. 263), preparing three times the recipe. If any of the wood is not covered, oil it well so that it will not burn. Put the steak on the plank. Bake at 375° until the steak is cooked and the potatoes are brown (about 15 minutes). Sprinkle the steak with salt and pepper.

Garnishes for Planked Steak

Stuffed Mushrooms (p. 250), with mounds of cooked cauliflower and peas.

Sautéed mushroom caps, broiled tomatoes topped with cucumber slices.

Glazed onions, buttered carrots in thin strips, sautéed mushroom caps.

Glazed onions, sautéed strips of green pepper.

Slices of cucumber and sections of tomato in French dressing.

Anchovies, stuffed tomatoes, asparagus tips.

Swiss Steak
(rump, round, chuck)

Have it cut about 1½ inches thick. A pound provides 3 servings, but prepare more at a time if you like — this dish reheats successfully.

Leave the meat in one piece or cut it in pieces for serving. Season with salt and pepper and sprinkle with flour, using about 3 tablespoons for each pound of meat. To make the meat very tender, pound the flour into it with a meat tenderizer or with the edge of a heavy plate.

Heat a heavy frying pan. Grease it thoroughly with suet or other fat. Put in the meat and brown it well on both sides. Add stewed tomatoes to cover (about 1 cup for each pound of meat).

Cover and cook very slowly until the meat is fork-tender (2 hours or more). Add a little water from time to time if necessary to keep the meat from sticking. Cook either on top of the stove or in the oven at 325°.

Vary by adding minced green peppers, sliced onions or mushrooms, or herbs.

Pressure-Cooked Swiss Steak. Have the meat cut about 1 inch thick. Brown in the pressure pan, add tomatoes, bring the pressure to 15 pounds and process 15 minutes. Let the pressure drop.

If the gravy is too thin, thicken it with flour or cornstarch (p. 156).

Braised Minute or Flank Steaks

Sprinkle lightly with flour, brown well in a greased frying pan, and add enough boiling water to just cover the meat. If you like, use tomato juice or red wine as part of the liquid.

Cook very slowly, covered, until fork-tender (about 45 minutes for minute steaks, 1 hour or longer for flank). Season with salt and pepper and sprinkle with chopped parsley.

London Broil (Flank Steak)

Flank steak must be top quality to cook tender by this method. Unless you are sure, braise it (p. 5) or treat it with meat tenderizer.

Peel and split
  1 clove garlic
Rub it over both sides of
  1 pound flank steak, about 1 inch thick
Sprinkle the steak with salad oil. Place in a preheated broiler, 1½ inches from the heat. Broil 5 minutes, turn and broil 5 minutes on the other side.

Spread with butter and sprinkle with salt and pepper. Cut in very thin slanting slices against the grain, so that all the tough fibers will be cut. *Serves 3 or 4.*

Beef Stroganoff

For a less expensive version, use round steak and cook it slowly about 20 minutes, so that it will be tender before adding the mushrooms and cream. But made with tenderloin, the meat is tender after only brief cooking and is still pink and rare when served. (See also Hamburg Stroganoff, p. 170.)

Cut in strips about 1 by 2½ inches
  2 pounds beef tenderloin or sirloin
Melt in a heavy frying pan
  2 tablespoons butter
Add
  1 tablespoon minced onion
Cook and stir until the onion is yellow. Add the beef. Cook quickly about 5 minutes, turning the meat to brown on all sides. Set aside.

Melt
  2 tablespoons butter
Slice into it the caps from
  ½ pound mushrooms (keep the stems for soup or Duxelles)
Cook and stir 5 minutes. Season with
  Salt and a trace of nutmeg
Add to the beef. Add
  ½ pint sour cream
Warm quickly. Season delicately to taste.

Serve with a border of
  Brown or wild rice
Serves 6.

Roast Beef Stroganoff. Cut rare roast beef in neat strips, removing all the fat. Add to the cooked onion, as above, but set aside without further cooking. Add the cooked mushrooms and sour cream and heat.

Braised Beef Gourmet

Richer than beef stew because the gravy cooks down more in a shallow pan than in a deep one.

Remove the fat from
  2 pounds bottom round steak or chuck
Cut the meat in 2-inch cubes. Dip in
  Flour
Brown on all sides in a heavy frying pan greased with the fat just enough to keep the meat from sticking. Add
  2 cups boiling water
Cover tightly. Simmer over very low heat until the meat is fork-tender and the gravy very thick and dark (about 3 hours). Add more water from time to time as needed. Season with
  Salt and pepper to taste
Put in a frying pan
  1 tablespoon butter
  ½ pound mushrooms, sliced
Cook and stir 5 minutes. Add to the beef. *Serves 4.*

To vary. Omit the sliced mushrooms and garnish the platter with a row of broiled mushroom caps.

Beef Bourguignonne

The standard recipe, but there are many versions. Add, if you like, more onion, a crushed clove of garlic, a small carrot (sliced), finely cut parsley. Another change is to omit the potatoes and serve with tiny boiled potatoes, noodles or rice.

Put in a deep heavy pan
  ⅛ pound salt pork, bacon or suet, diced

12 small white onions

Cook and stir until the onions are golden-brown. Remove the onions and set them aside.

Put into the pan
   2 pounds round steak, in 2-inch cubes
Brown well. Sprinkle with
   2 tablespoons flour
   Salt, pepper, marjoram and thyme
Stir and add
   1 cup red wine, preferably Burgundy
   1 cup bouillon or water
Cover and cook 4 or 5 hours over lowest possible heat or in a casserole or bean pot in a 250° oven.

Add the onions and
   12 small potatoes
   ½ pound sliced mushrooms
Cook until the vegetables are tender (about 45 minutes). Season to taste. *Serves 6.*

Old-Fashioned Beef Stew

Long slow cooking develops the fine flavor of a perfect beef stew. That makes it a practical dish to prepare well in advance — even the day before serving — since reheating improves it. Allow ¼ to ½ pound lean meat per person.

Use chuck, round, rump or shin. Have all the gristle and most of the fat cut off. Keep the fat and use some of it to brown the meat. Cook a piece of the cracked bone with the meat for good flavor, removing it before serving the stew.

Cut the meat in 1½-inch cubes. Sprinkle with salt and pepper and roll in flour. Melt some of the fat from the meat in a deep heavy pan. Brown the meat cubes thoroughly in the fat to a rich dark color.

For added flavor, cook a slice or two of onion with the meat.

Cover with boiling water, stock, or part tomato juice or red wine. The amount to use depends on the amount of gravy you want. For 2 pounds of meat, the usual amount is 1 quart. Bring to the boiling point. Cover, reduce the heat, and cook very slowly until the meat is fork-tender. This will take 2 to 3 hours.

Skim, if fat collects on the surface of the stew. Remove any pieces of fat. If the gravy is not as thick as you like it, mix 2 tablespoons flour (for about 2 cups of gravy) with ¼ cup water until it is smooth (or shake it in a swirl mixer), stir it into the stew, bring to a boil, and cook 3 minutes.

Season to taste with salt and pepper and any added seasonings you like such as thyme, Worcestershire, or chopped parsley. Serve with rice, noodles, or dumplings.

Beef and Vegetable Stew. After cooking the stew 1½ hours add, for each serving, 2 small whole carrots or 1 large carrot, sliced or cubed, and 3 tiny onions. One half hour later add 2 small whole potatoes or ½ cup sliced potatoes. Add, if you like, peas, whole green beans, cauliflowerets, or mushrooms.

Pressure-Cooked Beef Stew. Brown the meat in a pressure saucepan. For 2 pounds of meat, add 2 cups of liquid. Adjust the cover. Bring to 15 pounds pressure. Cook 15 minutes. Reduce the pressure immediately. Finish as above.

If you are cooking vegetables in the stew, reduce the pressure after 11 minutes, add the vegetables, raise again to 15 pounds, and cook 4 minutes.

Oven-Cooked Beef Stew. Put the browned meat in a casserole or bean pot. For 2 pounds meat, add only 2 cups liquid, which may be all water, or half red wine or tomatoes. Cover and bake 3½ hours at 250°. Add more liquid from time to time, if necessary. Finish as above.

Dumplings

For beef stew and other stews and fricassees.

Sift together
  1 cup flour
  2 teaspoons baking powder
  ½ teaspoon sugar
  ½ teaspoon salt
Stir in slowly
  Milk (about ½ cup)
until the batter is thin enough to take up by rounded spoonfuls with a wet tablespoon. To vary, add 1 tablespoon chopped parsley, or for savory dumplings, add ½ teaspoon poultry seasoning, ½ teaspoon celery seed, 1 teaspoon dried onion flakes and 2 tablespoons salad oil.

Heat the stew to the boiling point. The gravy should be shallow enough so that the dumplings rest on meat or vegetables as they cook. Put spoonfuls of batter on the stew. Cook, uncovered, 10 minutes. Cover and cook 10 minutes longer.

Steamed Dumplings. Use just enough milk for dough as stiff as for baking powder biscuits. Pat, roll out ½ inch thick, and cut with a biscuit cutter. Arrange, close together, in the buttered top part of a small steamer. Cover and cook 12 minutes. Place on the stew.

Rich Dumplings. Before adding the milk, cut in 2 tablespoons butter or other shortening as in making baking powder biscuits. Add a well-beaten egg.

Crunchy Dumplings. Mix ½ cup bread crumbs with 2 tablespoons melted butter. Roll tablespoons of the dough in this mixture and cook as directed above.

Hungarian Goulash

Use the best paprika for this famous dish. Never use pepper, because it would change the flavor of the paprika. Meat may be all beef (shin is excellent) or half beef and half veal and pork.

Remove any fat from
  2 pounds lean meat

Cut the meat in 1½-inch cubes.

Melt in a heavy skillet
  3 tablespoons bacon fat or beef suet
Add and cook until slightly browned
  2 large onions, chopped fine
Add the meat and brown thoroughly on all sides. Add
  3 tablespoons flour
  2 teaspoons paprika
  2 cloves garlic (on toothpicks)
Stir thoroughly. Add
  1 quart boiling water, stock, or stock and Burgundy or tomato juice
Cover. Cook slowly until fork-tender (about 2 hours). Remove the garlic. Add enough liquid to make about 2 cups. Stir and heat. The sauce should be dark and thick. *Serves 4 to 6.*

Pressure-Cooked Goulash. Brown the meat in a pressure cooker. Add only 1 cup of liquid. Cook 15 minutes at 15 pounds pressure.

Goulash with Sour Cream. Add ½ cup sour cream and reheat.

Goulash with Vegetables. Twenty minutes before serving, add cooked potato balls, tiny whole carrots, whole green beans, small onions or lima beans. Season with marjoram. Just before serving, add tomato wedges or 1 cup stewed tomatoes. If desired, cook 1 tablespoon chopped green pepper and 1 tablespoon chopped parsley with the onion.

Goulash Soup

Actually a thin stew. Serve it in the traditional way in deep bowls. Add marjoram and caraway seeds for further flavoring.

For each 2 cups of Goulash, fresh-made or leftover, add 3 cups boiling water and 1 cup diced peeled potatoes. Cover and cook until the potatoes are soft (about 10 minutes).

To add color, melt a tablespoon of fat, add ½ teaspoon paprika, 2 tablespoons water and 1 tablespoon tomato paste, bring to a boil, and stir into the soup.

Steak and Kidney Pie

Remove the fat from
    2 pounds round steak
Cut the lean meat in ¾-inch cubes.

Skin and split
    4 lamb kidneys or piece of beef kidney
Cut out and discard the fat and hard parts. Cut in ¼-inch cubes.

Put the fat from the steak in a frying pan. Heat until the fat melts. Add
    2 onions, sliced
Cook and stir until the onions are brown. Add the cubed meat and
    1 tablespoon butter
Brown well on all sides. Pick out and discard any bits of hard fat. Add
    2 cups boiling water
    1½ tablespoons Worcestershire
    2 tablespoons chopped parsley
    Salt and pepper to taste
Cover and cook very slowly until the meat is very tender (about 1½ hours). Add a little water from time to time as the juices cook away.

Mix together
    2 tablespoons butter
    2 tablespoons flour
Cook and stir until thick. Stir into the meat. Put in a casserole and cover with
    Pastry, baking powder biscuits or
        mashed potatoes
Bake at 400° until brown. *Serves 8.*

Braised Short Ribs

Allow at least 1 pound per person and select as meaty pieces as possible.

Cut in serving-size pieces. Dip in flour. Brown thoroughly in a heavy frying pan or Dutch oven, pouring off most of the fat as it accumulates. Add consommé or water (1 cup for each 4 pounds). Add seasonings such as chopped onion or a crushed clove of garlic or garlic salt and thyme, marjoram or rosemary. Cover and cook slowly until tender (about 2 hours).

Braised Oxtail

Add ½ pound sliced mushrooms with the vegetables, if you like. This dish is even better when reheated, so do not hesitate to make more than you need for one meal.

Wash and drain
    2 pounds oxtail, in 2-inch pieces
Roll in
    Flour
Melt in a heavy skillet
    2 tablespoons butter or other fat
Add the oxtail and
    2 onions, sliced
Cook until well browned. Add
    2 cups stock or consommé
    2 cups water
    2 cups canned tomatoes
    1 teaspoon salt
    ¼ teaspoon pepper
    1 bay leaf
    1 clove garlic (on a toothpick)
Cover and cook over very low heat (or in a casserole in a 300° oven) until the meat is fork-tender (about 3 hours). Remove the bay leaf and garlic. Add
    4 carrots, cubed
    1 small turnip, cubed
Cook until the vegetables are tender. Season to taste. *Serves 6.*

Corned Beef

Choose cuts that are not too fat. The best cuts are the brisket or a thick rib.

Wash under running cold water to remove the brine on the surface. Cover with cold water and bring slowly to the boiling point. Boil 5 minutes, remove the scum, reduce the heat, cover, and simmer until tender (3 or 4 hours).

Cool slightly in the water in which it was cooked. Drain. Serve hot or cold with Horseradish Sauce (p. 96) or Mustard Sauce (p. 97). *A 4-pound piece serves 8.*

Pressed Corned Beef. Cool completely in the broth. Drain. Cover with wax paper and put a weight on top to press the meat firmly. Chill and slice.

Corned Beef and Cabbage. When the meat is nearly tender, put 2 cups of the cooking water into another pan. In it cook a small cabbage, quartered and cored. Drain and serve on the platter with the beef.

Corned Beef Hash

Vary by adding chopped parsley, green or red pepper or pimientos. If you are heating canned hash, add a little cream to keep it moist.

Mix
  1½ cups chopped cooked or canned corned beef
  2 cups chopped boiled potatoes
  1 tablespoon chopped onion
  ⅓ cup cream, milk or stock
  Salt and pepper to taste
Melt in a heavy skillet
  2 tablespoons butter
Put in the hash and spread evenly. Cook very slowly until browned on the bottom (about 40 minutes). If you like crisp brown bits throughout the hash, stir and scrape along the bottom from time to time. Fold like an omelet and turn out onto a hot platter. *Serves 4.*

Red Flannel Hash. Add 1 cup finely chopped cooked or canned beets.

Baked Corned Beef Hash. Spread the hash in a buttered casserole. Bake 20 minutes at 325°. Serve from the casserole.

Corned Beef Hash with Eggs. Shape the hash in 3-inch patties 1 inch thick. Arrange in a buttered baking pan or put in individual casseroles. Press a hollow in each and break an egg into it. Sprinkle with salt and pepper. Cover. Bake at 325° until the egg white is set — about 25 minutes.

New England Boiled Dinner

Cook Corned Beef (p. 167). Remove the meat from the kettle. To the cooking broth add pared potatoes, carrots and turnips. If they are small, leave them whole. Otherwise, cut them in slices. Cook 15 minutes. Add cabbage, quartered and cored. (Some prefer to cook the cabbage separately instead of in the kettle with the other vegetables.) Cook until all the vegetables are tender (10 to 20 minutes longer). Put the meat back in the kettle long enough to reheat it.

Put the meat on a platter. Arrange the vegetables neatly around it. For added color and flavor, serve hot buttered beets or pickled beets.

Serve with Horseradish Sauce (p. 96) and Mustard Pickle (p. 521).

Chipped Beef

Separate the slices and remove any stringy bits.

For ¼ pound, melt 4 tablespoons butter in a frying pan. Add the beef and cook until the edges curl (2 or 3 minutes). Serve like bacon.

Creamed Chipped Beef. Tear ¼ pound dried beef in pieces and cook as above. Sprinkle with 3 tablespoons flour. Stir and add 2 cups milk or milk and cream. Cook and stir over low heat until thickened. Season and pour over toast or serve with baked potatoes or rice.

Savory Chipped Beef. Cook in the butter 1 tablespoon chopped onion and ¼ cup chopped celery until the onion is yellow. Continue as directed above, season with thyme, and sprinkle with chopped parsley.

Ground Beef

A whole cookbook could well be devoted to the multitude of good recipes using ground beef. Since there is no waste, it is comparatively economical, even when you buy the better grade, such as shoulder, bottom round or chuck ground to your order so that it will not be dried out.

For the best flavor, see that some fat is ground with the meat, but not so much that the meat looks heavily flecked with white. Salt pork (⅛ pound to 1 pound beef) adds flavor and juiciness. Have the meat ground medium fine, not too fine, unless you are making a special dish such as Spaghetti and Meat Balls (p. 170) or Swedish Meat Balls (p. 170).

Hamburgers

Shape ground beef into round patties about ½ inch thick. Handle lightly so that the meat will not be pressed solidly together.

Sprinkle a cold frying pan with salt. Put in the patties and cook over moderate heat until done to your taste (about 5 minutes on each side unless the meat is icy cold).

To the tasty juices in the pan, add ¼ cup water, red wine or sour cream, stir, bring to the boiling point and pour over the meat. As a variation, rinse out the pan with a tablespoon or two of sherry or Bourbon and pour it over the patties.

Broiled Hamburgers. Broil 2 inches from the heat, 5 minutes on each side. Sprinkle with salt and pepper.

Cheeseburgers. Cook patties on one side. Put on toasted split buns, cooked side down. Sprinkle with salt and pepper. Put a thin slice of cheese on each. Cook under the broiler until the cheese melts. For more piquant flavor, dot the hamburgers with prepared mustard, chili sauce or both.

Cincinnati Hamburgers. For 1 pound of ground beef, add 1 egg, slightly beaten, ¼ cup milk or tomato juice, 1 teaspoon prepared mustard, 1 teaspoon salt, ¼ teaspoon pepper and a few grains of nutmeg. Mix well and shape in 8 patties.

Hamburgers with Corn Flakes. To 1 pound of ground beef add 1 cup corn flakes (crushed fine), 1 teaspoon salt, ½ teaspoon pepper, ¼ teaspoon poultry seasoning and ½ cup milk. Shape in 10 patties and cook as above.

Hamburger Toast. Toast slices of bread on one side. Spread untoasted side well to the edges with a layer of ground beef about ¼ inch thick. Sprinkle with salt and pepper. Put under the broiler about 2 inches from the heat. Broil about 5 minutes. Dot with butter and serve immediately.

Salisbury Steak. Pat ground beef gently into one oval cake about 1 inch thick. Pan-broil or broil, turning carefully with two spatulas when half done. Sprinkle with salt and pepper. Garnish with parsley or watercress. Serve with Mushroom Sauce (p. 94) or Brown Gravy (p. 156) made with consommé.

Beef à la Lindstrom

Boil and mash
  2 potatoes
Add
  1½ pounds ground beef
  2 egg yolks, slightly beaten
  ½ cup cream
  2 pickled beets, diced
  1 tablespoon minced onion
  2 tablespoons capers
  Salt, pepper and paprika
Mix well. Shape in 8 or more patties.

Melt in a large frying pan
  2 tablespoons butter
Add the patties. Cook about 15 minutes,
turning once. *Serves 4 or 5.*

Cannelon of Beef

Mix and shape in a roll 6 inches long
  2 pounds ground beef (top round)
  Grated rind ½ lemon
  1 tablespoon finely cut parsley
  1 egg, slightly beaten
  ½ teaspoon lemon juice
  2 tablespoons melted butter
  Few gratings nutmeg
  1 teaspoon salt
  ¼ teaspoon pepper
Put on a rack in a baking pan. Lay over
the top
  5 slices salt pork or bacon
Bake 1 hour at 350°. Serve with
  Mushroom Sauce (p. 94)
Serves 6.

Spaghetti and Meat Balls

Mix
  1 pound finely chopped beef
  1 cup buttered bread crumbs
  2 tablespoons finely cut parsley
  1 tablespoon scraped onion or 1 tea-
    spoon dried onion flakes
Season to taste with
  Salt and pepper
Shape in 1-inch balls and brown well in
  Butter
Prepare, omitting the meat
  2 cups Italian Tomato Sauce (p. 298)
    (or use canned sauce)
Add the meat balls. Heat. Serve with

Spaghetti (p. 298)
using an 8-ounce package *to serve 4 to 6.*

Swedish Meat Balls

*Broad noodles are excellent with meat
balls. Do not hesitate to make more than
you need for one meal. Meat balls reheat
successfully and are popular cocktail fare.*

Put through the meat grinder twice
  1 pound lean beef, preferably shoulder
  ¼ pound salt pork
  6 slices whole wheat bread
Add
  1 egg, slightly beaten
  ½ teaspoon sugar
  ½ teaspoon allspice
  ½ teaspoon nutmeg
  1 teaspoon salt
  ¼ teaspoon pepper
Mix well. Shape lightly with your fingers
into 1-inch balls. Brown on all sides in a
lightly greased skillet.

Put in a deep pan
  2 cups consommé or stock, or 1 can
    consommé and ½ can concentrated
    tomato soup
Heat and add the meat balls. Cover and
cook over very low heat 1½ hours. Add
extra consommé or water from time to
time if necessary to keep the meat balls
from sticking. *Serves 4 to 6.*

If you like more gravy with this dish, add
extra consommé and thicken the gravy
with flour stirred with a little water until
smooth. Or add a can of beef gravy.

Hamburg Stroganoff

Melt in a heavy skillet
  ¼ cup butter
Add and cook slowly until soft
  ½ cup minced onion
Add
  1 pound ground beef
  1 clove garlic, peeled
Stir until lightly browned. Stir in
  2 tablespoons flour
  1 teaspoon salt
  ¼ teaspoon pepper
  ½ pound mushrooms, sliced
Cook 5 minutes. Add

1 can condensed cream of chicken or
   mushroom soup
Simmer 10 minutes. Stir in
   1 cup sour cream
Heat, taste and add more salt if needed.
Sprinkle with minced parsley, chives or
dill. *Serves 4.*

Chop Suey

Melt
   2 tablespoons butter
Add
   1 cup finely cut celery
   ½ cup minced onion
Cook slowly until tender. Add
   1 pound ground beef
Cook and stir 5 minutes. Add
   1 teaspoon thick soy sauce
   1 can bean sprouts
Mix well and heat. Serve with thin soy
sauce as a condiment. *Serves 4.*

American Chop Suey

Cook and drain
   ½ package egg noodles
Add
   2 cups canned tomatoes
   ¼ pound grated cheese
Cook and stir until the cheese melts.
Heat
   ¼ cup salad oil
Add
   1 large onion, sliced
Cook until soft. Add
   1 pound chopped beef
Cook and stir until browned. Add
   1 stalk celery, cut in fine strips 2 inches
      long
Add to the noodles and heat. Season to
taste with
   Soy sauce, salt and pepper
Serves 6.

Texas Hash

Chop
   1 onion
   3 stalks celery
Melt in a skillet
   1 tablespoon butter
Add the onion and celery. Cook until
soft. Add

1½ pounds chopped beef
Cook and stir until brown. Add
   1 cup cooked rice
   1 cup canned tomatoes
Cook and stir over low heat 15 minutes.
Season to taste with
   Worcestershire, Tabasco or chili sauce
Serves 4.

Revoltillos

*A highly seasoned Mexican dish to serve
immediately or to make ahead of time
and reheat.*

Steam (p. 394)
   1 cup rice
in
   2 cups bouillon
Heat in a heavy frying pan
   ¼ cup salad oil
Add
   3 green peppers, chopped
   3 onions, chopped
   2 cloves garlic, mashed
Cook until tender. Add
   2 pounds chopped beef
Cook and stir until brown. Add
   ¾ cup raisins
   ¾ cup ripe olives, pitted or not
   ½ box of bay leaves
Cover and cook slowly ½ hour. Pick out
most of the bay leaves. Stir in the rice.
Season to taste. *Serves 6.*

Chili con Carne

Heat in a skillet
   3 tablespoons bacon fat or salad oil
Add
   1 onion, sliced
Cook 2 minutes. Add
   1 pound ground beef
   1 clove garlic (on a toothpick)
Cook and stir 5 minutes. Add
   1 can red kidney or chili beans
   2 cups (or more) stewed or canned to-
      matoes or tomato sauce
   1 tablespoon chili powder
Simmer until thick (about 1 hour). Season to taste with
   Salt and paprika
Remove the garlic. *Serves 6.*

Chili con Carne with Dried Beans. Cook ½ pound dried beans (p. 236) and use in place of canned beans.

Corn Pone Pie. Put in a 1½-quart casserole. Over the top spoon Corn Bread batter (p. 314). Bake 20 minutes at 400°.

Beef and Corn Casserole

Melt in a frying pan
   2 tablespoons butter or bacon fat
Add
   1 green pepper, chopped
   2 onions, chopped
Cook until the onions are brown. Add
   1 pound ground beef
Cook and stir until brown. Place in a buttered baking dish in alternate layers with
   Cream-style canned corn (1 large can)
Sprinkle the layers with
   Salt and pepper
Put over the top a layer of
   Sliced tomatoes
Sprinkle with
   Buttered crumbs (p. 7) or toasted wheat germ
Bake at 350° until the crumbs are brown. *Serves 6.*

Beef Doves

An excellent way to use leftovers. Any cooked meat may provide the filling. Or use corned beef hash or sausage meat. Vary the seasoning by adding minced onion, chopped celery or pickle, or poultry seasoning.

Mix
   ½ pound ground beef
   ⅓ cup quick-cooking rice or ½ cup cooked rice
   ½ teaspoon salt
   ¼ teaspoon pepper
   Few grains cayenne
Open
   1 can condensed tomato soup
Moisten the beef and rice mixture with about 1 tablespoon of the soup and set the rest aside.

Cook 2 minutes in boiling water
   8 cabbage leaves
Drain. Put on each leaf 2 tablespoons of the meat mixture. Fold to enclose the meat, fasten with toothpicks, or tie with thread to make a tight bundle.

Put in a deep pan. Add the rest of the can of soup and a canful of water. Cover and simmer 1½ hours, or 20 minutes if you are using cooked meat and cooked rice. *Serves 4.*

Meat Loaf

This basic recipe is a fixture in most families. The variations are many and it can be served hot or cold. It is an appetizing way to use leftovers. See also other recipes for meat loaf on pp. 188 and 198.

Mix
   1 egg, slightly beaten
   2 teaspoons salt
   ¾ cup water or milk
   1 cup soft bread crumbs
   2 tablespoons minced onion or dried onion soup mix or flakes
   2 pounds lean ground beef, chuck or round
Taste and season more highly if you like. Pat into a greased loaf pan or shape in a roll and place in a shallow baking pan. Over the top lay
   4 strips bacon, if the meat is lean
Bake 1 hour at 350°. Serve hot with Tomato Sauce (p. 94) or Mushroom Sauce (p. 94). Or serve cold with pepper relish or chili sauce. *Serves 6 to 8.*

To shorten the baking time, bake in 3-inch muffin pans. Top with bacon squares. Bake at 400° about 25 minutes.

To use leftovers, add as part of the meat chopped cooked ham, beef, lamb, chicken or turkey. Add up to 1 cup cooked peas, diced carrots, or other cooked vegetables.

To vary

In place of milk or water, use canned tomatoes, gravy, undiluted canned soup (mushroom, celery, tomato or vegetable), or ½ cup catsup and ½ cup water.

For added flavor, add up to ½ cup grated cheese, chopped ripe or green olives, chopped parsley, chopped pimientos, or chopped celery, both stalk and leaves.

Season to taste with Worcestershire or Tabasco or a pinch of thyme and/or basil or other herbs.

In place of bread crumbs, use 2 cups rice flakes.

Miss Daniell's Meat Loaf. *Excellent flavor.* In place of 2 pounds ground beef use 1 pound mixed with ½ pound each of chopped fresh pork and veal.

Lamb and Mutton

Lamb is from young animals. The flesh should be pinkish, firm and fine-grained, the fat white, solid and flaky.

Mutton comes from mature animals. Young mutton has a mild, delicious flavor and may be as tender as lamb. Older mutton is darker red and has a stronger, distinctive flavor.

Lamb Cuts

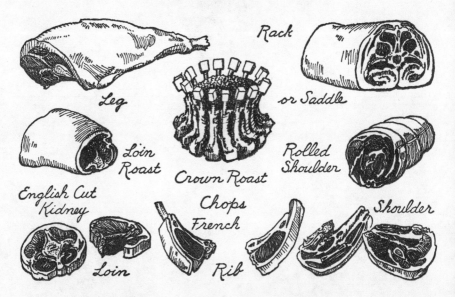

Leg

Rack

or Saddle

Loin Roast

Crown Roast

Rolled Shoulder

English Cut Kidney

Chops French

Shoulder

Loin

Rib

Roast Lamb

(leg, loin, saddle or whole loin,
crown roast, shoulder or cushion)

Except the crown roast, all these cuts may be boned at the market for easier carving. Stuffed roasts, p. 175.

Do not try to roast a piece weighing less than 3 pounds. It will be too dry. A whole leg provides 10 to 16 servings. For a smaller roast, order a half leg, a strip of the loin, or a piece of the shoulder. A heavy roast is a wise buy, since there is more meat in proportion to bone. There are many delicious recipes using leftover lamb (pp. 200ff.).

Do not sprinkle with salt, pepper or flour, but if you like garlic as a seasoning, make about 10 shallow slits in the roast with a sharp knife and tuck in each a tiny sliver of garlic. There are many other ways to season lamb — sprinkle with caraway seed, ginger, thyme or marjoram, or top with a few lemon slices. Experiment to find what you like best.

Put the roast on a rack in a shallow roasting pan without a cover. If the fat covering is very thin, lay several strips of bacon on top. Turn loin and saddle cuts over during the last half-hour of roasting so that they will brown.

Roast at 325°, 25 to 35 minutes per pound according to whether you like lamb pinkish or well done. If the roast is boned, allow 5 minutes more per pound. A meat thermometer registers 170° for pinkish lamb, 175° for medium, and 180° for well done. A 6-pound leg of lamb takes about 3 hours. A saddle or loin of lamb should always be pinkish — roast it about 2 hours.

Place on a hot platter. To carve (p. 176).

Lamb Gravy. Follow directions for making Brown Gravy (p. 156). Season with thyme, marjoram, lemon juice, red wine, or a trace of instant coffee.

To serve with roast lamb

> Brown Sauce (p. 93) flavored with
>   tarragon
> Cold Orange Sauce (p. 98)
> Currant Jelly (p. 512)
> Currant Jelly Sauce (p. 93)
> Currant Mint Sauce (p. 98)
> Littleton Sauce (p. 96)
> Mint Jelly (p. 512)
> Mint Sauce (p. 98)

Glazed Roast Lamb. Baste during the last hour of roasting with ½ cup currant or grape jelly in ½ cup boiling water, or with Mint-Apricot glaze. To prepare the glaze, cook 1 cup sugar with 2 cups water and ½ bunch mint 5 minutes, strain, add ⅔ cup cooked sieved apricots, continue cooking until well blended, and add 2 tablespoons butter.

Stuffed Roast Lamb. *Have a lamb leg or shoulder prepared at the market for stuffing.* Sprinkle inside with salt and pepper. Stuff lightly with Bread (p. 80), Onion (p. 81), or Celery Stuffing (p.

81). Sew edges together or fasten with skewers.

Barbecued Leg of Lamb

Have the butcher bone a leg of lamb and tie it firmly in shape. Make several shallow cuts in it and tuck into them bits of peeled garlic. Put the lamb on a spit in a rotisserie or over a charcoal fire. Cook until as well done as you like it (1½ hours or more). Baste frequently with a barbecue sauce (p. 100) or with a dry red or white wine.

Roast Crown of Lamb

Nothing is handsomer for a dinner party than a crown roast. Have it prepared at the market, allowing 2 ribs per person. A double piece of the loin has 14 chops. Have the butcher chop the trimmings for lamb patties or meat loaf for another meal.

Set the roast in a shallow roasting pan. To keep the tips of the bones from blackening, put on each a cube of salt pork or bread, or wrap with a bit of aluminum foil.

Roast at 325° about 2 hours (170° on a meat thermometer). A crown roast should be pinkish, not too well done.

Place on a hot platter. Put a chop frill or a pitted olive on each bone end. Fill the center with minted green peas or a big bouquet of watercress.

Stuffed Crown Roast. Mix the chopped trimmings with an equal amount of sausage meat or bread crumbs. Season to taste with salt, pepper and poultry seasoning. (Use packaged poultry stuffing, if you like.) Moisten with hot water. Spoon into the center of the roast after you have put it in the pan. Vary this stuffing as you like by adding chopped sautéed mushrooms, chopped celery or onion, or tomato paste, or moisten it with concentrated mushroom, celery or tomato soup in place of water.

Roast ½ hour longer than the unstuffed roast.

Roast Leg of Mutton

A young tender leg of mutton is delicious roasted. Remove most of the fat, leaving only a thin layer. Sprinkle with powdered garlic or rub with a cut clove of garlic.

Roast at 350°, 25 minutes to the pound. Mutton should be somewhat pink when served. *A 10-pound leg serves 12 generously.*

Carving Roast Lamb or Mutton

Leg. Cut a slice from the flatter side so that the roast will rest firmly on the platter. Slice thin at right angles to the bone.

Cut some slices from the thin side of a leg of lamb

Then slice the thick side in to the bone

And cut under the slices

Loin and crown. Cut between the chops or, if boned, cut in slices ½ inch thick.

Saddle. Make a cut along the backbone on each side to loosen the meat and slice at right angles to the bone, slipping the knife underneath to free the meat from the rib bones.

Broiled Lamb or Mutton Chops

For details about broiling, see p. 153. Broil chops cut 1 inch thick 12 to 15 minutes, 1½ to 2 inches thick 20 to 35 minutes, according to whether you prefer them rare or well done.

Loin lamb chops are usually cut 3 to the pound but may be cut thinner.

Kidney lamb chops are loin chops with the kidney attached.

Shoulder lamb chops should be cut about 1 inch thick.

Rib lamb chops. Have them Frenched (rib bone cleared of meat and fat) or not. Remove the solid piece of hard fat before cooking the chops.

Mutton chops. Have them cut 1½ to 2 inches thick. Broil rare.

Serving Lamb Chops

(1) Garnish with watercress, stuffed mushrooms, broiled tomato slices or slivers of ham.

(2) Arrange around a mound of Mashed Potatoes (p. 264), Green Peas (p. 253), or Turkish Pilaf (p. 296).

(3) Serve on thin slices of Broiled Ham (p. 187), Fried Eggplant (p. 246), or toast.

(4) Serve with any of the following:
Currant Jelly (p. 512)
Currant Mint Sauce (p. 98)
Mint Jelly (p. 512)
Mushroom Sauce (p. 94)
Soubise Sauce (p. 92)
Sauce Espagnole (p. 93)
Tomato Sauce (p. 94)

Stuffed Lamb Chops

Split thick (2-inch) lamb chops to the bone. Stuff with sausage meat or any stuffing (p. 81). Press together lightly. Dip in crumbs, egg and crumbs (p. 6). Arrange in a shallow pan. Bake 30 to 40 minutes at 450°. Turn after baking 15 minutes.

Roasted Lamb Chops

Actually individual roasts of lamb which need no last-minute attention.

Order loin lamb chops cut 2½ inches thick, boned and wrapped in bacon. Sprinkle with salt, pepper and flour. Brown well in a heavy frying pan. Transfer to a rack on a baking pan and bake at 350° until tender (about 40 minutes).

Tournedos of Lamb

Have loin chops boned and wrapped in strips of bacon. Broil or pan-broil. Sprinkle with salt and pepper.

Top each with a sautéed mushroom cap or a slice of tomato sprinkled with chopped parsley.

Braised Lamb Chops with Vegetables

Brown boned chops in a heavy frying pan. Put in a casserole and sprinkle with salt and pepper. Over the chops arrange small potato balls, tiny new carrots and tiny onions, or other vegetables such as mushrooms and quartered tomatoes. Sprinkle with salt and pepper. Add canned tomatoes, stock or consommé (1 cup for 6 chops).

Cover and bake at 350° until the chops are tender (about 40 minutes).

If you use canned potatoes and onions, add them after the chops have cooked 20 minutes so they will not be too soft.

Pressure-Cooked Lamb Chops. Brown in a pressure cooker (uncovered). Slip the rack under them, add the vegetables and enough liquid to cover the rack. Adjust the cover, bring the pressure to 15 pounds and cook 10 minutes. Reduce the pressure immediately.

Pan-Broiled Fillets of Lamb

Order
  2 pounds lamb steaks (below)
Have the butcher pound them so that they will be ¾ inch thick. Mix and pour over the lamb
  3 tablespoons olive oil
  3 tablespoons vinegar
  ½ teaspoon salt
  ½ onion, sliced
  1 tablespoon chopped parsley
Let stand several hours, turning the meat so that it will be well seasoned.

Heat a heavy frying pan. Put in it
  2 tablespoons butter or salad oil
Put in the meat and cook about 3 minutes on each side. *Serves 4 or 5.*

Lamb Steaks

Order 1-inch slices of lamb cut from the leg. Cut in serving-size pieces or in strips. Pan-broil like chops (p. 153). *One pound serves 3.*

Shaslik or Shish Kebab

Best of all cooked over a charcoal fire. Lean tender beef may be cooked this way, too.

Thread 1-inch cubes of lean lamb (shoulder, breast or leg) on long skewers or smooth green sticks (not dry ones, which might burn). (For Shaslik with tomatoes or other vegetables, see next page.) Brush with olive oil. Broil until fork-tender (10 to 15 minutes), turning frequently to brown evenly. Sprinkle with salt and pepper.

To marinate before broiling. Put the cubed lamb in a bowl and cover with French dressing, Burgundy or a marinade (p. 99). Let stand several hours and drain. Baste with the marinade during the cooking.

Shaslik with Vegetables. Prepare pieces of vegetable about the same size as the lamb cubes. Alternate on the skewers. Some good combinations are:

(1) Halved or quartered tomatoes, small cooked onions and squares of green pepper.
(2) Mushroom caps, sliced potatoes and carrots.
(3) Sweet potato chunks and pineapple cubes or wedges.
(4) Bacon squares, mushroom caps and eggplant.

Mixed Grill

Heat the broiler. Rub the rack with fat. For each person, put on the rack a lamb chop cut 1 inch thick, and a split lamb kidney or 2 small pork sausages which have been parboiled 5 minutes and drained.

Broil 7 minutes. Turn the meat over. Put on the broiler with the meat strips of bacon and vegetables such as tomato halves, mushroom caps, cooked or canned artichoke bottoms, and slices of cooked potatoes or frozen potato puffs. Brush the vegetables with butter or salad oil and sprinkle with salt and pepper.

Broil until the bacon is crisp, turning it to cook both sides (about 7 minutes).

Braised Lamb Shanks

Lamb shanks weigh about ½ pound each. Allow 1 or 2 per person.

Roll in flour. Brown well in fat or oil in a heavy pan. Add a bit of bay leaf, sliced onion, salt and pepper. Add just enough boiling water to cover the meat. Reduce the heat, cover, and simmer until tender (1½ to 2 hours). If more convenient, cook in the oven at 300°.

Lamb Shanks Savory Style. Brown shanks as above. For 4 shanks, mix 1 tablespoon cornstarch, 2 teaspoons salt, ½ teaspoon dry mustard and ¼ teaspoon each of pepper, ginger, cloves and onion salt. Add 3 cups hot water and pour over the meat. Simmer or bake. Season to taste. Sprinkle with chopped parsley.

Irish Stew

Authentic Irish Stew needs no thickening except the potato cooked in it, but if you prefer a thicker gravy, mix ¼ cup flour with ¼ cup cold water, pour into the finished stew, and cook and stir until the gravy is smooth and thick.

Cube or cut into serving-size pieces
  2 pounds stewing lamb
Cover with boiling water, cover, and simmer 1 hour. Add
  ½ cup cubed carrot
  ½ cup cubed turnip
  1 onion, sliced
  1 potato, cubed
Cover and simmer ½ hour. Add
  2 cups sliced potato
Cover, simmer ½ hour, and season to taste with
  Salt and pepper
Serves 6.

Irish Stew with Dumplings. See Dumplings (p. 166).

Fricassee of Lamb

Cut in 1½-inch cubes
  2 pounds stewing lamb
Dip in
  Flour
Heat a deep pan and grease it lightly with
  Salad oil or butter
Put in the meat and brown well on all sides. Add
  2 cups boiling water, tomato juice or tomato juice cocktail
  ¼ cup chopped onion or 1 package onion soup mix
  2 small carrots, chopped
  4 sprigs parsley
  Bit of bay leaf
  8 peppercorns

4 whole cloves
2 teaspoons salt (less if you use
  soup mix)

Cover. Reduce the heat. Simmer until the meat is fork-tender (about 2 hours). Add more liquid if needed to keep the meat from sticking. *Serves 6.*

To thin the gravy. Add water or Burgundy and reheat.

To thicken the gravy. Mix 1 tablespoon flour with ¼ cup water. Add slowly to the fricassee. Cook and stir 5 minutes.

To season more highly. Add Worcestershire or garlic salt, or cook a split clove of garlic in the fricassee.

Fricassee of Lamb with Vegetables. After the meat has been cooking for 1½ hours, add 2 cups diced potatoes (sweet potatoes are surprisingly good with lamb) and 2 cups of other vegetables such as small whole green beans, peas, cubed turnips, tiny onions, and diced celery. Add more water if necessary. Cook until the meat and vegetables are tender. If you prefer, cook the vegetables separately and arrange them around the fricassee on the platter.

As a time-saver, add canned new potatoes and canned onions to the finished stew, and simmer about 5 minutes to heat thoroughly.

Lamb Printanière. Make the fricassee with spring lamb. Add perfect young vegetables, such as tiny new potatoes, green beans, fresh peas, baby carrots and small onions. Season delicately.

Lamb Patties

Buy prepared lamb patties or season ground lamb with salt and pepper and shape like hamburgers. Wrap each patty in a strip of bacon and fasten with a toothpick.

Broil or pan-broil about 12 minutes, turning often.

Moussaka

A popular Greek dish.

Put in a deep pan
  3 tablespoons salad oil
Add and cook until brown
  3 tablespoons chopped onion
Add
  1 pound chopped lamb, veal or beef
Cook until the meat is brown and crumbly. Add
  1 cup tomato sauce or 1 can tomato
    paste and water to make 1 cup
  2 tablespoons chopped parsley
  1 cup dry white wine
  1 cup water
Season to taste with
  Salt, pepper and plenty of nutmeg
Cover and cook slowly 1 hour. While the meat is cooking, cut in ¼-inch slices
  3 or 4 small eggplants
Brown on both sides in
  2 tablespoons salad oil
Place in a large baking dish and set aside.

Melt in a double boiler top
  ¼ cup butter
Stir in
  1 cup flour
Add slowly, stirring constantly
  4 cups scalded milk
Stir until smooth. Cook over hot water 15 minutes. Add
  2 eggs, slightly beaten
Prepare
  1 cup grated cheese
  ½ cup dry bread crumbs (and a few
    more for the top)
  ¼ cup melted butter
Stir half the cheese and half the bread crumbs into the cooked meat mixture. Divide the rest of the crumbs into two parts, and sprinkle one part over the eggplant.

Spread the meat mixture over the eggplant, sprinkle with the rest of the cheese and another layer of crumbs. Spoon in the thick sauce, top with a few crumbs, and sprinkle with the melted butter.

Bake at 350° about ½ hour. *Serves 6.*

Savory Lamb Patties

Mix well
    1 pound ground lean lamb
    1 teaspoon salt
    ¼ teaspoon pepper
    1 egg
    ¼ cup chopped celery
    ½ cup chili sauce
    ¾ cup dry bread crumbs
Shape in flat patties or croquettes. Brown well on all sides in
    Shortening, any kind
Put on a rack in a shallow pan. Bake 40 minutes at 300°. Serve with
    Tomato sauce or relishes
Serves 4 or 5.

Pork

High-grade pork is fine-grained and firm. Lean pork from a young animal is nearly white; from an older animal, pinkish. The fat is white and softer than beef fat.

Pork Cuts

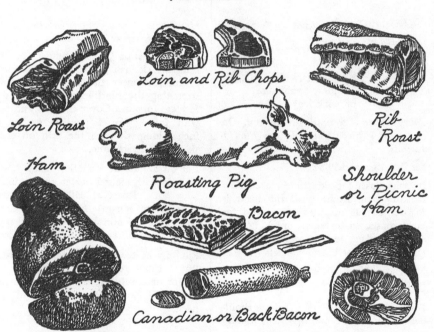

Loin and Rib Chops

Loin Roast

Rib Roast

Ham

Roasting Pig

Shoulder or Picnic Ham

Bacon

Canadian or Back Bacon

Accompaniments

Sweet potatoes, onions and tomatoes are particularly good with pork. Serve them in any of the ways suggested in the Vegetables chapter (p. 233).

Serve a tart fruit relish to heighten the bland flavor of fine pork:

Applesauce (p. 347)
Fried Apple Rings (p. 85)
Cinnamon Apples (p. 348)
Chutney (p. 525)
Tart jelly (p. 512)
Glazed Pineapple (p. 86)
Sautéed Pineapple (p. 86)

Cut away the severed chine of a pork rib roast

Then cut alternate rib and between-rib slices

Roast Pork
(loin, shoulder, fresh ham or pork leg)

Allow ½ to 1 pound per person. Do not roast a piece weighing less than 3 pounds.

Set the oven at 350°.

Put the roast fat side up in a shallow roasting pan. Roast until the meat is fork-tender (35 minutes per pound for large roasts, 45 for small ones). Pork is always cooked to the well-done stage (185° on a roast thermometer).

Make gravy (p. 156), using the fat in the pan.

Roast Shoulder of Pork. A whole shoulder weighs 8 to 12 pounds but is usually cut into smaller pieces called the butt and picnic shoulder or shoulder cushion. It may be boned to make carving easier or to be stuffed.

Roast Fresh Ham or Pork Leg. This large roast weighs 8 to 12 pounds. It may be boned or not.

Roast Loin of Pork. A whole loin weighs 10 to 14 pounds, but a smaller roast can be cut off. The center cut is the most expensive per pound, but there is less waste. To make carving easier, have the butcher separate the backbone from the ribs and saw through the bones.

Roast Crown of Pork. See Roast Crown of Lamb (p. 175), but roast to the well-done stage. Allow 2 chops per person.

Stuffed Roast Pork. Have fresh ham, butt or shoulder boned at the market. Stuff with Bread (p. 80), Apple (p. 81) or Celery Stuffing (p. 81). Skewer or sew together.

Roast Suckling Pig

Handsome holiday fare. A 10 to 12 pound pig serves 10 or more.

Prepare 8 cups Onion Stuffing (p. 81). Stuff the cleaned pig and sew or skewer together. Skewer the legs in position, stretching the hind legs backward, the forelegs forward. Cover the ears and tail with foil. Make 4 parallel gashes, 3 inches long, through the skin on each side of the backbone.

Put on a rack in a shallow pan. Brush all over with melted butter and sprinkle with flour. Roast at 350° until tender (4 hours or longer). For a crusty skin, baste every 15 minutes with melted butter or salad oil and sprinkle with flour.

Put on a heated platter. Remove the foil. Put a small red apple in the mouth, raisins or cranberries in the eyes, and a wreath of laurel or holly around the neck.

To carve. Cut off the legs. Cut along each side of the backbone, then at right angles to separate the ribs.

Pork Chops

Rib, loin or shoulder, cut about 1 inch thick. One pound serves 3.

Sprinkle with salt and pepper. Dust lightly with flour.

Pan-Broiled Pork Chops. Brown on both sides in a well-heated heavy frying pan (greased lightly, if the chops are lean). Pour off the fat. Reduce the heat, cover, and cook slowly 40 to 60 minutes or until tender, turning occasionally to cook evenly.

Baked Pork Chops. Arrange on an oven-proof platter. Put 1 tablespoon moist stuffing on each. Onion (p. 81), Apple (p. 81), Celery (p. 81), or Corn Stuffing (p. 80) are all delicious with pork. Bake at 350° about 2 hours or until very tender. Baste with water from time to time if the chops seem dry.

Stuffed Pork Chops. Stuff thick chops (see Stuffed Lamb Chops, p. 177) with Celery (p. 81), Apple (p. 81), or Apple and Prune Stuffing (p. 82). Bake as above.

Pressure-Cooked Pork Chops (stuffed or plain). Brown on both sides in hot fat in a pressure cooker. Put a rack under the chops. Add ¼ cup water. Put on the cover. Bring to 15 pounds pressure. Cook 15 minutes and reduce the pressure.

Broiled Pork Tenderloin

One pound serves 3.

Cut tenderloin in slices ½ inch thick. Pound with a potato masher, mallet, or the edge of a plate to flatten to about ¼ inch thick. Brush with melted butter. Pan-broil slowly until very tender (about 30 minutes).

Braised Pork Chops, Steak or Cutlet

Allow 1 or 2 chops for each serving. One pound of pork from the leg, sliced 1½ inches thick, serves 3.

Brown meat on both sides in a heavy skillet. Pour off the fat. Sprinkle with salt and pepper. Cover with a liquid — water, a barbecue sauce (p. 100), consommé or Sweet and Sour Sauce (p. 97). For heightened flavor, add chopped onion or a pinch of marjoram, sage, savory or thyme.

Cover and cook slowly until very tender (1 to 1½ hours). Or cook in a casserole at 350°.

Pork Goulash

Follow the recipe for Hungarian Goulash (p. 166), using pork.

City Chickens

See p. 196.

Spareribs

Spareribs are bony, so allow 1 pound per person. Loin ribs are meatier than regular ribs and so are more expensive. Spareribs are usually fresh pork, but in some parts of the country cured ribs are also marketed. Cured ribs must be cooked in water and drained to remove some of the salt before cooking in other ways. Stuffed Spareribs (p. 184).

Baked Spareribs. Cut into 2-rib pieces. Arrange in a shallow baking pan. Sprinkle with salt and pepper. On each piece put a slice of lemon and a teaspoon of chopped onion.

Bake 1½ hours at 350°, basting several times with a barbecue sauce (p. 100). Turn meat occasionally so that it will cook evenly.

Spareribs Chinese Style. Cut in single-rib pieces. For 2 strips of spareribs, prepare a sauce by mixing 1 teaspoon corn-starch, 1 cup vinegar, 1 teaspoon sugar, 1 cup sherry, 1 teaspoon thin soy sauce and 2 teaspoons salt. Beat 1 egg, add half the sauce, and dip each rib into the mixture.

Sauté slowly until brown and tender in hot peanut oil, ½ inch deep. Put the meat on a hot platter. Add the remaining sauce and 1 cup water to the pan. Cook and stir until thick. Serve with the meat.

Stuffed Spareribs

Order a pair of spareribs and have them cracked to make carving easier. Put one section on a rack in a baking pan. Cover with sauerkraut or Apple (p. 81), Onion (p. 81) or Bread Stuffing (p. 80). Put the other section on top.

Bake at 350° until tender (about 1¼ hours). Baste several times during the baking, using the fat in the pan.

Pigs' Feet (Hocks)

Often available already boiled or pickled. Allow 1 or 2 per person.

Clean thoroughly. Leave whole or split in half. To keep in shape, wrap tightly in cheesecloth. Put in a pan and cover with cold water. Add (for 8 pigs' feet) ½ onion, sliced, ½ carrot, sliced, ⅛ teaspoon whole peppercorns, a sprig of parsley, a bit of bay leaf and ½ teaspoon salt. Bring to the boiling point and simmer until tender. Do not cook so long that the meat falls apart.

Broiled Pigs' Feet. Wipe boiled pigs' feet. Sprinkle with salt and pepper. Broil 6 to 8 minutes. Serve with prepared mustard, Maître d'Hôtel Butter (p. 89) or Sauce Piquante (p. 93).

Pickled Pigs' Feet. Cook the pigs' feet in vinegar and water, allowing 1 cup vinegar to each 3 cups water and adding the seasonings suggested above.

Jellied Pigs' Feet. Prepare pickled pigs' feet. Strain the broth and remove the meat, discarding the skin and bones.

Taste the broth and add more salt if needed. Add the meat, pour into a mold and chill until firm.

Ground Pork

Ground pork is used in many tasty recipes such as the various meat loaf recipes (p. 172). It may replace the beef in Beef Doves (p. 172).

Jo Mazzotti

Excellent for a buffet supper. Even better if you make the sauce the day before and let it season. Use other meats in place of pork if more convenient — ground beef or pork sausage. If you use sausage you will not need extra fat.

Cook together until well browned
  ¼ cup butter or other cooking fat
  1½ pounds lean pork, ground
  8 large onions, sliced
Add
  3 cans condensed tomato soup or
    1 can tomato paste and 2 cups water
  1 pound mushrooms, sliced
  1 bunch celery, diced
  2 green peppers, cut fine
  Juice of ½ lemon
  Salt and pepper
  1 pound sharp cheese, cut small
Simmer 15 minutes to make a rich sauce. Meanwhile, in a deep kettle of boiling salted water (1 teaspoon to each quart of water), cook until just tender
  1 large package broad noodles
Drain and mix with the sauce. Cover closely and cook slowly 1 hour on top of the stove or in a 350° oven. *Serves 12 to 16.*

Ham, Bacon and Sausages

Smoked Hams

A whole ham weighs from 8 to 24 pounds. One pound with the bone serves 2, boneless it serves 3 or 4.

For a small family, buy a half ham (the butt end is meatier), a 5 or 6 pound "picnic" or "cottage" ham, or a piece of Canadian-style bacon (boned and smoked loin).

Tenderized or precooked hams need no soaking or boiling. The flavor is improved by baking (p. 185).

Home-cured, Smithfield and Virginia hams are especially salty. Scrub well with a brush under running water. To soak, cover with cold water and let stand overnight before cooking.

Polish or Polish-style hams have a distinctive flavor due to special feeding and aging. Follow the directions on the wrapping or tin.

Canned hams are excellent reserve items. Store in the refrigerator. Serve hot or cold with any of the sauces suggested for Baked Ham (below).

Using leftover ham. Ham is one of the most versatile of leftovers. Chop it and add to vegetable soups, sauces, mashed potato, potato salad, Welsh rabbit, scrambled eggs, omelets, soufflés or macaroni and cheese, or mix it with cottage or cream cheese, pickle relish or peanut butter for sandwiches or cocktail canapés. See pp. 188–189 for dishes using ground ham, and consult the index for further suggestions.

Boiled Ham
(home-cured, Virginia or Smithfield)

Tenderized or precooked hams are ready to bake without boiling first. Read the label.

Soak (above). Drain thoroughly. Put in a large kettle. Cover completely with boiling water. Reduce the heat so that the water barely simmers. Cover.

Simmer the ham gently until the small bone is loose enough to pull out easily (20 to 30 minutes to the pound). Cool the ham in the water in which it was cooked. Remove from the water and peel off the outer skin. Cut off most of the fat, leaving a ¼-inch layer. Bake (below).

For added flavor, replace part of the water with cider, wine or pineapple juice. Or add to the water ½ cup vinegar or 1 onion, 2 stalks celery, 4 cloves, a bit of bay leaf, 2 carrots and a few sprigs of parsley.

Baked Ham

Precooked hams are baked or glazed without boiling beforehand. Follow the directions on the wrapper. See next page for mild-cured ham, Daisy hams, etc.

Place the ham on a rack in a shallow roasting pan, fat side up, and bake at 325°. A meat thermometer will register 150° when the ham is done.

Precooked hams take about 10 minutes per pound to heat thoroughly.

Mild-cured hams (bone in) take about 2½ hours for a 5-pound half ham or shank or butt, 3½ hours for a 9 to 12 pound ham, and 4 hours for a 15 to 20 pound ham. A 5-pound boned piece takes 2½ hours, an 8-pound piece 3 hours.

Daisy ham, canned ham, Canadian-type bacon. Since these hams are already cooked, they need only an hour in a 350° oven to heat thoroughly. Follow any of the suggestions given for basting, glazing and serving Baked Ham (below). For easy serving, have your butcher cut a canned ham or a piece of Canadian bacon in thin slices and tie it firmly in shape. After baking, put it on a hot platter, snip and carefully remove the string.

To Glaze Baked Ham

Cut off all the skin from a precooked boiled or baked ham. Place the ham on a rack in a shallow roasting pan. With a long sharp knife, score the fat (make cuts about ¼ inch deep) in a diamond pattern. Spread with a glaze (below). Stick a whole clove in each square.

Bake at 400° about 30 minutes. Baste several times during the glazing with cider, cider mixed with brandy, or a special basting sauce (below). To make slicing easier, remove from oven about 15 minutes before serving.

To make the glaze, mix 1 cup brown sugar with ¼ cup strained honey, maple syrup, cider or fruit juice. Mix a little mustard with the sugar, if you like, or spread the ham with prepared mustard and pat on brown sugar mixed with fine cracker crumbs.

For the basting sauce, mix 1 cup brown sugar with 1 teaspoon dry mustard and ½ cup mild vinegar, or with 1 teaspoon ginger and ½ cup ginger ale, or with 1 cup honey and 1 cup orange juice.

To Serve with Ham

If you have basted the ham with a savory sauce, you may need no other accompaniment than prepared mustard. Otherwise, serve any of these.

Cole Slaw (p. 274)
Crushed pineapple
Fruit Relishes (p. 83)
Mustard Pickle (p. 522)
Mustard Sauce (p. 97)
Piccalilli (p. 522)
Raisin Sauce (p. 98)
Rochester Sauce (p. 97)
Spiced Fruit Sauce (p. 99)

Carving a Ham

Make a cut at right angles to the bone with a long straight knife. Cut several parallel slices. Slip the knife beneath to free the slices from the bone.

Tip the ham and cut some slices from the under side

Cut a small wedge from the shank end, slice down

And cut under the slices

Daisy Ham on a Spit

For out-of-door cooking.

Select a long, narrow daisy ham. Put it on a spit and wrap foil around it, folding the ends to keep in the juices. Cook over hot coals at least 1 hour or until tender. Serve with a tasty sauce (p. 186).

Broiled Ham

One pound serves 3.

Cut gashes in the fat so that it will not curl during the cooking. Broil ½-inch slices 3 minutes on each side.

Broiled Ham Epicurean Style. Have the ham cut in 1-inch slices. Broil on one side, turn, and spread with a thick layer of brown sugar. Broil until the sugar melts, reducing the heat so that the sugar will not scorch. Serve with sautéed pineapple slices.

Pan-Broiled Ham

Grease a frying pan with a little of the ham fat. Put in the ham and cook 3 minutes on each side. Thin slices of Canadian bacon take only 1 or 2 minutes on each side.

Ham with Mushrooms. Pile sliced sautéed mushrooms on the ham.

Barbecued Ham. When the ham is cooked, add to the fat in the pan 3 tablespoons vinegar, 1½ teaspoons mustard, ½ teaspoon sugar, ⅛ teaspoon paprika and 1 tablespoon currant jelly. Heat and pour over the ham.

Ham and Eggs. When the ham is cooked, fry eggs in the ham fat and serve on or with the ham.

Ham Steak with Glacéed Pineapple

Put in a baking dish
  1 slice ham (1 inch thick, about
    1½ pounds)

Spread with
  Prepared mustard
Pour over it
  1 cup syrup from canned pineapple
Sprinkle with
  ½ cup brown sugar
Stick with
  Whole cloves
Bake at 350° until tender (about 1 hour).
Over the ham lay
  6 slices canned pineapple
Bake until the pineapple is delicately brown, basting frequently with the juices in the pan. *Serves 4 or 5.*

Ham Casserole Country Style

Equally good made with bits of left-over ham. Put the ham and potatoes in layers.

Cut off the outside edge of fat from
  1 slice ham (2 inches thick, about
    2 pounds)
Put in a casserole and cover with
  1½ cups thinly sliced potatoes
  1 onion, sliced
Sprinkle with
  Thyme
Add
  2 cups milk
Cover and bake 1½ hours at 350°.
Serves 6.

Ham and Onion Casserole

Good variations are many — add herbs, chopped parsley or mushrooms to this basic dish. Or make it with bits of left-over ham.

Put in a casserole
  3 large onions, sliced thin
Lay over the onions
  1 slice ham (1 inch thick, about
    1½ pounds)
Pour over the ham
  1 can undiluted cream of celery soup
    or 1½ cups canned tomatoes
Bake 1 hour at 350°. *Serves 4.*

Ham Roll

Spread a thick (1 inch) slice of ham (1½ to 2 pounds) with Celery Stuffing (p. 81) or Bread Stuffing (p. 80). Roll up and skewer or tie in shape.

Put in a baking dish. Cover with stock, consommé or canned tomatoes. Cover. Bake 1½ to 2 hours at 350°. *Serves 6.*

Ground Ham

Ground ham is a major ingredient in the tasty meat loaf recipes below, but it is also a savory addition to many others. Add it to sauces and salads for extra flavor.

Ham Patties

Mix
  1 cup ground ham (about ½ pound)
  1 egg
  ¼ cup dry bread crumbs
Season to taste with
  Prepared mustard or Worcestershire
  Chopped parsley, stuffed olives or
    onion
Add
  Milk or water (enough so that you can
    shape the mixture)
Shape into patties. Brown on both sides in
  Bacon fat
Serve with
  Mustard Sauce (p. 97)
Serves 2 or 3.

Scalloped Ham

A tasty "second day" dish. Also excellent made with cooked chicken, veal or fish. Add vegetables, too, if you like. The amount of ham is only a suggestion — use more or less as convenient.

Prepare
  1 cup chopped or ground cooked ham
  2 hard-cooked eggs, chopped
  2 cups Cream Sauce (p. 90)
  ¾ cup fine bread crumbs, buttered
Butter a casserole and sprinkle with crumbs. Cover with half the eggs, then half the sauce and half the ham. Repeat, and cover with the rest of the crumbs. Bake at 375° until the crumbs are brown. *Serves 6.*

Ham and Veal Loaf

Order chopped together
  2 pounds ham
  1 pound veal
Add
  1 cup bread crumbs
  2 eggs, slightly beaten
  2 cups milk
  Salt and pepper to taste
Mix well. Shape in a roll. Put on a flat baking dish. Bake 2 hours at 350°. Serve with
  Tomato (p. 94) or Horseradish Sauce
    (p. 96)
Serves 8.

Ham Loaf

Grind together (or have it done at the market)
  1½ pounds ham
  1 pound fresh pork
Add
  ¼ teaspoon pepper
  ¼ teaspoon salt
  2 eggs, well beaten
  1 cup milk
  1 cup cracker crumbs
Mix well and shape into a loaf. Put in a shallow baking pan. Bake 2 hours at 350°. During the baking, baste frequently with the following basting sauce.

Basting Sauce. Cook and stir together for 5 minutes ½ cup brown sugar, 1 tablespoon prepared mustard, ½ cup boiling water, ½ cup mild vinegar.

Nancy's Ham Loaf

Delicious hot or cold.

Order ground together
  1 pound ham
  ½ pound beef
  ½ pound pork

Add
 1 cup bread, cut in ¼-inch cubes
 ¾ cup powdered milk
 ⅛ teaspoon pepper
 2 tablespoons minced onion
 1 egg, beaten
 1 cup tomato juice
Mix well. Pack into a loaf pan. Bake
1½ hours at 350°. *Serves 8.*

German Loaf

*Fussier than some recipes but delicious.
Cuts in handsome thin slices.*

Cut off the fat from
 1 pound ham
Set the fat aside. Grind the ham with
 1 pound fresh pork
 1 clove garlic
 1 small onion
Add
 1 tablespoon salt
 1 teaspoon pepper
 2 teaspoons curry powder
 1½ tablespoons sage
Grind again. Add
 1 egg white
 ½ cup cream
Mix thoroughly.

Put 4 strips of the ham fat on a square
of cheesecloth. Press the meat mixture
into a loaf shape and place on the fat.
Fold the cheesecloth tightly around the
meat and tie firmly. Put on a trivet in a
deep kettle. Add
 3 quarts boiling water
 ¼ cup vinegar
 1 teaspoon salt
Cover and simmer 2½ hours. Drain,
cool, and press under a weight.

Ham Mousse Alexandria

Party fare for lunch or supper.

Butter lightly 6 to 8 small molds. Set
the oven at 350°.

Mix to a smooth paste
 ½ pound ham, ground fine
 4 egg whites
Rub through a sieve or whirl in an
electric blender. Add

 ⅛ teaspoon pepper
 Few gratings nutmeg
Stir in, a little at a time
 ½ cup heavy cream
Fill the molds. Set in a pan of hot water.
Bake until firm (30 to 45 minutes). Turn
out onto a platter or plates. Coat with
 Allemande Sauce (p. 92)
Garnish with
 Parsley

Ham and Spinach Soufflé

Put in a bowl
 ½ cup dry bread crumbs
 Milk (enough to cover the crumbs)
Let stand until the crumbs are soft.
Drain off the milk. Add to the crumbs
 3 tablespoons butter
Cook and stir until smooth. Add
 1 cup chopped cooked spinach
 2 tablespoons finely chopped onion
 ¾ cup diced cooked ham
 ⅛ teaspoon pepper
 3 egg yolks, beaten until thick
 Salt to taste
Fold in
 3 egg whites, beaten stiff
Spoon into a straight-sided unbuttered
baking dish. Set in a pan. Put hot water
in the pan so that it is 1 inch deep.
Bake at 350° until firm (about 40 minutes). Serve with
 Hollandaise (p. 95)
*Serves 4 as a luncheon dish or 6 as a
vegetable.*

Vary by adding more ham or chopped
mushrooms or herbs.

Bacon

Bacon varies in flavor and in leanness.
It is marketed in one piece (slab bacon)
or in thick or thin slices. Buy only
enough for a week at a time, because
bacon is at its savory best when it is
fresh. It does not freeze well.

Bacon drippings. Store in a can or covered jar in the refrigerator. Use (within
two weeks) for frying eggs or potatoes
or for seasoning vegetables.

Pan-Broiled Bacon. Arrange strips in a single layer in a cold frying pan. If the strips are too cold to separate easily, put the bacon in the pan and separate it as it warms. Cook until crisp and brown, turning occasionally. Pour off the fat as it accumulates. Drain the bacon on a paper towel.

Oven-Broiled Bacon. Place thin slices close together on a rack in a shallow pan or on a special bacon cooker. Bake at 425° until crisp and brown, turning once.

Canadian bacon. See Broiled Canadian Bacon (p. 187, Pan-Broiled Ham) and Baked Canadian Bacon (p. 186).

Fried Salt Pork Country Style

Dip in flour to coat well
    ¼ pound lean salt pork (about 9 thin
        slices)
Heat a heavy frying pan. Put in the pork, lower the heat, and cook until crisp and brown, turning frequently. Remove the pork from the pan and put in a warm serving dish. If there is more than about 2 tablespoons of fat in the pan, pour off the extra.

Stir into the pan
    2 tablespoons flour
Blend well. Add
    1 cup milk
Cook and stir until thickened. Add
    Worcestershire, Tabasco, or a
        few grains of pepper
Pour into a bowl. Serve with
    Hot boiled potatoes
Serves 3.

For a richer gravy, add a little cream or butter just before serving.

Sausages and Sausage Meat

Bologna, salami (smoked and cooked), cervelat and other distinctively seasoned sausages are sold by the piece or in thin slices ready for sandwiches, a platter of mixed cold meats or a salad.

Liver sausage (liverwurst) discolors when sliced. Buy it in a piece and slice it as you serve it. See also Mock Foie Gras (p. 56).

Link sausages (frankfurters or pork) are sold by the pound or in packages.

Sausage meat is sold by the pound.

Store sausage in the refrigerator. For the finest flavor, use within a few days of purchasing.

Pan-Broiled Sausages

Some sausages need only browning. Follow directions on the package.

Cut sausages apart but do not prick. Put in a cold frying pan. Cook about 10 minutes over moderate heat, turning with tongs to brown evenly. Pour off the fat as it accumulates.

Serve with eggs, pancakes or waffles, or on squares of corn bread or a bed of mashed potato. Any of the accompaniments suggested for pork (p. 181) are good with sausage.

To reduce the fat, cover the sausages with boiling water, simmer 5 minutes and drain before browning.

Toad-in-the-Hole. Cook 1 pound sausages. Put them with the fat in the pan into a 9 by 9 inch shallow casserole or baking pan. Set the oven at 450°. Prepare Yorkshire Pudding batter (p. 156) and pour it over the sausages. Bake until puffed and brown (about 30 minutes). Serves 4.

Cornell Sausage Meat

Meat for sausage should not be too lean. One-third fat is about right. If you make more than enough for one meal, store it in the freezer and use it within two or three weeks.

Mix thoroughly
    1 pound pork chopped for sausage
    1 teaspoon salt
    ½ teaspoon freshly ground pepper
    ½ teaspoon sage

Sausage Cakes

Shape sausage meat in flat round cakes like small hamburgers. Put in a cold frying pan. Set over moderate heat. Cook about 10 minutes on one side, turn and cook 10 minutes on the other side. Pour off the fat as it accumulates. Sausage cakes should be well browned and thoroughly cooked but not dry.

To remove some of the fat before browning, cover the patties with boiling water, cover, and simmer 5 minutes. Drain and cook as above.

Sausage-Stuffed Apples

Cook together 15 minutes
  1 pound sausage meat
  1 clove garlic, crushed
  1 tablespoon chopped onion
Stir with a fork. Core and stuff with the sausage
  8 firm baking apples
Put in a baking dish. Sprinkle with
  Brown sugar
On each apple put a strip of
  Bacon
Bake at 350° until the apples are soft (about 40 minutes).

Sausage and Apple Casserole

Shape into 8 balls
  1 pound sausage meat
Cook in a skillet until brown.

Core and peel halfway down
  8 small tart apples
Fill with
  Cinnamon sugar
Pare and cut in quarters
  2 large sweet potatoes
Put in the center of a casserole
  Bread Stuffing (p. 80)
Arrange around it the sausage, apples and sweet potatoes. Bake at 350° about 1 hour. *Serves 4.*

Pineapple Rabbit with Sausage Cakes

Spread
  6 slices canned pineapple

with
  Horseradish
Shape in 6 flat patties
  1 pound sausage meat
Put a patty on each slice of pineapple. Put in a baking dish. Add
  1 cup sherry
Bake 30 minutes at 350°, basting 4 times. Put on each patty a slice of
  Cheese
Bake until the cheese begins to melt. Dust with
  Paprika
Serves 6.

Sausage-Stuffed Prunes

A good luncheon dish or an attractive garnish on the turkey platter.

Put in a saucepan
  ½ pound large prunes
Cover with water. Cook until just tender. Drain and pit.

Mix
  ½ pound sausage meat
  ½ cup soft bread crumbs
  Salt and pepper to taste
Stuff the prunes generously. Put in a lightly greased pan. Bake at 400° until the sausage is well browned (about 25 minutes). As a luncheon dish, serve the prunes with the sauce below. *Serves 3 or 4.*

To make the sauce. Mix 1 tablespoon fat with 1 tablespoon flour. Add 1 cup prune juice, 1 tablespoon lemon juice, 1 teaspoon grated lemon rind and salt to taste. Cook and stir until the sauce boils.

Bubble-and-Squeak

An old-fashioned English supper dish.

Put in layers in a casserole
  1 pound cooked sausage meat
  2 cups cooked chopped cabbage
Pour over the top
  2 cups Cream Sauce (p. 90)
Sprinkle with
  Bread crumbs
Bake at 350° for 30 minutes. *Serves 4 to 6.*

Frankfurters or Wieners

Frankfurters may be all beef or a mixture of beef, pork and veal. There is no cereal in the best ones. They are already cooked but need brief heating to be appetizing.

Pan-Broiled Frankfurters. Heat slowly in just enough butter to keep them from sticking. Turn with tongs to keep from pricking the skin.

"Boiled" Frankfurters. Cover with boiling water. Cover the pan and lower the heat or turn it off so that the water no longer boils. Let stand 5 minutes and drain.

Frankfurters Grilled with Cheese. Cut a long slit in each frankfurter. Tuck in a piece of cheese. Broil, cheese side up, until the cheese melts.

Frankfurters in Buns. *Standard fare for picnics and cookouts but good any time.* Split buns without cutting all the way through. Toast on the cut side and tuck in a heated frankfurter. Serve with prepared mustard or piccalilli or both.

Frankfurters and Sauerkraut. Simmer sauerkraut (p. 240) until thoroughly heated. Lay frankfurters over it and serve as soon as they are hot. **To vary,** for each pound of sauerkraut, add 1 teaspoon caraway seeds and 1 tablespoon water.

Frankfurters Southern Style

Melt
    1 tablespoon butter or bacon fat
Add
    1 medium onion, diced

    ½ cup diced celery
    ½ green pepper, diced
Cook slowly until the vegetables are tender. Add
    1 pound frankfurters, cut in pieces
    1 large can tomatoes (2½ cups)
Season to taste with
    Thyme and orégano
Simmer 10 minutes. Pour into a large casserole. Set the oven at 425°. Spread over the top of the casserole
    Corn bread batter (p. 314)
Bake until the corn bread is brown and crusty (about 25 minutes). *Serves 6.*

Scrapple

It is seldom worth while to make scrapple for a small family. It is marketed by the pound or in cans.

Put in a deep pan
    1 pound pork (inexpensive bony cut)
    2 fresh pigs' feet
    1 quart boiling water
    2 teaspoons salt
Cover the pan, reduce the heat, and cook until the meat drops from the bones. Strain the broth into a large double boiler top. Grind the meat. Stir into the broth
    ⅔ cup corn meal or buckwheat flour
Cook and stir over direct heat 5 minutes. Add the meat and
    2 tablespoons chopped onion
Season to taste with
    Salt and pepper
Cook over boiling water 1 hour. Pack into a small loaf pan rinsed with cold water. Chill.

Fried Scrapple. *Serve hot with syrup for a satisfying winter breakfast or lunch.* Cut scrapple in slices ½ inch thick. Pan-fry until crisp and brown. Unless the pork is very lean you will need no added fat in the pan.

Veal

Veal is young beef. It is almost as delicately flavored as chicken and so combines well with other foods. It is usually very lean and needs to be cooked by moist heat or with some added fat.

Roast Veal
(leg, cushion, loin, rump, shoulder, breast)

Veal is usually boned at the market and cut in a piece of the desired size, 4 to 6 pounds or more.

If you wish to stuff the roast, use Onion (p. 81), Mushroom (p. 81) or other savory stuffing. For added flavor, rub lightly with a cut clove of garlic or make shallow gashes in the meat and squeeze into them a little anchovy paste.

Place on a rack in a shallow roasting pan. Place strips of fat salt pork on the meat. Roast 40 minutes to the pound at 325°. A roast thermometer will read 180° when the veal is done. Veal should always be well done.

Serve with Brown Gravy (p. 156) made with the fat in the pan and either milk or water as the liquid. Add chopped parsley to the gravy.

Braised Leg of Veal

Veal done this way is tender and moist.

Cream together
   2 tablespoons shortening
   1 clove garlic, crushed
   1 teaspoon salt
   ¼ teaspoon sage
   ¼ teaspoon pepper
Spread over
   Leg of veal (boned and tied)
Put in a heavy Dutch oven or casserole

   ½ cup butter
   2 onions, sliced
   2 stalks celery
Put in the meat, cover, and bake at 375° until the meat is fork-tender (about 2 hours). Turn the meat several times. Add a little water as needed to keep the meat from sticking.

Remove the meat. Strain the broth, measure it, and add enough
   Water to make 2 cups
Mix
   1 tablespoon cornstarch
   ¼ cup sherry or Marsala
Add to the broth and cook and stir until smooth. Put the meat back in the pan. Add the gravy and heat, turning the meat to glaze the surface. *Serves 8 to 10.*

Broiled Veal Chops

Broil only young tender chops which will not take too long to cook. Cook others like cutlets (p. 194).

Sprinkle chops 1 to 1½ inches thick with salad oil and broil 10 minutes on one side, turn and sprinkle with more oil or top with a strip of bacon, and cook until thoroughly done (test by making a tiny slit in the meat).

Cheese-Topped Veal Chops. After turning, sprinkle with salt, pepper and orégano, and top with a slice of cheese. Broil until the cheese melts.

193

Sautéed Veal Cutlets

In Europe, veal is much more generally available than beef, and the many delicious ways of preparing it are among the famous dishes of the finest restaurants.

Veal cutlets are usually slices from the leg cut ½ inch thick. One pound serves 3.

Remove any bits of the bone and skin. Cut in pieces for serving. Pound with a meat tenderizer or the edge of a heavy saucer until ¼ inch thick. Roll up irregular pieces and fasten with toothpicks. Sprinkle with salt, pepper, and flour.

Sauté slowly until evenly browned and tender, in butter, olive oil, or a mixture of one-third butter and two-thirds bacon fat. Cook 2 split garlic cloves and/or ¼ cup chopped onion with the cutlets if you like.

Veal Cutlets with Mushrooms. Cut the meat in 3-inch pieces. Sauté a few at a time with sliced mushrooms. When all are cooked, put back into the pan and add ½ cup cream for 1 pound meat. Heat and season.

Veal Cutlets aux Fines Herbes. Sprinkle with chopped parsley and chives (3 tablespoons parsley to 1 teaspoon chives). Sprinkle with lemon juice.

Veal Cutlets Flambé. Sauté wafer-thin pieces, sprinkle with warm brandy, light with a match, and ladle the juice over the meat. Serve with Béarnaise Sauce (p. 95).

Veal Cutlets with Cheese Soufflé. Arrange cooked cutlets in a casserole. Pour Cheese Soufflé mixture (p. 115) over the meat and bake.

Veal Cutlets Hollandaise. Sauté. When almost tender, sprinkle with dry vermouth, cover, and simmer 10 minutes longer. Serve with Hollandaise (p. 95).

Veal Cazapra. Sauté. When almost tender, sprinkle with dry vermouth (¼ cup for each pound). Cover and simmer 10 minutes. Sprinkle with pine nuts (pignolia), cover, and cook 5 minutes longer.

Veal Cutlets Paradiso. Spread tomato paste in a shallow baking dish. Put in the sautéed cutlets. Put a slice of cheese on each. Set under the broiler until the cheese melts.

Veal Cutlets au Vin

Prepare for sautéing (above)
  1 pound veal cutlets
Melt in a heavy skillet
  1 tablespoon butter
Add the cutlets and cook 5 minutes on each side. Add
  1 tablespoon chopped onion
  1 teaspoon chopped parsley
  1 tablespoon chopped ham
  1 clove garlic, split
Cover and cook slowly 20 minutes. Remove the garlic. Add
  ¼ cup dry wine, white or red
Cover and cook slowly 10 minutes. Put the meat on a hot platter. Add to the pan
  ¼ cup water
Boil, season with
  Salt and pepper
Pour over the meat. *Serves 3.*

Braised Veal Cutlets

Follow the recipe for Sautéed Veal Cutlets (above), but after browning, surround with stock, gravy, sour cream, tomato sauce or canned tomato soup. Cover and cook slowly on top of the stove or bake in a casserole at 300° until tender — 35 to 60 minutes. Add more liquid from time to time as it cooks away. Season the sauce to taste, adding salt, pepper, onion juice, and sherry or Marsala.

Veal Cutlets with Claret Sauce. Without browning, put the cutlets in a baking dish, cover with claret, and let stand 30 minutes. Take out, dip in flour, and put in a buttered pan. Add the claret, an equal amount of stock or consommé, and (for 1 pound meat) the juice of ½ lemon. Cook as above.

Scallopini alla Marsala. Before browning, sprinkle with grated Parmesan cheese. Brown in olive oil. Braise in a mixture of one-third Marsala wine and two-thirds stock or consommé. Add a pinch of marjoram or orégano. As a variation, add sautéed mushrooms and tiny cubes of ham.

Veal Paprika. *Never use pepper in a paprika-flavored dish.* Sauté a cut clove of garlic with the meat. Simmer the meat in water or stock. Remove the garlic. Put the meat on a hot platter. Add sour cream (½ cup for 1 pound meat) to the pan and enough paprika to make the sauce very pink. Cook and stir until well heated and pour over the meat.

Breaded Veal Cutlets

Cover cutlets with boiling water. Cover and simmer until tender (about 35 minutes). Add various seasonings to the cooking water if you like — a slice or two of onion and carrot, a stalk of celery, a few peppercorns and whole cloves. Drain. Save the broth to use in a soup or a sauce.

Dip the cutlets in flour, egg, and crumbs (p. 6). Chill 20 minutes or longer to make the coating firmer and help keep it from slipping off as the cutlets cook.

Sauté or fry in deep fat heated to 385°.

Wiener Schnitzel. Garnish with anchovies and thin slices of lemon.

Veal Holstein

Dip cutlets in flour, egg, and crumbs (p. 6). Sauté slowly until brown in mixture of two-thirds bacon fat and one-third butter. Cover with Brown Sauce (p. 93). Cover and simmer until tender.

For traditional German service, top each piece with a poached egg. Garnish with cucumber pickles, pickled beets, sliced lemon, and olives stuffed with capers and anchovies.

Veal Cordon Bleu

Pound veal cutlets very thin. Sprinkle with salt and pepper. Cut in even pieces and put together like a sandwich with a thin slice of ham and a slice of Swiss cheese as the filling.

Dip in egg, beaten slightly with a tablespoon of water, then in grated cheese. Let stand 20 minutes.

Sauté slowly in a mixture of half olive oil and half butter until brown (about 20 minutes).

For a crisp crust, dip in seasoned flour, egg and crumbs (p. 6) instead of egg and cheese.

Veal Birds

Cut well-pounded veal cutlets in pieces about 2 by 4 inches. Spread with Bread Stuffing (p. 80) or a variation. (Use packaged stuffing if you like.) Roll up and fasten with toothpicks or skewers. Sprinkle with salt, pepper and flour.

Sauté in butter or bacon fat until brown. Add enough cream or gravy to half cover the meat. Cover and cook slowly until tender. Cook on top of the stove or bake in a casserole at 350°.

Veal Birds with Meat Stuffing. Grind the trimmings with a small piece of salt pork or bacon. Measure. Add half the quantity of crumbs. Season to taste. Moisten with beaten egg and hot water. Spread on the meat.

Veal Olives. Do not stuff the cutlets, but roll them up wrapped in strips of bacon or prosciutto ham. Brown. Cook in water or stock. Make a Brown Sauce (p. 93), using the stock in the pan.

Veal and Onion Casserole

Mix
> 2 tablespoons flour
> 2 teaspoons salt
> ⅛ teaspoon pepper

Roll in it
> 1½ pounds veal cutlets, cut in squares

Heat 5 minutes
> 2 tablespoons fat or salad oil
> 1 clove garlic, split

Remove the garlic. Add the meat and
> 1½ cups chopped onions

Cook and stir over low heat until the onions are golden. Put in a casserole. Add
> 1 cup sour cream

Cover and bake at 350° until the veal is fork-tender (1½ to 2 hours). *Serves 4 or 5.*

City Chickens

Allow 1 pound lean veal and 1 pound lean pork for 6.

Have the meat cut in 1½-inch cubes. Alternate cubes of veal and pork on skewers, 4 or 5 cubes to each. Sprinkle with salt and pepper, dip in flour, then in slightly beaten egg and then in crumbs (p. 6).

Sauté in butter, bacon fat or other shortening until well browned. Add ½ cup water to the pan, cover closely, and cook until tender (about 30 minutes).

Blanquette of Veal

On the platter with the veal, arrange sliced sautéed mushrooms, tiny potato balls and well-seasoned whole green beans or young carrots. Use any leftovers to make a veal and vegetable stew for another meal.

Put in a deep pan
> 3 pounds stewing veal, cut in 2-inch squares

Cover with
> Cold water or cold water and white wine

Add
> 6 small white onions
> 4 sprigs parsley
> 1 stalk celery with tops
> ½ bay leaf
> 1 sprig thyme
> 2 cloves
> 1 teaspoon salt
> ¼ teaspoon pepper

Cover and cook slowly until the meat is fork-tender (about 40 minutes). Remove the meat and strain the broth.

Melt
> 3 tablespoons butter

Add
> 3 tablespoons flour

Stir well and add 3 cups of the strained broth. Cook 5 minutes.

Just before serving, heat the sauce to the boiling point and pour slowly over
> 3 egg yolks, beaten with the juice of 1 lemon

Season with
> A few grains nutmeg

Put the meat in a heated serving dish and pour the sauce over it. *Serves 6.*

English Veal Pie

Remove the meat from
> A knuckle of veal (about 5 pounds) or other piece for stewing

Cover the bones with
> Cold water

Add
> 1 slice onion
> 1 slice carrot
> Bit of bay leaf
> Sprig of parsley
> 12 peppercorns
> Blade of mace or ½ teaspoon ground mace
> 2 teaspoons salt

Heat slowly to the boiling point. Add the veal and
> ½-pound piece lean ham

Cover and simmer until the meat is fork-tender (about 1½ hours). Take out the veal and ham and cook the broth until it is reduced to 2 cups.

Melt
    ¼ cup butter
Cook until brown. Add
    ¼ cup flour
Cook and stir until again well browned. Add the broth. Cut the veal and ham in neat cubes and add to the sauce. Simmer 20 minutes. Taste, and add more seasonings if needed.

Put in a casserole. Cover with
    Pastry top (Plain p. 407, or Puff, p. 409), baked separately
Serves 8 or more.

Ground Veal

Ground veal is usually combined with other more highly flavored foods in such recipes as Miss Daniell's Meat Loaf (p. 173) and Ham and Veal Loaf (p. 188). Use it also in Moussaka (p. 179) or in place of beef in Beef Doves (p. 172). Herbs add zest to this bland meat. Try adding a trace of chervil, marjoram, rosemary, tarragon or thyme.

Veal and Almond Patties

Cover with water
    1½ pounds lean veal
Add
    1 teaspoon salt
Cook slowly 30 minutes. Drain, reserving the liquid. Chop the meat fine. Add to 1 cup of the liquid
    4 slices bread, broken in pieces
    2 tablespoons butter
Cool and add the meat and
    ¼ cup sliced almonds
Season to taste. Shape in flat oval patties about 2½ inches long. Dip in
    Egg and cracker crumbs (p. 6)
Sauté in
    Butter
over low heat until well browned, turning once. Serve with
    Mushroom Sauce (p. 97)
Serves 6.

Vienna Steaks

Stuffed or broiled mushrooms add the right touch.

Mix
    ½ pound ground veal
    ½ pound ground beef
    1½ teaspoons salt
    ¼ teaspoon paprika
    ½ teaspoon celery salt
    Few gratings nutmeg
    1 teaspoon lemon juice
    Few drops onion juice
    1 egg, well beaten
Shape in 12 oval cakes, ½ inch thick. Cook like hamburgers. Remove the meat to a heated serving dish.

Heat in the pan
    ½ cup sour cream
Pour over the meat. *Serves 3 or 4.*

Veal-Stuffed Zucchini

See also Stuffed Zucchini (p. 261).

Cover with boiling salted water
    2 or 3 zucchini
Cook 10 minutes, drain, cool, and cut in half lengthwise. Scoop out the pulp and chop it.

Heat in a skillet
    2 tablespoons olive oil
Add
    ½ pound lean veal
Cook until well browned. Take out the veal and chop it.

Put in the skillet
    2 tablespoons chopped onion
    1 clove garlic, crushed
Cook until the onion is yellow. Add the zucchini pulp and cook 5 minutes. Cool slightly and add the chopped veal and
    2 eggs, well beaten
    ⅓ cup grated Italian cheese
Season to taste with
    Salt and pepper
    Marjoram or thyme
    Minced parsley
Fill the zucchini shells. Sprinkle with
    Buttered crumbs (p. 7)
Bake at 350° until the zucchini is tender (about 30 minutes). *Serves 4 to 6.*

Pressed Veal

A handsome dish for a summer buffet.

Cover with boiling water
   Knuckle or shin of veal (about 4
      pounds)
   1 pound lean veal
   1 onion
Cover and cook slowly until the meat is
tender (about 1½ hours). Drain, reserving the broth. Grind the meat and season
it with
   Salt, pepper and marjoram
Hard-cook, cool, and slice
   3 eggs
Garnish the bottom of a mold or loaf
pan with slices of egg and
   Chopped parsley
Put in a layer of the meat and a layer
of sliced egg, sprinkle with parsley, and
cover with the rest of the meat. Cook the
broth until it is reduced to 1 cup and
pour it over the meat. Press down firmly
and chill.

Turn out onto a serving dish and garnish with
   Sprigs of parsley

Quartered tomatoes
Serves 6.

Veal Loaf

*See also Miss Daniell's Meat Loaf (p.
173) and Ham and Veal Loaf (p. 188).*

Mix
   2 pounds ground veal
   ½ pound ground fresh pork
   ½ green pepper, cut fine
   1 onion, chopped
   1 tablespoon lemon juice
   1 teaspoon salt
   ½ cup cracker meal or wheat germ
   1 egg
   ½ cup milk
   1 teaspoon Worcestershire
Press firmly into a loaf pan. Lay over
the top
   6 strips bacon
Cover with a piece of foil and bake 40
minutes at 300°. Uncover and bake 30
minutes longer. Serve with
   Mushroom Sauce (p. 94)
Serves 8.

Venison

Fresh-killed venison is apt to be tough. It will be tenderer and of better flavor if you have your butcher hang it at least 2 weeks in his refrigerator before you cook it. He will cut it in pieces for you. Use immediately or wrap, freeze, and store for later use.

Broiled Venison

Cut ½-inch slices from the loin. Sprinkle with salt and pepper. Brush with melted butter or olive oil. Broil or sauté 5 minutes on each side. Serve with Maître d'Hôtel Butter (p. 89), Chestnut (p. 93) or Currant Jelly Sauce (p. 93), seasoned to taste with port or Madeira.

Roast Venison
(leg, loin, saddle)

Put the meat in a pottery bowl or an enameled dish. Cover with French dressing made with lemon juice or with a special marinade (below). Cover and refrigerate 12 to 24 hours to tenderize the meat and improve the flavor. Turn occasionally so that the marinade reaches all parts of the meat.

Drain and put in a shallow baking pan. Put slices of bacon over the meat. Roast like lamb (p. 174). Allow 20 minutes per pound for rare venison, 22 minutes for medium rare. Increase the heat to 450° for the last 15 minutes to brown the surface.

Marinade for venison. Heat 1 cup red wine or cider with 2 tablespoons oil, a slice of onion, 2 bay leaves and ½ teaspoon salt. For a more savory marinade, add sliced celery, onions or carrot and a sprig of thyme or rosemary. Cool.

Braised Venison

Cut the venison into serving-size pieces. Dip in flour seasoned with salt and pepper.

Heat fat (about ¼ inch deep) in a Dutch oven or a heavy frying pan with a tight cover. Brown the meat slowly in the fat, turning to brown the pieces evenly. Put a rack under the meat, add about ¼ cup water and cover tightly. Cook over very low heat or in a slow oven (300°) until tender (1½ to 2 hours). Add a little more water from time to time if necessary.

Recipes Using Cooked Meats

Cooked or canned meats can be presented in many appetizing ways. They are especially convenient for meals which must be made ready ahead of time with no last-minute tasks for the hostess. Cut the meat in neat, attractive pieces, free of bits of skin, fat, gristle and bone.

In addition to the recipes in this section, consider also suggestions in other chapters, such as Poultry and Game Birds, that can be adapted to cooked meats, and general recipes such as Fashion Park Salad (p. 273), Filled Biscuits (p. 311), Omelets (p. 105), Pilaf (p. 339), Rissoles (p. 202), Sandwiches (p. 337), Scalloped Ham (p. 188), Stuffed Peppers (p. 255) and Stuffed Tomatoes (p. 259).

Sliced Roast Meat

Cut roast or canned meat in neat slices and serve cold, attractively garnished with watercress, sliced tomatoes or pickled fruits. Or heat gravy or tomato sauce piping hot and pour it over the meat. Do not warm meat in the gravy over high heat, as that toughens it.

Ragout of Meat

Vary by seasoning with claret or Marsala, or by adding sliced sautéed mushrooms, tiny whole onions or sliced olives.

Heat
  1½ cups Brown Sauce (p. 93) or gravy or 1 can undiluted mushroom or celery soup
Add
  2 cups cubed cooked meat
Season to taste with
  Worcestershire, onion juice and cayenne
Heat but do not let the sauce boil. *Serves 4.*

Meat and Vegetable Casserole

With this good basic recipe, you can create a tasty dish no matter what you have on hand.

Cut in small, neat pieces
  Cooked or canned meat, fish, chicken or turkey
Add to it an equal amount of
  Cooked vegetable, such as carrots, peas, or lima beans
If you like, add also
  Cooked rice or diced boiled potato
Mix well and moisten with
  Gravy, Cream Sauce (p. 90) or undiluted canned cream soup
If the mixture seems too thin, stir in
  Bread crumbs or cracker crumbs
If it is too thick, add
  Gravy, milk or tomato juice
Season to taste with
  Salt and pepper
Season more highly, if you like, with
  Onion juice, Worcestershire or herbs
Spoon into a casserole. Put on the cover, or sprinkle over the top

Buttered crumbs, crushed corn flakes
or potato chips
Bake at 375° about 30 minutes.

Casserole Provençale

Cook and drain
  2 to 4 ounces noodles
Melt
  2 tablespoons fat
Add
  ½ cup sliced onion
  ½ cup diced green pepper
  1 cup sliced mushrooms
Cook until tender. Add
  1 to 2 cups cubed cooked meat
Cook slowly 10 minutes. Add
  2 small tomatoes cut in pieces
  1½ cups gravy
Heat. Season to taste with
  Salt and pepper
Add the noodles. Put in a casserole.
Sprinkle with
  Grated cheese
Bake 30 minutes at 325° or 20 minutes
at 375°. *Serves 3 to 6, according to the
amount of meat and noodles used.*

Casserole of Meat and Rice

Prepare
  2 cups cooked meat, chopped fine
Season to taste with
  Salt, pepper, cayenne and celery salt
  Onion juice or lemon juice
Add
  1 egg, slightly beaten
  Hot water or broth to moisten
Prepare
  2 cups Steamed Rice (p. 294)
Butter a casserole. Line with part of the
rice. Spoon in the meat and cover with
the rest of the rice. Cover and bake 45
minutes at 350°. Serve with
  Tomato Sauce (p. 94)
Serves 6.

Rice and Meat Loaf

Melt
  2 tablespoons butter
Stir in
  2 tablespoons flour

Add
  ¾ cup gravy or consommé
Cook and stir until thick. Add
  2 cups chopped cooked meat
  3 tablespoons chili sauce
  1 tablespoon chopped onion
Season more highly, if you like, with
  Worcestershire or Tabasco
Cook and drain
  ¾ cup rice (1½ cups, cooked)
Spread half the rice in a well-greased loaf
pan. Spread the meat over the rice. Cover
with the rest of the rice. Press down
firmly. Set in a pan of hot water ½ inch
deep. Bake 40 minutes at 350°. Turn out
on a platter and serve with
  Tomato Sauce (p. 94)
Serves 6.

Meat Pie

*Vary the amount of meat according to
what you have on hand. Cooked vegetables are a tasty addition — mushrooms,
peas, carrots, okra or green beans, for
example.*

Remove the fat from cooked meat. Cut
the meat in neat cubes. Cover with
gravy, adding water or consommé if
needed. Add, if you like, chopped onion,
celery or parsley.

Cook slowly until the meat is very tender. If the gravy is too thin, blend 2
tablespoons flour and ¼ cup water, stir
it in, and cook and stir until smooth.

Cover with a topping (below). Bake at
450° until brown (about 15 minutes).

Biscuit Topping. Cover with 2-inch
rounds made from Baking Powder Biscuit dough (p. 311). Or cover with packaged biscuits.

Pastry Topping. Roll out Plain Pastry
(p. 407). Cut to fit the top of the pie.
Place on the pie and make slits to let out
the steam. Or cut the pastry in strips and
lay them over the pie. Or bake the top
separately and put it on the heated pie
when you serve it.

Meat Croquettes and Timbales

Follow the recipes for Chicken Croquettes (p. 227) and Chicken Timbales (p. 227), using chopped cooked or canned meat. Season to taste, adding parsley and onion or herbs, if you like.

Rissoles

Follow the recipe for Turnovers (p. 426), using as the filling chopped cooked meat, chicken or ham, seasoned highly and moistened with gravy. Serve hot with gravy.

Savory Meat or Chicken Roll

Roll
    Baking Powder Biscuit dough (p. 311)
into an oblong ¼ inch thick. Mix
    Chopped cooked meat or chicken (1 cup or more)
    Gravy or cream, to moisten
    Chopped onion, green pepper or olives
    Salt and pepper to taste
Spread over the dough. Roll up and put in a buttered baking pan with the fold underneath. Bake at 425° until well browned (20 to 30 minutes). Cut in slices and serve with
    Gravy or Mushroom Sauce (p. 94) or Tomato Sauce (p. 94)
Serves 4 to 6.

Roast Beef Hash

Follow the recipe for Corned Beef Hash (p. 168), using chopped roast beef.

Julienne of Roast Beef

Serve for lunch or as an appetizer. For another way to present rare roast beef, see Roast Beef Stroganoff (p. 165).

Cut lean roast beef in match-shaped pieces. Moisten with sour cream. Season highly with Worcestershire or A-1 sauce. Serve with lemon wedges. Capers are good, too.

For added zest, stir in bits of pimiento, chopped green pepper or chopped ripe olives, or a little of each.

Cottage Pie

Also called Shepherd's Pie.

Chop or cube cooked beef, lamb or veal. Season with salt, pepper and onion juice or onion salt. Moisten with gravy. Put in a baking dish. Cover with a thin layer of mashed potato. Bake at 425° until thoroughly heated.

Beef, Lamb or Veal Creole. Add chopped green pepper and tomatoes, quartered. Arrange the mashed potato in a border in the baking dish.

Lamb Cardinal

Mix in a saucepan
    ¼ cup tarragon vinegar
    ¼ cup currant jelly
    ½ cup tomato catsup
Add
    1 cup cubed roast lamb
Simmer about 20 minutes and season to taste with
    Salt and paprika or cayenne
Serves 2 or 3.

Veal or Ham Cardinal. Substitute cooked veal or ham for lamb.

Curry of Lamb

If the dish is made the day before or must stand several hours before serving, it may need more curry. Taste and see. Lamb is traditional, but other meats can be prepared the same way — beef, pork, veal or mutton.

Melt in a deep pan
    2 tablespoons bacon fat or salad oil
Add and cook slowly until golden
    2 large onions, chopped
Stir in
    2 tablespoons flour
    ½ teaspoon sugar
    ½ teaspoon salt
    1 tablespoon curry powder (or more)
Add
    2 cups gravy or consommé
Cook and stir until thick. Taste and, if needed, add

Salt and pepper
Add
  3 to 4 cups cubed cooked lamb
Heat, but do not let the gravy boil. *Serves 6.*

To vary. Add ½ cup diced celery or 1 tablespoon chopped parsley. Or tuck in a bay leaf.

To serve. Have ready a large bowl of fluffy rice and small bowls of at least 4 of the condiments listed below. Each person takes a serving of rice, spoons curry over it, and sprinkles over the top some of the condiments.

  Crisp bacon, crumbled
  Sliced bananas sautéed in butter
  Mango chutney
  Toasted coconut flakes
  Chopped cooked egg whites
  Crumbled cooked egg yolks
  Chopped ham
  French-fried onions
  Chopped salted peanuts or almonds
  Green pepper, chopped fine
  Sliced pineapple, cut small

Lamb Hash

Remove the fat from cooked lamb. Cut the meat in small even pieces. Mix with an equal amount of cooked potatoes, cut small. Moisten with gravy and season to taste.

Put in a shallow baking dish and bake at 350° until thoroughly heated (about ½ hour). Sprinkle the top with cream, then with grated Parmesan cheese, and set under the broiler until the cheese melts.

Lamb Burgundy

A tasty way to present leftover roast lamb.

Cook 5 minutes
  2 tablespoons butter
  ¼ cup chopped onion
Add
  1 tomato, cut small, or 1 tablespoon tomato paste

  2 or 3 cups diced cooked lamb
  1 cup lamb gravy
  ½ cup Burgundy or claret
Season to taste with
  Salt, garlic salt, Worcestershire or rosemary
Simmer ½ hour, stirring occasionally. *Serves 3 or 4.*

To vary. Omit the tomato and season with prepared mustard and cayenne.

Parmesan Lamb. Make a border of mashed or Duchess Potatoes (p. 263) on a baking platter or in a shallow casserole. Sprinkle with melted butter. Pour the meat and gravy in the center. Sprinkle generously with grated Parmesan cheese. Bake at 400° until the potatoes are browned.

Lamb à la Breck

Butter a casserole. In it put
  1 cup cooked and drained macaroni
Mix and spread over the macaroni
  1 cup cooked lamb, chopped fine
  ½ teaspoon salt
  ⅛ teaspoon celery salt
  ⅛ teaspoon pepper
  Few drops onion juice
Mix and pour over the meat
  2 eggs, slightly beaten
  1½ cups milk
Bake at 350° until firm (to test custard, p. 363, Baked Custard). *Serves 4 to 6.*

Lamb Milanese

Put a layer of well-seasoned chopped cooked spinach in a shallow baking dish. Put sliced cooked lamb on the spinach. Pour Cheese Sauce (p. 91) over the meat.

Bake at 350° until well heated and lightly browned (20 to 30 minutes).

Veal or Ham Milanese. Substitute veal or ham for lamb.

Lamb-Stuffed Zucchini

Cooked chicken or veal may be substituted for lamb.

Cover zucchini with chicken broth and cook 10 minutes. Drain, reserving the broth. Cool and cut in half, lengthwise, or, if the zucchini are very large, in 2-inch slices. Scoop out some of the centers and stuff with well-seasoned chopped cooked lamb mixed with cooked rice and moistened with gravy.

Put in a casserole and sprinkle with buttered crumbs. Bake at 350° about 30 minutes. Serve with Lemon Sauce (p. 92), made with the reserved broth.

Veal Tetrazzini

Follow the recipe for Chicken Tetrazzini (p. 225), using veal in place of chicken and seasoning with thyme, tarragon or grated lemon rind instead of nutmeg.

Variety Meats

Brains, hearts, kidneys, liver and sweetbreads are high in protein, minerals and vitamins and therefore should be served frequently. It is important that these meats be absolutely fresh, so cook them promptly.

Brains

Calves' brains are considered the choicest. Allow about ¼ pound for each serving.

Precook before using in the following recipes. Hold under running water and remove the membranes. Cover with boiling water. Add 1 teaspoon salt and 1 tablespoon vinegar. Cover and simmer 20 minutes.

Drain, cover with cold water, let stand 10 minutes, and drain again.

Use at once or store in the refrigerator, well wrapped.

Brains with Black Butter. Slice cooked brains. Sauté in butter until delicately brown. Put on a hot platter. Add a little more butter to the pan and heat until dark brown. Add a little lemon juice and pour over the brains.

Brains Sautéed with Bacon. Slice cooked brains and sauté in bacon fat until delicately brown. Serve with crisp bacon. Watercress is an attractive garnish.

Scrambled Brains. Beat 4 eggs slightly. Add ½ pound cooked brains, broken in ½-inch pieces. Add 1 teaspoon salt, ¼

teaspoon pepper, 1 tablespoon Worcestershire and 2 tablespoons tomato catsup. Melt 2 tablespoons butter, add the mixture, and cook and stir over low heat until just firm.

Brains à la York. Break cooked brains in ½-inch pieces. Sprinkle with sherry (½ cup for 1 pound), cover, and let stand 1 hour. Add to 1½ cups Mushroom Sauce (p. 95). Serve on toast.

Hearts

Veal hearts weigh about ¾ pound, beef hearts 3 to 3½, lamb hearts ¼ pound, and pork hearts ½ pound. Allow about ⅓ pound per serving.

To prepare for cooking, cut out the coarse fibers at the top and inside the heart. Wash in cold water. A large beef heart may be tough — soak it overnight in 1 quart water and 2 tablespoons vinegar.

Hearts on Toast. Cover with boiling salted water. Simmer until tender. Drain, chop, season to taste, and serve on toast.

Pan-Broiled Hearts. Slice ½ inch thick. Sprinkle with flour or crumbs and cook slowly in butter (about 15 minutes).

Stuffed Heart

Prepare (above)
  2 veal hearts or 1 beef heart
Stuff with
  Bread Stuffing (p. 80)
Sprinkle with
  Salt and pepper
Roll in
  Flour
Brown evenly in
  Bacon fat
Put in a casserole. Add
  ½ cup boiling water
Cover. Bake 2 hours at 350°, adding more water from time to time if the liquid cooks away.

Put the heart on a serving dish and keep warm. Pour the broth into a saucepan. Stir in
  1 tablespoon flour, mixed with ¼ cup cold water
Bring to the boiling point. Season to taste and pour around the heart. *Serves 4 or 5.*

Fruit-Stuffed Heart. Instead of Bread Stuffing, fill with a mixture of pitted prunes and diced apricots.

Liver

Store fresh liver in the refrigerator loosely wrapped, and use within 24 hours. Store frozen liver in the freezer and thaw in the refrigerator before cooking. Calves' liver is the most expensive, but young beef, pork and lamb liver are excellent. One pound serves 4.

To prepare for cooking, wipe with a damp cloth and remove the thin outside skin and veins. If beef liver is tough, cover with boiling water, simmer 5 minutes, and drain.

Broiled Liver. Cut in slices ¼ to ½ inch thick. Broil 5 minutes. Spread with butter and sprinkle with salt and pepper.

Liver Sautéed in Butter. Sprinkle with salt and pepper. Dip in flour. Sauté in butter, allowing 2 tablespoons for 1 pound liver. Turn frequently. Cook ½-inch slices about 5 minutes (overcooking toughens liver) or until red color is gone. Serve with crisp bacon, or add a little sour cream to the juices in the pan, heat, and pour over the liver.

Liver and Bacon. Pan-fry bacon and drain on paper towel. Cook sliced liver (seasoned and dipped in flour) in bacon fat and serve with a piece of bacon on each slice.

Liver and Onions. Sauté thinly sliced onions in butter or bacon fat. Sauté the liver in the same fat and serve with the onions on top.

Liver Venetian Style

Popular even with those who think they don't like liver.

Heat in a skillet
  2 tablespoons salad oil
Add
  4 onions, sliced thin
Cook slowly until the onions are soft and golden. Add
  1 pound liver, cut with scissors in matchlike pieces
Cook and stir until the liver is just browned (about 3 minutes). Season to taste with
  Salt and pepper
Serves 4.

Liver Loaf

See also Liver Pâté (p. 56).

Cover with hot water
  1 pound beef or calves' liver
Simmer 5 minutes, drain, and reserve the stock. Chop the liver with
  ½ pound fresh pork
  1 onion
Add
  1 cup bread crumbs
  1 egg, well beaten
  1 teaspoon salt
  ¼ teaspoon pepper
  2 tablespoons tomato catsup
  Juice ½ lemon

Tomato juice or the reserved stock
to moisten
Mix thoroughly. Line a loaf pan with
Bacon
Pack in the mixture. Lay bacon over the
top. Bake 1 hour at 350°. Serve hot or
cold. *Serves 6.*

Kidneys

*For each serving, allow 1 veal kidney or
1½ lamb kidneys.*

To prepare for cooking, split and remove the white tubes and the fat. Cover
with cold water. Let stand 30 minutes.
Drain and pat dry with paper towels.
Cook briefly — overcooking toughens
kidneys.

Broiled Kidneys. Dip in French dressing.
Broil 10 minutes, turning frequently.
Serve on toast. Season melted butter with
salt, cayenne and lemon juice and pour
over the kidneys.

Pan-Broiled Kidneys. Cut in ¼-inch
slices. Sprinkle with salt and pepper.
Cook in butter until tender (about 5
minutes). Add a little lemon juice or
wine to the butter in the pan and pour
over the kidneys.

Kidneys en Brochette. Cover with stock
or consommé and cook 10 minutes.
Drain, reserving the stock. Slice and arrange on skewers with squares of bacon,
mushroom caps and quartered small tomatoes. Broil until the bacon is crisp,
turning to cook evenly. Baste with
French dressing several times. Serve with
slices of lemon or with Brown Sauce (p.
93) made with the stock.

Kidney Stew

See also Steak and Kidney Pie (p. 167).

Prepare (above)
1½ pounds veal or lamb kidneys
Cut veal kidneys in ½-inch slices. Split
lamb kidneys. Roll in flour.

Heat in a skillet
2 tablespoons bacon fat

Add and cook until onion is yellow
¼ cup chopped onion
1 clove garlic, split
Add the kidneys and cook and stir until
lightly browned. Add
4 peppercorns or ¼ teaspoon pepper
½ teaspoon salt
1 can consommé
½ cup red wine or Madeira
Cover and simmer until the kidneys are
tender (about 30 minutes). *Serves 4.*

Pressure-Cooked Kidney Stew. Brown
kidneys in a pressure pan and add other
ingredients as above. Cover and cook
12 minutes at 15 pounds pressure. Turn
off the heat and let the pressure drop
to normal.

Sweetbreads

*Sweetbreads are as tender and delicate
as chicken and combine pleasantly with
other ingredients. Veal sweetbreads are
the most expensive. They are marketed
fresh or frozen. Use fresh sweetbreads
promptly. Store frozen sweetbreads in
the freezer. One pound serves 4.*

To prepare for cooking. Cover with
boiling water. For each quart of water,
add 1 teaspoon salt and 2 tablespoons
vinegar or lemon juice. Cover and simmer 20 minutes. Drain. Cover with cold
water and let stand until cooled. Drain.
Slip off the thin membrane with the
fingers and cut out the dark tubes and
the thick membrane.

Sautéed Sweetbreads. Pan-fry in melted
butter until brown on all sides (about 5
minutes).

Braised Sweetbreads. Cut in slices. Sauté.
Cover wth Brown Gravy (p. 156), canned
or made with consommé (1 cup for each
pound). Heat. Season with sherry. Add,
if you like, sautéed mushrooms, cooked
vegetables or sliced olives.

Broiled Sweetbreads. Split and brush
with melted butter. Broil 5 minutes,
turning once.

Sweetbreads en Brochette. Cut in cubes and put on skewers, alternating with squares of bacon. Brush with melted butter or olive oil. Sprinkle with crumbs. Set the skewers on a cake tin so that the ends rest on the rim of the tin. Broil slowly 10 minutes or until the bacon is crisp, turning to brown evenly. Serve on the skewers or push onto plates.

Sweetbreads Country Style. Split or slice. Sprinkle with salt, pepper and flour. Put in a casserole. Sprinkle with melted butter, allowing 2 tablespoons to a pound of sweetbreads. Cover with thin slices of salt pork or bacon. Bake 25 minutes at 450°, basting twice during the cooking with the juices in the pan.

Sweetbread and Spinach Soufflé. Substitute cooked sweetbreads for ham in Ham and Spinach Soufflé (p. 189).

Creamed Sweetbreads

Delicious in place of chicken in any variation of Creamed Chicken (p. 224).

Prepare sweetbreads (p. 207). Cut in small pieces. For 1 pound of sweetbreads, prepare 1 cup of Cream Sauce (p. 90) or Velouté Sauce (p. 92) and season it highly with meat extract such as B–V. Heat the sweetbreads in the sauce. Serve on toast, in patty shells or on thin slices of broiled or baked ham, or fill individual baking dishes, sprinkle with buttered crumbs, and bake at 375° until brown.

Vary by doubling the amount of sauce and adding 1 cup cooked peas, sautéed mushrooms, asparagus tips, chopped ham or chicken. Sprinkle over the top toasted slivered almonds or buttered crumbs.

Tongue

Tongue is sold fresh, smoked, corned or pickled. In cans or jars, it is a convenient emergency shelf item. It is solid meat and yields 4 to 6 servings to the pound.

Follow directions on the wrapper in preparing smoked or pickled tongue.

To cook fresh tongue. Scrub with warm water. Cover with boiling water. Add 1 sliced onion, 2 bay leaves, 1 teaspoon salt, 6 peppercorns and 6 cloves. Cover and simmer until tender (2 to 4 hours, according to size). Drain, dip in cold water, slit the skin and peel it off. Cut off the bones and gristle at the thick end.

To serve cold tongue. Arrange thin slices on a platter. Garnish with watercress, cole slaw in lettuce cups, sliced tomatoes or stuffed olives. Other meats may be served with the tongue, such as sliced ham, chicken or cold roast meats. Serve with any of the sauces suggested for ham (p. 186) or with mustard, horseradish, currant jelly or sliced fruit.

Tongue and Mushroom Casserole

Melt
    2 tablespoons butter
Add
    1 pound mushrooms, sliced
Cook 5 minutes. Add
    2 cans undiluted mushroom soup
Heat. If you like a thinner sauce, add
    A little water
Season to taste with
    Nutmeg and sherry or brandy
Slice and put in a shallow baking dish
    1 pound cooked or canned tongue
Cover with the sauce and keep warm in a 300° oven. *Serves 6.*

To vary the seasoning, add herbs instead of nutmeg.

Braised Tongue

Cook (above)
    1 fresh tongue
Reserve the liquid for the sauce. Put the tongue in a deep pan. Add
    ⅓ cup diced carrot
    ⅓ cup diced celery
    ⅓ cup chopped onion
    1 sprig parsley
Melt
    ¼ cup butter

Cook until brown. Add
 ¼ cup flour
Brown well. Add
 4 cups of the reserved liquid (or part
  tomato juice)
Stir well. Season with
 Salt, pepper and Worcestershire
Pour over the tongue. Cover and bake
2 hours at 300°, turning after the first
hour. Remove the tongue and put it on
a hot platter. Strain the sauce (or not),
to serve with the tongue. *Serves 8 to 10.*

Sweet and Sour Tongue

An excellent dish for a buffet supper.

Put in a shallow pan
 1 lemon, sliced paper-thin
 1 cup mild cider vinegar
 1 cup dark brown sugar
 12 gingersnaps, rolled
 1 bay leaf
 ½ cup raisins
 1 cinnamon stick
 8 whole cloves
 ⅓ cup blanched almonds, halved
 1 small onion, sliced thin
Cook slowly 10 minutes. Add
 1 cooked or canned beef tongue, cut in
  thin slices
Heat thoroughly. *Serves 8 to 10.*

Tripe

*There are three kinds of tripe — honey-
comb (the choicest), pocket and smooth.
It is marketed fresh, pickled or canned.
Fresh tripe and pickled tripe need further cooking. Use fresh tripe within 24
hours. Store it, covered, in the refrigerator. Canned tripe is ready to heat and
serve. One pound serves 4 or 5.*

Cover with cold water, bring to the boiling point and drain. Cover with boiling
salted water. Simmer until tender (1
hour or more). For additional flavor,
add, after the first half-hour, 1 clove
garlic (split) or ¼ cup chopped onion, a
few sprigs parsley and ½ cup chopped
celery. Drain, reserving the liquid.

Serve with Tomato Sauce (p. 94) or
Espagnole Sauce (p. 93) made with the
reserved liquid.

Broiled Tripe. Cut cooked tripe in
pieces for serving. Dip in fine cracker
dust, then in olive oil or melted butter.
Place, smooth side up, on the broiler
rack 3 inches from the heat. Broil 5
minutes. Turn and broil until lightly
browned (about 5 minutes). Serve,
honeycomb side up, spread with butter
and seasoned with salt and pepper.
Good with broiled tomato slices and
bacon as a mixed grill.

Tripe Lyonnaise

Cook 5 minutes over moderate heat
 2 tablespoons butter
 1 tablespoon chopped onion
Add
 1 pound cooked tripe, cut in pieces
  about ½ by 2 inches
Cook 5 minutes. Sprinkle with
 Salt, pepper, lemon juice and
  chopped parsley
Serves 4.

Tripe in Batter

Cut cooked fresh or pickled tripe in 1½-
inch squares. Dip in batter (below).
Sauté in bacon fat or fry in deep fat at
370°. Serve with sliced lemon and chili
sauce.

Batter for tripe. Sift 1 cup flour with ¼
teaspoon salt and 1 teaspoon baking
powder. Beat 1 egg, add ⅓ cup milk
or water and 1 teaspoon salad oil or
melted butter. Stir into the flour and
beat until smooth.

Poultry and Game Birds

Poultry can be prepared in so many ways that it is one of our most valuable foods. It is available at popular prices throughout the year — fresh or frozen, whole or in parts.

Top-quality birds are plump, with broad meaty breasts. Young poultry has soft thin skin, older birds have coarse thick skin. Capons and caponettes are especially tender and meaty. **Fowl** is a good buy for salads and creamed dishes, but must be cooked by moist heat to become tender.

For each person to be served, buy ¾ to 1 pound of chicken, guinea chicken or turkey, 1 to 1½ pounds of duck or goose, and 1 pigeon, squab or small Cornish game hen. Larger birds have more meat in proportion to bone and so are often a more economical buy.

Leftovers are no problem. There are many easy and delectable recipes using cooked chicken or turkey (pp. 223–228).

Plucking and cleaning. Modern markets sell poultry ready to cook, so that this old and tedious task is over for most of us. However, the United States Department of Agriculture and State Extension Services have bulletins describing the process and also telling how to cut up a bird for fricasseeing or broiling. Poultry shears are a convenience for cutting poultry in pieces.

Game birds include grouse, partridge, pheasant, wild duck, wild goose, quail, woodcock, snipe and plover. The flesh of game birds, except partridge and quail, is dark in color, and all, except some wild ducks and geese, contain less fat than domestic poultry.

Rabbit is included here because it is cooked like chicken. Young and tender rabbits, domesticated or wild, have soft ears and paws, short necks and smooth sharp claws.

To Prepare Poultry for Cooking

If all the feathers have not been removed, pull them out with tweezers or a small sharp knife and burn off the fine hairs over the gas flame or with burning paper. Remove any red, spongy bits that may remain inside the bird.

Let cold water run through the bird, but do not soak it in water. Wipe inside and outside.

If the giblets have not been cleaned at the market, remove the thin membrane, the arteries, veins, and clotted blood around the heart. Separate the gall bladder from the liver, cutting off and discarding any of the liver which has a greenish tinge. Cut the fat and membranes from the gizzard. Make a gash through the thickest part of the gizzard, and cut as far as the inner lining, being careful not to pierce it. Remove the inner sac and discard it. Wash the giblets.

To stuff. Stuffing recipes are on pp. 80–82. Packaged stuffings are convenient and good. Prepare the stuffing the day before, if you like, but do not stuff the bird until just before you roast it.

Put the stuffing into the neck opening by spoonfuls, using enough to fill the skin so that the bird will look plump when served. Cracker stuffing expands during cooking, so fill more loosely. Put the rest of the stuffing in the body. Fasten with skewers and lace with string.

To truss. Draw the thighs close to the body. Tie firmly to the tail with string. Lace the string along the skewers and tie.

Place the wings close to the body and hold them in place with a long skewer. Draw the neck skin under the back and fasten it with a toothpick.

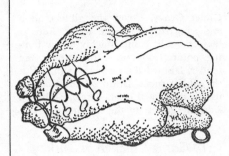

Chicken and Turkey

Roast Chicken or Capon

Allow ¾ to 1 pound as purchased per person. Follow directions on the package when using a frozen bird.

Select a plump, meaty bird for roasting, either a young roasting chicken or a capon. Clean, stuff and truss (above).

Allow about 4 cups of stuffing for a 4-pound chicken. Celery (p. 81), Corn Bread (p. 80), and Mushroom Stuffing (p. 81) are particularly delicious for chicken.

Place, breast side up, on a rack in an open roasting pan. Rub the skin with soft butter or salad oil. Put over the bird a piece of foil large enough to cover it loosely. Do not let the foil touch the heating unit in an electric oven.

Roast at 325° until tender. Test by moving the drumstick gently. When the bird is done, the joint will move easily. A 3-pound chicken will take 1½ to 2 hours, a 4-pound chicken about 3 hours, and a 6-pound chicken about 4. Times are approximate. Tender birds may take a shorter time, so begin to test for doneness well before the suggested time is up so that you will not overcook the chicken. Half an hour before the roasting time is up, turn back the foil so that the skin will brown prettily.

Keep the bird warm while you make the gravy. It will be easier to carve if it stands 20 minutes or so after roasting.

Chicken or Turkey Gravy

If there is much fat in the pan, pour it off into a cup. If you plan to make 1 cup of gravy, pour about ¼ cup of fat back into the pan. Giblet Gravy, p. 212.

Pan Gravy. Add 1 cup boiling water. Set over moderate heat. Scrape and stir to get the good brown glaze. Taste, and add salt and pepper if needed. Strain.

Thickened Gravy. Stir in 2 tablespoons flour. Set the pan over moderate heat and stir and scrape until the flour and fat are smoothly blended and nicely browned. Add 1 cup cold water, milk or cream. Cook and stir until smooth. Season to taste. Strain or not, as you prefer.

Giblet Gravy. Cover the giblets, neck and wing tips with cold water. Add ½ teaspoon salt. Bring quickly to the boiling point. Cook until the giblets are tender. Discard the neck and wings. Cut the giblets small. Drain off the stock to use in making thickened gravy (above). Add the giblets to the finished gravy.

To Carve Chicken or Turkey

The bird should be on the platter breast up, legs to the right. Insert the carving fork across the breastbone, hold it firmly in the left hand, and with the carving knife in the right hand cut through the skin between the leg and body, close to the body. Hold the leg by the bone and pull it away from the body. Find the joint with the tip of the knife and cut through it. Cut through the joint which separates the drumstick from the second joint. Cut off the wing.

Carve chicken and turkey slices sloping downward

Carve the breast meat in thin slices. Just above the tail, on each side of the backbone, are two small, oyster-shaped pieces of dark meat, which are delicious tidbits.

Roast Turkey

Allow 1 to 1½ pounds per person. This is a generous amount which will usually provide leftovers for another meal.

New breeds have been developed so that you can buy a meaty turkey even if you buy a small one. A hen turkey has more breast meat than a tom. A half turkey is often an economy buy. Roast it cut side

down. Thaw frozen turkeys to room temperature overnight before stuffing.

Stuff and truss (p. 210). Allow 8 cups of stuffing for a 10-pound turkey. Use Bread Stuffing (p. 80) or any of the following stuffings (pp. 81–82): Apple and Prune; Celery; Chestnut; Giblet; New England; Oyster; Sausage and Chestnut.

Follow directions for roasting chicken (p. 211). A turkey weighing 8 to 12 pounds will take 4 to 5 hours; one 12 to 16 pounds will take 5 to 6 hours (breast side down for the first 2 hours); larger birds take up to 7 hours. Roast large birds breast side down so that they will not dry out. Carving will be easier if the roasting is finished a half-hour before serving time. Set the roasted turkey in a warm place while you make the gravy (p. 211).

Herbed Roast Chicken

This French method is delicious. Vary it by using dill or a sprig of rosemary or tarragon in place of thyme.

Prepare for roasting
   2½ to 3 pound chicken
Put inside the chicken
   1 carrot, sliced
   1 teaspoon dried thyme
   ⅓ teaspoon salt
   1 tablespoon butter
Tie or skewer the legs and wings to the body. Put the chicken in a shallow roasting pan. Lay over the breast
   3 slices bacon
Dot the chicken with
   2 tablespoons butter
Dust with
   Salt, paprika and thyme
Roast at 450° until lightly browned, then reduce the heat to 350° and roast until tender (total time up to 1¾ hours).

Mix
   ½ cup beef bouillon
   ¼ cup water
Spoon some over the chicken every 15 minutes during the cooking.

Put the roasted chicken on a hot platter and remove the skewers or string. To the

drippings in the pan add
   Juice of 1 lemon
Scrape and stir, heat, season to taste, and serve as a sauce with the chicken. *Serves 4.*

Broiled Chicken

Allow ½ or ¼ chicken per person, depending on the size of the bird.

Order young chicken split or quartered for broiling.

Preheat the broiler oven to 550°. Place the broiler rack so that the top of the chicken will be 4 inches from the heat. Place the chicken on the rack, skin side down. Sprinkle with salt and pepper. Brush with salad oil or melted butter or other fat.

Broil 10 minutes. Turn over, brush with fat, and broil 10 minutes. Turn again and continue cooking until the chicken is very tender (35 to 60 minutes in all, depending on size of chicken). Dot with butter 3 times during broiling.

Put on a hot platter. Pour the drippings from the pan over the chicken.

To vary flavor. Sprinkle each broiler with a few drops of onion juice and a few grains of ginger before broiling, or spread sparingly with anchovy paste mixed with a little prepared mustard, or slice ripe olives over the chickens.

Sally's Broiled Chicken. Broil on each side only long enough to brown, then transfer to a baking pan. Add enough water or chicken stock to the pan to keep the chicken from burning. Dot with butter or put strips of bacon on each piece of chicken. Cover. Bake at 300° until tender (30 minutes or longer). Baste several times with the liquid in the pan. The chicken will be very tender.

Orange Broiled Chicken. Make a basting sauce of ½ cup orange juice, ½ cup salad oil, 3 tablespoons grated orange rind, and salt, mustard, paprika and

Tabasco to taste. Brush the chickens with it before broiling and when you turn them. Baste with the sauce several times during broiling.

Barbecued Chicken

For outdoor cooking.

Take the bird out of the refrigerator 2 or 3 hours before cooking. Truss securely. Rub all over with fat or oil. Put on a revolving spit or turn often during cooking. Roast over hot coals about 30 minutes to the pound, basting often with Herbed Barbecue Sauce (p. 100).

Barbecued Caponette or Turkey may be cooked the same way.

Delmonico's Deviled Chicken

Broil the chicken 8 minutes (above). For each broiler, cream ¼ cup butter with 1 teaspoon prepared mustard, ½ teaspoon salt, 1 teaspoon vinegar and ½ teaspoon paprika. Spread over the bird.

Put the chicken in a baking pan and sprinkle with ¾ cup soft buttered crumbs. Bake at 350° until the chicken is tender and the crumbs are brown (about 30 minutes).

Barbecued Broilers

Allow ½ broiler or ¼ (or more) frying chicken per person.

Broiler halves or quartered frying chickens are tasty and tender cooked this way.

Dip the pieces in Chicken Barbecue Sauce (p. 100) and put on the grill, skin side up. Turn about every 8 minutes. Each time you turn them, brush a little of the sauce over them. They will be done in about 45 minutes. To test, take hold of the leg bone and twist slightly. If the joint moves easily, the chicken is done.

Oven-Broiled Chicken

No added fat for this method.

Put pieces of chicken in a shallow baking dish in a single layer, skin side up. Cover tightly with a piece of heavy aluminum foil. Bake 30 minutes at 325°. Remove the foil and broil the chicken two inches from the heat until it is browned (about 15 minutes).

Sprinkle with salt, pepper and, if you like, a little ginger.

Fried Chicken
(in deep fat)

Sprinkle chicken halves (if very small) or quarters with salt and pepper. Dip in Fritter Batter (p. 429).

Fry until golden-brown in deep fat heated to 350° (about 15 minutes). Drain on a paper towel.

For very tender chicken, but not as crisp, fry only 10 minutes, drain, put on a rack in a baking pan, cover, and bake 1 hour at 325°.

Serve with any of the following:

Chicken Gravy (p. 211), made with chicken stock and cream or tomato juice.

Cream Gravy (*traditional with Southern Fried Chicken*). Use half milk and half cream as the liquid.

Hungarian Paprika Sauce. Cook 2 sliced onions in 4 tablespoons butter until yellow, stir in 1 tablespoon flour, ½ teaspoon salt and 1 tablespoon paprika. Stir in 1 cup sour cream and cook until smooth.

Pan-Fried Chicken

Order young broilers cut in halves, fryers or small young roasting chicken cut in serving-size pieces. Dip in cold water or milk. Drain but do not wipe dry. Sprinkle with salt and pepper. Coat with flour by shaking in a paper bag with about ½ cup flour.

Melt fat in a heavy frying pan to a depth of ½ to 1 inch. For delicious flavor use ⅓ butter and ⅔ olive oil, lard or vegetable fat, but any cooking fat or salad oil is satisfactory. Heat fat well but not so hot that it smokes.

Put in the chicken. Brown quickly on all sides. Cook until tender (30 minutes to 1 hour, depending on the size of the bird).

For a crisp crust, cover, cook half the required time, and remove the cover for the last half of cooking.

For a tender crust, cook uncovered half the time, then cover to finish cooking.

Serve with any of the sauces suggested under Fried Chicken (above).

Southern Fried Chicken. *Cream Gravy (above) is traditional.* Dip pieces of chicken in batter (p. 429). Or, for a very crisp crust, dip in water or milk, then coat as thickly as possible with flour to which has been added baking powder (½ teaspoon to each cup of flour). Have the fat 1½ to 2 inches deep.

Maryland Fried Chicken. Dip floured chicken in slightly beaten egg mixed with 2 tablespoons cold water, then in soft bread crumbs. Have the fat 1½ to 2 inches deep.

Baked Crisp Chicken. Brown the chicken quickly on both sides. Place in a single layer in a baking dish. Brush generously with melted butter or salad oil. Bake at 350° until tender (about 40 minutes). After the first 15 minutes, brush with butter or oil and again when the chicken is ready to serve.

Savory Fried Chicken

Dip in flour
    2 young chickens, cut in pieces
Pan-fry (above). Put the pieces in a casserole and cover with
    ¼ cup chopped onion
    ¼ cup chopped celery
    1 tablespoon chopped green pepper

1½ cups milk, tomatoes or tomato
  juice
Sprinkle with
  Salt and pepper
  Orégano or thyme, if liked
Cover and bake 1 hour at 325°. Uncover
and bake 10 minutes longer. *Serves 4 or 5.*

Fried Chicken with Mushrooms. Slice
and sauté ½ pound mushrooms and add
to the casserole 20 minutes before the
chicken is done.

Chicken or Turkey Breasts

One pound serves 2 or 3.

Cut chicken breasts in half, turkey
breasts in serving-size pieces. Bone, and
pound to flatten slightly. Sprinkle with
salt and pepper and roll in flour.

Sautéed. Sauté in butter or salad oil
until delicately browned. Cover and cook
slowly until tender.

Baked. Put in a pan and dot with 2 tablespoons butter. Cover with foil and bake
at 375° until tender (about 20 minutes).

Pressure-cooked. Brown in butter or
bacon fat in a pressure saucepan. Season
with salt and pepper. Add ¼ cup boiling water. Bring to 15 pounds pressure
and cook 5 minutes. Let the pressure
drop normally. Add ½ cup cream to the
juices, stir, and pour over the fillets.

Suprême of Chicken or Turkey. Cook
(above) and serve on cutlet-shaped pieces
of hot broiled ham. Garnish the top of
each with 3 asparagus tips or a large
broiled mushroom cap. Surround with
Suprême Sauce (p. 92).

Chicken or Turkey Lake Como. After
dipping in flour, dip in slightly beaten
egg mixed with 1 tablespoon water, then
in ¼ cup grated Parmesan cheese mixed
with ½ cup dry bread crumbs. Sauté the
chicken and serve on a layer of chopped
spinach seasoned with lemon juice and
nutmeg. Add a little cream or wine to
the juices in the pan, heat, and pour over
the chicken.

Baked Chicken Maryland

*The Maryland custom is to pour Cream
Sauce (p. 90) over the chicken, but it is
moist and tasty without a sauce.*

Trim chicken pieces (all breasts, or both
white and dark meat), removing loose
ends of skin. Bone or not, as you like.
Shake in a paper bag with flour, salt and
pepper. For 6 or 8 pieces, break an egg
into a pie pan, add 2 tablespoons water,
and beat with a fork until blended. Dip
the chicken pieces into the egg, then
coat well with crumbs. Place in a well-
greased shallow baking pan.

Bake at 400° until tender (35 to 50 minutes), basting several times with melted
butter (⅓ cup for 6 to 8 pieces).

Chicken Kiev

*A famous recipe. Be careful when you
cut into the cooked chicken rolls — the
butter may spurt out.*

Cut in half
  2 chicken breasts
Bone and skin. Place each piece between
sheets of wax paper and pound with a
rolling pin until thin. Peel off the paper.
Season with
  Salt, pepper, and mace or rosemary
Cream together
  ¼ pound butter (preferably unsalted)
  Juice and grated rind of ½ lemon
  1 tablespoon finely chopped parsley
Shape into a roll and chill in the refrigerator to harden; then cut into 4 finger-
shaped pieces and put one on each piece
of chicken. Roll up like a package, folding in the ends. Roll lightly in
  Flour, salt and pepper
Put in a pie pan
  1 egg
  2 tablespoons water
Beat with a fork until blended. Dip the
chicken rolls in the egg, then in
  Bread crumbs
Chill 1 hour or more before frying. Fry
(p. 5) in deep fat (350°) until golden-
brown (about 7 minutes). *Serves 4.*

Stuffed Chicken Rolls

Cut chicken breasts in half. Bone, skin, and pound (see Chicken Kiev, p. 215).

Put stuffing (below) on each piece of chicken and fold tightly to make a package. Place in a buttered baking dish. Brush with melted butter. Sprinkle with fine crumbs. Pour a little cream into the dish. Bake at 350° until tender (about ½ hour).

For the stuffing, use Duxelles (p. 249); or buttered crumbs (p. 7) seasoned with salt, pepper, dillseed or marjoram, chopped chives and grated lemon rind. Add more melted butter if needed.

Poached (Boiled) Chicken, Fowl or Capon

Less dry in a salad than roast chicken. Also delicious served hot with a sauce.

Truss but do not stuff. Put in a deep kettle. Add boiling water to half cover the bird. Cover and simmer until tender (2 to 3 hours). Turn occasionally. Add salt the last hour of cooking.

Drain off the liquid and strain it to use in the sauce or for soup.

Chicken à la Providence. Remove the cooked chicken and boil the strained liquid until it is reduced to 2 cups. Thicken with 2 tablespoons each of butter and flour cooked together. Just before serving, stir in 2 egg yolks, slightly beaten, and 1 teaspoon lemon juice. Season with salt, pepper and nutmeg.

Place the chicken on a hot platter, pour the sauce around it, and sprinkle with chopped parsley. Carve like roast chicken.

To vary, add to the sauce sliced sautéed mushrooms or ½ cup cubed cooked carrots and ½ cup cooked peas.

Herbed Chicken. Add to the cooking water ½ onion, sliced, 1 small carrot, cubed, 2 sprigs thyme, 1 sprig parsley and 1 bay leaf.

Poached Chicken or Turkey Breasts

Bone and skin chicken or turkey breasts. Cut chicken breasts in halves, turkey breasts in serving-size pieces. Put in a heavy pan and cover with chicken broth. Simmer, covered, until tender (½ hour or more). Drain, reserving the liquid, and keep warm.

Using the reserved liquid, make Soubise (p. 92), Mushroom Velouté (p. 92) or Suprême Sauce (p. 92).

Place the chicken on a platter and coat with the sauce. For an attractive touch, use a heatproof platter and brown the chicken lightly under the broiler.

Garnish with bits of pimiento or truffle or with a light sprinkling of paprika or chopped parsley. Arrange around the platter small browned potatoes and a colorful vegetable such as peas or tiny whole carrots or whole green beans. Pass extra sauce to spoon over the chicken.

Smothered Chicken

Excellent party fare, since you can prepare the chicken in advance and keep it warm in a casserole. Serving is simple too, and you need only to add a tossed salad and crusty rolls or French bread for an interesting and savory meal.

Select chicken breasts, chicken thighs, split broilers or fryers, or young roasting chickens cut in pieces. Bone or not. Sprinkle with salt, pepper and flour. Melt butter or salad oil in a heavy pan, using about ½ cup for 2 broilers. Put in the pieces of chicken and brown well on all sides. Cover and cook slowly until tender (30 to 60 minutes).

Smothered Chicken with a Sauce. Take the cooked chicken out of the pan and keep warm. Add a small amount of liquid to the pan. The liquid may be water, stock, wine, tomato juice or a mixture of several. Scrape and stir to get the good brown glaze. Heat and season to taste. Pour over the chicken.

Smothered Chicken with Sour Cream. Take the cooked chicken out of the pan. To the juices in the pan add sour cream (1 cup for 2 broilers). Stir well. Heat quickly, but do not boil. Season to taste, pour over the chicken, and serve immediately.

Smothered Chicken Swedish Style. Omit the butter. Sprinkle the chicken sparingly with flour and cook in 1 cup heavy cream (adding more cream if needed, while browning). Serve with gravy made with 3 tablespoons of the fat remaining in the pan, 3 tablespoons flour, 1½ cups chicken stock and ½ cup heavy cream.

Chicken Contadine

Put in a large pan
   2 onions, chopped fine
   ½ cup butter or salad oil
Cook slowly until the onions are soft. Add
   2 young chickens, quartered
Cook slowly until the chickens are browned. Remove the pieces of chicken. Add to the pan
   ½ cup Italian vermouth
Light with a match, and when the flame dies down, add
   1 teaspoon tomato paste
   ⅛ teaspoon cinnamon
   1 teaspoon salt
Stir well, add the chicken, cover, and cook slowly until tender (30 to 60 minutes). *Serves 6.*

Chicken Cacciatora

A famous Italian dish with many possible variations. Add chopped green peppers, mushrooms or pimientos, if you like. Add rosemary, thyme, a bit of bay leaf or chopped parsley to vary the seasoning.

Have ready
   2 young chickens, quartered, or
      4-pound chicken, cut in pieces

Sprinkle with
   Salt, pepper and flour
Brown lightly in
   ¼ cup olive or salad oil, butter or chicken fat
Take the chicken out of the pan. To the juices in the pan add
   1 large onion, chopped fine
   1 stalk celery, chopped fine
   1 clove garlic
Stir and cook until the onion is yellow. Add the chicken and
   ¼ teaspoon sugar
   Pinch of allspice or cinnamon
   ¼ cup sherry or ½ cup red wine
Cook and stir 5 minutes. Remove the garlic. Add to the pan
   1 cup tomato juice or 3 tomatoes, cut in pieces
Cover and cook slowly until the chicken is tender (40 to 60 minutes). If necessary, add more liquid from time to time, using
   Chicken broth, tomato juice, red wine or water
Season to taste. *Serves 6.*

Coq au Vin

Melt in a large pan
   ¼ pound butter
Dredge with flour
   5-pound roasting chicken, cut in serving pieces
Brown the chicken thoroughly in the butter; then put the chicken and juices in a large casserole and add
   ½ cup chopped ham
   10 small white onions
   1 crushed clove garlic
   ¼ teaspoon thyme
   1 sprig parsley
   1 bay leaf
   8 whole mushrooms
   Salt and pepper to taste
Pour over the chicken
   2 ounces warm Cognac
Light the Cognac with a match. When the flame dies down add
   1 cup red wine
Cover. Bake at 275° until the chicken is tender (about 2½ hours). *Serves 6.*

Chicken Marengo

Have ready
 4-pound chicken, cut in pieces
Sprinkle with
 Salt, pepper and flour
Brown in
 ¼ cup olive or salad oil
Take the chicken out of the pan and set aside. Cook in the pan juices
 1 chopped onion
 ½ clove garlic
Add the pieces of chicken and
 ¼ cup dry white wine
 ½ cup stewed or chopped fresh tomatoes
 8 small whole mushroom caps or ½ cup sliced mushrooms
Cover closely and cook slowly until tender (40 to 60 minutes). *Serves 6.*

Mexican Chicken

Have ready
 2 young chickens, cut in pieces
Sprinkle with
 Salt and pepper
Brown in
 3 tablespoons oil or chicken fat
Add
 1 teaspoon salt
 8 canned pimientos, puréed
 1 chopped onion
 2 crushed cloves garlic
 Boiling water to cover
Cover and cook slowly until the chicken is tender (about 1 hour). Put the chicken on a serving dish.

Cook together until smooth
 3 tablespoons butter
 3 tablespoons flour
Thicken the juices in the pan with this mixture and pour over the chicken. *Serves 6.*

Chicken Paprika

Cook together 10 minutes
 1 tablespoon chicken fat or butter
 3 red onions, cut fine
Stir in
 1 tablespoon paprika

Cook until red. Add
 1 young roasting chicken, cut in pieces, or 2 broilers, quartered
 1 teaspoon vinegar
 ¼ teaspoon sugar
 Salt to taste
Cover and cook slowly 20 minutes. Sprinkle with
 2 teaspoons flour
Add
 ½ cup chicken stock or tomato juice
Cover and cook slowly until the chicken is tender (20 to 30 minutes), adding more stock or water if necessary to keep the chicken from sticking. Remove the chicken and take off the skin. Strain the sauce. Add the pieces of chicken. Stir in
 ½ cup sour cream
Reheat. Season to taste. *Serves 4 to 6.*

Viennese Chicken

Cook together in a large pan
 2 tablespoons butter
 1 minced onion
When the onion is yellow, add
 1 roasting chicken, cut in serving pieces
Cook until the chicken is brown, turning to brown evenly. Add
 1 green pepper, chopped
 2 carrots, chopped
 6 mushrooms, chopped
 1 fresh tomato or ¼ cup canned tomatoes
 1 cup water
 Salt and paprika
Cover and simmer until tender (about 1 hour). Mix together
 1 tablespoon flour
 ½ cup sour cream
Stir into the chicken and sauce. Cook and stir 3 minutes. *Serves 6.*

Chicken Fricassee

Browning the chicken first improves both flavor and appearance, but many cooks omit this step. For the most appetizing flavor, make the fricassee a day ahead.

Melt in a deep pan
 ¼ cup fat

Add
   5-pound stewing chicken, cut for fricassee

Brown the pieces evenly on all sides, adding more fat if necessary. Add
   Boiling water to cover
   ½ small onion, sliced
   Few stalks or tops celery
   1 small carrot, sliced
   Bay leaf
   3 peppercorns or ⅛ teaspoon pepper

Cover and let simmer over low heat.

After the chicken has cooked 45 minutes, add
   2 teaspoons salt

Cover and continue cooking until the chicken is tender when tried with a fork (another 45 minutes). Remove from the heat and let stand until the fat collects on the surface. Spoon off the fat and set it aside. Remove the chicken and keep it warm.

Melt
   ¼ cup chicken fat

Blend in
   ¼ cup flour

Add slowly, stirring constantly
   2 cups chicken broth or broth and milk or cream

Heat to the boiling point, stirring so that it will thicken evenly. Season to taste with
   Salt and pepper
   Few drops Worcestershire or lemon juice, if liked

Pour some of the sauce over the chicken and pass the rest in a bowl. Serve with hot Baking Powder Biscuits (p. 311), Dumplings (p. 166), toast, fluffy rice or mashed potatoes. *Serves 6.*

For a richer sauce, beat 1 or 2 egg yolks slightly, add ½ cup cream, and stir in just before serving.

Chicken Fricassee with Mushrooms. Add 1 cup sliced sautéed mushrooms or put a row of sautéed mushroom caps around the platter.

Chicken Fricassee with Meat Balls. Mix ½ pound chopped beef with 1 slice bread ½ inch thick soaked in water, ½ teaspoon salt, a few drops of onion juice, a few grains of ginger. Form into small balls. Bring the sauce to the boiling point, add the meat balls, cover closely, turn off the heat, and let stand 15 minutes. Reheat if necessary.

Chicken Pie

Follow the recipe for Chicken Fricassee (above) without browning the chicken. Before making the sauce, remove the skin and bones from the pieces of chicken. Put the chicken in a baking dish not more than 3 inches deep. Add cooked vegetables, if you like, such as potato balls, peas or carrots, and pour the sauce over the chicken. Cool to room temperature but do not chill.

Roll out Plain Pastry (p. 407). Cut a piece to fit the top of the dish, make cuts in it to let out the steam as the pie bakes, and lay it over the pie. Or cover the pie with crisscross strips of pastry. Bake extra pastry in rounds or diamonds to serve with second helpings.

Bake 10 minutes at 450°. Reduce the heat to 350° and bake 15 minutes longer or until the pastry is a delicate brown. *Serves 6.*

Louisburg Chicken Pie. Add 12 mushroom caps, sliced and sautéed in butter, ½ pound sausage meat, made into tiny balls and sautéed, and 1 cup tiny potato balls, cooked. *Serves 8.*

Chicken Pie Country Style. Instead of a pastry top, cover with Baking Powder Biscuit mixture (p. 311) rolled ½ inch thick. Cut a 2-inch round from the center to allow the steam to escape during the baking. Or cut the dough in small rounds and place close together over the top of the pie. Bake extra biscuits for second servings. Bake at 450° until brown (15 to 20 minutes).

Chicken Casserole

Cut in pieces for serving
2 small chickens
Put in a casserole. Sprinkle with
Salt and pepper
Melted butter
Add boiling water until 1 inch deep.
Cover. Bake at 375° until tender (1 hour
or more).

Pour over the chicken
1 cup chicken gravy, cream or undiluted canned mushroom or chicken
soup
Cook 10 minutes longer. Season to taste.
Serves 4 or 5.

To vary, add sliced sautéed mushrooms
or strips of pimiento.

Chicken and Vegetable Casserole. After
baking ½ hour, add young whole carrots,
peas, potato balls or whole green beans,
or a combination of several vegetables.
Parboil carrots, potatoes and beans 10
minutes before adding to the casserole.

Chicken and Onion Stew

Put in a large pan
1 chicken, cut for fricassee
12 tiny onions
Barely cover with water. Cover and cook
slowly until tender (1 to 1½ hours). Take
the chicken and onions out of the stock
and keep them warm. Boil the stock until
it is reduced to one cup.
Melt
1 tablespoon butter or chicken fat
Add
2 tablespoons flour
Stir in slowly the stock and
½ cup heavy cream
Just before serving, add
1 egg yolk, slightly beaten
Salt and pepper to taste
Lemon juice to taste
Heat thoroughly. Pour the sauce over
the chicken and onions. *Serves 4 or 5.*

For a more savory stew, add chopped
parsley, chopped celery and a pinch of
thyme or marjoram.

Brunswick Stew

*Vary this famous Southern dish in many
ways. It is often made in huge quantities
for an out-of-doors get-together and can
be made of squirrel and rabbit as well as
stewing chicken. Sometimes pork spareribs and pieces of stewing beef are
cooked with the chicken, and other vegetables are added, such as green beans,
okra, diced potatoes and peas.*

Cover with boiling water
1 stewing chicken, cut in pieces
Cover and let simmer over low heat for
45 minutes. Add
2 teaspoons salt
Cover and continue cooking until tender
(about another 45 minutes). Take out
the pieces of chicken. Remove the bones
and cut the meat in 1-inch pieces. Put
back in the kettle and add
1 can condensed tomato soup, 3 tomatoes or 1 cup canned tomatoes
1 onion, sliced thin
1 cup green lima beans
3 potatoes, sliced thin
1 tablespoon sugar
Salt and pepper
Cook until the beans and potatoes are
tender. Add
1 cup corn, cut from the cob, or canned
whole-kernel corn
¼ pound butter
Cook 5 minutes. *Serves 6 to 8.*

Paella

*This tasty Spanish dish is an ideal cas-
serole supper for company. Vary it by
adding canned chick peas and cooked
green peas. As convenient, add any of
the following: thin strips of ham, chunks
of cooked lobster meat, or mussels. Stir
in 1 teaspoon capers for added zest.*

Heat in a large pan
¼ cup olive oil
Add
3 to 5 pound chicken, cut in serving
pieces
Brown well on all sides. Add
¼ cup water
1 teaspoon orégano
Cover and cook until the chicken is

tender (30 minutes or more). Remove the pieces of chicken and set them aside. To the juices in the pan, add

   ½ cup chopped onion
   1 split clove garlic

Cook slowly 5 minutes. Melt in a pan

   3 tablespoons butter

Add

   2 cups uncooked rice
   Pinch of saffron (not more than ¼ teaspoon)

Stir over low heat 5 minutes. Add

   4 cups chicken broth or water

Bring to the boiling point, cover, and cook slowly 17 minutes. Stir into the pan with the onion. Arrange in layers in a 4-quart casserole the rice, chicken and

   1 pound shrimp, cooked and shelled
   12 thin slices Italian or Spanish sausage or 1 cup chopped ham
   2 dozen cherrystone clams (in the shell)

Have a few of the clams on top. Bake at 350° until thoroughly heated and the clams are open. *Serves 8 generously.*

Chicken Gumbo

See also Chicken Gumbo Soup (p. 74).

Prepare for cooking

   3-pound chicken, cut in pieces

Sprinkle with

   Salt and pepper

Melt in a large pan

   3 tablespoons bacon fat

Brown the chicken thoroughly in the fat and set it aside. Add to the pan

   ½ onion, chopped

Cook until yellow. Add

   Sprig parsley
   4 cups sliced okra, cooked or canned
   ¼ sweet red pepper, chopped, or 1 pimiento, chopped

Cover and cook slowly 15 minutes. Add the chicken pieces and

   1½ cups chopped tomatoes, fresh or canned
   3 cups boiling water
   1½ teaspoons salt

Cover and cook slowly until the chicken is tender (40 minutes or more). Stir in

   1 cup boiled rice

Serves 4.

Chicken Californian

For added zest, add ⅓ cup capers.

Put in a deep pan

   ½ cup salad oil

Heat until it sizzles. Add

   4 to 5 pound chicken, cut in pieces
   1 tablespoon chopped parsley

Brown the chicken nicely on all sides. Remove it and add to the pan

   2 cups uncooked rice

Cook and stir until the rice is brown. Add

   2 cups water
   1 can consommé
   2 teaspoons salt
   2 bay leaves

Put in the chicken, cover, and simmer until the rice and chicken are tender (about 1 hour). Add

   ½ cup pitted green olives
   ½ cup pitted black olives
   2 cups cooked peas

Serves 6.

Chinese Chicken

One secret of fine Chinese cooking is to cut everything small, so that it cooks rapidly and is crisp and fresh when served.

Cut in matchlike pieces the meat from

   6 raw chicken breasts

or slice frozen chicken breasts paper-thin. Cook slowly until the meat is white in

   ¼ cup butter or salad oil

Add

   1 cup sliced water chestnuts
   1 cup bamboo shoots
   2 cups sliced celery
   ½ pound green beans, slivered
   3 cups boiling chicken broth or stock
   ¼ cup soy sauce
   2 teaspoons salt
   2 teaspoons monosodium glutamate
   1 teaspoon sugar
   1 teaspoon pepper

Cover and cook 5 minutes. Taste and add more salt, if necessary. Mix with a little of the broth

   2 tablespoons cornstarch

Pour into the pan and stir until the sauce thickens. Serve with Steamed Rice (p. 294). *Serves 6 to 8.*

Chinese Chicken with Nuts. Sauté 1 cup Chinese almonds or walnut meats quickly in butter and scatter over the finished dish.

Chop Suey

Specialty shops and Chinese groceries sell water chestnuts, bamboo shoots, soy sauce and Chinese almonds.

Cube the lean meat from
    2 pork chops
Prepare
    2 cups cubed cooked or raw chicken
Heat in a heavy frying pan
    ¼ cup peanut oil
Add the meat and stir over low heat until the meat is white (about 10 minutes). Add
    ½ cup chicken stock or water
    1 cup celery, in julienne strips
    ½ teaspoon thin soy sauce
    ½ teaspoon sugar
    Salt to taste
Cover and cook slowly until the celery is tender but still crisp. Mix
    1 teaspoon cornstarch
    ½ cup chicken stock or water
Stir into the pan and bring to the boiling point. Add
    1½ cups water chestnuts, sliced paper-thin
    1½ cups bamboo shoots, in julienne strips
Cover and heat well. Season to taste. Serve with
    Chinese almonds
    Chinese fried noodles (canned)
Serves 6.

Hawaiian Chicken

Canned or cooked chicken may be prepared this way, too.

Heat in a frying pan
    1 tablespoon salad oil
Add
    1 cup uncooked rice
Stir until the rice is brown. Put into a 2-quart casserole and stir in
    1¼ cups chicken broth or stock

Cover and bake 1 hour at 350° (adding a little broth if the rice dries).

Put in the frying pan
    2 tablespoons salad oil
Add
    1½ cups uncooked chicken, cut in small strips
Cook and stir until the chicken is white. Add
    2 cups sliced celery
    1 cup coarsely chopped onion
    ½ cup coarsely chopped green pepper
    1 tablespoon soy sauce
Heat
    1 cup syrup from a can of pineapple
Dissolve in this
    1 chicken bouillon cube
Add to the chicken, cover and simmer 5 minutes. Mix this into the rice. Put over the top
    Pineapple slices
Heat thoroughly in the oven. *Serves 6.*

Chicken Mousse

Follow the recipe for Fish Mousse (p. 124), using chicken breasts in place of fish. You will need two or three whole breasts, according to their size. There should be 2 cups of chicken after it has been ground.

For mousse made with cooked chicken, see Chicken Loaf (p. 227) and Macédoine Loaf (p. 227).

Chicken Livers

One pound serves 4.

Cut in half. Sprinkle with salt and pepper.

Sautéed Chicken Livers. Dip in flour or in fine crumbs, or egg and crumbs (p. 6). Sauté in butter or bacon fat until tender (about 10 minutes). Do not overcook.

Serve on toast with strips of crisp bacon or on broiled tomato halves. Or make Brown Sauce (p. 93), season to taste with Madeira or sherry and add the sautéed livers and a few slices of stuffed olives.

Curried Chicken Livers. Reheat sautéed livers in Curry Sauce (p. 93) made with chicken stock. Serve with steamed rice.

Chicken Livers en Brochette. Cut the livers in quarters. Wrap each piece in a thin slice of bacon and arrange on skewers or alternate with squares of bacon. Arrange on a rack in a baking pan. Bake at 425° until the bacon is crisp, turning to brown evenly.

Chicken Livers with Mushrooms

Cook together for 5 minutes
  1 slice bacon, cut in pieces
  2 tablespoons butter
Remove the bacon bits. Add
  1 shallot, chopped, or ½ tablespoon chopped onion
Cook 2 minutes. Add
  1 pound chicken livers
Cook 2 minutes. Add
  2 tablespoons flour
  1 cup Brown Stock (p. 70) or bouillon
  1 teaspoon lemon juice
  ¼ cup sliced mushrooms
Cook 2 minutes more. Sprinkle with
  Chopped parsley
Serves 4.

Recipes Using Cooked Chicken or Turkey

Cooked chicken is one of the most useful leftovers. If there is only a small amount, combine it with chopped ham or hard-cooked eggs in a casserole dish such as Scalloped Ham (p. 188), or add it to a salad or sandwich filling. If there is enough chicken to slice into neat pieces, you may prefer to arrange a cold platter with an attractive garnish of small whole tomatoes or asparagus tips topped with mayonnaise.

If the cooked chicken is to be cut in pieces, remove all the skin and bits of gristle or fat. White meat is more attractive in any creamed dish in fairly large pieces or in neat, even cubes. Chop dark meat unless the directions with the recipe suggest another method. In an electric blender, you can grind the skin very fine and add it to the sauce or gravy to deepen the flavor.

In addition to the recipes which follow, see Hawaiian Chicken (p. 222) and Chicken Mousse (p. 222); also use cooked chicken in any of the following ways:

Filled Biscuits (p. 311)

Chicken Roll (p. 202)

Crêpes Nicholas (p. 306)

Stuffed Peppers (p. 255)

Stuffed Tomatoes (p. 259)

Scalloped Ham (p. 188)

Filled Omelet (p. 106)

Chicken Salads (p. 278)

Fashion Park Salad (p. 273)

Pilaf (p. 296)

Rissoles (p. 202)

Deviled Chicken Bones

*For extra zest, add 1 tablespoon walnut
catsup to the sauce.*

Mix in a large saucepan
　2 tablespoons butter, melted
　1 tablespoon chili sauce
　1 tablespoon Worcestershire
　1 teaspoon prepared mustard
　Few grains cayenne
Cut 4 small gashes in
　Drumsticks, second joints and wings of
　　a cooked chicken
Sprinkle them with
　Salt, pepper and flour
Brown thoroughly in the prepared mix-
ture. Add
　1 cup Chicken Stock (p. 72)
Simmer 5 minutes. Sprinkle with
　Chopped parsley
Serves 4.

Creamed Chicken

*The sauce must be satin-smooth, thought-
fully seasoned and not too thick. Stir
frequently as you make it and add more
liquid if necessary.*

In a large saucepan or double boiler
top, melt
　2 tablespoons butter or chicken fat
Add
　3 tablespoons flour
Stir until evenly blended. Add gradually,
stirring constantly
　1 cup milk or chicken broth, or half
　　each
Cook and stir over low heat until the
sauce thickens. Bring to the boiling
point and cook 2 minutes. Add
　⅓ cup cream
　1½ cups cubed cooked chicken
　Salt and pepper to taste
Heat at least ½ hour over low heat on
an asbestos mat or in the double boiler,
so that the chicken will absorb some of
the sauce and be moist.

Serve on toast, waffles or hot biscuits or
with rice. Add a curl of crisp bacon or a
sprig of parsley or watercress. Or decorate with paprika or a strip of pimiento.
Serves 4.

To vary. Add diced cooked ham,
chopped hard-cooked eggs, sliced cooked
celery, cooked peas, sautéed mushrooms
or Duxelles (p. 249).

Blanquette of Chicken. Just before serving, stir in 1 egg yolk slightly beaten with
1 tablespoon milk or cream. Sprinkle
with minced parsley.

Scalloped Chicken. Spoon into a buttered
baking dish. Sprinkle with buttered
crumbs. Bake at 375° until the crumbs
are brown.

Creamed Chicken
and Mushrooms

Cook and stir together for 5 minutes
　2 tablespoons butter
　6 mushrooms, cut in pieces
　1 cup cubed cooked chicken
Blend in
　2 tablespoons flour
Add
　1 cup chicken stock or broth
Simmer 10 minutes. Season with
　Salt, cayenne and nutmeg
Mix
　1 slightly beaten egg
　1 tablespoon cream
　1 tablespoon sherry
Stir in and heat 1 minute. *Serves 4.*

Chicken Curry

Follow recipe for Curry of Lamb (p.
202), using chicken in place of lamb, and
Chicken Stock (p. 72) as the liquid.
Or season Creamed Chicken (above)
with curry powder and onion salt.

Chicken à la King

Heat in a double boiler
　1½ cups Velouté Sauce (p. 92)
　1 cup cubed cooked chicken
　½ cup sliced sautéed mushrooms
　¼ cup canned pimientos, cut in strips
Just before serving, beat together and
stir in
　1 egg yolk
　2 tablespoons sherry
Serve in Patty Shells (p. 410) or on toast.
Serves 3 or 4.

Chicken Scallop

Fill a buttered baking dish with alternate layers of sliced cooked chicken and cooked macaroni or rice. Over the top, pour hot Cream (p. 90), Brown (p. 93) or Tomato Sauce (p. 94), or undiluted cream of chicken, mushroom or celery soup. Sprinkle with buttered crumbs.

Bake at 375° until the crumbs are brown.

Chicken Almond Suprême

If Chinese almonds are available, sprinkle them over the top without slivering them.

Put in a shallow baking dish
   2 cups cooked chicken, cut in fairly large pieces
Spread over the chicken
   1 cup sautéed sliced mushrooms or small whole mushroom caps
Make another layer of
   1 cup water chestnuts, sliced paper-thin
Pour over the top
   2 cups Suprême Sauce (p. 92)
Cover the top with
   Slivered almonds
Bake at 375° until thoroughly heated and the almonds are browned. *Serves 4 or 5.*

Chicken Poulette

Put slices of cooked chicken in a shallow baking dish. Add sliced sautéed mushroom caps. Make Velouté Sauce (p. 92), omitting the cream. Pour it over the chicken. Bake 15 minutes at 375°.

Mix 1 egg yolk with ⅓ cup cream and stir into the mixture. Bake 10 minutes longer.

Just before serving, stir in ½ teaspoon lemon juice.

Chicken or Turkey Divan

Put in a shallow baking dish
   4 stalks cooked broccoli or 8 stalks cooked asparagus
Sprinkle with
   1 tablespoon melted butter
   1 tablespoon grated Parmesan or Romano cheese
   2 tablespoons sherry
Lay over the vegetable
   4 thick slices cooked turkey or chicken breast
Sprinkle with
   1 tablespoon grated Parmesan or Romano cheese
   2 tablespoons sherry
Prepare
   1 cup Cream Sauce (p. 90)
Stir in
   2 egg yolks, slightly beaten
Season to taste with
   Salt and pepper
Fold in
   1 tablespoon whipped cream
Pour over the chicken or turkey. Sprinkle with
   1 tablespoon grated Romano or Parmesan cheese
   2 tablespoons sherry
Bake at 350° until delicately brown (about 12 minutes). *Serves 3 or 4.*

Chicken Tetrazzini

Equally good with turkey, veal or lobster.

Have ready
   4 or more slices cooked chicken breast
   Velouté Sauce (p. 92)
Cook and drain
   ¼ pound spaghetti, in ¼-inch pieces
Melt
   2 tablespoons butter
Add
   ½ cup sliced mushrooms
Cook 5 minutes. Season with
   Few grains nutmeg
   1 tablespoon sherry
   Salt to taste
Put the spaghetti in a shallow baking dish. Pour half the sauce over it. Arrange the mushrooms and chicken on top of this and cover with the rest of the sauce. Sprinkle with
   ⅓ cup grated Italian cheese
Bake at 400° until well heated and browned. *Serves 4.*

Chicken and Noodles

Cook according to directions on the package
  ½ pound broad egg noodles
Drain. Stir in (reserving 2 tablespoons for the top)
  ¼ pound grated Parmesan cheese
Add
  Salt and pepper to taste
Put in a buttered baking dish. Place on the noodles
  2 cups cubed cooked chicken
Blend together in a saucepan over low heat
  2 tablespoons butter
  2 tablespoons flour
Add gradually
  1 cup cream
  1 cup Chicken Stock (p. 72) or broth
Bring to the boiling point, stirring constantly. Add
  2 egg yolks, slightly beaten
Pour the sauce over the chicken and sprinkle with the reserved cheese. Bake at 375° until thoroughly heated and well browned. *Serves 6.*

Chicken Hollandaise

Cook together for 5 minutes
  1½ tablespoons butter
  1 teaspoon onion, chopped fine
Stir in
  2 tablespoons cornstarch
Add gradually
  1 cup chicken broth or stock
Add
  1 teaspoon lemon juice
  ⅓ cup chopped celery
  ¼ teaspoon salt
  Few grains paprika
  1 cup cubed cooked chicken
Heat thoroughly. Add
  1 egg yolk, slightly beaten
Cook 1 minute. *Serves 3 or 4.*

Chicken Soufflé

Add diced pimientos or sliced sautéed mushrooms to the mixture, if you like. To make a particularly fluffy soufflé, use an extra egg white and stir a spoonful of the beaten white in thoroughly before folding in the rest.

Cook together until the onion is yellow
  1 tablespoon chopped onion
  2 tablespoons butter or chicken fat
Stir in
  2 tablespoons flour
Add
  2 cups Chicken Stock (p. 72) or 1 cup stock and 1 cup milk or cream
Cook and stir until smooth. Add
  ½ cup soft bread crumbs
Cook 2 minutes. Season to taste with
  Salt and pepper
  Worcestershire
Add
  2 cups chopped cooked chicken
  3 egg yolks, well beaten
  1 tablespoon chopped parsley
Fold in
  3 egg whites, beaten stiff
Pour into an unbuttered straight-sided baking dish. Bake 35 minutes at 325°. Serve with
  Mushroom Sauce (p. 94)
Serves 6.

Minced Chicken or Turkey

Put in a saucepan
  1 cup chicken or turkey gravy
Add
  1 cup minced cooked chicken or turkey
  ⅓ cup soft stale bread crumbs
  Few drops onion juice
  Salt and pepper to taste
Heat thoroughly. Serve on
  Toast or cooked rice
Serves 2 or 3.

Chicken or Turkey Hash

Chop cooked chicken or turkey. Moisten with gravy and season to taste. Add finely chopped parsley or pimiento, if you like.

Cook in a hot buttered omelet pan or a shallow baking dish until thoroughly heated but not dry.

Serve from the baking dish or turn out onto a serving dish and surround with peas, asparagus tips or broiled pork sausages.

Charleston Chicken Hash. Cube white meat of cooked chicken and put in a shallow baking dish. Sprinkle with salt, pepper and nutmeg. Pour enough heavy cream over the chicken to just barely cover it. Sprinkle with grated Parmesan. Bake at 350° until the cheese melts (about 15 minutes).

Chicken or Turkey Cakes

Chop cooked chicken or turkey. To each cup add 1 tablespoon cream and 1 egg, slightly beaten. Season to taste. Shape in 2-inch flat cakes and dip in flour or egg and crumbs (p. 6).

Sauté in butter until well browned. Serve with Mushroom Sauce (p. 94).

Chicken Chartreuse

Follow the recipe for Rice and Meat Loaf (p. 201), using chicken in place of meat. Season the chicken with salt, pepper, celery salt, onion juice and ½ teaspoon finely chopped parsley.

Macédoine Loaf

Mix thoroughly
    1 cup undiluted cream of mushroom
        soup
    ½ cup soft bread crumbs
    2 egg yolks
    1 cup cooked macaroni in ½-inch
        pieces
    ½ cup cubed cooked chicken
    1 tablespoon canned pimiento, cut
        small
    ½ cup heavy cream, beaten stiff
    1½ teaspoons salt
    1 teaspoon chopped parsley
Fold in
    2 egg whites, beaten stiff
Bake like Chicken Loaf (below). Serve with
    Tomato (p. 94) or Mushroom Sauce
        (p. 94)
Serves 6.

Chicken Loaf, Ring or Timbales

Season with ¼ teaspoon marjoram or thyme if you like a delicate herb flavor.

Mix thoroughly
    1 cup soft stale bread crumbs
    2 cups milk
    2 eggs, slightly beaten, or 3 egg yolks
    ½ teaspoon salt
    ¼ teaspoon paprika
    1 teaspoon Worcestershire
    3 cups diced cooked chicken
    ½ cup chopped celery
    1 green pepper, chopped
    Juice of ½ lemon
Pack into a buttered 1½-quart mold or 6 or 8 timbale molds. Set in a pan of hot water. Bake at 325° until firm (about 40 minutes). Let stand 10 minutes before unmolding. *Serves 6 or more.*

Chicken Croquettes

For delicious flavor, make the sauce of ¾ cup chicken stock and ¼ cup heavy cream and season with curry to taste.

Mix thoroughly
    2 cups chopped cooked chicken
    ½ teaspoon salt
    ¼ teaspoon celery salt
    Few grains cayenne
    1 teaspoon lemon juice
    Few drops onion juice
    1 teaspoon finely chopped parsley
    About 1 cup Croquette Sauce (p. 5)
Use enough sauce to keep the mixture soft but stiff enough to hold its shape. White meat absorbs more sauce than dark. Chill the mixture; then shape, egg and crumb, and fry (p. 5). Serve with
    Cream Sauce (p. 90) or Wine Jelly
        (p. 378), made with Sauterne
Serves 6.

Chicken and Almond Croquettes. Add ½ cup chopped nut meats to the mixture. Serve with Brown Almond Sauce (p. 90).

Chicken and Mushroom Croquettes. Use 1⅓ cups chicken and ⅔ cup chopped mushrooms.

Chicken Croquettes Macédoine

Cook together 3 minutes, stirring constantly
  3 tablespoons butter
  1 shallot, chopped fine, or 1 tablespoon chopped onion
Blend in
  ¼ cup flour
  1 teaspoon salt
  ¼ teaspoon paprika
  Few gratings nutmeg
Add gradually, stirring constantly

  1 cup Chicken Stock (p. 72) or broth
Bring to the boiling point and add
  3 egg yolks, slightly beaten
  1 cup diced cooked chicken
  ½ cup diced cooked ham
  ¼ cup chopped mushrooms
Cook 5 minutes. Chill.

Shape, egg and crumb, and fry (p. 6).
Serve with
  Cream Sauce (p. 90) or Velouté Sauce (p. 92)
Serves 6.

Other Poultry

Roast Duck

Allow at least 1 pound per person. Long Island ducklings weigh about 5 pounds.

Roast with a stuffing or not; either way is good. Apple (p. 81) and Onion Stuffing (p. 81) are excellent with duck. Instead of stuffing, put 2 cored and quartered apples inside, or a handful of celery leaves. Some cooks prefer to bake the stuffing in a separate pan, so that it will not be overmoistened by the duck fat; baste occasionally with a little fat from the roasting pan.

It is not necessary to truss ducks as they have short legs and wings.

Place on a rack in an open roasting pan. Roast at 325° until tender (about 30 minutes per pound). Do not baste, since ducks are fat. Prick in several places so that some of the fat will drain off. Turn often to brown evenly. Pour off the fat as it accumulates.

Serve with Gravy (p. 156) or with Olive Sauce (p. 93). Traditional with duck are Applesauce, Stewed or Brandied Apples (p. 348); Baked or Broiled Oranges (p. 86); Onion and Orange Salad (p. 275); also tart jelly such as currant or cranberry.

To carve. Cut off the legs and wings. Slice the breast meat at right angles to the surface.

Carve duck slices directly inward and then cut under them

Roast Duck Bigarade. Put a sliced orange in the duck. Make the gravy with one-third orange juice and two-thirds water. Cook the peel of 1 orange in boiling water 3 minutes, drain, scrape out the white pulp, cut the peel in thin strips and add to the gravy. Season to taste. Garnish the platter with thin slices of orange.

Salmi of Duck. Cut roast duck in pieces for serving. Reheat in Sauce Espagnole (p. 93).

Broiled Ducklings, Guinea Hens, Squabs and Turkey Broilers

Follow directions for Broiled Chicken (p. 213).

Braised Duck à l'Orange

Prepare for cooking (p. 210)
1 duck (about 6 pounds)
Rub with
Salt and pepper
Brown in a heavy pan in
¼ cup butter
Peel and cut in quarters
2 oranges
Scrape the white inner pulp from the peel and cut enough peel in thin strips to make 1 tablespoonful. Add to the duck with the orange quarters and
½ cup stock or strong consommé
Cover closely and simmer until tender (about 1½ hours). Remove the duck and keep it warm while you make the sauce.

Pour off all but ½ cup of the juice in the pan. Add to the pan
½ cup white wine, Italian vermouth or orange juice
Heat to the boiling point. Mix
1 teaspoon cornstarch
Water (enough to pour)
Add to the sauce and stir until slightly thickened. Pour it over the duck. Garnish with
Thin slices of unpeeled orange
Serves 6.

Roast Goose

Allow 1½ pounds or more per person, as goose has much bone and fat in proportion to the meat.

Stuff (preparing 8 cups stuffing for a 10-pound goose). Use Bread (p. 81), Apple (p. 81) or Apple and Prune Stuffing (p. 82). Roast like Roast Duck (p. 228).

Roast Guinea Hen

Allow about 1 pound per person.

Guinea hen is usually roasted without stuffing. Put a piece of bacon inside the bird, tie the legs close to the body, and set on a rack in a roasting pan. Lay 2 or 3 pieces of bacon over the breast. Roast at 325° until tender (45 minutes to 1 hour).

Squabs en Casserole

Allow 1 squab per person.

Truss squabs. Put in a casserole and brush with melted butter. Cover and bake 10 minutes at 375°. Add chicken stock (½ cup for 2 or 3 squabs). Cover, reduce heat to 325°, and cook until the squabs are tender (about 25 minutes).

When they are almost tender, add any cooked vegetables you like — potato balls, whole green beans, tiny carrots, onions or asparagus tips. Malaga grapes are delicious with squab. Split, seed, and add 5 minutes before squabs are done.

Roast Squab

Allow 1 squab per person.

Stuff with cooked wild rice or with Mushroom Stuffing (p. 81), allowing ⅓ cup for each bird. Truss. Season with salt and pepper and brush with melted butter. Roast at 325° until tender (about 45 minutes). Baste frequently with ⅓ cup butter melted in ⅔ cup boiling water or with melted currant jelly.

Game Birds and Hare

Game birds vary in meatiness, so that it is difficult to say how much to allow for each serving. In general, 1½ pounds will yield a generous serving.

Roast Game Birds

Clean, and let stand long enough to be at room temperature before roasting. Sprinkle the inside of the bird with salt. Tie the legs together and fasten them close to the body with skewers. Roast the required length of time (below).

Wild Goose. Do not stuff. Put celery leaves inside. Allow at least 3 hours, as wild geese are often old and very tough.

Wild Duck. Stuff with sliced apple or onion or with celery tops. Put slices of bacon or fat salt pork over the breast. Roast at 450° for 20 minutes for very rare duck with the juice still red. If you prefer duck that is still rare but slightly better done, roast it about 10 minutes longer. For well-done duck, roast 15 minutes to the pound at 350°, basting every 5 minutes with the fat in the pan or with melted butter or red wine or with a mixture of the two.

Grouse, Quail, Partridge, Plover and Woodcock. Brush with butter. Roast at 350° until tender (12 to 20 minutes). Baste 3 times with melted butter during roasting.

Pheasant. Put strips of bacon over the breast. Roast 30 to 40 minutes at 350° (or longer if you like pheasant well done). Remove the bacon.

Broiled Game Birds

Game birds (quail, plover, woodcock, young pheasant, partridge, grouse, young wild duck) tend to be dry, so rub well with butter or oil and baste often during broiling. Split and broil like chicken (p. 213), allowing 8 to 20 minutes according to size.

Braised Game Birds

Split small birds. Cut larger ones in serving-size pieces. Sprinkle with salt, pepper and flour. Brown well in butter or bacon fat. Cover with cream to a depth of 1 inch. Cover and cook over low heat or in a 325° oven until tender.

Thicken the juices in the pan with potato flour or cornstarch. Season to taste with salt, pepper and sherry.

Game Birds Chasseur (Hunter's Style). Add to each cup of sauce ⅓ cup tomato juice, lemon juice to taste, 1 teaspoon chopped parsley and ⅓ cup sliced sautéed mushrooms.

Rabbit and Hare

Allow 1 pound per person. A rabbit weighs 1½ to 4 pounds, a hare 4 to 10. The meat is like chicken or veal.

Soak wild rabbit 1 hour in salted water to which has been added 2 tablespoons vinegar for each 2 quarts of water. Cut in pieces.

Fricassee (p. 218) or fry (p. 214) like chicken, using bacon fat.

Braised Hare in Sour Cream

Ask the butcher to lard the hind legs and back of the hare, or lay strips of salt pork over it as it cooks.

Prepare for cooking
    1 hare (5 to 6 pounds), split

Sprinkle it with
   Salt and pepper
Melt in a saucepan
   2 tablespoons bacon fat
Add
   1 carrot, cut in small pieces
   ½ small onion
Cook 5 minutes. Add
   1 cup Brown Stock (p. 70) or con-
      sommé
Pour around the hare in a baking pan.
Bake at 400° until tender (45 minutes
or more), basting 4 times with the pan

juice. Add
   1 cup heavy sour cream
Cook 15 minutes longer, basting every
5 minutes. Take the hare out of the pan
and keep it warm. Strain the sauce.

Cook together
   2 tablespoons butter
   2 tablespoons flour
Thicken the sauce with this mixture.
Season to taste with
   Salt and pepper
Pour around the hare. *Serves 6.*

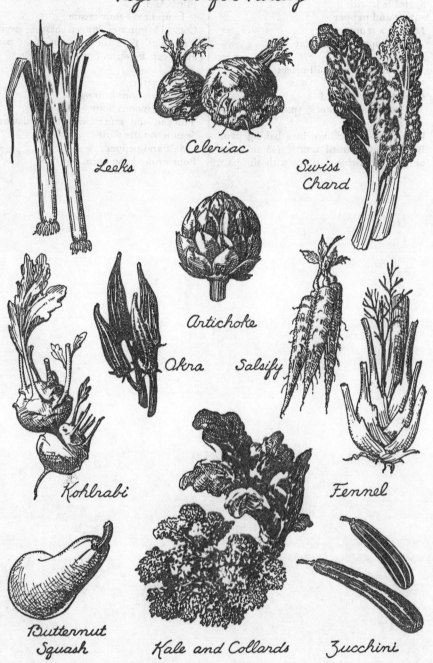

Vegetables for Variety

Leeks

Celeriac

Swiss Chard

Artichoke

Okra

Salsify

Kohlrabi

Fennel

Butternut Squash

Kale and Collards

Zucchini

Vegetables

Freshly picked vegetables from your own garden or from a road-side stand are so much better than those available at most stores that it is worth an effort to have them, at least occasionally. Some markets, however, make a specialty of offering the finest in vegetables and deserve the patronage of discriminating customers.

Serve vegetables in various ways so that they will continue to appeal to your family. Provide a contrast in color or texture by sprinkling with croûtons or by garnishing with sprigs of water-cress or parsley or bits of pimiento, chopped toasted almonds, or fried onion rings (canned or frozen ones are delicious).

Store fresh vegetables in a cool place and use promptly. Defrost frozen vegetables slightly just before cooking, so that they will cook evenly and quickly.

Season vegetables to taste before serving. Vegetables vary in flavor, so that a recipe can only suggest the average amount of salt or other seasoning to use. Let your imagination suggest an occasional change in seasoning — add curry or nutmeg, sherry or brandy, or a suggestion of herbs. But remember that seasoning should enhance, not overwhelm!

Vegetables Poulette

Heat a combination of cooked vegetables in Suprême Sauce (p. 92). Peas with cubed carrots and turnips make a good combination.

Casserole of Mixed Vegetables

An attractive way to serve vegetables for a buffet supper party. Cook vegetables especially for this dish or use leftovers.

Alternate layers of well-seasoned cooked rice and cooked vegetables, adding to each layer a bit of scraped onion or onion juice.

Pour consommé over the vegetables and dot with butter. Bake at any convenient temperature until thoroughly heated. Sprinkle with crumbled cooked bacon or paprika. If you like, sprinkle over the top, before baking, buttered crumbs or grated cheese, or both.

Vegetable Casserole à la Bishop

The amount and proportion of the vegetables may be varied.

Cook separately until just tender
  2 pounds fresh green peas or 1 package frozen peas
  2 bunches carrots, diced
  1 package frozen baby lima beans
Prepare, separating stems and caps
  1 pound mushrooms
Chop the stems and put them in a large casserole. Add
  3 cans condensed mushroom soup
  ⅓ cup milk
Add the cooked vegetables and stir well, adding a little more milk if necessary to moisten. Sprinkle over the top
  ½ cup grated Romano or Parmesan cheese
  Buttered crumbs to cover
Over the crumbs arrange the mushroom caps. Sprinkle with
  Melted butter
Half an hour before serving, bake at 350°. *Serves 10 or more.*

Vegetable Soufflé

In place of milk or cream, use part stock or the water in which the vegetable was cooked. Mix leftover vegetables if you like, such as peas and carrots, celery and carrots, or mushrooms and cauliflower.

Put in a saucepan
  3 tablespoons butter
  1 teaspoon chopped onion
Cook slowly until yellow. Add
  3 tablespoons flour
Blend well. Add
  1 cup milk or cream
Cook and stir until thick. Add
  1 cup cooked vegetable, mashed, chopped or cut fine
Stir in
  3 egg yolks, well beaten
Cook over low heat 1 minute. Season to taste, adding more onion if needed. Cool at least 10 minutes. Beat until stiff
  3 egg whites
Fold gently into the vegetable mixture. Spoon into a baking dish. Do not butter the dish unless the soufflé is to be turned out on a serving dish (as in a ring mold). Bake at 350° until firm (about 30 minutes). *Serves 6.*

Anise

See Fennel (p. 248).

Globe Artichokes

Also called French or Italian artichokes. Allow 1 to a person (or half, if they are very large). Choose smooth, dark green, tightly closed heads.

Wash thoroughly. Cut off the stem close to the leaves and pull off the tough outer leaves. Cut off the prickly tops with scissors.

Put in a deep saucepan with 1½ inches of boiling water. Add 2 tablespoons lemon juice or vinegar. Cover the pan and cook until you can easily pull off an outer leaf (25 to 45 minutes). Drain upside down.

Set upright on a serving dish. Serve hot with individual dishes of melted butter or Hollandaise (p. 95) in which to dip each leaf as it is eaten. Or serve cold with Vinaigrette Sauce (p. 97) or mayonnaise seasoned highly with lemon juice and prepared mustard.

Two ways of serving individually

Stuffed Artichokes. *A good luncheon dish.* Cook until just barely tender. Cut out the prickly center (choke) with a teaspoon. Spread the leaves apart to make a cup. Fill with creamed chicken, crab meat or lobster. Sprinkle with buttered crumbs or grated cheese. Bake in a covered dish 30 minutes at 350°. Uncover to brown the tops.

Canned and Frozen Artichokes

Both hearts and tiny whole artichokes, quartered, are excellent.

Drain canned artichokes. Cook frozen artichokes according to the directions on the package. Add them to a salad or prepare them à la Vinaigrette (p. 274) to serve as a cocktail accompaniment.

Sautéed Artichokes. Sauté in butter until delicately brown. Sprinkle with salt, pepper, lemon juice and chopped parsley.

Artichokes with Mushrooms. Slice into a baking dish. Add half the amount of sliced mushrooms. Season with salt, pepper and garlic salt. Sprinkle with salad oil or dot with butter. Cover. Bake about 20 minutes at 350°.

Artichokes à la Barigoule

Serve hot as a vegetable or cool in the sauce and serve as an appetizer or salad.

Mix in a saucepan
  1 cup water
  1 cup dry white wine

⅓ cup olive oil
1 tablespoon tomato sauce

Simmer 10 minutes. Season to taste. Add

   1 package frozen artichokes or 1 can
     artichoke hearts (drained)

Cook slowly until thoroughly heated. *Serves 4.*

Jerusalem Artichokes

One pound serves 6. Jerusalem artichokes are tubers like potatoes but sweeter and more watery. Serve in place of potatoes.

Scrub. Leave whole or pare and slice. Cook, covered, 15 to 35 minutes in boiling salted water or 2 minutes in a pressure saucepan (overcooking toughens this vegetable).

Drain. Pare if necessary. Add ½ cup butter, 2 tablespoons lemon juice, 2 tablespoons finely chopped parsley, ¼ teaspoon salt and a few grains cayenne. Cook 3 minutes.

Asparagus

One pound serves 2 or 3. Choose fresh-looking, very green stalks with smooth tight tips.

Until ready to cook, stand asparagus upright in cold water 2 inches deep. Snap off and discard the tough lower part of the stalks. Wash. Remove the scales, which often hold bits of sand.

Lay the stalks flat in a shallow pan. Add just enough boiling salted water to keep from burning. Cover and cook until tender (15 to 20 minutes). Drain, but there should be almost no water left when the asparagus is done. Spread with soft butter or serve with melted butter, Beurre Noir (p. 89), Hollandaise (p. 95), Suprême (p. 92) or Cheese Sauce (p. 91). Serve, if you like, on buttered toast or sprinkle with browned crumbs or toasted slivered almonds.

Creamed Asparagus. Cut in 2-inch pieces. Boil, adding the tips after cooking 10 minutes. Drain. Serve in Cream Sauce (p. 90) or Cheese Sauce (p. 91), or heat a little cream, yogurt or sour cream and pour it over the asparagus.

Asparagus au Gratin. Put creamed asparagus in a buttered baking dish. Sprinkle with buttered crumbs or with crumbs mixed with grated cheese. Bake at 350° until the crumbs are brown.

Asparagus Vinaigrette. Serve hot or cold with Vinaigrette Sauce (p. 97).

French-Fried Asparagus. Drain fresh-cooked or canned asparagus tips. Dip in egg and fine crumbs or flour (p. 6). Chill. Fry, a few at a time, for about 3 minutes in deep fat heated to 380°. Drain on a paper towel.

French-Fried Asparagus with Cheese. Mix grated Parmesan with the crumbs for dipping, using half cheese and half crumbs.

Asparagus Canton Style. *Easy to cook at the table in an electric skillet. Crisp and flavorful.* Cut uncooked asparagus in very thin slanted slices. Cook over low heat in melted butter (1 tablespoon for 1 pound of asparagus) in a covered frying pan until the asparagus is just barely tender (about 5 minutes). Season to taste. Add more butter, if you like.

Green Beans

One pound serves 4. Select beans that are crisp enough to snap when broken and are fresh-looking, with a bright, clear color.

Wash thoroughly. Cut off the ends. Cut with a sharp knife or scissors in 1-inch pieces. Or cut in very thin diagonal strips with a bean cutter; or cut lengthwise and then crosswise in thin pieces about 1½ inches long.

Cook about 2 minutes in a pressure saucepan, or 15 to 20 minutes in a covered pan in boiling salted water ½ inch deep. Drain. Add salt and butter to taste. Sour cream is delicious in place of butter. Season with finely cut dill or chives, if you like. Or see variations, next page.

Green Beans Amandine. Sprinkle slivered toasted almonds over the buttered cooked beans. For an especially delicious flavor, cook the slivered almonds in butter until the butter is brown, and pour over the beans.

Green Beans with Mushrooms. Add sliced sautéed mushrooms.

Green Beans Polonaise. Reheat beans with ¼ cup cream and sprinkle with croûtons.

Green Beans Texas Style. Season cooked beans with chili sauce to taste. Reheat and sprinkle crumbled crisp bacon over the top.

Uruguayan Green Beans. Sprinkle with chopped parsley and lemon juice.

Panned Green Beans. Cut the beans in lengthwise strips and cook gently in melted butter (1½ tablespoons per pound of beans) in a covered frying pan until just tender. Season to taste with salt and pepper.

Green Beans au Gratin. *An easy dinner party item since it can be prepared ahead and put into the oven half an hour before serving time.* Cook fresh or frozen green beans until just tender but still crisp. Drain and put in a casserole in layers. Dot each layer with butter and sprinkle with salt, pepper and grated cheese. Pour over the beans light or heavy cream (¼ cup for each 2 cups of beans).

Bake at 400° until the cheese melts (about ½ hour).

Beans Panaché

A different way with frozen vegetables. Partially defrost the vegetables before cooking.

Melt in a frying pan or electric skillet
    1 tablespoon butter
Add
    ½ cup water
    1 package frozen baby limas
    ¼ teaspoon salt
Cover. Cook 5 minutes. Add
    1 package frozen French-style green
    beans

1 package frozen green peas
Cover and cook until all the vegetables are tender (about 15 minutes). Stir in
    1 tablespoon butter
Season to taste. *Serves 6 to 8.*

Wax Beans

One pound serves 4. Select crisp, small beans.

Prepare and cook like green beans (above). To add a bit of color and zest, chop canned pimientos fine and sprinkle over the cooked beans.

Shell Beans
(lima, green soy, fava, etc.)

One pound, shelled, or 3 pounds, unshelled, serves 4 or 5.

Cut off the thin outer edge of the pods with a sharp knife. Squeeze out the beans. Wash.

Cook 1 minute in a pressure saucepan or 15 to 25 minutes, tightly covered, in boiling salted water, 1 inch deep.

Season with butter, salt and pepper. Add a little cream or top milk or sprinkle with chopped parsley or chives.

To shell soy beans. Drop into boiling water, cover, and let stand 5 minutes. Drain. Press the beans out of the pods with thumb and finger. Old soy beans (brownish pods) take longer to cook than other beans.

Dried Beans
(lima, kidney, navy, soy, pinto and black-eyed peas)

Dried beans double in bulk when cooked. One cup serves 4. They may be seasoned and served in a great variety of ways, so you may wish to cook more than enough for one meal.

Wash. Pick over and discard discolored beans. Cover with boiling water, cook 2 minutes, and remove from the heat. Soak 1 hour or more. If you are using packaged processed beans, follow the directions on the package.

Bring to the boiling point and simmer until just tender (about 45 minutes for limas, 2 to 3 hours for soy beans and the others). Add more water from time to time as it boils away. Add salt after the first hour.

Drain. Season with salt, pepper and butter. Save some for Bean Soup (p. 64), Beans Bretonne or Boston Baked Beans (below).

Boston Baked Beans

Boston baked beans are always flavored with molasses and baked to a rich dark brown. The preferred beans to use are small California or New York pea beans, but kidney beans are delicious, too, baked in the same fashion.

Wash, discarding imperfect ones
  2 pounds California or New York pea
  beans
Cover with
  2 quarts water
Bring to the boiling point, boil 2 minutes, then let soak 1 hour or more.

Without draining, cook slowly until the skins burst when you take a few on the tip of a spoon and blow on them. Drain, reserving the cooking water.

Cover with boiling water
  ½ pound fat salt pork
Let stand 2 minutes, drain, and cut 1-inch gashes every ½ inch without cutting through the rind.

Put the beans in the bean pot. Push the pork down into the beans until all but the rind is covered. Mix
  2 teaspoons salt
  1 cup molasses
  1 teaspoon dry mustard
  2 tablespoons sugar, brown or white
Add 1 cup of the reserved water and bring to the boiling point. Pour over the beans and add enough more water to cover the beans. Cover the bean pot.

Bake 6 to 8 hours at 250°. Add water as needed to keep the beans moist. Uncover

the last hour of baking so that the rind will be brown and crisp. *10 or more servings.*

To flavor the beans with onion, rub the inside of the pot with onion and add a few slivers of onion. If you like a pronounced onion flavor, put a peeled onion in the pot with the beans and remove it when you serve the beans.

Baked Beans New York Style. Omit the molasses and sugar. Arrange the slices of salt pork over the top. Bake uncovered in a shallow pan. Do not add water during the last hour of baking.

Canned or frozen baked beans. The beans may suit you just as they are. Otherwise, season to taste with salt, mustard and molasses. Heat in a bean pot for a homemade look.

Beans Bretonne

Put in a baking dish
  1½ cups cooked pea beans
Add
  1 cup stewed and strained tomatoes
  1 cup Chicken Stock (p. 72) or canned
  chicken broth
  6 pimientos, puréed
  1 onion, chopped fine
  ¼ cup butter
  2 teaspoons salt
Cover. Bake at 300° until the beans have nearly absorbed the sauce. *Serves 6.*

Lima Beans Fermière

Put in a casserole
  2 cups cooked dried lima beans
Season to taste. Add water to half the depth of the beans.

Put in a small frying pan
  2-inch cube fat salt pork, diced
Cook slowly until the fat melts and the lean bits are crisp and brown. Add
  1 small onion, sliced thin
  ½ carrot, cubed
Cook and stir until the onion is brown. Add to the beans. Cover. Bake at 300° until the beans are soft. *Serves 4.*

Beets

One pound serves 3 or 4. Select beets with fresh-looking leaves.

Wash. Cut off all but 1 inch of the tops. Do not cut off the root and do not pare.

Cook beets whole, without salt, until tender (5 to 10 minutes in a pressure saucepan, or 30 to 60 minutes in boiling water to cover). Very old, woody beets will never cook tender.

Drain, drop in cold water for a moment, and slip off the skins with your fingers. Leave whole, cut in quarters, or slice (an egg slicer does the job quickly). Dot with butter, and season, or serve in one of the following ways.

Sugared Beets. Cut hot boiled beets in thin slices. For each 4 beets, add 3 tablespoons butter, 1½ tablespoons sugar, and ½ teaspoon salt. Reheat.

Pickled Beets. Slice cooked beets and cover with mild cider vinegar or 1 cup vinegar boiled 5 minutes with ½ cup sugar. Add a few caraway seeds for extra zest. Serve lukewarm or cold in small individual sauce dishes.

Shredded Beets

Wash young beets. Shred into a frying pan. For 1 pound beets add 3 tablespoons butter, bacon fat or oil, and 1 tablespoon boiling water, lemon juice or vinegar. Cover. Cook over moderate heat until tender (5 to 10 minutes). Season to taste.

Beets and Greens

Very young beets — no larger than marbles — are delicious cooked with their tender leaves.

Wash thoroughly to remove every trace of sand. Cut off the root tips. Cook the beets covered, with just enough water added to the pan to keep them from burning. Sprinkle with salt and cook until the beets are tender. Drain. Cut the greens coarsely with the kitchen scissors. Add salt and butter to taste.

Baked Beets

Wash. Cut off the tops. Brush with oil. Bake at 350° until tender (1 hour or more). Peel, unless they are very young. Slice or chop. Season with butter, salt and pepper.

Sweet and Sour Beets

Melt in a saucepan
  2 tablespoons butter
Blend in
  2 tablespoons flour
Stir in
  ½ cup water in which the beets were cooked or liquid from the can
  ¼ cup vinegar
  ¼ cup cream
  1 teaspoon sugar
  ½ teaspoon salt
  Few grains pepper
Cook until smooth, stirring constantly. Add
  2 cups cooked or canned beets, drained and cubed
Heat thoroughly. *Serves 4.*

Harvard Beets

Mix in a saucepan
  ½ cup sugar
  1½ teaspoons cornstarch
Add
  ¼ cup mild vinegar
  ¼ cup water
Boil 5 minutes. Add
  12 small cooked beets, sliced or cubed
Let stand 30 minutes or more. Just before serving, bring to the boiling point. Add
  2 tablespoons butter
Serves 6.

Broccoli

One pound serves 2 to 4. Select stalks with dark green, tightly closed buds and short crisp stems.

Cover with cold salted water. Soak 30 minutes. Drain. Cut off the tough part of the stalk and the coarse outer leaves. Peel the stalks and slit large ones lengthwise for an inch or two so they will cook evenly. If the stalks are too large for individual portions, split into pieces of attractive size and shape.

Cook about 1½ minutes in a pressure saucepan or about 15 minutes in 1 inch of boiling water in a tightly covered pan. Do not overcook.

Serve with melted butter, Hollandaise (p. 95) or Cheese Sauce (p. 91). Sprinkle with buttered bread crumbs, if desired.

Puréed Broccoli. Chop fine or put through a purée strainer. Reheat. Cover with Hollandaise (p. 95).

Broccoli au Gratin. Mix puréed broccoli with Cream Sauce (1 cup to 1 pound of broccoli). Season highly. Place in a baking dish. Sprinkle with buttered crumbs or crushed corn flakes and freshly grated cheese. Bake 15 minutes at 350°.

Broccoli in Cheese Custard

Cook, drain and chop
    1 package frozen broccoli or 1 pound
        fresh broccoli
Put in a buttered casserole. Mix
    2 eggs, slightly beaten
    1½ cups milk
    ½ cup grated Cheddar cheese
    2 tablespoons lemon juice
    1 teaspoon salt
    ⅛ teaspoon pepper
Pour over the broccoli. Set the casserole in a pan of hot water. Bake at 325° until the custard is firm (about 35 minutes). *Serves 6.*

Brussels Sprouts

One pound serves 3 or 4. Select light green, compact heads with no yellow spots.

Remove wilted leaves, cut off stems, and soak 15 minutes in cold salted water. Drain.

Cook, covered, in boiling salted water 10 to 20 minutes or until just tender. Drain.

Serve with melted butter or Hollandaise (p. 95).

For a change, add 1 cup sliced sautéed mushrooms.

Brussels Sprouts en Casserole. Season cooked sprouts with melted butter. Put in a casserole, sprinkle with buttered crumbs and bake at 350° until the crumbs are browned.

Scalloped Brussels Sprouts. Follow the recipe for Cabbage Huntington (p. 240), using 1 pound sprouts in place of cabbage.

Brussels Sprouts with Chestnuts. Cook 2 tablespoons butter with 1 teaspoon sugar until golden-brown. Add ½ cup cooked (p. 244) or canned chestnuts and brown well. Add 1 pound cooked sprouts which have been sautéed in butter. Moisten with stock or the water in which the sprouts were cooked. Season to taste.

Cabbage

Young green cabbage, solid white cabbage, loose crinkly Savoy, deep red cabbage, pale mild Chinese — each has its special characteristics. Select a firm head, heavy for its size. One small head serves 4 to 6, or 1 pound serves 3.

Cole Slaw, p. 274.

Take off the outside leaves, cut in quarters and remove the tough center. Hold firmly, cut side down, on a board and slice thin with a long sharp knife.

Cook quickly in a covered pan with just enough water to keep from burning. Cook until just tender but still crisp — 5 to 15 minutes for green or white cabbage, 20 to 25 minutes for red. Drain. Season with butter, salt and pepper. Or use one of the variations on the next page.

Creamed Cabbage. Heat in cream or Cream Sauce (p. 90). Curry powder or grated cheese is a tasty addition.

Scalloped Cabbage. Put Creamed Cabbage in a buttered baking dish. Cover with buttered crumbs. Bake at 350° until brown. If desired, add grated cheese to the crumbs.

Chinese Cabbage and Bacon

Cook 8 strips of bacon in a large frying pan until crisp. Remove and drain on a paper towel. Add to the fat in the pan a shredded head of Chinese cabbage, cover, and cook until just tender (5 to 10 minutes). Crumble the bacon and stir it into the cabbage. Season to taste. Serve with soy sauce. *Serves 4 to 6.*

Chinese Cabbage and Tomatoes

To 4 cups shredded Chinese cabbage add ½ cup cooked or canned tomatoes and 1 small onion, chopped fine. Cook until tender, adding a little water if necessary to keep the cabbage from sticking. Season to taste. *Serves 4.*

Cabbage Huntington

Cook (p. 239)
  1 small crisp white or green cabbage
Drain thoroughly. Season with
  Salt and pepper
Put in a saucepan
  2 tablespoons butter
  ¼ cup finely cut celery (or more)
Cook slowly 5 minutes. Stir in
  2 tablespoons flour
Stir in gradually
  1 cup thin cream or milk and cream
Cook until thick, stirring constantly (about 5 minutes). Season to taste. Add the cabbage. Spoon into a baking dish. Cover with
  Buttered crumbs
Bake at any convenient temperature (325° to 375°) until well heated and browned on top. *Serves 4 or 5.*

Braised Red Cabbage and Apples

Caramelized chopped onion gives this dish its special flavor. To season more highly, add nutmeg and cayenne or allspice and clove.

Melt in a frying pan
  4 tablespoons bacon fat
Add
  2 tablespoons sugar
Stir until brown. Add
  1 small onion, chopped
Cook slowly until golden. Add
  4 cups shredded red cabbage
  2 tart apples, sliced
  2 tablespoons mild vinegar
  ½ teaspoon caraway seeds
  Salt and pepper
Cook slowly until very tender, adding
  A little water, stock or red wine
as necessary to keep from sticking. *Serves 4 to 6.*

Braised White Cabbage and Apples. Use ¼ cup sugar and only 1 tablespoon vinegar.

Hot Slaw

Cole Slaw (p. 274).

Shred
  ½ cabbage
Mix in a double boiler top
  2 egg yolks
  ¼ cup cold water
  1 tablespoon butter
  ¼ cup hot vinegar
  ½ teaspoon salt
Cook over hot water, stirring constantly, until thick. Add the cabbage and reheat. *Serves 4.*

Sauerkraut

Sauerkraut is marketed uncooked or cooked, ready to heat, season and serve. For an old-fashioned meal, serve sauerkraut with spareribs, ham or frankfurters. One pound serves 4.

To cook, cover with boiling water, stock or consommé. Cook slowly at least 35 minutes. Drain. Season to taste with salt, if needed, and pepper.

Many old German recipes suggest cooking with the sauerkraut a grated raw potato, or a tart apple cut fine. For an interesting flavor, add ¼ to 1 teaspoon caraway seeds, or season to taste with vinegar or brown sugar, or both.

Sauerkraut with Onions. Dice 1 onion and sauté in 2 tablespoons fat until soft. Add drained sauerkraut, stir well, cover, and cook slowly at least 30 minutes over moderate heat or in a 300° oven. Season to taste.

Sauerkraut with Wine. Cook sauerkraut in white or red wine, using 1½ cups to a pound. Use onion or not, as preferred.

Cardoon

Like coarse, prickly celery.

Wash and scrape. Cut in 2 or 3 inch lengths.

Cook until tender, 2 minutes in a pressure saucepan or 20 minutes in boiling salted water in a covered pan. Drain. Serve with melted butter.

Carrots

Young carrots have fresh green tops. Winter carrots should be firm and unblemished. One pound serves 3 or 4.

Wash. Scrub young carrots with a stiff brush. Scrape old carrots with a vegetable parer. Slice, cube, cut in slivers, or leave whole, if they are small.

Cook until tender (2 to 4 minutes in a pressure saucepan or 10 to 25 minutes in boiling salted water).

Season with butter, salt, pepper, a trace of sugar and a shake of nutmeg. Chopped mint or parsley is delicious with carrots, stirred in or sprinkled on top.

Carrots with Onion Butter. Cook 2 tablespoons butter with 2 tablespoons finely cut onion until the onion is yellow. Add to cooked chopped or sliced carrots.

Riced Carrots. Put cooked carrots through a potato ricer. Season with butter, salt and pepper. Sprinkle with chopped parsley.

Candied Carrots. Cut in halves or quarters, if large. Melt ½ cup butter in a heavy pan and add ½ cup brown sugar. Stir until melted, add the cooked carrots, and cook slowly until the carrots are well glazed.

Carrots Poulette. Reheat in Suprême Sauce (p. 92) made with the water in which carrots were cooked instead of stock.

Sweet and Sour Carrots. Make a sauce of the water in which the carrots were cooked, using 1 tablespoon fat and 1 tablespoon flour to each cup. Season the sauce to taste with brown sugar and vinegar or lemon juice. Add the sliced or cubed carrots and reheat.

Creamed Carrots and Celery. Cube cooked carrots, add finely cut cooked celery, and heat in Cream Sauce (p. 90) or a little heavy cream. Season to taste.

Carrots and Peas. Combine finely cut cooked carrots with an equal quantity of cooked green peas, and season with butter, salt and pepper. Heat thoroughly.

Mint-Glazed Carrots with Peas

Slice lengthwise, ¼ inch thick
  3 medium-sized carrots
Cut in strips. Cook (above) and drain. Add
  ½ cup butter
  ½ cup sugar
  1 tablespoon chopped fresh mint leaves
Cook slowly until well glazed. Add
  2 cups peas, cooked or canned
Heat and season to taste. *Serves 4.*

Slivered Carrots

Easy to prepare at the table in an electric skillet.

Cut carrots in thin shavings with a "knee-action" peeler. Sprinkle with salt. Cook 5 minutes in a covered pan with just enough water to keep from burning. Add melted butter and plenty of chopped parsley.

Vary as you like by cooking finely chopped onion in butter before adding the carrots to the pan or by seasoning with vermouth, Cointreau or nutmeg.

Baked Carrots

Melt
    3 tablespoons butter
Add
    ¼ cup chopped onion
Cook slowly until soft. Add
    2 cups shredded, scraped carrots
    1 teaspoon sugar
    Salt to taste
Put in a casserole. Add
    ½ cup water
Cover. Bake at 350° until tender (about 30 minutes). *Serves 4.*

Huntington Carrots

Melt in a heavy pan
    ½ cup butter
Add
    4 cups carrots, cut in 1½-inch strips
Turn over and over in the butter until well coated. Sprinkle with
    Salt
    ½ teaspoon sugar
Cover and cook slowly until tender (about 35 minutes). Turn occasionally. Season to taste. Just before serving, add
    ½ cup cream
Reheat. *Serves 4.*

Carrots Vichy. Use tiny young carrots and leave them whole. Instead of adding cream, sprinkle with lemon juice and chopped parsley.

Carrot Ring

Fill the ring with peas, Brussels sprouts or green beans, or, as a main dish, with creamed chicken, ham or tuna.

Mix
    2½ cups mashed cooked carrots
    2 teaspoons onion juice or minced onion
    2 tablespoons melted butter
    2 eggs, well beaten
    1 tablespoon flour
    1 cup milk or cream
Season to taste with
    Salt, pepper and paprika
Spoon into a buttered 1-quart ring mold. Set in a shallow pan of hot water. Bake at 350° until firm (40 to 50 minutes). *Serves 6.*

Carrot Ring with Cheese. Use 2 cups carrots and 1½ cups freshly grated Parmesan cheese. Add 1 cup bread crumbs.

Cauliflower

Choose a white head with fresh green leaves and no spots or bruises. If you like, set aside a few uncooked flowerets to use another day in a salad (p. 273) or on a relish tray. A medium-sized head serves 4 to 6.

Remove the leaves and cut off the stalk. Wash well. Leave whole or separate into flowerets.

Cook in boiling salted water, not more than 12 to 15 minutes for flowerets, 20 to 25 for a whole head. Drain.

Pour over the cauliflower melted butter seasoned with lemon juice and finely chopped parsley, or Hollandaise (p. 95), thin Cream Sauce (p. 90), Cheese Sauce (p. 91) or Lemon Sauce (p. 92).

Cauliflower au Gratin. Place a whole cooked cauliflower on an ovenproof dish. Cover with buttered crumbs. If you like, sprinkle with grated cheese before covering with the crumbs. Brown in a 350° oven. Remove from the oven and pour over the cauliflower 1 cup Cream Sauce (p. 90) or Cheese Sauce (p. 91).

Cauliflower Allemande. Place cooked cauliflower in a baking dish. Cover with Allemande Sauce (p. 92), sprinkle with ¼ cup grated Parmesan cheese, and bake at 350° until the cheese is melted.

French-Fried Cauliflower. Separate cooked cauliflower into flowerets, dip in egg and crumbs (p. 6), and fry in deep fat heated to 370° until brown (about 5 minutes).

Cauliflower with Mushrooms. Separate cooked cauliflower into flowerets. Cover with Mushroom Sauce (p. 97). If desired, leave the onion juice and beef extract out of the sauce and season it with ¼ teaspoon nutmeg.

Celeriac (Celery Root)

A variety of celery with a large turnip-like root. One pound serves 4.

Scrub thoroughly. Scrape or pare. Slice lengthwise or dice.

Cook 2 minutes in a pressure saucepan or 20 minutes in a covered pan in boiling salted water. Drain. Mash or not.

Serve with melted butter or Hollandaise (p. 95).

Celery

Green pascal celery has a more pungent flavor than white celery. A pound serves 2 or 3. If you like, save some of the small tender hearts to use as a relish or in salad.

Wash thoroughly. Cut off any discolored parts. Cut in 1-inch to 3-inch pieces.

Cook 2 minutes in a pressure saucepan or 15 to 20 minutes, covered, in just enough boiling salted water to keep the celery from burning. Drain. Add butter to taste.

Creamed Celery. Heat 2 cups cooked celery in 1 cup Cream Sauce (p. 90). To vary, add 1 or 2 green peppers, seeded, parboiled, and cut in small pieces. *Serves 4 to 6.*

Far East Celery

Cook (above) until just tender but still crisp (about 8 minutes)

    4 cups celery, in 1-inch pieces

Put in a 1-quart casserole. Stir in

    1 5-ounce can water chestnuts, drained and sliced thin

    1 can condensed cream of chicken soup

    1 pimiento, sliced

Mix lightly together and sprinkle over the casserole

    ½ cup soft bread crumbs

    ¼ cup toasted, slivered almonds

    2 tablespoons melted butter

Bake at 350° 35 minutes. *Serves 6.*

Braised Celery

Wash. Cut off the leaves. If the bunches are small, split the stalks in half or cut in even lengths. Put in a frying pan and add just enough boiling salted water, consommé or stock to keep the celery from burning. Cover and cook until tender (15 to 20 minutes).

Put the celery in a serving dish. Add a little water, consommé or cream to the liquid in the pan. Pour over the celery.

Braised Celery au Gratin. Arrange the cooked celery in a shallow baking dish. Sprinkle with melted butter, salt, pepper and plenty of grated Italian cheese. Broil or bake until the cheese melts.

Chayote

This pale green member of the cucumber family is similar to summer squash. One pound serves 4.

Cut in half or in quarters or slice without removing the edible seed. Peel before or after cooking.

Cover with boiling salted water. Cover the pan and cook until tender (15 to 20 minutes). Drain.

Serve with melted butter or Tomato Sauce (p. 94).

French or Italian Chestnuts

See also Chestnut Stuffing (p. 81) and the famous dessert, Mont Blanc (p. 381). One pound serves 3, but often there are imperfect nuts, so allow a little more to be sure. Canned cooked chestnuts are a convenience.

Shell chestnuts (p. 13). Cover with boiling salted water. Cover the pan and cook gently until tender when tested with a toothpick (15 to 20 minutes). Drain.

Creamed Chestnuts. Heat in a small amount of heavy cream. Season to taste.

Riced Chestnuts. Put through a ricer or strainer. Pile lightly on a serving dish or beat until light with hot milk or cream. Season to taste.

Sautéed Chestnuts. Cook 5 minutes in butter. Serve as a garnish with ham or roast turkey.

Corn

Corn is at its best fresh-picked just before cooking. Fresh corn looks moist and juicy. The kernels are well filled but still soft and milky. Old corn looks hard and dull. Keep ears of corn in the refrigerator until cooking time.

Just before cooking time, husk, pull off the silky threads, and cut out any blemishes with a pointed knife.

Scraped Corn. Cut uncooked corn from the cob with a long sharp knife. Scrape the cob with the dull edge of the knife to get all the sweet "milk." Add a small amount of cream or milk, cover and simmer until just tender (about 5 minutes). Add salt to taste.

Corn on the Cob. Have ready a deep kettle of unsalted water or half milk and half water. Bring to the boiling point and put in enough ears of corn for the first serving. Let the water come to the boiling point again and boil 5 minutes.

(A large quantity of corn will be cooked enough as soon as the boiling point is reached.) Serve with plenty of butter.

Steamed Corn on the Cob. Put the ears in the upper section of a steamer, not more than two layers deep. Steam 5 minutes.

Foil-Roasted Corn on the Cob. Wrap husked ears of corn individually in foil. Bake at 400° about 15 minutes. At a picnic or barbecue, roast over hot coals, turning once after 10 minutes.

Broiled Corn on the Cob. Turn the husks back without removing them. Pull off the silky threads. Dip the corn in cold water and replace the husks. Broil on the grill over a picnic fire, turning often, until thoroughly heated (about 15 minutes). Watch carefully so that the corn will not scorch. Season with salt, pepper and butter.

Buttered Corn. Cut freshly cooked corn from the cob with a long sharp knife and season with butter and salt.

Succotash. *(Fresh-cooked corn cut from the cob is better for succotash than canned corn.)* Heat together equal quantities of cooked corn and lima or shell beans. Season with salt and butter.

Corn Pudding

Irresistible with ham or chicken.

Beat for 3 minutes
   2 cups raw scraped corn
   1 cup heavy cream
   ½ teaspoon salt
Pour into a baking dish. Bake at 325° until firm (about 45 minutes). *Serves 4.*

Southern Corn Pudding

Mix
   2 cups fresh grated corn or chopped canned, frozen or cooked corn
   2 eggs, slightly beaten

1 teaspoon sugar
1½ tablespoons melted butter
2 cups scalded milk
1 teaspoon salt
⅛ teaspoon pepper

Put in a buttered baking dish. Set in a pan of hot water. Bake at 325° until firm (about 45 minutes). *Serves 4 to 6.*

Corn Soufflé

Melt
1 tablespoon butter
Stir in
2 tablespoons flour
Add gradually
1 cup milk
Stir and bring to the boiling point. Add
2 cups corn, fresh grated, canned, frozen or cooked
2 egg yolks, beaten thick
Season with
1¼ teaspoons salt
Few grains pepper
Cook about 10 minutes. Fold in
2 egg whites, beaten stiff

Spoon into an unbuttered baking dish. Bake 30 minutes at 350°. *Serves 6.*

Corn Fritters

Chop and drain
1 cup fresh or whole kernel canned corn
Add
1 egg yolk, beaten thick
Sift together
½ cup plus 2 tablespoons flour
½ teaspoon baking powder
½ teaspoon salt
Few grains paprika
Stir into the corn. Fold in
1 egg white, beaten stiff

Drop from a tablespoon into fat heated to 370°. Cook until delicately brown. Drain on a paper towel. *Serves 4 to 6.*

Corn Oysters. Make the batter with only ¼ cup flour or ½ cup soft bread crumbs. Cook by spoonfuls on a hot griddle in bacon fat or drippings.

Scalloped Corn

Put in a saucepan
2 tablespoons butter
½ onion, chopped fine
Cook 5 minutes. Mix
2 tablespoons flour
1 teaspoon salt
¼ teaspoon paprika
¼ teaspoon mustard
Few grains cayenne
Stir into the butter and onion. Add, stirring constantly
½ cup milk
Bring to the boiling point. Stir in
1 cup fresh or drained canned whole kernel corn
1 egg yolk, slightly beaten
Melt
1 tablespoon butter
Add
½ cup dried bread, broken in small pieces
Stir until brown and add to the corn mixture. Put in a buttered baking dish. Cover with
⅔ cup buttered cracker crumbs
Bake at 400° until the crumbs are brown. *Serves 4 to 6.*

To season more highly, add a few drops Worcestershire or Tabasco, or chop a small green pepper and cook it with the onion.

Cucumbers

Select firm slender cucumbers, dark green and glossy. Yellow spots show they are too mature and will be seedy and spongy. One large cucumber serves 3.

In salads (p. 274). On the relish tray (p. 83). Wilted Cucumbers (p. 274).

Stewed Cucumbers. Pare the cucumbers unless they are very young and tender. Cut in pieces. Put in a saucepan with just enough water, chicken stock or bouillon to keep from burning. Cover and cook gently until tender (5 to 15 minutes). Season with butter, salt and pepper.

Fried Cucumbers. Wipe and pare the cucumbers. Cut in slices at least ¼ inch thick. Dry on a paper towel. Sprinkle with salt, pepper and flour and sauté in butter; or season, dip in crumbs, egg and crumbs (p. 6), and fry in deep fat heated to 390°. Drain on paper towels.

Stuffed Cucumbers. Wipe the cucumbers. Pare if the skin is tough. Cut in 2-inch pieces, crosswise. Remove the seeds. Stuff with bread crumbs mixed with finely chopped ham and cheese and moistened with tomato sauce or canned tomato soup. Or stuff with any well-seasoned mixture of bread crumbs or cooked rice combined with bits of cooked meat, chicken, lobster, crab meat or cheese.

Put in a baking dish. Surround with stock or consommé. Bake about 30 minutes at 350°. Cover with buttered crumbs and bake until brown.

Dandelion Greens

See Greens (p. 248).

Dasheens

This uncommon vegetable is violet-colored when cooked. One pound serves 4.

Scrub thoroughly with a brush. Do not pare before cooking, as the raw juice is irritating to the skin.

Cover with boiling salted water. Cook until tender (15 to 30 minutes). Peel. Put through a ricer or vegetable mill.

Season with salt and pepper and plenty of butter.

Eggplant

Choose one that is satin-smooth and firm. A medium-sized eggplant (1½ pounds) serves 4.

Peel only if the skin is very tough. Cut in slices ¼ to ½ inch thick. Dry on paper towels.

Pan-Fried or Sautéed Eggplant. Dip in seasoned flour or fine bread crumbs. Brown slowly in butter or bacon fat, turning to cook evenly. Or dip in flour, egg and fine crumbs and fry in fat about ½ inch deep, using bacon fat or oil.

Oven-Fried Eggplant. Prepare as for pan-frying. Put in a baking pan in a single layer. Bake at 450° until tender (about 20 minutes). During the baking, sprinkle three times with melted butter or salad oil.

Baked Eggplant. Marinate 15 minutes in French dressing and drain. Or spread with softened butter. Bake until tender at 400° (about 15 minutes), turning once. Sprinkle with lemon juice.

French-Fried Eggplant. Dip in Fritter Batter (p. 425), or flour, egg and crumbs (p. 6). Fry at 370°. Delicious cut in julienne strips instead of slices.

Scalloped Eggplant

Pare and cut in ½-inch cubes
 1 eggplant
Cover with
 Boiling water or ½ cup dry white wine
Cook until just tender, and drain. Melt
 2 tablespoons butter
Add
 ½ onion, chopped fine
Cook until yellow. Add the eggplant and
 1 tablespoon finely chopped parsley
Put in a buttered baking dish. Cover with
 Buttered crumbs
Bake at 375° until the crumbs are brown.
Serves 4 to 6.

Scalloped Eggplant de Luxe. Cook the eggplant in dry white wine. Do not drain. Beat 2 eggs slightly, add ½ teaspoon salt and ¼ teaspoon pepper, and add to the eggplant with 2 tablespoons minced onion and 1 cup soft bread crumbs mixed with ⅓ cup melted butter. Put in a shallow buttered baking dish. Top with ½ cup freshly grated cheese. Bake at 350° until firm (about 25 minutes). *Serves 4 to 6.*

Eggplant and Mushrooms

Put in a saucepan
    1 tablespoon butter
    1 large onion, minced
Cook until yellow. Add
    ½ pound mushrooms, cut small
Cover and cook 5 minutes. Add
    1 eggplant, peeled and cubed
    ½ cup bouillon
    ½ clove garlic
    Salt to taste
Cover and cook slowly 1 hour. Remove the garlic. *Serves 4.*

Eggplant Istanbul

Perfect with roast lamb.

Put in a saucepan
    ½ cup salad oil
    1 eggplant, peeled and cubed
    1 onion, chopped fine
Cook 10 minutes. Add
    2 cloves garlic, crushed
    2 tomatoes, peeled and cut in eighths
    1 can tomato paste
    Juice of 1 lemon
Simmer 15 minutes. Add
    Salt to taste
Serve with lemon wedges or spoon over fluffy steamed rice and add an extra squeeze of lemon juice. *Serves 6.*

Eggplant and Okra

Put in a saucepan
    1 eggplant, peeled and cubed
    1 onion, sliced
    3 tomatoes, quartered
    12 okra pods, sliced
    Salt and pepper
Cover. Cook slowly 30 minutes. Sprinkle with
    1 tablespoon finely chopped parsley
Serves 4 to 6.

Eggplant Soufflé

Peel and cube
    2 eggplants (about 3 pounds)

Cover with boiling salted water. Add
    1 slice onion
Cover and cook until soft. Remove the onion. Drain and mash the eggplant. Add
    2 tablespoons butter
    ½ cup bread crumbs
    ½ cup milk
Season to taste with
    Salt, pepper and nutmeg
Stir in
    3 egg yolks, slightly beaten
Cool.

When ready to bake, fold in
    3 egg whites, beaten stiff
Put in an unbuttered baking dish and sprinkle with
    2 tablespoons buttered crumbs
    2 tablespoons shredded toasted almonds
Bake 30 minutes at 400°. *Serves 6 to 8.*

Eggplant and Mushroom Soufflé. Add ½ cup chopped sautéed mushrooms.

Baked Stuffed Eggplant

Cover with boiling salted water
    1 eggplant
Cook 15 minutes. Drain. Cut in half lengthwise. Carefully remove the pulp with a spoon so that you will not break the skin. Chop the pulp and add
    1 cup soft bread crumbs
Melt in a frying pan
    2 tablespoons butter or bacon fat
Add
    ½ tablespoon finely chopped onion
       (or more)
Cook 5 minutes. Add the pulp and crumbs, season to taste, and moisten with
    A little stock or water
Cook 5 minutes. Cool. Add
    1 egg, well beaten
Refill the eggplant. Cover with
    Buttered crumbs
Bake at 375° for 25 minutes. *Serves 4 (or 6, if the eggplant is large).*

To vary. Add finely chopped ham, mushrooms or toasted almonds.

Ratatouille Niçoise

A famous French dish, excellent as the main course at lunch or as the vegetable for a buffet supper.

Peel and cube
　1 eggplant
Peel (if skin is tough) and cube
　1 zucchini or summer squash
Cook 10 minutes in boiling water and drain.

Peel and cut in pieces
　6 tomatoes
Put in a saucepan
　¼ cup oil
Add
　1 onion, chopped fine
Cook until brown. Add the vegetables and
　1 clove garlic, crushed
　1 tablespoon chopped parsley
　1 bay leaf
　Salt and pepper
Cook until the vegetables are tender (about 20 minutes). Season to taste. Place in a shallow baking dish, and sprinkle with
　½ cup freshly grated Parmesan or
　　Romano cheese
Brown under the broiler. *Serves 6.*

Braised Endive

Allow 1 or 2 stalks per person.

Wash under running water and cut off any discolored parts. Leave stalks whole unless they are very large, in which case split them in two pieces.

Place in a skillet, add bouillon or chicken broth until ½ inch deep. Sprinkle with salt, cover, and cook slowly until tender (about 20 minutes). Drain. Add butter, cover, and cook 10 minutes longer.

Fennel (Anise)

Like celery with a licorice flavor. One pound serves 3.

Peel and slice the bulb and as much of the stalk as is tender. Wash and drain.

Cook in a covered pan in salted boiling water until tender (15 to 25 minutes). Drain. Sprinkle with salt and pepper and melted butter or olive oil and lemon juice.

As a relish. Cut in strips and serve raw, like celery.

Fiddleheads

Such an unusual vegetable that it adds a touch of glamor to a dinner party menu. Fiddleheads (young fern shoots) occasionally appear in market in the spring. Frozen ones are also available.

Wash fresh fiddleheads, drain, and peel off the woolly skin. Partially defrost frozen ones.

Cook like asparagus (about 5 minutes). Season with salt and melted butter.

Greens

Young tender beet tops, Swiss chard, dandelion greens, collards, kale, chicory, escarole, lettuce, spinach, turnip tops, mustard greens. One pound serves 3, though some greens cook down more than others.

Remove any discolored leaves. Wash greens thoroughly, using slightly warm water at first. Cut off the roots and tough stems and wash again, lifting the greens out of the water to let the sand settle in the pan. Sprinkle with salt.

Cook, covered tightly, until just barely tender, in a steamer or in the smallest amount of boiling water possible. The water that clings to the leaves from washing is usually enough.

Drain. Chop fine or cut through a few times. Season with butter, pepper and salt.

Gumbo

See Okra (p. 251).

Kohlrabi

Select small, pale green bulbs. Allow 1 or 2 to a person.

Cut off the tops, peel, and slice. Cook, uncovered, in boiling salted water until tender (25 to 35 minutes). Drain thoroughly. Season with melted butter, salt and pepper. If the tops are young and tender, cook in boiling salted water, drain, chop, and add to the sliced bulbs.

Leeks

One large bunch serves 4. See also Leek and Potato Soup (p. 68) and Vichyssoise (p. 68).

Wash and trim, leaving about 1½ inches of the green top. Cook until tender 2 or 3 minutes in pressure saucepan or 15 to 20 minutes in boiling salted water. Drain. Serve with melted butter.

Leeks au Gratin. Arrange cooked stalks in a baking dish, sprinkle with salt, pepper and freshly grated cheese. Set under the broiler to melt the cheese.

Dried Lentils

Follow directions for cooking Dried Beans (p. 236). See also Lentil Soup (p. 68).

Braised Lettuce

Soak in cold water 1 hour
    3 small firm lettuce hearts or 1 large
        heart, quartered
Drain. Tie firmly with string. Cook 10 minutes in boiling salted water. Drain and cut off the string.

Melt in a heavy frying pan
    2 tablespoons butter
Add the lettuce. Season with
    Salt, pepper and nutmeg
Cook slowly 35 minutes.

Pour over the lettuce
    1 tablespoon lemon juice
Serves 2 or 3.

Wilted Lettuce

Add onion juice, if you like, or sprinkle the lettuce with 1 teaspoon finely cut onion. Use the same dressing for endive or dandelion greens or for young cabbage, shredded and cooked 5 minutes in boiling water and drained.

Wash and dry thoroughly
    2 small heads tender lettuce (not
        iceberg)
Tear into pieces and put in a large salad bowl.

Fry until crisp
    4 strips bacon
Drain on a paper towel and crumble into bits. Add to the fat in the pan
    2 tablespoons vinegar
    2 tablespoons water
    Salt and pepper
    1 tablespoon brown sugar
Heat to the boiling point. Add the bacon and pour the hot dressing over the lettuce. Toss to wilt the lettuce. Slice hot hard-cooked eggs over the top if you like. *Serves 4.*

Vegetable Marrow

See summer squash recipes, p. 256.

Mushrooms

Select firm, unspotted mushrooms. One pound serves 4 (or 2 if served as the main dish).

Wash, but do not peel unless the skin is tough and brown. Cut off any discolored parts and the tough ends of the stems.

Duxelles. Chop fine, or, if you are using the tops in another way, chop the stems only and sauté in butter until the moisture is absorbed. Season delicately to taste with onion salt and nutmeg. Add a touch of Madeira or brandy, if you like. Store, covered, in the refrigerator, to use as the basis for sauce or soup or to add to sauces, gravies, stews and vegetables.

Sautéed Mushrooms. Wash and slice 1 pound mushrooms. Put in a heavy frying pan with ¼ cup butter. Season with salt, pepper, and a trace of nutmeg. Cover and cook over low heat 10 minutes, stirring occasionally.

Creamed Mushrooms. Sprinkle Sautéed Mushrooms with 1 tablespoon flour, stir, and add 1 cup cream or milk. Cook until slightly thickened. Season to taste with more nutmeg or sherry.

Mushrooms Flambé. Just before serving Sautéed Mushrooms add ⅓ cup warmed brandy and light with a match. Serve with steak or chicken. Add ½ cup heavy cream to make a rich sauce.

Broiled Mushrooms. Reserve the stems for soup or Duxelles (p. 249). Dip the caps in milk, oil or melted butter and let stand ½ hour. Arrange in a shallow pan, smooth side up. Broil 3 minutes on each side. Put a small piece of butter in each cap. Sprinkle with salt and pepper. Serve on buttered toast or as a border on the meat platter. Pour the pan juices over the mushrooms.

Sausage-Stuffed Mushrooms. After turning Broiled Mushrooms, fill with sausage meat, and broil or bake at 375° until the sausage is cooked (about 20 minutes). Serve as a luncheon or supper dish or with roast turkey.

Mushrooms Baked in Cream. Reserve the stems for soup or Duxelles (p. 249). Put the caps in a shallow buttered pan, smooth side down. Sprinkle with salt and pepper. Dot with butter and pour a little cream or milk around them. Bake 10 minutes at 450°. Place on dry toast. Pour the juices over the mushrooms.

French-Fried Mushrooms. Wash and dry perfect mushrooms. Cut off the stems and keep them for soup or Duxelles (p. 249). Beat an egg with 1 tablespoon water. Dip each cap in the beaten egg, then in salted bread crumbs. (For a thicker coating, dip the mushrooms in Fritter Batter, p. 429.) Let stand 1 hour.

Fry until brown in deep fat heated to 375°. Serve as a vegetable, as a garnish or appetizer, or for lunch with strips of crisp bacon.

Stuffed Mushrooms

Wash and dry on a paper towel
  12 large mushrooms
Cut off the stems and chop them fine. Melt
  3 tablespoons butter
Add the mushroom stems and
  ½ tablespoon finely chopped shallot or onion
Cook 10 minutes. Add
  1½ tablespoons flour
  Chicken Stock (p. 72), tomato juice, or cream to moisten
  Few gratings nutmeg
  ½ teaspoon finely chopped parsley
  Salt and pepper
Cool. Fill the caps, rounding well over the top. Cover with
  Buttered cracker crumbs
Bake 15 minutes at 425°.

To vary. Add finely chopped cooked chicken or turkey liver, ham, celery or cheese.

Mushroom Ring

Melt in a frying pan
  2 tablespoons butter
Add
  1 tablespoon chopped onion
Cook slowly until golden. Add
  ½ pound mushrooms, chopped
Cook and stir 5 minutes. Add
  ½ teaspoon salt
  ⅛ teaspoon nutmeg
  Few grains pepper
  2 tablespoons flour
Add slowly, stirring constantly
  ½ cup milk
Cook and stir until thickened. Add
  2 beaten eggs
Pour into a buttered ring mold. Bake at 350° until firm (about 30 minutes). Turn out onto a serving dish and fill with buttered green peas or green beans. Serves 6.

Mushroom Flan. *Most attractive done in a flan ring, but a pie plate will do. Flan rings are available in shops selling French cooking equipment.* Increase the onion to one whole chopped onion. Pour the filling into an 8-inch pie plate or flan ring lined with Plain Pastry (p. 407). Bake at 400° until delicately browned (about 30 minutes). *Serves 6.*

Okra (Gumbo)

Select small, crisp green pods. One pound serves 6.

Wash well and cut off the stems. If very young and small, leave whole. Otherwise, cut in ½-inch slices.

Cook 3 minutes in a pressure saucepan or until tender in salted boiling water to cover (10 to 20 minutes). Drain. Season with salt, pepper, butter and vinegar.

Okra with Tomatoes. Stew ½ pound okra (or 1 can) with 2 cups stewed or canned tomatoes. Season to taste.

Okra Baked in Tomato Sauce. Brown 1 sliced onion in 2 tablespoons butter. Add 1 pound sliced okra. Cook 3 minutes. Season to taste. Put in a casserole, pour over the okra 1 cup Tomato Sauce (p. 94) or concentrated tomato soup. Bake 30 minutes at 350°.

Onions

Tiny button onions, white, yellow and red cooking onions, mild Italian, Spanish and Bermuda onions — all are good. Select firm onions with dry crackly skins and no green sprouts. Buy a few at a time unless you have a cool dry place to store them. One pound serves 4.

Peel, holding the onion under running water to keep the eyes from watering, or cover with boiling water, drain, dip in cold water, and slip off the skins. Make two crossed gashes on the root end.

Cook until tender (10 minutes in a pressure saucepan or 20 to 40 in boiling salted water in a deep, uncovered pan). Drain. Add a little milk or cream, simmer 5 minutes and season with butter, salt and pepper.

Creamed Onions. Cook small onions 15 minutes. Drain. Add thin cream (1 cup for 3 cups onions) and cook in a double boiler until tender. Add salt to taste when the onions are nearly done. If you like, sprinkle with chopped roasted peanuts or almonds.

Scalloped Onions. Put in a buttered baking dish 2 cups cooked onions (quartered). Cover with 1 cup Cream Sauce (p. 90) or canned cream of celery or mushroom soup. Sprinkle with buttered crumbs. Bake at 400° until brown. Mix grated cheese with the sauce if you like.

Glazed Onions. Drain cooked or canned tiny onions. For each cupful, melt 1 tablespoon butter with 2 teaspoons sugar or 1 tablespoon honey. Add the onions. Cook over very low heat until brown (about 20 minutes). To be sure the onions do not burn, set the pan on an asbestos mat. Turn the onions occasionally so that they will brown evenly. If more convenient, put in a casserole and bake at 350°.

Broiled Onions

Cut large mild onions in ½-inch slices. Put in a shallow pan. Season with salt and pepper. Dot with butter. Broil until tender (about 15 minutes), turning once.

Smothered Onions

Peel 4 medium-sized onions and cut in thin slices. Sauté very slowly in butter until delicately brown. Turn occasionally with a fork so that the onions will not burn. Sprinkle with salt. *Serves 4.*

Onions Baked in Cream

Two large onions serve 4 to 6.

Cut large sweet onions in thin slices. Arrange in a baking dish. Sprinkle with salt and pepper. Add enough cream to cover. Bake at 325° until tender.

French-Fried Onions

Heat canned or frozen fried onion rings in the oven before serving.

Peel 4 large mild sweet onions. Cut in ¼-inch slices and separate into rings. Dip in milk, drain, and dip in ½ cup flour mixed with ½ teaspoon salt.

Fry 4 to 6 minutes in deep fat heated to 370° (p. 5). Drain on a paper towel and sprinkle with salt.

Serve with cocktails or on steak.

Stuffed Onions

Spanish onions are ideal for this dish. Allow 1 for each serving.

Cover the onions with lightly salted boiling water and cook 10 minutes. Drain and dip in cold water. Drain and scoop out the centers to make cups ½ inch thick. Chop the centers and mix with cooked sausage meat or with any well-seasoned cooked meat or chicken, chopped mushrooms and soft bread crumbs. Moisten with cream or melted butter and season to taste. Stuff the onions and sprinkle with buttered crumbs.

Put in a baking dish with a small amount of water or stock. Bake at 375° until tender (30 to 45 minutes).

Almond-Stuffed Onions. *A gourmet version for a dinner party.* Instead of the filling suggested above, add for each cup of chopped onion ½ cup chopped toasted almonds, ¼ cup bread crumbs and ¼ cup melted butter. Add salt and pepper to taste. Continue as above, but use cream as the liquid in the baking dish.

Onions and Green Peppers

Remove the seeds and the white membrane from
   1 or 2 green peppers
Cut in very thin slivers. Sauté slowly until tender in
   2 tablespoons butter
Stir in
   2 tablespoons flour

Blend well. Add
   1 cup milk or thin cream
Cook and stir until thickened. Add
   1 pound small onions, cooked or canned
Heat slowly. Season to taste with
   Salt and pepper
Serves 6.

Cheese and Onion Casserole

Cut in quarters
   6 slices bread
Have ready
   2 cups drained small white onions, cooked or canned
   1 cup grated Cheddar cheese
Put the bread, onions and cheese in a buttered casserole in layers. Mix
   4 eggs, beaten slightly
   2 cups milk
   ½ teaspoon salt
   Few grains pepper
Pour over the mixture in the casserole. Set in a pan of hot water. Bake at 350° until firm (about 45 minutes). *Serves 6.*

Green Onions or Scallions on Toast

Trim off any wilted parts.

Cook in boiling salted water until just tender (about 10 minutes). Drain.

Serve on buttered toast. Season melted butter with salt and pepper and pour it over the onions.

Green Onion Pie

Wonderful with sliced ham or tongue. If you prefer, bake as you would custard, without bothering with the pastry shell, and spoon it from the baking dish.

Put in a saucepan
   3 tablespoons butter
   3 cups sliced green onions or scallions
Cook slowly until tender. Put in an
   Unbaked pie shell (8 or 9 inches)
Mix and pour over the onions
   2 eggs, slightly beaten
   ½ cup cream
   1 teaspoon salt

Pepper or nutmeg to taste
Bake at 425° until firm (about 20 minutes). *Serves 6.*

Oyster Plant (Salsify)

Similar to parsnip but darker, with a flavor somewhat like oysters. One bunch (about 6 roots) serves 6.

Wash, scrape, and put in cold water with a little vinegar or lemon juice to prevent discoloration. Cut in inch slices or strips. Do not salt before cooking.

Cook until tender (10 minutes in a pressure saucepan or 20 to 45 minutes in boiling water in a covered pan). Drain. Season with butter, salt and pepper.

Oyster Plant aux Fines Herbes. Add 1 teaspoon finely chopped parsley and ¼ teaspoon finely chopped chives. Sprinkle with salt and pepper.

Oyster Plant Fritters. Mash. Season with butter, salt and pepper. Shape in small flat cakes, roll in flour, and brown in butter.

Parsnips

Parsnips are at their best in the spring, either freshly dug or from storage. Large ones may have woody cores. One pound serves 3 or 4.

Wash, scrape, and slice or cut in strips. Remove the cores, if woody.

Cook until tender (30 to 40 minutes in boiling salted water, 4 to 10 minutes in a pressure saucepan). Drain. Season with salt, nutmeg and butter.

Sautéed Parsnips. Boil small whole parsnips. Drain and cut in eighths lengthwise. Brown delicately in butter. Sprinkle with salt and pepper. To candy, sprinkle with brown sugar before sautéing.

Caramel Parsnips. Scrape small whole parsnips. Cook 20 minutes and drain. Put in a shallow baking dish. Dot with butter. Sprinkle with brown sugar. Bake at 400° about 20 minutes.

Parsnip Fritters. Mash cooked parsnips. Season with butter, salt and pepper. Shape in 3-inch patties. Dip in flour and sauté on both sides in butter.

Green Peas

Fresh peas have shiny green pods. Open a pod and taste to see if the peas are young and sweet. Do not shell until time to cook them. Store in the refrigerator. Young peas from a nearby farm — or your own garden — are best of all. One pound serves 2.

Frozen peas are good, too, and so are canned tiny French peas, which are very tender and delicious.

Shell the peas. Put in a saucepan. Add just enough water to keep the peas from burning. Cover and cook until tender but not mushy. A pressure cooker is too fast for young peas. Season with salt, pepper and butter. Add a trace of sugar if the peas are not young and sweet.

Peas on Artichoke Bottoms. Serve on canned artichoke bottoms, sprinkled with lemon juice. Pour a little heated cream over them.

Peas with Lemon-Mint Butter. *Also good with carrots.* Cream together ½ cup butter, 1 tablespoon lemon juice and ¼ teaspoon grated lemon peel. Add 2 tablespoons chopped fresh mint leaves and dot over cooked peas. Enough for 3 or 4 cups of peas.

Peas with Celery and Olives

Easily done in an electric frying pan.

Put in a frying pan
  2 tablespoons salad oil
  2 cups celery (sliced thin at an angle)
Cover and cook 10 minutes. Add
  2 packages frozen peas, slightly defrosted
Cover and cook 10 minutes longer. Add
  ½ cup pitted ripe olives, cut in halves lengthwise
Season to taste with
  Salt and pepper
Serves 6.

Petits Pois à la Française

Very young and tender peas are perfect cooked this way.

Put in a deep pan
    1 tablespoon butter
    2 pounds peas, shelled
Lay over the peas
    2 or 3 leaves of lettuce, rinsed in cold water
Cover. Cook over low heat until the peas are just tender (10 minutes or more). Season with
    Salt and pepper
    Butter
Serves 4 or 5.

Petits Pois with Onions. Brown 12 tiny cooked or canned onions lightly in butter. Over them lay ½ head of lettuce, shredded, and the shelled peas. Vary by adding a few sliced sautéed mushrooms. Cook as above. Moisten with a little heavy cream. *Serves 6.*

Purée of Green Peas

Successful, too, with old or tough peas; put through a strainer after puréeing if the tough skins are still in evidence.

Put cooked or canned peas through a vegetable mill or strainer or whirl in a blender. Beat until light and smooth with hot milk or cream. Season to taste. Keep hot in a double boiler. Dust with paprika. Vary the seasoning by cooking a slice of onion and a sprig or two of parsley with the peas.

Ring Mold of Green Peas. To 2 cups puréed peas, add 2 well-beaten eggs and 2 tablespoons melted butter. For a fluffier mixture, add the beaten whites last. Fill a buttered ring mold. Set in a shallow pan of hot water and cover with buttered paper.

Bake at 350° until firm (about 25 minutes). Fill the center with creamed shrimp, chicken or mushrooms, or Carrots Vichy (p. 242).

Snow Peas

Snow peas have tender edible pods. The tiny ones are delicious cooked, covered with French dressing, chilled and served as a salad. One pound serves 4 or 5.

Wash but do not shell. Cook, shells and all, until tender (15 minutes or longer) in a covered pan in just enough salted water to keep them from burning. Drain. Serve with Hollandaise (p. 95) or melted butter.

Purée of Split Peas

Cover 1 pound of split peas with boiling water and cook 2 minutes. Remove from the heat and let stand 1 hour or more. Add a ham bone or a piece of salt pork and cook slowly, covered, until the peas are soft. Drain and remove the bone or pork. Put the peas through a purée strainer.

Season to taste. Add butter or heavy cream. *Serves 6.*

Peppers

Sweet peppers, green or red, are the ones usually cooked as a vegetable. The hot green or red or chili peppers are used chiefly for seasoning. Pimientos are sweet red peppers preserved in oil.

Sautéed Peppers. Cut in half. Remove the seeds and the tough white membrane. Cut in small pieces. Put in a frying pan with butter, salad oil or bacon fat (2 tablespoons for 4 to 6 peppers), cover, and cook over moderate heat 5 to 10 minutes. Sprinkle with salt and pepper.

Serve as a vegetable or as a garnish.

French-Fried Pepper Rings. Slice green sweet peppers in thin rings. Remove the seeds. Cover with boiling water, cook 5 minutes, and drain on a paper towel.

Dip in egg slightly beaten with 1 table-spoon water, then in fine crumbs.

Fry, a few at a time, in deep fat, heated to 370° (p. 5). Drain on a paper towel.

Stuffed Green Peppers

If the peppers are small, leave them whole and cut off a slice from the stem end. Cut large peppers in half length-wise. Remove the seeds and tough white membrane. Cook in boiling water 5 min-utes and drain. Sprinkle with salt. Cool.

Fill generously with any of the fillings suggested below. Cover with grated cheese or buttered bread crumbs. Bake 15 minutes at 350°. Raise the temper-ature to 400° and bake until the tops are brown.

Corn Filling. Use Scraped Corn (p. 244) or canned corn, sprinkled with salt and pepper.

Cheese Filling. Mix freshly grated Ched-dar cheese with an equal quantity of buttered bread crumbs. Season to taste with salt, pepper, paprika and chopped onion or onion salt.

Chicken, Ham or Veal Filling. Chop cooked meat. Mix with an equal quantity of bread crumbs. Moisten with melted butter, concentrated tomato soup or consommé. Season to taste. Add chopped sautéed mushrooms, if you like.

Hamburg and Rice Filling. Sauté in 2 tablespoons butter 1 small onion, chopped, ½ pound ground beef and 2 peeled and diced tomatoes (or ½ cup canned tomatoes). Add 1 cup cooked rice and season with salt and pepper. *Enough for 4 peppers.*

Potatoes

Potatoes, both white and sweet (pp. 262–269).

Radishes

Piquant and unusual as a cooked vege-table. Allow about ⅓ cup per person. As a relish or garnish (pp. 84, 270).

Scrub in cold water. Cut off leaves, stems, and any long roots.

Creamed Radishes. Slice. Add to Cream Sauce (p. 90), using 1 cup sauce for 1 to 1½ cups radishes. Cook over hot water until the radishes are tender (about 25 minutes).

Radishes Hollandaise. Cover sliced rad-ishes with boiling salted water. Cover and cook until tender but still crisp (about 25 minutes). Drain. Serve with Hollandaise (p. 95).

Salsify

Another name for Oyster Plant (p. 253).

Spinach

Select spinach with small, dark green, fresh-looking leaves. Frozen or canned spinach is less crisp than fresh spinach. One pound serves 2 or 3. Eggs Florentine (p. 104).

Prepare and cook like other greens (p. 248). Chop or leave in sprays or cut through several times. Season to taste with butter, salt and pepper, or with French dressing. Add, if you like, a little vinegar or a trace of sugar, a sprinkling of nutmeg or grated lemon peel.

Serve with Hollandaise (p. 95), or gar-nish with toast points or sliced hard-cooked eggs, cut in eighths or chopped fine.

Spinach Ring. Spoon hot drained and chopped cooked spinach or creamed spinach into a serving dish. Push to the edge to make a ring. Fill with tiny but-tered beets or creamed mushrooms, chicken, fish or eggs.

Creamed Spinach French Style

An excellent luncheon dish, served on French Toast (p. 344) made without sugar.

Melt

   3 tablespoons butter

Add

   2 cups finely chopped cooked spinach, well drained

Cook 3 minutes. Sprinkle with

   1 tablespoon flour

Stir well. Add

   ½ cup cream

Cook 5 minutes. Season to taste with

   Salt, pepper, nutmeg and a trace of sugar

Garnish with

   Pastry crescents or chopped sautéed almonds

Serves 4 or 5.

To prepare in a blender. (With dried cream, no flour is needed, yet the spinach will not be watery.) Drain cooked spinach thoroughly. Whirl in an electric blender until smooth. Stir in powdered cream and seasonings to taste.

Spinach à la Béchamel. Instead of cream, use canned chicken broth or Chicken Stock (p. 72).

Spinach Custard

Mix

   2 cups cooked spinach, drained and chopped fine

   2 tablespoons melted butter

   2 eggs, slightly beaten

   1 cup milk

   ⅛ teaspoon sugar

   Few drops onion juice

   Few grains nutmeg

   Salt and pepper

   Vinegar or lemon juice to taste

Put in a buttered casserole. Bake at 300° until firm (about 25 minutes). *Serves 4.*

Spinach Soufflé. Beat the egg whites until stiff and fold them in last.

Summer Squash

Select small young squash of any of the many types available — smooth yellow crooknecks, dark green zucchini, striped vegetable marrow, or scalloped, pale green pattypan squash. One pound serves 3.

See also zucchini recipes, pp. 260–261.

Wash, quarter, or cut squash in thick slices. Do not peel unless rough and old.

Cook until tender (2 minutes in a pressure saucepan; 10 to 20 minutes in a covered pan) with just enough water to keep from burning.

Drain thoroughly. Mash and season with butter, salt, and pepper.

To vary, add a grating of nutmeg or a bit of chopped fresh dill, or sprinkle with grated cheese.

Creamed Summer Squash. Cut in cubes, cook until nearly done but still firm, drain, and reheat in cream. Season.

Fried Summer Squash

Cut in ½-inch pieces. Sprinkle with salt and pepper. Dip in crumbs, egg and crumbs (p. 6), fry in hot fat (375°), and drain.

Sautéed Summer Squash

Slice. Sprinkle with salt, pepper and flour. Sauté slowly in salad oil or butter until crisp and brown. Especially with zucchini, you will like the flavor if you put a clove of garlic in the pan. If you wish, add a spoonful or two of catsup, cover and heat 5 minutes, then serve.

Baked Summer Squash and Onions

Slice squash into a baking dish (removing the seeds if they are large). Add sliced onion separated into rings. Dot with butter, salt and pepper. Repeat. Cover and bake 30 minutes at 400°. Uncover and add cream (½ cup for about 2 pounds of squash). Bake until delicately brown (about 10 minutes).

Squash Ring

Mix

3 cups cooked summer squash (drained and put through a coarse sieve before measuring)
¼ cup melted butter
¼ cup milk
3 eggs, well beaten
Salt, pepper, cayenne
1 tablespoon grated onion
¼ cup buttered crumbs

Spoon into a buttered 1-quart ring mold. Set in a pan of hot water. Bake at 350° until firm (about 25 minutes). Turn onto a serving dish. Fill with buttered peas, tiny white onions or creamed mushrooms. *Serves 6.*

Winter Squash

Hubbard squash weigh 5 pounds or more. Buy a whole squash or part of one. Butternut squash weigh 2 or 3 pounds and are very dry and mealy. Acorn squash weigh 1 pound or less and are perfect for the small family or for individual service. Allow ½ pound per person. If you cook more than you need for one meal, you will have some for a spicy Squash Pie (p. 416).

Mashed Winter Squash. Cut in pieces. Remove the seeds and fibers.

Cook until tender (6 to 10 minutes in a pressure saucepan, 20 to 30 minutes in boiling salted water in a covered pan). Drain, pare, and mash. Season with butter, salt and pepper and a trace of sugar.

If you like, put in a baking dish, cover with marshmallows or strips of bacon, and bake at 400° until the marshmallows melt or the bacon crisps.

Baked Hubbard Squash. Put a whole squash in a large pan, a half squash cut side down. Bake at 350° until soft (2 hours or more). Cut in half. Remove the seeds. Scoop the squash out of the shell. Mash and season with butter, salt and pepper.

Baked Squash in Squares. Cut in 2-inch squares. Remove the seeds and fibers. Put in a baking pan, skin side down. Brush with butter or bacon fat. Sprinkle with salt and pepper. Put ½ teaspoon molasses on each piece or sprinkle with brown sugar. Bake at 350° until soft (about 50 minutes). Cover for the first half hour of the baking. Serve in the shell.

Baked Acorn Squash

One squash serves 2 people.

Cut in half but do not remove the seeds. Put on a cooky sheet, cut side up. Bake at 400° until soft (30 to 45 minutes).

Scrape out the seeds and fibers and discard. Sprinkle with salt and pepper. Put a bit of butter in each.

Glazed Acorn Squash. Just before serving, sprinkle with brown or maple sugar. Set in the oven again and bake until the sugar melts.

Stuffed Acorn Squash. Fill the baked squash with Tomatoes Creole (p. 258) or, as a lunch or supper dish, with creamed chicken or ham. Sprinkle with buttered crumbs. Bake until brown.

Tomatoes

At their succulent best when they are vine-ripened to a brilliant red or yellow but are still firm. Tiny round or pear-shaped ones are attractive additions to a salad or a relish tray. Broiled or curried green tomatoes are delicious. Hothouse tomatoes add color to a salad but are often disappointing in flavor. If the skins are tender, you do not need to peel them.

Wash tomatoes and cut out the stem.

To peel, dip in boiling water for 1 minute, then into cold water, and slip off the skin.

Sautéed Tomatoes. Cut ripe or green tomatoes in thick slices. Dip in flour seasoned with salt, pepper and a trace of sugar. Pan-fry in salad oil, bacon fat or butter. Turn once with a wide spatula.

Add a little sour cream or evaporated milk to the pan juices, heat, season, and pour over the tomatoes.

Stewed Tomatoes. Wipe, peel, cut in pieces, and cook slowly 20 minutes, stirring occasionally. Season with butter, salt, pepper and a few grains of sugar. Sprinkle with croûtons.

Scalloped Tomatoes. Season stewed or canned tomatoes to taste with salt, pepper and onion juice. Orégano adds a pleasant flavor. Many like to add a little white or brown sugar. For 4 cups of tomatoes, prepare 1 cup of buttered bread crumbs or croûtons. Put a layer of crumbs in a buttered casserole and cover with tomatoes. Repeat. Sprinkle the top with a thick layer of crumbs. Bake at 400° until the crumbs are brown. *Serves 6.*

Tomatoes aux Fines Herbes

Simmer chopped green onion in butter with an assortment of finely chopped herbs — parsley and basil, thyme or marjoram — chosen with discretion. Add small peeled tomatoes, sprinkle with salt and pepper, cover, and cook very slowly 15 or 20 minutes.

Lift out carefully to keep the tomatoes whole. Pour the pan juice over the tomatoes.

Tomatoes Creole

Melt in a large pan
   2 tablespoons butter
Add
   1 green pepper, seeded and cut in tiny
     shreds
   1 large onion, chopped fine
Cook slowly until the onion is yellow.
Add
   6 to 8 tomatoes, quartered

Cook slowly 20 minutes. Season to taste with
   Salt and pepper
Serves 4 or 5.

Tomato Curry

Put in a large frying pan
   2 tablespoons butter
   ½ tablespoon chopped onion
Cook until the onion is yellow. Add
   1 tart apple, pared, cored, and cut in
     small pieces
Cook 8 minutes. Add
   ½ cup stock or consommé
   2 cups tomatoes, cut in pieces, or
     canned tomatoes
   ½ tablespoon curry powder
   1 teaspoon vinegar
   Salt and pepper
Bring to the boiling point. Add
   1 cup boiled rice
Cook 5 minutes. *Serves 4.*

Curried Green Tomatoes

Melt in a saucepan
   2 tablespoons butter
Add
   2 tablespoons minced onion
Cook slowly until yellow. Add
   1 teaspoon curry powder
   2 cups green tomatoes, sliced or cut in
     pieces
Cook slowly until well heated. Season with
   Salt and pepper
Serves 4.

Tomato Fritters

Put in a saucepan
   1 can tomatoes (about 3½ cups)
   6 cloves
   ½ cup sugar
   3 slices onion
Cook 20 minutes. Rub through a sieve to strain out the seeds. Add
   1 teaspoon salt
   Few grains pepper
Melt
   ½ cup butter

Stir in
½ cup cornstarch
Add the tomato slowly, stirring constantly. Cook 2 minutes. Stir in
1 egg, slightly beaten
Pour into a buttered pan about 7 by 7 inches. Cool. Turn out onto a board. Cut in squares, diamonds or strips. Roll in crumbs, egg and crumbs (p. 5). Fry in deep fat at 385°. Drain. *Serves 6 to 8.*

Tomato Soufflé Napoli

Melt in a saucepan
2 tablespoons butter
Stir in
2 tablespoons flour
Add slowly, stirring constantly
½ cup milk or cream
1 can tomato paste
Bring to the boiling point and simmer 2 minutes. Add
⅔ cup grated cheese
½ teaspoon salt
Few grains pepper
Cook in boiling salted water until soft
½ cup macaroni, in 1-inch pieces
Drain. Add
1 tablespoon butter
Add to the tomato mixture.

Beat until stiff and set aside
3 egg whites
Without washing the beater, beat until thick
3 egg yolks
Stir into the tomato mixture and fold in the beaten whites. Turn into an unbuttered casserole. Bake at 300° until firm (about 45 to 60 minutes). Serve immediately. *Serves 6.*

Baked or Broiled Tomatoes

Serve as a relish on the meat platter, as an important part of a vegetable plate, or as the main dish at luncheon or supper with a curlicue of crisp bacon on top.

Cut unpeeled tomatoes in half. Put in a buttered shallow pan, cut side up. Season with salt, pepper, a trace of sugar and chopped onion or onion salt, or a few grains of curry powder or orégano. Dot with butter or cheese, or sprinkle buttered crumbs on top. Bake (at whatever temperature you are using for other baking) until thoroughly heated and brown. Or broil 6 to 8 minutes (cut side towards the heat) with whatever meat or fish you are broiling.

Tomatoes à la Crème. Heat sweet or sour cream, season highly to taste, and pour it over broiled tomatoes.

Deviled Tomatoes. Mix 2 teaspoons confectioners' sugar, 1 teaspoon mustard, ¼ teaspoon salt, few grains cayenne and 1 hard-cooked egg yolk, crumbled. Add to 4 tablespoons creamed butter. Add 1 egg, slightly beaten, and 2 tablespoons vinegar. Cook and stir over hot water until thick. Pour over baked or broiled tomatoes.

Baked Stuffed Tomatoes

For other suggestions, see Stuffed Peppers (p. 255).

Cut a thin slice from the stem end of smooth medium-size tomatoes. Take out most of the pulp with a spoon. Discard the seeds. Add to the pulp any juice remaining in the tomato shells. Sprinkle the tomatoes with salt, invert, and let stand half an hour or longer.

Add to the pulp an equal quantity of bread crumbs. Season with salt, pepper and a few drops of onion juice. Add chopped green pepper and onion, if you like. Stuff tomatoes with the mixture. Place in a buttered pan. Sprinkle with buttered crumbs. Bake 20 minutes at 400°.

Tomatoes Stuffed with Mushrooms. Stuff with finely chopped mushrooms, mixed with thick Cream Sauce (p. 90) or tomato pulp and seasoned to taste.

Tomatoes Stuffed with Crab Meat. Stuff with Crab Meat à la King (p. 139) and sprinkle with buttered coarse bread crumbs.

Tomatoes Stuffed with Meat. *An excellent way to use small amounts of leftover cooked meat. Good with chicken or fish, too.* Cook a little chopped onion in butter until soft, add the meat (chopped), some of the tomato pulp and enough crumbs to make the amount needed to fill the shells. Season well. For a firmer stuffing, stir in 1 egg, slightly beaten. Stuff tomatoes and bake as above.

Tomatoes Stuffed with Spinach and Mushrooms. Sauté chopped onions and chopped mushrooms until just soft. Mix with well-drained chopped cooked spinach and add garlic salt and grated Parmesan cheese to taste. A few nuts are a welcome addition — toasted pine nuts or slivered almonds. Top with grated Parmesan cheese and sprinkle lightly with olive oil. The proportions of the ingredients may be varied.

Turnips

White turnips are milder than yellow rutabagas and cook in a shorter time. Select clean firm roots. One pound serves 3 or 4.

Wash and pare. Slice, dice, or quarter. Cook until tender (5 minutes in a pressure saucepan, 10 to 30 minutes in boiling water in a covered pan). Drain thoroughly.

Mashed Turnip. Mash drained, cooked turnip. Cook a minute or two longer to dry thoroughly. Season with butter, salt and pepper. For variety, fold in ¼ cup heavy cream, whipped, and season delicately with rum or sherry.

Creamed Turnip. Reheat diced cooked turnip in a little heavy cream.

Turnips Bordelaise. Season diced cooked turnips with butter, salt and pepper. Add garlic salt or a little crushed garlic if you like. Put in a casserole and sprinkle with buttered bread crumbs mixed with chopped parsley (1 tablespoon to each ½ cup of crumbs). Heat in the oven at any convenient temperature until lightly browned.

Turnip Soufflé. Follow the recipe for Vegetable Soufflé (p. 234).

Yams

See Sweet Potatoes (p. 268).

Zucchini

A delicious Italian summer squash. Do not pare young zucchini — the dark green skin adds a pleasant texture. For other ways to cook zucchini, see Summer Squash (p. 256). See also Ratatouille Niçoise (p. 248). Zucchini is good raw, too, cut in finger-shaped pieces and served like celery either as a relish or as a cocktail accompaniment. One pound serves 3.

Wash zucchini and cut in cubes or slices. Cook, covered, in boiling salted water until just tender (10 to 20 minutes). Drain, and add butter, salt and pepper to taste. Sprinkle, if you like, with chopped chives or parsley or with grated Parmesan cheese, or serve with Lemon Sauce (p. 92).

Shredded Zucchini. Shred on a coarse grater directly into a saucepan. Add just enough salted boiling water to keep from burning (¼ cup for 2 pounds of zucchini). Cover and cook until tender (3 or 4 minutes). Drain and season as above.

Zucchini Italian Style. Sauté 1 sliced onion in butter until yellow, add 1 pound zucchini, sliced, and cook and stir 5 minutes. Add 1 cup fresh or canned tomatoes, season with salt and pepper, cover, and cook 5 minutes. Reduce the heat and cook until tender (25 minutes), or put in a casserole, sprinkle with freshly grated Parmesan cheese. Bake at 375° until brown. *Serves 4.*

Baked Zucchini

Allow 1 small zucchini per person.

Cut in half lengthwise. Put in a buttered baking dish cut side up. Dot with butter or bits of bacon. Sprinkle with salt and pepper. Bake at 375° until tender. Serve with Tomato Sauce (p. 94) or Hollandaise (p. 95).

Zucchini with Tomato. Scoop out some of the center. Fill with tomato, cut in pieces. Season and bake as above.

Stuffed Zucchini

Allow ½ small zucchini per person. See also Veal-Stuffed Zucchini (p. 197) and Lamb-Stuffed Zucchini (p. 204).

Cook 10 minutes in boiling salted water. Drain and cool. Cut in two lengthwise. Scoop out the pulp, chop, and add to it an equal quantity of bread crumbs or crumbs and chopped sautéed mushrooms. Moisten with stock, consommé or gravy, and season with salt and pepper. Add freshly grated cheese, minced parsley, marjoram or thyme to taste.

Stuff the zucchini with the mixture. Sprinkle with buttered crumbs and grated cheese. Bake at 350° until the zucchini is tender (about 30 minutes).

Potatoes

Choose firm large potatoes for baking, French-frying and mashing. Small new potatoes are at their best boiled. For a small family, buy only enough potatoes for one or two weeks at a time. To store in quantity, keep in a dry cellar, cool but not freezing. Look over frequently and remove sprouts as they appear. Or dust with a commercial powder which prevents sprouting. Allow 1 medium-sized potato per serving or 1 pound new potatoes for 5.

Baked Potatoes

Use firm smooth potatoes with no blemishes. New potatoes will not bake well.

Bake potatoes of uniform size, or start the larger ones earlier. Scrub with a vegetable brush. Place in a shallow pan, on a potato baker or directly on an oven rack. (It is easier to take them out if they are in a pan or on a baker.)

Bake until soft at any convenient temperature from 350° to 450°. At 350° medium-sized potatoes take about 1 hour and 10 minutes, at 450° about 40 minutes. To test, pick up one potato in a folded towel and squeeze gently. If it feels soft, the potatoes are done.

Cut a cross in the top of each potato and press the sides of the potato so that steam will escape. Put a bit of butter in each or serve plain. Potatoes will remain dry and fluffy if the serving dish is left uncovered.

West Coast Baked Potatoes. Serve with the potatoes a bowl of sour cream, a dish of chopped chives, salt and pepper.

Stuffed Baked Potatoes

Bake potatoes (above). Cut in half lengthwise. Scoop out and mash thoroughly. Beat well, adding hot milk until the mixture is soft and fluffy (1 teaspoon or more for each potato). Season to taste with butter, salt and pepper. Add, if you like, freshly grated cheese, minced green pepper sautéed in butter, minced pimiento or ham.

Refill the shells. Brush with butter or sprinkle with grated cheese. Set on a baking sheet.

Shortly before serving time, put in a 450° oven to reheat and brown (8 to 10 minutes unless the potatoes are very cold).

Boiled Potatoes

Scrub well. Do not peel. Leave small potatoes whole. Cut large ones in half. Put in a pan with about 1 inch of boiling water. Sprinkle with salt, cover, and cook quickly until just tender (12 minutes for tiny new potatoes, 20 minutes or more for old ones). Add more water from time to time to keep the potatoes from burning.

Drain, if necessary, and shake over the heat a moment to dry. Peel old potatoes. Serve young potatoes unpeeled, peeled, or with a band of peel.

Tuck a dish towel over the potatoes to keep them warm and to absorb the steam so they will not be soggy. When ready to serve, put the potatoes in a heated serving dish. Pour melted butter over them and dust with paprika or sprinkle with chopped parsley or finely cut chives, unless you are serving a sauce or gravy.

Parsley, Dill or Minted Potatoes. For 1 pound of potatoes, add 1 tablespoon lemon juice to ½ cup melted butter. Sprinkle the cooked potatoes with chopped parsley, fresh dill or mint, or roll small whole potatoes in parsley, dill or mint, and pour the melted butter around them.

Potatoes with Caraway Seeds. For 2 pounds of new potatoes, prepare Velouté Sauce (p. 92), adding 1 tablespoon caraway seeds to the melted butter. Pour the sauce over the hot potatoes.

Brabant Potatoes. Pare small potatoes and parboil 10 minutes. Drain and put in a single layer in a shallow baking dish. Bake at any convenient temperature until soft, basting 3 times with melted butter.

Spring Potatoes with Peas. Scrub tiny new potatoes but do not peel. Boil for 10 minutes. Drain and add cream to half cover them. Cover and cook slowly until tender. Add an equal quantity of cooked peas. Season with salt, pepper and butter.

Potatoes Hollandaise

Save the drained chicken broth to use in soup.

Slice or cube
    2 cups potatoes, pared or not
Cover with
    Chicken Stock (p. 72) or canned
      chicken broth
Cook until tender. Drain.
Cream
    ½ cup butter
Beat in
    2 teaspoons lemon juice
Season with
    Salt and cayenne

Add to the potatoes. Stir and cook 5 minutes. Sprinkle with
    1 teaspoon chopped parsley
Serves 4.

Potatoes au Gratin

Rub a baking dish with
    1 split clove garlic
    Butter
Grate
    ¼ pound Cheddar cheese
Sprinkle half of it in the baking dish. Cover evenly with
    2 cups sliced cooked peeled potatoes
Sprinkle with
    Salt and pepper
Mix
    2 eggs, beaten slightly
    1 cup milk
    ½ teaspoon salt
    ¼ teaspoon nutmeg
Pour over the potatoes. Cover with the rest of the cheese. Dot with
    Butter
Bake 45 minutes at 350°. *Serves 4.*

Riced Potatoes

Do not prepare new potatoes this way — they will not be fluffy.

Drain hot boiled potatoes and put through a ricer directly into a heated serving dish. Dot with butter and sprinkle with paprika.

Duchess Potatoes. *For planked steak or fish. See also Mashed Potato Border (p. 264).* Mix 2 cups Riced Potatoes with 2 tablespoons butter and 3 slightly beaten egg yolks. Beat well. Make into a border on the plank, using a tablespoon or a pastry bag.

Cheese Potatoes. Mix 3 cups Riced Potatoes with 1½ cups cottage cheese, ½ cup sour cream, 1 tablespoon grated onion and salt and pepper to taste. Beat well and spoon into a buttered casserole. Brush the top with melted butter. Bake 30 minutes at 350°. Brown the surface lightly under the broiler. *Serves 6.*

Mashed Potatoes

Do not try to mash new potatoes. Firm old potatoes make the fluffiest mashed potatoes.

Peel the potatoes. Cut in pieces and cook, covered, in just enough boiling water to keep the potatoes from burning. Drain, put the potatoes back in the pan, and set over very low heat.

For 6 potatoes, heat ½ cup milk with about 2 tablespoons butter. Crush the potatoes with a blending fork or a potato masher or put through a ricer. Beat until snowy white and as fluffy as whipped cream, adding the hot milk, little by little, as you beat. Use enough milk so that the potatoes will not be dry, but be careful not to use so much that they are too soft to stand up in peaks.

For very fluffy potatoes, use a portable electric beater. Do not transfer potatoes to a bowl — beat them right in the pan over low heat.

Season to taste with salt and pepper. Spoon lightly into a heated dish and put a dab of butter on top. Serve immediately, if possible. If necessary, keep hot in a double boiler, uncovered.

Mashed Potato Border. Using a large tablespoon, put spoonfuls of mashed potato around a heated serving platter to make a scalloped edge. Dust with paprika or sprinkle with chopped parsley or chives. Or, if you are using a heatproof platter, brush potato with egg yolk (slightly beaten with 1 tablespoon water) and brown 5 minutes at 400°.

Savory Potatoes. For each 2 potatoes, beat in 1 teaspoon chopped watercress and ⅓ teaspoon finely cut mint.

Spanish Potatoes. For each 2 potatoes, beat in 1 teaspoon canned pimiento, puréed or cut in small pieces.

Potatoes Fondante. Pile in a baking dish. For 5 potatoes, pour over ½ cup heavy cream. Sprinkle with ¾ cup coarse dry bread crumbs. Bake at 425° until crumbs are brown. *Serves 6.*

Potato Cakes. Shape cold mashed potato in small flat cakes. If the potatoes are too dry to make firm cakes, stir in an egg, slightly beaten. Dip lightly in flour. Brown on both sides in bacon fat or butter.

Chantilly Potatoes

Spoon lightly into a baking dish
   3 cups Mashed Potatoes (above)
Beat until stiff
   ½ cup heavy cream
Fold in
   ½ cup freshly grated cheese
Season with
   Salt and pepper
Spread over the potatoes. Bake at 350° until delicately brown. *Serves 6.*

Pittsburgh Potatoes

Cook 10 minutes in boiling salted water to cover
   2 cups potato cubes
   1 teaspoon (or more) chopped onion
Drain. Put in a buttered baking dish. Mix
   1 or 2 canned pimientos, cut in small pieces
   1 cup Cheese Sauce (p. 91)
Pour over the potatoes. Bake at 350° until the potatoes are soft. *Serves 6.*

Franconia Potatoes
(pan-roasted)

Pare medium potatoes. Cook 10 minutes in boiling salted water. Drain and place in the pan in which meat is roasting. Bake until soft (about 1 hour), basting several times with the fat in the pan. Turn the potatoes occasionally so that they will brown evenly.

Broiled Potatoes with Cheese

Cut cooked peeled or unpeeled potatoes in thick slices. Brush with butter and broil on the buttered side until brown. Turn, brush with butter, and put a thin wedge of mozzarella cheese on each slice. Broil until the cheese melts and bubbles.

Broiled New Potatoes

Pare small potatoes. Boil 10 minutes in salted water. Drain. Brush with melted butter. Broil until tender (10 to 15 minutes), turning to brown evenly.

Scalloped Potatoes

Melt
   2 tablespoons butter
Stir in
   1 tablespoon flour
Add slowly, stirring constantly
   1½ cups milk
Cook and stir over low heat until thickened. Season to taste with
   Salt and pepper
Put in a buttered baking dish
   4 potatoes, peeled and sliced
   1 onion, chopped fine
Pour the sauce over the top.

Bake at 350° until tender (about 1¼ hours). *Serves 4 to 6.*

To vary, sprinkle grated cheese or buttered crumbs over the top before baking.

Scalloped Potatoes Country Style

The easiest method, but the milk may curdle if you are making a large amount.

Pare the potatoes and cut in thin slices. Put a layer in a buttered baking dish. Sprinkle with salt, pepper and flour. Dot with butter. Repeat, having no more than 3 layers. Add milk until it can be seen through the top layer.

Bake 1¼ hours at 350° or until the potatoes are tender.

Scalloped Potatoes with Onion. Sprinkle each layer with 1 teaspoon minced onion.

German-Fried Potatoes

Allow 1 medium-sized potato per person.

Wash, pare, and slice thin, using a vegetable slicer. Let stand ½ hour in cold water.

Drain and dry between towels. Heat fat ½ inch deep in a heavy frying pan. Put in the potatoes and sprinkle with salt. Sauté slowly until evenly browned (about 15 minutes), turning occasionally. Cover and cook slowly 15 minutes longer or until tender.

To vary, cook minced onion in the fat before adding the potatoes.

Chambéry Potatoes. Instead of frying the sliced potatoes, arrange them in layers in a well-buttered shallow baking dish. Season each layer with salt and pepper and brush over with melted butter. Bake at 350° until tender and well browned (about 45 minutes).

Hashed Brown Potatoes

Chop or dice raw or cooked potatoes. Season with salt and a few grains of pepper.

For 2 cups potatoes, melt 3 tablespoons bacon fat or butter in a heavy pan. Put in the potatoes, stir and lift until the potatoes are well coated with fat. Reduce the heat and cook until the potatoes are tender and there is a crisp brown crust on the bottom (20 minutes for cooked potatoes, 30 or more for raw potatoes). Add more fat from time to time if necessary to keep the potatoes from sticking. Fold like an omelet.

Potato Pancakes

Grate
   3 medium-sized raw potatoes
Drain. Add
   1 tablespoon flour or 2 tablespoons dry
      bread crumbs
   1 tablespoon cream, sweet or sour
   1 egg, beaten light
   1 teaspoon salt
   Grated onion or onion salt to taste
Stir well. Cook by spoonfuls in
   Hot bacon or other fat
turning once. Or cook in one big pancake. Serve with
   Applesauce, cranberry sauce or sour
      cream
to spoon over the pancakes. *Serves 4 or 5.*

French-Fried Potatoes

Wash and pare firm potatoes. Cut in eighths lengthwise, or with a special cutter or in balls or 1-inch cubes. Cover with cold water. Let stand at least 30 minutes.

Drain. Dry thoroughly on a paper towel so that water will not make the fat sputter.

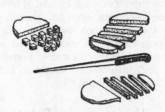

Heat fat to 370° (p. 6). Put a single layer of potatoes in the frying basket. Fry 5 minutes. Keep the basket in motion so that the potatoes will fry evenly. Drain on a paper towel.

Repeat until all are done. Just before time to serve, heat the fat to 390°. Put the potatoes in the frying basket. Fry until crisp and brown. Keep the basket in motion. Drain; sprinkle with salt.

Oven-Fried Potatoes. Dip the prepared potatoes in melted butter, bacon fat or suet. Spread in a shallow pan. Bake at 400° for 40 minutes or till delicately brown, turning occasionally. Sprinkle with salt.

Potato Chips. *Unpeeled sweet potatoes are delicious this way as a vegetable or as a cocktail tidbit.* Slice as thin as possible, using a vegetable cutter. Soak 2 hours in cold water, changing the water twice. Fry at 390°. Keep the chips warm but omit the second frying.

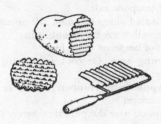

Fried Potatoes Burgoyne. Melt 1 tablespoon butter in a heavy frying pan. Add 1 teaspoon finely cut chives and 2 cups French-fried potatoes. Stir gently until the butter is absorbed. *Serves 4.*

O'Brion Potatoes. Cook a slice of onion in 1 tablespoon butter 3 minutes. Remove the onion. Add 2 canned pimientos, cut small. Add 2 cups fried potato cubes. Stir gently to blend. Sprinkle with chopped parsley. *Serves 4.*

Souffléed Potatoes

To create these astonishing little balloons (often called Potato Puffs), use well-ripened Idaho potatoes and work with two kettles of fat.

Pare potatoes. Cut in even slices, ⅛ inch thick, using a vegetable slicer. Do not use the ends of the potatoes, since it is necessary to have even pieces to make perfect puffs. If the slices seem large, cut out rounds with a small biscuit cutter. Soak in ice water 5 minutes, drain, and dry thoroughly on paper towels.

Prepare two kettles of fat, one heated to 250°, the other to 425°. Fry the potato slices, a few at a time, at the lower temperature for 3 minutes. Keep well submerged during frying and turn at least once. At the end of 3 minutes, lift in a wire basket and put immediately into the 425° kettle. (*The potatoes will puff instantly if they are the right type. If not, it is hopeless to try to prepare them this way; cut the rest of the slices in strips and fry according to directions on page 6.*) Continue to fry until delicately brown.

Remove and drain on paper toweling in a 350° oven until all are ready for serving. Sprinkle with salt and serve immediately.

Potato Croquettes

Boil potatoes. Drain, mash well, or put through a ricer or food mill. For each cup (*1 cup serves 3*) add 1 tablespoon butter. Beat well and season to taste with salt, pepper and a few grains of cayenne. Season more highly, if you like, by adding celery salt, onion salt or chopped parsley.

Chill. Shape by tablespoonfuls into balls. Roll quickly into cylinders or cones. Egg and crumb (p. 6). Fry in deep fat at 390° and drain (p. 6). Keep warm in a 350° oven until ready to serve.

For a richer mixture, stir in 1 egg yolk for each cup of potatoes.

Creamed Potatoes

One cup of cubed potatoes serves 2 or 3.

Boil or bake potatoes until just barely tender, not too soft. For additional seasoning, put a stalk of celery in the water in which you boil the potatoes. If you bake them (for exceptionally delicious flavor) take the potatoes from the oven while they are still firm.

Peel and cube the potatoes. For each cup, heat ½ cup cream in a double boiler. (Or make Cream Sauce, p. 90, but cream is far more delicious.) Add the potatoes. Season to taste. Add, if you like, chopped pimiento, parsley or grated cheese. Cook at least 30 minutes to develop the best flavor.

Baked Creamed Potatoes. Put in a baking dish. Sprinkle with buttered crumbs. For **Delmonico Potatoes** arrange in layers, sprinkling each layer with grated cheese. About half an hour before serving time, put in a 350° oven and bake until nicely browned.

Skillet Creamed Potatoes

An electric frying pan does creamed potatoes to perfection — on the buffet for a party, if you like.

Peel and dice into a frying pan
    4 or 5 potatoes
Add

½ cup boiling water
½ teaspoon salt
Cover and cook 10 minutes. Uncover and simmer until the water has almost evaporated. Add
    ½ cup milk or cream
Season to taste. Cook until slightly thickened, stirring gently with a fork. Sprinkle with
    2 tablespoons chopped parsley
Serves 4 or 5.

Potatoes Hashed in Cream

Perhaps the best flavor of all.

Bake at 350° until barely tender but still firm
    4 medium-sized potatoes
Cool, peel, and chop in a chopping bowl.

Melt
    2 tablespoons butter
Stir in
    1 tablespoon flour
Add slowly
    1 cup heavy cream
Cook and stir until the cream bubbles. Season with
    Salt and freshly ground pepper
        (plenty)
Add the potatoes, mix well, and spoon into a baking dish. Dot with
    2 tablespoons butter
Bake at 350° until brown (about 30 minutes). *Serves 4.*

Curried Potatoes

Melt in a large saucepan
    ¼ cup butter
Add
    1 small onion, chopped fine
Cook until yellow. Add
    3 cups cooked potato cubes
Cook until the butter is absorbed. Add
    ½ cup Chicken Stock (p. 72) or
        canned chicken broth
    1 teaspoon curry powder (or to taste)
    2 teaspoons lemon juice
    Salt and pepper
Cook until the potatoes have absorbed the stock. *Serves 6.*

Lyonnaise Potatoes

Put in a large frying pan
   3 tablespoons butter
   1 small onion, chopped fine
Cook until yellow. Add
   2 cups cooked potato cubes
   Salt and pepper
Stir until well mixed. Add
   2 tablespoons consommé or stock
Cover and cook slowly until the potato is
brown underneath. Fold like an omelet.
Sprinkle with
   Finely chopped parsley
Serves 6.

Alphonso Potatoes

Cook 6 minutes in boiling water
   1 green pepper, seeded
Drain and mince. Add to
   2 cups cooked potato cubes
Add
   ¾ cup milk
   ½ teaspoon salt
Simmer 15 minutes. Put in a buttered
baking dish. Sprinkle with
   1½ tablespoons grated Parmesan
      cheese
Bake 10 minutes at 400°. *Serves 6.*

Cottage-Fried Potatoes

Dice or slice cooked potatoes. Season
with salt and pepper. Brown on both
sides in a well-greased heavy frying pan.
See also Hashed Brown Potatoes (p. 265).

Sweet Potatoes and Yams

*Sweet potatoes contain more sugar and
fat than white potatoes. They are particularly delicious with ham, roast pork and
roast goose. Yams are sweeter and juicier
than sweet potatoes. Cook them in any
of the ways suggested below except frying.*

Baked Sweet Potatoes. Scrub. Bake at
375° until soft (about 50 minutes).

Sherried Sweet Potatoes. Bake potatoes.
Scoop out and mash. Moisten with cream.
Season with salt, butter and sherry to
taste. Refill the skins. Bake 5 minutes at
425°.

Boiled Sweet Potatoes. Scrub well. Cover
with boiling salted water. Cover. Cook
until soft (about 20 minutes). Drain.
Peel.

Fried Sweet Potatoes. Boil 10 minutes.
Drain, peel, and cut in strips. Fry in deep
fat at 375° (p. 6). Drain on a paper
towel. Sprinkle with salt.

Sautéed Sweet Potatoes. Boil, drain, and
dice or slice. Sauté in butter until lightly
browned. Sprinkle with orange juice and
grated orange rind.

Franconia Sweet Potatoes. Pare. Cover
with boiling salted water. Cook 10 minutes. Drain and put in the pan with
roasting meat about 1 hour before it is
done. Baste every 10 minutes with the
fat in the pan.

Mashed Sweet Potatoes

Allow 1 potato per serving.

Boil sweet potatoes and drain. Crush
with a blending fork or a potato masher
or put through a ricer.

Moisten with hot milk or orange juice
and beat until light. Add salt and butter
to taste, and, if you like, a few grains of
nutmeg, allspice and cinnamon, or a few
grains of ginger. Chopped candied ginger
is delicious in any sweet potato dish.

Sweet Potatoes Calypso. Moisten with
rum and add ½ teaspoon vanilla (for 6
potatoes).

Sweet Potatoes de Luxe. To 6 potatoes
add ½ cup drained crushed pineapple or
½ cup chopped pecan nut meats. Put in
a buttered baking dish. Dot with marshmallows. Bake at 375° until the marshmallows melt and brown.

Sweet Potatoes Georgian. Put in a buttered baking dish, leaving a rough surface. Mix 2 tablespoons molasses and 1 teaspoon butter in a small pan and heat 5 minutes. Pour over the potatoes. Bake at 400° until delicately brown.

Sweet Potatoes in Orange Cups. Cut oranges in half. Remove the pulp and white membrane. Use the juice to moisten the potatoes. Add some orange pulp, cut small, if you like. Flavor with sherry, Cointreau or rum.

Fill the orange shells and sprinkle with brown sugar. Bake at 350° until slightly glazed.

Sweet Potato Puffs. Shape in 2-inch balls. Brush with melted butter. Roll in corn flakes, chopped crisp bacon, or chopped almonds. Arrange on a baking sheet. Bake at 350° until brown.

To vary, mold the balls around marshmallow halves. When baked, the marshmallow melts and blends with the potato to make a soft creamy center.

Sweet Potato and Apple Scallop

Have ready
  2 cups boiled sweet potatoes, sliced
    thin
  1½ cups tart apples, cored, peeled,
    and sliced thin
  ½ cup brown sugar
  ¼ cup butter
  1 teaspoon salt
Put half the potatoes in a buttered baking dish. Cover with half the apples, sprinkle with half the sugar, dot with half the butter, and sprinkle with half the salt. Repeat.

Cover and bake ½ hour at 350°. Uncover and bake until the apples are soft and the top is brown. *Serves 6.*

To vary. In place of apple use 1 cup pineapple, chunk-style or crushed. Add ¾ cup pineapple juice before baking.

Candied Sweet Potatoes

Canned sweet potatoes are usually too soft to prepare this way. Instead, make a syrup of the butter, sugar and water, add the sliced potatoes and heat.

Boil until tender but still firm
  4 medium-sized sweet potatoes
Pare and cut in half lengthwise.

Put in a heavy frying pan
  ¼ cup butter
  ⅓ cup brown sugar
Heat until melted. Add the potatoes and turn until brown on both sides. Add
  ¼ cup water
Cover closely, reduce the heat, and cook about 20 minutes. If you prefer, bake at 300°. *Serves 4.*

Sweet Potatoes Flambé. Pour ½ cup brandy over the potatoes, light with a match, and serve.

Sweet Potatoes Vermont. Heat ½ cup maple syrup with ¼ cup butter and 1 teaspoon Angostura bitters. Add the potatoes, cover and cook about 20 minutes.

Sweet Potato Croquettes

Mix
  2 cups hot riced (p. 268) sweet potatoes
  2 tablespoons butter
  ½ teaspoon salt
  Few grains pepper
  1 egg, slightly beaten
If very dry, moisten with
  Hot milk or cream
Shape in croquettes. Roll in flour or dip in crumbs, egg and crumbs (p. 6). Fry in deep fat at 375° (p. 6) or sauté in butter. *Serves 6.*

Sweet Potato Balls. Shape in small balls instead of croquettes.

Sweet Potatoes Amandine. Add to the mixture ¼ cup chopped almonds, ⅛ teaspoon nutmeg and 1 teaspoon sugar. Croquettes may be rolled in chopped almonds instead of crumbs.

Salads

Salad may appear at almost any point in the menu for lunch or dinner. Serve it as the first course in the California fashion, with the main course or immediately following it. A colorful fruit salad, especially a frozen one, is often served as dessert. A hearty salad is perfect for a buffet meal, summer or winter. In any case, suit the salad to the situation — the rest of the menu, the weather and your guests. Serve from a generous bowl or on chilled plates.

Salad Garnishes

Garnish a salad casually, so that the effect is natural and not ornate.

For vegetable salads. Sprays of watercress, mint or parsley, thin strips of pimiento or green pepper, grated raw carrot, chopped olives, chopped truffles or capers.

For fruit salads. Tiny seedless grapes (fresh or canned), red or green cherries, chopped candied orange peel or candied fruits.

Cheese Garnishes and Accompaniments (p. 111).

Carrot Curls. *Good, too, with cocktails or as a relish with fish or meat.* Make thin shavings with a "knee action" knife. Drop into ice water to crisp. Drain.

Celery. Save the tough outer stalks for soup or to cook as a vegetable. Serve the hearts whole ("club style") or separate into individual stalks. Crisp in a covered container in the refrigerator or in ice water with a little lemon juice, a lemon rind or a dash of vinegar.

Celery Curls. *The cut ends will curl back and the celery will be very crisp.* Cut celery hearts in 3-inch pieces. Beginning at one end, make 5 parallel cuts, one third the length of the piece. Make cuts at both ends if you like. Cover with ice water and let stand overnight or several hours. Drain.

Green or Red Peppers. Cut out the stem and remove all the seeds. Cut in thin rings or strips. Wash your hands at once — pepper juice is irritating.

Radishes. Wash. Cut off the tip. Leave a bit of the stem and a tiny leaf, if you like. Crisp in ice water until serving time. Radishes may be cut to represent tulips or roses or in other fancy ways.

Some Common Salad Greens

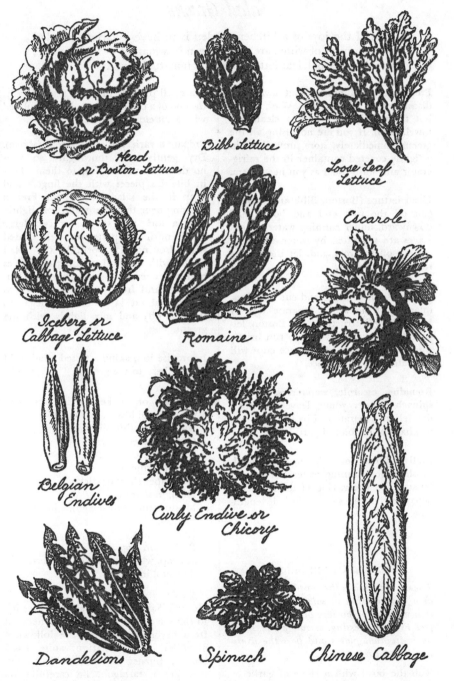

Head or Boston Lettuce

Bibb Lettuce

Loose Leaf Lettuce

Iceberg or Cabbage Lettuce

Romaine

Escarole

Belgian Endives

Curly Endive or Chicory

Dandelions

Spinach

Chinese Cabbage

Salad Greens

One of the joys of a kitchen garden is to have a variety of salad greens, many of which are seldom seen in a market — for example, peppergrass, oak leaf lettuce, and mignonette lettuce.

Preparing salad greens. Cut away any discolored or wilted parts. Wash gently but thoroughly. Dry with a clean soft towel. Chill. If you are not using all the greens immediately, store, unwashed, in a tightly covered container in the refrigerator and wash them as you need them.

Head lettuce (Boston, Bibb and others). Cut off the root end and hold, head downward, under running water so that leaves are separated by water. Or, after cutting off the root end, let the lettuce stand in cold water.

Iceberg lettuce. Wash and cut in halves, quarters or slices. To separate leaf by leaf, follow instructions for Boston lettuce or allow warm water to run briefly through the head. The lettuce cups will separate perfectly at once.

Romaine, escarole, watercress, parsley, spinach (tender young leaves), chicory, dandelion. Separate leaf by leaf. Remove any hard or discolored part. Wash.

Endive, French or Belgian, and fennel. Wash under running water but do not let stand in water. Cut off the root end. Separate the leaves or cut in half lengthwise.

Tossed Green Salad

The classic salad is the simplest — lettuce or a combination of salad greens tossed in a wooden or pottery bowl with a perfect French dressing. Arrange the salad on individual plates and pass the dressing, if you prefer.

Rub the bowl with a clove of garlic or toss a chapon with the salad. (A chapon is a small piece of bread — traditionally, the end of a crusty French loaf — rubbed with a cut clove of garlic.)

Prepare a variety of salad greens (above). Dry gently and thoroughly so that no drops of water cling to them. Tear in bite-size pieces with the fingers and heap in the salad bowl. Pour French dressing over the greens and toss lightly with a fork and spoon (or two large forks) until all parts are well coated with dressing. Or sprinkle the salad lightly with olive oil, turning the leaves over and over until each glistens. Then add salt and freshly ground pepper to vinegar (about ¼ as much vinegar as there is oil) and mix lightly with the greens.

Improvise in making a tossed salad. Add any of these to the greens:

Canned or cooked artichokes or artichoke hearts, cut small.
Avocado, in thin slices.
Carrot, grated raw.
Cauliflowerets, raw.
Cheese, crumbled.
Cucumber slices or sticks.
Ham, in slivers.
Mushrooms (uncooked), in thin slices.
Radish slices.
Red onion rings.
Shrimp, whole or broken in pieces.
Tomato, in wedges.

Herbed Salad. Before adding dressing to the salad, add 1 tablespoon finely cut fresh herbs. Use any of the following, alone or in combination: anise, basil, borage, burnet, chervil, chives, mint, rue, sorrel, tarragon. Be careful! You can overdo herbs.

Caesar Salad

Sometimes called California Salad.

Have ready
  1 cup croûtons, packaged or home-
    made (p. 58)
Combine and let stand several hours
  1 clove garlic
  ½ cup olive oil
Tear in bits and heap in a bowl
  2 heads romaine or other lettuce
Sprinkle with
  Salt and pepper
Add
  ½ cup grated Parmesan or Romano
    or crumbled bleu cheese
Squeeze the juice from
  2 lemons
Pour it over the salad bowl. Add ¼ cup
of the oil (removing the garlic). Pour
the rest of the oil over the croûtons and
stir well. Break over the salad
  1 egg
Mix gently until well blended. Taste
and add more salt and pepper or a drop
or two of
  Worcestershire
Add the croûtons and toss again. *Serves
6 generously.*

Chef's Salad

*Delicious as the main dish for a summer
lunch party.*

Make Tossed Green Salad (p. 272). Add
julienne-shaped pieces of cheese and
cooked ham, chicken, turkey or tongue
or a combination of meats. Cheese with
anchovies or bits of sardine is a good
combination, too.

Fashion Park Salad

*Also hearty enough to be served as the
main dish.*

Arrange a bed of shredded iceberg lettuce in a big salad bowl. For an attractive presentation, arrange on the lettuce
neat piles of match-shaped pieces of ham
or tongue, chicken or turkey, and plain
Cheddar or American cheese.

Have ready a generous bowl of Russian
dressing.

When ready to serve, pour the dressing
over the salad and blend well.

Vegetable Salads

Here is room for improvising. When you cook vegetables for dinner, save some for a salad. They should be crisp and unbuttered.
Cover cooked vegetables with French dressing (marinate). Chill
and drain. Serve on any salad green. Garnish attractively.

See also molded vegetable salads (pp. 280 ff.).

Asparagus tips, cooked or canned, on
thick slices of tomato. French dressing
or Vinaigrette Sauce (p. 97).

Beets, cooked, sliced thin, sprinkled with
chopped mint. French dressing.

Broccoli, cooked. French dressing or
Vinaigrette Sauce (p. 97.)

Carrots, raw, chopped with a few
blanched toasted almonds or raisins and
mixed with mayonnaise.

Cauliflower, raw, sliced paper-thin, or
cooked and separated into flowerets.
French dressing or mayonnaise.

Celeriac, cooked, cut in halves. French
dressing.

Celery, tender stalks cut fine, mixed with mayonnaise or Cream Dressing (p. 291).

Green beans, cooked, preferably whole, garnished with a few rings of mild onion or crumbled crisp bacon — or both. French dressing.

Hearts of palm, canned, cut in slices. French dressing.

Mixed Vegetable Salad

Marinate cooked vegetables separately with French dressing. Chill and drain. Arrange attractively on a salad plate or in a salad bowl. Garnish. Serve with French dressing or mayonnaise.

Russian Salad. Combine any cooked vegetables. Add Boiled Dressing (p. 290), Cream Dressing (p. 291) or Russian Dressing (p. 290). Mix well. Arrange in salad bowl on bed of lettuce. If desired, garnish as follows.

Spread the entire surface with dressing. Divide the top in three sections with lines of chopped parsley, chopped green pepper, chopped pimiento or pepper or pimiento strips. Garnish each section differently, with small pieces of smoked salmon, finely chopped cooked egg white, and cooked egg yolks forced through a strainer.

Artichoke Salad

Tiny canned or frozen artichokes or artichoke hearts are also delightful in green salads.

Chill whole cooked artichokes and serve with mayonnaise seasoned highly with lemon juice and prepared mustard. Or serve with tiny individual cups of French dressing. Dip the leaves in the dressing as you eat them. Serve a whole artichoke to each person.

Artichokes Vinaigrette. Use Vinaigrette Sauce (p. 97) instead of dressing.

Stuffed Artichoke Salad. Fill the centers with a hearty salad — chicken, tuna or shrimp.

Cabbage Salad (Cole Slaw)

Shred cabbage or chop fine. Chill in the refrigerator. Just before serving, mix with Boiled Dressing (p. 290) or Cream Dressing (p. 291), using ½ cup for 2 cups cabbage. If you like, add ½ teaspoon caraway or celery seeds, or 1 tablespoon minced onion and ¼ cup finely cut green pepper. *Serves 4.*

For variety, add grated raw carrot or a few sliced stuffed olives. Finely cut celery, apple or drained crushed pineapple (a third to half the amount of cabbage) make tasty combinations.

Cabbage Salad Bowl

Remove the outside leaves from a small, solid white cabbage. Cut off the stalk close to the leaves. Cut out the center, leaving a shell three or four leaves thick. Cut the edge in points. Pin each point with a long clove. Fill with any cabbage or vegetable salad.

Cucumber Salad

Pare if the skin is tough or discolored. Slice thin, dice or cut in julienne pieces.

To cut slices with a fancy edge, pare with a fluted knife or make parallel grooves lengthwise with a silver fork.

To crisp, soak ½ hour (no longer) in salted water and drain. Serve on lettuce with French dressing or a variation (p. 287).

Wilted Cucumbers

Pare and cut in paper-thin slices
    1 cucumber
Mix and pour over the cucumber
    1 cup cold water
    1 tablespoon salt

Let stand 15 minutes. Drain and rinse with cold water. Pour over the cucumber
   ¼ cup French dressing
Sprinkle with
   ¼ teaspoon celery seed
Serves 3 or 4.

Allerton Salad

Mix
   ½ cup cucumber, cut in tiny cubes
   ½ cup thinly sliced celery
   ¼ cup broken walnut meats
   3 tablespoons chopped red or green
      pepper
Moisten with
   Boiled Dressing (p. 290) or
      mayonnaise
Mound on
   Tomato slices on lettuce
Serves 6.

Onion Salad

Cut in thin slices Bermuda, Italian or Spanish onions. Separate into rings, if you like. Serve on lettuce with French dressing.

Onion and Orange Salad. *Particularly good with duck.* Alternate slices of onion with thin slices of unpeeled orange.

Potato Salad

Vary the seasoning by adding chopped chives, parsley, olives or pickles. Use plenty of dressing so the salad will not be dry.

Mix and let stand several hours
   2 cups cubed cooked potatoes
   1 teaspoon grated onion
   ½ cup chopped celery
   1 teaspoon salt
   ½ cup French dressing
Just before serving, add
   1 hard-cooked egg, sliced
   Mayonnaise or Boiled Dressing
      (p. 290)
Arrange in a large bowl on
   Lettuce

Garnish with
   Tomato sections, radishes or sliced
      hard-cooked egg
Serves 4.

Potato Salad Garni. Put in a large bowl. Divide the top into quarters with lines of chopped parsley. Garnish one quarter with finely chopped cooked egg white, the opposite one with crumbled egg yolk, and the others with chopped pickled beets.

Bolivia Salad. Add 3 hard-cooked eggs, finely chopped, 1½ tablespoons minced pimientos and ½ tablespoon chopped olives. Mix with Cream Dressing (p. 291).

Hot Potato Salad

Cook, cool and slice into a baking dish
   6 potatoes
Season with
   Salt and pepper
Sprinkle with
   ¼ cup chopped celery
   1 tablespoon chopped parsley
Mix
   2 tablespoons tarragon vinegar
   2 tablespoons cider vinegar
   ¼ cup olive oil or bacon fat
   1 thick slice lemon
Heat to the boiling point. Remove the lemon and pour the dressing over the potatoes. Cover and let stand in a 350° oven until heated (about 10 minutes). *Serves 6.*

German Potato Salad

Cover with boiling water
   2 cups diced potato
   1 onion
Cook until the potatoes are tender. Drain, remove the onion, and add
   1 teaspoon grated onion
   1 slice bacon, cooked and crumbled
   2 tablespoons hot bacon fat
Let stand until cold. Mix with
   French dressing
Season to taste and serve on
   Lettuce
Serves 4.

Tomato Salad

If the skin is thin and tender, do not peel. Cut in slices, quarters or eighths. Leave tiny tomatoes whole or cut them in half. Serve on lettuce with French dressing, mayonnaise (add curry if you like) or Avocado Mayonnaise (p. 290). Garnish with watercress or parsley or sprinkle with chopped chives.

For a festive look, cut in eighths without cutting all the way through. Open like the petals of a flower. In the center put a spoonful of mayonnaise or any of the fillings suggested for Stuffed Tomato Salad (below).

Stuffed Tomato Salad

Peel tomatoes, unless the skin is very thin and tender. Remove a thin slice from the top of each. Spoon out the seeds and some of the pulp. Sprinkle the inside with salt. Invert and let stand 30 minutes. Fill, garnish, and serve on salad greens.

Use any of these fillings:

Chicken (p. 278), Crab Meat (p. 279), Lobster (p. 280) or Shrimp Salad (p. 280).

Russian Salad (p. 274) or any mixed vegetable salad.

Shrimp, diced pineapple and cucumber with mayonnaise.

Diced cucumbers with mayonnaise.

Shredded pineapple, mixed with one-third the amount of nut meats and with mayonnaise.

Finely cut celery and apple mixed with mayonnaise.

Cottage cheese, well seasoned, mixed with chopped chives.

Roquefort and cream cheese worked together and moistened with French dressing.

Chopped broiled bacon, diced sardines and tomato.

Cream cheese, chopped stuffed olives and tomato pulp moistened with French dressing and seasoned with prepared mustard.

Russian Tomato Salad

A tasty way to use small amounts of cooked meats and vegetables.

Prepare as for Stuffed Tomato Salad (above), reserving the pulp
  6 tomatoes
Drain the juice from the pulp and mix ⅓ cup of the pulp with
  ⅓ cup diced cucumber
  ⅓ cup cooked peas or lima beans
  ¼ cup chopped pickles
  2 tablespoons capers
Season with
  Salt, pepper and vinegar
Add
  ½ cup diced cooked chicken, ham, pork or veal
Mix with
  Mayonnaise or Russian dressing
Stuff the tomatoes and serve on
  Lettuce
Sprinkle with
  Chopped parsley
Serves 6.

Fruit Salads

Prepare fruit, chill, and serve on salad greens. For molded fruit salads, see Grapefruit Jelly Salad (p. 283) and other molded fruit salad recipes (pp. 282, 283).

Avocado or Alligator Pear. Cut in half, remove the pit, peel and slice, or cut in wedges. Alternate, if you like, with sliced cucumber or tomato, or with orange or grapefruit sections. French or Thousand Island Dressing (p. 288). Stuffed (p. 277).

Banana, in 2-inch chunks rolled in finely chopped peanuts. Use French dressing or mayonnaise.

Cherries, fresh or canned. Pit and stuff with whole nut meats for a delicious salad or garnish.

Grapefruit. Sections, sprinkled with chopped mint, thin slivers of sweet onion or chopped ripe olives and celery. French dressing.

Melon. Balls or cubes of watermelon, cantaloupe or honeydew, separately or mixed. Sprinkle with salt, cover and chill at least 1 hour. French dressing.

Orange. Sections garnished with watercress, finely chopped mint, or a few thin rings of sweet onion. French dressing. Or alternate orange and grapefruit sections and use Lime Dressing (p. 288).

Peach. Fresh or canned halves (pitted). Fill with chopped celery and nuts, well-seasoned cottage cheese, or Cream Cheese Balls (p. 111). French, Lime (p. 288), or Cream Dressing (p. 291).

Pear. Canned or ripe fresh pear halves (peeled, cored, sliced or in halves). French, or Roquefort, or Cream French Dressing (pp. 287–288). Stuff, if you like, with Waldorf Salad (p. 278) or chopped pecans, raisins, and finely cut celery mixed with mayonnaise or a cooked dressing.

Pineapple. Sliced, with French dressing. Garnish with green pepper rings or Cream Cheese Balls (p. 111).

Prune. Cooked or canned, stuffed with highly seasoned cream or cottage cheese. French dressing.

Stuffed Avocado Salad

Cut avocado in half and remove the seed. Serve a half to each person. Fill with a sharp French dressing or a special fruit salad dressing (pp. 288ff.). Or stuff with diced orange and grapefruit sections mixed with French, Lime (p. 288) or Chutney Dressing (p. 287), or with Crab Meat, Chicken, Cooked Fish or Shrimp Salad (pp. 278ff.), as a main luncheon dish.

Mixed Fruit Salad

As the basis, prepare grapefruit or orange sections, or cut crisp tart (but not sour) apples in neat pieces. Small fruits add an attractive touch. Pit cherries. Leave strawberries and raspberries whole. Use seeded or seedless grapes, canned or fresh (Malaga, Tokay or Muscatel types are best), and canned mandarin orange sections. Slice kumquats very thin without peeling. Bits of dried fruits, raisins or candied orange peel are tasty additions. Add to the fresh fruit and let stand several hours to soften.

Chill the fruit. Mix or arrange in separate piles on a handsome glass or pottery serving plate. Add the dressing before serving or pass it in a bowl. French dressing is always good but other dressings are also popular, especially when the salad is to be served as dessert. For suggestions, see p. 288.

Some successful combinations are:

Two oranges in sections, 3 bananas in thin slices, 1 cup seeded or seedless grapes and ¼ cup nut meats, broken in pieces. Cream Mayonnaise (p. 290).

One grapefruit and 2 oranges in sections, ½ cup seeded or seedless grapes and ⅓ cup pecan meats, broken in pieces. Lakewood Dressing (p. 288).

One cup each of orange and/or tangerine sections, banana slices and crushed or cubed pineapple. Nut Pascagoula Dressing (p. 288).

Waldorf Salad

Cut well-flavored apples, peeled or not as you prefer, into small even cubes. To each cupful add ⅔ cup finely cut celery and 5 tablespoons mayonnaise or Boiled Dressing (p. 290). Mix well. Taste and season further, adding a shake of nutmeg or more salt or a little lemon juice. Add a few chopped walnut or pecan meats just before serving. Serve on lettuce.

Pineapple Waldorf Salad. Instead of celery, add cubed pineapple.

Frozen Fruit Salad

Prepared in advance, frozen salads can simplify summer entertaining.

Drain, reserving the juice
    2 cups fresh or canned fruit, cut in small pieces
Put ½ cup of the fruit juice in a small saucepan. Sprinkle over it
    1 envelope gelatine (1 tablespoon)
Stir over low heat until the gelatine dissolves. Add slowly to
    ⅓ cup mayonnaise
Stir in gently
    ⅔ cup heavy cream, beaten until stiff

Fold in the fruit. Season to taste with
    Salt and paprika
Freeze (below). Serve on
    Lettuce
with
    French dressing
Serves 6.

To freeze. Fill oiled molds and seal tightly. Put in the freezer or in equal parts of crushed ice and salt. Let stand until firm (about 4 hours). Serve before the fruit is icy hard. Another way is to pack the salad in a refrigerator tray to freeze.

Frozen Tropical Salad

Mix gently
    1 cup mayonnaise or Boiled Dressing (p. 290)
    1 cup heavy cream, whipped
Stir in
    5 oranges, peeled and cut in small pieces
    5 bananas, peeled and sliced
    1 cup diced pineapple
    ½ cup Maraschino cherries, cut in pieces
Freeze (above). *Serves 6.*

Meat, Fish and Egg Salads

For other main-dish salads, see the molded salad recipes using meat, fish and eggs, pp. 284–286; also Chef's Salad and Fashion Park Salad (p. 273).

Chicken Salad

The meat of a plump poached fowl (p. 216) is the tastiest for salad. Leftover roast chicken may be used, but it is less moist. For a small amount, steam a chicken breast or use canned chicken.

Prepare
    2 cups cooked chicken, cut in neat cubes
Sprinkle over it

    ¼ cup French dressing or the juice of ½ lemon
Cover and let stand at least 1 hour. Add
    ¾ cup mayonnaise, mixed with chutney if desired, or Cream Dressing (p. 291)
Mix thoroughly. Serve on
    Lettuce
Garnish with
    Watercress or a dusting of paprika
Serves 2 or 3.

To vary, add diced celery or canned artichokes, cut small. A delicious combination is chicken, cubed cucumber, chopped nut meats and tiny canned peas.

Other garnishes are crumbled crisp bacon, sliced stuffed olives or toasted slivered almonds.

Sweetbread Salad. In place of chicken, use cooked sweetbreads with an equal amount of diced cucumber or celery.

Curried Chicken Salad

Whip until stiff
    ¾ cup heavy cream
Blend into the cream
    ¾ cup mayonnaise
    1 teaspoon curry powder
    Salt and pepper to taste
Mix
    2 cups diced cooked chicken
    1 cup diced celery
    1 cup diced peeled apple
    2 tablespoons minced onion
    ½ cup diced drained cucumber
Add the dressing and mix well. Serve on
    Lettuce
Serves 8.

Stuffed Egg Salad

Cut hard-cooked eggs in half lengthwise. Remove the yolks, mash, and season with French dressing, mayonnaise or Boiled Dressing (p. 290). Refill the whites. Serve on lettuce with extra dressing.

Vary this basic pattern many ways. For example, add to the yolk mixture bits of crumbled crisp bacon, finely chopped chicken, chopped sweet pickles or Roquefort crumbs. Serve on slices of tomato or thin rounds of cooked ham. See also Egg Salad Sandwiches (p. 339).

Crab or Tuna Salad

Use about two-thirds as much finely cut celery as you have crab meat or tuna

(remove the hard tendons from crab meat before measuring). Mix together with mayonnaise, season to taste, and serve on lettuce or in avocado halves. Garnish with tomato wedges and watercress or sliced stuffed olives or pickles.

Crab Louis

Remove the hard tendons from
    2 cups crab meat
Heap on a bed of
    Shredded lettuce
Mix
    ⅓ cup chili sauce
    ½ cup French dressing
    2 tablespoons mayonnaise
Season to taste with
    Salt, pepper and Worcestershire
Pour over the crab meat. Serves 4.

Crab Ravigote

Mix
    2 cups crab meat (tendons removed)
    1 teaspoon salt
    ⅛ teaspoon cayenne
    1 teaspoon prepared mustard
    ½ teaspoon minced parsley
    1 hard-cooked egg, chopped fine
    3 tablespoons vinegar
    1 tablespoon olive oil
Spoon into scallop shells, ramekins or other small dishes. Spread evenly with
    Ravigote Mayonnaise (p. 290)
Serves 4.

Herring Salad

Mix
    1 cup flaked cooked salt herring
    1 cup cooked potato cubes
    ¼ cup chopped cooked egg white
    ¼ cup French dressing
Chill 1 hour. Beat until stiff
    ¼ cup heavy cream
Add
    2 tablespoons pimiento purée (sieved canned pimiento)
    ¼ cup mayonnaise
Add the herring mixture. Serve on
    Lettuce
Serves 4.

Lobster Salad

At its luscious best made with lobster meat alone, but added celery makes a good salad, too. Allow ½ cup lobster meat for each serving or a little less if you are adding celery. Two pounds of lobster in the shell yields 1 cup.

Cut lobster meat, cooked or canned, in neat pieces. Sprinkle with lemon juice or French dressing, cover and let stand at least 1 hour. Add celery, cut fine, and mix with mayonnaise. Serve on lettuce.

In the shell. Cook lobsters and remove the meat carefully, leaving the body and tail in one piece (p. 141). Crack the claws and remove the meat. Make the salad (above) and pile it in the shells. Spread with mayonnaise and sprinkle with paprika. To vary, mix the lobster liver and coral, rub it through a sieve, add a few drops of anchovy essence and enough mayonnaise to cover the top of the salad.

Shrimp Salad

Clean cooked or canned shrimp. Break in pieces and moisten with mayonnaise or Cream Dressing (p. 291). Arrange on lettuce or in avocado halves on lettuce. Garnish with whole shrimp, capers or sliced stuffed olives.

Salad Sandwich Loaf

A festive creation to prepare ahead of time for a company lunch or supper.

The same salad may be used for all three layers or each layer may be different. Chop the ingredients fine, so that the layers will be firm enough to cut easily.

Prepare
  3 cups salad, such as chicken, tuna,
    salmon or mixed vegetable
Remove the crusts from
  1 small loaf of firm bread, unsliced
Cut in 4 slices lengthwise. Spread 2 slices on one side (for the top and bottom) and 2 on both sides with
  Creamed butter or mayonnaise
On 3 slices put a layer of
  Lettuce, cut small

Spread prepared salad on the lettuce. Put the layers together. Top with the fourth slice, buttered side down. Set a weight (a pan or platter) on top to press the loaf firmly. Mash
  ½ pound cream cheese
with enough
  Mayonnaise or cream
to spread easily. Spread the top and sides of the loaf evenly. Garnish and chill. Cut in 1-inch slices. *Serves 6.*

Molded Salads

Molded salads are perfect for the buffet table, whether main-dish salads such as Chicken and Almond Mousse (p. 284) and Molded Salmon (p. 285), or tasty accompaniments like Cucumber Aspic (p. 282) and Bing Cherry Mold (p. 282). You can prepare them well in advance, and serving them is very simple.

To mold. See p. 12.

To garnish. Put a ½-inch layer of the

jelly mixture in the mold and chill until the jelly begins to stiffen. Arrange on it any desired garnish, such as parsley sprigs, slices of stuffed olives, bits of pimiento or truffle or nut meats. Spoon the jelly carefully over the decorations and chill until firm before adding other ingredients. If the jelly has stiffened too much to pour, melt it in a double boiler.

To serve. Serve individual molds on any salad green. An attractive plate may be arranged with a small mold of a simple jelly (tomato or grapefruit), a few stalks of endive dressed with French dressing, and a spray of watercress.

Decorate a large mold with fruit or with cooked vegetables, pimientos or truffles or slices of stuffed olives. Fill the center of a ring mold with salad dressing or with another salad; for example, Tomato Aspic (below) with Chicken Salad (p. 278); Grapefruit Jelly (p. 283) with Mixed Fruit Salad (p. 277).

Simple Jellied Salads

Dissolve 1 package flavored gelatine in 1 cup boiling water. Add 1 cup cold liquid (water, fruit juice, tomato juice, consommé or wine). Season to taste. Chill.

When the jelly begins to thicken, fold in 1½ cups prepared fruit, vegetables or cooked meat or fish. Season to taste and mold.

Some suggested combinations are:

Lemon or lime gelatine with grated or diced cucumber and 1 teaspoon grated onion or 3 tablespoons chopped chives.

Apple gelatine with finely cut celery and ¼ cup chopped walnuts.

Lemon or apple gelatine with 1 cup uncooked cranberries chopped with 1 orange (seeded but not peeled). Add 2 tablespoons sugar.

Lemon gelatine with 1 cup diced or shredded cooked beets, 2 tablespoons minced onion, 1 tablespoon horseradish and ¾ cup diced celery. Use ¾ cup beet juice and 3 tablespoons vinegar as the required cup of cold liquid.

Lemon, lime or apple gelatine with 1 cup chopped nut meats and ½ cup sliced stuffed olives.

Lemon gelatine (made with tomato juice as the liquid) with shredded cabbage and celery, 1½ teaspoons chopped onion and 1½ tablespoons finely cut pimiento or green pepper (Quick Perfection Salad).

Aspic gelatine with chopped cooked ham, chicken, shrimp or lobster, and with or without vegetables such as finely cut celery or grated carrot.

Tomato Aspic (Tomato Jelly)

A ring mold may be filled with lettuce, watercress, mayonnaise, diced celery mixed with mayonnaise, or a mixture of chopped hard-cooked egg and sliced raw mushroom caps in mayonnaise.

Mix in a saucepan
    1 envelope gelatine (1 tablespoon)
    ½ teaspoon sugar
    ¾ cup tomato juice
Stir over moderate heat until the gelatine dissolves. Add
    1 cup tomato juice
Season to taste with
    Lemon juice, lime juice or vinegar
    Salt and pepper
    Few drops Worcestershire
Fill a 1-pint ring or other mold or a set of individual molds. Chill until firm. Turn out on a serving dish. *Serves 4.*

For a more highly seasoned jelly, use canned tomato juice cocktail or 1 cup canned tomato sauce diluted with ¾ cup water. Or heat the tomato juice first with orégano, a few sprigs of basil or thyme or a bay leaf, and strain it before mixing with the gelatine.

Anchovy Tomato Aspic. Fill the mold half full. Chill until firm. Spread with a thin layer of anchovy paste. Pour in the rest of the jelly and chill.

Caviar Tomato Aspic. Sprinkle caviar in the mold before pouring in the jelly.

Cottage Cheese Tomato Aspic. As the jelly begins to thicken, stir in ½ cup cottage cheese by the spoonful. Do not make the mixture too smooth.

Shrimp and Tomato Aspic. Put a layer of cooked or canned shrimp in the mold. Pour the aspic over them. Or break the shrimp in pieces and fold in as the aspic begins to thicken. Add cubed avocado, too, for color and flavor contrast. Make **Lobster Aspic** or **Crab Meat Aspic** the same way.

Perfection Salad

Chill Tomato Aspic (above) in a bowl. As the jelly begins to thicken, fold in ½ cup shredded cabbage, ½ cup shredded celery, 1½ teaspoons chopped onion and 1½ tablespoons finely cut pimiento or green pepper. Mold.

For a heartier salad, add finely cut ham, chicken or cheese.

Cucumber Aspic

Put in a small saucepan
　　½ cup cold water
Sprinkle over it
　　1 envelope gelatine (1 tablespoon)
Stir over low heat until the gelatine dissolves. Put in an electric blender. Add
　　½ cup undiluted frozen orange juice
　　2 tablespoons lemon juice
　　2 cups sliced cucumber
　　½ small onion, sliced
　　4 sprigs parsley
　　1 teaspoon salt
Whirl until smooth. Chill until the mixture begins to set. Stir well and pour into an oiled mold. *Serves 4.*

Cheese Salad Mold

Mash until smooth
　　½ pound cream cheese
Stir in
　　¼ cup milk or cream
　　½ cup grated Italian or Cheddar cheese
Whip and fold in
　　½ pint heavy cream
Put in a small saucepan
　　½ cup cold water
Sprinkle over it
　　1 envelope gelatine (1 tablespoon)
Stir over low heat until the gelatine dissolves. Stir gently into the cheese mixture. Season to taste with
　　Salt and paprika
Mold. Serve on
　　Lettuce
with
　　French dressing seasoned with curry
Serves 6.

Bing Cherry Mold

Delicious with hot or cold chicken or turkey.

Drain, reserving the juice
　　1 #2 can pitted Bing cherries
Put them in a ring mold. Add to the juice enough
　　Cold water to make 2 cups
Put ½ cup in a saucepan. Sprinkle over it
　　1 envelope gelatine (1 tablespoon)
Stir over low heat until the gelatine dissolves. Add the rest of the juice. Pour over the cherries. Chill until firm and unmold.
Beat until as light as whipped cream
　　½ pound cream cheese
　　Pineapple juice (about ¼ cup)
Pile in the center of the ring. Garnish with
　　Watercress
Serves 6.

Walnut Cherry Mold. Stuff each cherry with a piece of walnut meat.

Cranberry Jelly Salad I

Mold Cranberry Jelly (p. 85) in cylindrical tin or use canned cranberry jelly. Slice 1 inch thick. Arrange on lettuce. Scoop out the centers to form rings. Fill with chopped apple and celery or other salad. Serve with Cream Dressing (p. 291) or mayonnaise.

Cranberry Jelly Salad II

Prepare 2 cups Cranberry Jelly (p. 85) or melt canned cranberry jelly. Let stand to thicken slightly. Fold in ½ cup finely cut apple or celery and ¼ cup chopped nut meats. Mold. Chill. Serve on lettuce with Cream Dressing (p. 291) or mayonnaise. *Serves 4 to 6.*

Grapefruit Jelly Salad

Garnish with Cream Cheese Balls (p. 111) or grapefruit sections and watercress.

Mix in a saucepan
  1 envelope gelatine (1 tablespoon)
  1 tablespoon sugar
Add
  ½ cup cold water
Cook and stir over low heat until the gelatine dissolves. Add
  1 cup grapefruit juice
  1 tablespoon lemon juice
  Sugar and salt to taste
Mold in a pint mold or 4 small molds. *Serves 4.*

Grapefruit and Cucumber Salad. Chill the jelly until it is as thick as unbeaten egg white. Stir in ½ cup each of grapefruit sections, cut small, and chopped drained cucumber.

Pineapple and Cucumber Salad. Use canned pineapple juice in place of grapefruit juice. As the jelly begins to stiffen, fold in ½ cup each of chopped drained cucumber and drained crushed pineapple.

Molded Fruit Salad. For each cup of jelly prepare 1 cup of fruit such as cubed apple, seeded or seedless grapes and pineapple cubes. Chopped celery is good, too. As the jelly begins to thicken, fold in the fruit. Serve with mayonnaise or any fruit salad dressing (pp. 288ff.).

Ginger Ale Fruit Salad. In place of grapefruit juice, use ⅔ cup ginger ale. Add an extra tablespoon of lemon juice. To heighten the ginger flavor, add 1 tablespoon chopped candied ginger.

Avocado Mousse

Put in a small saucepan
  ½ cup cold water
Sprinkle over it
  1 teaspoon gelatine
Set over low heat and stir until the gelatine dissolves. Set aside. Peel
  1 large avocado
Remove the pit and mash the pulp. Season with
  ½ teaspoon salt
  Few drops onion juice
  1 teaspoon Worcestershire
Mix gently together
  ¼ cup heavy cream, whipped
  ¼ cup mayonnaise
Add the dissolved gelatine and fold in the avocado pulp. Mold. Serve on
  Lettuce
with
  Mayonnaise
and a garnish of
  Tomato wedges
Serves 4.

Jellied Garden Special

Drain (reserving the liquid)
  1 pint Garden Special (p. 532)
Measure the liquid and add enough water to make 1 cup. Put in a saucepan and sprinkle over it
  1 envelope gelatine (1 tablespoon)
Stir over low heat until the gelatine dissolves. Chill until as thick as unbeaten egg white. Add the drained vegetables and mold. *Serves 4.*

Jellied Vegetable Ring

Vary the vegetables according to what is on hand. For example, use 2 canned pimientos, cut small, in place of peas and beets.

Mix in a saucepan
    1 envelope gelatine (1 tablespoon)
    ¼ cup sugar
Add
    1 cup cold water
Stir over low heat until the gelatine dissolves. Add
    ¼ cup vinegar
    3 tablespoons lemon juice
    1 teaspoon salt
Chill until as thick as unbeaten egg white. Stir in
    1 cup celery, cut in small strips
    ½ cup shredded cabbage
    ⅓ cup cucumber cubes
    ¼ cup cooked green peas
    ¼ cup cubed cooked beets
Mold. Serve on
    Lettuce or watercress
with
    Mayonnaise or Denver Cream
        Dressing (p. 291)
Serves 6.

Chicken or Turkey Aspic

Put in a small saucepan
    ¾ cup water
Sprinkle over it
    1 envelope gelatine (1 tablespoon)
Stir over low heat until the gelatine dissolves. Cool. Stir into
    ¾ cup mayonnaise, Boiled or Cream
        Dressing (pp. 290–291)
Blend well. Add
    1 cup cooked chicken or turkey, cut
        in small pieces
    ½ cup chopped celery
    ¼ cup chopped green pepper,
        pimientos or stuffed olives
Mix well. Season to taste with
    Salt and paprika
Mold and chill. *Serves 4 or 5.*

Molded Seafood Salad. In place of the chicken, use crab meat, lobster, shrimp, tuna, salmon or a combination of sea foods. Curry powder added to the mayonnaise is particularly good with seafood.

Chicken and Almond Mousse

Vary this party dish by adding chopped pimientos or sautéed mushrooms or by seasoning more highly.

Put in a saucepan
    1 cup cold chicken broth
Sprinkle over it
    1 envelope gelatine (1 tablespoon)
Stir over low heat until the gelatine dissolves. Pour it slowly over
    3 egg yolks, slightly beaten
Pour back into the saucepan and cook and stir until slightly thickened (about 5 minutes).

Grind fine
    1 cup cooked chicken (white meat)
    ½ cup blanched almonds
Add to the gelatine mixture. Season highly to taste with
    Salt and cayenne
Chill until as thick as unbeaten egg white. Fold in
    ½ pint heavy cream, beaten stiff
Mold and chill. *Serves 6.*

Epicurean Ham Mousse

Put in a small saucepan
    ¾ cup cold water
Sprinkle over it
    1 envelope gelatine (1 tablespoon)
Stir over low heat until the gelatine dissolves. Mix
    2 cups chopped cooked ham
    1 teaspoon prepared mustard
    Few grains cayenne
Stir in the gelatine. Chill until as thick as unbeaten egg white. Fold in
    ½ cup heavy cream, beaten until stiff
Mold. Garnish with
    Parsley
Serve with
    Epicurean Sauce (p. 97)
Serves 4 to 6.

Jellied Sweetbreads and Cucumber

Parboil (p. 207)
    1 pair sweetbreads
    Bit of bay leaf
    1 slice onion
    1 blade mace
Drain and dice the sweetbreads.

Put in a small saucepan
    1 cup cold water
Sprinkle over it
    1 envelope gelatine (1 tablespoon)
Stir over low heat until the gelatine dissolves. Add
    3 tablespoons mild vinegar
Cool 10 minutes. Stir gently into
    ½ pint heavy cream, whipped stiff
Add the sweetbreads and
    1½ cups cucumber cubes
Season to taste with
    Salt and paprika
Mold. Serve on
    Lettuce
with
    French dressing
Serves 6 to 8.

Jellied Crab Meat and Celery

Dissolve
    1 package lemon gelatine
in
    1 cup boiling water
Add
    1 can tomato sauce (8 ounces)
    1 teaspoon grated onion
    1½ tablespoons vinegar
    ½ teaspoon salt
    ⅛ teaspoon pepper
    1 can crab meat (8 ounces) or ½
        pound fresh crab meat (flaked)
    1 cup diced celery
Stir well and mold. Serves 4.

Molded Salmon

Mix
    2 teaspoons salt
    2 tablespoons sugar
    2 teaspoons flour
    1 teaspoon mustard
    Few grains cayenne
    2 egg yolks, slightly beaten
    2 tablespoons melted butter
    1 cup milk
    ¼ cup mild vinegar
Cook until thick over hot water (or in a heavy pan over low heat), stirring constantly.

Put in a small saucepan
    ½ cup water
Sprinkle over it
    1 envelope gelatine (1 tablespoon)
Stir over low heat until the gelatine dissolves. Stir into the sauce. Add
    2 cups cooked salmon separated into
        flakes
Mold. Serve with
    Cucumber Sauce (p. 98)
Serves 6.

Aspic

Classic aspic is made of homemade stock, but canned bouillon is what most of us use these days. Chicken broth is best if you are making a vegetable or chicken aspic.

Aspic-flavored gelatine is on the market. Before molding it, season it more highly by adding tomato paste, sherry, Burgundy or brandy.

Put in a saucepan
    ½ cup stock or bouillon
Sprinkle over it
    1 envelope gelatine (1 tablespoon)
Stir over low heat until the gelatine dissolves. Add
    1 cup stock or bouillon
    Lemon juice, sherry or brandy to taste
Add enough more stock or water to make 2 cups in all. Mold. *Makes 1 pint.*

For a more savory aspic, add 1 teaspoon tomato paste or simmer the stock for 20 minutes with a sprig of parsley, a bit of thyme, a clove and a teaspoon each of diced carrot, onion and celery. Strain.

If the chilled stock is firm, you will need only 1 teaspoon gelatine. Soften the gelatine in cold water instead of stock.

Eggs in Aspic

The amount of aspic you need depends on whether you arrange the eggs close together. It is simple to make more aspic and add it later to fill the mold.

Prepare highly seasoned Stuffed Eggs (p. 101), adding to the stuffing, if you like, chopped mushrooms, ham, crab meat or caviar.

Pour Aspic (above) into a shallow serving dish or mold, ½ inch deep. Chill until the jelly begins to stiffen. Arrange stuffed egg halves on it and add other garnishes, if you like, such as sprigs of parsley or watercress. Spoon in more aspic until the eggs are covered. Chill. Serve from the dish or unmold onto a serving dish.

Cooked Meat in Aspic

Excellent as party fare or as a reserve for unexpected summer guests. The meat stays moist and appetizing even if you store it in the refrigerator for many days.

Prepare Aspic (p. 285). Pour it into a chilled mold until it is ½ inch deep.

Chill until it begins to stiffen. Arrange the meat on it and fill the mold with another layer of aspic. If the aspic has become too stiff to pour, reheat it. Chill until firm.

Chicken or Turkey in Aspic. Arrange cooked sliced breast meat in layers.

Ham in Aspic. Cut off the fat. Trim the slices in neat, even pieces.

Tongue in Aspic. Slice, or use a whole cooked tongue.

Chicken Salad in Aspic

Cut cooked chicken in neat cubes. Prepare 1 cup Aspic (p. 285) for each cup of chicken and chill until it begins to stiffen. Fold in the chicken and season to taste. Mold in custard cups or individual molds. Serve on lettuce or other salad green with mayonnaise.

To vary. Use a combination of chicken and diced celery or chicken and chopped ham or hard-cooked egg. For added color and seasoning, add chopped green pepper, pimientos, or a few capers.

Salad Dressings

Affinity between a salad and its dressing makes for perfection. A light French dressing (oil, vinegar or lemon juice, and seasonings) is right with almost any salad. Use mayonnaise, a boiled dressing or a whipped cream dressing with discretion. Vary the seasoning to suit the ingredients and your individual taste. Experiment with your salad dressings — you may produce a masterpiece!

Oils. To the epicure, high-grade olive oil is essential. Some prefer a fruity Italian oil, others the more delicate French type. Vegetable oils — made from corn, cottonseed, peanuts and soy beans — are excellent too.

Vinegars vary in strength, so add gradually until the dressing is as sharp as you like. Old-fashioned cider vinegar has a mild, delicious flavor. Other vinegars add a distinctive taste to dressings — tarragon, wine, pear, garlic or other specially seasoned ones (p. 16).

Seasonings. *Pepper* is at its pungent best if you grind whole peppercorns fresh in a pepper mill. To add *garlic* flavor, use cloves of garlic (to crush, see p. 16), garlic salt or powdered dry garlic. Fresh or dried *herbs* in discreet amounts are delicious with some salads. Special suggestions are given with the recipes.

French Dressing

The classic formula for green salads, but modifications are many. With wine vinegar, garlic- or herb-flavored vinegar (p. 16), you may need nothing more. If the vinegar is very sharp, add a trace of sugar.

It is convenient to have French dressing on hand; make it in quantity, but do not leave garlic in the dressing longer than a day. Do not chill; French dressing tastes best at room temperature.

Mix in a bottle or a jar with a cover
    ½ cup olive or salad oil
    2 tablespoons mild vinegar
    1 teaspoon (or less) salt
    ½ teaspoon freshly ground pepper
    ½ clove garlic
Cover. When ready to serve, remove the garlic and shake hard to blend. *Makes ½ cup.*

To vary. Add a few drops of onion juice, Tabasco or Worcestershire, or a teaspoon of strained tomato juice, or season delicately with mustard or curry powder or add Dijon mustard to taste. For a slightly thicker dressing add 1 tablespoon mayonnaise just before serving and shake well.

Chiffonade Dressing. Add 1 tablespoon each of chopped parsley and chopped red pepper, ½ teaspoon chopped onion or shallot, and 1 hard-cooked egg, chopped fine.

Chutney French Dressing. Add ¼ to 1 cup finely chopped chutney.

Cream French Dressing. Just before serving, add 1 tablespoon heavy cream or sour cream and shake well.

Cumberland French Dressing. Use lemon juice in place of vinegar. Add 1 tablespoon currant jelly and ¼ teaspoon grated lemon rind. *For fruit salads.*

Fruit Salad French Dressing. Use lemon juice or grapefruit juice in place of vinegar. Add finely chopped pistachio or other nuts, chopped candied fruit or fresh mint leaves. For a thicker dressing, add ½ cup strained honey or ⅓ cup sour cream, yogurt or heavy cream, whipped or not. See also Lime Dressing (below) and the others which follow it.

Martinique Dressing. Add 1 teaspoon finely chopped parsley and 1 tablespoon finely chopped green pepper.

Puerto Rico Dressing. Use half lemon juice and half vinegar. Add 2 tablespoons chopped olives and 1 tablespoon tomato catsup.

Roquefort or Bleu Cheese Dressing. Add 1 to 4 tablespoons dry cheese crumbs and a few drops onion juice. If you like, add 2 tablespoons mayonnaise and a dash of Worcestershire.

Russian French Dressing. Add 2 tablespoons chili sauce, 1 tablespoon finely chopped red or green pepper and a few drops onion juice.

Vermouth French Dressing. Use dry vermouth in place of vinegar.

Herb Dressing

Add 1 teaspoon finely crushed dried marjoram and 1 tablespoon chopped parsley to French dressing made with lemon juice. Season more highly, if desired, with a few drops Angostura bitters, Worcestershire or A–1 sauce. Or omit marjoram and add 1 tablespoon finely chopped fresh herbs, using one of the following or a combination: anise leaves, basil, borage, burnet, chervil, chives, mint, rue, sorrel, tarragon. *For green salads.*

Thousand Island Dressing

Mix
  ⅓ cup olive or salad oil
  Juice ½ orange
  Juice ½ lemon
  1 teaspoon salt
  ¼ teaspoon paprika
  1 teaspoon onion juice
  1 tablespoon chopped parsley
  8 stuffed olives, sliced
  1 teaspoon Worcestershire
  ¼ teaspoon dry mustard
Shake well. *For green salads.*

Lime Dressing

Mix
  ¼ cup olive or salad oil
  2 tablespoons lime juice
  5 drops Tabasco
  Few grains cayenne
  ⅛ teaspoon pepper
  ¼ teaspoon salt
  1 teaspoon celery salt
  2 teaspoons sugar

Lakewood Dressing. Instead of lime juice, use 1 tablespoon grapefruit juice and 1 teaspoon vinegar. Add 1 tablespoon crumbled Roquefort cheese. *For fruit salads.*

Nut Pascagoula Dressing

Pound into a paste (or whirl in a blender)
  10 pecan halves
  10 blanched almonds
Mix
  ¼ teaspoon dry mustard
  ¼ teaspoon paprika
  ¼ teaspoon salt
  ¼ teaspoon sugar
Add
  1 tablespoon vinegar
Stir in slowly
  5 tablespoons olive or salad oil
Add gradually to the nut mixture. *For fruit salads.*

Pineapple Honey Dressing

Mix, and shake well
  ½ cup honey
  ¼ cup lemon juice
  ¼ teaspoon salt
  3 tablespoons crushed pineapple
For fruit salads.

Sour Cream or Yogurt Dressing

Season sour cream or yogurt with lemon juice, salt and pepper to taste. *For vegetable or fruit salads.*

Roquefort Cream Dressing. *Especially good stirred into iceberg lettuce, cut in small cubes.* Add at least ¼ cup crumbled Roquefort to each cup of sour cream or yogurt.

Mayonnaise

Olive oil has a delicious flavor, but the mayonnaise is more likely to separate than if made with other oils. If you do not plan to use mayonnaise the day it is made, add 1 teaspoon of hot water. If mayonnaise separates (usually because the oil was added too rapidly), put an egg yolk in a bowl and add the mayonnaise to it, beating it in gradually. Add mayonnaise to a salad just before serving.

Have all the ingredients at room temperature, not icy cold. Have ready
  ¾ cup olive or salad oil
Put in a small deep bowl
  ½ teaspoon dry mustard
  ½ teaspoon sugar
  ½ teaspoon salt
  Few grains cayenne
Mix well. Add
  1 egg yolk
Mix thoroughly. Add, stirring constantly
  1 tablespoon vinegar
Beat in 1 tablespoon oil, a drop or two at a time (using a small wooden spoon or an electric or hand beater). Beat in the rest of the oil, a teaspoonful at a time, until the dressing is as thick as whipped cream. Have the mixture perfectly smooth each time before you add more oil. Stir in

  1 tablespoon lemon juice
Add more lemon juice if the mayonnaise is too thick.

To vary. Add chutney or curry powder (especially for chicken salad), or color with tomato paste or tomato catsup. Or see the variations below and on p. 290.

To add zest to commercial mayonnaise. Add more seasonings or stir in a little lemon juice or heavy sweet or sour cream. **For a special variation,** put in a jar ½ cup mayonnaise, ½ cup lemon juice and ¼ cup sugar (more seasonings if you like) and shake well.

Whole-Egg Mayonnaise

The easiest method, especially with an electric mixer or blender.

Beat until thick
  1 egg
Beat in
  ½ teaspoon dry mustard
  ½ teaspoon salt
  2 tablespoons lemon juice or vinegar
Add, ¼ cup at a time
  1½ cups olive or other oil
Beat until thick and smooth before adding each ¼ cup of oil.

To thin, stir in more lemon juice.

To make in a blender. Put the egg, seasonings and ¼ cup oil in the blender and whirl until well mixed (20 to 30 seconds). Pour in the rest of the oil in a steady stream. Stop as soon as blended smoothly.

Astoria Dressing

Mix
  ¼ cup mayonnaise
  ¼ cup French dressing
  1 tablespoon tomato catsup
  Tabasco to taste
For green salads or as a cold sauce with fish and shellfish.

Carlton Mayonnaise

Mix
1 cup mayonnaise
2 tablespoons tomato paste
½ tablespoon lemon juice
1½ teaspoons sugar
½ teaspoon Worcestershire
½ teaspoon A-1 sauce
For any meat or vegetable salad.

Cream Mayonnaise

Beat until stiff
⅓ cup cream
Stir gently into
1 cup mayonnaise
For fruit salads.

Chinese Mayonnaise. Before adding the cream, stir into the mayonnaise ¼ cup chopped almonds and ¼ cup currant jelly.

Ravigote (Green Mayonnaise)

Cover with boiling water
10 sprigs watercress
10 leaves spinach
4 sprigs parsley
Let stand 5 minutes. Drain, put in cold water, and drain again. Rub through a fine sieve or whirl in a blender. Add to
1 cup mayonnaise
Season to taste with
Salt and nutmeg
For seafood salads.

Russian Dressing

Mix
½ cup mayonnaise
½ cup chili sauce (drained)
¼ cup India relish or 1 tablespoon each of minced celery, pimiento and green pepper
Taste, and if needed add
Salt
For green salads or seafood salads.

Cream Russian Dressing. Just before serving, fold in ¼ cup cream, beaten stiff.

Green Goddess Dressing

Mix in a bowl
1 egg yolk
½ teaspoon salt
2 tablespoons tarragon vinegar
1 tablespoon (or less) anchovy paste
Beat in, 2 tablespoons at a time
1 cup salad oil
Stir in
¼ cup cream
1 tablespoon lemon juice
1 teaspoon onion salt
Dash of garlic salt
2 tablespoons chopped chives
2 tablespoons chopped parsley
For green salads.

Avocado Mayonnaise

Delicious on small whole tomatoes or shrimp or as a dip with cocktail wafers.

Mash with a fork the flesh of
1 small avocado
Add
2 tablespoons evaporated milk
1 tablespoon lemon juice
1 teaspoon prepared mustard
Beat well. Season to taste with
Paprika, salt and Tabasco

Boiled Dressing

This excellent old-fashioned dressing is not actually boiled but cooked slowly over low heat. Especially good on vegetable salads.

Sift into a double boiler top or a small heavy saucepan
½ teaspoon salt
1 teaspoon dry mustard
2 teaspoons sugar
Few grains cayenne
2 tablespoons flour
Stir in slowly
1 egg or 2 egg yolks
2 tablespoons butter
¾ cup milk
¼ cup vinegar
Stir and cook over boiling water or over low heat until slightly thick. Cool. *For vegetable and fruit salads.*

Cream Dressing. Use cream or evaporated milk in place of milk and butter.

Tango Dressing. Add ¼ teaspoon celery seed. Thin with orange juice.

Cleveland Dressing

Mix
    1 teaspoon salt
    ½ cup sugar
    1 teaspoon dry mustard
    1 teaspoon paprika
    ¼ cup vinegar
Chill overnight in the refrigerator. With an electric or rotary hand beater, beat in slowly
    1 cup salad oil
Beat until as thick as honey. *For fruit salad.*

Poppyseed Dressing. Use lemon juice in place of vinegar and add 1 tablespoon poppyseed.

Sour Cream Dressing

Mix thoroughly
    1 egg, slightly beaten
    ¼ cup vinegar
    2 teaspoons salt
    2 teaspoons sugar (1 teaspoon for vegetable salads)
    1 teaspoon prepared mustard
    ⅛ teaspoon pepper
Add to
    1 cup sour cream
Cook and stir until thick in a double boiler or in a small heavy pan over low heat. *For vegetable and fruit salads.*

Bacon Dressing

Melt in a small heavy saucepan
    3 tablespoons bacon fat
Stir in
    2 tablespoons flour
    1 teaspoon grated onion
Cook and stir 1 minute. Add
    ½ teaspoon salt
    ¼ teaspoon pepper
    ¼ teaspoon sugar
    2 teaspoons prepared mustard
    2 teaspoons vinegar
Cook until well blended. Add slowly
    1 cup water
Cook and stir until thick. Cool. *For vegetable salads.*

Whipped Cream Dressing

Beat until stiff
    ½ cup heavy cream, sweet or sour
Beat in slowly
    ¼ teaspoon salt
    3 tablespoons vinegar or 2 tablespoons lemon juice
    Few grains pepper
    ½ teaspoon sugar (if sour cream is used)
For fruit salads.

Denver Cream Dressing. Add prepared mustard or grated horseradish to taste. *For ham, tongue or beef, as well as for vegetable salads.*

Cereals and Grains

Cereals are marketed in various forms — whole grain (cracked or ground), coarse, fine, or flaked. Have a variety on hand to serve for breakfast or to use as ingredients. For the highest food value buy whole grain cereal rather than cereals from which the outer layer has been removed, or else buy enriched cereals.

Store, tightly closed, in air-tight containers or in the original packages. In warm weather, buy in small amounts and store in a cool place.

Breakfast Cereals

To cook. The first time, follow directions on the package. Then modify to suit your taste. You may prefer cereal thicker or thinner than the standard, and with more or less salt.

To make 4 servings (about 2 cups cooked), use 1 cup of any of the rolled cereals (oats or wheat) to 2 cups of water. For all others, use ½ cup to 2 cups of water.

Over direct heat. Only satisfactory for quick-cooking cereals, because cereals stick easily and need constant stirring. Measure the water into the pan. Add ½ teaspoon salt (for 2 cups water). Bring to the boiling point. Stir in the cereal very slowly. Lower the heat and cook, stirring frequently. Quick-cooking cereals require only 3 to 5 minutes but are improved by further cooking in a double boiler.

In a double boiler. Cook 5 minutes in a double boiler top over direct heat (see above). Then set over the lower part of the double boiler and continue cooking for the required time — 15 to 20 minutes for finely ground cereals and regular oatmeal, or 2 to 3 hours for cracked wheat,

hominy, or steel-cut oats. (The length of time is only a general guide — the longer the better.) Add more water from time to time if it evaporates so much that the cereal is too dry and thick.

To serve. Brown sugar and shaved maple sugar are delicious on breakfast cereal. Stir raisins or cut-up dates, figs, prunes or apricots into cooked cereals. Slice bananas or peaches over cooked or ready-to-eat cereals.

Corn Meal Mush

See also Hasty Pudding (p. 366)

Stir together until smooth
   1 cup corn meal
   1 cup cold water
   1 teaspoon salt
In a heavy saucepan or double boiler top, bring to a boil
   4 cups water
Add the soaked corn meal, stirring constantly. Cook and stir 2 minutes. Cover. Set over an asbestos mat or over hot water. Reduce the heat and cook until the mush tastes thoroughly cooked (30 to 45 minutes).

Hominy Grits. Substitute for corn meal.

Fried Mush. Rinse a small loaf pan or a refrigerator storage dish with cold water. Fill with the cooked mush and cover to prevent a crust from forming. Chill. Cut in ½-inch slices. Dip in flour. Sauté slowly in butter or bacon fat. Serve hot with maple syrup or Mock Maple Syrup (p. 400) as a breakfast dish, a dessert, or an accompaniment to ham or chicken.

Corn Meal or Hominy Cakes. Shape cooked corn meal or hominy grits in 3-inch patties. Dip in flour and cook as above. Serve in place of potato or other starchy vegetable.

Hominy

Canned whole hominy is a convenience. Drain, season to taste with butter, salt and pepper, and heat over low heat or in a double boiler. Serve instead of potato. As a variation, serve hominy with tomato sauce.

For uncooked hominy and hominy grits, allow plenty of time for long slow cooking, as in Hominy Southern Style (below).

Hominy Southern Style

Put in a double boiler top
   1 cup water
   1 teaspoon salt
Set over direct heat and bring to a boil. Add, stirring constantly
   ¾ cup fine hominy grits
Boil 2 minutes, then set over hot water and continue cooking until thick. Add
   1 cup milk
Stir thoroughly and cook 1 hour. Add
   ¼ cup butter
   1 tablespoon sugar
   1 egg, slightly beaten
   1 cup milk
Turn into a buttered casserole. Bake 1 hour at 325°. *Serves 4 to 6.*

Buckwheat groats may be cooked in the same way.

Hominy Croquettes

Put in a double boiler top
   ½ cup boiling water
Set over direct heat. Add slowly, stirring constantly
   ¼ cup fine hominy grits
Set over boiling water and cook until the hominy absorbs the water. Add
   ¾ cup milk
Cook until the hominy is tender. Add
   2 tablespoons butter
   ½ teaspoon salt
Cool. Shape into croquettes. Roll in flour, dip in beaten egg, then in crumbs, and fry (p. 5). *Serves 6.*

Spoon Bread

White corn meal makes a crusty top and a soft center. Yellow corn meal gives an even texture throughout.

Butter a casserole and keep it warm. Put in a saucepan
   2 cups boiling water
Add slowly
   1 cup white or yellow corn meal
   ½ teaspoon salt
Cook and stir 1 minute. Remove from the heat. Add
   2 tablespoons butter
Beat well. Beat in
   4 eggs, well-beaten
   1 cup milk
Pour into the casserole. Bake 25 minutes at 400°. *Serves 6.*

Alace's Spoon Bread

Mix
   2 eggs, well beaten
   1 cup milk
   1 cup water
Stir in
   ½ cup white or yellow corn meal
   ½ cup cooked hominy or rice
   1 teaspoon baking powder
   2 tablespoons softened or melted
      butter
   ½ teaspoon salt
Put in a buttered casserole. Bake at 400° until the top is brown (30 to 40 minutes). *Serves 4.*

Buttermilk Spoon Bread. Use buttermilk in place of sweet milk and baking soda in place of baking powder.

Batter Bread

Beat until light
    1 egg
Add
    1 teaspoon salt
    ½ cup cold cooked hominy or rice
    1 cup white corn meal
Stir in
    Boiling water
to make the batter as thick as heavy cream.

Put in a deep baking dish
    1 tablespoon lard or bacon fat
Heat the dish until the fat smokes. Pour in the batter. Bake 40 minutes at 350°. *Serves 4.*

Bulgur

A cracked wheat widely used in Middle Eastern cooking. Good with chicken or lamb.

Follow the directions on the package. To make bulgur especially tasty, cook it in chicken or lamb broth.

Wheat Pilaf. Put in a pan 2 tablespoons butter, 1 tablespoon chopped onion and 1 cup uncooked bulgur. Set over low heat and cook and stir until the onion is yellow. Add the required liquid and cook.

Rice

Long-grain rice cooks into separate fluffy grains, and is excellent as an accompaniment to meat.

Short-grain rice is tender and moist when cooked. It is delicious in puddings.

Converted rice retains many of the food values lost in polished white rice.

Precooked rice is partially cooked before packaging and is handy for quick meals; read the directions on the package.

Brown (natural) rice retains some of the outer coating. It is rich in food value and has a pleasant nutty flavor.

Wild rice is actually the seed of a marsh grass. It is a luxury item, and especially good with game and poultry.

Steamed Rice

For rice desserts, see p. 369.

Put in a special rice cooker or a heavy saucepan with a tight-fitting cover
    2 cups cold water
    1 cup rice
    1 teaspoon salt
    1 teaspoon butter
Bring quickly to the boiling point. Reduce the heat so that the water just simmers, cover closely, and cook 14 minutes. Uncover and let stand until the rice is dry and fluffy (about 5 minutes). Toss with a fork. *Makes 3 cups (5 or 6 servings).*

For more tender rice, use 2⅓ cups water and cook 20 minutes.

Steamed Brown Rice. Cook for 40 minutes or more after the water boils. To be sure it does not burn before it is tender, cook in a double boiler.

Rice Ring. Season Steamed Rice with butter and pack in a ring mold. Set in a pan of hot water to heat. Turn out onto a serving dish. Fill with creamed chicken or seafood, ragout of veal, sautéed mushrooms, or any creamed dish.

Gullah Goober Rice. *Delicious with chicken or ham.* Mix 2 cups Steamed Rice with 1 cup finely chopped celery and ½ cup finely chopped salted peanuts. Cover and set over low heat 10 minutes. *Serves 4.*

Mushroom Rice. Mix 2 cups Steamed Rice with ½ cup sautéed chopped mushrooms and a few grains of nutmeg. *Serves 4.*

Curried Rice

Delicious with lamb or chicken.

Mix lightly with a fork
  2 cups hot Steamed Rice (p. 294)
  1 egg yolk, slightly beaten
  1 teaspoon anchovy paste
  ½ teaspoon curry powder
  Cayenne and salt to taste
If convenient, add
  1 chopped green chili
Serves 4 or 5.

Green Rice

For an attractive luncheon dish, bake in a ring mold, turn onto a serving dish, and fill with creamed chicken or fish.

Mix and put in a buttered casserole
  1 cup Steamed Rice (p. 294)
  1 cup milk
  ¼ cup melted butter or olive oil
  ½ cup grated cheese
  ½ medium onion, chopped fine
  ¼ to 1 cup chopped parsley
  1 egg, well beaten
  ½ teaspoon salt
  ¼ teaspoon paprika
  2 tablespoons chopped pimiento, if
    desired
Bake at 350° until firm (about 45 minutes). *Serves 6.*

Rice with Tomato Sauce

Melt in a heavy frying pan
  2 tablespoons butter
Add
  3 cups Steamed Rice (p. 294)
Cook until delicately browned, stirring lightly with a fork. Spoon into a hot serving dish. Pour over the rice
  1 cup hot Tomato Sauce (p. 94)
Sprinkle with
  ½ cup grated cheese
Lift the rice with a fork to coat each kernel with sauce and cheese. *Serves 6.*

Baked Rice

Put in a buttered baking dish
  2 cups Steamed Rice (p. 294)

Beat together
  1 egg
  1 cup milk
Pour over the rice. Dot with
  Butter
Sprinkle with
  Salt, pepper and paprika
Bake until brown at 350° (about 20 minutes). *Serves 3 or 4.*

To season more highly, add chopped parsley, crumbled crisp bacon, bits of pimiento or sautéed mushrooms, or top with grated or sliced cheese.

Baked Rice with Cheese

A basic recipe which can be used as a main dish or to accompany meat or chicken. Allow about ½ cup cooked rice for each serving.

Butter a baking dish. Put in it layers of Steamed Rice (p. 294), dotting each layer with butter and thinly sliced mild cheese (about ⅛ pound for each 2 cups of rice). Add milk to about half the depth of the rice. Cover with crumbs. Bake at 350° until the cheese melts and the crumbs are brown.

To vary, add chopped parsley, chopped pimiento or grated onion. For a heartier dish, add chopped ham, cooked chicken or hard-cooked eggs.

Fried Rice

Melt in a saucepan
  ¼ cup salad oil or butter
Add
  1 cup rice
Cook and stir over low heat until the rice browns delicately (about 20 minutes). Add
  2½ cups boiling water, stock or consommé
  1½ teaspoons salt
Bring to the boiling point. Cover. Cook over low heat 20 minutes. Season to taste with
  Salt and pepper
Serves 4.

Sauterne Rice

Especially good with chicken.

Put in a small pan
 ½ cup dried currants
 Water to cover
Bring to a boil. Remove from the heat,
let stand 5 minutes, and drain.

Put in a large saucepan
 ⅓ cup butter
 2 cloves garlic, split
Cook 5 minutes. Remove the garlic. Add
 1½ cups dry white wine
 3 cups water
Bring to a boil. Add slowly
 2 cups rice
 2½ teaspoons salt
 ¼ teaspoon pepper
 ¼ teaspoon nutmeg
 ¼ teaspoon allspice
 2 teaspoons sugar
Bring to a boil again. Cover tightly. Reduce the heat. Simmer 25 minutes. Stir
in the currants and
 ⅔ cup chopped or slivered Brazil nuts
Serves 8 generously.

Spanish Rice

*There is no "classic" recipe for Spanish
rice. Start with cooked rice and add
tomatoes, cheese, sautéed celery, onion,
peppers and seasonings until the rice is
as savory as you like. Or follow this
recipe.*

Put in a large frying pan
 2 tablespoons bacon fat or butter
 2 onions, sliced thin
Cook until the onion is soft. Add
 1 cup uncooked rice or 1⅓ cups precooked rice
Stir until the rice is lightly browned.
Add
 3 cups boiling water or stock (1⅓
  cups for precooked rice)
 2 cans tomato sauce (8 ounces each)
  or 2 chopped green peppers and 1
  cup canned or fresh tomatoes
 Salt and pepper to taste
 Chili powder or prepared mustard to
  taste

Stir well with a fork, cover, and cook
slowly until the rice is tender (10 minutes for precooked rice, 30 to 40 for uncooked rice). Season to taste. Spoon into
a serving dish. Sprinkle with
 Grated cheese
Serves 4 to 6.

Turkish Pilaf

Put in a frying pan
 2 tablespoons butter, bacon fat or
  chicken fat
 ½ cup uncooked rice
Cook and stir over moderate heat until
the rice is brown (the rice will pop as it
browns). Add
 1 cup boiling water, tomato juice or
  canned bouillon
Cook slowly until the liquid is absorbed.
Add
 1¾ cups drained canned tomatoes
Cook until the rice is soft. Season to taste
with
 Salt and pepper
Serves 4 to 6.

Chicken or Lamb Pilaf. Add ½ cup (or
more) diced cooked meat. Lamb and
chicken are the traditional choice, but
other meats are good, too. If you make
the pilaf with chicken, cook the rice in
chicken stock.

Rice Croquettes

*As a luncheon or supper dish, serve with
a tangy cheese sauce. Cook the rice in
consommé if you prefer, but use less salt.*

In a saucepan, put
 ½ cup boiling water
 ½ cup rice
 1 teaspoon salt
Cover and cook slowly until the water is
absorbed (about 10 minutes). Add
 1 cup milk
Stir lightly with a fork, cover, and cook
until the rice is tender. Stir in
 2 egg yolks or 1 egg
 1 tablespoon butter
Spread on a shallow plate to cool. Shape,

egg and crumb, and fry (p. 6). *Makes 6 or more.*

To season more highly, add tomato catsup and paprika to taste, or use highly seasoned tomato juice in place of milk. Add ¼ cup grated cheese.

Wild Rice

Definitely a luxury dish which adds a distinctive touch to a dinner party menu.

Canned cooked wild rice saves the long cooking time.

Put in a double boiler top
  1 cup wild rice, thoroughly washed
  2 cups cold water
  1 teaspoon salt
Set over direct heat and bring quickly to the boiling point. Cover and cook over hot water until tender but still firm (1 to 1½ hours). Serve plain or add butter or chopped sautéed mushrooms.

Spaghetti, Macaroni, Noodles and Other Pastas

The best Italian pastas are creamy rather than white and break with a clean sharp edge. There are many attractive forms — elbows, shells, twists and letters as well as macaroni, spaghetti and vermicelli.

Noodles are usually enriched with eggs or egg yolks. Green noodles have spinach added to the dough to give them a fine color.

Spaghetti

1 package (8 or 9 ounces) serves 4 or 5 as the main dish.

Have ready a deep kettle of rapidly boiling salted water (1 teaspoon salt to each quart). Do not break spaghetti in pieces. Take a handful of it, dip the ends in the water, and as the ends soften, coil the spaghetti under the water. Cook until

just tender (about 7 minutes). Drain in a colander. Arrange in layers in a heated serving dish, spreading each layer generously with sauce (below). Serve with extra sauce and plenty of freshly grated Parmesan or Romano cheese.

Spaghetti and Meat Balls (p. 170).

Garlic Sauce

Heat ¼ cup olive oil with 2 or 3 split cloves of garlic. Remove the garlic. Pour the oil over cooked spaghetti. Toss until well blended.

Anchovy Garlic Sauce. Just before pouring the oil over the spaghetti, add 6 anchovies, cut in pieces.

Mushroom Garlic Sauce. Add ½ to 1 cup sliced sautéed mushrooms.

Clam Garlic Sauce. Add ½ cup fresh or canned minced clams.

Italian Tomato Sauce

Canned tomato sauce is a convenience. Add extra meat for a richer sauce. Leftover sauce is good over poached eggs or added to a soup or gravy.

Put in a large skillet or a saucepan
   3 tablespoons olive oil or 2 tablespoons oil and 1 tablespoon butter
   1 or 2 onions, sliced thin
   1 clove garlic, split
Cook until the onion is golden. Add
   ½ to 1 pound ground beef
Cook and stir 5 minutes. Add
   1 can tomato paste
   1 large can tomatoes (about 2½ cups)

1 tablespoon sugar
Salt, pepper, cayenne, orégano and
    basil to taste
Simmer at least 1 hour. Add water as
needed, but the sauce should be thick
and smooth. For the finest flavor, let the
sauce mellow for a day before using it.
For ½ pound spaghetti.

Variations

Add other seasonings such as thyme,
    chopped parsley, a few grains of
    mace or allspice or a few drops of
    Worcestershire or Tabasco.
Omit the meat for a simpler sauce.
Substitute for the tomatoes 2½ cups
    tomato juice, water or consommé.
In place of olive oil, use other salad
    oil, bacon fat, or 2 slices bacon,
    diced.
Omit the onion, garlic and sugar.

Truman's Sauce

*Good also made with leftover chopped
cooked lamb, pork, veal or beef.*

Put in a large skillet or a heavy saucepan
    2 slices bacon, diced
    ½ green pepper, seeded and chopped
    1 or 2 onions, chopped
    1 clove garlic, split
Cook until the onion is golden. Add
    ½ to 1 pound ground beef
Cook and stir until the meat is browned.
Add
    2 cans tomato paste
    1 can consommé, undiluted
    1 tablespoon Worcestershire
    2 tablespoons freshly grated Parmesan
        or Romano cheese
    Salt, pepper and orégano to taste
Simmer 2 or 3 hours, adding water if the
sauce gets too thick. For finest flavor, let
the sauce mellow a day. *For ½ pound
spaghetti.*

Quick Tomato Sauce

Empty a can or two of tomato paste into
a pan. Stir in hot water until the sauce is
as thin as you like it. Season to taste,
adding a trace of sugar and a shake of

powdered garlic. Serve hot but not
boiling.

Spaghetti Carbonara

*Not all Italian pasta recipes include to-
matoes and garlic. This one is popular,
especially in northern Italy.*

Sauté until crisp
    1 pound bacon, diced
Pour off all but 3 tablespoons of the fat.
Add to the pan
    ½ cup chopped green pepper
    ½ cup chopped onion
Cook slowly until the vegetables are
tender.

Cook in a large kettle
    1 pound spaghetti
Drain and rinse the spaghetti. Put it
back in the kettle and keep it warm. Add
    2 eggs
    ¼ cup freshly grated Parmesan cheese
        (or to taste)
Stir well. Reheat the bacon and vegeta-
bles and stir them into the spaghetti.
Reheat. Serve with
    Grated Parmesan cheese
Serves 6 to 8.

Macaroni

*Allow 1 to 3 ounces per person, accord-
ing to whether the macaroni is to be
served as an accompaniment or as the
main dish.*

Break into 1 or 2 inch pieces. Have ready
a deep kettle of rapidly boiling salted
water (1 teaspoon salt to each quart).
Add the macaroni slowly so that the boiling will not stop. Boil until just tender
but still firm — *al dente,* as the Italians
describe it. Be careful not to overcook,
especially if there is to be further cooking in a sauce.

Drain in a strainer and rinse with cold
water to remove excess starch which
would make the pasta sticky.

Reheat in cream, Cream Sauce (p. 90),
Tomato Sauce (p. 94) or Cheese Sauce
(p. 91).

Macaroni alla Milanese. Heat 2 cups cooked macaroni in 1 cup Italian Tomato Sauce (p. 298) with 6 sautéed sliced mushrooms and 2 slices cooked smoked tongue cut in strips. Serve with freshly grated Parmesan cheese.

Macaroni and Cheese

Cook and drain
    9-ounce package macaroni
Put half of it in a buttered baking dish.
Sprinkle with
    ½ cup (or more) grated cheese
Cover with the rest of the macaroni.
Sprinkle with
    ½ cup (or more) grated cheese
Cover with
    2 cups Cream Sauce (p. 90)
Sprinkle with
    ½ cup buttered bread crumbs
Bake at 400° until brown. *Serves 6.*

For a very creamy dish, make 2 cups Cheese Sauce (p. 91) and spread it on the layers of macaroni instead of cheese and Cream Sauce.

Macaroni and Cheese with Chipped Beef. Cover ¼ pound dried beef (separated in pieces) with boiling water. Drain. If the beef is very salty, let it stand a few minutes before draining. Put half the beef on each layer of macaroni.

Macaroni and Cheese with Spiced Ham. Cut canned spiced ham in strips. Put half on each layer of macaroni. Other meats are good this way, too — sliced cooked frankfurters or bits of cooked ham or chicken.

Macaroni Mousse

Cook and drain
    1 cup elbow macaroni
Add
    1½ cups milk
    ¼ cup melted butter
    2 eggs, well beaten
    1 pimiento, chopped fine
    1 sweet green pepper, chopped fine

    1 tablespoon chopped onion
    ½ tablespoon salt
    ½ cup mild or sharp cheese, cut small
    ½ cup soft bread crumbs
Mix well. Put in a buttered loaf pan, 9 by 5 inches. Bake at 350° until firm (about 40 minutes). Turn out onto a serving plate.

Serve with any creamed dish such as Creamed Chicken (p. 224), Creamed Fish (p. 128) or Creamed Mushrooms (p. 250). *Serves 6.*

Macaroni Ring. Bake in a 10-inch ring mold. Turn out onto a round serving dish.

Homemade Noodles

Beat slightly
    1 egg
    ½ teaspoon salt
Mix in
    Flour (about 2 cups)
to make a very stiff dough. Knead 5 minutes on a slightly floured board. Roll paper-thin. Cover with a towel and set aside 20 minutes.

Cut in strips of any desired width. Spread the strips out on a table to dry thoroughly.

Store in a tightly covered jar. Cook like spaghetti (p. 298).

Noodles for soup. Cut in 3-inch strips; pile the strips on each other and cut in fine shreds.

Buttered Noodles

Cook noodles according to directions on the package or like spaghetti (p. 298). Stir in butter to taste and season with salt and pepper.

Noodles with Poppyseed. For ½ pound noodles, melt 2 tablespoons butter, add 3 tablespoons poppyseed and ¼ cup chopped almonds. Cook and stir 5 minutes and stir into the cooked noodles.

Sautéed Noodles

Cook ½ pound noodles according to the instructions on the package or like spaghetti (p. 298). Dry thoroughly on a towel. Melt ¼ cup butter, add the noodles and toss over moderate heat until the noodles are delicately brown.

Serve sprinkled with croûtons or arrange in a ring on a platter and fill with creamed chicken or other creamed dish. *Serves 6.*

Alfredo's Noodles

Plenty of butter and plenty of cheese make this dish memorable.

Have ready a deep kettle of boiling salted water (1 teaspoon to each quart). Add slowly
    ½ pound broad noodles
Cook until the noodles are just barely tender. Drain. Add
    ¼ pound unsalted butter, soft but not melted
Turn over and over with a large fork and spoon until the butter is melted and the noodles are well coated. Heap on a large heated platter. Sprinkle with
    ¼ pound freshly grated Parmesan cheese
Toss with a fork and spoon until the cheese melts. *Serves 4 to 6.*

Sour Cream Noodles

Cook according to directions on the package or like spaghetti (p. 298)
    ¼ pound broad noodles
Drain. Add
    1 cup cottage cheese
    1 cup sour cream
    1 egg, slightly beaten
    ½ teaspoon salt
    ⅛ teaspoon pepper
    ¼ cup butter, melted
Mix. Put in a well-buttered baking dish. Bake 1½ hours at 300°. *Serves 4 to 6.*

Noodle Pudding. *Excellent with ham or chicken.* Add ½ cup raisins.

Noodle Ring

For a simple version, butter cooked noodles, pack into a ring mold, and set in a pan of hot water in a 300° oven until serving time.

Bake Sour Cream Noodles (above), or Baked Noodles (below) in a well-buttered 1-quart ring mold. Turn out onto a serving dish. Fill with creamed chicken or seafood or with sautéed mushrooms or buttered green beans. *Serves 4 or 5.*

Margery's Noodles

For a more pungent flavor, add a clove of garlic, cut fine.

Cook according to directions on the package or like spaghetti (p. 298)
    ½ pound fine noodles
Mix
    1 cup cottage cheese
    1 cup sour cream
    ¾ cup finely chopped onion
    1 teaspoon Worcestershire
    Few drops Tabasco
    Salt and pepper to taste
Add the noodles and mix well. Put in a buttered casserole. Bake 20 minutes at 350°. Spread over the top
    ½ cup grated Parmesan cheese
    ½ cup sour cream
Bake 10 minutes longer. *Serves 6.*

Baked Noodles

Cook according to directions on the package or like spaghetti (p. 298)
    ¼ pound noodles
Drain. Add
    1 tablespoon butter
    ½ teaspoon salt
    ⅛ teaspoon pepper
    Few grains nutmeg
    ¼ cup hot milk
    2 egg yolks, well beaten
Mix lightly with a fork and spoon. Fold in
    2 egg whites, beaten stiff
Pour into a buttered baking dish. Set in a pan of hot water. Bake 30 minutes at 325°. *Serves 4 to 6.*

Baked Noodles with Cheese. Increase the milk to ½ cup. Add ½ cup grated cheese (or ¼ cup grated cheese and ½ cup chopped cooked ham). Add 2 tablespoons each of shredded green pepper and finely cut celery.

Lasagne

Mix in a large kettle
  1 large can tomato purée
  2 cans tomato paste
  2 cups water
  1 teaspoon orégano
  1 teaspoon sugar
  1 teaspoon salt
  ¼ teaspoon freshly ground pepper
Let the mixture simmer. Meanwhile, heat in a skillet
  2 tablespoons olive oil
When the oil is hot, sauté in it
  1 cup minced onion
  1 clove garlic, crushed
When the onion is golden, add
  1½ pounds ground beef, preferably chuck
  1 teaspoon salt
Cook until the meat has lost its red color, then add to the kettle mixture. Simmer for about 2 hours or until the sauce is thick.

Cook as directed on the package
  1 pound lasagne noodles
Drain thoroughly, rinse and separate the noodles, spreading them on a towel to dry. Cut into thin slices
  1 pound mozzarella cheese
Have ready
  1 pound ricotta cheese
  ¼ pound fresh grated Romano cheese
Spoon some of the sauce into two 8-inch square pans or one large casserole. Put in a layer of noodles, then a layer of mozzarella and a layer of ricotta. Put in another layer of noodles, crosswise, then more sauce, and layers of noodles, mozzarella and ricotta. Top with a last layer of noodles and the rest of the sauce. Sprinkle generously with Romano cheese.

Bake at 375° for 30 minutes. Let stand in a warm place for 15 minutes before serving. *Serves 8 to 10.*

Cannelloni

Cook like spaghetti (p. 298)
  1 8-ounce package lasagne noodles
Drain. Spread on a cloth to dry. Mix
  1 pound ricotta cheese
  ½ pound cream cheese
  1 egg, slightly beaten
  ¼ cup chopped chives or parsley
  ¼ cup butter, creamed
  Salt and pepper to taste
Spread a tablespoonful on each cooked noodle. Roll tight. Place the rolls, close together, on shallow baking dishes. Pour over the rolls
  Italian Tomato Sauce (p. 298) or
  2 cans tomato paste mixed with
  3 cups water
Cut in thin slices
  1 pound mozzarella cheese
Put a slice of cheese on each roll. Sprinkle with
  Grated Parmesan cheese
Bake 30 minutes at 375°. *Serves 4 to 6.*

For a heartier dish, add any chopped cooked meat to the filling.

Ravioli

Sift onto a breadboard
  1½ cups flour
  ½ teaspoon salt
Make a depression in the center. Drop in
  1 egg yolk
Mix with a knife. Moisten with
  Warm water

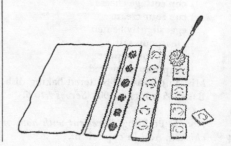

to make a stiff dough. Knead until smooth. Cover with a warm bowl. Let stand 30 minutes.

Roll paper-thin and cut in strips 2 inches wide. Put teaspoonfuls of filling (below) on half the strips, 2 inches apart. Cover with the other strips. Seal by pressing along the edges and between the mounds with your thumbs. Cut apart. Dry 2 hours.

Cook 20 minutes in
    Rapidly boiling water, stock or
      bouillon
Take up with a skimmer. Arrange in layers in a heated serving dish. Sprinkle each layer generously with
    Grated Parmesan cheese
Cover with
    Italian Tomato Sauce (p. 298)
Serves 6.

Spinach and Cheese Filling. Mix ¼ cup cracker crumbs, ½ cup grated Parmesan or Romano cheese, ¼ cup chopped cooked spinach and 1 egg, slightly beaten. Moisten with chicken stock or broth. Season with salt and pepper.

Spinach and Meat Filling. Mix ½ cup chopped cooked meat or chicken, ½ cup chopped cooked spinach, 1 egg and 2 tablespoons grated Romano or Parmesan cheese. Season to taste with salt, pepper and orégano or nutmeg.

Gnocchi alla Romana

Especially good with Sautéed Veal Cutlets (p. 194), Smothered Chicken (p. 216) or Chicken Cacciatora (p. 217). Convenient to prepare in advance ready for the final browning just before serving time.

Put in a saucepan
    ¼ cup butter
Heat until bubbling. Take from the stove. Add
    ¼ cup flour
    ¼ cup cornstarch
    ½ teaspoon salt
Stir well. Stir in slowly
    2 cups milk
Cook 8 minutes over low heat, stirring constantly. Add
    2 egg yolks, slightly beaten
    ½ cup grated Parmesan cheese
Pour into a buttered shallow pan, about 10 by 14 inches. Chill.

Turn out on a board. Cut in squares, strips or diamonds. Arrange on a buttered ovenproof platter. Sprinkle with
    ¼ cup melted butter
    ¼ cup grated Parmesan cheese
Bake at 400° until brown (about 15 minutes). *Serves 6.*

Pancakes, Waffles and Doughnuts

Although traditionally served at breakfast, pancakes, waffles and doughnuts appear at other times as well. With crisp bacon or tasty country sausage, pancakes and waffles are hearty enough for lunch. Waffles are a welcome dessert after a simple main course.

Pancakes (Griddlecakes)

Put in a mixing bowl
    ½ cup milk
    2 tablespoons melted butter
    1 egg
Beat lightly. Sift
    1 cup all-purpose or pastry flour
    2 teaspoons baking powder
    2 tablespoons sugar
    ½ teaspoon salt
Add to the milk mixture all at once. Stir just enough to dampen the flour. Add enough more milk to make the batter about as thick as heavy cream.

To cook. Heat the griddle or frying pan over moderate heat. To test the griddle for correct heat, pour a few drops of water on it. When the griddle is hot enough, the water will boil up immediately and form rapidly moving globules. Most modern griddles need no greasing, but if necessary, grease lightly with butter.

Put the batter on the griddle by tablespoonfuls; or, for larger pancakes, use a ¼-cup measure to dip the batter onto the griddle.

Cook until the cakes are full of bubbles and the undersurface is nicely browned. Lift with a pancake turner or spatula and brown the other side.

Serve immediately with plenty of melted butter and warmed maple syrup. Other good accompaniments are Honey Sauce (p. 400), Mock Maple Syrup (p. 400), honey, molasses, sour cream and applesauce. *Makes 6 or 8.*

To vary, use buttermilk, sour milk or yogurt in place of milk. Use ½ teaspoon baking soda instead of baking powder. Or sift a tablespoon of corn meal with the flour.

Whole Wheat Pancakes. Use ⅓ cup whole wheat flour and ⅔ cup white flour. Sweeten with molasses instead of sugar.

Oatmeal Pancakes. Heat ½ cup milk, add ½ cup quick oatmeal, and let stand 10 minutes. Add the rest of the ingredients, reducing the flour to 2 tablespoons.

Buckwheat Cakes. Use half buckwheat flour and half white flour.

Apple Pancakes. Peel 1 tart juicy apple. Cut in thin slices and stir into the batter. Serve with Cider Syrup (p. 307).

Blueberry Pancakes. Add ½ cup blueberries to the batter. If you use canned blueberries, strain off the juice.

Pancake Sandwiches

A tasty way to make leftovers into a hearty luncheon dish.

Put pancakes together sandwich fashion with any of the fillings suggested below.

Serve immediately or keep warm in the oven.

Creamed chicken or tuna.

Creamed mushrooms.

One can condensed cream of chicken soup diluted with about ¼ cup cream or milk. Add extra chicken and mushrooms, if you like. Season to taste with nutmeg or sherry.

One can condensed cream of celery soup, diluted with about ¼ cup cream or milk. Add ½ cup chopped ham.

Corn Meal Griddlecakes

Put in a saucepan
  ¾ cup water
Bring to a boil. Stir in
  ¼ cup corn meal
Cook 5 minutes. Remove from heat. Stir in
  ¾ cup sour milk
Sift together
  1 cup all-purpose flour
  2 tablespoons sugar
  ½ teaspoon salt
  ½ teaspoon baking powder
  ¼ teaspoon baking soda
Add to the corn meal mixture. Stir in
  1 egg, well beaten
  1 tablespoon melted butter
Cook (p. 304). *Makes 12.*

With sweet milk. Omit the soda and use 1 teaspoon baking powder.

Sour Cream Pancakes

Mix
  1 pint sour cream
  1 cup yellow corn meal
  ½ cup flour
  1 teaspoon soda
  ½ teaspoon baking powder
  ½ teaspoon salt
Cook (p. 304). *Makes 12 or more.*

Rice Griddlecakes

Mix
  1 cup milk
  1 cup warm cooked rice
  ½ teaspoon salt
Stir in
  2 egg yolks, beaten until thick
  1 tablespoon melted butter
  ⅞ cup all-purpose flour
Fold in
  2 egg whites, beaten stiff
Cook (p. 304). *Makes 15 to 18.*

French Pancakes

Internationally famous for dessert. Also the basis for some exceptional luncheon dishes (p. 306) and an epicurean way to use leftovers.

Put in a bowl
  2 eggs
Beat only until well blended. Add
  1 cup milk
  ½ teaspoon salt
  1 cup all-purpose or pastry flour
Stir until smooth. Cover and let stand at least ½ hour. The batter should be thin — just thick enough to coat a spoon dipped in it. If the batter is too thick, stir in a little more milk.

Heat a 5 or 6 inch frying pan and grease lightly with salad oil. Pour in just enough batter to cover the pan with a very thin layer. Tilt the pan so that the batter spreads evenly. If there is a little too much, tip the pan over the mixing bowl and pour the extra back.

Cook on one side, turn with a spatula, and brown the other side. Cook the pancakes one by one. Roll up or fold in quarters.

Keep warm if you are serving them immediately, or set aside and reheat in the oven. *Makes 18 to 24.*

Crêpes Napoleon. Add 1 tablespoon sugar and 1 tablespoon melted butter to the batter. Spread each cooked pancake with a thin layer of warmed raspberry jam and pile the pancakes evenly in a shallow baking dish. Sprinkle lightly with sugar and keep warm in a slow (200°) oven. Serve in wedges.

Normandy Pancakes. Cook small pork sausage links. Wrap one in each pancake. Heat in the oven. Serve with maple syrup and Fried Apple Rings (p. 85).

Crêpes Nicholas. Put a tablespoon of chopped cooked chicken on each pancake. Add a dab of Duxelles (p. 249), if you like. Roll up and put close together in a shallow baking dish. When ready to serve, pour piping hot Cheese Sauce (p. 91) over the pancakes and brown lightly in the broiler.

Mushroom Crêpes. *Use Duxelles (p. 249) as a filling if more convenient.* Slice ¾ pound mushrooms thin. Cook 5 minutes in 3 tablespoons butter. Add 2 egg yolks beaten with ¾ cup sour cream. Cook 2 minutes. Put a spoonful on each pancake and roll up. Put in a baking dish and reheat in a 350° oven.

Seafood Crêpes. Flake crab meat or tuna, or cut shrimp or lobster in small pieces. Mix with undiluted cream of celery soup. Season to taste with orégano, curry powder or paprika. Add sherry, too, if you like. Put a spoonful on each pancake. Roll up and put in a buttered baking dish. Sprinkle with melted butter or salad oil. Bake at 350° until well heated (about 20 minutes). Serve with tomato sauce and grated Parmesan cheese.

Cocktail Crêpes. Cook the batter by teaspoonfuls. Put on each pancake a dab of any savory filling such as cheese, curried chicken, ham or lobster. Roll up, keep hot, and serve on toothpicks.

Crêpes Gruyère. Put a small piece of Gruyère cheese on each pancake. Fold to cover the cheese completely. Egg and crumb (p. 6) and fry in deep fat heated to 370° until lightly browned (about 1 minute). Serve with drinks or with tomato sauce for lunch.

Blini. *Attractive as a first course or as the main dish for supper or lunch.* Serve the pancakes with melted butter, sour cream, and smoked salmon, smoked whitefish, caviar or salt herring.

Cheese Blintzes. For the filling, beat together 1 pound moist cottage cheese, 1 beaten egg, 2 tablespoons sugar (or more, to taste), and ½ teaspoon cinnamon. Add, to taste, grated lemon rind or orange rind and a few drops of vanilla. Add 1 tablespoon melted butter to the pancake batter. Brown the pancakes on one side only. As each is browned, turn it out onto a double layer of kitchen towels, browned side up. When all are done, put a spoonful of filling on each one and roll up, tucking the ends firmly. Brown in butter. Serve with sour cream and apricot jam or stewed blueberries or cherries.

Crêpes María

A modification of Italian manicotti. If you prefer, cook and drain packaged manicotti, then fill and bake in the same way.

Make French Pancakes (p. 305). Mix
   1 pound ricotta or dry cottage cheese
   1 cup chopped cooked ham
   2 eggs, well beaten
   3 tablespoons chopped parsley
   ¼ cup grated Romano cheese
Spread on the pancakes. Roll up and put close together in a baking dish. Mix
   2 cans tomato paste
   2 cups water
Pour over the pancakes. Sprinkle with
   ¼ cup grated Romano cheese
Bake about 30 minutes at 350°. *Serves 6.*

Crêpes Suzette

For a gala effect, make Crêpes Suzette at the table in a chafing dish or electric skillet. Otherwise, put them on a warmed serving dish and pour sauce over them. At serving time sprinkle with sugar and warmed brandy and light with a match.

Sift together
   1 cup flour

¼ cup fine sugar
½ teaspoon salt
Put in a mixing bowl
  2 eggs
  1 cup milk
  1 tablespoon brandy or 1 teaspoon
    vanilla
Beat well. Stir in the flour mixture. Cover and let stand at least ½ hour.

Follow the directions for cooking French Pancakes (p. 305).

Heat in a chafing dish
  3 tablespoons Suzette Sauce I or II
    (below)
Add 6 of the pancakes and heat slowly, spooning the sauce over the pancakes several times. Add more sauce as needed. When the sauce is syrupy and the pancakes are very hot, sprinkle with
  Sugar and warmed brandy or Curaçao
Light with a match. Cook the rest of the crêpes the same way. *Serves 6 (18 or more small pancakes).*

Jelly Pancakes. Spread the crêpes with any jelly and roll up. Sprinkle with confectioners' sugar.

Crêpes Vert Galant. Keep the crêpes warm. Whip ½ cup heavy cream, fold in ½ cup chopped toasted almonds, hazelnuts or walnuts, and sweeten to taste. Put a spoonful on each pancake, roll up, sprinkle with sugar and Cointreau, and serve immediately.

Sauces for Crêpes Suzette

Make the sauce ahead of time. It does not need to be perfectly smooth.

I. Cream ½ cup sweet (unsalted) butter. Beat in ½ cup confectioners' sugar. Add the grated rind and juice of 2 tangerines or 1 orange, and ¼ cup Cognac or Curaçao or a mixture of maraschino, kirsch and Curaçao.

II. Mix the grated peel and juice of 1 orange and 1 lemon. Add 1 cup sugar, ½ cup water and ¼ cup brandy.

Cottage Cheese Pancakes

Easy to make on a table grill as a show-off dessert.

Put in a bowl
  3 eggs
Beat well. Add
  1 cup dry cottage cheese
  2 tablespoons butter
  ¼ cup flour, sifted
  ¼ teaspoon salt
Beat only until well blended. Cook by tablespoonfuls on a heated griddle. Spread with tart jelly, roll up, sprinkle with confectioners' sugar. *Makes 12.*

Waffles

For a heartier dish, serve with small broiled sausages, creamed chicken, mushrooms, bacon or fried chicken.

Sift together and set aside
  1½ cups flour
  3 teaspoons baking powder
  2 teaspoons sugar
  ½ teaspoon salt
Put in a bowl
  2 eggs
Beat well. Add
  1 cup milk or milk and cream
  3 tablespoons melted butter or
    salad oil
Add the flour mixture and beat with a rotary or electric beater. The batter need not be perfectly smooth. If it is thicker than heavy cream, add more milk. Thin batter makes tender waffles. *Makes 8.*

To cook. Heat the waffle iron but do not grease it. Pour about 1 tablespoon of the batter into each compartment near the center (the batter will spread to fill the iron), cover, and leave closed until steaming stops. Waffles should be well puffed and delicately brown. Lift from the iron with a fork. Bake the first waffle a little longer; they sometimes stick.

Serve with melted butter and warmed maple syrup or **Cider Syrup** (1 cup cider and ½ cup sugar simmered 5 minutes).

Sour Milk Waffles. Use 1¼ cups sour milk or cream, buttermilk or yogurt, and add ¼ teaspoon soda. Use only 2 tablespoons butter if you use sour cream.

Coconut Waffles. After pouring the batter onto the iron, sprinkle with a tablespoon or more of shredded coconut.

Ham Waffles. Add to the batter ½ to 1 cup chopped cooked ham.

Corn Waffles. Add to the batter 1 cup cooked corn or drained whole kernel canned corn.

Raised Waffles

The best ever — crisp but tender. To serve at breakfast, start them the night before.

Put in a large mixing bowl
  ½ cup lukewarm water
  1 package yeast
Let stand 5 minutes. Add
  2 cups lukewarm milk
  ½ cup melted butter or salad oil
  1 teaspoon salt
  1 teaspoon sugar
Beat in
  2 cups flour
Cover the bowl. Let stand overnight or at least 8 hours (but not in the refrigerator).

When time to cook the waffles, add
  2 eggs
  Pinch of baking soda
Beat well. The batter will be very thin. Cook on a waffle iron. *Makes 6 or more large waffles.*

Corn Meal Waffles

Good with sausage, bacon or ham.

Follow the recipe for Corn Meal Griddlecakes (p. 305), but fold in the egg white, beaten stiff, at the last. Cook on a waffle iron (p. 307).

Rice Waffles

Sift together into a mixing bowl
  1¾ cups flour
  4 teaspoons baking powder
  ¼ teaspoon salt
  2 tablespoons sugar
Add
  ⅔ cup cold cooked rice
Mix evenly with a fork. Add
  1½ cups milk
  1 egg yolk, well beaten
  1 tablespoon melted butter or salad oil
Stir thoroughly. Fold in
  1 egg white, beaten stiff
Cook on a waffle iron (p. 307). *Makes 6 to 8.*

Doughnuts

Sift
  1¾ cups flour
  2 teaspoons baking powder
  ¼ teaspoon nutmeg
  ½ teaspoon salt
Put in a mixing bowl
  1 egg, beaten
  ½ cup milk
  ½ cup sugar
  1 tablespoon melted butter or salad oil
Add the dry ingredients. Add enough more flour to make the dough just firm enough to handle, but keep the dough as soft as possible. Chill.

Put a third of the mixture on a floured board, knead slightly, pat, and roll out ⅓ inch thick. Shape with a floured doughnut cutter and put the doughnuts on a floured piece of wax paper. Add the trimmings to half the remaining mixture. Roll and shape as before; repeat until all the dough is cut out. Let the doughnuts stand 5 or 10 minutes before frying.

To fry. Heat the fat to 360° (p. 6). Doughnuts will absorb fat if the fat is too cool, and will brown before they are done in the center if it is too hot. Lower the doughnuts, three or four at a time, gently into the fat. When brown on one side, turn and brown on the other side. Lift from the fat with a fork or tongs (without piercing). Drain on paper towels. *Makes 18.*

To sugar. Roll in fine or confectioners' sugar. Or put the sugar in a paper bag, add the doughnuts, two or three at a time, and shake gently until well coated.

To frost. Spread one side of unsugared doughnuts with Portsmouth Frosting (p. 491). Sprinkle with chopped nut meats, if desired.

Sour Milk Doughnuts. *These doughnuts are especially tender.* Use half pastry flour and half all-purpose flour, and use sour milk or buttermilk in place of sweet milk. Add ½ teaspoon baking soda and use only ½ teaspoon baking powder.

Cream Doughnuts. Use cream in place of milk and butter. With sour cream (best of all) add ½ teaspoon baking soda and use only ½ teaspoon baking powder.

Lemon Doughnuts. In place of 1 whole egg, use 2 egg yolks. Add 1 tablespoon lemon juice and ½ teaspoon grated lemon rind. Season with nutmeg.

Chocolate Doughnuts. Sift ½ cup cocoa with the flour. Sugar the doughnuts with confectioners' sugar or spread with Chocolate or Orange Portsmouth Frosting (p. 491).

Raised Doughnuts

Put in a mixing bowl
> 1 cup lukewarm milk
> 1 package yeast
> 1 teaspoon salt
> 2 cups all-purpose flour

Beat thoroughly. Cover and let rise ½ hour. Add
> ¼ cup melted butter or salad oil
> 1 cup light brown sugar
> 2 eggs, well beaten
> ½ teaspoon nutmeg
> 1½ cups flour

Beat well. Cover and let rise again until dough is light. Punch down (p. 323). Add more flour if the dough is too soft to handle.

Turn out onto a well-floured board. Divide the dough in two parts, cover each with a bowl, and let "rest" 10 minutes to make the dough easier to work with.

Roll about ½ inch thick. Cut with a floured biscuit cutter and shape into a ball, or cut with a 3-inch doughnut cutter. Set on the board, uncovered, and let rise about 1 hour. Fry (p. 308) and sugar (above). *Makes 24.*

Jelly Doughnuts. Cut out the dough in 2½-inch rounds. On half of them place heaping teaspoons of jam or jelly. Brush the edges with slightly beaten egg white and cover with the other rounds. Press the edges together. Let rise, fry, and sugar.

Doughboys

Serve in place of hot rolls or with maple syrup or Mock Maple Syrup (p. 400) as a breakfast dish or a dessert.

After bread dough has risen, punch down (p. 323) and roll out the desired amount ⅛ inch thick. Cut in strips 2½ inches wide and cut the strips in squares or in diamond-shaped pieces. Cover and let stand 10 to 15 minutes. Fry like doughnuts (p. 308).

Afternoon Tea Doughnuts

Also delicious with coffee. Serve with julienne strips of cheese.

Beat until light
    1 egg
Add
    2 tablespoons sugar
    ½ teaspoon salt
    3 tablespoons milk
    1 tablespoon melted shortening or oil
Sift together
    1 cup flour
    2 teaspoons baking powder
Stir into the first mixture.

Shape dough by teaspoonfuls, or force through a pastry bag (using the small ladyfinger tube) directly into the fat.

Heat fat to 370°. Fry and drain (p. 308). *Makes 24 or more.*

Crullers

See also French Crullers (p. 429).

Mix batter for Doughnuts (p. 308) or Raised Doughnuts (p. 309). Roll it ⅓ inch thick. Cut in strips 8 inches long and ¾ inch wide. Let rise (10 minutes for doughnut batter, 1 hour for raised doughnut batter).

Twist each strip several times and pinch the ends. Fry and roll in sugar (p. 309). *Makes 3 dozen.*

Jiffy Crullers

These midget-sized crullers are perfect for a mid-morning coffee party.

Cut ready-to-bake packaged baking powder biscuits in half. Twist each piece to make a tiny cruller. Fry at 370° and roll in sugar or cinnamon sugar (see Cinnamon Toast, p. 343).

Quick Breads, Biscuits and Coffee Cakes

Hot breads give the menu a lift, and you can make quick breads in no time since they are raised with baking powder rather than yeast. (To reheat, see p. 326.)

Baking Powder Biscuits

The shortening may be all butter or margarine, all lard or other cooking fat or oil, or half of each. Lard makes very flaky biscuits. For richer biscuits, double the amount of shortening.

To serve piping hot, bake and serve in a glass pie plate.

Split leftover biscuits, toast lightly, butter, and serve for breakfast or tea.

Sift into a mixing bowl
    2 cups all-purpose flour
    4 teaspoons tartrate-type baking powder or 2 teaspoons "double-action" type
    1 teaspoon salt
With fingertips or a pastry blender or fork, work in
    2 tablespoons shortening
With a fork, quickly stir in
    ⅔ cup milk
Add more milk, little by little, until the dough is soft and light but not sticky. (Flours differ so much that it is impossible to tell exactly how much milk you will need.)

Turn out onto a floured board. With floured hands, pat down or knead about 20 strokes until smooth. Roll lightly ¾ inch thick. Shape with a biscuit cutter or roll out into an oblong and cut in diamonds with a knife. Place on an ungreased cooky sheet, close together for soft biscuits, 1 inch apart for crusty ones. Prick with a fork.

Bake 12 to 15 minutes at 450°. *Makes 12 to 15.*

Bacon Biscuits. Cook bacon until crisp. Crumble to make about ⅓ cupful. Add to the batter.

Butter Sticks. Melt ¼ cup butter in an oblong pan about 12 by 10 inches. Roll the dough into an oblong about ½ inch thick. Cut in 16 finger-shaped pieces. Put in the pan and turn so that all sides are buttered.

Buttermilk Biscuits. Use buttermilk in place of sweet milk and use only half the quantity of baking powder. Add ¼ teaspoon baking soda.

Cheese Biscuits. Add ½ cup grated cheese to the dry ingredients.

Cream Biscuits. Use 1 cup heavy cream in place of shortening and milk. Whip the cream stiff before adding.

Drop Biscuits. Increase the milk to 1¼ cups. Drop by spoonfuls in buttered muffin tins or on a buttered cooky sheet.

Filled Biscuits. Roll the dough ½ inch thick. Cut out rounds. Spread half of them with melted butter, then with chopped cooked ham, sausage meat, orange marmalade, shaved maple sugar or grated cheese. Press other rounds lightly on top. Brush with milk.

Maple Tea Biscuits. Roll Cream Biscuits (above) about ½ inch thick, and cut out with a small cutter. Sprinkle with shaved maple sugar before baking.

Orange Biscuits. Before baking, put ½ teaspoon orange marmalade on each.

Peanut Butter Biscuits. Work in 2 tablespoons peanut butter, leaving it in large enough bits so that it will show when baked.

Pinwheel Biscuits

Roll Baking Powder Biscuit (p. 311) dough into an oblong ¼ inch thick. Brush with melted butter. Roll up like a jelly roll. Cut off pieces ¾ inch thick. Set on a baking sheet, cut side down.

Bake 15 minutes at 450°. *Makes 12 to 15.*

Butterscotch Biscuits. Cream ½ cup butter with ¾ cup brown sugar. Spread part on the dough before rolling it up. Spread the remainder on the bottom of a 9-inch pan. Brush the sides of the biscuits with melted butter. Place close together in the pan, flat side down. Sprinkle pecan nut meats on the dough and in the pan, if desired.

Cheese Pinwheels. Sprinkle the dough with ½ cup grated cheese and roll.

Onion Pinwheels. *Serve hot, as an accompaniment for cocktails.* Spread the dough with 1 cup finely chopped onion. Scatter sesame seed over the onion. Roll, cut, and brush with slightly beaten egg white. Sprinkle a few more seeds on each.

Orange Marmalade Pinwheels. Spread the dough with orange marmalade before rolling it up.

Orange Pinwheels. Cream ¼ cup butter with ½ cup sugar. Add ½ cup orange juice and 2 tablespoons grated orange rind. Distribute in 12 buttered muffin tins. Sprinkle the dough with ¼ cup

sugar mixed with ½ teaspoon cinnamon before rolling it up. Arrange the pieces in the muffin tins.

Irish Bread

Follow the recipe for Baking Powder Biscuits (p. 311), adding 1 tablespoon shortening, 1 tablespoon sugar, ½ cup raisins, ½ cup currants and 1 tablespoon caraway seed. Spread in a buttered heavy frying pan or 9-inch round tin.

Bake about 30 minutes at 350°. Increase the heat to 400° the last 5 minutes of baking. Serve in wedges.

Cream Scones

Traditional at English tea parties.

Sift into a mixing bowl
> 2 cups flour
> 4 teaspoons tartrate-type baking powder or 2 teaspoons "double-action" type
> 2 teaspoons sugar
> ½ teaspoon salt

Using fingertips, a pastry mixer or fork, work in
> ¼ cup butter

Into another bowl, break
> 2 eggs

Reserve a small amount of the egg white for the topping. Beat the rest and add to the flour mixture with
> ½ cup cream or milk

Add a little more cream or milk if needed to make the dough just firm enough to handle but still soft.

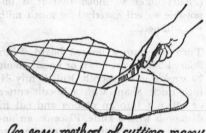

An easy method of cutting many biscuits and cookies

Turn out onto a floured board. Knead ½ minute. Pat and roll into an oblong ¾ inch thick. Cut in diamonds by making diagonal cuts with a long sharp knife. Brush with the reserved egg white diluted with

1 teaspoon water

Sprinkle with

Sugar

Bake 15 minutes at 450°. *Makes 12 or more.*

Muffins

The famous basic Twin Mountain recipe. For the tenderest muffins, use pastry flour and avoid overbeating.

Sift into a mixing bowl

2 cups pastry flour or 1⅞ cups all-purpose flour
3 teaspoons baking powder
½ teaspoon salt
2 tablespoons sugar (or up to ½ cup)

Mix in another bowl

1 or 2 eggs, slightly beaten
1 cup milk
¼ cup melted butter

Pour over the flour mixture. Stir only enough to dampen the flour. (The batter should not be smooth.) Spoon into buttered muffin tins, having the tins about two-thirds full.

Bake at 400° about 15 minutes. *Makes 12.*

Bacon Muffins. Use bacon fat as the shortening. Add 3 tablespoons cooked crumbled bacon.

Berry Muffins. Reserve ¼ cup of the flour. Sprinkle it over 1 cup blueberries or huckleberries. Stir into the batter last. Use ½ cup sugar.

Date or Raisin Muffins. Add ½ cup sliced pitted dates or ¼ cup raisins.

Orange Muffins. Add ¾ cup candied orange peel, cut in small pieces.

Peach Muffins. Add to the milk ¾ cup fresh peaches, peeled and cut small, or drained and chopped canned peaches.

Pecan Muffins. Use ¼ cup sugar. Add ½ cup chopped pecans. After filling the pans, sprinkle with sugar, cinnamon and more nuts.

Quick Sally Lunn. *See also the variations suggested for Sally Lunn made with yeast (p. 335).* Spread in a buttered 8 or 9 inch square tin. Sprinkle with cinnamon sugar. Bake at 375° about 25 minutes. Cut in squares.

Whole Wheat Muffins. Substitute ¾ cup coarse whole wheat flour for 1 cup of the flour. Do not sift it. Add it after sifting the other dry ingredients.

Berkshire Muffins

Scald

⅔ cup milk

Pour slowly on

½ cup corn meal

Let stand 5 minutes. Add

½ cup cooked rice

Stir. Sift together

½ cup all-purpose flour
2 tablespoons sugar
3 teaspoons baking powder
½ teaspoon salt

Add to the first mixture with

1 egg yolk, well beaten
1 tablespoon melted butter

Stir and fold in

1 egg white, beaten stiff

Spoon into buttered muffin pans.

Bake at 400° about 25 minutes. *Makes 12.*

Bran Muffins

Sift into a mixing bowl
  1 cup all-purpose flour
  3 teaspoons baking powder
  ¼ cup sugar
  ½ teaspoon salt
Mix in another bowl
  1 egg, slightly beaten
  1 cup milk
  2 tablespoons melted butter
  1 cup bran
Let stand 10 minutes. Add the flour mixture. Stir just long enough to dampen the flour. Spoon into buttered muffin tins.

Bake at 400° about 25 minutes. *Makes 12.*

Popovers

A perfect popover is crisp on the outside, tender and moist inside. The secret of success is simple — do not overbeat the batter, and be sure the popovers are thoroughly baked when you take them from the oven. Test one to be sure.

Set the oven at 450°. Butter muffin pans or glass or pottery custard cups.

Put in a bowl
  2 eggs
Beat until light. Add
  1 cup milk
  1 tablespoon melted butter
  1 cup all-purpose flour
  ¼ teaspoon salt
Beat until evenly blended (30 seconds with an electric beater). The batter should be like heavy cream. Add more milk if necessary. Pour into the pans, having them ⅓ full.

Bake 20 minutes. Reduce the heat to 350° and bake about 20 minutes longer. *Makes 8 to 12.*

To make in a blender. Put all the ingredients in the blender jar. Mix at high speed 15 seconds.

Bacon Popovers. Add to the batter ¼ cup crumbled cooked, crisp bacon.

Corn Bread

The shortening may be butter, bacon fat, chicken fat or beef drippings.

Sift together
  ¾ cup corn meal
  1 cup flour
  ⅓ cup sugar
  3 teaspoons baking powder
  ¾ teaspoon salt
Mix in
  1 cup milk
  1 egg, well beaten
  2 tablespoons melted shortening
Spoon into a shallow buttered pan 8 inches square. Bake 20 minutes at 425°.

Rich Corncake. In place of baking powder, use 1 teaspoon soda and 2 teaspoons cream of tartar. In place of milk, use 1 cup heavy sour cream or yogurt and ¼ cup milk.

Molasses Corncake. Omit sugar. Use ¾ cup milk and ¼ cup molasses. If desired, add ½ to 1 cup ripe peaches peeled and cut small, or drained and chopped canned peaches.

Forest Hall Corn Sticks. Omit sugar. Add ½ cup hot boiled hominy to the mixture. Increase shortening to ¼ cup. Turn into buttered bread stick pans. Bake 20 minutes at 350°.

Johnnycake

Mix
  1 teaspoon salt
  ½ cup white corn meal
Gradually stir in
  1 cup scalded milk or boiling water
Spread ¼ inch deep in a buttered shallow pan. If desired, dot with
  Butter, in small bits
Bake at 350° until crisp.

White Corncake

Cream together
  ¼ cup butter
  ½ cup sugar

Add
 ⅓ cup milk
Sift together
 1¼ cups white corn meal
 1¼ cups flour
 4 teaspoons baking powder
 1 teaspoon salt
Add one-fourth of the dry ingredients to the first mixture. Add the rest alternately with
 1 cup milk
When all is added, beat thoroughly. Fold in
 3 egg whites, beaten stiff
Spoon into a buttered pan 9 by 9 inches. Bake 30 minutes at 425°.

Littleton Spider Corncake

Sift together into a bowl
 1⅓ cups corn meal
 ⅓ cup flour
 1 teaspoon baking soda
Stir in
 1 cup sour milk
 2 eggs, well beaten
 1 cup sweet milk
 ¼ cup sugar
 ½ teaspoon salt
In a heavy shallow baking dish or iron frying pan, melt
 1½ tablespoons butter
Pour in the mixture. Over the top, pour
 1 cup sweet milk
Bake 50 minutes at 350°. Cut in wedges. *Serves 6.*

Quick Coffee Cake

Lightning Cake (p. 470) also makes a delicious coffee cake. Use it for any of the variations below.

Butter a pan about 6 by 10 or 9 by 9 inches. Set the oven at 375°.

Cream
 ¼ cup butter
Beat in
 1 cup sugar
 1 egg, well beaten
Sift together
 1½ cups all-purpose flour
 2 teaspoons baking powder
 ¼ teaspoon salt
Add to the first mixture alternately with
 ½ cup milk
Unless you are putting on a more elaborate topping, sprinkle with
 2 tablespoons melted butter
and then with
 1½ teaspoons cinnamon mixed with
 3 teaspoons sugar
Bake about 20 minutes. Cut in squares or oblongs.

For a crunchy topping, sprinkle with ½ cup soft bread crumbs mixed with 2 tablespoons sugar, ¾ teaspoon cinnamon and 2 tablespoons chopped nuts.

Streusel Coffee Cake. Mix ½ cup brown sugar, 2 tablespoons flour, 2 teaspoons cinnamon, ½ cup melted butter and ½ cup chopped walnut meats. Sprinkle over the batter.

Fruit Kuchen

Make the batter for Quick Coffee Cake (above) or Lightning Cake (p. 470). Put into a shallow buttered pan about 6 by 10 inches. Arrange prepared fruit over the batter. Sprinkle with sugar and cinnamon. Bake at 375°. Cut in squares and serve plain or, as a dessert, with whipped cream.

Apple Kuchen. Slice tart apples very thin. For a glazed effect, simmer the apple slices gently for 5 minutes in ½ cup water and ½ cup sugar cooked together; then arrange on the batter. Sprinkle a few walnut meats over the apples, or cover the apples with thin slices of cheese, or pour over the apples 1 egg beaten with ½ cup cream or milk.

Plum or Prune Kuchen. Drain cooked or canned fruit, reserving the juice. Arrange close together in even rows on the batter. Sprinkle first with ½ cup juice, then with ¼ cup sugar mixed with 1 teaspoon cinnamon.

Quick Loaf Breads

A recipe using about 2 cups of flour will fill a loaf pan 9 by 5 inches or, for party sandwich bread, two small pans. Butter the pans lightly, dust with flour, and fill. Let stand 20 minutes before baking to start the action of the baking powder or soda.

Make the bread the day before it is to be used, to make neat slices. Very fresh bread crumbles easily.

Quick Whole Wheat Bread

Sift into a bowl
  ½ cup all-purpose flour
  1 teaspoon baking powder
  1 teaspoon baking soda
  1 teaspoon salt
Add
  2 cups whole wheat flour
  ¼ cup melted shortening
  1½ cups sour milk
  ½ cup molasses
Stir well. Spoon into a buttered loaf pan 9 by 5 inches. Let stand 20 minutes.

Bake about 50 minutes at 375°.

Whole Wheat Nut Bread. Add ½ cup nut meats, broken in pieces.

Nut Bread

Vary this good bread by substituting chopped dates or candied orange peel for the nuts.

Sift into a bowl
  2 cups all-purpose flour
  ½ cup brown or white sugar
  2 teaspoons baking powder
  1 teaspoon salt
Add
  1 egg
  1 cup milk
  2 tablespoons melted butter
  ½ cup walnut or pecan meats, broken in pieces
Beat thoroughly. Spoon into a buttered loaf pan 9 by 5 inches or two small pans.

Bake at 350° about 45 minutes.

Whole Wheat Nut Bread. Instead of all-purpose flour, use 1 cup whole wheat flour and 1 cup pastry flour.

Orange Nut Bread. In place of sugar use ½ cup orange marmalade. Reduce the milk to ½ cup.

Winchester Nut Bread

Put in a bowl
  ½ cup brown sugar
  ¾ cup cold water
Stir until the sugar dissolves. Add
  ½ cup molasses
  ¾ cup milk
Sift together
  1 cup all-purpose flour
  1 teaspoon salt
  2½ teaspoons baking powder
  ¾ teaspoon baking soda
Add to the dry ingredients
  2 cups whole wheat flour
Combine the mixtures. Stir in
  ¾ cup walnut meats, in large pieces
Spoon into two buttered pans 9 by 5 inches. Bake 2 hours at 275°.

Apricot Almond Bread

For tea sandwiches, bake in two small pans. If you make half the recipe, use 1 egg yolk in place of a whole egg.

Chop fine or put through food chopper
  1½ cups dried apricots
Add
  1½ cups boiling water
  2 tablespoons butter
  1 cup sugar
  1 teaspoon salt
Sift together
  1½ cups pastry flour
  1 teaspoon baking soda

Add to the apricot mixture. Add
  1 cup whole wheat flour
  1 cup almonds, chopped
  1 egg, well beaten
  1 teaspoon orange extract
Stir well and put in a buttered loaf tin 9 by 5 inches.

Bake 1¼ hours at 350°.

Banana Nut Bread

Some like to add 2 tablespoons melted butter to the batter.

Mix in a bowl
  3 ripe bananas, well mashed
  2 eggs, beaten until light
Sift together
  2 cups flour
  ¾ cup sugar
  1 teaspoon salt
  1 teaspoon baking soda
Add to the first mixture. Add
  ½ cup nut meats, coarsely chopped
Stir well. Put in a buttered loaf pan 9 by 5 inches.

Bake 1 hour at 350°.

Cranberry Nut Bread

Grate the rind of
  1 orange
Squeeze the juice and add enough boiling water to make
  ¾ cup liquid
Add the grated rind. Add
  2 tablespoons butter
Stir to melt the butter.

Put in another bowl
  1 egg
  1 cup sugar
Beat well and stir into the orange mixture. Add
  1 cup cranberries, chopped
  ½ cup walnuts, chopped
Sift together
  2 cups flour
  ½ teaspoon salt
  ½ teaspoon baking soda
Stir into the first mixture. Spoon into a buttered loaf pan 9 by 5 inches.

Bake 1 hour at 325°.

Date and Nut Bread

For a sweeter, richer bread, double the amount of sugar and nuts. For an interesting flavor, add 1 tablespoon rum. Black walnuts are especially delicious in this bread.

Mix in a bowl
  1 cup dates, cut fine
  ½ cup sugar
  ¼ cup butter
  ¾ cup boiling water
Stir until the butter melts. Cool.

Stir in
  1 egg, well beaten
  1 teaspoon baking soda
  1¾ cups flour
  ½ teaspoon salt
  ½ cup chopped nuts
Put in a buttered loaf pan 9 by 5 inches.

Bake about 50 minutes at 350°.

Orange Peel Bread

When you double the recipe, use a whole egg.

Put in a small saucepan
  ½ cup prepared orange peel (below)
  Water to cover
Cook until the orange peel is tender. Add
  ½ cup sugar
Boil until the syrup is as thick as honey and the orange peel glossy and transparent.

Put in a mixing bowl
  1 tablespoon soft butter
  ¼ cup sugar
  1 egg yolk
  1 cup milk
Sift together and add
  2 cups all-purpose flour
  2 teaspoons baking powder
  Few grains salt
Beat well and add the orange peel and syrup. Spoon into a buttered loaf pan 9 by 5 inches.

Bake about 45 minutes at 325°.

To prepare orange peel. Discard all the white part and cut the yellow part in small bits.

Peanut Butter Bread

Sift into a mixing bowl
   2 cups all-purpose flour
   ⅓ cup sugar
   2 teaspoons baking powder
   1 teaspoon salt
Add
   ¾ cup peanut butter
Blend with a fork. Stir in
   1 cup milk
   1 egg, well beaten
Spoon into a buttered loaf pan 9 by 5 inches.

Bake at 350° about 50 minutes.

Pecan Bread

Mix in a bowl
   2 cups unsifted coarse whole wheat
      flour
   1 cup pastry or cake flour
   ¾ cup brown sugar
   1 teaspoon salt
   3 teaspoons baking powder
   1 teaspoon baking soda
Add
   2 cups buttermilk
   1 cup pecan meats, cut fine
Stir well. Spoon into a buttered loaf pan 9 by 5 inches.

Bake about 1 hour at 325°.

Prune Bread

Mix
   1 cup sugar
   2 tablespoons melted butter
   1 egg, well beaten
   1 cup cooked prunes, cut small
   ½ cup prune juice
   1 cup sour milk or buttermilk
Sift together
   1 cup fine whole wheat flour or rye
      flour
   2 cups all-purpose flour
   1 teaspoon baking soda
   ¼ teaspoon baking powder
   ½ teaspoon salt
Add to the first mixture and mix thor-

oughly. Put in two buttered loaf pans 9 by 5 inches.

Bake about 1 hour at 350°.

Honey Bread
(Spice Bread; Pain d'Épice)

Long beating makes the fine texture which distinguishes this bread, the famous French pain d'épice. Add 1 tablespoon rum to the mixture, if you like. Cut in thin slices, spread with unsalted butter, and serve with tea or coffee.

Sift into a mixing bowl
   2 cups all-purpose flour or half rye
      flour
   1 teaspoon baking powder
   1 teaspoon baking soda
   1 teaspoon salt
   ½ teaspoon cinnamon
   1 teaspoon ginger
Add
   ½ cup strained honey
   1 egg, slightly beaten
   1 cup milk
Beat thoroughly, 15 minutes at the very least. If you have an electric beater, beat ½ hour. Spoon into a buttered loaf pan 9 by 5 inches, or into bread stick pans.

Bake at 350°, about 50 minutes for a loaf, 25 for bread sticks.

Boston Brown Bread

The proper New England recipe.

Mix
   ½ cup rye meal or all-purpose flour
   ½ cup corn meal
   ½ cup coarse whole wheat flour
   1 teaspoon baking soda
   ½ teaspoon salt
Stir in
   ⅜ cup molasses
   1 cup sour milk or ⅞ cup sweet milk
      or water
Mix well. Grease a 1 or 1½ quart mold or two smaller ones. Fill not more than two-thirds full. Put on the cover.

Place on a rack in a deep kettle. Add boiling water to come halfway up around the mold. Cover. Set over the heat and steam 3½ hours in a large mold, 1½ to 2 in smaller ones. Keep the water boiling, and add more as needed to keep the water at the proper level.

Take the mold from the water, remove the cover, and set in a 300° oven for 15 minutes to dry out somewhat. Remove the bread from the mold.

To cut with string. Old-fashioned cooks make neat slices by drawing a string around the hot loaf, crossing the ends, and pulling them to cut off slices.

To cook in a pressure cooker. Set the mold on a rack in the cooker. Have the water 2 inches deep. Steam 15 minutes with the petcock open. Close and steam 1 hour longer for a large mold, 40 minutes for small ones.

Raisin Brown Bread. Add to the batter ½ cup seedless raisins.

Yeast Breads

Making bread at home is a joy to the creative cook who knows that it is far superior to most bakery products. Fragrant, crusty rolls and bread are not hard to make and, once you have tried, will lead to many interesting variations.

Since bread-making is a somewhat lengthy process, it pays to make the full amount in the recipes, even if your family is small. You can divide the dough and make it up in several different ways — part for a loaf of bread, part for tiny rolls or sweet buns, and part for a coffee cake. Bake them all at once and store them in the freezer.

Reheat the stored breads before you serve them so that they will taste fresh-baked.

Ingredients

Yeast is a living plant which grows when it has warmth and moisture. Granular yeast and yeast cakes are equally satisfactory. Store granular yeast on the pantry shelf, yeast cakes in the refrigerator. Note the date on the package so that you will use the yeast while it is at its best.

To soften yeast so that it will blend evenly with the dough, sprinkle or crumble it over lukewarm (110°) water or milk and allow to stand a few minutes while the other ingredients are measured. If the liquid is too cold, the yeast will not grow. If it is too hot, the yeast will be killed.

The standard amount of yeast to use is 1 package to each 2 cups of liquid in the recipe. This makes bread which is finished in 5 hours with two risings, or about 3½ hours with one rising. To complete bread in 3 hours (or in 2½ hours with one rising), use 2 packages of yeast. To raise bread overnight, use only ¼ package of yeast. Using the larger amount of yeast does not give bread a "yeasty" taste — overrising does.

Flours rich in gluten make the best bread because gluten makes the dough strong and elastic and able to expand with the growth of the yeast and the bubbles it makes. Bread flour is richest in gluten, but all-purpose flour is widely used and is quite satisfactory. Other flours, such as rye or buckwheat, should be combined with wheat flour to make good bread. One secret of making deliciously tender rolls and bread is to use as little flour as you can and still be able to handle the dough.

Milk or potato water makes bread which browns better, keeps fresh longer and is more nutritious than bread made with plain water. It is unnecessary to scald pasteurized milk.

Shortening makes bread more tender and adds to its flavor and keeping quality. Use butter, lard or any bland cooking oil or fat. If the dough is especially rich

To knead bread push

and pull

Test the risen dough by poking it

and if it is ready punch it down

Divide into two parts and shape for pans

or for French loaves

(with eggs or extra shortening), the action of the yeast is slower.

Sugar makes the dough rise more quickly and helps brown the crust, but too much sugar slows the yeast action.

Salt is added for flavor. It slows the action of the yeast somewhat, so if you are making salt-free bread, remember that it will rise more rapidly.

Mixing Dough

Thorough mixing at the start is important so that the yeast will be evenly distributed and the strength of the gluten in the flour developed. Beating the flour into the liquid with an electric mixer or a strong rotary egg beater is very successful.

Add the flour a little at a time until the dough is too stiff to beat. Then remove the beater and scrape the dough from the blades. If you are making a soft dough, add the rest of the flour and beat with a wooden spoon until thoroughly blended. If you are making a firm bread dough, work in the rest of the flour with your hands.

Kneading Dough

It is essential to knead bread thoroughly and correctly, so that the yeast will be evenly distributed and the bread will have the perfect texture which marks the superior loaf. Watching an experienced person is the quickest way to learn to knead. But you can teach yourself by following directions carefully.

Put ½ cup flour on the mixing board or cloth and use some of it to dust the board very lightly, pushing the rest aside to work into the dough if needed. Turn the ball of dough out onto the board, leaving a clean bowl. Cover with the inverted bowl and let "rest" 10 minutes, which makes the dough easier to work with.

Rub your hands lightly with melted shortening. Fold the ball of dough

double, then push it lightly and quickly away from you, using the "heel" of your hands. Pull it towards you again with your fingertips. Repeat these two motions, turning the dough as you work, until the surface is smooth and elastic (5 to 8 minutes). When the dough is light enough, you can hold the palm of your hand on it for 30 seconds without having it stick to your hand.

Raising Dough

The time is based on dough made with 1 package of yeast to 2 cups of liquid.

Use a mixing bowl which will hold three times the bulk of the dough. Grease the mixing bowl lightly, put in the ball of kneaded dough, and turn it so that the top is greased. Cover with a clean, slightly damp cloth. Set in a warm place (80°–85°), and let rise until doubled in bulk (about 1½ hours).

If your oven has a pilot light, it will be warm enough. Otherwise, set the mixing bowl in a cold oven with a pan of warm water on the shelf beneath it. Add warm (not hot) water from time to time to keep the temperature up to 80°. If the room is about 80°, keep the water at about 75°. The purpose is to keep the dough itself at 75° to 85°, the temperature at which yeast grows best. A higher temperature kills the yeast and a low temperature retards growth. You may insert a dairy or bath thermometer into the dough in order to watch the temperature precisely.

For perfect bread it is important to let the dough rise exactly the right amount. If you let it rise too long, the bread will be full of large holes; if not long enough, the bread will be heavy and soggy. To test it, press your finger into the dough. If the dent remains, the dough is just right, ready to punch down and shape.

If the dough rises before it is convenient for you to shape it, punch it down and let it rise again or store it in the refrigerator. Chilling the dough does no harm.

To punch down. When the dough has risen long enough, punch it down with your fist to let some of the gas escape and let fresh oxygen reach the yeast. Fold the edges towards the center. Put the dough on a floured mixing board and slap it hard to force out all the gas.

To make bread of very fine grain, put the dough back into the greased bowl, turn it so that the top is greased, and let it rise again (about 1 hour with 1 package of yeast, 30 to 45 minutes with 2).

Shaping Dough into Loaves

Divide the dough into two equal parts. Knead each part to make a smooth ball. Cover with a cloth and let "rest" 10 or 15 minutes.

Fold and pull to shape into loaves. Put into two greased bread pans with the "seam" underneath. Cover and let rise until double in bulk (about 1 hour). Do not have the pans in a place warmer than 80° or there will be a heavy streak near the bottom of the loaf.

Baking Bread

Heat the oven to 400°. Bake the bread 40 to 60 minutes. Bake at 350° if you are using glass bread pans, since they hold heat longer than metal ones. The loaves should begin to brown after the first 15 minutes.

To test. Tap the bottom of the bread pan lightly. When the bread is done, the bottom will sound hollow when you tap it. A thoroughly baked loaf shrinks from the side of the pan and slips out easily.

For a softer crust, brush the bread with melted butter 3 minutes before taking it from the oven.

Care of Bread After Baking

Remove the loaves at once from the pans and place, side down, on a wire cooling rack. Otherwise the crust will be tough and the bread soggy. For a crisp crust, do not cover the bread. For a soft crust, cover with a dish towel during cooling. When cool, store in a clean, well-aired breadbox not too near heat.

To avoid mold in hot weather, wrap the bread tightly in wax paper and store in the refrigerator.

Chill bread if you plan to cut it in thin slices.

White Bread

As an introduction to bread-making, read pages 320ff., which describe the necessary ingredients and explain each step in making bread.

Rinse a large mixing bowl with hot water (a cold bowl delays the action of the yeast). Put in it
  ½ cup lukewarm (110°) water
  1 package yeast
Let stand 5 minutes, then stir to dissolve the yeast. Put in another bowl
  1 cup milk
  1 cup boiling water
  2 tablespoons butter or other
    shortening
  2 tablespoons sugar
  1 tablespoon salt
Stir until lukewarm; then combine with the yeast mixture. Add
  3 cups bread or all-purpose flour
Mix thoroughly with a spoon or knife. Add another
  3 cups flour
Stir vigorously. Add a little more flour if needed to make the dough firm enough to keep it from sticking to the bowl.

Knead, let rise, shape and bake (p. 322–323).

To vary. Add fruit or nuts or shape part of the dough into rolls, braids or twists.

Bran Bread. Use 1 cup bran and 5 cups flour. Omit the sugar and use ¼ cup molasses instead.

Cheese Bread. To half the recipe, add ¾ cup grated Cheddar cheese, mixing it with the last flour added. Use a whole yeast cake, if you like, to hasten the rising.

Date or Raisin Bread. Double the amount of shortening and sugar. After adding the first 3 cups of flour, add 1½ cups raisins or dates (pitted and cut in small pieces).

Cornell Bread. *A high-protein bread.* With the first 2 cups of flour add 6 tablespoons soy flour, 6 tablespoons powdered skim milk and 2 tablespoons toasted wheat germ. (These ingredients replace 1 cup of flour.)

Rye Bread. Use brown sugar in place of white and 3 cups sifted rye flour in place of part of the white flour. Rye bread takes longer to rise than white bread and need not quite double in bulk.

German Rye Bread. Use 2 cups sour milk in place of milk and water. Add 2 tablespoons caraway seeds after the first rising. Bake 2 hours at 300° to make the characteristic firm texture.

Whole Wheat Bread

Whole wheat flour makes bread somewhat heavy. If you prefer a lighter bread, use 4 cups all-purpose flour and 2 cups whole wheat flour. See also the recipe for Cornell Bread (above).

Put in a mixing bowl
    ½ cup lukewarm water
    1 package yeast
Let stand 5 minutes. Stir. Put in a separate bowl
    1 cup milk
    ½ cup boiling water
    ¼ cup sugar or molasses
    2 teaspoons salt
Mix well, cool to lukewarm and add to the yeast mixture. Stir in
    3 cups all-purpose flour
Beat thoroughly. Add

    3 cups whole wheat flour
Stir with a heavy spoon or add a little more flour and knead. When smooth, let rise until double in bulk (about 1 hour).

Shape into two loaves. Place in greased tins and let rise again to almost double in size (about 50 minutes).

Bake about 50 minutes at 375°. *Makes 2 loaves or 1 loaf and 1 to 2 dozen rolls.*

Colonial Bread. *If you like, make part of the dough into this attractive teabread.* Knead into half the dough (after the first rising) ½ cup finely cut candied orange peel and ½ cup pecan meats broken in pieces. Shape into 2 or 3 small loaves. Let rise and bake (30 to 40 minutes).

Oatmeal Bread

Put in a large mixing bowl
    2 cups boiling water
    1 cup rolled oats, regular or quick
Stir thoroughly. Let stand 1 hour. Add
    ½ cup molasses
    2 teaspoons salt
    1 tablespoon butter
Put in a small bowl
    ½ cup lukewarm water
    1 package yeast
When dissolved, add to the oatmeal. Stir in
    4½ cups flour
Beat thoroughly and let rise until double in bulk. Add enough more flour to make the dough just firm enough to knead. Shape into loaves and put into buttered pans. Let rise until almost double in bulk.

Bake about 50 minutes at 350°. *Makes 2 loaves.*

Prune Oatmeal Bread. After the first rising, add ½ cup chopped nuts and 1 cup prunes cut in pieces.

Anadama Bread. Use ½ cup corn meal in place of the cup of oatmeal.

French Bread

These long thin loaves with chewy crisp crusts are perfect for French or Italian style meals. If you like, shape part of the dough into small rolls. This dough is also good for English muffins or pizza (p. 336).

Put in a large mixing bowl
    1 cup lukewarm water
    1 package yeast
Let stand 5 minutes. Add
    1 tablespoon sugar
    1½ teaspoons salt
    2 tablespoons melted lard or other
        shortening
Stir well. Add
    1 cup all-purpose or bread flour
Beat thoroughly with a rotary beater or an electric mixer. Add
    2 cups flour (or enough to make a stiff
        dough)
Sprinkle a board with flour. Put the dough on it and let "rest" 10 minutes. Knead well, let rise, punch down, and let rise again (pp. 322–323).

Turn the dough out on a floured surface and divide into two or three parts. Let "rest" 10 minutes. Flatten each part with a rolling pin to about ¼ inch in thickness. Roll up each sheet of dough tightly to make a long slender loaf. Press firmly along the rolled edges to seal.

Sprinkle cooky sheets with
    Corn meal
Put the loaves on the sheets, leaving enough space between them so that they will be crusty on all sides. Cut diagonal gashes in the loaves about ½ inch deep.

Beat together
    1 egg white
    1 tablespoon water
    1 teaspoon salt
Brush over the top of the loaves. If you like, sprinkle with
    Sesame or poppyseed
Let rise uncovered until double in bulk (about 1 hour).

Put a large pan of boiling water in the bottom of the oven with the pans of bread on a rack above. Bake at 425° for 10 minutes. Brush again with the egg white mixture. Reduce the heat to 375° and bake until the bread sounds hollow when you tap it (about 25 minutes). Cool on a rack. *Makes 2 or 3 loaves.*

Ways to Serve French or Italian Bread

Serve in a bread basket or on a plate covered with a napkin, or serve on a breadboard. Prepare crusty hard rolls in any of the ways suggested below.

Cut the loaf diagonally into thick or thin slices. Wrap in foil. Heat in a 400° oven. Serve very hot.

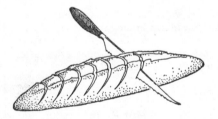

Buttered. Slice as above but without cutting all the way through. Spread creamed butter (preferably unsalted) between the slices. Wrap and heat as above.

Cheesed. Spread with soft cheese instead of butter or with butter creamed with grated Cheddar cheese.

Garlic Bread. Peel and slice a clove of garlic and put it in a bowl with ¼ cup butter. Cover and let stand ½ hour before spreading.

Herb Bread. Spread with Herb Butter (p. 19).

Saffron Bread. Spread with butter creamed with saffron to taste. Especially good with bouillabaisse.

Yeast Rolls and Coffee Cakes

Yeast rolls, especially the type made without kneading, are simpler to make well than baking powder biscuits. If you are a beginner, start with Feather Rolls, Raised Whole Wheat Muffins and Brioche. As your experience increases, make Dinner Rolls, Potato Biscuits, Sweet Rolls and Coffee Cakes, for these delicious breads rise quickly.

Reheat rolls in a bun warmer or in the top part of a double boiler over hot water. Or put in a paper bag, sprinkle very lightly with water, close the bag tightly, and set in a 400° oven for 5 minutes.

If the rolls have been stored in the freezer, reheat in the oven.

Frost sweet buns and coffee cakes after they have been reheated.

Hot Rolls

The basic recipe from which you can make many different types of rolls and buns according to the way they are shaped and seasoned. Instead of making all the dough into rolls, you may prefer to make part of it into a small loaf of bread.

Put in a mixing bowl
  1 cup lukewarm milk
  1 package yeast
Let stand 5 minutes. Stir. Add
  2 tablespoons soft butter
  1 tablespoon sugar
  1 teaspoon salt
Mix in gradually
  2½ cups all-purpose or bread flour
Beat thoroughly 5 minutes, or 2 minutes with an electric beater on slow speed. Add enough more flour to make the dough just barely firm enough to handle.

Knead (p. 322). Shape immediately in any of the ways suggested below, or let rise about 1 hour before punching down and shaping (below). With two risings, the rolls will be of finer grain, especially if you are using bread flour.

Arrange in buttered pans. To make rolls with plenty of crust, place them on the baking sheet with space between. Brush with
  Melted butter
Cover with a clean dish towel. Let rise until double in bulk (about 1 hour).

Bake at 425° until well browned (12 to 20 minutes). *Makes about 18.*

To make richer rolls, use ¼ cup sugar and ⅓ cup butter. Shape (below).

Buttermilk Rolls. Use buttermilk in place of milk, sifting ½ teaspoon baking soda with the flour. These rolls have a delicious flavor and fine grain.

Shaping Rolls and Biscuits

Place the dough on a lightly floured pastry cloth or board. Flour the rolling pin lightly.

Biscuits. Roll about ⅓ inch thick. Cut with a small round cutter. If you prefer, shape the dough into a long thin rope and cut off small pieces. Fold the ends under to make smooth balls.

Making Rolls and Biscuits

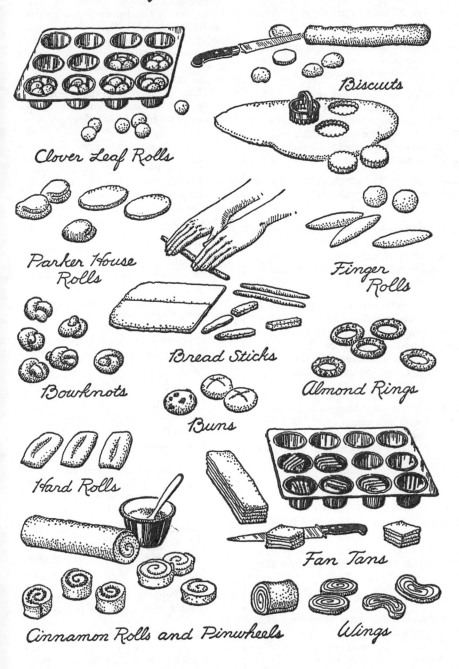

Clover Leaf Rolls

Biscuits

Parker House Rolls

Finger Rolls

Bread Sticks

Bowknots

Buns

Almond Rings

Hard Rolls

Fan Tans

Cinnamon Rolls and Pinwheels

Wings

Clover Leaf Rolls. Shape bits of dough into 1-inch balls. Put three in each muffin tin.

Finger Rolls. Shape balls of dough, then roll under one hand on an unfloured board to the desired length.

Parker House Rolls. Cut with a special oval or round cutter. Let cut-out rolls "relax" on the board for 10 minutes. Crease through the center with a floured knife handle. Brush with melted butter and fold double.

Bowknots or Twists. Shape like Bread Sticks (below) and twist or tie loosely in knots.

Almond Wreaths. Shape like Bread Sticks (below) in 6-inch lengths. Curve into rings. Brush with melted butter, then dip the upper surface in almonds, blanched, chopped, and seasoned with salt.

Butter Rolls or Fantans. Roll the dough into a rectangle about 12 by 16 inches. Spread with softened butter. Cut into 4 strips, lengthwise. Stack evenly in a pile. Cut in 1-inch pieces and fit into buttered muffin tins (see illustration, p. 327).

Wings. Divide the dough in four parts. Roll each into an oblong 6 inches wide. Spread with soft butter. Roll up tightly like a jelly roll. Cut each roll in three pieces. Make a deep crease in the center of each with a floured knife handle. Each roll looks like a butterfly.

Pinwheel Biscuits

Prepare Hot Roll dough (p. 326). Roll ¼ inch thick. Spread with softened butter. Roll up like a jelly roll. Cut in ¾-inch pieces. Place in a buttered pan, cut side down.

Bake at 375° about 25 minutes.

Cinnamon Rolls. After spreading with butter, sprinkle with ¼ cup sugar mixed with 1 teaspoon cinnamon. Sprinkle with seeded raisins, chopped citron or nuts, if you like.

Butterscotch Biscuits. Cream ½ cup butter with ¾ cup brown sugar. Spread part on the dough before rolling it up. Spread the rest in a 9-inch round pan. Brush the sides of the rolls with melted butter. Place close together in the pan, cut side down. Let rise until double in bulk. Bake. Remove from the pan immediately after baking, before the syrup hardens. Serve butterscotch side up.

Hard Rolls

Prepare Hot Roll dough (p. 326), adding 1 egg white with first 1½ cups flour. Sprinkle a buttered pan with corn meal and arrange the shaped rolls on it 2 inches apart. Let rise.

Bake at 400° with a pan of boiling water on the shelf beneath the rolls, so that the oven is steamy throughout the baking time.

Sesame or Poppyseed Rolls. Brush unbaked rolls with egg white blended with 2 tablespoons water, and sprinkle with sesame or poppyseed.

Bread Sticks

Make Hot Roll dough (p. 326), adding 2 tablespoons butter and 1 egg white. When ready to shape, roll the dough into a rectangle about 8 by 12 inches. Cut in half lengthwise, then into 16 strips. Roll under the palms of your hands on an unfloured board to make smooth even sticks 8 to 10 inches long. Arrange 1 inch apart on a buttered cooky sheet. Let rise.

Bake 5 minutes at 425°, then reduce the heat to 350° and bake 15 minutes. The slower baking makes the sticks crisp and dry.

Sesame or Poppyseed Sticks. Before baking, sprinkle with sesame or poppyseed.

Salt Sticks. Add 1 tablespoon salt to Hot Roll dough (p. 326). Shape and bake like Bread Sticks, but before baking, brush with an egg yolk, slightly beaten and diluted with ½ tablespoon cold water. Sprinkle with coarse salt or salt crystals. Bake about 20 minutes at 300° until crisp and dry.

Cheese Sticks

Roll Hot Roll dough (p. 326) into a rectangle ¼ inch thick. Spread with butter, sprinkle with flour, and fold from the ends to make 3 layers. Repeat three times, ending with the rolled-out rectangle. Cut in finger-shaped pieces. Arrange on a buttered cooky sheet, cover, and let stand 15 minutes.

Bake at 425° for 10 minutes. Remove from the oven, brush the tops with egg white and dip in grated Parmesan cheese seasoned with salt and cayenne. Return to the oven and bake 4 minutes.

English Muffins

For breakfast or tea, or to use as the base for quick pizzas (p. 344). Toasted English Muffins (p. 344).

Prepare Hot Roll dough (p. 326) or reserve part of the dough for muffins when you make White Bread (p. 323) or French Bread (p. 325).

After the dough has risen, place it on a board sprinkled with corn meal. Flatten with a rolling pin until the dough is ½ inch thick. Cut out 3-inch circles. Chill until ready to cook.

Cook the muffins 15 minutes on a hot griddle, turning several times during the cooking. *Dough made with 2½ to 3 cups of flour will make 12 muffins.*

Crescent Rolls

Divide Hot Roll dough (p. 326) in two parts. Roll each into a 12-inch circle. Spread lightly with soft butter. Cut like a pie into 12 parts. Roll each, beginning with the outer edge. Pull the points and tuck them under so that the crescents will not unroll during baking. Let rise and bake (p. 326).

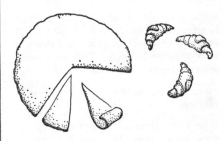

Cinnamon Crescents. Before baking, sprinkle with 2 tablespoons sugar mixed with ½ teaspoon cinnamon.

French Croissants

True croissants are as rich as pastry. Serve them for breakfast in Continental fashion or with coffee as an afternoon or evening treat.

Put in a mixing bowl
    1 cup lukewarm milk
    1 package yeast
Let stand 5 minutes. Stir. Add
    1 tablespoon sugar
    1 teaspoon salt
    1 tablespoon soft lard or butter
    1 cup all-purpose flour
Beat thoroughly. Mix in
    1 cup flour
Pat the dough into a ball. Cover the mixing board with
    ½ cup flour
Turn out the dough, rolling it lightly in the flour. Cover with a bowl and let "rest" for 5 minutes. Knead the dough (p. 322). Place in a greased bowl, cover, and let rise until doubled in bulk (about 1 hour). Punch down (p. 323), cover, and chill 1 hour or longer.

Cream or wash (p. 8)
    1 cup butter
Put the ball of dough on a slightly floured cloth or board and roll into a rectangle ¼ inch thick. Spread with ¼ cup of the butter and fold from the ends toward the center, making three layers. Turn a quarter way round, pat, roll out as before, and again spread with ¼ cup butter. Repeat twice. Chill at least 2 hours.

Divide the dough in half. Shape like Crescent Rolls (p. 329), or shape half in crescents and chill the other half to make into a coffee cake (p. 333) or Cheese Squares (below) for another meal.

Place on a buttered cooky sheet. Chill 20 minutes.

Bake 10 minutes at 400°, preheating the oven if necessary. Decrease the heat to 350° and bake 20 minutes longer. *Makes 24 croissants or 12 croissants and 1 coffee cake.*

Cheese Squares

Roll French Croissant dough as above, but use only half the amount of butter. Each time you spread the dough with butter, sprinkle it with any tasty cheese, grated or cut fine.

Roll the finished dough into an oblong ½ inch thick. Cut in squares, tiny for cocktails, larger ones to serve as luncheon bread. Place on a cooky sheet and chill 20 minutes.

Bake 10 minutes at 400°, then reduce the heat to 350° and bake 10 minutes longer.

Potato Biscuits

Put in a mixing bowl
    ½ cup lukewarm milk (not hot)
    1 package yeast
Let stand 5 minutes. Stir in
    ¼ cup melted shortening
    ¼ cup sugar
    ½ cup lukewarm mashed potatoes
    ¾ teaspoon salt
    ¼ cup flour
Beat thoroughly. Cover. Let rise until light. Add
    2 cups flour
Mix thoroughly. Cover and again let rise to about double in size. Turn onto a floured board, pat and roll ¼ inch thick. Shape in any of the ways suggested under Hot Rolls (p. 326). Let rise.

Bake at 425°, 12 to 20 minutes according to size of the biscuits. *Makes about 18 biscuits.*

Rich Potato Biscuits. After adding the yeast, add 1 egg (yolk and white beaten separately).

Refrigerator Rolls

You do not need a special recipe for Refrigerator Rolls, although the recipe for Potato Biscuits (above) is especially successful. Rich sweet doughs slow the action of the yeast, so if you wish to use the recipe for Hot Rolls (p. 326), increase the sugar and butter to ¼ cup each. Double the entire recipe, except the yeast, to have enough for 3 or 4 dozen rolls.

Put the mixed or kneaded dough in a well-buttered bowl, turn the dough so that the top is greased, and cover tightly with wax paper, foil or plastic, so that a crust will not form on top. Cover with a dampened towel.

Store in the refrigerator. If the dough rises, cut through it with a knife, press it down, turn it over, and cover it again. Set a plate on top to help hold it down. A sweet dough will keep for 3 or 4 days.

When you wish to use some of the dough, cut off a piece, knead, shape, let rise, and bake (p. 326). The dough may take longer to rise if it is very cold.

Twice-Baked Rolls

These are the popular "brown and serve" rolls to finish baking at mealtime. Store on the pantry shelf for as long as 1 week, in the refrigerator 2 weeks, or in the freezer up to 3 months.

Put in a mixing bowl
    3 cups lukewarm milk
    2 packages yeast
Let stand 5 minutes. Stir well. Add
    5 teaspoons salt

¼ cup sugar
6 cups flour
Beat as long as possible. Stir in
4 cups flour (about)
or enough to be able to knead the dough
thoroughly. Let rise until about double
in size. Punch down and shape like Hot
Rolls (p. 326). Let rise until slightly less
than double in bulk.

Bake 40 minutes at 275°. Leave in the
pans 20 minutes. Cool at room temperature and wrap in plastic freezer bags.
Makes 8 dozen rolls.

When ready to serve, place on an unbuttered cooky sheet. Bake at 400° until
brown (7 to 15 minutes according to the
size you make).

Raised Whole Wheat Muffins

*Enriched with added protein and so
just right with fruit salad as a complete
luncheon. As a variation, add ½ cup
chopped apple or chopped nuts or both.*

Put in a mixing bowl
½ cup warm water (not hot)
2 packages yeast
Let stand 5 minutes. Stir well. Add
1 cup warm milk (not hot)
3 tablespoons dark molasses
1 egg
3 tablespoons bacon fat, melted butter
or salad oil
Beat well. Sift together
2½ cups whole wheat flour
⅓ cup powdered milk
1 teaspoon salt
Beat into the yeast mixture, adding a
little more flour if necessary, to make a
stiff batter. Stir in
½ cup wheat germ
When ingredients are blended well,
spoon into 12 large greased muffin tins,
filling them half full. Let rise until
doubled (about 40 minutes).

Bake about 20 minutes at 350°. *Makes 12.*

Sour Cream Rolls

Put in a mixing bowl
¼ cup warm (not hot) water

1 package yeast
Let stand 5 minutes and stir. Add
¼ cup melted butter or oil
2 tablespoons sugar
1 teaspoon salt
1 egg
1 cup sour cream
Beat thoroughly. Beat in
3 cups sifted flour (about)
Add a little more flour if needed to make
the dough stiff enough to handle. Grease
the top lightly with
Melted butter or oil
Cover the dough and let rise until light
and nearly double in size (about 50
minutes).

Put on a floured board, pat to ½ inch
thick. Cut and shape in any of the ways
suggested on p. 326. Let rise.

Bake at 375° about 20 minutes. *Makes
about 36 small rolls.*

Feather Rolls

*These light and delicate rolls are very
easy and quick to make and require no
kneading or shaping.*

Put in a mixing bowl
1 cup warm milk (not hot)
1 package yeast
Let stand 5 minutes. Stir well. Add
¼ cup soft butter
2 tablespoons sugar
½ teaspoon salt
1 egg
Beat with a rotary egg beater or electric
beater until the ingredients are thoroughly blended. Add
2 cups all-purpose flour
Continue to beat as long as possible,
then finish mixing with a spoon. Cover
the bowl, set in a warm place and let rise
for about 45 minutes.

Stir down the batter and fill buttered
muffin pans a little more than half full.
Let rise in a warm place until the pans
are full (about 30 to 45 minutes).

Bake 15 to 20 minutes at 400°. *Makes
8 to 12 rolls.*

Grilled Muffins. Put buttered muffin rings on a hot greased griddle. Fill half full with the mixture and cook slowly until well risen and browned underneath. Turn the muffins and rings over and brown the muffins on the other side. Watch carefully and adjust the heat so the muffins do not brown too quickly.

Crumpets. Omit the sugar and egg and increase the butter to ½ cup. Cook like Grilled Muffins (above).

Brioche

A touch of Continental elegance for Sunday breakfast or a morning or afternoon coffee party. The distinctive texture of brioche is due to its rising twice, once in the refrigerator.

Put in a mixing bowl
  ½ cup lukewarm milk (not hot)
  1 package yeast
Let stand 5 minutes. Stir well. Add
  ⅓ cup butter or salad oil
  1 egg
  2 egg yolks
  ¼ cup sugar
  ¼ teaspoon salt
  ¼ teaspoon lemon extract or carda-
    mon seeds
  1¼ cups all-purpose flour
Beat thoroughly 10 minutes, or 3 minutes in an electric beater. Add
  1 cup flour
Mix thoroughly. Let the dough rise in the bowl for 3 hours. Stir down, chill in the refrigerator overnight or at least 3 hours. Butter heavy muffin pans and fill one-third full. Let rise until double in bulk.

Bake about 15 minutes at 375°. *Makes 20.*

Flûtes. Shape the dough like Bread Sticks (p. 328). Place on a buttered sheet, cover, and let rise until light. Brush over with an egg white, slightly beaten and diluted with 1½ teaspoons cold water. Sprinkle with fine sugar. Bake 10 minutes at 350°.

Apricot or Strawberry Buns. Put half the chilled dough on a pastry cloth dusted with flour. Pat it into a narrow rectangle ¼ inch thick. Spread with ¼ cup soft butter. Using the pastry cloth to help, roll into a long cylinder like a jelly roll. Cut off pieces ¾ inch wide. Place cut side down on a buttered pan and bake at 375° about 15 minutes. Spread with Lemon Frosting (p. 491) and top with a dab of apricot or strawberry jam. *Half the recipe makes 12 buns or 24 tiny ones.*

Coffee Twists. Shape like Apricot or Strawberry Buns. Instead of baking immediately, cover with a towel and let rise (about 1 hour). Twist each piece several times and shape into a coil. Place in buttered pans, cover, let rise, and bake. Spread with Lemon Frosting (p. 491).

Sweet Rolls

The basic sweet dough to use for sweet buns and coffee cakes. It is a small recipe. You may like to double it and put some of the dough in the refrigerator to use another time or bake all of it and put some rolls in the freezer.

Put in a mixing bowl
  1 cup lukewarm milk
  1 package yeast
Let stand 5 minutes. Stir. Add
  ¼ cup sugar
  1 teaspoon salt
  ¼ cup soft butter
  2 eggs
Beat thoroughly with a heavy egg beater or electric mixer. Beat in
  1½ cups all-purpose flour
Remove the beater. Let the dough rise about 40 minutes.

Mix in
  1 cup flour
Add enough more flour, if necessary, to make the dough just barely firm enough to handle. Cover and chill ½ hour in the refrigerator.

Knead (p. 322) and shape in any of the ways below, or into tea rings, coffee cake, or rolls. See also suggestions for using Hot Roll dough (p. 326). Arrange in buttered pans. Brush with

Melted butter

Cover with a clean dish towel. Let rise until double in bulk (about 1 hour).

Bake at 400° until delicately brown (12 to 20 minutes, according to size). Frost with confectioners' sugar moistened with water and flavored with vanilla.

Sweet French Rolls. When the rolls are nearly done, brush with an egg white slightly beaten and mixed with 1 tablespoon water and ½ teaspoon vanilla. Sprinkle with sugar.

Cinnamon Buns. Flavor the dough with ½ teaspoon cinnamon. Cut out with a 3-inch cutter.

Raisin Buns. Add to Cinnamon Bun dough ¼ cup seeded raisins, cut small.

Hot Cross Buns. Mark hot Raisin Buns when they come from the oven with a cross of Portsmouth Frosting (p. 491).

Orange Rolls. Use orange juice in place of milk and add 1 tablespoon grated orange peel. Shape like Parker House Rolls (p. 328). Put in each 1 navel orange section, drained and dipped in sugar. Fold and bake. Frost with Orange Confectioners' Frosting (p. 491).

For simpler Orange Rolls, roll out the dough and sprinkle with grated orange rind, roll lightly to press the rind into the dough, and cut out small rounds. Press into each roll a small sugar cube dipped in orange juice. Let rise and bake.

Coffee Cakes (Kuchen)

You may prefer to make only one small coffee cake and use the rest of the dough for French Croissants (p. 329). Add a little sugar to the dough if you like. See also Quick Coffee Cakes (p. 315).

Prepare Sweet Roll dough (p. 332). After kneading, divide it into two parts and spread in two buttered layer cake tins, or put the whole amount in a shallow pan about 9 by 15 inches, or make half into buns. Spread with desired topping (see recipes below). Let rise until double in bulk (about 1 hour).

Bake 20 to 25 minutes at 375°.

Apple Kuchen. After spreading the dough in pans, brush with melted butter. Pare 5 tart apples and cut in eighths. Press close together into the dough, sharp edge down. Sprinkle with the following topping: ¼ cup sugar mixed with ½ teaspoon cinnamon and 2 tablespoons currants or seedless raisins. Cover and let rise. Bake 30 minutes at 350°.

Raisin Kuchen. Add to the dough ½ cup raisins, cut in pieces. Before baking, brush over with beaten egg and cover with the following topping: Melt 3 tablespoons butter, add ⅓ cup sugar and 1 teaspoon cinnamon. Stir and add 3 tablespoons flour.

Honey Twist. Add slightly more flour to make the dough firm enough to roll into a long cylinder about 1 inch in diameter. Coil in a buttered 9-inch layer cake tin, beginning at the outer edge and cover-

ing the bottom. Spread the following topping over the hot twist after it is baked: Cream ¼ cup butter with 2 tablespoons honey and stir in 1 egg white and 1 cup confectioners' sugar.

Christmas Coffee Cake. Make a roll as for Honey Twist and shape on a cooky sheet like a Christmas tree. Bake. Frost and decorate with colored candies.

Cincinnati Coffee Cake. After putting the dough in pans, sprinkle over it the following topping: Mix ¼ cup sugar, 1½ teaspoons cinnamon, 1 cup soft stale bread crumbs, ¼ cup melted butter and ¼ cup chopped blanched almonds.

Streusel Coffee Cake. Sift ⅓ cup sugar with ⅓ cup flour. Work in ⅓ cup butter and mix until all is crumbly. Spread this topping over the coffee cake before the last rising, pressing in slightly with the fingers.

Ruth's Coffee Cake. Make a roll as for Honey Twist. Cut off 1-inch pieces, shape into balls, and dip in melted butter, then in sugar mixed with cinnamon (½ cup to 1 teaspoon). Arrange in 2 layers in a tube pan, sprinkling chopped nuts or raisins on each layer.

Christmas Stollen

Make Sweet Roll dough (p. 332). After mixing and raising, turn the dough onto a mixing board and pat or roll out flat. Cover with ½ cup slivered almonds, ½ cup chopped candied fruit, and 1 tablespoon grated lemon rind. Fold and knead the fruit into the dough. Flatten the dough into an oblong. Brush with melted butter and fold double lengthwise. Press the edges together. Place on a greased baking sheet. Let rise to double its size.

Bake at 375° for 35 minutes. Frost with Confectioners' Frosting (p. 491) and decorate with almonds and candied fruit.

Cinnamon Bread

Make Sweet Roll dough (p. 332), increasing the flour to about 3 cups. After the first rising, punch down and knead. Roll into a rectangle ½ inch thick. Spread with softened butter, sprinkle with ¼ cup sugar mixed with 1½ teaspoons cinnamon. Roll like a jelly roll. Place in a buttered loaf pan, brush with melted butter, cover with a clean cloth, and let rise.

Bake 30 minutes at 400°.

Danish Pastry

The dough is folded repeatedly to make several flaky layers. The process is similar to that used in making Puff Paste. See the illustration on p. 410.

Prepare Sweet Roll dough (p. 332), adding to it
   ¼ teaspoon vanilla
   ¼ teaspoon mace
After kneading the dough thoroughly, roll it into an oblong ¼ inch thick.

Wash (p. 8)
   ⅞ cup butter
Divide into small bits and place half in the center of the dough. Fold one end of the dough to cover the butter, place the remaining butter on top, and fold over the other end of the dough, pressing the edges firmly together.

Turn a quarter way around, pat with a rolling pin, and roll into an oblong as thin as possible, lifting the dough frequently to keep it from sticking. Fold each end to the center, pat and fold to make four layers.

Turn a quarter way around, and again pat, roll and fold. Repeat twice more, making four turns in all. Cover and let rise 20 minutes.

Roll ½ inch thick. Shape into pinwheels or horns (below). Arrange on a cooky sheet covered with brown paper. Brush with an egg, slightly beaten. Sprinkle with coarsely chopped nut meats, if desired. Let rise until light and about double in size.

Bake 25 minutes at 375°. Brush with Confectioners' Frosting (p. 491).

Pinwheels. Cut in 4-inch squares. Make a cut from each corner almost to the center. Fold each alternate point to the center, pressing them down firmly. Put a bit of jam in the center.

Horns. Cut in triangles 5 inches long and 3 inches wide at the base. Spread with a little jam or Cream Filling (p. 495). Press the long edges together and shape like horns.

Swedish Bread

Put in a mixing bowl
  1 cup lukewarm milk
  1 package yeast
Let stand 5 minutes. Add
  ½ cup flour
Beat well, cover, and let rise. Add
  2 cups flour
Beat and let rise again. Add
  ¼ cup melted butter
  ⅓ cup sugar
  1 egg, well beaten
  ¼ teaspoon salt
  ½ teaspoon almond extract
Mix thoroughly. Add enough
  Flour
to knead the dough well. Let rise until about double in size. Shape in a braid or ring (below). Let rise until light, and about double in size. Bake about 20 minutes at 350°.

Swedish Braid. Divide the dough in thirds. Roll each part between the hands into long thin ropes of uniform size. Braid. Form in a ring, if desired. Put on a buttered cooky sheet, cover, and let rise. Beat an egg yolk with 1 teaspoon cold water. Brush it over the braid. Sprinkle with finely cut blanched almonds.

Swedish Ring. Shape with hands in a long roll. Roll as thin as possible on an unfloured board with a rolling pin. Lift with a knife to keep the dough from sticking to the board. Spread with melted butter. Sprinkle with sugar and chopped

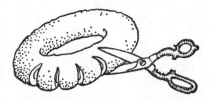

blanched almonds or cinnamon. Roll like a jelly roll. Join the ends to form a ring. Place on a buttered cooky sheet. Snip with scissors, holding the scissors at right angles to the roll.

Sally Lunn

See also Quick Sally Lunn (p. 313).

Put in a mixing bowl
  1 cup lukewarm milk
  1 package yeast
Let stand five minutes. Stir. Add
  ½ cup softened butter or oil
  ⅓ cup sugar
  ½ teaspoon salt
  3 eggs
Beat with a strong rotary beater or electric mixer, gradually adding
  3½ cups flour
Leave the mixture in the bowl and let rise until very light and about double in size. Spoon into a buttered 10-inch angel cake pan or Turk's head pan or 2 dozen 2-inch muffin pans. Let rise about 1 hour.

Bake about 50 minutes at 350° in a large pan or 20 minutes at 425° in muffin pans.

To vary, add raisins and chopped citron or other fruits to the batter; or put a layer of brown sugar and pecans in the buttered pans; or sprinkle the top before baking with cinnamon sugar (½ cup sugar mixed with 2 teaspoons cinnamon) or with ½ cup sugar mixed with 1 teaspoon cinnamon and 1 teaspoon nutmeg.

Pizza

*Cut in wedges and serve hot as a lunch-
eon dish or an evening snack with coffee,
beer or red wine.*

Put in a mixing bowl
  1 cup lukewarm water
  1 package yeast
Let stand 5 minutes. Stir. Add
  1 teaspoon sugar
  1 teaspoon salt
  1 tablespoon shortening
Beat well. Add
  1½ cups all-purpose flour or bread
    flour
Beat until smooth. Add
  About 1½ cups flour
using enough to make the dough just
barely firm enough to handle.

Knead until smooth. Divide in thirds.
Knead each piece into a ball. Flatten,
then pull and stretch gently to fit 9-inch
layer cake tins, lightly greased. Press up
around the edges to make a slight rim.
Let rise 15 minutes.
Brush lightly with
  Olive oil
Sprinkle with
  Parmesan cheese, grated
Cover with
  Fresh tomatoes or drained canned
    tomatoes
  Slivers of mozzarella or other Italian
    cheese
  Chopped anchovies or meat
  Sprinkling of orégano or basil
Bake 25 minutes at 425°. *Makes three
9-inch pizzas.*

Sandwiches and Toast

A perfect sandwich is more than a filling and two slices of bread. The bread must be neatly sliced and evenly spread, the filling appropriate to the occasion and well seasoned, and the finished sandwich properly stored until serving time so that it looks its appetizing best. Then serve it with satisfaction as a picnic standby, a sturdy lunch or an appealing accompaniment to a party beverage.

Sandwich breads should be firm-textured. White, whole wheat, Boston brown and pumpernickel are all suitable. The bread should not be too fresh — day-old bread cuts evenly. Use thick or thin slices as you prefer for lunchbox or picnic sandwiches, but make party sandwiches of thinly sliced bread. If you are using an unsliced loaf, be sure you have a very sharp bread knife. A loaf weighing about 1 pound will make 8 to 12 sandwiches.

Butter for sandwiches should be soft enough to spread easily. Let it stand at room temperature. If you are making a large number of sandwiches, beat the butter with a spoon or an electric beater until it is soft and fluffy. Then beat in ½ cup milk for each pound of butter. Allow about ¼ cup butter for 16 whole slices of bread.

Storing sandwiches. Wrap tightly in cellophane, plastic, or wax paper or in aluminum foil. If you are preparing party sandwiches in advance, arrange them on plates, cover with wax paper, then with a slightly dampened cloth, and store in the refrigerator or other cool place.

Storing sandwiches in the freezer (p. 540).

Making Sandwiches

Make the sandwiches just before you serve them if the filling is very moist; otherwise, it may soak into the bread.

Prepare the filling (pp. 338–341).

Prepare the bread. Cream the butter. Slice the bread. Cut off the crusts or not, as you prefer. Spread the slices with butter or mayonnaise. If you are using a smooth filling like cream cheese, butter only one slice for each sandwich. If sandwiches are being made hours in advance of serving or to put in the freezer, butter all the slices of bread, then chill them to harden the butter before spreading with the filling so that the filling will not soak through.

Spread half the slices with the filling, spreading it evenly to the edges and corners. For tea sandwiches, have the layer of filling thin, so that it will not press out. For heartier sandwiches, have the layer a generous one. Cover with the other slices and press firmly together.

Making sandwiches in quantity. Arrange slices of bread in rows on a large table. Distribute dabs of butter on the slices in alternate rows. Then spread all those slices evenly. Distribute and spread the filling in the same way on the bread in the other rows. Fold together.

337

Party Sandwiches

In addition to Ribbon, Rolled and Pin-wheel Sandwiches (below), see other suggestions for tea party and cocktail sandwiches under Hot Sandwiches (p. 341).

Small sandwiches. Use thinly sliced bread. Make full-size sandwiches. Cut off the crusts with a long sharp knife. Cut in any of the ways shown below. Or cut sliced bread in rounds and make into sandwiches. (Dry the scraps of bread in a slow oven, roll, and save to use as bread crumbs.)

Open sandwiches. See also Canapés (p. 48). Cut the bread in any shape you choose. Spread with creamed butter, then with filling. Decorate with nut meats, chopped nuts, bits of cherry, a leaf of watercress or parsley, or a slice of stuffed olive.

Fillings for party sandwiches. Almost any filling (below) is adaptable to party sandwiches. For tea and coffee parties, see especially the suggestions under Cream Cheese (p. 340), Ginger Pecan Filling (p. 340), and the various salad fillings (p. 339). For cocktail parties, see Chicken-Ham and Liver Sausage (p. 339) and other meat and fish fillings.

Ribbon Sandwiches

Put three or more slices of bread together with creamed seasoned or tinted butter or other soft filling. Have the bread ¼ inch thick. Wrap tightly in a damp cloth and press under a weight. Cut in ¼-inch slices just before serving. Use all white bread or alternate slices of white and dark bread.

Chicken and Ham Ribbon Sandwiches. Use chopped ham highly seasoned and moistened with cream, chopped cooked chicken or turkey moistened with mayonnaise, and chopped nut meats moistened with mayonnaise.

Pepper Ribbon Sandwiches. Chop red and green peppers separately very fine. Wring in a piece of cheesecloth. Moisten with mayonnaise. Use in alternate layers.

Tongue and Gruyère Ribbon Sandwiches. Use brown and white bread alternately. Make alternate layers of cold boiled tongue and Gruyère cheese.

Rolled Sandwiches

Cut the crusts from thin slices of very fresh fine-grained bread. Spread with creamed butter or other filling, such as seasoned cream cheese or Mushroom Dip (p. 47). Roll, fasten with picks, and chill.

When ready to serve, remove the toothpicks. Tuck a sprig of parsley, mint or watercress in the ends of the sandwiches as a garnish.

Asparagus Rolls. Spread slices of bread with mayonnaise or with butter seasoned with lemon juice. Wrap tightly around small asparagus tips (cooked or canned), letting the tip end show.

Watercress Rolls. Fill with sprays of watercress, letting a few small perfect leaves show at each end.

Pinwheel Sandwiches

Cut a lengthwise slice from a loaf of bread. Spread with creamed butter and filling (below). Roll up like a jelly roll. Wrap tightly in a dry towel, then in a slightly moist one, and put in a cold place. To serve, cut in thin slices.

Simple Sandwich Fillings

For other fillings, see Hearty Fillings (p. 339), as well as dips, butters and spreads (pp. 48–49).

Creamed butter, cream cheese or cottage cheese, plain or seasoned with lemon juice, anchovy paste, honey, grated horse-radish, Roquefort cheese crumbs, chopped parsley, chives or watercress. Other cream cheese fillings (p. 340).

Peanut butter, plain or moistened with salad dressing. Or sprinkle lightly with sugar or spread with jam or jelly. Or sprinkle with chopped sweet pickle or crumbled crisp bacon.

Jelly, jam or marmalade, plain or with chopped nuts. Marmalade is especially good on nut bread, with or without cream cheese.

Hearty Sandwich Fillings
Good luncheon or supper fare.

See also the suggestions for cheese sand-wiches (below), for Fish Fillings (p. 340) and Hot Sandwiches (p. 341). For salad sandwiches, spread the bread with mayonnaise before putting on the filling. Add a layer of shredded lettuce to the sandwich.

Egg Salad. Chop hard-cooked eggs fine and mix with mayonnaise, Cream Dress-ing (p. 291) or melted butter. Add chopped pickles, olives or chives. Season to taste with salt and pepper, anchovy paste or chutney.

Chicken or Turkey. Cut cooked chicken or turkey in neat slices. Sprinkle with salt and pepper. Add a leaf of lettuce or a sprig of watercress.

Chicken or Turkey Salad. Chop cooked chicken or turkey and moisten with mayonnaise. Add crumbled crisp bacon or chopped celery.

Ham, Beef, or Lamb (or other cooked meat). Slice or chop and moisten with Tartare Sauce (p. 97).

Ham and Cheese. Top a slice of ham with a slice of cheese, preferably Swiss. Dot with prepared mustard, if you like.

Ham Salad. Mix chopped ham and chopped hard-cooked egg and moisten with mayonnaise or Cream Dressing (p. 291). Add finely chopped green or red pepper or prepared mustard.

Corned Beef or Tongue. Cut thin. Spread with mustard, if you like. Rye bread is particularly good.

Almond-Chicken Filling

Mix 1 cup chopped cooked chicken, ¼ cup chopped blanched almonds, and ½ cup finely chopped celery. Moisten with mayonnaise and season to taste with lemon juice, salt and paprika.

Chicken-Ham Filling

Cream
    ⅓ cup butter
Mix with
    ½ cup finely chopped cooked chicken
    ½ cup finely chopped cooked ham
    Salt and paprika to taste

Liver Sausage Filling

Remove the skin from
    ½ pound liver sausage
Add to the meat
    1 small cream cheese (3 ounces)
    3 hard-cooked eggs, chopped
    3 tablespoons mayonnaise
    ½ teaspoon chopped chives
    Salt and pepper
Cream thoroughly. Add more mayon-naise, if needed, to spread easily.

Shrimp and Chicken Liver Filling

Mix and put through food chopper
    ½ cup cooked or canned shrimp
    ½ cup cooked chicken livers
    ½ red pepper, seeded
    ½ large sweet onion
Season with
    Salt
Moisten with
    Mayonnaise

Spanish Filling

Chop very fine or pound in a mortar

2 anchovies
2 pickles
1 sprig parsley
3 tablespoons capers
1 teaspoon prepared mustard
2 tablespoons salad oil
2 tablespoons vinegar

Add

2 hard-cooked eggs, chopped fine

Mix and season to taste with

Salt and paprika

Ginger Pecan Filling

For small tea party sandwiches.

Mix together

¼ cup chopped Canton ginger
¼ cup chopped pecan nut meats
2 tablespoons orange pulp, cut fine
1 tablespoon ginger syrup
1 teaspoon vinegar
Few grains salt

Cheese Fillings

Many cheeses make excellent sandwiches, on plain or toasted bread. Add a little mustard or other seasoning if you like. See also Toasted Cheese Sandwiches and other hot sandwiches (p. 341).

Cream Cheese. Season. Moisten with mayonnaise, French dressing or cream, or mix with any of the following:

Honey and grated orange rind. Use 1 tablespoon of each to a small package of cream cheese.
Black walnut meats, coarsely cut, coconut, chutney or Deviled Almonds (p. 87).
Chicken or ham, chopped fine.
Chopped olives, ripe or stuffed, or nut meats, or a combination of both.
Canton ginger, chopped.
Crushed pineapple and chopped pecan nut meats.

Shrimp, mashed with a fork.
Watercress, chopped or in sprays.
Strawberry jam spread on the cheese.
Guava jelly spread on the cheese.
Pimiento and green pepper, cut fine, with a few drops of onion juice added.

Cottage Cheese. Use plain or seasoned cottage cheese in any of the ways suggested for cream cheese. Spring Salad (p. 111) is delicious on dark bread.

Gruyère Cheese. Grate, mix with chopped walnut meats, and season with salt and cayenne.

Swiss Cheese. Slice and dot with prepared mustard. Use rye bread.

Cheese and Anchovy. Cream 2 tablespoons butter, add ¼ cup grated mild cheese and 1 teaspoon vinegar. Season with salt, paprika, mustard and anchovy paste.

Fish Fillings

Flake any cooked white fish and mix with finely cut celery, pickle or cucumber. Moisten with mayonnaise.

Salmon or Tuna (cooked or canned). Flake and mix with mayonnaise and chopped cucumber or pickle or finely cut celery.

Sardine. Skin, bone, and mash to a paste. Mix with chopped hard-cooked egg. Season with salt, cayenne and a few drops lemon juice. Moisten with olive oil or melted butter.

Shrimp. Mash with a fork and season to taste with French dressing or mayonnaise or both.

Lobster. Chop and season with salad dressing or cayenne, mustard and lemon juice. Spread on lettuce if desired. As a variation, add an equal quantity of chopped hard-cooked egg.

Vegetable Fillings

See also BLT Sandwiches (p. 342).

Carrot. Grate raw carrot and mix with mayonnaise. Spread on a leaf of lettuce or shredded lettuce.

Cucumber. Chop and moisten with mayonnaise; or cut in thin slices, sprinkle with salt and freshly ground pepper.

Lettuce. Cut in strips with scissors. Season with a small amount of mayonnaise.

Olive. Chop ripe or stuffed green olives and mix with mayonnaise.

Tomato. Slice, drain, and sprinkle with salt or dip in French dressing. Dot with mayonnaise (open or closed sandwich).

Watercress. Sprinkle with salt, or chop and mix with mayonnaise.

Hot Sandwiches

For luncheon or supper. Hot roast beef sandwiches, covered with gravy, Hamburgers (p. 342), Toasted Cheese Sandwiches (below), Club Sandwiches (p. 342), Chicken Sandwiches (p. 339) are all popular as main dishes for luncheon or supper. These will suggest other suitable combinations.

For a tea party. Make small plain or rolled sandwiches on unbuttered bread. When ready to serve, brush with melted butter, place on a cooky sheet, and toast in the broiler. Toast a few at a time so that you can serve them piping hot. The filling may be orange marmalade, sliced cheese or chopped chicken, or chopped sautéed mushrooms moistened with cream. See also Baking Powder Biscuit Sandwiches (below) and Waffle Sandwiches (below).

For a cocktail party. Make sandwiches as for a tea party (above) but do not use sweet fillings. See also Baking Powder Biscuit Sandwiches (below) and Waffle Sandwiches (below).

Baking Powder Biscuit Sandwiches

Make tiny Baking Powder Biscuits (p. 311). Split, butter, and put together with deviled ham spread, shaved maple sugar, halved and sugared strawberries, jam, thin slices of cheese, or chopped chicken moistened with hot gravy or cream sauce.

Waffle Sandwiches

Make small sandwiches with a filling of orange marmalade or a bit of cheese dotted with mustard or a few drops of Worcestershire. Keep the filling away from the edges. Spread the outside of the sandwiches lightly with butter and toast in a waffle iron.

Toasted Sandwiches

Make sandwiches without buttering the bread. Spread one side of each sandwich lightly with soft butter. Toast in the broiler, buttered side toward the heat. Turn the sandwich over and spread the other side with butter. Toast. Serve piping hot.

Good fillings for toasted sandwiches are peanut butter, marmalade, chopped ham, sliced tomato or chopped cooked meat, fish or chicken mixed with mayonnaise and seasoned to taste. French Toast Sandwiches (p. 342) are good with any of these fillings, too.

Toasted Cheese Sandwiches

Use 2 slices of bread for each sandwich. Lay thin slices of cheese on half the slices of bread. Arrange all the slices in the broiler 2 inches from the heat.

Toast until the cheese begins to melt and the plain bread to brown. Cover the cheese with the plain bread, toasted side down. Spread tops sparingly with soft butter and toast until delicately brown. Turn over, butter again, and toast. Cut in half and serve very hot.

Open Toasted Cheese Sandwiches. Toast bread on one side. Put sliced cheese on the untoasted side, sprinkle with paprika, and, if desired, with bits of uncooked bacon and rings of sweet onion. Toast in the broiler until the cheese melts.

Open Cheese and Bacon Sandwiches

Combine and mix well
  3 eggs, beaten until light
  ¾ pound Cheddar cheese, grated or put through food chopper
  1½ teaspoons Worcestershire
  ¾ teaspoon salt
  ½ teaspoon paprika
  Few grains cayenne
Spread on
  8 slices bread, ⅓ inch thick
Cut into tiny squares
  ¾ pound bacon
Sprinkle over the cheese. Bake 8 to 10 minutes in 400° oven. *Makes 8 sandwiches.*

Western Sandwiches

For each sandwich, put in a small frying pan
  1 teaspoon butter
  1 tablespoon minced onion
Cook slowly 5 minutes.
Beat until just blended
  1 egg
  1 tablespoon water
Add
  1 tablespoon minced ham (or more)
Pour into the pan with the onion and cook until lightly browned on the bottom. Turn and cook a moment on the other side. Put between halves of a toasted bun or slices of buttered bread.

Eastern Sandwiches. Make in the same way, but omit the onion.

Hamburger Sandwiches

Split and toast hamburger buns.

Shape hamburgers ½ inch thick and the size of the buns. Cook the hamburgers 4 minutes on one side, put on half of the split buns, cooked side down. Sprinkle with salt and pepper. Broil until the meat is browned. Top with the other bun halves.

For a more piquant flavor, dot the hamburgers with prepared mustard, chili sauce, or both.

Cheeseburgers. After putting the hamburger on the bun, top with a slice of cheese. Broil until the cheese melts.

Club Sandwiches

Club sandwiches are usually made wtih three slices of hot buttered toast filled with plenty of sliced chicken or other meat, lettuce, sliced tomato and mayonnaise. Top with a strip or two of crisp bacon, if you like.

If you are planning to serve a club sandwich on a plate with a fork, cut the toast diagonally in quarters so that the sandwich will be easier to manage.

BLT Sandwiches

Put sliced tomato, lettuce, a dab of mayonnaise and crisp strips of bacon between slices of hot buttered toast.

French Toast Sandwiches

Make sandwiches with a filling of cheese, sliced white meat of chicken or turkey, or chopped chicken, turkey or ham. Press the edges firmly together.

For 4 sandwiches, beat 1 egg slightly and add ¼ cup milk. Dip the sandwiches in the mixture, turning to coat both sides. Sauté on both sides in butter. Serve immediately with a garnish of crisp bacon.

Croque Madame. *A French version.* Make the filling of sliced white meat of chicken and a thin slice of Gruyère cheese. Or of chicken with a layer of sautéed mushrooms or Duxelles (p. 249).

Croque Monsieur. Make the filling of a thin slice of broiled or baked ham and a thin slice of Gruyère cheese.

Devonshire Sandwiches

A versatile recipe, excellent for a Sunday night supper party. Bake in a large shallow baking dish, if you prefer.

Butter individual shallow baking dishes. In each put
    Buttered toast, cut to fit
On the toast, arrange
    Sliced white meat of chicken or turkey
    Ham or Canadian bacon, sliced thin
Top with
    Cream Sauce (p. 90)
Sprinkle with
    Sharp Cheddar cheese, grated

    Paprika
Dot with
    Butter
Bake at 350° about 15 minutes. Garnish with
    Strips of cooked bacon
Put under the broiler long enough to brown lightly.

To vary. Use Cheese Sauce (p. 91) or Mushroom Sauce (p. 94) in place of Cream Sauce. Or put a spoonful of sautéed mushrooms on the meat before covering with the sauce. Use only chicken or turkey, if you prefer.

Toast

Which does your family prefer? Thick slices of fresh bread, toasted quickly so that they are crisp on the outside but soft inside, or thin slices browned slowly so that the toast is crisp all the way through?

To make toast at the table or a few pieces at a time, an electric toaster is ideal.

To make toast in quantity, put the slices of bread on a cooky sheet and toast them in the broiler. Butter and set in the oven a moment to reheat.

Melba Toast

The bread for Melba toast must be fine-grained so that you can cut it in very thin even slices. Chilled bread 2 or 3 days old will cut more easily than fresh bread.

Put the slices on a cooky sheet and bake at 250° until delicately brown and completely dry. Serve unbuttered.

Toast for Tea

Cut sliced bread (preferably thin) in halves or thirds. Toast, butter, reheat, and serve with jam, marmalade or honey, or make one of the special toasts listed below. If you make toast in an electric toaster, cut the slices in pieces after toasting.

Butterscotch or Maple Toast. Sprinkle buttered toast lightly with brown sugar or soft maple sugar. Set in the oven until the sugar melts.

Cinnamon Toast. Toast bread on one side. Butter the untoasted side and sprinkle with cinnamon sugar (¼ cup sugar mixed with 1 teaspoon cinnamon). Toast, buttered side up, until the sugar melts. For a party, prepare early in the day and do the final toasting at teatime.

Coconut Toast. Toast bread on one side. Spread the untoasted side with shredded or grated coconut mixed with creamed butter. Toast.

Orange Toast. Follow directions for making Cinnamon Toast, but instead of cinnamon sugar, sprinkle with ½ cup sugar mixed with ¼ cup grated orange rind and 2 tablespoons orange juice.

Herbed Melba Rye

For cocktails or salad. Keeps fresh for days and reheats successfully.

Cut in thin slices
    1 loaf party rye
Spread on cooky sheets in single layers and bake at 250° until thoroughly crisp and dry (about 1 hour). Melt
    ½ cup butter
Add to it
    1 teaspoon dried marjoram or 2 tea-
        spoons chopped fresh herbs
    2 teaspoons lemon juice
Brush over the toast. Return to the oven for 10 minutes.

Toasted English Muffins

Pull English muffins (packaged or home-made) apart with a fork or your fingers so that the surface is rough. Spread generously with butter. Toast quickly in the broiler, buttered side only. Serve hot with jam, marmalade or honey.

English Muffins with Cheese. Before toasting, sprinkle with grated cheese, or put a thin round slice of soft cheese on each.

Quick Pizzas. Dot hot toasted muffins with bits of fresh or canned tomato and very thin slices of onion. Sprinkle with salt and pepper and a pinch of orégano. Put a slice of mozzarella cheese on top. Set under the broiler until the cheese melts.

Butter Toasties

An easy and delectable bread for dinner, tea or lunch.

Cut firm bread in slices 2 inches thick. Remove the crusts and cut each slice in halves or thirds. Dip in melted butter. Bake at 400° until well browned, turning from time to time to brown evenly.

Butterscotch or Cinnamon Toasties. Before browning, sprinkle with brown sugar or cinnamon sugar (¼ cup sugar mixed with 1 teaspoon cinnamon).

Seed Toasties. Before browning, sprinkle lightly with celery seed, poppyseed or sesame.

Tea Toasties. Cut 1-inch slices of bread in cubes. Continue as above, but bake at 325°.

Coconut Squares. Cut the bread in 1½-inch cubes. Dip in condensed milk, then in shredded coconut. Put on a cooky sheet and bake at 350° until lightly browned.

Croustades

Cut the crusts from slices of bread. Butter the bread and press into muffin tins. Bake at 325° until brown. Use in place of patty shells for creamed chicken or other creamed dishes.

Milk Toast

Prepare
    Hot milk or Thin Cream Sauce (p.
        90)
Dip in it
    4 to 6 slices toast
Place the toast on plates or a serving dish and pour the rest of the sauce over it. Sprinkle with
    Chopped parsley, ham or hard-cooked
        egg

French Toast

As a heartier dish for luncheon or supper, omit the sugar and top with creamed eggs, chicken, tuna, dried beef or mush-rooms. French Toast Sandwiches (p. 342).

Mix
    1 egg, slightly beaten
    Few grains salt
    1 teaspoon sugar
    3 tablespoons milk
Dip in it, turning to coat each side
    4 slices bread (not too soft)
Heat a griddle or heavy frying pan. Butter it well and brown the dipped bread on each side. Serve with maple syrup, jam or marmalade, or sprinkle with cinnamon sugar (¼ cup sugar mixed with 1 teaspoon cinnamon).

Fruits and Fruit Desserts

Fruit is a piquant addition to any meal of the day — refreshing at breakfast, zestful as an accompaniment to the main dish at lunch or dinner, welcome as dessert, especially after a hearty meal, and good as a snack any time. Fruits are low in calories compared with puddings and pies, and are rewardingly high in important food values.

In this section are suggestions for fruit cups and compotes as well as information about selecting, storing and preparing fruit. Consult the index for other fruit recipes. Many variations are possible, such as different combinations of fruits; using brown sugar, maple syrup or honey in place of white sugar; and adding zest with a bit of lemon juice, brandy or rum.

Fresh fruits. Store in a cool place, preferably spread out so the pieces do not touch.

Frozen fruits and fruit juices. Often of better flavor than out-of-season fresh fruits. Use promptly after defrosting. Shake juices in a closed jar to blend.

Canned fruits and fruit juices. Read the labels to compare can sizes and quality as well as prices. Sliced fruit is cheaper than whole fruit of the same quality.

Dried fruits. Small fruits are less expensive than large ones but may be equally good. Buy unsulphured fruit whenever possible. Packaged dried fruits do not need soaking before cooking. To cook very quickly, use a pressure saucepan (8 to 10 minutes).

Fruit Bowl

An ideal centerpiece, especially for a holiday dinner.

Choose the large fruits for contrast in color and shape. Arrange them in an at-tractive pattern in a large bowl. Then scatter over them seedless grapes, large raisins and unshelled walnuts and pecans. Let each person help himself — you will need to supply fruit knives and nutcrackers.

Fruit Cup (Fruit Cocktail)

There is no finer dessert or first course than a medley of perfect fruits, carefully selected and prepared. Use all fresh fruit or combine fresh and canned fruit.

Choose fruits for contrast in color, texture and flavor. Citrus fruits add zest — oranges, grapefruit, kumquats, canned mandarin oranges. Small fruits add an attractive touch — berries, grapes, Bing cherries. Peaches, pears, bananas, apricots, cantaloupe, watermelon, pineapple — all are delicious.

See also special recipes such as Ambrosia (p. 355) and Melon Suprême (p. 354).

Allow at least ½ cup of prepared fruit for each serving. Follow the directions in this chapter for preparing each fruit.

Cut large fruit in even pieces, not too small. Seed grapes, unless they are the seedless variety. Pit cherries. Sprinkle cut peaches with lemon juice to prevent darkening. Add bananas just before serving, as they discolor after cutting.

Put the fruit in a bowl, sprinkle lightly with salt, then with sugar and mix gently.

To vary the flavor, tuck in a few mint leaves or sprinkle with lemon juice, rum, sherry or brandy. Taste the juice and add more salt, sugar or lemon juice if needed. Cover and refrigerate an hour or more to blend the flavors. Just before serving time, remove mint leaves, if used, and replace them with fresh ones.

To serve as a first course. Spoon into sherbet glasses. Top with a sprig of mint, a perfect cherry or strawberry, or a tiny scoop of lemon or orange ice.

To serve as dessert. Serve from the bowl, or arrange in sherbet glasses as above. Other good toppings are Gervaise (p. 405) or sour cream or yogurt sprinkled lightly with brown sugar. Crisp cookies are especially good with fruit — Coffee Cookies (p. 435), Chocolate Walnut Wafers (p. 436), Brandy Wafers (p. 442), and Lace Cookies (p. 443) are perfect.

Macédoine of Fruit

A handsome way to present fruit as a dessert. Fruits particularly attractive served this way are avocado in slices or cubes, orange or grapefruit sections, melon balls, seeded white grapes, cherries (canned or fresh), strawberries, raspberries, wedges of fresh pineapple, sliced peaches, pears and nectarines.

Prepare the fruit as for Fruit Cup (above), but do not mix it together. Arrange separately on a large flat serving dish in an attractive pattern. Squeeze lemon juice over the fruit to keep it from darkening. Sprinkle sparingly with confectioners' sugar and Kirsch or Cointreau. Chill thoroughly.

Cottage Cheese Fruit Bowl

Circle a mound of cottage cheese with fresh, frozen or canned fruit such as peaches, plums, apricots or pears. As an extra fillip, serve little bowls of powdered coffee, grated chocolate, granulated sugar and cinnamon to be sprinkled over the fruit.

Sherried Frozen Fruit

For a refreshing summer dessert, thaw (enough to separate the fruit) a package of frozen raspberries or peaches. The fruit should still be somewhat icy when it is served. Sprinkle with ¼ cup sherry or vermouth. *Serves 3 or 4.*

Glazed Fruit

Wash and dry thoroughly strawberries, raspberries, white grapes or cherries. Dip in egg white beaten slightly with water (½ teaspoon to 1 egg white). Drain and roll in fine sugar. Dry until crusty. Pass with summer afternoon drinks or with after-dinner coffee. See also Glacéed Fruit (p. 508).

Hot Fruit Compote

Beautiful and satisfying as a winter dessert following a hearty roast. Easy to prepare in quantity for a big party.

Drain the juice from
   1 can pears
   1 can Bing cherries
   1 can whole apricots (pitted)
To the juice add
   1 tablespoon slivered orange peel
Simmer 30 minutes. Add the fruit. Heat. Stir in
   Brandy, rum or vanilla to taste
Serve plain or with
   Sweet or sour cream or Gervaise (p. 405)
Serves 6 to 8.

Other combinations

Peaches, raisins, plums and slivered almonds.
Peaches, pears, apricots and marrons.
Plums, apricots and cherries.
Pineapple, orange sections and black cherries.
Prunes and apricots.
Cooked apple slices, raisins and walnut halves.

Baked Fruit Compote

For an extra touch, sprinkle macaroon crumbs on each layer, or top each serving with a dab of sour cream.

Arrange layers of canned fruit (such as sour cherries, greengage plums, sweet black cherries and peaches) in a deep baking dish. Sprinkle each layer sparingly with brown sugar.

Bake 30 minutes at 350°. Arrange several thin slices of lemon over the fruit and bake 10 minutes longer. If the fruit is very juicy, spoon out some of the juice after the first 10 minutes of baking. Serve warm or cold.

Apples

New varieties of apples are constantly being developed and some of the fine old ones are no longer available. Learn to know and appreciate your local varieties. Sweet bland apples do not make good applesauce or pie. Some wonderful early fall apples do not keep well in storage. Add zest to apple dishes with a touch of nutmeg, cinnamon or allspice. Dried apples, canned apples and canned applesauce are often a convenience.

See the index for other apple recipes, such as Dutch Apple Cake (p. 333) and other apple desserts.

Apple Savories. Slice bright red apples but do not pare. Spread with cream cheese or Camembert and serve after the dessert course at dinner or as an evening snack.

Applesauce

Wash and quarter apples but do not pare or core. Cook slowly until soft with just enough water to keep from burning. Or cook in a pressure saucepan 5 minutes with ¼ cup water.

Put through a food mill or coarse strainer. Add a sprinkling of salt. Add sugar to taste. Stir until the sugar melts completely. Some cooks stir in a bit of butter.

If apples need more flavor, add spice and lemon juice.

If you like applesauce less smooth, pare and core the apples before cooking and beat only slightly with a fork when they are done.

Apple Snow

Best when prepared within half an hour of serving.

Beat until stiff
    2 egg whites
Beat in, little by little
    Applesauce (very cold)
adding as much as will keep the whip stiff enough to pile in a bowl or individual dishes. Serve very cold with
    Soft Custard (p. 362), made with brown sugar
Serves 4.

Apple Compote

Serve as dessert or as an accompaniment to roast duck or pork.

Quarter, core and pare
    8 tart cooking apples
Cook for 5 minutes
    1 cup sugar
    1 cup water
    Few shavings of lemon rind
Remove the lemon rind. Cook the apples in the syrup, a few at a time, until tender enough to pierce with a toothpick. Strain the syrup over the cooked apples.

Cinnamon Apples

Serve as a relish with pork or as dessert.

Core and pare tart apples. Stick each with 2 or 3 cloves. For 6 apples, cook together for 5 minutes 1 cup sugar, 2 tablespoons red cinnamon drops, and 1½ cups water. Add the apples, and simmer until tender but not mushy. Baste often with the syrup in the pan.

Apple Porcupine. Omit the cinnamon drops and cloves. Drain and cool. Fill with jelly, marmalade or preserved fruit. Stick with bits of sliced almonds. Serve with whipped cream as dessert.

Baked Apples

Only firm, tart cooking apples bake well.

Core the apples and put in a baking dish. In each apple put 1 tablespoon sugar and a dash of cinnamon or nutmeg. Cover the bottom of the baking dish with boiling water.

Bake at 400° until soft (30 minutes or more). Several times during the baking, spoon the pan juices over the apples.

If you prefer to pare apples before baking, core before paring, so that the fruit will keep its shape. Or make 2 circular cuts through the skin, leaving a ¾-inch band around the apple midway between the stem and blossom ends.

Apple Meringue. *Also delicious made with heated and drained canned peaches.* Pile Meringue (p. 411) on warm baked apples. Brown lightly in the oven at 450°. Cool. Serve with Soft Custard (p. 362).

Crusty Baked Apples

Core and pare halfway down
    6 tart apples
Put in a baking dish, pared side up.

Melt
    3 tablespoons butter
Stir in
    2 tablespoons flour
Mix well. Add
    ½ cup brown sugar
    ½ teaspoon vanilla
Spread over the apples.

Bake at 425° until the crust is set. Lower the temperature to 350°. Bake until the apples are tender (about 30 minutes).

Glazed Baked Apples

A dessert or a relish to serve with pork or ham.

Core tart apples. Pare one-third of the way down. Put close together in a saucepan, peeled side up. Add water ½ inch deep. Cover and cook slowly until tender when pierced with a toothpick.

Put in a baking dish, peeled side up. Sprinkle with sugar (½ cup or more for 4 apples). Bake at 425° until the sugar dissolves and the tops are crisp and delicately brown. Baste frequently with the water in which the apples were cooked.

Brandied Apples

Serve as a relish with pork, duck, chicken or turkey, or as a hot dessert with brown or confectioners' sugar and sour cream.

Core tart apples. Cut in ½-inch slices. Sprinkle generously with brandy or rum. Cover and let stand at least 4 hours.

Drain and dip in flour. Melt butter in a skillet or a chafing dish. Add the apple slices and cook until tender and brown on both sides.

Apple Brown Betty

Mix lightly with a fork
  2 cups bread crumbs or corn flakes
  ¼ cup melted butter
Prepare
  4 cups peeled sliced tart apples
Mix
  ½ cup sugar, brown or white
  ¼ teaspoon grated nutmeg or 1 tea-
    spoon cinnamon
  Grated rind and juice of ½ lemon
Butter a baking dish. Put a layer of
crumbs in it. Spread half the apples over
the crumbs, then half the sugar mixture.
Repeat, and cover with the rest of the
crumbs. Add
  ½ cup hot water
Bake 40 minutes at 350°. Cover at first
so that the crumbs will not brown too
quickly. Serve with
  Maryland Sauce (p. 403) or cream
Serves 6.

Apricot Brown Betty. Use 2 cups stewed
and drained apricots in place of apples.
Use apricot juice in place of lemon juice
and water.

Peach Brown Betty. Use equal quantities
of sliced peaches and bread crumbs. Omit
lemon and nutmeg. Syrup from canned
peaches may be used in place of water
(omitting sugar).

Rhubarb Brown Betty. Use equal quantities of cooked rhubarb and bread
crumbs. Season to taste. Omit water.

Apple Grunt
(Cape Cod Apple Pudding)

Put in a deep saucepan
  3 cups peeled sliced tart apples
  ¾ cup sugar
  ¼ teaspoon salt
  ½ teaspoon nutmeg or cinnamon (or
    both)
Cook until the apples are tender, adding
a little water, if necessary, to keep the
apples from burning.

While the apples are cooking, prepare
  Baking Powder Biscuit dough (p. 311)
Roll out and spread over the apples.

Cover tightly. Cook 15 minutes over
moderate heat. Turn out and serve with
  Cream
Serves 6.

Apple Crisp
(Apple Candy Pie)

Butter a deep baking dish. Put in it
  4 cups peeled sliced tart apples
  ½ cup water (less for juicy apples)
Mix with a fork
  ¾ cup flour
  1 cup white or brown sugar
  1 teaspoon cinnamon
  ½ cup butter
  ¼ teaspoon salt
Spread over the apples.

Bake at 350° until the apples are tender
and the crust brown (about 30 minutes).
Serve with
  Cream or whipped cream
Serves 6 to 8.

Corn Flake Apple Crisp. Use 1 cup
crushed corn flakes in place of flour.
Melt the butter and stir it in.

Peach Crumble Pie. Slice peaches into
a shallow baking dish. Sprinkle with the
crumb mixture and bake as above.

Apple Dumplings

Peaches make delicious dumplings too.

Roll or pat Shortcake (p. 384) or Baking
Powder Biscuit (p. 311) dough ¼ inch
thick. Cut in 4-inch squares.

Pare and core small tart apples and place
on the squares. Fill with sugar mixed
with cinnamon or nutmeg. Dot with butter. Draw the corners of the dough together on top of the fruit. Pinch the
edges together. Prick with a fork.

Bake 30 minutes at 350°. Serve, warm,
with Hard Sauce (p. 402), Foamy Sauce
(p. 403) or Lemon Sauce (p. 402).

Apple Fritters

See Fruit Fritters (p. 429).

Apricots

Ripe apricots are plump and firm and golden yellow.

Serve whole, or peel and slice and serve with cream and sugar. Also delicious in fruit cups and salads. Use canned apricots the same way.

To peel. Dip in boiling water, then in cold water. Slip off the skins with your fingers.

Dried Apricots

Cook according to directions on the package. Add sugar to taste. For excellent flavor, cook a sliced lime with each pound of apricots.

Apricots in Sour Cream. Drain cooked or canned apricots. Cover with sour cream. Chill. Sprinkle with brown sugar or chopped nut meats.

Apricot Charlotte. Mash cooked apricots. Fold into whipped cream. Spoon into serving dishes and sprinkle crushed peanut brittle over the top.

Avocados (Alligator Pears)

Choose fruit that is beginning to soften. Shake — the stone will rattle slightly if the fruit is ripe. The flesh should be evenly green with no dark soft spots. Allow one half for each serving.

Cut in half, lengthwise, and remove the seed but do not pare. Unless you are filling them immediately, sprinkle with lemon juice to prevent darkening.

As a first course (p. 44). See also Guacamole (p. 53).

As the main dish for luncheon or supper. Fill with chicken or lobster salad or with seasoned cooked or canned shrimp or crab meat.

Bananas

For immediate use, select yellow fruit flecked with brown. If bananas are green, let them ripen thoroughly before using. Bananas slightly green at the ends are best for cooking. For the finest flavor, store at room temperature, not in the refrigerator.

Serve bananas whole, sliced (with orange juice or cream and sugar) or cut in half lengthwise, and sprinkled with lemon juice and sugar.

Sautéed Bananas

Serve with curry or chicken, or as dessert.

Peel, cut in half lengthwise, and again cut in half crosswise. Sprinkle with flour. Sauté in butter until delicately brown. Drain. Sprinkle with confectioners' sugar.

Bananas au Rhum. *A delicious dessert.* Sprinkle Sautéed Bananas with sugar and pour warm rum over them (¼ cup for 3 bananas). Light with a match and baste with the flaming syrup.

Baked Bananas

Serve with ham or chicken or as a dessert.

Peel. Leave whole or cut in halves or quarters. Arrange on a buttered ovenproof dish. Sprinkle with brown sugar and a few gratings of lemon peel. If you like, sprinkle with orange juice, sherry or rum. Dot with butter.

Bake at 350° (15 to 20 minutes).

Bananas Berkeley. Pour Melba Sauce (p. 404) over cooled baked bananas. For a richer dessert, garnish with whipped cream.

Banana Whip

Peel and scrape
   3 bananas
Force through a sieve. Add
   ¾ cup sugar
   ¼ cup lemon juice
Cook just to the boiling point. Chill and fold into
   ½ pint heavy cream, whipped

Spoon into dessert glasses. Sprinkle with
   Chopped salted peanuts
Serves 4.

Blackberries

Prepare blackberries like raspberries (p.
359). Serve with sugar and heavy cream.
Or use in pie (p. 411), Blackberry Rolypoly (p. 485), or other berry desserts.

Blueberries and Huckleberries

*Blueberries are bright blue with a slightly
frosted look. Huckleberries are larger,
darker, and have more seeds. Cultivated
berries are larger than wild ones but wild
ones have the finer flavor. Frozen and
canned blueberries are convenient for
pies and puddings.*

Remove bits of leaf and stem. Wash
carefully.

Serve with sugar and cream or milk. Delicious with sour cream and confectioners' sugar mixed with ginger.

Stewed Blueberries or Huckleberries.
Cook until soft with just enough water
to keep them from burning. Sweeten to
taste. Serve with cream or not.

Blueberry Muffins (p. 313).

Blueberry Pie (p. 413).

Maine Blueberry Pudding

*If you use cultivated berries, add lemon
juice to taste.*

Cook 10 minutes
   3 cups blueberries
   ¾ cup sugar
   ½ cup water
Butter
   6 slices bread
Sprinkle with
   Cinnamon
Put the bread and the berries in a loaf
pan in layers. Chill in the refrigerator
several hours. Serve with
   Heavy cream
Serves 6.

Blueberry Grunt

An old-fashioned Cape Cod recipe.

Cook until soft
   2 cups blueberries
   ½ cup water
   ⅛ teaspoon allspice
Sweeten to taste. Put in a deep baking
dish and cover with
   Baking Powder Biscuit dough (p. 311)
      or unbaked biscuits
Set the dish in a pan of boiling water.
Cover. Cook 1 hour, keeping the water
boiling constantly. Add more water as
needed to keep it within 1 inch of the
top of the dish.

Serve from the dish with
   Heavy cream
Serves 4.

Cantaloupe

See Melons (p. 354).

Cherries

*Cherries are at their best in June and
July, the sweet ones for eating fresh and
the sour ones for stewing, for pies, and
for canning and pickling. Large black
Bing cherries are fine additions to a fruit
cup.*

To serve fresh, select sweet cherries that
are ripe but not oversoft. Wash and
shake dry in a colander. Do not remove
the stems. Chill. Serve heaped in a bowl
or on a bed of grape leaves in a flat
basket.

Stewed Cherries. *Serve as a relish with
meat or as dessert.* Wash sweet or sour
cherries. Remove stems, and pit or prick
well. (To pit, use a cherry pitter or the
curved end of a paper clip.) Cook with a
small amount of boiling water until
nearly tender. Add sugar to taste and
cook 3 minutes longer.

For a richer dessert, serve with sour
cream.

Black Cherries Jubilee

For a dramatic effect, prepare in a chafing dish at the table.

Drain stewed or canned black cherries, reserving the juice. For 2 cups of cherries, mix 1 tablespoon sugar and 1 tablespoon cornstarch and add 1 cup of the juice, a little at a time. Cook gently 3 minutes, stirring constantly. Add the cherries.

Warm ½ cup brandy, pour it over the cherries, and light with a match. Spoon the juices in the pan over the cherries and serve, flaming, over vanilla ice cream or orange sherbet. *Serves 6.*

Currants

Currants are used principally for jelly and jam, but they are delicious eaten fresh, especially mixed with raspberries.

Wash. Remove the stems. Sprinkle thickly with granulated sugar.

Dates

Packaged dates are usually pitted.

Consult the index for recipes using dates. Also, cut them small and add to fruit cups and salads, or put on each salad plate a date stuffed with a nut meat or with cream cheese.

Figs

Store fresh figs in the refrigerator. Pare off the outer skin with a sharp knife. Cut in slices and serve with cream. Fully ripe figs need no sugar.

Stewed Figs

Put in a saucepan
  1 pound dried figs
  Cold water to cover
  1 tablespoon lemon juice
Cover. Simmer until the figs are tender. Take out the figs and add to the juice
  ½ cup sugar

Cook until thick. Flavor to taste with
  Sherry, vanilla or more lemon juice
Pour over the figs. Cool. Serve with cream. *Serves 6.*

Figs Gourmet. Sprinkle stewed or canned figs with Cointreau, rum or Curaçao. Serve with sour cream.

Grapes

Grapes are of many varieties, some with skins which slip off easily from the soft pulp, others the firm-fleshed ones which are usually eaten skin and all. Seedless grapes are excellent in a fruit cup or a mixed fruit salad.

In a fruit cup or salad. Peel (or not, as you like) Malaga (greenish) or Tokay (red) grapes. Cut in half and remove the seeds. Seedless white grapes (fresh or canned) are used whole without peeling or seeding.

As dessert. Wash the bunches in cold water. Drain. Discard imperfect grapes. Chill. Serve in a bowl with scissors (there are special grape scissors) so that each person may snip off his own. Grape leaves are an attractive garnish.

Grapes Gervaise. *An epicurean dessert.* Remove the stems from white seedless grapes. Pile in a bowl or in sherbet glasses. Top with Gervaise (p. 405) or sour cream with a sprinkling of brown sugar or a dash of crème de cacao.

Frosted Grapes. *Glitter for the Christmas fruit bowl.* Beat an egg white until frothy. Sprinkle it over a bunch of perfect Malaga grapes. Dust with granulated sugar. Let stand until dry.

Grape Juice Frappé

Whirl in an electric blender
  1 can frozen grape juice concentrate
  3 cans crushed ice
Serve immediately in fruit juice glasses as a first course or as party refreshment. *Serves 4.*

Orange Juice Frappé. Substitute frozen orange juice for grape juice.

Grapefruit

Select firm, smooth-skinned fruit, heavy for its size. Color is unimportant — greenish ones may be of excellent flavor.

Wipe and cut in half crosswise. With a small sharp-pointed knife (special curved ones are made for the purpose), cut the pulp away from the membrane in each section. Cut out the core with scissors or

with a grapefruit corer, or cut the membrane between the sections to remove it entirely. Sweeten or not, as desired. Serve very cold.

As a first course. You may like to add (for each portion) 1 tablespoon sherry or rum or ½ tablespoon apricot brandy or sloe gin.

Baked or Broiled Grapefruit. *Serve as first course or dessert.* Sprinkle each half with 1 tablespoon brown sugar. Dot with a bit of butter. Add, if you like, 1 tablespoon sherry or 1 teaspoon brandy. Bake at 450° or broil until the sugar melts and the surface is slightly browned.

Grapefruit or Orange Sections

Put the fruit on a cutting board. Hold it firmly with your left hand and pare off the skin with a long, very sharp knife. Cut away the white layer beneath the skin as you pare. Remove the pulp by sections, cutting it away from the membrane, first on one side of a section, then

the other. Cut off any white bits that remain, so that you have perfect sections of fruit.

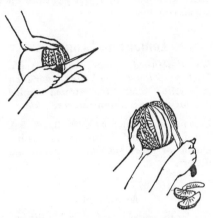

Grapefruit or Orange Coupe. Cut sections in pieces, sprinkle with sugar, and chill. Serve in sherbet glasses with a cherry or a sprig of mint on top. For a more pungent mint flavor, sprinkle with crème de menthe or put a few sprigs of mint with the fruit as it chills and remove them when the fruit is put in the glasses.

Rector Grapefruit Cup. Fill 4 sherbet glasses with grapefruit sections. Mix ½ cup powdered sugar, 2 teaspoons Curaçao, 1 teaspoon lemon juice, 1 teaspoon Kirsch and ⅛ teaspoon salt. Sprinkle over the fruit.

Grapefruit or Orange Baskets

Cut the fruit in half. Remove the pulp and scrape out the white membrane and the core. Scallop the edge with scissors or a special knife. Fill with Fruit Cup (p. 345), sherbet (p. 387) or fruit jelly (p. 378). Grapefruit halves may be used like individual casseroles, filled with creamed chicken or tuna.

Guava Shells

Spread cream cheese in preserved guava shells for a gourmet last course.

Kumquats

The whole fruit is edible, skin and all. Sliced kumquats are a pretty garnish on a fruit cup or salad.

Lemons and Limes

Smooth-skinned, heavy fruit is juicy. Dark-green limes have better flavor than pale yellow ones. Concentrated canned or frozen juice is a convenience.

Lemons and limes as garnish (p. 83). Consult the index for recipes using lemons or limes, such as lemonade and desserts.

Mangoes

Similar to cantaloupe but with a distinctive lemony flavor.

Cut in half lengthwise and eat with a spoon.

Melons

All the varieties of melon are delicious — cantaloupe and muskmelon, pale green Persian, honeydew, casaba and the rest. Ripe melons are fragrant and feel slightly soft when pressed with your thumb. To preserve the finest flavor, do not chill. See also Watermelon (p. 361).

Cut small melons in half, larger ones in sections. Discard the seeds and the stringy part. Do not chill or put ice inside as it changes the delicate flavor. Serve with salt or powdered sugar. With Persian, honeydew or casaba melons, you will like lemon or lime wedges to squeeze over the fruit. Or mix confectioners' sugar with a little ginger and put it in a shaker or a small bowl to sprinkle over the melon. Mint leaves are a pleasant garnish for melons.

Melon Suprême. Cut melons in balls with a ball cutter. Combine more than one kind of melon or use just one. Sprinkle with sugar and rum or maraschino. Serve in chilled sherbet glasses.

Raspberry-Stuffed Cantaloupe. In the hollow, heap fresh or partially thawed frozen raspberries. Sprinkle fresh berries lightly with sugar.

Cantaloupe Ring. Cut in 1-inch slices. Carefully cut off the peel. Put a slice on each plate. Fill with any fruit cup mixture, with melon balls or with vanilla ice cream.

Melon Frascati

Fruit cup with a Baked Alaska topping.

Cut small ripe cantaloupe in halves and remove the seeds. Fill with any fruit cup mixture — raspberries and nectarines or peaches are particularly delicious. Sprinkle with sugar and, if you like, a little rum, sherry or Cointreau. Cover with wax paper and chill at least 1 hour.

Cover with a 2-inch layer of Meringue (p. 411), spooned on lightly. Bake at 400° until delicately browned (about 5 minutes). Serve at once or chill until ready to serve.

Nectarines

Nectarines have a flavor similar to peaches but a smooth skin, like plums. Select unblemished fruit, ripe or nearly ripe. Green fruit will shrivel and not ripen.

Serve whole, without peeling, or peel, cut in pieces, and add to fruit cup.

Oranges

Select fruit heavy for its size and free from soft or spongy spots. Scars, scratches or greenish areas do not affect the flavor. Navel oranges have a bright color. Flor-

ida oranges are naturally a pale or greenish yellow.

Buy oranges by the pound, dozen, crate or half crate. If you buy them in quantity store them at 40° to 60°, sort over regularly, and remove any that develop soft spots. Small oranges are often an economical buy.

Wash. Serve whole or cut in half to eat with a spoon. Or peel and slice.

In addition to the following recipes using oranges, consult the index. Orange Fritters, see Fruit Fritters (p. 429).

Oranges Amandine. Sprinkle orange sections or sliced oranges with shredded toasted almonds and grated maple sugar. Serve icy cold.

Ambrosia. Mix sliced oranges or orange sections with sliced bananas. Chill and sprinkle with shredded coconut.

Orange Juice

Thin-skinned, heavy oranges are best for juice. Frozen concentrated juice is convenient as an ingredient as well as a breakfast beverage.

Cut in half or, if oranges are very small, cut a slice from the top. Squeeze out the juice. Strain or not. Serve immediately or cover tightly and store in the refrigerator. Garnish, if desired, with sprigs of fresh mint. If the juice is very sweet, add a little lemon or grapefruit juice.

Orange Mint Cup

Cut in halves
  4 large oranges
Remove the pulp with a spoon. Add
  2 tablespoons fine sugar
  2 tablespoons finely chopped mint
  1 tablespoon lemon juice
  1 tablespoon sherry
Chill. Pour off some of the juice if the oranges are very juicy.

Serve in sherbet glasses. Garnish with
  Sprigs of mint
Serves 4.

Guatemala Orange Cup

Do not make this fruit cup too sweet. It is served as a refreshing first course, not a dessert.

Cut in halves
  4 large oranges
Remove the pulp with a spoon. Add
  2 tablespoons chopped parsley
  1 tablespoon chopped chives
  1 tablespoon pimiento, cut small
Add
  Sugar and salt to taste
Spoon into sherbet glasses. Serves 4.

Baked Oranges

Wash seedless oranges, cover with boiling water, and cook until the skin is tender when pricked with a toothpick. Drain, cut in half, and remove the cores. Put in a baking dish. Fill the centers with sugar and sprinkle sugar over the top. Add 1 tablespoon brandy to each and dot with butter. Heat in the broiler until the sugar melts and browns delicately.

Serve warm with duck or turkey or, as a dessert, with cream, Zabaglione (p. 364) or Hot Orange Sauce (p. 402), flavored with brandy.

Papaya (Pawpaw)

Papaya is similar to muskmelon. Its flavor is at its best when the fruit is fully ripe (soft enough to dent with a slight pressure of your thumb).

Chill thoroughly and cut in wedges or quarters. Remove most of the seeds (the seeds are edible).

Serve with lemon or lime sections or with salt or sugar. Or use in a fruit cup with lime or lemon juice or combined with pineapple or orange sections.

Peaches

Select firm ripe peaches, free of bruises. Golden-yellow peaches are delicious and so are the juicy white ones.

Wash and dry. Serve whole or peeled and sliced. If they are hard to peel, dip in boiling water. Slice peaches just before serving, or sprinkle sparingly with lemon juice to prevent darkening.

Serve sliced peaches with cream or Gervaise (p. 405).

Peaches Riviera. Peel peaches. Leave whole and pour over them sieved strawberries or raspberries (or a mixture of both), sweetened to taste and flavored with lemon juice and Cointreau.

Peach Shortcake. See Strawberry Shortcake (p. 484).

Peach Meringue. See Apple Meringue (p. 348).

Peach Brown Betty (p. 349).

Peach Melba (p. 396).

Baked Peaches

Peel, cut in half, and remove stones. Place in a shallow baking dish, cut side up. Fill each cavity with chopped nuts, fruits or macaroon crumbs, or 1 teaspoon sugar, ½ teaspoon butter, few drops lemon juice and a slight grating of nutmeg.

Bake 20 minutes at 350°. Sprinkle a little sherry or brandy over the peaches for a particularly delicious flavor.

Serve warm with Hard Sauce (p. 402), or chilled with whipped cream or sour cream.

Peaches Flambé

Arrange canned peach halves in a shallow baking dish, cut side up. Pour a little of the syrup over the peaches. Sprinkle generously with maple syrup. Bake ½ hour at 350°. Just before serving, pour heated brandy or brandy and Kirsch over the peaches and light with a match.

Serve with Foamy Sauce (p. 403) or Floradora Sauce (p. 402), reducing the sugar to ¼ cup.

Pears

Summer pears do not keep well, so buy in small quantities. Ripen hard winter pears at room temperature. Pears are always picked green; otherwise they will be dark at the core.

Pears with Cheese. As a gourmet last course at dinner, serve perfect whole pears with Gruyère or Camembert cheese.

Pears with Chocolate Sauce

Peel, cut in quarters lengthwise, and remove the cores. Sauté in butter until browned. Canned pears drained from syrup may be used in place of fresh fruit.

Serve warm with Creamy Chocolate Sauce (p. 399).

Stewed or Baked Pears

Peel firm pears. Quarter large ones and cut out the cores, but leave small Seckel pears whole. Cook ½ cup sugar with ½ cup water 5 minutes (with a piece of lemon rind or stick cinnamon, if you like). Add the pears. Cook slowly, covered, on top of the stove or bake in a casserole at 300° until tender but still firm.

Serve warm or cold with cream or Soft Custard (p. 362).

Pears with Cointreau. Cook whole pears. Take out of the syrup. Cook the syrup until as thick as honey, add 1 tablespoon Cointreau, and pour over the pears. Chill. Flavor with vanilla in place of Cointreau if you prefer. Serve with cream.

Pears in Port Wine. *Serve as dessert.* Pour port wine over cooked pears. Cover and let stand at least 1 hour.

Pears Hélène. When the pears are tender, add vanilla or brandy to taste and cool in the syrup. Serve on vanilla ice cream with Creamy Chocolate Sauce (p. 399).

Pears Zabaglione. Serve cooked pears warm or cold with warm or chilled Zabaglione (p. 364).

Persimmons

This decorative fruit should be soft but still firm.

Chill thoroughly. Cut in half. Eat with a fork and spoon. Bits of persimmon are an attractive garnish on fruit salads.

Oriental and American Wild Varieties

Pineapple

The center spines of a ripe pineapple pull out easily. A medium-sized pineapple weighs 2 pounds and yields 2½ to 3 cups of diced fruit (4 to 6 servings). Canned pineapple is very popular.

Unless the pineapple is very ripe, sprinkle it with sugar after cutting or shredding, and let it stand in the refrigerator at least 1 hour.

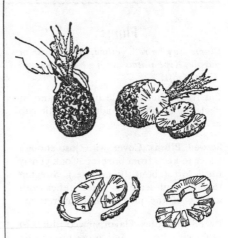

To cut pineapple. Cut out the crown with a sharp pointed knife, then cut crosswise in ¾-inch slices with a long sharp knife, cut off the rind, cut out the "eyes" and remove the core. Then cut as you like.

To shred pineapple. Hold upright, pare with a long sharp knife, dig out the "eyes," then tear out the pulp in bits with a fork.

Madeira Pineapple. Shred or cut in chunks. Sprinkle with sugar and cover with Madeira or white wine. Cover and chill at least 1 hour.

Pineapple in the Shell. Without paring, cut the pineapple in halves or quarters lengthwise, leaving on the top leaves. Cut out the core and carefully cut the flesh away from the rind in one piece. Slice or cut in wedges. Refill the shell. Sprinkle with sugar or Kirsch. Garnish, if you like, with cherries, strawberries or sprigs of mint.

Pineapple with Avocado. Prepare Pineapple in the Shell (above), slicing the pineapple and alternating it with slices of avocado when you refill the sections. Pour French dressing over the fruit. Serve as a first course or as salad and dessert in one.

Plums

Plums may be red, yellow, green, blue or purple. Ripe plums are deep-colored and slightly soft.

Eat fresh plums whole in your hand or peel, cut in bits, and add to a fruit cup or fruit salad.

Stewed Plums. Cover with just enough water to keep from burning. Cook gently until soft (about 10 minutes). Sweeten to taste and serve in sauce dishes with a little of the juice poured over them.

Brandied Plums. Flavor stewed plums to taste with brandy and serve on vanilla ice cream.

Pomegranates

Use this brilliant crimson fruit in a holiday centerpiece.

Cut in half and serve with a spoon. Use the tart-flavored seeds to accent a fruit salad.

Dried Prunes

Large prunes are more expensive than small ones, but the flavor is the same.

Stewed Prunes. Packaged prunes do not need soaking. Follow the directions on the package. Cover bulk prunes with hot water (2 cups to ½ pound), let stand 2 hours and cook slowly in the same water until plump and tender.

Refrigerator Prunes. Put prunes in a fruit jar. Add enough water to cover. Screw on the top. Store in the refrigerator 4 days or more. The prunes will be plump and delicious but with a different flavor and texture.

Prune or Apricot Whip

Rub cooked or canned fruit through a strainer, or use canned strained fruit to make
   ¾ cup prune or apricot pulp
Add
   Sugar to taste
Cook until as thick as marmalade. Add
   1 tablespoon lemon juice
   ⅛ teaspoon salt
Cool. Beat until stiff
   3 egg whites
Fold the fruit carefully into the egg whites. Spoon into a straight-sided un-buttered baking dish. Set in a pan of hot water.

Bake at 300° until firm when pressed lightly with a finger (about 45 minutes). Serve with
   Soft Custard (362), Sabayon Sauce
   (p. 401) or whipped cream
Serves 4.

To cook in a double boiler. Spoon into the top of a large double boiler and cook over hot water until firm (about 45 minutes).

Norwegian Prune Pudding

Put in a double boiler top
   1 cup prune pulp (see Prune Whip
     above)
   ½ cup prune juice
   ¾ cup sugar, brown or white
   ⅛ teaspoon salt
   ¼ teaspoon cinnamon
   1 cup boiling water
Simmer 5 minutes over low heat.

Mix until smooth
   4 tablespoons cornstarch
   ⅓ cup cold water
Add to the prune mixture and cook and

stir until thick. Set over hot water and cook 10 minutes longer. Add

2 tablespoons lemon juice (or to taste) Chill. Serve with cream. *Serves 4 to 6.*

Nut Prune Soufflé. Fold into the finished pudding 2 egg whites, beaten stiff, and ½ cup walnut meats, broken in pieces. Chill and serve as above.

Quinces

Ripe quinces are deep yellow. They are used principally for jellies and preserves.

Baked Quinces. Wipe, quarter, core, and pare. Put in a casserole, sprinkle with sugar (2 tablespoons to each quince), and add water ½ inch deep. For an interesting flavor, add 1 sliced orange (for 4 or more quinces). Bake at 300° until tender and deep red (about 2 hours). Serve cold.

Raspberries

Picked ripe, raspberries have an incomparable flavor. If you can, buy them from a grower. One pint serves 3.

Ripe raspberries are very delicate. Look them over carefully and remove all imperfect berries. Dip, a few at a time, in and out of cold water, holding them carefully in your hand or in a single layer in a coarse strainer. Drain well on a paper towel.

Serve with fine or confectioners' sugar and cream. Raspberry Shortcake (p. 484).

Rhubarb

Hothouse rhubarb is pink, with light green leaves. Rhubarb grown out of doors is darker and needs longer cooking. Select firm young stalks with fresh-looking leaves. One pound makes about 2 cups, cooked.

Stewed Rhubarb. Cut off the leaves and the stem ends. Wash. If the rhubarb is young and the skin is tender, do not peel. Cut in 1-inch pieces. Sprinkle generously with sugar and, if you like, a few gratings of orange or lemon peel. Add just enough water to prevent burning. Cover and cook gently until just barely tender (7 to 20 minutes). Taste and add more sugar if necessary.

Baked Rhubarb. Prepare 1 pound of rhubarb. Add ½ cup sugar. Put in a casserole, sprinkle with salt, cover, and bake at 325° until tender. Taste and add more sugar if needed. If more convenient, cook in a double boiler.

Rhubarb in Syrup. Prepare 1 pound of very tender rhubarb. Put ¾ cup sugar and ¾ cup water in a saucepan. Bring to the boiling point and add the rhubarb. Stir to mix well. Again bring to the boiling point. Cover and let stand until cool.

Rhubarb Compote. Add sliced strawberries or pineapple bits to cooled cooked rhubarb. Sprinkle with grated orange or lemon rind and a slight dusting of ginger.

Strawberries

Small, early strawberries often have exceptionally fine flavor, but delicious berries are available many months of the year. Tiny wild strawberries are gourmet fare imported from France. One quart serves 4 to 6.

Discard imperfect berries. Place perfect berries in a colander and pour cold water over them. Drain thoroughly and remove the hulls.

Serve with fine or confectioners' sugar and sweet or sour cream. If the berries are not very sweet, sprinkle with sugar and let stand ½ hour before serving. Large perfect berries are delicious served unhulled, ready to dip in confectioners' sugar.

Strawberries in Whipped Cream. Cut 1 quart of berries in halves and sprinkle with sugar. Whip ½ pint heavy cream until stiff, sweeten with sugar, and flavor with vanilla, brandy, Cointreau or sherry. Fold in the berries. *Serves 5 or 6.*

Strawberries in Claret. Pour ¼ cup claret over 1 quart berries. Sprinkle with sugar to taste. *Serves 4.*

Lenox Strawberries. Mix ½ cup orange juice, ½ cup sugar and 1 teaspoon Curaçao. Pour over 1 quart of berries, hulled. Serve with whipped cream.

Strawberry Shortcake (p. 484).

Glacéed Strawberries (p. 508).

Glazed Strawberries (p. 346).

Strawberry Whip

Also good made with raspberries.

Put in a bowl
  1½ cups strawberries, cut in halves
  1 cup confectioners' sugar
  1 egg white
Beat until stiff with a wire whisk or an electric beater.

Serve on pieces of sponge cake or angel food, or pile in a bowl and serve with Soft Custard (p. 362). *Serves 4.*

Strawberries Romanoff

A rich dessert but simple to prepare.

Wash, drain and hull
  2 quarts strawberries
Beat with a fork to soften slightly
  1 pint vanilla ice cream
Fold in
  ½ pint heavy cream, whipped
Stir in gently
  Juice of 1 lemon
  ¼ cup rum or Cointreau
Taste, and add if needed
  Confectioners' sugar

Fold in the berries and serve immediately. *Serves 8.*

Strawberries in Sherry Cream

A superb dessert, fit for a gala dinner.

Put in a double boiler top
  5 egg yolks
Beat with an electric or hand beater until thick and lemon-colored. Beat in
  1 cup sugar
  1 cup sherry
Cook and stir over hot water until thick. Cool.

Shortly before serving time, fold in
  ½ pint heavy cream, whipped
  3 pints strawberries, washed and
    hulled
Serves 6 to 8.

Strawberries Flambé

A handsome party dessert to prepare at the table in a chafing dish.

Wash, hull and dry
  1 quart strawberries
Put in a pan
  Peel of 1 lemon, cut in pieces
  Juice and peel of 2 oranges
  8 lumps sugar
Cook slowly 5 minutes, pressing the peel with a spoon to get all the flavor possible. Take out the peel and discard it. Add the berries.

Spoon the hot syrup gently over the berries until they are well coated. Add
  ½ cup brandy (warmed)
Light with a match. Serve over
  1½ quarts vanilla ice cream
Serves 8.

Tangerines

A variety of orange, with deep yellow skin which is easily pulled off. Mandarin oranges are similar but lighter in color.

Wipe fruit. Serve whole or pull off loose skin, separate sections, and remove all white stringlike parts.

Serve around simple desserts or cut in pieces, remove the seeds, and add to a fruit cup or fruit salad.

Watermelon

This refreshing fruit may be round or oval, large or small, according to the variety. Buy a whole melon or a section, by the pound.

Chill thoroughly. Cut in wedges or slices and serve with salt or fine sugar.

Watermelon Cocktail. Cut the ripe deep pink part in ¾-inch cubes or balls. Sprinkle with lemon juice and sugar. Cover and chill several hours in the refrigerator. Serve in sherbet glasses.

Watermelon Cocktail with Sherry Dressing. In place of lemon juice and sugar, mix ½ cup sugar, ½ cup sherry, 2 tablespoons sloe gin (if desired) and a few grains of salt. Let stand until the sugar is dissolved. *Serves 6.*

Custards and Other Puddings

A basic custard is made of eggs, milk, sugar and flavoring, cooked over low heat (soft custard) or in the oven. Slow, careful cooking is essential for smooth, velvety perfection. In addition to the variations which follow, there are many puddings of a similar type — Zabaglione, Rice Custard, Tapioca Cream, Bread Puddings, and so on. See also Custard Pie (p. 420).

Soft Custard

A classic with many names — "crème anglaise," "English cream," "boiled custard," to list a few. Satin-smooth, it is the basis for a whole group of beguiling desserts. A jar of custard in the refrigerator is a joy if you need to concoct a dessert in a hurry. Pour it over fresh, cooked or canned fruit (especially good over pears) or over squares of cake, or make Floating Island (below).

Beat enough to blend evenly
  3 eggs or 6 yolks
Add
  ¼ cup white or brown sugar
  ⅛ teaspoon salt
  2 cups scalded milk
Cook and stir over very low heat or in a double boiler over hot, but not boiling, water until the custard coats a spoon dipped into it (about 7 minutes). Chill. Flavor with
  Vanilla, sherry or brandy to taste

If the custard curdles (because the water boiled or the custard was overcooked), beat with an egg beater. It will be thinner than it should be, but smooth. It can be used as a sauce.

Custard Sauce. *Thinner than Soft Custard.* Use only 3 egg yolks or 1 egg and 1 egg yolk.

Coconut Custard. Pour the cooked custard into a baking dish. Beat 3 egg whites until stiff, fold in ½ cup sugar and ¾ cup shredded coconut and spread over the custard. Brown delicately in a 450° oven (about 5 minutes).

Floating Island. Top chilled custard with whipped cream or spoonfuls of Meringue (p. 411) poached in hot milk. Decorate with shaved sweet chocolate, bits of bright jelly, slivered toasted almonds or a dribble of Caramel (p. 14).

Chocolate Floating Island. Beat 1 egg white until stiff, beat in 2 tablespoons confectioners' sugar and Dutch cocoa to taste. Add a few drops vanilla. Put spoonfuls on chilled custard.

Chocolate Pots de Crème. Scald the milk with 2 ounces unsweetened chocolate. Pour the finished custard into small pottery bowls. Let stand until firm. When ready to serve, pour a thin layer of heavy cream over the top.

Tipsy Pudding

Put in a bowl
  ½ cup sherry or rum
Dip in it
  ¼ pound lady fingers or cubes of dry unfrosted cake
Put in a serving bowl. Cover with
  Soft Custard (above)
Chill. Garnish with
  Whipped cream, macaroon crumbs or chopped nut meats
Serves 4 to 6.

English Trifle. Spread over the lady fingers 1 cup sliced fruit such as fresh or canned peaches, pears, bananas or orange sections. For a particularly delicious trifle, spread canned Nesselrode sauce over the lady fingers. You will need only about ½ cup since the sauce is rich with marrons and brandied fruits.

Baked Custard

For a delicious variation, use brown or maple sugar.

Beat just enough to blend evenly
  3 eggs or 6 egg yolks
Stir in
  ½ cup sugar
  ¼ teaspoon salt
Add slowly, beating with a fork
  3 cups scalded milk
  1 teaspoon vanilla
Pour into buttered custard cups. Sprinkle with
  Nutmeg
Set in a shallow pan on a paper towel. Pour into the pan hot water about 1 inch deep.

Bake at 325° about 1 hour or at 350° about 45 minutes. Test by inserting a silver knife into the custard near the edge: if it comes out clean, the custard will be firm when it cools. Serve in the baking cups or turn out, upside down. *Makes 6 small custards.*

To make custard in one large dish, use 4 eggs so that it will be firm enough to turn out onto a serving dish without cracking.

Caramel Custard. Instead of adding sugar to the eggs, melt ¾ cup sugar in a small heavy pan over low heat and stir slowly into the scalded milk before blending with the eggs. Serve with Caramel Sauce (p. 398) or plain cream.

Crème Renversée. *The usual European version of caramel custard.* Caramelize (p. 14) 1 cup sugar and pour it into the cups or large dish, turning the dishes to coat them as well as possible. Add the custard mixture and bake as above. Cool and turn out onto serving dishes; the caramel will provide the sauce.

Coconut Custard. Add ½ cup shredded coconut. Omit the nutmeg.

Coffee Custard. Add instant coffee and vanilla or rum to taste. Omit the nutmeg.

Queen Anne Custard. Use 1 egg and 4 yolks. Bake in an ovenproof dish which can go to the table. Do not unmold. Spread the finished custard with tart jelly or sprinkle with 3 tablespoons Curaçao. Chill. Cover with Meringue (p. 411) made of 4 egg whites and ¼ cup sugar. Sprinkle with grated orange peel. Bake 5 minutes at 425°. *Serves 6.*

Macaroon Custard. Add about ½ cup dry macaroon crumbs to the ingredients.

Crème Brûlée

Heavy cream is used in the classic recipe, but half evaporated milk is successful and not as rich.

Scald in a double boiler
  1 pint heavy cream
Beat until smooth
  4 eggs or 8 yolks
  ¼ cup brown sugar
  ¼ teaspoon salt
Stir in the cream slowly. Put back in the double boiler and cook about 7 minutes or until the custard begins to thicken, beating constantly with an electric or hand rotary beater.

Pour into a shallow, heatproof dish, large enough so that the custard is not more than 2 inches deep. Cool, then chill in the refrigerator until the top is very firm — several hours or overnight.

To glaze. Sift evenly over the top
  Light brown sugar (¼ to ½ cup)
Set under the broiler in a cold oven. Turn on the heat and brown, moving the dish to make an even glaze. Watch carefully so that the sugar will not burn. Set in the refrigerator and chill at least 4 hours so that the glaze will be firm and crackly. *Serves 6.*

To glaze with a salamander. A French salamander is a long-handled glazing utensil with which the top can be browned without putting the dish in the broiler, so that you can use a fine china or glass bowl without danger of breaking it. Heat the salamander thoroughly over moderate heat (about 30 minutes). Starting along the edge of the bowl, move the salamander around just above the surface until the sugar browns and melts into a thin even glaze. Reheat the salamander as necessary.

Baked Crème Brûlée. After adding the cream, pour into a shallow, heatproof dish and bake like custard (p. 363). Glaze.

Puerto Rico Coconut Cream

Its Puerto Rican name, "bien me sabe," means "It tastes good to me."

Drain the milk from
   1 coconut
Set it aside. Grate the meat (p. 13). Heat the coconut meat and milk in a double boiler ½ hour. Squeeze through a piece of linen and discard the coconut meat. You should have about 1 cupful of the milk.

Beat until thick
   4 egg yolks
Beat in the coconut cream.

Put in a small pan
   ¾ cup sugar
   ¼ cup water
Boil 5 minutes and add slowly to the coconut mixture. Cook over hot water until thickened, stirring with a wooden spoon. Flavor with
   Vanilla or rum, to taste
Cool and serve over
   Sponge cake squares
Serves 6 to 8.

Zabaglione

Marsala is traditional for this famous Italian dessert, but you may use port, Tokay or sherry. Zabaglione is also delicious as a sauce over fruit (especially
drained canned or stewed pears), squares of cake, or coffee ice cream.

Beat until thick and lemon-colored
   4 egg yolks
   2 tablespoons fine sugar
Put in a heavy round-bottomed bowl. Set over hot (not boiling) water. Beat constantly with electric or rotary hand beater, adding little by little
   2 tablespoons Marsala
Beat until the mixture begins to hold its shape but is still smooth. Pile immediately into heated thick cups or sherbet glasses. (If a crust has formed from overcooking, do not scrape the bowl.)

Serve warm or very cold with simple wafers. *Serves 2 or 3.*

Coffee Rum Zabaglione. In place of wine, use ¼ cup strong cold coffee and 2 teaspoons rum.

Zabaglione Frappé (p. 392).

Blanc Mange

Old-fashioned cornstarch pudding, a favorite in many households, especially in one of the many variations.

Scald in a double boiler
   2 cups milk
Mix
   3 tablespoons cornstarch
   ⅓ cup sugar
   ¼ teaspoon salt
Stir in
   ¼ cup cold milk
Add to the scalded milk. Cook 15 minutes over hot water, stirring constantly until the pudding thickens, afterwards occasionally. Cool slightly and add
   1 teaspoon vanilla
Chill. *Serves 4.*

To vary. Add ½ cup shredded or grated coconut to the scalded milk, or add ¾ cup broken nut meats or crushed pineapple to the finished pudding.

For a more delicate pudding, beat 2 egg whites until stiff and fold them into the finished pudding.

Butterscotch Pudding. Omit the white sugar. Melt 1 tablespoon butter, add 1 cup brown sugar, cook and stir until the sugar melts. Add slowly to the hot scalded milk and stir until well blended. Mix the cornstarch and salt with the cold milk and continue as above.

Chocolate Pudding. Scald the milk with 2 ounces unsweetened chocolate. Beat until smooth and continue as above. Serve with cream, plain or whipped, or fold ½ cup heavy cream, whipped, into the finished pudding.

French Chocolate Mousse

The classic French pots de crème. See also Chocolate Pots de Crème (p. 362).

Put in a pan
  1 package (6 ounces) semisweet
    chocolate
  2 tablespoons water
Stir over hot water until melted. Cool slightly.

Separate
  4 eggs
Beat the whites until stiff and set aside. Beat the yolks until thick and lemon-colored. Beat in the chocolate and
  1 teaspoon (or more, to taste)
    vanilla, rum or brandy
Fold in the whites. Spoon into pot de crème cups, custard cups, or sherry or cocktail glasses. Chill (12 hours or more, if convenient). Top with chopped nuts, if you like, though this is contrary to the French way. *Serves 4 to 6.*

For an even richer version, add ¼ cup fine sugar to the melted chocolate, then ¼ pound unsalted butter, bit by bit. Use 6 eggs. *Serves 6 to 8.*

Chocolate Cream Squares

This rich dessert freezes successfully, so that you can make it days ahead of a party.

Melt in a double boiler
  1 package German sweet chocolate

  3 tablespoons cold water
Stir well and cool.

Mix
  2 cups vanilla wafer crumbs
  1 cup finely chopped nut meats
  ½ cup melted butter
Pat about half the crumb mixture over the bottom of a pan about 7 by 11 inches. Whip
  1 cup heavy cream
Add
  4 tablespoons confectioners' sugar
  1 teaspoon vanilla
Fold in the chocolate mixture. Spread over the crumbs. Pat the rest of the crumbs lightly into the cream. Chill several hours. Cut in squares. *Serves 8.*

Denver Chocolate Pudding

Sometimes called Fudge Pudding, this is pudding and sauce in one. Do not over-cook it. Serve it the day it is made, while the cakelike top is still somewhat moist. For a richer pudding, add ½ cup chopped nuts.

Sift together
  ¾ cup sugar
  1 cup flour
  2 teaspoons baking powder
  ⅛ teaspoon salt
Melt together over hot water
  2 tablespoons butter
  1 ounce unsweetened chocolate or
    3 tablespoons cocoa
Add to the flour mixture. Stir in
  ½ cup milk
  ½ teaspoon vanilla
Pour into a buttered baking dish about 9 by 9 inches. Over the top scatter, with-out mixing
  ½ cup brown sugar
  ½ cup white sugar
  4 tablespoons cocoa
Pour over the top
  1½ cups cold water or coffee
Bake 40 minutes at 350°. Let stand at room temperature and serve cool but not chilled. Serve plain or with
  Whipped cream or ice cream
Serves 6.

Indian Pudding

The classic New England Indian Pudding should be soft and should separate ("whey") somewhat. For the finest flavor use the best dark molasses.

Scald in a double boiler
    2 cups milk
Mix until smooth
    ¼ cup yellow corn meal
    ¼ cup cold milk
Stir into the hot milk. Cook over hot water 20 minutes, stirring frequently. Add
    ½ cup dark molasses (unsulphured)
    1 teaspoon salt
    ¼ cup sugar
    1 teaspoon cinnamon or ginger
    ¼ cup butter
    ½ cup raisins, if desired
Stir and pour into a buttered pudding dish. Pour over the top
    1¾ cups cold milk
Bake 3 hours at 250°. Let stand ½ hour. Serve with heavy cream or vanilla ice cream. *Serves 4 to 6.*

Club Indian Pudding

Similar to traditional Indian Pudding, but firmer and baked in a shorter time.

Scald in a double boiler
    1 quart milk
Stir in slowly
    5 tablespoons corn meal
Cook over hot water 20 minutes. Add
    2 tablespoons butter
    1 cup molasses
    1 teaspoon salt
    1 teaspoon cinnamon
    2 eggs, well beaten
Spoon into a buttered baking dish. Pour over it
    1 cup cold milk
Bake 1 hour at 350°. *Serves 6 to 8.*

To vary the seasoning, use ¾ teaspoon cinnamon and ¼ teaspoon ginger or nutmeg.

Apple Indian Pudding. Put 1 cup thinly sliced peeled apples into the baking dish before spooning in the pudding.

Hasty Pudding

Serve Corn Meal Mush (p. 292) with butter and finely shaved maple sugar.

Carrot Pudding

Mix
    ½ cup shortening
    ½ cup brown sugar
    1 egg, slightly beaten
    1 cup grated raw carrots
    2 teaspoons chopped candied lemon peel
    ½ cup seedless raisins
    1 cup currants
Sift together
    1¼ cups flour (preferably pastry)
    1 teaspoon baking powder
    ½ teaspoon salt
    ½ teaspoon nutmeg
    ½ teaspoon cinnamon
    ½ teaspoon baking soda
Stir into the first mixture. Put in a buttered casserole or 6 to 8 individual molds.

Bake, uncovered, at 350° until firm (1 to 1¼ hours in a casserole or about 45 minutes in small molds). Serve with
    Creamy Hard Sauce (p. 403)
Serves 6 to 8.

Honeycomb Pudding

For a richer pudding, add nut meats, raisins or dates.

Set the oven at 350°. Butter a 2-quart baking dish.

Mix
    1 cup sugar
    1 cup flour
    ½ teaspoon baking soda
Add
    1 cup molasses
    ½ cup butter, melted in 1 cup lukewarm milk
Beat thoroughly. Stir in
    4 eggs, well beaten
Pour into the baking dish. Bake until firm (about 45 minutes). Serve with
    Thin Lemon Sauce (p. 401) or

Floradora Sauce (p. 402) or
whipped cream
Serves 6.

Baked Lemon Pudding

*The top is cakelike. The soft lemon
custard beneath provides the sauce. For
a richer dessert, spread the chilled pudding with a thin layer of unsweetened
whipped cream.*

Set the oven at 350°. Butter a 2-quart
baking dish.

Sift together
1 cup sugar
½ cup flour
½ teaspoon baking powder
¼ teaspoon salt
Separate
3 eggs
Beat the whites until stiff. Beat in, a
spoonful at a time
½ cup sugar
Set aside. Without washing the beater,
beat the yolks until light. Add
2 teaspoons grated lemon rind
¼ cup lemon juice
2 tablespoons melted butter
1½ cups milk
Stir into the flour mixture. Beat until
smooth. Add the beaten whites and
fold gently until no white flecks show.
Pour into the baking dish. Set in a pan
of hot water ½ inch deep. Bake 45
minutes. Chill at least 1 hour. *Serves 6.*

Lemon Sponge

Also attractive in a baked pie shell.

Separate
4 eggs
Beat the whites until stiff with
¼ cup water
Set aside. Without washing the beater,
beat the yolks until thick with
½ cup sugar
⅛ teaspoon salt
Add
Grated rind and juice of 2 lemons
Stir and cook over hot water until thick.

Fold in the whites. Pour into a buttered
baking dish.

Brown lightly in a 375° oven. *Serves 4
to 6.*

Bread Pudding

*So many combinations make an excel-
lent bread pudding that a recipe is only
a general guide. If you prefer a sweeter
pudding, add more sugar. Season dis-
creetly with any spice. To make a firmer
pudding, use less milk, even as little as
2 cups. To make a fluffier pudding, separate the eggs and add the whites last,
beaten stiff.*

Butter a baking dish. Put in it
2 cups dry bread crumbs
¼ cup butter
1 quart hot milk
Cool. Set the oven at 325°.

Add to the crumbs and milk
½ cup sugar
2 eggs, slightly beaten
½ teaspoon salt
1 teaspoon vanilla
Stir to blend.

Bake 1 hour. Serve with plain or whipped
cream, Melba Sauce (p. 404), Yellow
Sauce (p. 401) or Hard Sauce (p. 402).
Serves 6.

Butterscotch Bread Pudding. In place of
white sugar, use 1 cup brown sugar.
Cook the sugar with the butter until it
melts to a syrup. Add to the crumbs.

Coconut Bread Pudding. Use 1½ cups
bread crumbs and ½ cup shredded or
grated coconut.

Coffee Bread Pudding. Mix 2 teaspoons
instant coffee with the sugar.

Rich Bread Pudding. Add 1 cup orange
marmalade, chopped raisins, dates or
figs, or add ½ cup chopped nut meats.
Zabaglione (p. 364) is a delicious topping
for a pudding made with nuts and raisins.

Meringue Bread Pudding

Make Bread Pudding (above), using 4 egg yolks instead of 2 whole eggs. Spread the baked pudding with a thin layer of jam or jelly and top with Meringue (p. 411) made of the 4 egg whites.

Bake at 425° until delicately brown (about 5 minutes).

Lemon Meringue Bread Pudding. Add grated rind of 1 lemon to the pudding mixture. Pour over the hot baked pudding the juice of 1½ lemons mixed with ½ cup sugar. Top with meringue as above.

Bread and Butter Pudding

To vary this good old-fashioned pudding, sprinkle between the layers ¾ cup raisins or ½ cup shredded coconut.

Put in a buttered baking dish, buttered side down
    4 slices buttered bread
Mix
    2 eggs, slightly beaten
    ⅓ cup sugar
    ¼ teaspoon salt
    3 cups milk
Pour over the bread. Let stand 30 minutes.

Bake 1 hour at 325°, with the dish covered during the first half hour of baking. The top of the pudding should be well browned. Serve warm with Hard Sauce (p. 402) or Creamy Hard Sauce (p. 403). *Serves 4 to 6.*

Bread and Butter Apple Pudding. Put a layer of applesauce in a shallow baking dish. Remove the crusts from sliced dry bread. Butter the bread, cut in triangles, and put over the applesauce, close together. Sprinkle generously with sugar and a few drops of vanilla or a shake or two of cinnamon. Bake at 350° about 30 minutes or until the top is brown. Serve with cream, plain or whipped.

Lemon Bread Pudding

Remove the crusts from
    8 slices firm bread
Spread with Lemon Cream (below) and put in a buttered baking dish.

Mix
    2 eggs, slightly beaten
    1 cup milk
    3 tablespoons sugar
    ⅛ teaspoon salt
    Grated rind 1 lemon
Pour over the bread. Cover. Set in a pan of hot water.

Bake 1 hour at 350°. *Serves 6.*

Lemon Cream. Put in a saucepan 3 tablespoons lemon juice, grated rind of 1 lemon and ¼ cup butter. Cook 2 minutes. Add 1 cup sugar and 3 eggs, slightly beaten. Cook and stir over low heat until thick. Cool.

Chocolate Bread Pudding

Put in a double boiler top
    1½ cups milk
    1 cup sugar
    1 cup soft stale bread crumbs
    1½ ounces unsweetened chocolate
Cook over hot water until smooth. Stir in
    2 tablespoons butter
Beat until light
    2 eggs
Add
    ¼ teaspoon salt
    ½ teaspoon vanilla
    ½ cup milk
Stir into the chocolate mixture and cook until thick. Pour into a serving dish. (For a firmer pudding, pour into a buttered baking dish and bake 20 minutes at 350°.) Chill. Serve with
    Whipped cream
Serves 4 to 6.

Chocolate Nut Bread Pudding. Before spooning into the dish, stir in ½ cup chopped walnut meats.

Rice Desserts

Some of the best rice desserts do not even need a recipe! Cold or freshly cooked and hot, rice is delicious served with Chocolate (p. 399) or Butterscotch Sauce (p. 398) or with cream and brown sugar, grated maple sugar, or confectioners' sugar mixed with a little cinnamon. Successful, too, is rice mixed with well-drained crushed pineapple and then folded into whipped cream. Short-grained rice is best for puddings.

Rice Cream

Heat in a double boiler
   2 cups milk
Add
   3 tablespoons uncooked rice
Cook until the rice is tender (about 30 minutes).

Mix
   1 envelope gelatine (1 tablespoon)
   1 tablespoon sugar
   ¼ teaspoon salt
Add to the rice. Mix thoroughly. Cool.

Fold in
   ½ pint heavy cream, whipped
   1 teaspoon vanilla
Mold (p. 12) or spoon into dessert dishes. Serve with any sauce suitable for ice cream, or pour maple syrup over the pudding and sprinkle with chopped nuts. *Serves 6.*

Pineapple Rice. Before molding, fold in 1 cup well-drained crushed pineapple.

Lemon Cream Rice

For a richer pudding, stir 1 tablespoon butter into the rice mixture and use 4 eggs instead of 2.

Put in a double boiler top
   3 cups milk
   ½ cup rice
Cook over hot water until the rice is soft (about 30 minutes). Add

   ½ cup sugar
   Grated rind of ½ lemon
   1½ tablespoons lemon juice
   ¾ teaspoon salt
   2 egg yolks, slightly beaten
Cook until thickened, stirring gently. Spoon into a buttered baking dish. Cool.

Beat until in soft peaks
   2 egg whites
Beat in
   2 tablespoons confectioners' sugar
   ½ teaspoon lemon juice
Spoon over the pudding.

Bake at 425° long enough to brown the meringue (about 5 minutes). *Serves 6.*

Rice Custard

Add ½ cup raisins, if you like.

Heat in a double boiler
   2 cups milk
   1 cup cooked rice (not quick-cooking)
Beat until smooth
   2 egg yolks
   ½ cup sugar
   ¼ teaspoon salt
Add the milk and rice slowly. Pour back into the double boiler and cook until thick. Fold in
   2 egg whites, beaten stiff
Add
   ½ teaspoon vanilla or lemon juice to taste
Serve warm or cold. *Serves 4 to 6.*

Rice Meringue. Set the oven at 425°. Without adding the egg whites, pour the cooked pudding into a baking dish. Beat the whites with 2 tablespoons fine sugar and ½ teaspoon lemon juice and spoon over the top. Bake until delicately brown (about 5 minutes). Serve from the baking dish. Meringue is at its best if served within an hour of baking. The pudding can be prepared ahead of time and the meringue added later.

Old-Fashioned Rice Pudding

Very soft and creamy. For a firm pudding, use ½ cup of rice. Brown rice gives a delicious flavor. For a richer pudding, stir in 1 or 2 well-beaten eggs 30 minutes before the pudding is done.

Put in a casserole
    4 cups milk
    ⅔ cup sugar
    ¼ cup uncooked rice (not quick-cooking)
    ½ teaspoon salt
    1 teaspoon vanilla or a dash of nutmeg or the grated rind of ½ lemon
Bake, uncovered, 3 hours at 300°. During the first hour, stir three times with a fork so that the rice will not settle. After the first hour, stir in
    ½ cup raisins, dates or figs, cut small
Serves 6.

Poor Man's Pudding. In place of sugar, use ⅓ cup molasses. Flavor with ½ teaspoon cinnamon. At the last stirring, add 1 tablespoon butter.

Tapioca Cream

Tapioca stiffens as it cools; it should be soft when you finish cooking it.

Break into a saucepan
    1 egg
Beat with a fork, just enough to blend the yolk and white. Add
    2 tablespoons tapioca (quick-cooking)
    ¼ cup white or brown sugar
    ¼ teaspoon salt
    2 cups milk
Cook and stir over moderate heat until the pudding boils. Let stand 15 minutes. Stir in
    ½ teaspoon vanilla
As a garnish, top each serving with
    Whipped cream or a dab of jelly
Serves 4.

For a fluffier pudding, separate the egg. Cook the yolk with the pudding. Beat the white until stiff, beat in 1 tablespoon sugar. Fold into the finished pudding.

Baked Tapioca. Add 1 tablespoon butter. Instead of cooking over direct heat, pour into a buttered baking dish and bake 45 minutes at 325°.

Chocolate Tapioca. Add ¼ cup cocoa and 1 tablespoon butter.

Coconut Tapioca. Add ¼ cup shredded coconut.

Coffee Tapioca. Add 2 teaspoons instant coffee.

Apple Tapioca

Set the oven at 350°.

Put in a baking dish
    3 cups sliced tart apples (peeled)
Mix
    ½ cup white or brown sugar
    ½ teaspoon cinnamon
Sprinkle over the apples. Bake 15 minutes.

Meanwhile, put in a saucepan
    2 cups boiling water
    ⅓ cup quick-cooking tapioca
    ⅛ teaspoon salt
    ¼ cup sugar
Cook and stir over moderate heat until the tapioca is transparent (5 to 10 minutes). Pour over the apples. Continue baking until the apples are tender. Serve warm or cold with
    Heavy cream, whipped or not
Serves 4 to 6.

Peach Tapioca. Drain canned peaches, reserving the juice. Slice the peaches into a baking dish. Sprinkle with fine sugar (¼ cup for 2 cups fruit). Let stand 1 hour. Heat the peach juice and enough water to make 2 cups, add the tapioca, and cook as above. Pour over the peaches and bake ½ hour at 350°.

Butterscotch Tapioca

Melt in a small heavy pan
    1 tablespoon butter
Add
    1 cup brown sugar

Cook and stir over low heat until the sugar melts.

Break into a saucepan
   1 egg
Beat with a fork just enough to blend the yolk and white. Add
   2 tablespoons quick tapioca
   2 cups milk
   ¼ teaspoon salt
Cook and stir over moderate heat until the pudding boils. Add the melted sugar slowly and stir until it dissolves evenly. Cool slightly and add
   1 teaspoon vanilla
Serves 4.

Peanut Butterscotch Tapioca. Omit the salt. Stir into the finished pudding ½ cup chopped, salted peanuts.

Date Butterscotch Tapioca. Stir into the finished pudding ½ cup chopped dates.

Newton Tapioca

A form of Indian pudding.

Put in a bowl
   ¼ cup corn meal
Scald in a double boiler
   1 quart milk
Pour it over the corn meal. Add
   ½ cup quick tapioca
   ¾ cup molasses
   3 tablespoons butter
   1½ teaspoons salt
Pour back into the double boiler and cook 20 minutes. Pour into a buttered baking dish. Without stirring it in, pour over the pudding
   1 cup cold milk
Bake 1¼ hours. Start the oven at 450°. When the pudding begins to separate like Indian pudding, reduce the heat to 350°. *Serves 6 to 8.*

Soufflés

Making a soufflé is actually an extremely simple process, in spite of all the warnings so often issued. If you can make a smooth cream sauce, you can easily produce a perfect soufflé. Most of the preparation can be done far ahead of time — all but folding in the beaten egg whites and the flavoring.

To bake. French soufflé dishes are ideal — straight-sided, fluted pottery ones, usually white. The soufflé must cling to the sides of the baking dish as it rises, so either do not butter the dish or butter it well, sprinkle thickly with sugar, then turn upside down to shake out the excess sugar.

Fill the dish two-thirds full, or, for a truly impressive effect, use a smaller dish and clip firmly around it a collar of well-buttered heavy wax paper within which the soufflé can rise. The collar should come 2 or 3 inches above the rim of the dish. Remove the collar before serving.

Another idea is to make a deep cut all around the soufflé mixture an inch from the edge; the center will rise higher as the soufflé bakes.

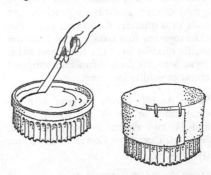

To make an even, fairly firm soufflé, bake 30 to 40 minutes at 325°.

To make a soufflé with a crusty top and a center soft enough to serve as a sauce, bake 20 minutes at 375°. This is the classic French method.

Dessert Soufflé

Serve a soufflé the moment it is baked. A soufflé sturdy enough to stand without falling is not delicate enough to be perfect.

Beat until thick and lemon-colored
    4 egg yolks
    ¼ cup sugar
Melt
    3 tablespoons butter
Stir in
    3 tablespoons flour
    ¼ teaspoon salt
Add gradually, stirring constantly
    1 cup milk
Bring to the boiling point and pour over the egg yolks. Stir well. Cool.

When it is time to bake the soufflé, set the oven at 325° or 375° (see above).

Beat until stiff
    4 egg whites (or 5 for a fluffier soufflé)
Beat in, a tablespoon at a time
    ¼ cup sugar
Stir a tablespoon of the beaten whites into the cooled mixture. Carefully fold in the rest. Add
    1 teaspoon vanilla or ¼ cup sherry
      and 1 tablespoon brandy
Bake (above). *Serves 6.*

Apricot or Peach Soufflé. Drain (reserve syrup) canned apricots or peaches. Cut fruit into quarters to make 2 cups. Put close together in a baking dish. Pour the soufflé mixture over the fruit, and bake. Serve with the fruit syrup and whipped cream or vanilla ice cream.

Coffee Soufflé. Flavor to taste with instant coffee or use ¾ cup strong coffee and ¼ cup cream in place of milk. Serve with cream or Coffee Cream Sauce (p. 400).

Hazelnut Soufflé. Chop 1 cup toasted hazelnuts. Pour the milk over them and heat to just below the boiling point.

Orange Soufflé. Before adding the egg whites, stir in ½ cup tart orange marmalade and 2 teaspoons grated orange rind.

Soufflé Grand Marnier. Soak 6 lady fingers or 2-inch squares of dry sponge cake in Grand Marnier or Cointreau 1 hour and arrange in a baking dish. Pour the soufflé mixture over the cake and bake.

Chocolate Soufflé

Melt over hot water
    1½ ounces unsweetened chocolate
Add
    2 tablespoons sugar
    2 tablespoons hot water
Stir until smooth. Melt
    2 tablespoons butter
Stir in
    2 tablespoons flour
    ¼ teaspoon salt
Blend well. Add gradually
    ¾ cup milk
Stir and cook to the boiling point. Add to the chocolate mixture. Pour over
    3 egg yolks, beaten until thick
Beat well and set aside to cool.

When it is time to bake the soufflé, set the oven (p. 371).

Beat until stiff
    3 egg whites
Beat in, a spoonful at a time
    3 tablespoons sugar
Add
    ½ teaspoon vanilla or ¼ cup brandy
      (or both)
Fold into the soufflé mixture. Bake. Serve with
    Cream, plain or whipped
Serves 4 or 5.

Fruit Soufflé

Rub peaches, apricots or quinces (if you use canned fruit, drain off the syrup) through a sieve to make
    ¾ cup fruit pulp
Heat. Add
    1 tablespoon lemon juice
    Few grains salt
    Sugar to taste
Add, hot, to
    3 egg whites, beaten stiff
Continue beating until evenly blended.

Butter 4 or 5 individual molds. Sprinkle sugar over the butter to coat the molds well. Fill three-quarters full with the soufflé mixture.

Bake at 325° until firm (20 to 25 minutes). Serve with

Sabayon Sauce (p. 401)

Serves 4 or 5.

Lemon Soufflé

Set the oven at 325°.

Separate

4 eggs

Beat the whites until stiff. Add by tablespoonfuls

⅓ cup sugar

Without washing the beater, beat the yolks until thick and lemon-colored. Beat in

⅓ cup sugar

Add

Grated rind and juice of 1 lemon

Fold in the whites. Pour into an unbuttered baking dish.

Bake 40 minutes. Serve warm. *Serves 4.*

Marmalade Soufflé

For an extra touch, sprinkle each serving with coarsely chopped toasted almonds.

Beat until stiff but not dry

3 egg whites

Beat in gradually

3 tablespoons sugar

Fold in

3 tablespoons orange marmalade
¼ teaspoon orange extract
Grated rind of 1 orange

Spoon into a buttered double boiler top. Cook 1 hour over boiling water. Serve with

Zabaglione (p. 364) or Floradora Sauce (p. 402), made with 3 egg yolks

Serves 4 or 5.

Soufflé au Rhum

Soufflé au Rhum should be very soft inside. For a gala touch, pour warmed rum around the soufflé on the serving dish and light it with a match just before serving.

Beat until stiff

4 egg whites

Beat in gradually

2 tablespoons confectioners' sugar

Without washing the beater, beat until thick and lemon-colored

2 egg yolks
2 tablespoons confectioners' sugar
Few grains salt
1 tablespoon rum

Fold in the whites.

Heat a 6-inch omelet pan. Butter it and pour in half the mixture. Brown on one side, turn with a spatula, brown on the other side, fold, and turn out onto a heated serving dish. Sprinkle wtih

Confectioners' sugar

Cook the rest the same way. *Serves 4.*

Steamed Puddings

Steamed puddings are especially appropriate for winter desserts. Fruit puddings made with suet are hearty and have a rich and distinctive flavor. When you buy beef, ask your butcher to give you the suet, or buy a piece especially for the pudding. Some steamed puddings are light and delicate, such as Chocolate Pudding, Orange Puff and Snow Balls.

To fill the molds. Butter pudding molds, large or individual size, or use any small tins or custard cups. Fill not more than two-thirds full to allow for expansion. Put on covers or cover tightly with aluminum foil.

To steam. Place a rack in a deep kettle. Set the filled molds on the rack. Add boiling water until it comes halfway up around the molds. Cover tightly. Adjust the heat to keep the water boiling throughout the steaming, adding more as it boils away. Steam the length of time required by the recipe. **Pressure-cooker steaming** is quick and satisfactory. Pressure cookers vary slightly, so follow the directions which come with the cooker.

To unmold. Set the molds in cold water for a few seconds. Uncover and turn out. If you like fruit puddings less moist, set in the oven for a few minutes to dry out.

To serve. Cut large puddings with a very sharp knife. Serve with the sauce suggested with the recipe, but see also the many other sauces (pp. 398–405).

Black Pudding

A simple, old-fashioned dessert.

Sift together
  2 cups flour
  ½ teaspoon salt
  ½ teaspoon baking soda
Add
  1 egg, slightly beaten
  1 cup molasses
  1 cup boiling water
Stir to blend evenly.

Steam 1 hour (above). Serve with
  Floradora Sauce (p. 402)
Serves 6.

Orange Puff

Melt
  3 tablespoons butter
Stir in
  ¼ cup flour
Blend well. Add gradually
  1 cup milk
Bring to the boiling point, stirring constantly, and remove from the heat.

Separate
  4 eggs
Beat the whites until stiff. Beat in
  ¼ cup sugar

Set aside. Without washing the beater, beat the yolks until thick with
  ¼ cup sugar
  1 tablespoon orange juice or frozen orange concentrate
  1 teaspoon grated orange rind
Add to the hot mixture. Fold in the whites.

Steam (above) 35 minutes. Serve with
  Orange Sauce (p. 404), or Creamy Hard Sauce (p. 403) flavored with orange juice and grated rind
Serves 6.

Snow Balls

Cream together
  ¼ cup butter
  ½ cup sugar
Add
  2 egg whites, beaten stiff
  ¼ cup milk
Sift together
  1 cup flour
  1 teaspoon baking powder
  ¼ teaspoon salt
Stir into the first mixture. Fill buttered custard cups.

Steam (above) 20 minutes. Take the puddings out of the cups and roll gently in
  Confectioners' sugar
Serve with
  Creamy Chocolate Sauce (p. 399) or crushed and sweetened fruit
Serves 4 or 5.

Steamed Chocolate Pudding

Melt over hot water
  1½ ounces unsweetened chocolate
  3 tablespoons butter
Stir in
  ½ cup sugar
  1 egg
Beat until smooth. Add
  ⅓ cup milk
  ½ teaspoon vanilla
Sift together
  1 cup flour
  1½ teaspoons baking powder
  ¼ teaspoon salt
Stir into the first mixture.

Steam (p. 374) 45 minutes in small molds or 1½ hours in a large mold. Serve with Yellow Sauce (p. 401), or whipped cream sweetened and flavored with vanilla or rum
Serves 4 or 5.

Ohio Pudding

Sift together
1 cup sugar
1 cup flour
2 teaspoons baking powder
1 teaspoon salt
1 teaspoon baking soda
Add
1 cup finely grated raw potato
1 cup finely grated raw carrot
1 cup currants
1 cup raisins
Mix thoroughly.

Steam (p. 374) 2 hours in small molds or 3 hours in a large mold. Serve with Ohio Sauce (p. 403)
Serves 8.

Steamed Berry Pudding

Cream together
⅓ cup butter
⅔ cup sugar
Add
2 eggs, well beaten
Sift together
2⅓ cups flour
2½ teaspoons baking powder
¼ teaspoon salt
Add to the first mixture alternately with
⅓ cup milk
Stir in
1 cup cranberries or blueberries, lightly floured
Steam (p. 374) 3 hours. Serve with Vanilla (p. 402), Lemon (p. 401) or Hard Sauce (p. 402)
Serves 6.

Fig Pudding

Rub with fingers or a wooden spoon until creamy
3 ounces suet, chopped

Add
½ pound dried figs, chopped fine
Put in a bowl
2½ cups bread crumbs
½ cup milk
Let stand ½ hour. Add
2 eggs, well beaten
1 cup sugar
½ teaspoon salt
Add the figs and suet.

Steam (p. 374) 3 hours. Serve with Yellow Sauce (p. 401)
Serves 4 or 5.

Steamed Date or Fig Pudding

Sift together
1⅞ cups flour
½ teaspoon baking soda
½ teaspoon each of salt, clove, allspice and nutmeg
Melt
3 tablespoons butter
Add
½ cup molasses
½ cup milk
Add the flour mixture and
½ pound pitted dates or dried figs, cut small
Steam (p. 374) 2½ hours. Serve with Foamy Sauce (p. 403) or Thin Lemon Sauce (p. 401)
Serves 6.

Suet Pudding

Sift together
3 cups flour
1 teaspoon baking soda
1½ teaspoons salt
½ teaspoon ginger
½ teaspoon clove
½ teaspoon nutmeg
1 teaspoon cinnamon
Add
1 cup finely chopped suet
1 cup molasses
1 cup milk
1½ cups seeded raisins, floured
Steam (p. 374) 3 hours. Serve with Sterling Sauce (p. 403)
Serves 8 or more.

Thanksgiving Pudding

Put in a bowl
  2½ cups bread crumbs
  ¾ cup milk
Let stand ½ hour. Add
  4 eggs, well beaten
  1 cup brown sugar
  1 teaspoon salt
  ¾ teaspoon cinnamon
  ½ teaspoon nutmeg
Work with fingers until creamy
  ⅓ cup chopped suet
Add to the first mixture. Add
  ½ cup chopped walnut meats, floured
  ½ cup seeded raisins, cut small and
    floured
Sift over the mixture
  2 teaspoons baking powder
Beat thoroughly.

Steam (p. 374) 3 hours. Serve with
  Yellow Sauce (p. 401)
Serves 8.

Sterling Fruit Pudding

*For a festive look, decorate the mold with
citron, sliced and cut in fancy shapes.*

Work with fingers or a wooden spoon
until creamy
  1 cup chopped suet
Add
  2⅔ cups dry bread crumbs
  1 cup grated raw carrots
Beat until light
  4 egg yolks
Beat in
  1⅓ cups brown sugar
Add to the first mixture. Add
  Grated rind 1 lemon
  1 tablespoon vinegar
Mix
  2 tablespoons flour
  1½ teaspoons salt
  1 teaspoon cinnamon
  ½ teaspoon nutmeg
  ¼ teaspoon clove
  1 cup seeded raisins, cut small
  ¾ cup currants
Add to the pudding. Fold in

  4 egg whites, beaten until stiff
Steam (p. 374) 3½ hours. Serve with
  Creamy Hard Sauce (p. 403)
Serves 8 or more.

Flaming Christmas Pudding

Steam Sterling Fruit Pudding (above) or
English Plum Pudding (below) in a
round mold. Put on a serving dish and
top with a holly sprig. Pour ¼ cup
warmed brandy over it, light with a
match, and carry to the table flaming.

Christmas Wreath

Steam any fruit pudding in a ring mold.
Turn out onto a serving dish and decorate with cherries and with leaves cut
from candied citron to look like a
Christmas wreath.

English Plum Pudding

*Rich and delicious — the climax of a
holiday dinner.*

Put in a bowl
  1 cup hot milk
  1 cup dry bread crumbs
Let stand until cool. Add
  ½ cup sugar
  4 egg yolks, well beaten
  ½ pound seeded raisins, cut in pieces
    and floured
  ¼ pound figs, chopped
  2 ounces citron, cut fine
Work with fingers or a wooden spoon
until creamy
  ½ pound suet, chopped
Add to the first mixture. Stir in
  ¼ cup wine, grape juice or currant
    jelly
  1 teaspoon nutmeg
  ¾ teaspoon cinnamon
  ¼ teaspoon clove
  ¼ teaspoon mace
  1½ teaspoons salt
Beat until stiff
  4 egg whites
Fold into the pudding.

Steam (p. 374) 6 hours.
Prepare
    Sterling Sauce (p. 403), omitting the
    cream
    Lemon Sauce (p. 402), adding 2 table-
    spoons brandy, drop by drop

Serve both sauces with the pudding. Traditionally, the Sterling Sauce was put
through a pastry bag and tube and garnished with green leaves and candied
cherries, and the Lemon Sauce tinted
with red coloring. *Serves 8.*

Gelatine Desserts

Simplicity is the present mode in gelatine desserts in contrast to
the elaborate affairs which were once popular. Mold in dessert
glasses if you like, and serve on each a bit of fruit or a spoonful of
whipped cream. A large mold of jelly can be presented very attractively with sweetened fresh fruit arranged around it. For general
information about using gelatine, see p. 12.

Lemon Jelly

Put in a bowl
    ½ cup cold water
    1 envelope gelatine (1 tablespoon)
Let stand 5 minutes. Add
    ½ cup sugar
    Few grains salt
    1 cup boiling water
Stir until the sugar dissolves. Add
    ½ cup lemon juice
Pour in molds or sherbet glasses. *Serves 4.*

Grapefruit Jelly. Use only ¾ cup boiling water. In place of lemon juice, use
¾ cup grapefruit juice.

Apricot and Wine Jelly

Mix well in a bowl
    2 envelopes gelatine (2 tablespoons)
    1 cup sugar
Add
    1½ cups boiling water
Stir until the gelatine dissolves. Add
    1 cup apricot juice
    1 tablespoon lemon juice
    1 cup sherry or port
Put, cut side up, in 8 individual molds
    Canned apricot halves
Fill the molds with the jelly mixture.
Chill. *Serves 8.*

Orange Jelly

Put in a bowl
    ½ cup cold water
    1 envelope gelatine (1 tablespoon)
Let stand 5 minutes. Add
    ¼ cup sugar
    Few grains salt
    ½ cup boiling water
Stir until the sugar dissolves. Add
    1 cup orange juice
Taste, and add more sugar if needed.
Pour in molds or sherbet glasses. *Serves 4.*

Coffee Jelly

Mix
    1 envelope gelatine (1 tablespoon)
    ¼ cup sugar
Add
    2 cups strong hot coffee
Stir until the gelatine dissolves. Mold
and chill. *Serves 4.*

Sherry Coffee Jelly. Use only 1½ cups
coffee. When the gelatine has dissolved,
add ½ cup sherry.

Brandy Coffee Jelly. Use only 1¾ cups
coffee. When the gelatine has dissolved,
add ¼ cup brandy.

Wine Jelly

A dessert or a delicious accompaniment for cold turkey or chicken.

Mix well in a bowl
    2 envelopes gelatine (2 tablespoons)
    1 cup sugar
Add
    2 cups boiling water
Stir until the gelatine dissolves. Add
    ⅓ cup orange juice
    3 tablespoons lemon juice
    1 cup sherry or Madeira or ¼ cup
        brandy and ⅓ cup Kirsch
Mold and chill. *Serves 6 to 8 as a dessert, 12 as an accompaniment.*

Jellied Fruit

Brush a mold lightly with salad oil. Chill Lemon, Orange or Wine Jelly (above) until as thick as unbeaten egg white. Add the prepared fruit (below) and pour into the mold.

To prepare the fruit. Prepare 1 to 2 cups of fruit for each 2 cups of jelly. Appropriate fruits are sliced bananas, whole strawberries and raspberries, pitted cherries, grapefruit and orange sections, peeled and seeded grapes, peeled and diced apples, peaches and pears and drained canned fruit of all kinds. Do not use fresh pineapple — it will prevent the jelly from stiffening.

To unmold. Dip the mold in warm water to the depth of the gelatine. Loosen around the edge with the tip of a knife. Put the serving dish, bottom up, on top of the mold. Quickly turn upside down. Shake slightly to loosen the jelly. If the jelly sticks, wipe the mold with a cloth wrung out of hot water.

To serve. Surround with more fruit and top with whipped cream.

Crème aux Fruits

Mix thoroughly in a saucepan
    1 envelope gelatine (1 tablespoon)
    ½ cup sugar
    Few grains salt
Add
    ½ cup milk
Cook and stir over low heat until the gelatine dissolves. Chill until as thick as unbeaten egg white.

Add
    2 egg whites
Beat until almost stiff. Stir in
    ½ cup cooked prunes, cut small
    ½ cup chopped figs
Fold in
    ½ pint heavy cream, whipped
Mold. *Serves 6 to 8.*

Snow Pudding

Mix well in a bowl
    1 envelope gelatine (1 tablespoon)
    1 cup sugar
    ¼ teaspoon salt
Add
    1½ cups boiling water
Stir until the gelatine dissolves. Add
    ¼ cup lemon juice
Cool until as thick as unbeaten egg white.

Beat until fluffy. Add
    3 egg whites
Beat until thick enough to hold its shape. Mold.

Chill until firm. Serve with
    Soft Custard (p. 362) or crushed fruit
Serves 6.

Macaroon Squares. Flavor the pudding with 1½ teaspoons vanilla instead of lemon juice. Before it is stiff enough to mold, pour it into a shallow pan (about 9 inches square) which has been dipped in cold water. Chill. Cut in 3-inch squares and dip them gently in dried macaroon crumbs. Serve with Sabayon Sauce (p. 401) or whipped cream flavored with lemon juice.

Coffee Sponge

Mix well in a bowl
    1 envelope gelatine (1 tablespoon)
    ⅓ cup sugar

Add
 1 cup strong hot coffee
Stir until the gelatine dissolves. Chill until as thick as unbeaten egg white.

Add
 1 egg white
Beat until thick enough to hold its shape and spoon into a mold or dessert glasses. Chill. Serve with
 Whipped cream
Serves 3 or 4.

Coffee Mallow

Put in a double boiler
 ½ cup hot coffee
 ¼ pound tiny marshmallows, or large ones cut in quarters with wet scissors
Cook over hot water until the marshmallows melt. Cool.

When slightly thickened, fold in
 ½ pint heavy cream, whipped
Add
 Vanilla or brandy to taste
Pour into dessert glasses. Chill. *Serves 6.*

Spanish Cream

For a gala dessert, flavor with sherry or brandy. Unmold and garnish with alternate spoonfuls of whipped cream and orange marmalade, Bar-le-Duc currants or marrons.

Mix in a saucepan
 1 envelope gelatine (1 tablespoon)
 Few grains salt
 2 tablespoons sugar
Beat together and pour over the gelatine
 2 egg yolks, slightly beaten
 1 cup milk
Cook and stir over low heat until the gelatine dissolves (about 5 minutes). Add
 1 cup milk
 ½ teaspoon vanilla
Chill until slightly firm.

Beat until they stand in soft peaks
 2 egg whites
Beat in, a tablespoon at a time
 ¼ cup sugar

Fold into the gelatine mixture. Pour into a bowl or into a mold dipped in cold water. As the cream cools, it divides prettily with a foamy top over a layer of smooth custard.

Serve from the bowl (a glass one is attractive) or unmold. *Serves 4.*

Chocolate Spanish Cream. Scald the milk with 1 ounce unsweetened chocolate. Beat until smooth. Sweeten the finished pudding to taste.

Coffee Spanish Cream. Flavor with instant coffee. Add sugar as needed.

Macaroon Spanish Cream. Before adding the egg whites, pour the pudding into a bowl set in ice water and add ½ cup dry macaroon crumbs. Stir until slightly thickened. Fold in the whites, mold, and chill. Change the flavoring by substituting almond flavoring for vanilla or by adding brandy to taste.

Bavarian Cream

Very impressive made in a mold lined with lady fingers or strips of sponge cake.

Mix in a saucepan
 1 envelope gelatine (1 tablespoon)
 Few grains salt
 ¼ cup sugar
Beat together until well blended
 2 egg yolks
 1¼ cups milk
Add to the gelatine. Cook and stir over low heat until the gelatine dissolves (about 5 minutes). Add
 ½ teaspoon vanilla
Chill until the mixture begins to stiffen. Beat until in soft peaks
 2 egg whites
Beat in, a little at a time
 ¼ cup sugar
Fold into the gelatine mixture. Fold in
 ½ pint heavy cream, beaten stiff
Mold in individual molds or one large mold. Unmold (p. 378), and garnish or flavor as suggested for Spanish Cream. *Serves 6.*

Charlotte Russe

Basically, a charlotte is merely sweetened whipped cream, usually stiffened slightly with gelatine. Variations are innumerable. Some suggestions are given below, but invent your own!

Mix in a saucepan
  ⅓ cup sugar
  1 tablespoon gelatine
  ½ cup milk
Cook and stir over low heat until the gelatine dissolves. Add
  1½ teaspoons vanilla
Chill until almost firm. Beat until fluffy. Whip until stiff
  ½ pint heavy cream
Beat one-third of the cream into the charlotte. Fold in the rest. Spoon into individual molds or one large mold. Chill.

Turn out and garnish with
  Lady fingers
  Whipped cream
Serves 4 to 6.

Other ways to serve Charlotte Russe. Line a large mold with slices of jelly roll. Or fill Mary Ann cakes (baker's or sponge cake baked in Mary Ann pans) with charlotte and decorate with whole strawberries and a border of whipped cream. Or chill in sherbet glasses and put a spoonful of cold Butterscotch Sauce (p. 398) on each. Add a few shavings of toasted almonds, if you like.

Caramel Charlotte. Caramelize all the sugar and add it slowly to the scalded milk. Stir until dissolved before adding the gelatine. Add confectioners' sugar to taste.

Burnt Almond Charlotte. Make Caramel Charlotte, adding ½ cup finely chopped blanched toasted almonds.

Chocolate Charlotte. Melt 1 ounce unsweetened chocolate over hot water, add 3 tablespoons hot water and ⅓ cup powdered sugar. Add to the gelatine mixture while hot. Sprinkle with slivers of milk chocolate and garnish with whipped cream around base of the mold.

Chocolate Rum Charlotte. Flavor with 3 tablespoons rum before adding the cream. Before molding, fold in 1 ounce unsweetened chocolate, grated.

Coffee Charlotte. Flavor with instant coffee or use strong hot coffee in place of scalded milk.

Marron Charlotte. Add to Caramel Charlotte ½ cup marrons, broken in pieces. Garnish with whipped cream and marrons. Pour over the charlotte marron syrup (from the jar or can) flavored with sherry or rum.

Peanut Charlotte. Scald 3 tablespoons peanut butter with the milk. Sprinkle with chopped peanuts.

Quick Charlotte Russe

Beat until stiff
  1 egg white
Fold in
  ¼ cup confectioners' sugar
  ½ cup heavy cream, whipped
Flavor to taste with
  Vanilla, instant coffee, brandy or
    sherry
Line dessert glasses with
  Lady fingers or thin strips of sponge
    cake
Fill with the charlotte. Put a bit of preserved fruit in each glass or sprinkle with chopped nuts. Chill. *Serves 4.*

Nut Brittle Whip. Omit the sugar. Add pounded peanut brittle or other brittle to taste.

Maple Charlotte

Top with chopped pecans to add a wonderful touch.

Put in a saucepan
  1 cup maple syrup
  1 envelope gelatine (1 tablespoon)
Stir over moderate heat until the gelatine dissolves. Chill until slightly thick. Fold in
  1 pint heavy cream, whipped

Line a mold or paper cups with
Lady fingers
Fill with charlotte and chill. *Serves 6 to 8.*

Orange Charlotte

Mix in a small saucepan
1 envelope gelatine (1 tablespoon)
1 cup sugar
⅔ cup water
Cook and stir over low heat until the gelatine dissolves. Cool. Add
3 tablespoons lemon juice
1 cup orange juice and pulp or
1 small can frozen orange juice
Chill until as thick as unbeaten egg white. Beat until frothy. Fold in
3 egg whites, beaten stiff
½ pint cream, whipped
Line a mold with sections of orange. Pour in the charlotte. Chill. *Serves 6.*

Marmalade Charlotte

Add Curaçao to taste, if you like.

Mix
4 tablespoons bitter orange
marmalade
Juice of 1 lemon
1 teaspoon vanilla
Beat until stiff
3 egg whites
Whip
½ pint heavy cream

Fold the cream gently into the egg whites. Stir in the marmalade mixture. Add
Sugar to taste
Line a bowl with
Lady fingers
Fill with the cream. Garnish with
Mandarin orange sections (canned)
Chill. Serve from the bowl. *Serves 6.*

Mont Blanc

A dramatic and very rich dessert called Monte Bianco in Italy. Canned cream of marrons can be found in shops that deal in imported delicacies. Taste, sweeeten and flavor.

Shell 1 pound French or Italian chestnuts (p. 244). Cover with milk and cook until soft. Drain, if necessary, and mash with a fork.

Sweeten to taste with confectioners' sugar (about 1 cup for 1 pound of nuts) and season with salt and vanilla, Kirsch, rum or maraschino. Beat thoroughly. Put through a vegetable mill or ricer.

Pile lightly on 3-inch rounds of baked pastry or in a pyramid on a serving dish. Decorate with whipped cream to look like a snow-capped mountain. Or use as a filling between pairs of Meringues (p. 449). *One pound serves 6.*

Frozen Desserts

Ice creams and sherbets are universally popular desserts. Crank freezing gives ice cream a velvety texture, but there are many excellent recipes for making frozen desserts in a refrigerator tray.

Crank Freezing

A 2-quart freezer, electric or hand-cranked, is the right size for most families. Scald the freezer can each time you use it and rinse with cold water.

Prepare the mixture to be frozen according to the recipe. Chill it in the refrigerator an hour or more.

When you are ready to begin freezing the mixture, put the ice in a canvas bag and crush with a heavy wooden mallet. Or buy ice crushed and ready to use.

Have ready a package of coarse rock salt.

Measure out the ice and salt beforehand, ready to use, or measure it as you go along, using 8 parts of ice to 1 of salt. A larger proportion of salt hastens the freezing but the ice cream will be less velvety.

Put the can in the tub and fit the dasher in place. Pour the chilled ice cream mixture into the can, filling it no more than two-thirds full (to allow for expansion). Put on the cover and adjust the top and the crank. Turn once or twice to be sure all is in place.

Fill the tub one-third full of crushed ice. Put in the rest of the ice and salt in layers until slightly above the level of the mixture in the can. Pack the ice down solidly with a wooden spoon. Let stand 5 minutes, then begin turning the crank. When the ice cream is frozen, the crank turns with difficulty (an electric freezer shuts off automatically).

To stiffen ice cream mixture. If a frozen dessert refuses to harden, it may be that the cream is too heavy or there is too much sugar or acid fruit in the mixture. To stiffen, stir in beaten egg whites when the ice cream is frozen to a mush and continue freezing.

To pack ice cream. Drain off the water. Wipe the lid of the can, remove it and lift out the dasher. Pack the ice cream down solidly with a spoon. Cover, putting a cork in the opening unless the freezer has a solid cover to replace the other. Repack, using 4 parts of ice to 1 part of salt. Cover with newspapers or a heavy cloth. Let stand at least ½ hour before serving.

Freezing in a Refrigerator Tray

Mousses and parfaits (p. 390) freeze successfully this way since they do not require stirring. Prepare the mixture and pack it into an ice-cube tray with the racks removed. Cover with wax paper.

Set the temperature according to the manufacturer's directions. Put the tray in place and freeze until firm. If it is harder than you like when you are ready to serve it, remove from the freezer compartment and let stand for a few minutes.

If you have a little mixture left over, fill small paper soufflé cups and freeze them in another tray. To freeze mousses and parfaits in ice and salt, see p. 390; bombes and molds p. 393.

Sherbets and ices freeze well in trays, too. Pack the mixture into the tray as for mousses (above). When the mixture is partially frozen but not solid, spoon it into a chilled bowl and beat until evenly blended, using a rotary hand or electric beater. Spoon back into the tray and freeze until firm.

Ice cream freezes better in a tray if the recipe is especially adapted to this method. See Refrigerator Ice Cream (p. 385). To modify a recipe for refrigerator freezing, keep the proportion of sugar low — not more than 1 to 4 — or substitute corn syrup for one-third of the sugar. Beaten egg whites help make a light mixture. One teaspoon of gelatine to each cup of liquid makes a smoother ice cream. Follow the instructions for sherbets (above).

Serving Ice Cream and Sherbet

See also Ice Cream with a Topping (below), Coupes and Parfaits (p. 390), and Desserts Made with Ice Cream (p. 396).

Homemade ice cream. Serve from the can with a large spoon or an ice cream scoop. Or remove the can from the freezer, wipe it carefully, let it stand 1 minute in cool water, remove the cover, run a knife around the edge of the cream and invert it in a serving dish. If the cream does not slip out easily, wipe the can with a cloth wrung out of hot water.

Ice cream bombes and molds. Invert the mold on the serving dish. Wipe with a cloth wrung out of hot water and lift the mold from the ice cream. Add a touch of decoration such as a frill of whipped cream, a sprinkling of chopped toasted nuts or toasted coconut, or bits of glazed fruit or marrons. Serve in slices, with a sauce if you like.

Ices and sherbets. Serve plain or in a mound surrounded by fruit. Lemon ice is delicious with preserved cherries or orange sections and strips of fresh pineapple. Or top individual servings with whipped cream decorated with chopped pistachios or other nuts. Or pour rum around the sherbet.

Commercial ice cream. Soften bulk ice cream slightly so that you can spoon it into a deep bowl as if it were fresh from a home freezer. Serve in any of the ways suggested below. To vary, soften the ice cream slightly and stir into it added flavoring as suggested below. Pack into a mold or an ice-cube tray and set in the freezer compartment to harden.

Stir instant coffee into vanilla, coffee or chocolate ice cream. Add vanilla or brandy to taste.

Swirl chocolate or butterscotch sauce or peanut butter through vanilla ice cream.

Add crushed and sweetened raspberries, strawberries or peaches to vanilla ice cream.

Add chopped toasted nuts or crushed nut brittle to vanilla, chocolate or coffee ice cream.

Ice Cream with a Topping

Perfect ice cream is delicious just as it is, but for a more elaborate dessert, serve it with a sauce. Serve the sauce separately in a bowl or over scoops of ice cream on dessert dishes. Or arrange ice cream and sauce (or other topping) in layers in tall coupe or parfait glasses, decorated if you like with a dab — but not too much — of whipped cream.

Sauces

Butterscotch Sauce (p. 398) on vanilla or chocolate ice cream.

Caramel Sauce (p. 398) on vanilla ice cream.

Chocolate Sauce (p. 399) on vanilla, chocolate, coffee or peppermint ice cream or on lemon sherbet.

Coffee Custard Sauce (p. 399) on vanilla, chocolate or coffee ice cream.

Fudge Sauce (p. 399) on vanilla ice cream.

Ginger Sauce (1 cup sugar, ½ cup water and ¼ cup chopped crystallized ginger boiled 10 minutes and cooled) on vanilla ice cream.

Holiday Sauce (p. 401) on vanilla ice cream.

Marshmallow Sauce (p. 400) on chocolate, mint or any fruit ice cream.

Marshmallow Mint Sauce (p. 400) on vanilla or chocolate ice cream.

Melba Sauce (p. 404) on vanilla or peach ice cream. See also Peach or Pear Melba (p. 396).

Peppermint Sauce (p. 401) on vanilla or chocolate ice cream.

Pineapple Mint Sauce (p. 406) on vanilla ice cream.

Other Toppings

Chopped salted nuts or toasted coconut on vanilla, butterscotch, caramel, chocolate, coffee or mint ice cream. Icebergs (p. 396).

Coffee, strong and hot, on vanilla, chocolate or coffee ice cream.

Crushed and sweetened fruit (peaches, raspberries or strawberries) on vanilla ice cream.

Maple syrup (plain or warmed with a little rum) on vanilla or coffee ice cream.

Whipped cream on any ice cream or as an added touch over a fruit sauce.

Zabaglione (p. 364) on coffee ice cream. A 4-egg zabaglione is enough for 6 servings.

Cordials and Other Liquors

Brandy or Benedictine on peach cream.

Cointreau or Cherry Heering on crushed fruit or fruit cup over vanilla ice cream.

Crème de menthe on vanilla or chocolate ice cream or lemon sherbet.

Crème de cacao on coffee ice cream.

Curaçao or Cointreau on vanilla or chocolate ice cream.

Rum on lemon sherbet.

Ice Cream

Ice cream is made of cream or of cream and milk thickened with eggs or gelatine. Vary any of the basic recipes which follow as suggested on p. 385.

Philadelphia Ice Cream

The richest mixture of all. Traditionally, it should be made with grated vanilla bean. Another way is to put a 1-inch piece of vanilla bean in the pan while you scald the cream.

Scald
  1 quart cream
Add
  ¾ cup sugar
  Few grains salt
Stir until the sugar dissolves. Chill. Add
  1½ tablespoons vanilla or 1 teaspoon grated vanilla bean

Freeze in a crank freezer (p. 382). *Makes 3 pints.*

Custard Ice Cream

Scald
  1½ cups milk
Mix until smooth
  1 tablespoon cornstarch or flour
  ¾ cup sugar
  ½ cup cold milk
Add the scalded milk slowly and cook and stir over hot water 8 minutes. Add
  1 egg or 2 egg yolks, slightly beaten
Cook 2 minutes. Cool. Add

1 pint cream
1 tablespoon vanilla
¼ teaspoon salt
Freeze (p. 382). *Makes 3 pints.*

French Vanilla Ice Cream

Mix
½ cup sugar
⅛ teaspoon salt
4 egg yolks, slightly beaten
Add, stirring constantly
2 cups scalded milk
Cook over hot water until the mixture
coats a spoon. Cool, strain, and add
1 pint cream
1 tablespoon vanilla
Freeze (p. 382). *Makes 3 pints.*

Refrigerator Ice Cream

Put in a double boiler top
¼ cup cold water
1 teaspoon gelatine
Let stand 5 minutes. Add
1 cup hot milk or cream
Mix
⅜ cup sugar or ¼ cup sugar and
3 tablespoons corn syrup
1 teaspoon flour
Few grains salt
Add to the gelatine and milk. Cook and
stir over low heat until thick. Cover and
cook over hot water 10 minutes. Stir in
slowly
1 egg yolk, slightly beaten
Cook 1 minute. Strain into a refrigerator tray and put in the refrigerator until
chilled.

Spoon into a chilled bowl and beat with
an egg beater until very light. Fold in
1 pint heavy cream, whipped
1 egg white, beaten stiff
1 teaspoon vanilla
Pour back into the tray and freeze (p.
383). *Makes about 1 quart.*

Ice Cream in Many Flavors

Vary any of the basic vanilla ice cream
recipes (above) in the following ways:

Bisque Ice Cream. Add to the mixture
1 cup finely chopped nut meats. Toasted
(not salted) almonds and hazelnuts are
especially good.

Butterscotch Ice Cream. Cook sugar
with 2 tablespoons butter until melted
and well browned. Dissolve in hot milk
or cream.

Caramel Ice Cream. Caramelize half the
sugar (p. 14). Add it slowly to the hot
mixture. For **Burnt Almond Ice Cream,**
add 1 cup finely chopped blanched and
toasted almonds.

Chocolate Ice Cream. Make Custard Ice
Cream (p. 384), melting 2 squares chocolate with the milk as it is scalded. Increase sugar to 1¼ cups.

Coffee Ice Cream. Flavor to taste with
instant coffee and brandy.

Frozen Tom and Jerry. Freeze French
Vanilla Ice Cream (above) to a mush.
Add 2 tablespoons rum and 1 tablespoon
brandy and finish freezing. Serve in
frappé glasses.

Ginger Ice Cream. Add ½ cup preserved
ginger cut in small pieces and 3 tablespoons ginger syrup from the jar. Add 2
tablespoons sherry, if desired.

Grape-Nut Ice Cream. Add 1 cup Grape-
Nuts. Flavor with almond extract instead
of vanilla.

Macaroon Ice Cream. Add 1 cup macaroon crumbs or 8 dry macaroons pounded.
Reduce sugar to ½ cup. Flavor with
sherry, if liked, instead of vanilla.

Maple Ice Cream. Use maple syrup or
maple sugar in place of sugar. If desired, add 1 cup nut meats, cut in pieces
or chopped, stirring them into the cream
when nearly frozen.

Marron Ice Cream. Add 1 cup canned
marrons, forced through a sieve. Reduce
sugar by one half. Flavor to taste with
sherry or vanilla.

Mint Ice Cream. Flavor with oil of peppermint instead of vanilla. Color delicately green with vegetable coloring. Serve with Chocolate Sauce (p. 399).

Peanut Brittle Ice Cream. Omit sugar. Pound ½ pound peanut brittle, roll, and sift. Add to mixture. Add sugar to taste.

Peppermint Candy Ice Cream. Omit sugar. Crush ½ pound peppermint stick candy and add to hot milk or cream.

Pistachio Ice Cream. Omit vanilla. Add 1 teaspoon almond extract and ½ cup pistachio nuts, chopped fine. Color green.

Praline Ice Cream. Add 1 cup almonds, blanched, toasted, and finely chopped. Caramelize half the sugar and add slowly to scalded milk or cream. Or add 1 cup Praline Powder (p. 14), made with pecans.

Chocolate Ice Cream

Smoother than some because the chocolate blends evenly with the cream during the freezing.

Cook until thick and smooth
  ½ pound semisweet cooking chocolate
  2 cups milk
Beat well
  3 eggs
  1 cup sugar
Add
  1 pint thin cream
  1 tablespoon vanilla
  ⅛ teaspoon salt
Add the chocolate mixture, stir well and strain. Freeze in a crank freezer (p. 382). *Makes 3 pints.*

Fresh Fruit Ice Cream

Mix
  2 cups thin cream
  2 cups prepared fruit (below)
  ¼ teaspoon salt
  Sugar to taste
Freeze until firm (p. 382). *Makes about 1½ quarts.*

Banana Ice Cream. Put 2 ripe bananas through a sieve and sprinkle with lemon juice.

Blueberry Ice Cream. Stew 1 quart blueberries until soft. Add 1 cup sugar, mash, strain, and cool.

Peach Ice Cream. Pare, slice, and crush fruit to make 2 cups. Sprinkle with ½ cup sugar. Add lemon juice or almond flavoring if the peaches are too bland.

Raspberry or Strawberry Ice Cream. Mash 1 quart berries, sprinkle with ½ cup sugar, cover, and let stand at least 20 minutes. Strain to remove the seeds.

Orange Ice Cream

Orange juice, sweetened to taste and combined with an equal amount of thin cream, is the simplest recipe, but a custard base makes a smoother ice cream.

Boil 5 minutes
  2 cups sugar
  1 cup water
Add
  2 cups orange juice
Scald
  ½ pint thin cream
Add
  2 egg yolks
Cook and stir over hot water or very low heat until thick. Cool. Add the first mixture. Fold in
  ½ pint heavy cream, beaten stiff
Freeze (p. 382). When nearly firm, stir in
  ¼ cup candied orange peel, cut in
    thin slivers
Makes 2 quarts.

Frozen Pudding

Prepare (using mixed candied fruits or candied pineapple with a small amount of preserved ginger)
  ⅔ cup fruit, cut small
Freeze to a mush
  Custard Ice Cream (p. 384)
Add the fruit and
  ½ cup chopped almonds
  3 tablespoons brandy or sherry
Freeze until firm. *Makes about 3 pints.*

Frozen Plum Pudding. Make the ice cream with 4 egg yolks, omitting the flour. In place of fruit and nuts, use ⅓ cup sultana raisins and ½ cup dry macaroon crumbs.

Nesselrode Pudding. In place of fruit and nuts, use 1 cup preserved marrons, forced through a sieve, or 1 cup marron purée. Flavor with maraschino. To vary, add bits of candied fruit.

Ices and Sherbets

Ices are made of sweetened fruit juices, usually diluted with water. They are also called sherbets, but sherbet is the old name for a frozen dessert made with cream or milk added to the fruit juice. Frappés and sorbets are frozen only to a mush. Freeze ices and sherbets in a crank freezer (p. 382) or in a refrigerator tray. Suggestions for serving (p. 383). They are delicious in bombes and molds (p. 393).

Lemon Ice

Put in a bowl
    2 cups sugar
    4 cups boiling water
Stir until dissolved. Cool. Add
    ¾ cup lemon juice
    1 tablespoon grated lemon rind
Freeze in a crank freezer (p. 382) or a refrigerator tray. *Makes 3 pints.*

To vary. In place of lemon juice and rind, use any of the following combinations, adding water to make about 4 cups.

Orange Ice. Use 3 cups orange juice, ¼ cup lemon juice, grated rind of 2 oranges, Sugar Syrup (p. 36) to taste.

Three Fruit Ice. Use 1½ cups grapefruit juice, 1½ cups orange juice, ½ cup lemon juice, Sugar Syrup (p. 36) to taste.

Grape Ice. Use 2 cups grape juice, ⅔ cup orange juice, ¼ cup lemon juice, Sugar Syrup (p. 36) to taste.

Mint Ice. Flavor Lemon Ice with oil of peppermint and color delicately green with vegetable coloring.

Raspberry and Currant Ice. Use ⅔ cup raspberry juice, 1⅓ cups currant juice, 2 cups Sugar Syrup (p. 36).

Lime Sherbet

Mix in a saucepan
    1 teaspoon gelatine
    ½ cup sugar
    1½ cups water
Boil 3 minutes. Add
    ⅓ cup lime juice
    Few grains salt
Freeze in a crank freezer (p. 382) or a refrigerator tray. *Makes about 1½ pints.*

Lemon Milk Sherbet

Very smooth and creamy.

Mix
    Juice of 3 lemons
    1½ cups sugar
    Few grains salt
    1 quart milk
(The mixture may look curdled but it will be smooth after freezing.) Freeze in a crank freezer (p. 382) or in a refrigerator tray. *Makes 3 pints.*

Lemon Cream Sherbet. Use 3 cups milk and 1 cup cream.

Orange Cream Sherbet. Use the juice of 2 oranges and 2 lemons.

Cranberry Sherbet

Refreshing as a dessert or as a relish with chicken or turkey.

Beat together
    1½ cups cranberry jelly
    Grated rind and juice of 1 lemon
    Juice of 1 orange
Freeze to a mush in a refrigerator tray (p. 382).

Fold in
    2 egg whites, beaten stiff, or ½ pint cream, whipped
Finish freezing. *Makes 1 quart.*

Lime Cream Sherbet

Put in a bowl
    1 package lime gelatine
    1 cup boiling water
Stir until dissolved. Add
    ½ cup sugar
    2 cups milk
    1 cup thin cream
    ¼ cup lemon juice
    1 teaspoon grated lemon peel
    Few grains salt
Mix well. Freeze in a refrigerator tray (p. 382). *Makes 1 quart.*

Pineapple Cream Sherbet

Boil 5 minutes
    ½ cup sugar
    1 cup water
Cool. Add
    1 cup crushed pineapple (canned, not fresh)
Freeze to a mush in a refrigerator tray (p. 382).

Fold in
    ½ pint heavy cream, whipped
Finish freezing. *Makes 1 quart.*

Pineapple Marquise. Use pineapple juice in place of pineapple. Add the juice of ½ lemon. Just before serving, stir in ½ teaspoon vanilla or 1 tablespoon rum and ½ cup crushed pineapple, sweetened to taste. Garnish with candied pineapple or chopped pistachios or pecans or both.

Fruit Sherbet

Gelatine keeps large crystals from forming, so this sherbet is particularly successful made in a refrigerator tray.

Put in a small saucepan
    1 cup water
    ¼ cup sugar
    1 tablespoon gelatine (1 envelope)
Stir over low heat until the gelatine dissolves. Heat
    2 cups puréed fruit, fresh or canned (below)
Stir in the gelatine. Mix well. Add
    Few grains salt
    Sugar to taste
    Lemon juice to taste (2 tablespoons or more)
Freeze in a refrigerator tray (p. 382). *Makes 1 quart.*

To prepare purée. Drain canned fruit or wash and peel fresh fruit and remove the pits or seeds. Put through a coarse sieve, ricer, or food mill. To keep peaches from darkening, sprinkle with ACO (a commercial ascorbic) or simmer 5 minutes in thin sugar syrup (¼ cup sugar to 2½ cups water) and drain.

Fruit Cream Sherbet. Before freezing, fold in 1 cup Soft Custard (p. 362) or ½ pint heavy cream, whipped.

Orange Cream Sherbet

Unless oranges are at their best, frozen orange juice may have a better flavor than fresh.

Mix
    1¼ cups sugar
    1½ cups orange juice
    Few grains salt
    2 cups milk
    ½ pint cream
Freeze in a crank freezer (p. 382) or a refrigerator tray. *Makes 3 pints.*

Raspberry or Strawberry Ice

Wash, drain and hull
    2 quarts raspberries or strawberries

Sprinkle with
   2 cups sugar
Cover and let stand 2 hours.

Mash and squeeze through cheesecloth
or a fine sieve. Add
   Few grains salt
   2 cups water
   Lemon juice, to taste
Freeze in a crank freezer (p. 382) or a
refrigerator tray. *Makes 3 pints.*

Pineapple Ice

*If you use fresh fruit, add more sugar
to taste.*

Boil 5 minutes
   2 cups water
   1 cup sugar
Add
   2 cups crushed or shredded pineapple
   ½ cup lemon juice
   Few grains salt
Cool. Freeze in a crank freezer (p. 382)
or in a refrigerator tray. *Makes 3 pints.*

Cardinal Punch

*A Victorian accompaniment for chicken
or turkey, but nowadays considered the
perfect finale to a rich dinner.*

Boil 10 minutes
   4 cups water
   2 cups sugar
Add
   ⅔ cup orange juice
   ⅓ cup lemon juice
   ¼ cup strong tea (strained)
Cool. Freeze to a mush in a crank freezer
(p. 382). Add
   ¼ cup brandy
   ¼ cup Curaçao
Freeze until firm. Serve in tall coupe
glasses. *Makes about 2 quarts.*

Roman Punch. Instead of brandy and
Curaçao, use ½ cup rum.

Club Punch

Boil 10 minutes
   2½ cups sugar
   3 cups water
Add
   1 cup lemon juice
   1 cup orange juice
   1 cup pineapple juice
Cut in pieces
   1 cup candied fruit (such as a mixture
     of cherries, pineapple and apricots)
Add
   ¼ cup rum
   ¼ cup brandy
Cover and let stand 1 hour.

Freeze the first mixture to a mush (p.
382), add the fruit, and freeze until
nearly firm. Serve in tall coupe glasses.
Makes 2 quarts.

Frozen Lime Pie

Beat until thick
   2 eggs
Beat in
   ½ cup sugar
Add
   ½ cup light corn syrup
   1 pint cream
   ¼ cup lime juice
   1 teaspoon grated lime peel
Freeze in a refrigerator tray (p. 382).
Beat until fluffy.

Mix
   1 cup graham cracker crumbs
   ½ cup butter, melted
   ½ cup sugar
Line a refrigerator tray or a pie pan with
wax paper. Spread with half the crumb
mixture, pour in the beaten lime mixture, and cover with the remaining
crumbs. Freeze (p. 382). *Serves 6 to 8.*

Mousses and Parfaits

Mousses and parfaits are frozen without stirring. Serve like ice cream or as a mold (p. 383); or use as a layer or the center in a bombe (p. 393). See also parfaits (coupes) on p. 395.

To freeze in the refrigerator (p. 382).

To freeze in ice and salt. Fill molds to overflowing with the mixture and cover with buttered paper, then with tight covers. It is important to keep the salt water out of the mold, so bind on the cover with a strip of cloth (finger bandage is practical) which has been dipped in melted fat, not oil. Cover individual molds with a double thickness of wax paper held with elastic bands.

Pack the molds in equal amounts of crushed ice and salt in the freezer tub or a large kettle. Be sure the ice and salt are *under, around* and *over* the molds. Pour off salt water as it forms so that it will not get into the molds. Leave small molds 2 hours, large ones 3 to 4 hours. To unmold. Take out the mold and wipe with a cloth wrung out of hot water, and remove the strip of cloth and the cover. Invert on the serving dish.

Vanilla Mousse I

Vary the flavoring as suggested on p. 385.

Beat until stiff
   2 egg whites
Beat in gradually
   ¼ cup confectioners' sugar
Whip until thick but not stiff
   1 pint heavy cream
   ¼ cup confectioners' sugar
   1 teaspoon vanilla
Fold in the egg whites. Freeze (p. 382). *Makes 1 quart.*

With whole eggs. Beat 2 egg yolks with half the sugar and the vanilla. Fold in the beaten whites and whipped cream. Add confectioners' sugar to taste. One cup of cream may be omitted, in which case reduce the sugar to ⅓ cup.

Biscuit Tortoni I. (*See also p. 391.*) Flavor with sherry. Add ½ cup dried macaroons, finely crushed. Pack in a mold or in paper cups, sprinkle with powdered macaroons, and set in a refrigerator tray to freeze.

Apricot Mousse. Press stewed apricots through a sieve. Spread a layer in a refrigerator tray and cover with the mousse. Freeze (p. 382). Cut in cubes and pile in dessert glasses.

Chantilly Mousse. Add 1 cup meringues, broken in pieces.

Chestnut Mousse. Add ½ cup marrons, broken in pieces.

Coffee Mousse. Add 2 tablespoons instant coffee dissolved in ¼ cup water.

Orange Mousse. Melt 1 can frozen orange concentrate and stir it into the mousse.

Vanilla Mousse II

Less expensive than the classic recipe and lower in calories, too. Vary the flavoring as suggested on p. 385.

Heat until thoroughly blended
   ¾ cup condensed milk
   ½ cup water
Chill. Add
   1½ teaspoons vanilla
Fold in
   ½ pint heavy cream, whipped
Freeze in a refrigerator tray (p. 382). *Makes 1½ pints.*

Peach Mousse. Add 1 cup crushed peaches to the chilled condensed milk and water. Sweeten to taste before folding in the cream.

Marshmallow Mousse

Cut in pieces with wet scissors (or use small marshmallows)
    20 marshmallows
Pour over them
    1 cup fruit juice
Cook in a double boiler until the marshmallows melt. Cool. Add
    Juice of ½ lemon
Fold in
    ½ pint heavy cream, beaten stiff
Freeze in a refrigerator tray (p. 382). *Makes 1 quart.*

Coffee Marshmallow Mousse. Use coffee in place of fruit juices. Flavor with vanilla, sherry or brandy to taste.

Biscuit Tortoni II

See also the variation following Vanilla Mousse I (p. 390). Some bakery supply houses sell macaroon crumbs.

Roll dry macaroons to make
    1 cup macaroon crumbs
Cover with
    1 pint thin cream
Soak 1 hour. Add
    ½ cup sugar
    ⅓ cup sherry
Freeze to a mush in a refrigerator tray (p. 382).

Fold in
    1 pint heavy cream, beaten stiff
Pack in fluted paper cups. Sprinkle over the tops
    Dried macaroon crumbs
Set in the freezer compartment and freeze until firm. *Makes 3 pints.*

Coffee Tortoni. In place of sherry, flavor with 1 teaspoon vanilla and 2 tablespoons instant coffee, dissolved in ⅓ cup water. Chopped toasted almonds are delicious instead of macaroons. You will need about ½ cup.

Chocolate Mousse

Cook over low heat or in a double boiler, stirring frequently

    1 cup milk
    2 ounces unsweetened chocolate
    ¾ cup sugar
    1 teaspoon gelatine
Beat until smooth and well blended. Chill until thick. Add
    1 teaspoon vanilla
Beat until light. Fold in
    1 pint heavy cream, whipped
Freeze in a refrigerator tray (p. 382). *Makes 1 quart.*

Coffee Mousse

See also coffee variations under Vanilla Mousse I (p. 390) and Marshmallow Mousse (above).

Put in a small saucepan
    1 cup strong coffee
    ¾ cup sugar
    Few grains salt
    1 teaspoon gelatine
Cook and stir over low heat until the gelatine and sugar dissolve. Stir well and pour into a refrigerator tray. Chill until thickened.

Fold in
    1 pint heavy cream, beaten stiff
Freeze until firm. *Makes 1 quart.*

Coffee Coconut Mousse. Melt 1 tablespoon butter. Stir in 1 cup flaked coconut and cook until lightly browned. Fold into the mousse with the whipped cream.

Pineapple Mousse

Put in a small saucepan
    1¼ cups syrup from canned pineapple
    ½ cup sugar
    1 teaspoon gelatine
    Few grains salt
Cook and stir over low heat until the gelatine and sugar dissolve. Add
    2 tablespoons lemon juice
Chill until thickened. Beat until light.

Fold in
    1 pint heavy cream, whipped
Freeze until firm in a refrigerator tray (p. 382). *Makes 1 quart.*

Fruit Mousse

Raspberries, strawberries and peaches are especially delicious, but other fruits are good, too. If the fruit is bland, add lemon juice to taste. Almond extract intensifies the flavor of peaches.

Prepare, by rubbing fruit through a sieve
    1 cup fruit pulp and juice
Add
    Few grains salt
    Sugar to taste
Put in a small saucepan
    ½ cup water
    ¼ cup sugar
    1 teaspoon gelatine
Cook and stir until the sugar and gelatine melt. Add to the fruit. Pour into a refrigerator tray or a bowl. Chill until thickened. Beat until very light.

Fold in
    1 pint heavy cream, whipped
Freeze in a refrigerator tray (p. 382) or in salt and ice (p. 390). *Makes 1 quart.*

Zabaglione Frappé

Stir together
    1 envelope gelatine (1 tablespoon)
    ½ cup cold water
Make double recipe of
    Zabaglione (p. 364)
Stir in the gelatine. Beat thoroughly. Pour into a bowl or paper soufflé cups. Place in the refrigerator freezing compartment. Chill until firm. *Serves 4 to 6.*

Vary by adding cognac and maraschino and toasted almonds, bits of brandied fruit or macaroon crumbs.

Frozen Apple Cream

For a richer dessert, fold in toasted flaked coconut or chopped nuts.

Mix in a refrigerator tray
    1 cup applesauce
    Few grains cinnamon
    Few grains nutmeg
    1 teaspoon melted butter
    2 teaspoons lemon juice

Chill. Fold in
    ½ pint heavy cream, whipped
Freeze in the tray (p. 382) until firm (2 to 4 hours). *Makes 1½ pints.*

Angel Parfait

Boil until the syrup spins a thread (about 5 minutes)
    1 cup sugar
    ½ cup water
Beating constantly, pour the syrup slowly over
    3 egg whites, beaten stiff
Beat until cool. Fold in
    1 pint heavy cream, whipped
    2 teaspoons vanilla
Spoon into a bombe mold lined with ice cream (p. 393) and freeze. Or freeze in a refrigerator tray (p. 382) and serve in dessert glasses, garnished with whipped cream, chopped nuts or fruit. *Makes about 1 quart.*

Vary as suggested for Vanilla Mousse I (p. 390).

Pistachio Parfait. Color delicate green. Add 1 teaspoon almond extract and ½ cup chopped pistachios.

Strawberry Parfait

Wash, hull, and mash
    1 quart strawberries
Sprinkle with
    1 cup sugar
Let stand several hours. Strain through a fine sieve. Pour into a refrigerator tray. Freeze until slightly icy.

Put in a saucepan
    1 cup sugar
    ½ cup water
Boil until the syrup spins a thread (about 5 minutes). Beat stiff
    3 egg whites
Beating constantly, pour the syrup slowly over the egg whites and keep beating until the mixture is cool. Fold in
    1 pint heavy cream, whipped

Fold into the strawberries and freeze (p. 382) until firm. *Makes 3 pints.*

Butterscotch Parfait

Put in a saucepan
 ⅓ cup brown sugar
 1 tablespoon butter
Cook until melted. Add
 ¼ cup boiling water
Stir and cook until blended. Pour slowly over
 2 egg yolks, well beaten
Cook over hot water until fluffy, beating constantly. Chill.

Fold in
 ½ pint heavy cream, whipped
Add
 Few grains salt
 1½ teaspoons vanilla
Use as the center for a bombe (p. 393) or freeze in a refrigerator tray (p. 382) and serve in dessert glasses with a topping of chopped nuts. *Enough for the center of a 2-quart mold or 4 small servings.*

Marron Parfait

Prepare
 1 cup preserved marrons, cut in small
  pieces

Add
 1 tablespoon vanilla
Boil 5 minutes
 ⅔ cup sugar
 ¼ cup water
Beating constantly, pour gradually over
 6 egg yolks, beaten thick
Cook over hot water, stirring constantly, until thick. Beat until cold. Add the marrons and fold in
 1 pint heavy cream, whipped
Freeze (p. 382). *Makes 1 quart or 8 small servings.*

To vary, use chopped nut meats or dry macaroon crumbs in place of marrons.

Maple Mousse

Extravagant, high-caloried, but a superb indulgence once in a while.

Beat slightly
 4 eggs or 6 egg yolks
Add, little by little
 ⅔ cup hot maple syrup
Stir and cook in a double boiler until thick. Cool. Fold in
 1 pint heavy cream, whipped
Freeze (p. 382). Serve in dessert glasses. Sprinkle with
 Pecan nut meats
Makes 1 quart or 8 small servings.

Bombes and Molds

A feast for the eye, too, especially when made with attention to color as well as flavor.

To fill mold. Chill a brick or melon mold or a refrigerator tray. Put in homemade or commercial ice cream, sherbet or mousse in layers. Or line with one flavor (using a spoon to smooth it in) and fill the center with a special mixture such as whipped cream, any mousse (p. 390), Charlotte Russe (p. 380), Angel Parfait (p. 392), or Butterscotch Parfait (above). Fill to overflowing. Put on the cover and press it down.

To freeze. Pack in salt and ice, using 4 parts ice to 1 of salt, if the center is unfrozen, or equal parts ice and salt if both are frozen.

If you are using a refrigerator tray (p. 382), set the temperature low enough for freezing until the cream is firm.

To unmold and serve (p. 390).

Suggested combinations (see also the recipes for molded ice cream desserts which follow):

Vanilla Ice Cream filled with Butterscotch Parfait (p. 393), Frozen Tom and Jerry (p. 385) or Coffee Mousse (p. 391).

Chocolate Ice Cream filled with Mint, Peppermint, Pistachio or Coffee Ice Cream (p. 385) or Orange Ice (p. 387) or Orange Ice Cream (p. 386).

Coffee Ice Cream filled with Burnt Almond (p. 385) or other nut ice cream or Angel Parfait (p. 392) or Marron Parfait (p. 393).

Orange Ice filled with Macaroon Ice Cream (p. 385) or Orange Ice Cream (p. 386).

New Year's Bombe

Put in a small saucepan
  ½ cup water
  ¼ cup sugar
  1 tablespoon gelatine (1 envelope)
Cook and stir over low heat until the gelatine dissolves. Cool slightly and stir gently into
  1 pint heavy cream, whipped
Fold in
  1 cup crushed nut brittle
  ⅓ cup chopped toasted almonds
  1 teaspoon vanilla
  ⅛ teaspoon salt
Line a 2-quart mold with
  1 quart French Vanilla Ice Cream
    (p. 385)
Fill the center with the prepared cream. Put on the cover and freeze (p. 393).
Serves 12.

Strawberry Bombe

Prepare
  1 cup sieved strawberries
Stir gently into
  1 cup heavy cream, whipped
Add
  1 tablespoon Kirsch
  2 teaspoons vanilla
  ¾ cup confectioners' sugar

Line a 2-quart mold with
  1 quart Strawberry Ice (p. 388)
Fill with the prepared cream, cover, and freeze (p. 393).

Garnish with
  Whipped cream
  Whole perfect strawberries
Serves 10.

Sultana Roll

Line molds with Pistachio Ice Cream (p. 386). Sprinkle with sultana raisins which have been soaked 1 hour in brandy. Fill the centers with Vanilla Ice Cream or whipped cream. Cover with Pistachio Ice Cream. Pack (p. 393). Serve with Melba Sauce (p. 404) or Claret Sauce.

Claret Sauce. Boil 1 cup sugar and ¼ cup water 8 minutes. Cool slightly and add ⅓ cup claret.

Spumone

Line a melon mold with Lemon Ice (p. 387) or French Vanilla Ice Cream (p. 385). Fill with Bisque Ice Cream (p. 385) and Chocolate Mousse (p. 391), one layer of each. Freeze (p. 393).

Neapolitan Ice Cream

Pack two or three flavors of slightly softened ice cream in layers in a brick mold. One layer is usually lemon or orange ice. Freeze until firm. (p. 393).

Cassata alla Siciliana

Pack a brick mold with layers of slightly softened Pistachio (p. 386) and Vanilla Ice Cream (p. 384) and Raspberry Ice (p. 389). Freeze until firm.

Cassata Flambé. Heat cognac, light with a match, and pour, flaming, over slices of cassata.

Manhattan Pudding

Mix
  1½ cups orange juice
  ¼ cup lemon juice

Sweeten to taste with
  Sugar
Pour into a refrigerator tray or a 1-quart
brick mold. Whip
  ½ pint heavy cream
  ¼ cup confectioners' sugar
  1 teaspoon vanilla
Add
  ⅔ cup chopped walnut meats or
    macaroon crumbs
Spoon over the first mixture. Freeze (p.
393) until just firm enough to cut in
slices. The orange layer should not be
icy. *Makes 1 quart.*

Standish Pudding. Prepare strawberries
as for Strawberry Parfait (p. 392). Add
lemon juice to taste and enough water to
make 2 cups. Use in place of orange and
lemon juice mixture.

Frozen Orange Whip

Boil until the syrup spins a thread
(about 5 minutes)
  1 cup sugar
  ⅔ cup water

Add
  Grated rind of 2 oranges
  ¼ cup orange juice
Cover and keep warm 1 hour, then cool
and beat gradually into
  1 pint heavy cream, whipped
Cut in half and remove the pulp of
  2 oranges
Cut the pulp in small pieces. Put alternate layers of the cream mixture and the
bits of orange into a refrigerator tray
until the tray is full. Freeze until firm
(p. 382). *Makes 1 quart.*

Peanut Coconut Mold

Blend thoroughly
  ½ cup peanut butter
  1 can sweetened condensed milk
  2 tablespoons lemon juice
  1 can flaked coconut
Soften slightly
  1 quart Vanilla Ice Cream (p. 384)
Spoon into refrigerator trays (or into a
mold) in layers, spreading each layer
with some of the peanut mixture. Cover.
Freeze (p. 382) until firm. *Makes about
3 pints.*

Coupes and Parfaits

For a party dessert, use tall parfait glasses. Put a scoop of ice cream
in each one and pour over the ice cream a spoonful of sauce or
crushed sweetened fruit. Garnish further, if you like, with
whipped cream, marshmallow cream, candied fruit, chopped
nuts, crushed nut brittle, marrons, candied orange peel or toasted
coconut. See suggestions on p. 384.

Orange Coupe. Spoon Orange Ice (p.
387) into hollowed-out orange halves.
Pour 1 teaspoon Curaçao over the ice
and decorate with sprig of mint or other
green leaves. Or stir a little Curaçao
into Vanilla Ice Cream (p. 384) and
serve topped with shaved toasted hazelnuts.

Orange Pistachio Cream. Garnish Orange Ice (p. 387) or Orange Ice Cream (p.

386) with whipped cream and chopped
pistachio nuts.

Chocolate Mint Coupe. Alternate layers
of Chocolate Ice Cream (p. 384) and
Mint Ice Cream (p. 386). Garnish with
squares of glacé mint or a sprig of fresh
mint. Or serve Chocolate Ice Cream garnished with whipped cream flavored
with oil of peppermint and colored
green. Or Chocolate Ice Cream with
Marshmallow Mint Sauce (p. 400).

Ice à la Margot. Flavor sweetened whipped cream with pistachio and tint pale green. Spoon over Vanilla Ice Cream (p. 384). Garnish with pistachio nuts or Malaga grapes, peeled, seeded and halved.

Coupe St. Jacques. Put any mixture of fresh fruits in a parfait glass. Spoon Lemon Ice (p. 387) over the fruit. Pear, grapefruit, orange and Malaga grapes or strawberries make a delicious combination.

Desserts Made with Ice Cream

Among the easiest yet most impressive and delicious are Black Cherries Jubilee, Strawberries Flambé and Strawberries Romanoff.

Ice Cream Roll. Make Chocolate Roll (p. 484). Spread with slightly softened ice cream instead of whipped cream and serve immediately.

Ice Cream Croquettes. Shape firm ice cream with an ice cream scoop. Roll in finely chopped toasted almonds, toasted coconut or macaroon crumbs.

Meringue Glacé. For each serving, press 2 Meringues (p. 449) around a scoop of ice cream. Serve with whipped cream, a sauce or crushed fruit.

Frozen Éclairs or Cream Puffs. Fill Éclairs or Cream Puffs (p. 428) with Vanilla Ice Cream (p. 384). Serve with Chocolate Sauce (p. 399) or Butterscotch Sauce (p. 398).

Icebergs. Mix finely chopped almonds, hazelnuts, pecans and walnuts in equal proportions. Sprinkle over Mint Ice (p. 387).

Profiteroles au Chocolat (p. 428).

Black Cherries Jubilee (p. 352).

Peach or Pear Melba. For each serving, put a peach or pear half, hollow side up, on a dessert plate and top with a scoop of Vanilla Ice Cream (p. 384). Serve with Melba Sauce (p. 404). This dessert is usually made with canned fruit; if you

use fresh fruit, cook 5 minutes in Heavy Syrup (p. 529).

Peanut Balls. Shape firm Vanilla (p. 384) or Chocolate Ice Cream (p. 384) with a scoop. Roll in chopped peanuts and serve with hot Chocolate Sauce (p. 399).

Strawberries Flambé (p. 360).

Strawberries Romanoff (p. 360).

Sorbet à la Bruxelles. Crush raspberries or strawberries and put through a strainer to remove the seeds. Sweeten to taste and flavor with brandy or Kirsch. Stir into slightly softened Vanilla Ice Cream (p. 384) and serve in goblets. This dessert should not be firm.

Butterscotch Ice Cream Ring

Cook (p. 498) to the soft ball stage
    1 cup brown sugar
    1½ tablespoons light corn syrup
    ⅓ cup milk
    3 tablespoons butter
Butter a mixing bowl and pour in the syrup. Add
    4 cups corn flakes
Stir until well mixed. Pack into a well-buttered 8-inch ring mold or 8 small ring molds. Let stand to cool but do not chill.

Turn out and fill with
    Ice cream (1 to 1½ quarts)
Serves 6 to 8.

Frozen Rum Cake

Put a thin layer of sponge cake in a refrigerator tray. Sprinkle generously with rum. Cover with a layer of Vanilla, Coffee, or Chocolate Ice Cream (pp. 384–386). Put another layer of cake on top and sprinkle it with rum. Leave in the refrigerator to become firm. Turn onto a serving dish. Slice and serve with Rum Sauce (p. 429) as made for Babas.

For variety, spread on the top layer chopped nut brittle or macaroon crumbs soaked in rum.

Baked Alaska

Always an impressive dessert but not difficult to prepare. With ice cream frozen firm, you can prepare it before dinner and set it in the refrigerator ready to be put in the oven to brown while the table is being cleared for dessert. As added decoration, you may like to sprinkle chopped toasted filberts or almonds on the meringue before baking. Do not double the amount of meringue when you make a 2-quart Alaska — one based on 6 whites will be enough.

Beat until stiff
  4 egg whites
  ⅛ teaspoon cream of tartar
Beat in gradually
  ½ cup sugar
Continue beating until very stiff.

Put several thicknesses of brown paper on a small board that will fit in your oven. Set on the paper
  1 quart ice cream, frozen hard

Baked Alaska on a cake

Cover completely with the meringue. When ready to serve, set in a 450° oven and brown lightly (about 5 minutes). *Serves 6 to 8.*

Baked Alaska on Sponge Cake. Put a ½-inch layer of sponge cake on the paper. Place the ice cream on the cake, leaving a ½-inch rim of the cake all round. The cake insulates, too.

Baked Alaska en Surprise. Before spreading the ice cream with meringue, make a hollow in it and fill with crushed sweetened fruit or marrons.

Frozen Meringue Pies. Fill baked pie shells or tarts with ice cream and continue as above.

Grapefruit Surprise. Cut grapefruit in half, remove the fruit pulp, and cut away the white part to make a clean bowl. Put in each a layer of grapefruit sections or a combination of fruits and cover with vanilla ice cream or lemon ice. Top with meringue and finish like Baked Alaska (above).

Gâteau Riche

A superb but simple Swedish dessert.

Set the oven and prepare the mixture as for Swedish Almond Wafers (p. 441). Butter and flour two 8 or 9 inch inverted layer cake pans. Put 1 tablespoon of the mixture on each and bake (the batter will spread to cover the pan). Let stand a few minutes until firm enough to remove from the pans. Repeat until the mixture is used. (The recipe will make 8 large circles, so bake part in small wafers to serve another time, if you prefer.)

Put one of the circles on a serving plate. Spread evenly with softened Vanilla Ice Cream (p. 384) in a layer about 1½ inches thick. Press another circle gently on top. Cut in wedges like a pie and serve with hot Chocolate Sauce (p. 399). *Serves 4 or 5.*

Dessert Sauces

Some desserts require a particular sauce to complete the blending of flavor and texture necessary to perfection, and when this is so the recipe refers to the special sauce required. Often you can concoct a delicious dessert out of leftover cake or pudding by adding an interesting sauce, such as Coffee Custard Sauce (p. 399) or Maple Cream Sauce (p. 400).

Sauces for ice cream. Some of the best are the various Butterscotch Sauces, Chocolate Sauces (including the popular Fudge Sauce), Peppermint Sauce, Holiday Sauce, Melba Sauce and other fruit sauces.

Amount to make. One cup of sauce serves 6 or 8, but of course this is a matter of individual taste. If the sauce is passed, you may need more than if you arrange each serving yourself.

To thin sauces. If a cooked sauce is too thick, add thin Sugar Syrup or cream, reheat in a double boiler or over low heat, and add more flavoring, if needed. Leftover sauces can often be eked out in this way to use on another day's dessert. To make thin Sugar Syrup, cook ¼ cup sugar and ¾ cup water for 5 minutes.

Butterscotch Sauce

Cook 10 minutes
    ½ cup brown sugar
    ½ cup light corn syrup
Add
    ¼ teaspoon salt
    2 tablespoons butter
    1 teaspoon vanilla
Stir well. *Makes about 1 cup.*

Cream Butterscotch Sauce. Add ½ cup thin cream to the sugar and syrup. Cook 30 minutes in a double boiler, stirring occasionally. Add the salt, butter and vanilla. Serve warm or cold.

Rich Butterscotch Sauce

Mix in a double boiler top
    ½ cup butter
    2⅔ cups light brown sugar (1 pound)
    1 tablespoon lemon juice or ½ teaspoon vinegar
    ½ cup heavy cream
    Few grains salt
Cook over simmering water 1 hour, stirring occasionally. *Makes 1 pint.*

Henri's Butterscotch Sauce

A de luxe sauce, almost transparent but very rich. Store in a covered jar in the refrigerator and reheat in a double boiler. If it is too thick, thin it with Sugar Syrup (p. 36).

Cook to 246° (firm ball stage)
    1½ cups sugar
    1¼ cups corn syrup
    ¼ teaspoon salt
    ¼ pound butter
    ½ pint cream
Remove from the heat. Stir in
    ½ pint cream
Cook to 224° (just barely thick). Add
    1 teaspoon vanilla
Cool. *Makes about 1 quart.*

Caramel Sauce

Put in a small heavy pan
    1 cup sugar
Heat over low heat, stirring constantly, until the sugar melts and is slightly brown. Add slowly

398

1 cup boiling water
Boil 6 minutes. Cool. *Makes about 1 cup.*

To make slightly less sweet, flavor with lemon juice to taste. For a change add crème de cacao or brandy as well.

Chocolate Sauce

Put in a small heavy saucepan
  2 tablespoons butter
  2 ounces unsweetened chocolate
Stir over low heat until the chocolate melts. Remove from heat. Stir in
  1 cup sugar
  Few grains salt
Add
  ½ cup water
Blend well. Cook, stirring constantly, until the sauce is as thick as you like it. Flavor to taste with
  Vanilla, vanilla and brandy, or peppermint
Makes about 1 cup.

Quick Chocolate Sauce

Melt over hot water
  2 ounces unsweetened chocolate
Add
  ¼ teaspoon salt
  1½ cups sweetened condensed milk (1 can) or 1 cup light corn syrup
Stir until thick. Add
  1 teaspoon vanilla
Add until as thin as you like
  Boiling water (½ to 1 cup)
Makes about 2 cups.

Creamy Chocolate Sauce

Creamy even when reheated.

Put in a saucepan
  1½ cups milk
  2 ounces unsweetened chocolate
Heat until the chocolate melts. Beat with a rotary beater until smooth.
Mix
  ½ cup sugar
  1 tablespoon flour
  Few grains salt
Stir slowly into the chocolate mixture.

Cook and stir 5 minutes. Add
  2 tablespoons butter
  ½ teaspoon vanilla
For Profiteroles (p. 428) or Cottage Pudding (p. 481). Makes about 1½ cups.

Chocolate Cream Sauce

Melt in a double boiler
  1 package semisweet chocolate (7 ounces)
Add
  1 tablespoon corn syrup
Stir until smooth. Add
  ⅓ cup cream
  Few grains salt
  Vanilla or peppermint essence to taste
Blend well. *Makes about 1 cup.*

Fudge Sauce

Mix in a double boiler top
  1 cup cocoa or 2 ounces unsweetened chocolate
  ¾ cup sugar
  ½ teaspoon salt
  1 tablespoon cornstarch
Add
  ½ cup light corn syrup
  ½ cup milk
Cook 15 minutes over hot water, stirring until thickened. Add
  2 tablespoons butter
Cool. Add
  2 tablespoons vanilla, sherry or brandy
Makes about 2 cups.

Coffee Custard Sauce

Beat slightly in a double boiler top
  3 egg yolks
Stir in
  ¼ cup sugar
  ⅛ teaspoon salt
Add gradually
  1 cup hot coffee
Cook over hot water until thick, stirring occasionally. Cool.

Fold in
  ⅓ cup heavy cream, whipped
For ice cream, puddings or Cream Puffs (p. 428). Makes about 2 cups.

Coffee Cream Sauce

Beat until thick
> 2 egg yolks

Cook to 234° (thread stage)
> 1 cup sugar
> ⅓ cup strong coffee

Pour over the yolks, beating constantly.
Add
> Few grains salt

Chill. Just before serving, whip
> ½ pint heavy cream

Fold in the coffee mixture. Add
> ½ teaspoon vanilla or brandy

Serve on any chocolate pudding or on squares of cake. Particularly delicious on Steamed Chocolate Pudding (p. 374). Makes about 2 cups.

Honey Sauce

Mix in a small saucepan
> 2 tablespoons melted butter
> 2 teaspoons cornstarch

Stir until smooth. Add
> ½ cup honey

Cook 5 minutes. *Makes about ½ cup.*

Honey Cream Sauce

Beat until thick
> ½ cup heavy cream

Beat in
> ½ cup strained honey
> 1 teaspoon lemon juice

Makes about 1 cup.

Maple Syrup

Delicious not only on pancakes and waffles but as a sauce on vanilla ice cream.

Warm the syrup slightly, and sprinkle a few nuts on top.

Rum Maple Sauce. Add rum to taste.

Maple Cream Sauce

Boil (p. 498) to the soft ball stage
> 1 cup maple sugar or syrup
> ½ cup cream

Beat 1 minute. Add

> 1 teaspoon vanilla

Add, if you like
> ½ cup chopped pecans or walnuts

Makes about 1½ cups.

Mock Maple Syrup

Boil until the sugar dissolves (1 minute)
> 1 cup light brown sugar
> ⅓ cup water

Add
> Few grains salt
> 1 teaspoon vanilla or maple flavoring

Serve hot or cold. *For pancakes and puddings. Makes about 1 cup.*

Marshmallow Sauce

Cut in pieces with wet scissors (or use very small marshmallows)
> ¼ pound marshmallows

Melt in a double boiler. Mix
> 1 cup confectioners' sugar
> ¼ cup boiling water

Add to the marshmallows. Stir until thoroughly blended. *Makes about 2 cups.*

Marshmallow Mint Sauce

Boil 5 minutes
> ½ cup sugar
> ¼ cup water

Add
> 1 cup tiny marshmallows, or large ones cut in pieces

Stir well. Pour slowly over
> 1 egg white, beaten stiff

Beat until well blended. Add
> 1 drop oil of peppermint

Tint with
> Green food coloring

Especially good on chocolate pudding or ice cream. Makes about 2 cups.

Molasses Sauce

Boil 5 minutes
> 1 cup molasses
> 1½ tablespoons butter

Remove from the heat. Add
> 2 tablespoons lemon juice or 1 tablespoon vinegar

Makes about 1 cup.

Thin Lemon Sauce

Put in a small saucepan
    ¾ cup sugar
    2 tablespoons light corn syrup
    ¼ cup water
Boil 5 minutes without stirring. Remove
from the heat. Add
    2 teaspoons butter
    1 tablespoon lemon juice
Makes about 1 cup.

Peppermint Sauce

Especially good on chocolate ice cream.

Mix in a saucepan
    ½ cup crushed peppermint stick candy
    ½ cup sugar
    1 cup water
    ¼ cup light corn syrup
Simmer until the candy dissolves.

Mix until smooth
    1 tablespoon cornstarch
    2 tablespoons water
Stir into the peppermint syrup. Cook
and stir until thick. Tint with
    Green food coloring
Cool. *Makes about 1½ cups.*

Holiday Sauce

A treat for Christmas or Thanksgiving.

Mix
    1 cup dates, cut small
    ½ pint jar maraschino cherries
    ½ pint jar green figs, cut small
    Syrup from the jars
Let stand over night or for several hours.

Add
    ¼ pound toasted almond halves
    Few grains salt
Boil 5 minutes
    ½ cup sugar
    ½ cup water
Add the fruit and
    Brandy or rum to taste
Spoon over servings of vanilla ice cream.
Makes about 3 cups.

Sabayon Sauce

*Zabaglione, the Italian version (p. 364),
is a wonderful sauce, too.*

Mix in a double boiler top
    Grated rind and juice of ½ lemon
    ½ cup orange juice or white wine or
        ¼ cup sherry
    ⅓ cup sugar
    2 egg yolks
Set over hot water and beat with a whisk
until thick. Cut and fold into
    2 egg whites, beaten until stiff
*Delicious over fresh fruit or a hot fruit
compote. Makes about 1½ cups.*

Cream Sabayon Sauce

Heat in a double boiler top
    ½ cup milk
    ½ cup cream
Beat together until thick
    2 egg yolks
    2 tablespoons sugar
Pour the hot milk and cream over the
egg yolks, beating constantly. Pour back
into the double boiler top and cook over
hot water, beating constantly with a
whisk until thick. Add
    2 tablespoons sherry
    ½ teaspoon vanilla
    Few grains salt
Cut and fold into
    2 egg whites, beaten stiff
*For fresh fruit or fruit puddings. Makes
about 2 cups.*

Yellow Sauce

Beat until stiff
    2 egg whites
Beat in gradually
    ½ cup confectioners' sugar
Without washing the beater, beat until
thick
    2 egg yolks
    ¼ cup confectioners' sugar
Combine. Flavor with
    1 teaspoon vanilla or ½ teaspoon
        vanilla and 1 teaspoon brandy
*For steamed puddings. Makes about 1½
cups.*

Floradora Sauce. Fold in ¾ cup heavy cream, whipped. Flavor with rum or sherry to taste.

Vanilla Sauce

The standard old-fashioned sauce for Cottage Pudding (p. 481).

Mix in a small saucepan
  ½ cup sugar
  1 tablespoon cornstarch
Add, stirring constantly
  1 cup boiling water
Boil 5 minutes. Remove from the heat.
Stir in
  2 tablespoons butter
  1 teaspoon vanilla
  Few gratings nutmeg
  Few grains salt
Makes about 1 cup.

Lemon Sauce. Omit the vanilla. Add 1½ tablespoons lemon juice.

Hot Orange Sauce. Use orange juice in place of water.

Maraschino Sauce. Use 2 tablespoons cornstarch. Add ¼ cup halved maraschino cherries and ½ cup maraschino syrup.

Thin Sauce (for Plum Pudding, p. 376). Use only ½ tablespoon cornstarch and omit the butter. Flavor with 1 tablespoon lemon juice and 2 tablespoons brandy. Tint with red coloring.

Roxbury Sauce

Beat until thick and lemon-colored
  1 egg yolk
Beat in gradually
  ¾ cup confectioners' sugar
Mix in a double boiler top
  ¼ cup fine sugar
  1 teaspoon cornstarch
  ⅛ teaspoon salt
Add gradually
  ½ cup milk
Cook over hot water 10 minutes, stirring constantly until thick. Add the egg mixture and
  ½ teaspoon vanilla

  1 tablespoon lemon juice
  1 teaspoon grated lemon rind
Fold in
  1 egg white, beaten stiff
For steamed puddings. Makes about 1½ cups.

Sea Foam Sauce

Cream
  2 tablespoons butter
  2 tablespoons flour
  ½ cup sugar
Beat together
  1 egg yolk
  ½ cup water
Add to the butter mixture. Cook over low heat or in a double boiler until thick, stirring constantly. Cool. Just before serving, stir in lightly
  1 teaspoon vanilla
  1 egg white, beaten stiff
For steamed puddings. Makes about 1½ cups.

Hard Sauce

Traditional with holiday plum pudding but excellent with all steamed puddings. For a perfect sauce, beat long enough to make it fluffy and smooth.

Let stand at room temperature until soft but not melted
  ⅓ cup butter
Cream thoroughly. Beat in gradually
  1 cup confectioners' sugar (sifted)
Beat until as light as whipped cream.
Beat in, drop by drop
  ½ teaspoon vanilla
If the sauce separates, add a teaspoon of boiling water, drop by drop. If you use an electric mixer, scrape down the sides of the bowl occasionally. Chill or serve at room temperature. *Makes about 1 cup.*

For a richer sauce, beat in ¼ cup heavy cream (lukewarm).

Brandy or Wine Hard Sauce. Flavor with 1 teaspoon brandy or 1 to 3 tablespoons sherry or Madeira.

Creamy Hard Sauce. Add 3 tablespoons warm milk, drop by drop.

Lemon Hard Sauce. Add ⅓ teaspoon lemon extract or 1 teaspoon lemon juice and 1 tablespoon grated rind.

Mocha Hard Sauce. Flavor with 2 tablespoons strong coffee and 2 teaspoons dry cocoa. Add cream.

Orange Hard Sauce. Flavor with 2 tablespoons orange juice and add 2 tablespoons grated orange rind.

Raspberry Hard Sauce. Beat in 2 or 3 tablespoons strained raspberry juice, fresh or canned, adding it drop by drop to prevent separating.

Strawberry Hard Sauce. Wash, hull, and drain ⅔ cup strawberries. Beat in one at a time. If desired, beat 1 egg white into the sugar and butter mixture before adding berries.

Sterling Sauce

The brown sugar version of hard sauce.

Follow the recipe for Hard Sauce (p. 402), but use ⅔ cup light brown sugar in place of white sugar. Add 2 tablespoons heavy cream, drop by drop. Flavor with 1½ tablespoons sherry and 2 teaspoons brandy, added drop by drop. *Makes about 1 cup.*

Ohio Sauce. Add 2 tablespoons chopped nut meats and 2 tablespoons chopped dates. Flavor with lemon extract.

Cambridge Sauce

Cream
⅓ cup butter
Beat in gradually
1 cup confectioners' sugar
Mix until smooth
2 teaspoons flour
2 tablespoons cold water
Stir into
½ cup boiling water
Boil 5 minutes. Cool.

Just before serving, combine the two mixtures and add

1 teaspoon vanilla
For steamed puddings or Cottage Pudding (p. 481). Makes about 1 cup.

Yankee Sauce. Add 1 teaspoon vinegar.

Monroe Sauce

Boil 12 minutes
2 cups brown sugar
1 cup boiling water
Mix until smooth
2 teaspoons cornstarch
¼ cup cold water
Add gradually to the syrup. Simmer 40 minutes, stirring occasionally. Just before serving, add
¼ cup butter
1 teaspoon vanilla
Slight grating of nutmeg
Few grains salt
For steamed puddings. Makes about 1½ cups.

Foamy Sauce

Cream
½ cup butter
Beat in gradually
1 cup confectioners' sugar
1 egg or 2 egg yolks, well beaten
Few grains salt
Set over hot water and beat until smooth and light (about 7 minutes). Flavor with
Vanilla, sherry or brandy
For steamed puddings. Makes about 1½ cups.

Foamy Sauce with Cream. Fold in ½ cup cream, whipped until stiff.

Maryland Sauce

Cream together
½ cup butter
1 cup sugar
Beat in gradually
4 egg yolks, well beaten
6 tablespoons hot water
3 tablespoons brandy
Put in a bowl and spoon over the top
4 egg whites, beaten stiff
Mix while serving. *For holiday steamed puddings. Makes about 3 cups.*

Hot Brandy Sauce

Cream together
    ¼ cup butter
    1 cup confectioners' sugar
Add
    2 egg yolks, well beaten
    ½ cup cream
Cook over hot water until the mixture coats a spoon, stirring occasionally. Fold gently into
    2 egg whites, beaten stiff
Add
    2 tablespoons brandy
For holiday steamed puddings. Makes about 2 cups.

Fruit Sauces

Crush fresh or thawed frozen peaches, raspberries, strawberries or blueberries. Sweeten to taste. Serve over ice cream or simple puddings or squares of sponge cake.

Currant Jelly Sauce

Beat slightly with a fork
    ½ cup currant jelly
Add
    2 tablespoons hot water
    2 teaspoons lemon juice
    Few grains salt
For a smooth sauce, heat until the jelly melts. *Makes about ½ cup.*

Fruit Juice Sauce

If the fruit juice is very sweet, use less sugar.

Mix in a saucepan
    1 cup sugar
    1 tablespoon cornstarch
    Few grains salt
Add slowly
    ½ cup boiling water
Boil 5 minutes. Cool and add
    1 cup fruit juice, fresh or canned
    2 tablespoons lemon juice
For ice cream and simple puddings. Makes about 2 cups.

Melba Sauce I

The simplest version.

Crush 1 cup canned, frozen or fresh raspberries. Strain to remove the seeds. Add ¼ cup sugar and cook slowly 10 minutes.

Melba Sauce II

Thicker than Melba Sauce I.

Crush
    2 cups fresh raspberries or 1 package
        frozen raspberries
Strain to remove the seeds. Add
    ½ cup currant jelly
Bring to the boiling point. Add
    Sugar to taste
Mix until smooth
    1 teaspoon cornstarch or arrowroot
    1 tablespoon cold water
Add to the berries. Cook and stir until thick. Strain and cool. *For fruit (see especially Peach Melba, p. 396) as well as puddings and ice cream. Makes about 1½ cups.*

Orange Sauce

Beat until stiff
    3 egg whites
Beat in gradually
    1 cup confectioners' sugar
Blend in
    Juice and grated rind of 2 oranges
    Juice of 1 lemon
For simple puddings. Makes about 1½ cups.

Orange Custard Sauce

Mix in a saucepan
    Grated rind of ½ lemon
    Juice of ½ lemon
    ½ cup orange juice
    ⅓ cup sugar
    Few grains salt
    2 egg yolks, slightly beaten
Cook and stir over low heat until thick. Add gradually, beating constantly, to
    2 egg whites, beaten stiff
Cool. Add

1 teaspoon vanilla
For Cottage Pudding (p. 481), fruit or sponge cake. Makes about 1½ cups.

Orange Cream Sauce

Put in a double boiler top
1 egg
Grated rind of 1 orange
2 tablespoons orange juice
¾ cup sugar
3 tablespoons flour
Stir thoroughly. Cook and stir over hot water until thick. Cool.

Fold in
1 cup heavy cream, whipped
For sponge cake squares or any simple pudding. Makes about 1½ cups.

Pineapple Mint Sauce

Mix
1 small can crushed pineapple
1 cup sugar
¾ cup water
Simmer 10 minutes. Cool.

Tint with
Green food coloring
Add
3 drops oil of peppermint
For ice cream or puddings. Makes about 2 cups.

Strawberry Sauce

Mash berries, sprinkle with sugar and let stand 1 hour. Taste, and add more sugar if necessary. See also Strawberry Whip (p. 360).

Strawberry Cream Sauce

Beat until stiff
1 egg white
Without washing the beater, beat
1 egg yolk
Stir gently together. Add
1 cup confectioners' sugar
1 cup mashed strawberries
½ cup heavy cream
¼ cup milk

Beat just enough to blend well. *For Cottage Pudding (p. 481) or squares of sponge cake. Makes about 2 cups.*

Whipped Cream

Whip cream, adding confectioners' sugar to taste as the cream begins to thicken. For ½ pint of cream the average amount to use is 1 tablespoon, but to serve with a very sweet dessert unsweetened cream is delicious. Add a few grains of salt and vanilla to taste. Whip until fluffy but not stiff. For details about whipping cream (p. 11).

Frozen Whipped Cream. *Particularly good on warm apple or blueberry pie.* Pack in a refrigerator tray and chill until firm. Serve in cubes.

Molasses or Honey Cream. *For hot gingerbread and spice or fruit puddings.* Sweeten with molasses or honey instead of sugar.

Whipped Dry Milk

A light fluffy topping which can substitute for whipped cream.

Mix in a bowl
½ cup powdered skim milk
½ cup water
1 tablespoon lemon juice
Whip until light. Add, to taste
Confectioners' sugar
Vanilla

Devonshire Cream

Delicious with hot scones and raspberry jam or on fresh or stewed fruit.

Mash until soft
1 package cream cheese (3 ounces)
Beat in
½ cup heavy cream
Beat until smooth. *Makes about ¾ cup.*

Gervaise. *Particularly good on peaches or on a hot fruit compote.* Use thick sour cream and add 1 tablespoon brandy.

Pie Crusts

Lining the Pie Plate or Tin. Filling and Applying the Top Crust

Two Methods for Making a Single Crust

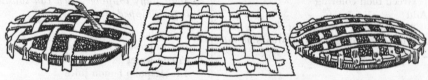

Three Methods for Making a Lattice Top Crust

Two Methods for Making a Baked Shell

Making Patty Shells

Pastry and Pies

Perfect pastry is a triumph. Made by the standard method, it is superbly flaky, but Hot Water Pastry (p. 409) and Stirred Pastry (p. 409) are easier for the beginner to make and are tender and delicious. Puff Paste (p. 410), the queen of pastries, is used for patty shells and small pastries. It is satisfying to have a ball of pastry in the refrigerator, ready for hurry-up desserts, cocktail snacks and meat or chicken pies.

Pies are usually served as dessert, but in New England warm apple pie is sometimes presented at breakfast as a special Sunday morning treat. An 8 or 9 inch pie may be cut into 6 generous pieces. Very rich pie — Pecan Pie, for example — should be cut in narrower wedges and so will provide as many as 8 servings.

Plain Pastry

Save the scraps of pastry for Cheese Straws (p. 52), or Petites Galettes (p. 426), or cut with a cooky cutter, bake, and spread with jelly or jam.

Measure accurately until you can judge by the "feel." Work very quickly and with a light touch. Beginning cooks can be too conscientious about pastry making and blend it so thoroughly that the layers of shortening and flour cannot separate into tender sheets.

Sift into a mixing bowl
    2 cups pastry flour or 1¾ cups all-purpose flour
    1 teaspoon salt
Add
    ⅔ cup vegetable shortening or lard
    or ⅓ cup lard and ⅓ cup butter
Mix (cut in) with a pastry blender, a blending fork or two knives (one in each hand) until the mixture is in even bits about the size of peas. (*Old-fashioned cooks use their fingers and work very quickly so that the shortening does not soften.*)

Put in a cup
    ⅓ cup ice water
Sprinkle it over the flour by tablespoonfuls, stirring it in with a fork until just enough has been added so that you can pat the dough lightly into a ball (*flours vary, so you may not need all the water*). Handle the dough as little as possible and do not knead it.

Wrap the dough in wax paper or foil and chill it. *Enough for a 9-inch two-crust pie or a one-crust pie and some tarts.*

Pie Making

Dust a canvas pastry cloth or a board very lightly with flour. Too much flour makes pastry tough. Well-chilled pastry dough needs very little to keep it from sticking.

Set the ball of chilled dough on the cloth. Tap it with a few light strokes of the rolling pin to flatten it but do not press it hard.

Roll with quick light strokes, working outward from the center. Lift the pastry occasionally with a broad spatula and

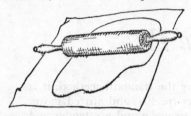

dust under it with just enough flour to keep it from sticking. Roll as evenly as possible so that the baked pastry will be the same thickness throughout. Piecrust should be about ⅛ inch thick.

Two-crust pie. Divide the pastry in two parts, one slightly larger. Put the smaller one in the refrigerator. Roll the larger piece into a circle about ⅛ inch thick and an inch larger than the pie pan. Fold double and lift gently into the pan. Unfold and fit lightly in place. Do not stretch. Trim the edge evenly with scissors or a sharp knife, allowing about ½ inch extra all around.

Put in a generous amount of filling.

Roll out the other piece of pastry the same way. Fold double and cut several slits or a fancy design near the center to let out steam during the baking. Or prick well with a fork after you have set it on the pie.

Brush the edge of the undercrust with water, fit the top crust over the filling, and press the edge of the top crust lightly over the undercrust. Trim the edges evenly and crimp with the fingers or the tines of a fork.

One-crust pie. Line a pie pan as for a two-crust pie. Press the pastry to the edge of the pan with the tines of a fork.

For a higher crust, as for pumpkin or custard pies, turn under ½ inch of crust, making it stand upright. Press into a fluted edge with the fingers.

Chill thoroughly. Put in the filling.

Lattice crust. Cut pastry in strips as long as the width of the pie and about ¾

inch wide. Weave them directly onto the top of the pie or weave them onto wax paper, chill, and transfer to the pie. Trim off the ends. Finish the edge with the tines of a fork or crimp with the fingers.

Another way to make a lattice top is to lay half the strips in rows across the pie and the rest across them to make a diamond pattern without actually weaving them.

To glaze pies. Before baking, spread softened butter very lightly over the top crust; or brush the crust with ice water, milk or cream 10 minutes before the pie is done.

Baking pies. See individual recipes for correct temperature and time. The length of time is approximate: test fruit pies by pricking with a fork to see if the fruit is tender. If the upper crust begins to brown too quickly, cover it with a piece of brown paper.

To keep the juices from dripping in the oven, put a piece of aluminum foil under the pie pan and fold the edges up.

Ways to Vary Plain Pastry

Cheese Pastry. Add 5 tablespoons grated cheese, cutting it in with shortening. *For fruit pies.*

Coffee Pastry. Add 1 tablespoon instant coffee. *For cream pies.*

Nut Pastry. Substitute ½ cup finely ground nut meats for ½ cup of the flour. *For cream pies.*

Sesame Pastry. Add ¼ cup sesame seeds. *For cream pies.*

Catherine's Pastry

Almost as flaky as Puff Paste (p. 409). Especially good for Cream Pie (p. 419).

Sift into a bowl
    2 cups sifted pastry flour
    1 teaspoon salt
    ½ teaspoon baking powder
Work in, following directions for Plain Pastry (p. 407)

⅓ cup lard
⅓ cup ice water
Have ready
⅓ cup butter
Roll out the pastry. Dot with a third of the butter, roll up like a jelly roll, pat, and again roll out. Repeat twice. Chill. *For a 9-inch pie.*

Hot Water Pastry

A quick and easy method. The pastry is less flaky than pastry made by the standard method (above), but it is crisp and tender.

Put in a bowl
½ cup shortening (lard is best)
¼ cup boiling water
Stir until the shortening melts. Add
1½ cups sifted pastry or cake flour
¼ teaspoon salt
¼ teaspoon baking powder
Stir with a knife until well blended. Pat into a ball, wrap in wax paper and chill. *For an 8-inch pie.*

Stirred Pastry

Easy, crisp and delicious but not as flaky as Plain Pastry (p. 407) or Catherine's Pastry.

Sift into a bowl
2 cups pastry or all-purpose flour
1½ teaspoons salt
1½ teaspoons sugar
Put in a cup
½ cup salad oil (corn, cottonseed, peanut or soy)
¼ cup milk
Stir with a fork. Pour over the flour and stir until no dry flour shows.

Pat the dough into two balls for a two-crust pie or into one ball for a large one-crust pie and a few tarts. If you are making a two-crust pie, put the dough for the top crust in the refrigerator and roll it out after you fill the pie.

To roll the pastry. Place a ball of dough on a sheet of wax paper, flatten with the palm of your hand, cover with another sheet of wax paper and roll out with a rolling pin. Peel off the top paper and ease the crust into the pie pan, with the other sheet of paper on top. Peel off the paper. If it sticks, set the pastry in the refrigerator for a few minutes.

Galette Pastry

Sweeter and richer than plain pastry but less flaky. Especially for open fruit pies or tarts of the European type.

Sift into a bowl
1 cup pastry or all-purpose flour
½ teaspoon salt
1 tablespoon sugar
Blend in as for Plain Pastry (p. 407)
6 tablespoons butter
Beat together and stir in
1 egg yolk
1 tablespoon water
1½ tablespoons lemon juice or rum
Pat together and chill. Roll ¼ inch thick and fit into a pie pan or a flan ring. Trim the edge evenly.

Puff Paste

The classic recipe requires washing the butter (p. 8) and patting it into a thin square about 5 by 5 inches. However, the following method is so simple that it will stimulate you to make this delectable flaky pastry often. If you need more than this amount, make it in two batches for easier handling. For small pastries made with Puff Paste see pp. 426–428.

Cut in 3 slices
1 stick of butter (¼ pound), preferably unsalted
Put on a piece of foil and chill.

Put in a bowl
¾ cup sifted all-purpose or bread flour
¼ teaspoon salt
Sprinkle over the flour
¼ cup ice water
Blend with a fork, adding an extra tablespoon of water if necessary so that you can pat the dough into a ball. Put on a lightly floured board, cover with the bowl, and let "rest" 5 minutes.

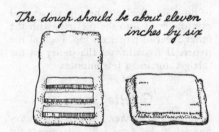

The dough should be about eleven inches by six

Knead until smooth and elastic (about 5 minutes). Roll out to make a neat oblong about 11 by 6 inches. Place the pieces of butter on the dough as in the illustration. Fold the dough to cover the butter. Press the edges firmly. Wrap in foil and chill in the refrigerator at least 30 minutes.

Unwrap the dough and put on the pastry board with the fold to your left. Tap with the rolling pin to flatten the dough and roll it into an oblong 18 by 6 inches, keeping it of even thickness and rolling with long light strokes. Lift the dough occasionally and dust the board lightly with flour. Fold into three layers, turn it clockwise so that the fold is not facing you, and roll out as before. This completes two "turns." Repeat until you have made six turns.

Unless you are working in a very cold room, wrap the dough in foil and chill it after each two turns.

Shape, chill, and bake according to the recipe.

Patty Shells. *Party fare filled with creamed chicken or lobster or other rich creamed dish.* Roll into an oblong about 18 by 6 inches. Cut out 12 rounds with a 3-inch cutter. Remove the centers from half the rounds with a smaller cutter to make rims and tops.

Put the plain rounds on a cooky sheet covered with two thicknesses of brown paper. Moisten the edges of the large rounds and set the rings on them. Press gently. Chill at least 20 minutes.

Heat the oven to 500°. Put in the pastry. Reduce the heat 50° every 5 minutes and bake until the shells are well risen and browned (about 25 minutes). Turn as necessary to brown evenly.

Baked Pie Shell

Line a pan with Plain Pastry (p. 407) or Hot Water Pastry (p. 409) as for a one-crust pie. Set another pan inside to hold it in shape or prick it well all over.

Bake at 450° until well browned (about 12 minutes).

Crumb Pie Shell

Especially for chiffon or cream pies. For a richer crust, add chopped nut meats.

Prepare
   1½ cups fine crumbs (graham cracker, gingersnap, rusk, zweibach, or vanilla wafers)
Add
   ½ cup sugar (or less)
   ½ cup melted butter or margarine
Mix well. If you will need crumbs for the top of the pie, set ½ cup aside and line a 9-inch pie pan with the rest, patting firmly with your fingers or the back of a spoon.

Chill until firm in the refrigerator or bake 8 minutes at 375° and chill.

Chocolate Crumb Shell. Make the crumbs of chocolate wafers. Add no sugar.

Coconut Pie Shell

For any fruit or cream filling or for ice cream.

Beat until stiff
   1 egg white
Beat in gradually
   2 tablespoons sugar
   1 tablespoon light corn syrup
   ½ teaspoon vanilla
Add
   2 cups shredded coconut, chopped fine
Line a pie pan as directed for a Crumb Pie Shell (above).

Bake 15 minutes at 350°. Chill.

Chocolate Coconut Pie Shell

Especially for ice cream pies.

Melt in a double boiler or over very low heat
2 squares chocolate
2 tablespoons butter
Mix together
⅔ cup confectioners' sugar
3 tablespoons hot water
Add this to the chocolate mixture and add
1½ cups shredded coconut
Mix well and press into an 8-inch pie plate. Chill.

Meringue
(for pies and other desserts)

At its best when put on the pie shortly before serving. If it must be baked ahead of time, set the pie in the refrigerator until serving time.

Put in a bowl
2 egg whites
Beat with a whisk or an egg beater until in soft peaks when you lift out the beater. Beat in gradually
¼ cup sugar
1 teaspoon lemon juice or ¼ teaspoon vanilla
Few grains salt
Spoon the meringue evenly over the pie but do not make it too smooth. Spread well to the edge so that the meringue will not shrink as it bakes. (For a different effect, spread part of the mixture and put the rest through a pastry bag and tube to make a pattern.) Bake at 425° until delicately brown (about 5 minutes).

Spread meringue on pies to the very edge

If a meringue "weeps," too much sugar was used or the sugar was too coarse.

If a meringue shrinks or is tough, the oven was too slow.

To cut a meringue pie easily, dip the knife in hot water.

Fruit Pie
(general recipe)

Remove the skin and pits from fresh or canned fruit. Cut in pieces to make about 2½ cups. If the fruit is hard (pears, for example), cook gently in Sugar Syrup (p. 36) until just tender and drain.

Line a 9-inch pie plate with
Plain Pastry (p. 407)
Fill with the prepared fruit. Mix
½ cup sugar (more or less, according to the sweetness of the fruit)
⅛ teaspoon salt
2 tablespoons flour
Cinnamon, allspice or ginger
Sprinkle over the fruit. Put on the top crust or a lattice top (p. 408).

To bind (for juicy pies). You may need to bind the edge with pie tape or foil to keep the juice in while the pie bakes.

Bake at 425° until the fruit is tender when pricked with a fork and the crust is nicely browned (about 40 minutes for most fruits). If the edges brown too quickly, cover with strips of foil. Remove foil or tape before serving.

Apricot Pie. Mash cooked or canned apricots to make 3 cups. Sweeten to taste.

Blackberry Pie. Cook 2½ cups berries with just enough water to keep from burning. Sweeten to taste. Add ⅛ teaspoon salt.

Cranberry Pie. Mix 2 cups berries, ¾ cup sugar, ½ cup water and 1½ tablespoons flour. Cook 10 minutes. Cool.

Cranberry and Raisin Pie. Add ½ cup seeded raisins to cranberry filling.

Date Pie. Cook 2 cups pitted dates with 1 cup water until thick. Add 2 tablespoons orange juice. Cool. Serve with whipped cream or sour cream.

Peach Pie. Cooked dried peaches or canned peaches make a delicious pie. Mash and sweeten to taste.

Meringue Fruit Pie
(in a crumb shell)

Prepare, setting aside ½ cup of the crumbs, a
  Crumb Pie Shell (p. 410)
Fill with prepared fruit as for Fruit Pie (above). Cover with
  Meringue (p. 411)
Sprinkle with the reserved crumbs.

Bake at 425° until the meringue is set (about 5 minutes).

Galette (French Fruit Pie)

Also delicious made with stewed and strained apples or plums, sweetened to taste.

Line a flan ring or 9-inch layer cake tin (square or round) with Galette Pastry (p. 409). Fill with cut fresh fruit, such as plums, apricots, peaches or apples. Sprinkle generously with brown or white sugar. Unless the fruit is tart, squeeze a little lemon juice over it. Bake at 425° until the fruit is tender (25 minutes or more). Cool. *Serves 6 or 8.*

To glaze. Melt currant jelly and pour over the finished pie.

Apple Pie

When apples are at the peak of their flavor they need very little seasoning — perhaps only a whiff of cinnamon. If they are somewhat bland, add lemon juice, grated lemon rind and nutmeg, or even a little rum.

Prepare
  Plain Pastry (p. 407)

Pare, core and slice
  6 to 8 firm, tart cooking apples (about 3 cups)
Line a 9-inch pie pan with pastry and fill evenly with the apples, piling them slightly higher in the center.

Mix and sprinkle over the apples
  Brown or white sugar (½ to ¾ cup, according to the apples)
  ¼ teaspoon salt
  ½ teaspoon cinnamon
  ¼ teaspoon nutmeg
If the apples are very juicy, add
  1 tablespoon flour
Dot with
  1 tablespoon butter
Cover with the upper crust.

Bake at 425° until the apples are tender (about 50 minutes). If your oven browns the pie too much at this temperature, bake the pie at 450° for 10 minutes, then reduce the heat to 375° until the pie is done.

Serve either warm or cold. Sharp cheese is the classic accompaniment, but also delicious — especially on warm pie — is heavy cream or Frozen Whipped Cream (p. 405).

Apple Pie à la Mode. Top warm pie with scoops of vanilla ice cream.

Deep Dish Apple Pie. Pack sliced apples closely in a buttered baking dish. Season as above. Put on a top crust. Bake at 350° until the apples are tender and the crust is brown (about 50 to 60 minutes). Serve warm with cheese, cream, whipped cream (plain or frozen), ice cream or Molasses Sauce (p. 400).

Apple-Cranberry-Raisin Pie

Line a 9-inch pie pan with
  Plain Pastry (p. 407)
Core, peel and slice into the pan
  4 large tart apples
Scatter over the apples
  1 cup cranberries
  ½ cup raisins

Mix
 ½ cup sugar
 ¼ teaspoon salt
 2 tablespoons flour
Sprinkle over the fruit. Dot with
 2 tablespoons butter
 Grated lemon rind
Put on the top crust.

Bake at 425° about 45 minutes.

Banana Cream Pie

Prepare a Baked Pie Shell (p. 410). Slice ripe bananas into the shell. Cover with cold Soft Custard (p. 362). Chill.

Just before serving, cover with whipped cream or sprinkle with shredded coconut or chopped peanuts.

Banana Custard Pie

Mix in a double boiler top
 ⅓ cup sugar
 1 tablespoon flour
 ⅛ teaspoon salt
Add
 2 egg yolks, slightly beaten
Stir in gradually
 1 cup scalded milk
Cook 15 minutes over hot water, stirring constantly until thick, and afterwards occasionally. Chill.

When the custard is cold, stir into it
 ¼ cup thin cream
 1 tablespoon lemon juice
 1 large banana, cut in thin slices
Just before serving, spoon into a
 9-inch Baked Pie Shell (p. 410)
Cover with
 Meringue (p. 411)
Bake at 425° until delicately brown (about 5 minutes).

Blueberry Pie

Wild blueberries have the finest flavor — tart and fresh.

Prepare
 3 cups berries, fresh or frozen
(Fresh berries need to be picked over;

discard the stems and leaves. Wash and drain well.) Add
 2 tablespoons flour
 ¾ cup sugar
 ⅛ teaspoon salt
Mix well. Line a 9-inch pie pan with
 Plain Pastry (p. 407)
Fill with the berries. Except for wild berries, sprinkle over them
 1 tablespoon lemon juice
Dot with
 1 tablespoon butter
Put on the top crust and prick well.
Bake at 425° about 45 minutes.

Open Blueberry Pie

The uncooked berries give this pie its distinctive flavor.

Prepare a
 9-inch baked Pie Shell (p. 410)
Wash and drain thoroughly
 1 quart blueberries
Mix 1 cup of the berries in a pan with
 1 cup sugar
 3 tablespoons cornstarch
 ⅛ teaspoon salt
 1 cup water
Cook and stir over low heat or over hot water until thick. Add the uncooked berries and
 1 tablespoon butter
Mix well and cool. Just before serving, pour into the shell. Spread over the top
 1 cup heavy cream, whipped and
 sweetened

Cherry Pie

Frozen cherries are excellent for pie.

Pit
 1 quart cherries (preferably sour)
Line a 9-inch pie pan with
 Plain Pastry (p. 407)
Fill with the cherries. Sprinkle over them
 ⅛ teaspoon salt
 1 cup sugar (¾ for sweet cherries)
 1 tablespoon flour
Put on the top crust or a lattice crust.
Bind (see Fruit Pie, p. 411).
Bake at 425° about 45 minutes.

Sweet Cherry Pie

Line a 9-inch pie pan with
    Plain Pastry (p. 407)
Fill with
    3 cups canned cherries, pitted
Mix
    ¼ cup cherry juice
    2 tablespoons sugar (or to taste)
    2½ tablespoons quick-cooking
        tapioca (or 1½ tablespoons
        for a softer filling)
Pour over the cherries. Dot with
    1 teaspoon butter
Put on the top crust or a lattice top.
Bake at 425° about 45 minutes.

Glacé Cherry Pie

Prepare a
    9-inch Baked Pie Shell (p. 410)
Drain, reserving the juice
    1 large can Bing cherries, pitted
Put the cherries in the shell.

Measure the juice and add water if necessary to make 1 cup. Add
    Salt and sugar to taste
Put in a small saucepan. Add
    1 teaspoon gelatine
Cook and stir until the gelatine dissolves. Pour over the cherries.

Chill. Cover with
    1 cup heavy cream, whipped and
        sweetened

Lemon Meríngue Pie

*The classic recipe, but there are ex-
cellent variations. Some like it very tart,
others sweeter. Some like it stiff enough
to cut in neat pieces, others prefer it
soft and creamy. Try it various ways until you have the version you like best.
For a softer filling, reduce the flour and
cornstarch or use fewer egg yolks. But always have a high fluffy meringue made
of 4 whites.*

Mix in a double boiler top
    4 tablespoons cornstarch
    4 tablespoons flour

    ½ teaspoon salt
    1½ cups sugar
Add
    1½ cups boiling water
Cook and stir over direct heat until the
mixture boils. Set over hot water, cover,
and cook 20 minutes. Add
    1 tablespoon butter
    Few gratings lemon rind
    ⅓ cup lemon juice
    4 egg yolks, slightly beaten
Cook and stir until thick. Cool.

Prepare and cool a
    9-inch Baked Pie Shell (p. 410)
Using 4 egg whites, make
    Meringue (p. 411)
Pile the filling into the shell. Spoon the
meringue on top, spreading well to the
edge.

Bake at 425° until delicately brown (5
minutes).

Lemon Meringue Tarts. Make large
Tart Shells (p. 424) instead of a pie
shell. Especially attractive and easy to
serve if the filling is soft.

Lemon Crumb Pie

Prepare, reserving ¼ cup of the crumbs
for the top, a
    9-inch Crumb Pie Shell (p. 410)
Set the oven at 325°. Separate
    3 eggs
Beat the yolks until thick. Stir in
    Grated rind and juice of 1½ lemons
    1 can sweetened condensed milk
    ⅛ teaspoon salt
Beat the whites until stiff and fold them
in. Pour into the crumb shell. Sprinkle
the reserved crumbs over the top.

Bake 40 minutes.

Lime Crumb Pie. In place of lemon
juice and rind, use the grated rind and
juice of 4 limes or ½ cup frozen or fresh
lime juice.

Orange Pie

Prepare a
9-inch Baked Pie Shell (p. 410)
Separate
3 eggs
Beat the yolks until thick. Stir in
½ cup sugar
3 tablespoons flour
1 cup orange juice
Juice of 1 lemon
Cook and stir over hot water until thick
(about 10 minutes). Pour into the pie
shell.

With the 3 egg whites, make
Meringue (p. 411)
Spread over the pie.

Bake at 425° until delicately brown
(about 5 minutes).

Glacé Peach or Strawberry Pie

Prepare a
9-inch Baked Pie Shell (p. 410)
Mix in a saucepan
1 cup sugar
3 tablespoons cornstarch
¼ teaspoon salt
¾ cup fruit juice or water
1 teaspoon lemon juice
Stir and cook over low heat until thick;
then simmer in a double boiler 20 minutes.

Fill the pie shell with
Hulled strawberries or sliced peaches
(about 3 cups)
Cover with the cornstarch mixture.

Chill. Spread with
1 cup heavy cream, whipped and
sweetened

Peach Pie

Follow the recipe for Apple Pie (p. 412),
using peeled sliced peaches in place of
apples. If the peaches are very sweet,
use only ½ cup sugar.

Open Peach Pie. See Galette (p. 412).

Fresh Peach Pie. Prepare a Baked Pie
Shell (p. 410), Crumb Pie Shell (p. 410)
or Coconut Pie Shell (p. 410) and fill
with sweetened sliced peaches.

Pineapple Pie

Prepare a
9-inch Baked Pie Shell (p. 410)
Heat in a double boiler top
2 cups crushed or shredded pineapple
Mix
2 tablespoons cornstarch
½ cup sugar (2 tablespoons for
canned pineapple)
¼ teaspoon salt
Add to the pineapple. Cook 20 minutes
over hot water, stirring constantly until
thick. Cool. Stir in
1 tablespoon butter
1 tablespoon lemon juice
1 tablespoon grated lemon rind
Fill the pie shell. Cover with
Meringue (p. 411)
Bake at 425° until delicately brown
(about 5 minutes).

Prune Pie

Cook, pit, and cut in quarters
1 pound dried prunes
Add
½ cup sugar
1 tablespoon lemon juice
Drain off the juice and cook until it
is reduced to 2 tablespoonfuls.

Line a 9-inch pie pan with
Plain Pastry (p. 407)
Fill with the prunes and pour over the
juice. Dot with
1½ tablespoons butter
Sprinkle with
1 tablespoon flour
Put on the top crust or a lattice top.

Bake at 425° about 45 minutes.

Raisin Pie

Put in a bowl
 ¾ cup raisins
 2 cups water
Let stand 2 hours. Mix
 1½ cups sugar
 ¼ cup flour
 1 egg, well beaten
 3 tablespoons lemon juice
 3 tablespoons grated lemon rind
 ⅛ teaspoon salt
Add the raisins and the liquid. Cook over hot water or over low heat until thickened (about 15 minutes), stirring occasionally. Cool.

Line a 9-inch pie pan with
 Plain Pastry (p. 407)
Fill with the raisin mixture. Cover with a lattice top.

Bake at 425° about 45 minutes.

Rhubarb Pie

For a softer filling, omit the egg.

Prepare
 3 cups rhubarb cut in pieces
Mix
 1 cup sugar
 2 tablespoons flour
 1 egg
Add to the rhubarb.

Line a 9-inch pie pan with
 Plain Pastry (p. 407)
Spoon in the filling. Put on a top crust or a lattice top.

Bake at 425° about 40 minutes.

Rhubarb and Raisin Pie. Before putting on the top crust, sprinkle ½ cup raisins over the rhubarb.

Pumpkin Pie

For a spicier filling, add ¼ teaspoon clove or nutmeg.

Set the oven at 450°.

Use canned pumpkin or cut raw pump-kin in pieces, peel, steam, drain well, mash, and put through a strainer.

Mix
 1½ cups cooked or canned pumpkin
 ⅔ cup brown sugar
 1 teaspoon cinnamon
 ½ teaspoon ginger
 ½ teaspoon salt
 2 eggs, slightly beaten
 1½ cups milk
 ½ cup cream or evaporated milk
Line a 9-inch pie pan with
 Plain Pastry (p. 407)
Pour in the filling.

Bake 10 minutes, then lower the heat to 300° and bake until firm (about 45 minutes).

With Whipped Cream. Spread the pie with whipped cream, sweetened slightly and flavored with vanilla or brandy.

With Ginger Meringue. Make Meringue (p. 411). Fold into it 2 tablespoons chopped preserved ginger. Spread on the finished pie and bake at 425° until delicately brown (about 5 minutes).

Pecan Pumpkin Pie. Flavor the filling with brandy. Decorate the top of the pie with pecan halves. Sprinkle with ½ cup Caramel Syrup (p. 14) to glaze the nuts.

Squash Pie

When you have squash as a vegetable, cook enough for a pie, too.

Set the oven at 450°.

Mix
 3 cups cooked mashed winter squash
 ½ cup sugar
 1 teaspoon salt
 ½ teaspoon cinnamon
 ½ teaspoon ginger
 ½ teaspoon nutmeg
 1 egg
 1¾ cups milk
Line a 9-inch pie pan with
 Plain Pastry (p. 407)
Pour in the filling.

Bake 10 minutes, then lower the heat to 300° and bake until firm (about 45 minutes).

Rich Squash Pie

Set the oven at 450°.

Mix
  1 cup steamed, well-drained, strained winter squash
  1 cup heavy cream
  1 cup sugar
  3 eggs, slightly beaten
  ¼ cup brandy
  1 teaspoon cinnamon
  1 teaspoon nutmeg
  ½ teaspoon ginger
  ½ teaspoon salt
  ¼ teaspoon mace
Line a 9-inch pie pan with
  Plain Pastry (p. 407)
Brush with slightly beaten egg white. Put in the filling.

Bake 10 minutes. Reduce the heat to 300° and bake until firm (45 to 60 minutes).

Sweet Potato Pie

Set the oven at 425°.

Line a 9-inch pie pan with
  Plain Pastry (p. 407)
Mix
  1½ cups mashed cooked sweet potatoes
  1 egg, well beaten
  1 cup milk
  1 teaspoon vanilla or 1 tablespoon rum
  Sugar, salt and spices to taste
  2 tablespoons melted butter
Spoon into the pie shell.

Bake until brown (about 30 minutes).

Sweet Potato Pudding. Pile into a buttered baking dish instead of a pie shell. Bake as above.

Mince Pie

Mincemeat recipes follow. Commercial mincemeat is improved by adding to it a few raisins, some chopped fresh apple or applesauce, a dab of butter, and brandy to taste. Add to any mincemeat chopped cooked meat, bits of jelly, ground orange or lemon peel and extra liquor.

Set the oven at 425°.

Line a 9-inch pie pan with
  Plain Pastry (p. 407)
Fill to the level of the edge of the pan with
  Mincemeat (about 2 cups)
Put on a top crust or cover with a lattice top (p. 408). Bake until the top is evenly brown (30 minutes). Serve warm, with pieces of sharp Cheddar cheese. Reheat if necessary.

For a gala effect, sprinkle the pie with warmed brandy, light with a match, and serve flaming.

Mincemeat I

A fine old recipe, but so large that you may prefer to make only half of it. Vary this basic recipe in any of the ways suggested in the recipe for Mince Pie (above).

Put into a large kettle
  4 pounds lean chopped beef
  2 pounds chopped beef suet
  3 pounds brown sugar
  2 cups molasses
  2 quarts cider
  3 pounds dried currants
  4 pounds seeded raisins
  ½ pound citron, chopped
Cook slowly, stirring occasionally, until the sugar and citron melt. Meanwhile, prepare
  2 quarts peeled sliced apples
Add to the mincemeat and cook until the apples are tender. Add
  1 quart brandy
  1 tablespoon cinnamon
  1 tablespoon mace
  1 tablespoon powdered clove
  1 teaspoon nutmeg
  1 teaspoon allspice
  2 teaspoons salt (or to taste)
Pour into jars, seal, and store. *Makes 20 pints.*

Mincemeat II
(without meat)

Put through a meat grinder
  1 pound suet
Add
  1½ pounds apples, pared, cored, and
    chopped coarsely
  1 pound dried currants
  1 pound sultana raisins
  1 pound seedless raisins
  4 ounces candied lemon peel, diced
  4 ounces candied orange peel, diced
  4 ounces citron, diced
  Rind of 2 lemons, grated
  Juice of 3 lemons
  1 teaspoon cinnamon
  ½ teaspoon nutmeg
  ½ teaspoon mace
  1 teaspoon allspice
Mix thoroughly with your hands. Add
enough brandy to moisten well. Pack
into jars or a crock and store in a cool
place. As you use the mincemeat in pies
or tarts, add more brandy to taste. *Makes
about 4 pints.*

California Mincemeat
Quick and delicious.

Put through the food chopper, using the
coarse blade
  1 cup seeded raisins
  3 tart apples, cored
  ½ orange
  ¼ lemon
Add
  ½ cup cider
Heat to the boiling point. Simmer 10
minutes. Add
  1 cup brown sugar
  ½ teaspoon salt
  ½ teaspoon cinnamon
  ½ teaspoon nutmeg
  ½ teaspoon powdered clove
Simmer 15 minutes longer. *For one pie.*

Green Tomato Mincemeat

Put in a deep kettle
  6 cups chopped apples
  6 cups chopped green tomatoes
  4 cups brown sugar

  1½ cups vinegar
  3 cups raisins
  1 tablespoon cinnamon
  1 teaspoon powdered cloves
  ¾ teaspoon allspice
  ¾ teaspoon mace
  ¾ teaspoon pepper
  2 teaspoons salt
Bring slowly to the boiling point. Simmer
3 hours. Add
  ¾ cup butter
Pour into 6 one-pint jars, seal, and store.
For 6 pies.

Coconut Macaroon Pie

Butter and flour a 9-inch pie pan. Set
the oven at 350°.

Beat until stiff
  4 egg whites
Beat in, a spoonful at a time
  1 cup sugar
  1 teaspoon vanilla
Mix together and fold in
  1 cup graham cracker crumbs
  1 teaspoon baking powder
  ¼ teaspoon salt
  ½ cup shredded coconut
  ½ cup chopped walnuts
Spread in the pan and bake 30 minutes.
Top with
  Whipped cream or vanilla ice cream
Serves 6.

Chocolate Pecan Pie. Use crumbs of
chocolate wafers in place of graham
crackers and 1 cup pecan nut meats instead of coconut and walnuts.

Pecan Pie
Serve this very rich pie in small wedges.

Set the oven at 450°.
Line a 9-inch pie pan with
  Plain Pastry (p. 407)
Mix and pour into the pie pan
  3 eggs, slightly beaten
  ½ cup brown or white sugar
  ¼ teaspoon salt
  1 cup light corn syrup
  ½ teaspoon vanilla
  1 cup pecans, broken in pieces

Bake 10 minutes. Reduce the heat to
350° and bake 35 minutes longer. Chill.
When ready to serve, spread over the
top
  ½ cup heavy cream, whipped
Garnish with
  Pecan halves

Southern Nut Pie

Line a 9-inch pie pan with
  Plain Pastry (p. 407)
Chill. Set the oven at 450°.

Cream together
  ¼ cup butter
  ¾ cup sugar
  1 teaspoon vanilla
Add
  2 tablespoons flour
  ½ teaspoon salt
Mix well. Beat in, one at a time
  3 eggs
Stir in
  1 cup dark corn syrup
  ¾ cup evaporated milk
  1 cup chopped pecans or walnuts
Mix well. Pour into the pie pan.

Bake 10 minutes. Reduce the heat to
325° and bake until firm (about 50 minutes).

Norfolk Treacle Tart

Another English delicacy.

Set the oven at 350°.

Line an 8-inch pie pan with
  Galette Pastry (p. 409)
Warm in a saucepan
  6 tablespoons golden syrup
Stir in, bit by bit
  3 tablespoons butter
When the butter is melted, add
  3 tablespoons cream
  1 whole egg and 1 egg yolk, beaten
  1 teaspoon grated lemon rind
Pour into the pastry shell.

Bake until the shell is brown and the
filling is set (about 25 to 30 minutes).
After the first 10 minutes, prick the tart
gently with a skewer so that the pastry
will not puff up too much in the bottom of the plate.

Cornish Treacle Tart

A traditional English delicacy.

Set the oven at 400°.

Line an 8-inch pie pan with
  Catherine's Pastry (p. 408)
reserving enough for a lattice top.

Mix
  ¾ cup golden syrup
  4 tablespoons fresh white bread
  crumbs
  2 teaspoons lemon juice
  2 teaspoons grated lemon rind
Pour into the pie shell (it will not be
quite full), and cover with the lattice.

Bake until brown (about 35 minutes).

Cream Pie

Prepare a Baked Pie Shell (p. 410) or
a Crumb Pie Shell (p. 410). Make a
Cream Pie Filling (below) and pour into
the baked shell. Or bake two or three
9-inch circles of pastry (Catherine's
Pastry, p. 408, is especially good), put
them together with the filling, and sprinkle powdered sugar over the top.

Meringue Cream Pie. Make Meringue
(p. 411; use the egg whites left after making Cream Pie Filling, below), spread it
over the top, and bake at 425° until
delicately brown (about 5 minutes).

Cream Pie Filling

Also delicious as a pudding.

Mix in a double boiler top
  1 cup sugar
  ½ cup flour
  ¼ teaspoon salt
Stir in
  3 cups milk
Cook 15 minutes over hot water, stirring
constantly until thick. Add
  3 egg yolks, slightly beaten
Cook 3 minutes. Add
  2 tablespoons butter
Cool. Add
  1 teaspoon vanilla

Butterscotch Cream Pie. Use brown sugar in place of white. Cook the sugar over low heat with 6 tablespoons butter until it melts to a golden-brown syrup. Add to 2½ cups of scalded milk. Add ½ cup cold milk to the flour, stir into the hot mixture, and continue as above.

Chocolate Cream Pie. Scald the milk with 2 ounces unsweetened chocolate (3 if you like a more pronounced chocolate flavor). Beat until smooth before adding the flour mixture.

Coconut Cream Pie. Add ½ cup coconut. Sprinkle the top of the finished pie with coconut, plain or toasted.

Frangipan Cream Pie. Add 6 tablespoons macaroon crumbs and ½ teaspoon lemon extract.

Devonshire Cream Pie

Cut out three 9-inch circles of Plain Pastry (p. 407). Cut the center from one, leaving a 1½-inch ring. Bake. Put the 2 circles together with Cream Pie Filling (above). Spread with a thin layer of the filling. Place the ring on top.

Fill with fresh strawberries or other fruit, sweetened to taste.

Garnish with whipped cream or glaze with melted currant jelly poured over the fruit.

Custard Pie

Baked this way, the pie has a crisp, dry crust. Easier to do than it sounds.

Set the oven at 375°. Butter a 9-inch pie pan.

Beat until well blended
    4 eggs
Stir in
    ½ cup sugar
    ¼ teaspoon salt
    3 cups milk, scalded
    1 teaspoon vanilla
Pour into the pan. Set in a larger pan

and pour hot water into the outer pan ½ inch deep.

Bake until firm (about 45 minutes). Cool on a wire cake rack. Prepare a
    9-inch Baked Pie Shell (p. 410)
Half an hour before serving, loosen the edge of the custard with a sharp knife. Shake gently to loosen the bottom. Hold over the pie shell with both hands, tilt, and ease the filling gently into the shell. Sprinkle with
    Nutmeg

To bake by the old-fashioned method, line the pie pan with pastry, brush with slightly beaten egg white, put in the uncooked filling, and bake 10 minutes at 450°. Then reduce the heat to 300° and bake until firm (45 to 50 minutes).

Caramel Custard Pie. Caramelize the sugar (p. 14) and stir it into the hot milk. Continue stirring until the sugar melts.

Coconut Custard Pie. Add ½ cup grated coconut to the custard.

Chiffon Pie

For a richer pie, whip ½ cup heavy cream and fold it into the filling before you spoon it into the pie shell.

Prepare a
    9-inch Baked Pie Shell (p. 410) or
        Crumb Pie Shell (p. 410)
Separate
    4 eggs
Put in a heavy saucepan
    1½ cups milk
    1 envelope gelatine (1 tablespoon)
    ½ cup sugar
    ¼ teaspoon salt
Add the egg yolks and beat with a rotary egg beater to blend thoroughly. Cook and stir over low heat until as thick as custard. Add the flavoring (below). Chill until slightly thickened.

Beat the egg whites until they stand in soft peaks when you lift out the beater. Fold into the gelatine mixture. Spoon into the pie shell. Chill.

Chocolate Chiffon Pie. Add to the hot custard 6 tablespoons cocoa or 2 ounces melted chocolate. Flavor with rum, brandy or vanilla. Particularly good in Chocolate Crumb Shell (p. 411). Sprinkle with chocolate shot.

Chocolate Chip Chiffon Pie. Stir into the hot custard 1 cup chocolate chips.

Coffee Chiffon Pie. Instead of milk, use strong coffee or flavor the custard with instant coffee. Add a tablespoon of lemon juice and sugar to taste. Spread the finished pie with a thin layer of unsweetened whipped cream.

Eggnog Chiffon Pie. Add 3 tablespoons rum. Cover the finished pie with a thin layer of unsweetened whipped cream. Sprinkle with nutmeg.

Chiffon Candy Pie. Stir crushed peppermint stick candy, butter crunch or nut brittle into the hot custard.

Black Bottom Pie

Follow the recipe for Chiffon Pie (p. 420) but after making the custard, divide it in half. To one part add 1½ ounces unsweetened chocolate, melted, and ½ teaspoon vanilla. To the other part add 1 tablespoon rum. Cool about 5 minutes. Add half the beaten egg whites to each part. Cool.

When the mixtures begin to thicken, pour the chocolate part into the pie shell and cover with the rum-flavored custard. Top with a thin layer of sweetened whipped cream and sprinkle with thin shavings of chocolate.

Lemon Chiffon Pie

Prepare a
    9-inch Baked Pie Shell (p. 410) or
        Crumb Crust (p. 410)
Separate
    4 eggs
Put in a small heavy saucepan
    1 envelope gelatine (1 tablespoon)

½ cup sugar
⅛ teaspoon salt
¼ cup water
½ cup lemon juice
Add the egg yolks and beat with a rotary egg beater until well blended. Cook and stir over low heat until the gelatine dissolves (about 5 minutes). Stir in
    1 teaspoon grated lemon rind
Chill until the mixture begins to thicken.

Beat the egg whites until foamy. Beat in gradually
    ½ cup sugar
Beat until stiff. Fold in the gelatine mixture and spoon into the pie shell. Chill.

Lime Chiffon Pie. Use lime juice and grated lime rind.

Orange Chiffon Pie. Use 2 tablespoons lemon juice and ½ cup orange juice. Use orange rind in place of lemon.

Strawberry Chiffon Pie

For a richer pie, fold in ½ cup heavy cream, whipped, or spread the finished pie with sweetened whipped cream.

Prepare a
    9-inch Baked Pie Shell (p. 410) or
        Crumb Pie Shell (p. 410)
Wash and hull
    1½ cups strawberries
Save a few perfect berries to garnish the finished pie. Slice the rest and cover with
    ⅓ cup sugar
Let stand ½ hour.

Mix in a saucepan
    1 envelope gelatine (1 tablespoon)
    ¼ cup sugar
    ¾ cup water
    1 tablespoon lemon juice
    ⅛ teaspoon salt
Cook and stir over low heat until the gelatine dissolves. Add to the berries, stir well, and chill until the mixture begins to thicken. Fold in
    2 egg whites, beaten stiff
Pour into the pie shell. Garnish with berries. Chill.

Raspberry Chiffon Pie. Use raspberries in place of strawberries. Taste and add more sugar, if needed.

Coconut Almond Pie

Follow the recipe for Chiffon Pie (p. 420), adding to the filling ½ teaspoon almond extract and ½ cup shredded coconut. Pour into the pie shell. Pat into the surface ¼ cup chopped toasted almonds mixed with ¼ cup chopped shredded coconut.

Angel Pie

Butter a 9-inch pie pan. Set the oven at 275°.

Beat until stiff
   4 egg whites
   ¼ teaspoon salt
   ¼ teaspoon cream of tartar
Beat in, a spoonful at a time
   1 cup granulated sugar
   ½ teaspoon vanilla
Spread in the pan, having the edge higher to make a rim. Bake until dry and firm to the touch but not brown (about 1 hour). Turn off the heat and cool in the oven with the door open. Spread with
   ½ cup cream, whipped
Let stand several hours or overnight in the refrigerator. Cover with
   Filling (below)
Spread with
   ½ cup cream, whipped but not
      sweetened
Serves 6.

Lemon Filling. Beat 4 yolks until thick with ¼ cup sugar and ¼ cup lemon juice. Cook over hot water until thick and smooth. Cool.

Strawberry or Raspberry Filling. Spread a layer of halved strawberries or whole raspberries over the cream. Sprinkle lightly with sugar and cover with the second layer of cream.

Florentine Meringue Pie

Roll Puff Pastry (p. 409) into an oblong about 6 by 18 inches. Cut off ½-inch strips from the ends and sides. Place the oblong on a cooky sheet. Wet the edges with cold water. Press the strips around the edge to make a rim. Prick in several places with a fork.

Bake at 450° until well puffed and lightly browned (about 10 minutes). Cool.

Spread with any tart jam. Cover with Meringue (p. 411). Sprinkle with shredded toasted almonds, dust with powdered sugar. Bake 5 minutes at 425°.

To serve, cut in oblongs or squares.

Cheese Cake

The best of the many good versions of this popular dessert.

Mix
   1 cup zweibach crumbs
   ¼ cup melted butter
   ¼ cup sugar
   ¼ teaspoon cinnamon
   ¼ teaspoon nutmeg
Pat over the bottom of a 9-inch spring pan and up about 1 inch on the sides. Chill.

Set the oven at 325°.

Separate
   4 eggs
Beat the whites until stiff with
   ¼ cup sugar
Set aside. Without washing the beater, beat the yolks until thick. Add
   1 cup sour cream
   1 teaspoon vanilla
Beat in
   ¾ cup sugar
   2 tablespoons flour
   ¼ teaspoon salt
Stir in, bit by bit
   1 pound cream cheese (softened)
Beat until smooth. Fold in the egg whites. Spoon into the pan.

Bake until firm to the touch (about 1 hour). Cool, then chill in the refrigerator.

Turn out onto a serving plate. Serve in wedges, plain or with crushed sugared strawberries, raspberries or sliced peaches. *Serves 8.*

Cheese Pie Royale. Do not add the sour cream and vanilla to the mixture. Bake the pie at 375° for 20 minutes and cool. Stir the vanilla and 2 tablespoons sugar into the sour cream and spread it over the pie. Sprinkle with cinnamon and bake 5 minutes at 400°. Cool.

Cottage Cheese Pie

Set aside ½ cup of the buttered crumbs while making a
   Crumb Pie Shell (p. 410)
Set the oven at 350°.

Press through a fine sieve or whirl in a blender

1 pound cottage cheese (not creamed)
Add
   ⅓ cup sugar
   ½ teaspoon salt
   ½ cup light cream or milk
   3 eggs, well beaten
   2 tablespoons melted butter
   Grated rind and juice of 1 lemon
Pour into the crumb shell. Bake until firm (about 1 hour). *Serves 6.*

Raisin Cottage Cheese Pie. Add ½ cup raisins.

Strawberry Cheese Pie

Spread a Baked Pie Shell (p. 410) with cream cheese softened with sour cream. Cover evenly with perfect strawberries. Melt a small glass of currant jelly, cool until almost firm, and spoon over the berries. Chill.

Tarts, French Pastries, Cream Puffs and Fritters

Small pastries make excellent desserts which can be prepared well in advance. They are delicious, too, served with afternoon tea or morning coffee. At large parties they are most satisfactory because you can replenish the plate on which they are served at frequent intervals so that it always looks attractive.

Pastries are adaptable. When you make a pie, it is simple to put away a little of the pastry to use another day for a few tarts or for a cocktail accompaniment (p. 50). See also Cheese Straws (p. 52), Cheese Pastries (p. 52) and Cheese Wafers (p. 52), which are made of a cheese pastry.

Tarts

Roll out Plain Pastry, Hot Water Pastry or Stirred Pastry (pp. 407–409). Cut out with a pastry wheel or, a cooky cutter, or shape in any of the ways described below.

Bake at 450° until delicately brown (5 to 15 minutes). Fill with jam, jelly, marmalade, or any cake filling (pp. 495–497) or cream pie filling (p. 419).

Rounds. Cut with a large or small cooky cutter. Cut the centers out of half of them with a smaller cutter to make rims. Brush the plain rounds with cold water. Set the rims in place and press gently.

Squares. Cut out 2½-inch squares. Wet the corners and fold toward the center.

Deep Tart Shells. Cut in rounds large enough to cover inverted muffin pans. Press gently onto the pans. Prick all over with a fork. Or line the pans with pastry, press gently so there will be no air under the pastry, and prick well. Cool slightly before easing from the pans.

Fruit Tarts

See also Petites Galettes (p. 426).

Make Deep Tart Shells (above) in cupcake tins or special tart pans. Fill with sweetened fresh fruit or drained canned fruit. Top with Meringue (p. 411) or whipped cream, or garnish with chopped nuts or jelly.

To glaze (Glacé Fruit Tarts). Cook and stir ¾ cup water or fruit juice with 2 tablespoons sugar until thick. Cook 20 minutes longer over hot water, stirring occasionally. Pour over the fruit. Or pour melted currant jelly over the fruit.

Glacé Strawberry Tarts. Bake tart shells in tiny cupcake tins. Put a single perfect strawberry in each. Glaze (see above).

Lemon Tarts

Bake Tart Shells (above). Fill with Lemon Pie (p. 414) filling. Top with Meringue (p. 411) and bake. Or make tiny tart shells and fill with Lemon Cheese (p. 425).

Lemon Cheese
(for tarts)

Also delicious spread between lady fingers or slices of sponge cake.

Put in a double boiler top
¼ pound butter
1½ cups sugar
Grated rind of 2 lemons
Juice of 3 lemons
6 eggs, slightly beaten
Stir well. Cook over hot water until thick, stirring occasionally. Store in a covered jar in the refrigerator.

Pecan Tarts

Tiny ones are delicious sweets for a tea party. Serve larger ones as dessert.

Line muffin pans with Plain Pastry (p. 407). Fill with Pecan Pie (p. 418) filling. Bake at 450° until the filling is firm (15 to 30 minutes). Top with whipped cream.

Coconut Tarts

If you need only 12 tarts, set aside half the mixture, add ½ cup flour to it, and make into cookies, baking them like Sugar Cookies (p. 434).

Cream together
¼ cup butter
1¼ cups sugar
Add
1 egg
Beat until light. Stir in
⅓ cup milk
1 cup moist coconut
Line deep cupcake tins with
Plain Pastry (p. 407)
Fill about a third full with the mixture. Bake 15 minutes at 350°. *Makes 24 tarts or 12 tarts and 24 small cookies.*

Banbury Tarts

Prepare
Plain Pastry (p. 407)
Roll ⅛ inch thick and cut in pieces 3 by 3½ inches. Mix
1 cup seeded raisins, chopped
1 cup sugar

1 egg, slightly beaten
1 tablespoon cracker crumbs
Juice and grated rind of 1 lemon
Put 2 teaspoonfuls on each piece of pastry. Moisten the edges with cold water, fold over, and press the edges together with a 3-tined fork dipped in flour. Prick the tops well. Bake 20 minutes at 350°. *Makes 12 tarts.*

Cheese Banbury Tarts. Place a thin square of cheese on the filling before folding. Start baking at 450°. After 5 minutes, reduce the heat to 350°.

Raisin Tarts

Serve these thin tarts like cookies.

Roll very thin
Plain Pastry (p. 407)
Cut out 3-inch rounds (at least 60). Mix
¾ cup chopped seeded raisins
2 tablespoons chopped citron
3 tablespoons honey
2 tablespoons melted butter
1 tablespoon grated orange peel
¼ cup brown sugar
Put teaspoonfuls on half the pastry circles. Moisten the edges with
Milk
Cover with the other circles. Roll flat and prick the tops with a fork. Bake 15 minutes at 450°. *Makes about 30.*

Strawberry Almond Tarts

Line 8 muffin tins with
Plain Pastry (p. 407)
Put in each
1 teaspoon strawberry jam
Cream together
¼ cup butter
⅔ cup sugar
Stir in
⅛ teaspoon salt
2 eggs, well beaten
1 tablespoon flour
1 teaspoon almond extract
Fill the tins two-thirds full. Bake at 425° until golden-brown (about 13 minutes). Garnish, if you like, with
Whipped cream and chopped toasted almonds
Serve warm or cold. *Makes 8.*

Swedish Almond Tarts

Line 12 muffin tins with
  Galette Pastry (p. 409)
Mix
  ½ pound almond paste
  1 egg white
Divide in the tins. Put 2 strips of pastry over the top of each tart. Bake 25 minutes at 425°. Cool. *Makes 12.*

Petites Galettes

Cut out rounds of Plain (p. 407) or Galette Pastry (p. 409) with a small cooky cutter. Brush with egg white. Sprinkle with cinnamon and sugar. Bake at 450° until delicately brown. Serve plain or spread with jelly or jam.

Lemon or Orange Sticks

Bake pastry oblongs at 450° until pale brown. Put together with Lemon or Orange Filling (p. 496).

Nut Pastry Sticks

Cut pastry in strips 5 inches by 1 inch. Bake at 450° until pale brown.

Cool slightly. Brush with egg white slightly beaten and diluted with 1 teaspoon cold water. Sprinkle generously with chopped pecans and press lightly with fingers. Return to the oven and bake 2 minutes.

Orange Pastries

Roll Puff Paste (p. 409) ¼ inch thick. Cut out 2½-inch rounds. Bake at 450° until pale brown.

Split. Fill with orange marmalade, cover the tops with Orange Frosting (p. 491), and sprinkle a border of chopped candied orange peel around the edge.

Coconut Tea Cakes

Bake pastry rounds until nearly done. Cool slightly, brush with beaten egg white, sprinkle with shredded coconut, and finish baking.

Swedish Tea Circles

Roll Plain (p. 407) or Puff Pastry (p. 409) ⅓ inch thick. Spread generously with chopped blanched almonds, mixed with sugar, using half as much sugar as nut meats. Pat and roll ⅛ inch thick and shape with a small round cutter dipped in flour. Bake at 450° about 10 minutes.

Nut Pastry Rolls

Cut pastry in strips 5 by 3 inches. Spread with a thin layer of tart jelly, beaten with a fork. Sprinkle with chopped pecan meats. Roll like jelly roll. Place the rolls on a cooky sheet, with the edges on the bottom so that the rolls will stay firm. Bake about 8 minutes at 450°.

Bouchées

Make very small Tart Shells or Cream Puff Shells (p. 424). Fill with Cream (p. 495) or Lemon Filling (p. 496).

Condés

Roll ¼ inch thick
  Plain (p. 407) or Puff Pastry (p. 409)
Cut in strips 3½ by 1½ inches.

Beat until stiff
  2 egg whites
Beat in gradually
  ¾ cup fine sugar
Stir in
  ⅔ cup chopped blanched almonds
Spread on the pastries, leaving a space around the edges. Sprinkle with confectioners' sugar. Bake 15 minutes at 350°. *Makes 30 or more.*

Turnovers

Prepare Plain Pastry (p. 407). Cut out squares or rounds. Put a spoonful of filling on each, slightly off center. Wet the edges with cold water, fold over to form rectangles, triangles or half-circles, and press lightly together. Prick the tops well. Bake at 450° until brown (about 15 minutes).

Fruit Turnovers. Make 4-inch squares. Fill with applesauce, mincemeat, jam or jelly, or with fruit prepared as for any fruit pie. Apple and peach turnovers are very popular.

Tea Party Turnovers. Make tiny turnovers with any filling. Serve hot.

Cream Cheese Turnovers

Cream until smooth
   ⅓ cup butter
   2 3-ounce packages cream cheese
Blend in
   1 cup sifted pastry or cake flour
   ¼ teaspoon salt
Chill. Roll ⅛ inch thick. Cut in 2-inch rounds or squares. Put on each a dab of
   Tart jelly or jam
Fold double. Bake at 450° until brown (about 10 minutes). *Makes 30 or more.*

Miniature Cheese Cakes

Cream together until smooth
   3-ounce package cream cheese
   ¼ pound butter
Blend in
   1 cup flour
Divide in 24 small balls. Put one in each of 24 small muffin tins. Press against the sides with your fingers to line each tin evenly. Spoon filling (below) into each. Bake 20 minutes at 350°. Cool. Spread each with
   Sour cream
Top with a bit of
   Raspberry or cherry jam
Makes 24.

Cheese Cake Filling. Crush 2 3-ounce packages cream cheese. Beat in 2 tablespoons sugar, 1 teaspoon vanilla and 1 egg.

Palm Leaves (Palmiers)

Delicate French pastries that are ideal with coffee or with a simple dessert.

Sprinkle a pastry cloth or board with granulated sugar. On it roll out Puff Pastry (p. 409) into an oblong ¼ inch thick. Turn it over, sprinkle lightly with granulated sugar, and roll out to make an oblong 6 by 18 inches. Fold each end towards the center, making two layers on each side. Fold double, like a book, to make four layers.

Cut in ¼-inch slices. Pinch the centers slightly together. Place, cut side down, on a cooky sheet covered with brown paper. Chill 10 minutes.

Bake 4 minutes at 450°. Turn the palm leaves over and bake until crisp and brown (about 5 minutes).

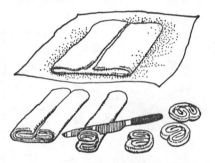

Cream Horns

Roll Puff Paste (p. 409) into a rectangle about 8 by 10 inches. Cut into twelve 10-inch strips. Roll over special forms, having the edges overlap. Chill 20 minutes.

Bake at 450° until well puffed and slightly brown. Brush with slightly

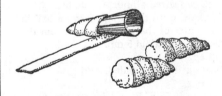

beaten egg white diluted with 1 teaspoon water. Reduce the heat to 350° and bake until glazed and brown.

Slip from the forms and cool. Fill with whipped cream or Cream Filling (p. 495). *Makes 12.*

Napoleons

Roll Puff Paste (p. 409) into a rectangle 6 by 15 inches. Cut into six pieces 6 by 2½ inches. Put on a baking sheet covered with two layers of brown paper. Prick well.

Bake 10 minutes at 450°. Reduce the heat to 350°. Bake until well puffed and brown (about 15 minutes longer). Cool.

Put together in pairs or in three layers with whipped cream or Cream Filling (p. 495). Sprinkle with confectioners' sugar or spread with Confectioners' Frosting (p. 491). Cut in half with a saw-toothed knife.

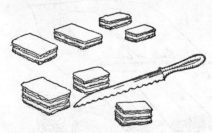

Cream Puffs (Pâte à Choux)

For other ways to use this basic paste, see Cocktail Bouchées (p. 50) and Choux Puffs (p. 59).

Set the oven at 425°. Put in a saucepan
    ½ cup boiling water
    ¼ cup butter
Heat until the butter melts. Add, all at once
    ½ cup sifted all-purpose flour
Stir hard until the dough forms a ball in the center of the pan. Remove from the heat and let stand 5 minutes. Add
    1 egg
Beat until well blended. Add
    1 egg
Beat as before. *The mixture should be very stiff. If it is not, let it stand 10 minutes before shaping.*

Take up by spoonfuls and arrange on a cooky sheet, 2 inches apart. Use a tablespoon for large puffs, a teaspoon for small ones.

Bake until there are no beads of moisture on the puffs, about 20 minutes for small puffs. For large puffs, reduce the heat after 20 minutes to 375° and continue baking 10 to 20 minutes or until the puffs are firm and crusty.

If the puffs are not baked long enough they will be soft rather than crisp. Test by taking one out of the oven. If it does not flatten down the puffs are done.

Prick small puffs and slit large ones with a sharp knife to let out the steam so that the puffs will be dry inside.

Cool. Fill with ice cream, whipped cream or any cream filling (p. 495). *Makes 8 large puffs, 18 or more small ones.*

Éclairs. Shape in finger-shaped oblongs, 1 by 4½ inches. For perfect shaping, use a pastry bag and tube. Bake. Split and fill. Frost with Confectioners' Frosting (p. 491), or add ⅓ cup melted Fondant (p. 504) to the frosting and dip the tops of the éclairs in the hot frosting.

Chocolate Pâte à Choux Rings. Shape in rings, 3½ inches in diameter. Bake, cool, split, and fill with whipped cream. Cover with Chocolate Portsmouth Frosting (p. 492) and sprinkle with blanched and shredded almonds.

Profiteroles. Shape tiny puffs with a teaspoon. Cool, fill with vanilla ice cream, and serve with Creamy Chocolate Sauce (p. 399). Allow 4 to 5 puffs for each serving.

Gâteau Praline. Shape in a ring (about 8 inches across) on a cooky sheet. Bake. Split and fill with whipped cream. Spread the top with Caramel (p. 14) and sprinkle with toasted almonds, cut small. *Serves 6.*

Queen Fritters

Make Cream Puff mixture (above). Drop by spoonfuls into deep cooking fat or oil heated to 375° and fry until delicately brown. The fritters will turn over as one side browns. Drain well on paper towels. Slit and fill with preserve or marmalade or Chocolate Cream Filling (p. 495). Sprinkle with confectioners' sugar or serve with Vanilla Sauce (p. 402). *Makes 18 fritters.*

Beignets (French Crullers). Drain and sprinkle lightly with confectioners' sugar.

Sfogliatelle. Brush with honey and sprinkle with chopped nuts.

Fritter Batter

For a thinner coating, add more milk and omit the baking powder. For a fluffier coating, beat the egg white separately and add it to the batter last.

Sift together
  1 cup flour
  1 teaspoon baking powder
  ¼ teaspoon salt
Beat until fluffy
  2 eggs
Add
  2 teaspoons sugar (for sweet fritters)
  ⅔ cup milk
  1 teaspoon salad oil
  Dash of lemon juice or 1 teaspoon brandy
Add the flour and stir only enough to dampen it.

Fruit Fritters

A dash of cinnamon goes well with fruit fritters.

Heat fat (p. 6) to 370°. While it is heating, prepare Fritter Batter (above) and the fruit. Dip pieces of fruit in the batter and lift out with a long-handled fork, letting the batter drain off into the bowl. Lower carefully into the fat and fry until delicately brown (3 to 5 minutes).

(It is impossible to give the exact amount of flour for perfect fritters. Keep the batter thin for delicacy and crispness. Test one fritter — if the batter does not cling as the fritter fries, add a small amount of flour to the batter and try again.)

Drain on paper towels. Keep hot until all are done. Sprinkle with
  Confectioners' sugar
Serve hot with meat or chicken, or as a dessert with
  Thin Lemon Sauce (p. 401), Melba Sauce (p. 404) or whipped cream

To prepare fruit for fritters. Peel and core apples and cut in ½-inch slices. Cut bananas in chunks and sprinkle with lemon juice and sugar. Drain canned peaches, apricots, pineapple and other fruit and cut in convenient pieces. Sprinkle lightly with flour.

Baba Cakes

An outstanding dessert.

Put in a mixing bowl
  ½ cup lukewarm water
Sprinkle over it
  1 package yeast
Let stand 5 minutes. Add
  ½ cup flour
Beat well with an egg beater or an electric mixer. Beat in
  4 eggs, one at a time
  ¼ cup sugar
  ⅛ teaspoon salt
  1 cup flour
Cover and let rise until light (about 45 minutes). Beat in, bit by bit
  ½ cup butter, soft but not melted
Butter deep cupcake tins or special baba tins. Put a tablespoon of batter in each tin. Cover and let stand 10 minutes.

Bake at 400° until brown. Finish as suggested below. If you do not need so many for one occasion, put some away in the freezer for another time, or bake part of the batter in a ring mold to serve as a Savarin (p. 430). *Makes 24.*

Babas au Rhum (with Rum Sauce). Boil 1 cup water with 1 cup sugar for 10 minutes. Cool to lukewarm and add ½ cup rum. Dip cooled Baba Cakes in this sauce and pour more sauce around them. As a variation, add ¼ cup raisins (or raisins and currants) to the dough when the butter is added.

Marmalade Babas. Cut a circular piece from the top of each Baba and scoop out a small quantity of the inside. Fill with apricot or orange marmalade. Replace tops. Serve with Thin Lemon Sauce (p. 401).

Savarin

Half the recipe makes one ring, enough for 6 servings.

Mix Baba Cake dough (p. 429), adding ½ cup flour. Bake about 30 minutes in two ring molds. Turn out onto a serving plate and spoon rum syrup (see Babas au Rhum) generously over the cakes. Fill the center with sliced and sweetened strawberries, a macédoine of fruit, ice cream or whipped cream, sweetened and flavored with rum. Vary the liquor as you like. Cointreau is delicious with strawberries, and Kirsch or brandy with mixed fruit. *One ring serves 6.*

Swedish Timbales and Rosette Cases

You will need special irons for making these professional-looking pastries. The deep ones make perfect patty shells for creamed chicken or lobster. The large rosettes are delicious with crushed fruit and whipped cream or merely sprinkled with confectioners' sugar and served with coffee.

Sift together
¾ cup flour

½ teaspoon salt
1 teaspoon sugar
Stir in
¾ cup milk
2 egg yolks, slightly beaten
1 tablespoon salad oil
Pour into a small deep bowl or cup. Let stand several hours so that the air bubbles will disappear.

Put enough vegetable oil in a small heavy pan to cover the iron completely. Put the iron into the cold fat and heat to 375°. Lift out the iron, drain it slightly on a paper towel and dip into the batter to about three-quarters its depth. Lift out, lower into the hot oil, and fry until delicately brown.

Timbale irons come in various shapes

(The first timbale case may not cling to the iron. Try having the oil a trifle hotter or cooler. You will soon find the perfect temperature.)

Pry off the timbale case with a fork. Drain, upside down, on a paper towel. Pry the rosettes off the iron with a skewer as soon as they are firm and drop into the oil to finish browning, turning them over to brown evenly. Lift out with a flat wire whisk. *Makes 18 or more.*

Cookies, Cooky Bars and Small Cakes

Cookies are favorites in most families. For one thing, they are easier to make successfully than most cakes. The dough may be thicker or thinner, the baking time may vary slightly — all without ruining the cookies. Most cookies are successful thick or thin, crisp or chewy.

A batch of plain cooky dough can produce a variety of cookies: divide the dough into several parts and flavor each differently; or use part for drop cookies, then add flour to the rest of the dough, chill, and make into rolled cookies.

Pastry flour makes cooky dough that spreads out during the baking to make thin delicate cookies. All-purpose flour makes firm cookies which hold their shape while baking. The amount of flour suggested in each recipe is approximate. Bake a sample cooky, then add more flour to the dough if you prefer thicker cookies. But do not add too much or the cookies will be hard and tough.

Preparing Cooky Pans

Select cooky sheets the correct size for your oven. They should be small enough to allow good heat circulation.

To grease pans (unnecessary for most cookies if you bake them on a heavy pan). Crush a piece of wax paper or paper toweling. Dip it in soft or melted butter or vegetable shortening. Rub lightly over the pan. If the cooky mixture is very thin, dust the pan with flour and shake off any that does not cling to the butter. It will be easier to remove the baked cookies from the pan.

Shaping Cookies

A cupful of cooky dough will make as many as 3 or 4 dozen thin small cookies or half that number if you make large thick cookies. The number suggested with each recipe is based on the way that particular recipe is usually made, but vary it as you prefer.

Drop Cookies. Take up even teaspoonfuls of cooky dough and push them off onto the cooky sheet. Leave space between the cookies for them to spread. A very thin mixture will need 2 inches between the cookies. If the mixture is firm you may prefer to press each cooky flat with a floured fork or the bottom of a glass or spread it with a knife dipped in cold water. Or shape with your fingers into balls.

Rolled Cookies. Put the dough in a covered bowl or wrap firmly in wax paper. Chill. Dust the board lightly with flour or confectioners' sugar. Put no more than a cupful of dough on the board at a time. Keep the rest cold.

Pat and roll to about ⅛ inch thick. Cut

Shaping Cookies

Dropping from a spoon

Making little balls

And flattening if wished

Cutting rolled dough with a knife or cutters

Pressing with a pastry bag or tube

Cutting after baking

out cookies with a floured cutter. Put on an unbuttered cooky sheet, close together.

Lay the scraps of dough on top of each other, roll and cut out or pat together and shape with your fingers into balls and flatten with a floured fork. To simplify the shaping, roll the dough into an oblong and cut with a long knife or a pastry wheel into squares or diamonds.

Refrigerator Cookies. Pack the dough in special molds or shape firmly into rolls about 2 inches in diameter and wrap in wax paper, twisting the ends to close. Chill thoroughly. With a long sharp knife, cut in slices ⅛ to ½ inch thick, as you prefer. Bake on unbuttered pans.

Cooky Bars. Butter a pan with a 1 or 2 inch rim. Spoon in the dough and spread it evenly. Cut the cookies in bars or squares after they are baked.

Cooky Press Cookies (p. 439).

Baking Cookies

Preheat the oven to the required temperature.

Watch carefully during baking. Turn the cooky sheet as necessary so that the cookies will brown evenly. If some bake more quickly than others, take them from the pan with a spatula and continue baking the rest.

Bake very thin cookies 5 to 7 minutes. Thick cookies and bars take longer. A slight variation in baking time does no harm, which is one reason why cookies are easier to make than cake. Most cookies are equally delicious whether they are slightly soft or are baked longer and become more crisp.

As a general rule, bake cookies until they are delicately brown, with a dry glossy surface and firm edges. Dark-colored cookies (ginger and chocolate) are sufficiently baked when the surface is dry

and the edges firm. If cooky dough is spread in a pan to be cut after baking, it is baked enough when it begins to shrink from the edges and when the top springs back when you press it.

To remove cookies from pan. Lift with a thin spatula. Let very delicate cookies cool slightly to stiffen so that you can

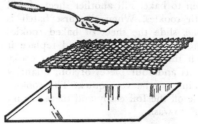

lift them without breaking them. If they become too stiff, hold the pan over moderate heat to soften the cookies slightly. Place the cookies on a wire cake cooler in a single layer, not touching.

Cut bar cookies according to the recipe. Some need to become firm before cutting while others cut more easily when warm.

Storing Cookies

Cool thoroughly. Pack in a tightly covered jar or metal box, or wrap in freezer paper and store in a freezer. If the cookies are very delicate, put sheets of wax paper between the layers. To keep soft cookies from drying out, put a slice of bread or a cut section of apple into the jar with them.

To store cooky dough. See Refrigerator Cookies (p. 438).

Decorating Cookies

Sprinkle unbaked cookies with sugar, plain or colored, or press lightly on each cooky a few nut meats, raisins or bits of citron, coconut, angelica, or dates, figs, candied fruit, or fruit peel. For special occasions, decorate baked cookies with Confectioners' Frosting (p. 491) or Portsmouth Frosting (p. 491), put through a pastry bag and tube to make jack-o'-lantern faces, hearts, initials, or other appropriate designs.

Quantity Cooky Baking

Assembly-line technique.

Put a sheet of aluminum foil on a cooky sheet. Put cookies on it and put it in the oven to bake. Fill another sheet of foil with cookies. When the first batch is done, slide the sheet of baked cookies onto a wire cake cooler and replace it with the second one. With two cooky sheets and four pieces of foil, quantity baking can be very quick. The cookies slide off the foil easily and there are no pans to wash.

Christmas Cookies

A variety of Christmas cookies is a gay touch for holiday entertaining. Wrapped in bright paper, they are always welcome gifts. Cookies made with honey or fruit keep so well that you can make them weeks ahead. Bake thin ginger cookies and other rolled cookies a week or two in advance. In the last few days before the holidays make macaroons, meringues and butter cookies. Make Orange Cookies (p. 435) to use leftover yolks.

There are countless delicious cookies, but some of the best liked are:

Cookies for the Christmas Tree. Cut green string in 3-inch pieces, fold double, and press the cut ends into unbaked cookies on the underside. The baked cookies will have a loop so that you can hang them on the tree.

Sugar Cookies

Old-fashioned sugar cookies need the distinctive flavor of butter, but you may use a substitute successfully for the variations. For richer cookies, use more butter (up to 1 cup). To deepen the color, add an extra egg yolk. To emphasize the butter flavor, brush the baked cookies lightly with melted butter while they are still warm.

Set the oven at 375°.

Cream until light and fluffy
    ½ cup butter
Beat in
    ¾ cup sugar
Add
    1 egg or 2 egg yolks
    ½ teaspoon vanilla
Beat thoroughly. Add
    1 tablespoon cream or milk
Sift together
    1¼ cups flour
    ¼ teaspoon salt
    ¼ teaspoon baking powder

Stir into the butter mixture and blend well. Arrange by teaspoonfuls on a buttered cooky sheet, 1 inch apart. Bake about 8 minutes. *Makes 50 to 60.*

Almond Cookies. Add ⅓ cup almonds, blanched and finely chopped, ½ teaspoon each of cinnamon, clove and nutmeg, and the grated rind of ½ lemon.

Butterscotch Cookies. Use brown sugar in place of white. Melt butter, add sugar, and heat slowly until well blended. If desired, add ¼ cup chopped nut meats (black walnuts are especially good).

Chocolate Cookies. Before adding flour, add ⅓ cup dry cocoa, ½ cup chocolate bits, melted or not, or 2 ounces unsweetened melted chocolate. Bake at 325°.

Frost with Chocolate Frosting (p. 492) if desired.

Coconut Cookies. Add ½ cup shredded coconut chopped fine.

Date Cookies. Add ½ cup dates, cut fine with wet scissors.

Lemon Sugar Cookies. Omit vanilla. Add ½ teaspoon lemon extract and 2 teaspoons grated lemon rind.

Maple Cookies. Use maple sugar, crushed fine, in place of white.

Marmalade Cookies. Reduce the sugar to ⅔ cup. Add 6 teaspoons marmalade.

Nut Cookies. Add ½ cup chopped nut meats.

Orange Cookies. Use orange juice in place of milk. Add the grated rind of ½ orange. To heighten the color, use 2 to 4 egg yolks instead of a whole egg.

Raisin Cookies. Add ½ cup chopped seeded raisins.

Seedcakes. Add 1½ tablespoons caraway seeds.

Spiced Sugar Cookies. Add ¼ teaspoon nutmeg or cinnamon for very delicately flavored cookies. Add more if you prefer.

Rich Cookies

Cream until light and fluffy
    1 cup butter
    1 teaspoon vanilla
Beat in gradually
    ⅔ cup sugar
    2 eggs, well beaten
Stir in
    1½ cups flour (pastry flour for very delicate cookies)
Arrange by teaspoonfuls on a cooky sheet. Spread thin with a knife dipped in cold water. On each cooky place
    Raisins, nut meats or bits of citron

Bake like Sugar Cookies (p. 434). *Makes about 60.*

Sour Cream Cookies

Vary in any of the ways suggested for Sugar Cookies (p. 434).

Beat thoroughly
    2 eggs
Add
    1 cup sugar, white or brown
    ½ cup sour cream
    ⅓ cup butter, melted
    ½ teaspoon vanilla
Mix well. Sift together
    2 cups flour
    ½ teaspoon baking soda
    ¼ teaspoon nutmeg
Add to the first mixture. Bake like Sugar Cookies (p. 434). *Makes about 60.*

Chocolate Chip Cookies

Set the oven at 375°.

Cream
    ½ cup butter
Beat in until light and smooth
    ⅜ cup brown sugar
    ⅜ cup white sugar
Stir in
    1 egg, slightly beaten
    ½ teaspoon salt
    ½ teaspoon baking soda in 1 tablespoon hot water
    1⅛ cups flour
    ½ cup chopped nut meats
    1 teaspon vanilla
    1 package chocolate bits (6 ounces) or a 6-ounce semi-sweet chocolate bar, cut small
Mix well. Bake like Sugar Cookies (p. 434). *Makes about 40.*

Chocolate Oatmeal Cookies. Use quick oatmeal in place of nuts.

Date and Nut Cookies. Instead of chocolate chips, use ½ cup chopped dates. See also cookies made of the mixture for Date and Nut Bars (p. 445).

Chocolate Walnut Wafers

Set the oven at 350°.

Melt over very low heat
    2 ounces unsweetened chocolate
Cream until light and fluffy
    ½ cup butter
Beat in
    1 cup sugar
    2 eggs, well beaten
Stir in the chocolate. Add
    1 cup chopped walnut meats
    ¼ teaspoon salt
    ¼ teaspoon vanilla
    ⅔ cup flour (preferably pastry)
Mix well. Arrange by teaspoonfuls on cooky sheets. Bake 10 minutes. *Makes about 36.*

Coffee Cookies

Also delicious without the nuts.

Butter a cooky sheet. Set the oven at 350°.

Cream together until very light
    ½ cup shortening
    ⅔ cup sugar
    2 tablespoons instant coffee
Add
    1 egg, slightly beaten
    ¾ cup flour
    ¼ teaspoon salt
    ½ teaspoon vanilla
    ½ cup chopped nuts
Mix well. Put on the cooky sheet by teaspoonfuls. Bake until the edges are firm and the tops dry (about 12 minutes). Remove from the tin immediately. *Makes about 36.*

Rolled Sugar Cookies

Prepare Sugar Cooky dough (p. 434), adding just enough flour to make the dough stiff enough to roll out — about ¼ cup. Be careful not to add too much flour or the cookies will be hard and tough.

Chill 1 hour or more. Roll ¼ inch thick and cut out (p. 431).

Sugar Cooky Shells. Cut out in 4-inch rounds. Press on the outside of scallop shells or fluted tins. Bake. Serve filled with ice cream or fruit.

Sand Tarts. See also Virginia Sand Tarts (p. 438). Cut out with a doughnut cutter. Brush the circles with slightly beaten egg white and sprinkle with cinnamon sugar (1 tablespoon sugar mixed with ¼ teaspoon cinnamon). Split blanched almonds and arrange 3 halves on each cooky. Decorate the cut-out centers the same way or put a raisin, nut meat or a piece of citron on each to make cookies that are a bit different.

Filled Cookies

Follow the recipe for Rolled Sugar Cookies (above), cutting them in 3-inch circles. On half the circles put teaspoons of filling (below) or bits of jam, jelly or mincemeat (well drained, if necessary). Cover with the other circles. Press the edges together with a fork. Prick well or make 2 or 3 slashes in the top so that the filling will show.

Bake at 325° until delicately brown (about 12 minutes).

Jumbles. Before putting the top circles in place make 3 small openings in each, using a thimble like a tiny cooky cutter.

Fruit and Nut Filling. Mix ½ cup chopped seeded raisins, ½ cup dates, cut fine, ¼ cup chopped walnuts, ½ cup water, and ½ cup sugar mixed with 1 teaspoon flour. Cook slowly until thick.

Date or Fig Filling. Mix 1 cup chopped dates or figs, ⅓ cup sugar, ⅓ cup boiling water, 1½ teaspoons lemon juice, ½ tablespoon butter. Cook slowly until thick.

Lemon Butter Cookies

Cream thoroughly
    1 cup butter
Add gradually, creaming well
    1 cup light brown sugar

Add
   2 eggs, well beaten
   Grated rind of 1 lemon
   Juice of ½ lemon
   1 teaspoon cinnamon
   ¼ teaspoon powdered clove
   ¼ teaspoon salt
Mix well. Blend in
   2 cups flour
Add more flour, if necessary, to make the dough thick enough to roll out. Chill. Roll ⅛ inch thick and cut out. Bake until delicately brown at 350° (about 10 minutes). *Makes about 60.*

Peanut Butter Cookies

Set the oven at 350°.

Cream together
   ½ cup butter or margarine
   ½ cup peanut butter
Beat in
   ½ cup white sugar
   ½ cup brown sugar

Stir in
   1 egg
   ½ teaspoon vanilla
   ½ teaspoon salt
   ½ teaspoon baking soda
   1 cup flour (preferably pastry)
Arrange by teaspoonfuls on cooky sheets. Press flat with a floured spoon or mark with a floured fork. Bake until firm (about 10 minutes). *Makes about 60.*

Scotch Shortbreads

Shortbreads have a distinctive texture — sandy and somewhat crumbly.

Set the oven at 350°.

Cream thoroughly
   1 cup butter
Add gradually, while beating
   ½ cup confectioners' or light brown sugar
Sift together
   2 cups flour
   ¼ teaspoon salt
   ¼ teaspoon baking powder
Add to the mixture. Mix well and roll out ¼ inch thick. Cut in squares or rounds. Prick with a fork. Bake at 350° until delicately brown (20 to 25 minutes). *Makes 24 or more.*

Royal Fans. Cut in rounds (2 to 5 inches). Cut in quarters and mark with the back of a knife like a fan. Brush with egg yolk diluted with water. Bake.

Piñon Cookies. Cut out. Cover thickly with pine nuts, pressing them firmly into the cookies. Bake.

Jubilees

Cream thoroughly
   ½ cup butter
Add gradually, creaming well
   1 cup sugar
Beat until light and fluffy.

Beat together
   2 eggs
   1 teaspoon vanilla
   1 teaspoon baking powder
Add to the butter mixture.

Sift together
   1½ cups flour
   ¼ teaspoon soda
   ½ teaspoon salt
Stir into the first mixture and blend until evenly mixed. Let stand until firm enough to handle. Shape with fingers into 1-inch balls. Roll in
   Flaked cereal (corn or rice)
Put on a cooky sheet 1½ inches apart. Poke a hole in each with your finger or the handle of a small wooden spoon. Fill with
   Jam or jelly
Bake at 350° until firm (about 20 minutes). *Makes about 40.*

Butter Stars

Cream thoroughly
    1 cup butter
Add
    1 egg yolk
    6 tablespoons confectioners' sugar
    3 cups flour
    1 tablespoon sherry or brandy
Mix thoroughly. Chill. Roll ½ inch thick. Cut out with a star cutter.

Beat until stiff
    1 egg white
Fold in
    ½ cup sugar
Put a spoonful on each cooky. Prepare
    ⅓ cup chopped almonds
Sprinkle on the cookies.

Bake 30 minutes at 325°. *Makes 36.*

Refrigerator Cookies

Other cooky doughs may be successfully stored, too, if the recipe calls for at least ¼ cup of shortening to each cup of flour. A dough with less shortening will dry out and crumble. By refrigerating part of the dough you can bake cookies as you need them, a few at a time.

Cream thoroughly
    ½ cup butter
    1 teaspoon vanilla
Beat in
    ⅔ cup brown sugar
    ⅓ cup white sugar
    1 egg, slightly beaten
Sift together
    1½ cups flour (preferably pastry)
    ¼ teaspoon cream of tartar
    ¼ teaspoon salt
Add to the first mixture. Shape in a roll

about 2 inches in diameter or in several small rolls. Wrap lightly in wax paper. Store in the refrigerator.

With a very sharp, long thin knife, slice in rounds about ⅛ inch thick. Bake at 400° about 8 minutes or at 250° about 15 minutes. Both ways are delicious. *Makes about 60.*

To vary the flavoring, add ⅓ teaspoon cinnamon or nutmeg or 2 ounces chocolate, melted. Or add a package of chocolate bits or ½ cup broken or chopped nut meats, whole blanched almonds, raisins or coconut.

Pinwheel Cookies. Divide the mixture in half. Melt 1 ounce unsweetened chocolate, cool slightly, add to one part, and mix well. Chill. Roll each part separately into equal oblongs ⅛ inch thick. Place one on top of the other and roll up like jelly roll. Chill, slice, and bake as above.

Pecan Cookies. Add ½ cup chopped pecans.

Virginia Sand Tarts

Similar to a very rich shortbread.

Set the oven at 325°.

Cream until light and fluffy
    1¼ pounds butter (or part margarine)
Beat in
    2 pounds dark brown sugar
Beat well (setting 1 white aside for the top)
    3 eggs
Add to the butter-sugar mixture. Add
    2 teaspoons vanilla
    2 pounds flour (about 7½ cups)
Beat to blend thoroughly. Pat evenly into a lightly buttered jelly roll pan. The dough should be about 1 inch thick. If your pan is too small, put the extra in a cake pan. Beat the egg white slightly and brush it over the top of the dough. Sprinkle lightly with
    Cinnamon sugar
Press evenly into the dough
    ½ pound blanched almonds,
        separated in halves

Bake until delicately brown and firm to the touch (about 20 minutes). Cut in squares. *Makes about 60.*

Cooky-Press Cookies

Some of the best mixtures for cooky-press cookies are Norwegian Butter Cookies (below), Refrigerator Cookies (p. 438), and Peanut Butter Cookies (p. 437), made with 1½ cups flour.

Pack the mixture into a cooky press and push out onto an unbuttered cooky sheet. Bake about 10 minutes at 375°.

Norwegian Butter Cookies

Cream thoroughly
  ½ cup **butter**
Add
  2 hard-cooked egg yolks, pressed
    through a sieve
Beat in
  ¼ cup **sugar**
Add
  1 cup **flour**
  ½ teaspoon lemon or vanilla extract
Mix well. Shape and bake (see Cooky-Press Cookies, above). *Makes about 40.*

Chocolate Cooky-Press Cookies

Cream thoroughly
  ¾ cup **shortening**
Add gradually, creaming well
  1 cup **sugar**
Beat until fluffy. Add
  1 egg, **well beaten**
  ½ teaspoon **vanilla**
  ¼ teaspoon **salt**
  2 ounces **unsweetened chocolate,**
    melted
  2 tablespoons **milk**
Beat well. Stir in gently
  2 cups **pastry or cake flour**
Mix, shape and bake (see Cooky-Press Cookies, above). *Makes about 60.*

Peg's Molasses Cookies

No spice in these delicious cookies.

Set the oven at 350°. Butter a cooky sheet.

Sift together
  1 cup **flour**
  ½ teaspoon **salt**
  ½ teaspoon **baking soda**
Mix in a bowl
  ¼ cup **molasses**
  ½ cup **vegetable shortening, softened**
  ¾ cup **brown sugar**
  1 egg, **well-beaten**
Stir in the flour mixture.

Shape and bake like Sugar Cookies (p. 434). *Makes 30 or more.*

Molasses Cookies (Spice Cookies)

The old-fashioned kind — so good with a glass of milk.

Set the oven at 375°.

Cream together
  ¼ cup **shortening**
  ¼ cup **butter**
  ⅓ cup **brown sugar**
Add
  1 egg, **slightly beaten**
  ½ cup **molasses**
  ¼ cup **milk, coffee or water**
Sift together and add
  2 cups **flour**
  ½ teaspoon **salt**
  ½ teaspoon **ginger or cloves**
  ½ teaspoon **cinnamon**
  1 teaspoon **baking soda**
Beat well and add more flour if needed.

For crisp cookies, keep the mixture as thin as possible. For thick soft cookies, add more flour (about ¼ cup), but avoid using too much, which will make the cookies hard and dry. Flours vary, so test the mixture by baking a sample cooky.

Put spoonfuls on a cooky sheet. Bake about 10 minutes. *Makes 30 to 60.*

To vary, add ¼ teaspoon each of nutmeg, cloves and allspice. Or add ½ cup floured raisins.

Molasses Bars. Spread in two square cake tins, 9 by 9 inches. Bake about 12 minutes. While hot, sprinkle with sugar. Cut in squares or bars.

Rolled Molasses Cookies. Add enough more flour (about ½ cup) to make the mixture just stiff enough to handle. Chill. Roll (p. 431) and cut out, or shape and cut like Refrigerator Cookies (p. 438).

Molasses Crinkles

Very pretty with grains of sugar glistening on top.

Set the oven at 350°.

Mix well
    1 cup vegetable shortening (not oil)
    ¾ cup sugar
    ¼ cup molasses
    1 egg
Sift together
    1¾ cups flour
    2 teaspoons baking soda
    ½ teaspoon salt
    1 teaspoon ginger
    1 teaspoon cinnamon
    ½ teaspoon powdered clove
Stir into the first mixture and blend well. Shape in 1-inch balls with your fingers. (If the dough is too soft to shape easily, cover and chill in the refrigerator about 1 hour.) Dip tops in granulated sugar. Arrange on a cooky sheet.

Bake about 12 minutes. *Makes 50 or more.*

Gingersnaps

Old-fashioned gingersnaps keep so well that you will want to make them in quantity. Follow the "assembly line" technique (p. 434) to do them in a hurry.

Set the oven at 350°.

Heat to the boiling point
    1 cup molasses
Pour it over
    ½ cup shortening

Sift together and stir in
    3¼ cups flour
    ½ teaspoon baking soda
    1 tablespoon ginger
    1½ teaspoons salt
Shape one-fourth of the mixture at a time, keeping the rest of the dough in the refrigerator until you are ready to cut it out. Roll as thin as possible and cut with a small round cutter.

Bake until crisp and dry (8 to 10 minutes). *Makes 100 or more.*

Gingerbread Men

Also excellent made into cookies. Follow directions for Sugar Cookies (p. 434).

Heat to the boiling point
    ½ cup molasses
Add
    ¼ cup sugar
    3 tablespoons butter or other
      shortening
    1 tablespoon milk
Sift together
    2 cups flour
    ½ teaspoon each of baking soda, salt,
      nutmeg, cinnamon, powdered cloves
      and ginger
Add to the first mixture. Add more flour if necessary to make dough thick enough to roll out. Follow directions for Rolled Cookies (p. 431). Cut with a special cutter or with a very sharp knife.

Bake. Frost with Confectioners' Frosting and decorate with candies, raisins or bits of citron.

Crunchy Ginger Cookies

Set the oven at 350°. Cream
    ½ cup shortening
Add
    1 egg, well beaten
    ½ cup molasses
    ½ cup grape-nuts or toasted wheat
      germ
Let stand 10 minutes. Beat in
    ½ cup sugar
    ½ teaspoon vanilla

Sift together
  1½ cups flour
  1 teaspoon baking soda
  ½ teaspoon salt
  2 teaspoons ginger
Add to the batter.

Shape and bake like Sugar Cookies (p. 434). *Makes about 50.*

Swedish Nut Wafers

Set the oven at 325°. Prepare
  ⅓ cup chopped nut meats
Cream
  ¼ cup butter
Beat in
  ¾ cup sugar
Add
  1 egg, well beaten
  2 tablespoons milk
  1 teaspoon vanilla
Sift together
  1⅓ cups flour
  1 teaspoon baking powder
  ½ teaspoon salt
Stir into the first mixture. Spread evenly with a knife on the bottom of a lightly buttered inverted loaf pan. One tablespoon will cover a pan 7 by 3 inches. Sprinkle with nut meats. Press them gently into the cooky dough. Mark in strips 1 inch wide. Bake until delicately brown (about 12 minutes).

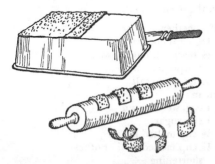

Cut the strips apart and lay immediately over a rolling pin to shape. Repeat until all the dough is used, baking a few at a time so that the wafers will be soft enough to shape. If they stiffen too much

to shape, put them in the oven a moment to reheat and soften. *Makes about 100.*

Swedish Almond Wafers

Serve these delicate wafers plain or put together in pairs with Paris Cream (p. 447).

Set the oven at 350°.

Mix in a small heavy saucepan
  ¾ cup finely ground almonds
    (unblanched)
  ½ cup butter
  ½ cup sugar
  1 tablespoon flour
  2 tablespoons light cream
Cook and stir over moderate heat until the butter melts. Arrange by teaspoonfuls, 3 inches apart, on a heavy cooky sheet or on a sheet of foil on a cooky sheet.

Bake until delicately brown around the edges but still bubbling slightly in the center (about 7 minutes). Cool until the edge is firm enough so that you can lift the cookies with a long, thin, sharp knife or a spatula. Repeat until all are baked. *Makes about 36.*

Hazelnut Wafers. Use unblanched hazelnuts in place of almonds.

Nut Cookies

Set the oven at 350°.

Beat until thick and lemon-colored
  2 egg yolks
Beat in gradually
  1 cup brown sugar
Add
  1 cup chopped nut meats
  Few grains salt
Fold in
  2 egg whites, beaten stiff
Stir in
  6 tablespoons flour
Place teaspoonfuls on cooky sheets and flatten with a knife.

Bake until firm (5 to 8 minutes). *Makes 50.*

Brandy Wafers

The only tricky part of making these delicate wafers is removing them from the pan. They must be firm enough to lift but not so stiff that they crumble.

Set the oven at 300°.

Heat to the boiling point
   ½ cup molasses
Add
   ½ cup butter
Sift together
   1 cup flour
   ⅔ cup sugar
   1 teaspoon ginger
Stir slowly into the molasses and butter. Arrange by teaspoonfuls on heavy cooky sheets or the back of a shallow baking pan.

Bake until dry on top (about 15 minutes). Let stand about 3 minutes before removing from the pans. *Makes about 60.*

To shape in tubes. Roll the baked wafers over the handle of a wooden spoon while they are still warm.

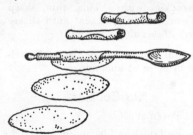

Boston Cookies

Set the oven at 350°.

Sift together
   1 cup flour
   ¼ teaspoon baking soda
   Few grains salt
   ½ teaspoon cinnamon
Cream together
   ¼ cup butter
   ½ cup sugar
Add
   1 egg, well beaten

Mix well. Stir in half the flour. Add
   ⅓ cup chopped nut meats
   ⅓ cup seeded raisins, chopped
Add the rest of the flour. Arrange by spoonfuls 1 inch apart on buttered cooky sheets.

Bake until delicately brown (about 12 minutes). *Makes about 36.*

Charleston Benne Wafers

True benne is wild sesame seed.

Set the oven at 350°.

Put in a small heavy pan
   ½ cup sesame seeds
Stir over moderate heat until slightly brown. Remove from the heat. Add
   1 tablespoon butter
   1 cup light brown sugar
   3 tablespoons flour
   1 egg, beaten
   1 teaspoon vanilla
   ¼ teaspoon salt
Arrange by teaspoonfuls on well-buttered cooky sheets about 2 inches apart.

Bake until firm (5 to 8 minutes). Remove carefully while still warm. *Makes about 30.*

Cape Cod Oatmeal Cookies

Set the oven at 350°.

Sift together
   1½ cups flour
   ½ teaspoon baking soda
   1 teaspoon cinnamon
   ½ teaspoon salt
Stir in
   1 egg, well beaten
   1 cup sugar
   ½ cup melted butter
   ½ cup melted lard or other
      shortening
   1 tablespoon molasses
   ¼ cup milk
   1¾ cups oatmeal
   1 cup seeded raisins or nut meats, cut
      fine, or ½ cup of each

Arrange by teaspoonfuls on buttered cooky sheets. Bake until the edges are brown (about 12 minutes). *Makes about 75.*

Date Oatmeal Cookies

Cook slowly until thick and smooth
 1 cup pitted dates
 ½ cup sugar
 ½ cup water
Set aside.

Cream together
 ½ cup shortening
 ½ cup brown sugar
Sift together and add
 1½ cups flour
 ¼ teaspoon baking soda
 ½ teaspoon salt
Add
 1¼ cups oatmeal
Mix well and add enough water to make the dough the right consistency to roll.

Roll ⅛ inch thick. Cut in 2-inch rounds. Put together in pairs with the date mixture as filling. Press the edges firmly together.

Bake at 350° until browned (about 15 minutes). *Makes about 24.*

Scottish Fancies

Butter cooky sheets. Set the oven at 325°.

Beat until light
 1 egg
Beat in
 ½ cup sugar
Stir in
 2 teaspoons melted butter
 1 cup oatmeal
 ¼ teaspoon salt
Arrange by teaspoonfuls 1½ inches apart on the cooky sheets. Spread into rounds with a knife dipped in cold water.

Bake until delicately brown (about 10 minutes). *Makes about 36.*

To shape in tubes, see Brandy Wafers (p. 442).

Aunt Amy's Cookies

Set the oven at 350°.

Sift together
 1 cup flour (preferably pastry)
 ½ teaspoon baking soda
 ¼ teaspoon baking powder
 ½ teaspoon salt
Cream
 ½ cup shortening
Beat in
 ½ cup white sugar
 1 cup brown sugar
Beat until light and fluffy. Stir in
 1 egg, slightly beaten
 1 teaspoon vanilla
 1 cup Grape-Nuts Flakes
 1 cup oatmeal
Stir in the flour mixture. Arrange by teaspoonfuls on buttered cooky sheets. Flatten with a knife or fork dipped in cold water. For very delicate cookies, flatten until almost paper-thin.

Bake until delicately brown (8 to 10 minutes). Take from the cooky sheet while still warm. *Makes 60.*

For a delicately spicy flavor, sift ½ teaspoon cinnamon with the flour.

Lace Cookies

These cookies spread to make very thin wafers, almost transparent. Make large ones and use them for a dessert like Gâteau Riche (p. 397).

Set the oven at 375°. Mix in a bowl
 2¼ cups oatmeal
 2¼ cups light brown sugar (1 pound)
 3 tablespoons flour
 1 teaspoon salt
Stir in
 1 cup butter or margarine, melted
Add
 1 egg, slightly beaten
 1 teaspoon vanilla

Blend well. Arrange by half-teaspoonfuls (6 to a tin), at least 2 inches apart, on heavy cooky sheets or on foil (see Quantity Cooky Baking, p. 434).

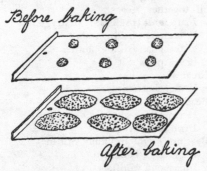

Before baking

After baking

Bake until lightly browned (about 7 minutes). Cool slightly. As soon as firm enough, remove from the cooky sheets. *Makes about 90.*

Brownies

Everyone seems to have an idea about how to bake brownies — at 300°, 325°, 350° or even 425°. All are good. The thing to avoid is overbaking — brownies should be moist and chewy.

Butter a shallow pan 9 by 9 inches. Line the bottom with wax paper cut to fit. Butter the paper. Set the oven at 325°.

Put in a double boiler top or a saucepan large enough to use as the mixing bowl
    2 ounces unsweetened chocolate
    ¼ cup butter or margarine
Stir over hot water or low heat until melted. Remove from the heat. Stir in
    1 cup sugar
    2 eggs, unbeaten
    ⅛ teaspoon salt
    ½ cup pastry or all-purpose flour
    ½ cup walnut meats, cut in pieces
    1 teaspoon vanilla
Spread in the pan.

Bake until dry on top and almost firm to the touch (30 to 35 minutes). Turn upside down on a cake cooler. Cool. Peel off the paper. Cut in squares. *Makes 16.*

Sultana Sticks. Add ¼ cup raisins to the mixture. Cut in fingers.

Chocolate Orange Squares. Add ½ cup slivered orange peel (candied or fresh) to the mixture.

Harvard Brownies. *Especially rich and chewy.* Use only one egg. Bake in a pan 8 by 8 inches at 300° about 35 minutes.

Butterscotch Brownies

Butter a shallow pan about 8 by 8 inches. Set the oven at 350°.

Mix
    ¼ cup melted butter
    1 cup brown sugar
    1 egg
    ¼ teaspoon salt
    ¾ cup flour
    1 teaspoon baking powder
    ½ teaspoon vanilla
    ½ cup nut meats, broken in pieces
Spread in the pan.

Bake about 25 minutes. Cut in squares or strips while warm. *Makes 16 or more.*

Peanut Butter Brownies

Especially popular with the youngest set.

Butter a pan about 9 by 9 inches. Set the oven at 350°.

Put in a bowl
    2 eggs
    1 cup sugar
    ½ cup light brown sugar
    ¼ cup crunchy peanut butter
    1 teaspoon vanilla
    2 tablespoons butter (soft)
Beat thoroughly with a mixer or a rotary beater.

Sift together
    1½ cups flour
    2 teaspoons baking powder
    ½ teaspoon salt
Stir into the first mixture. Spread in the pan. Sprinkle over the top and press in lightly
    ¼ cup chopped salted peanuts
Bake about 30 minutes. Cut in squares while warm. *Makes 60 or more.*

Coconut Bars

A rich coconut topping on a pastry base.

Line a pan 8 by 8 inches with wax paper. Set the oven at 350°.

Blend thoroughly
  ½ cup butter
  2 tablespoons confectioners' sugar
  1 cup cake flour
Spread evenly in the pan. Bake 15 minutes.

Beat together until thick
  2 eggs
  1¼ cups light brown sugar
  1 teaspoon vanilla
Sift together
  2 tablespoons flour
  ¼ teaspoon salt
  1 teaspoon baking powder
Add to the egg mixture. Stir in
  1 cup broken nut meats
  1 cup moist shredded coconut
Spread over the first mixture and bake 30 minutes longer. Cool in the pan. Cut in bars. *Makes 16.*

Coconut Squares

Butter a pan 8 or 9 inches square. Set the oven at 350°.

Beat until foamy
  2 eggs
Beat in
  2 cups brown sugar
  ⅛ teaspoon salt
  ½ teaspoon vanilla
Stir in
  2 cups shredded coconut
  ¼ cup broken walnut meats
Sift over the batter
  6 tablespoons flour
Stir lightly and spoon into the pan.

Bake about 30 minutes. Cut in squares while warm. Cool and remove from the pan. *Makes 16.*

Almond Spice Bars

Butter a jelly roll pan, about 9 by 13 inches. Set the oven at 300°.

Mix together
  1¼ cups sifted confectioners' sugar
  ¾ teaspoon ground cardamon
  ½ teaspoon cinnamon
  1 egg white
  1 tablespoon water
  1¼ cups unblanched almonds, chopped fine
Sift together
  2¼ cups sifted flour
  2 teaspoons baking powder
  ¾ cup sugar
Cut in
  ¾ cup butter
Beat together
  1 egg yolk
  2 tablespoons milk
Add to the flour mixture and blend well.

Press two-thirds of the dough into the pan. Spread the almond mixture over the top. Roll the remaining dough into a rectangle about ¼ inch thick. Cut in ½ inch strips. Place crisscross over the filling.

Bake until brown, about 45 minutes. Cool and cut in strips, 1 by 2 inches. *Makes 54 bars.*

Date and Nut Bars

Butter a pan about 14 by 8 inches. Set the oven at 350°.

Mix in the order given
  ¼ cup melted butter
  1 cup sugar
  3 eggs, well beaten
  1 cup flour
  ½ teaspoon baking powder
  Few grains salt
  1 cup dates, cut fine
  1 cup chopped nut meats
Spread in the pan and bake until firm and delicately brown (about 30 minutes).

Cut in finger-shaped pieces and roll while still warm in
  Confectioners' sugar
Makes about 40.

Honey Date Bars. Use honey in place of sugar. Increase the flour to 1¼ cups and the baking powder to 1 teaspoon.

Date and Nut Cookies. Arrange by teaspoonfuls on buttered cooky sheets. Bake until delicately brown (about 12 minutes).

Linzer Schnitten

A wonderful Christmas cooky but delicious any time.

Beat until light
  2 eggs
Beat in gradually
  1½ cups sugar
Melt and add
  ¾ cup butter
Sift together
  3½ cups flour
  1 teaspoon baking powder
  2 teaspoons cinnamon
  1 teaspoon powdered cloves
  ¼ teaspoon salt
Blend into the first mixture. Add
  Grated rind and juice of 1 lemon
Turn out on a floured board and knead until smooth and no longer sticky. Let stand at least 1 hour.

Roll ½ inch thick. Cut in strips 1½ by 10 inches. Mark a groove down the center of each strip with the handle of a wooden spoon. Fill the grooves with
  Jelly (any kind)
Put on a cooky sheet. Bake at 375° until light brown (about 15 minutes).

Beat together
  1 egg
  ¾ cup sugar
Brush over the baked strips while they are still hot and cut immediately into diagonal pieces. *Makes 40 or more.*

Date Lebkuchen

Moist and delicious for weeks after baking.

Grate the peel and extract the juice of
  1 lemon
  1 orange
Add
  1 pound dates, cut small
Cover and let stand at least 12 hours.

Butter a pan about 12 by 15 inches. Set the oven at 375°.

Beat until light
  4 eggs
Beat in gradually
  1 pound brown sugar
Sift together and add
  2 cups flour
  ¼ teaspoon salt
  1 teaspoon instant coffee
  2 teaspoons baking powder
  2 teaspoons cinnamon
Stir in the date mixture and
  1 cup chopped nut meats
Spread in the pan. Bake 30 minutes. Cool in the pan.

Put in a bowl
  3 tablespoons orange juice
Add gradually until thick enough to spread
  Confectioners' sugar
Stir in
  1 teaspoon melted butter
Spread over the lebkuchen. Cut in 1½-inch squares. *Makes about 80.*

Hermits

Set the oven at 350°. Butter a pan about 7 by 14 inches. For thinner hermits, use a larger pan.

Mix
  ¼ cup raisins, cut fine
  ¼ cup currants
  3 tablespoons citron or candied orange peel, cut small
  ¼ cup chopped nut meats
  ¼ cup flour
Cream together
  ¼ cup butter
  ½ cup sugar
Add
  ½ teaspoon salt
  2 eggs, well beaten
  ½ cup molasses
Beat well. Sift together
  1¾ cups flour
  1 teaspoon baking soda
  ½ teaspoon cream of tartar
  1 teaspoon cinnamon
  ½ teaspoon powdered cloves

¼ teaspoon mace
¼ teaspoon nutmeg
Add to the butter, sugar and egg mixture and beat thoroughly. Stir in the fruit and nuts. Spread in the pan or make drop cookies (p. 431).

Bake until the top is firm (15 minutes or more). Cut in squares or bars while warm. *Makes 36.*

Concord Hermits. Use 1 cup brown sugar in place of white sugar and molasses. Add ½ cup coffee, sour cream or sour milk.

Pecan Squares

Butter a jelly roll pan about 9 by 13 inches. Set the oven at 375°.

Cream together
    ½ cup butter (or up to 1 cup for
        richer cookies)
    1 cup sugar
Beat in
    1 egg yolk
    1 teaspoon vanilla
Stir in
    2 cups flour
Blend well. Pat evenly in the pan. Brush over the cooky dough
    1 egg white, beaten slightly
Scatter evenly over the top
    1 cup chopped pecans
Press in slightly.

Bake until golden-brown (10 to 20 minutes). Cut in squares. *Makes about 36.*

Paris Cakes

Butter a pan about 8 by 14 inches. Line it with wax paper. Set the oven at 350°.

Melt over hot water
    2 ounces unsweetened chocolate
Stir in
    ½ cup butter or margarine
When the butter is melted, stir in
    2 egg yolks
    ½ cup sugar
    1 teaspoon vanilla

¾ cup flour
    ¼ teaspoon salt
Fold in
    2 egg whites, beaten stiff
Spread in the pan. Bake 25 minutes. Spread with
    Paris Cream (below)
Pat evenly over the top
    1 cup nut meats, cut small
Cut in 1½-inch squares. *Makes about 50.*

Paris Cream. *Especially for these cakes, but also a delicious frosting for other cakes.* Put ½ pint heavy cream in a small heavy saucepan. Add 4 ounces unsweetened chocolate, ¼ cup sugar and a few grains of salt. Heat slowly to the boiling point. Boil 2 minutes, stirring constantly. Cool to lukewarm and beat until smooth.

Walnut Meringue Bars

Butter a shallow pan about 8 by 12 inches. Set the oven at 300°.

Cream together
    ½ cup butter
    1 cup light brown sugar
Add
    ½ teaspoon salt
    1 teaspoon vanilla
Beat in
    2 egg yolks
Sift together
    1¼ cups flour
    1½ teaspoons baking powder
Add to the butter and sugar. Stir until blended. Spread evenly in the pan.

Beat until stiff
    2 egg whites
Beat in
    1 cup light brown sugar
Add
    1 cup chopped walnut meats
    1 teaspoon vanilla
Spread over the cooky mixture. Bake 35 minutes. Cool. Cut in squares with a very sharp knife. Lift out carefully with a spatula. *Makes about 50.*

Jelly Meringue Bars. Before covering with the meringue, spread with a thin layer of tart jelly. For a change of flavor, make the meringue with white sugar and add to it 1 teaspoon cinnamon.

Jam Bars

Butter a shallow pan 8 or 9 inches square. Set the oven at 400°.

Cream together
  ½ cup shortening
  ½ cup sugar
  ½ teaspoon vanilla
  ½ teaspoon almond flavoring
Stir in
  1 egg
Sift together
  1½ cups flour
  1 teaspoon baking powder
  ½ teaspoon cinnamon
  ¼ teaspoon powdered cloves
  ½ teaspoon salt
Add to the first mixture and blend well. Spread half in the pan. Cover with a layer of
  Raspberry jam, tart jelly, marmalade
    or Lemon Cheese (p. 425)
Pat the rest of the dough on top. Bake 25 minutes. Cool. Cut in bars. *Makes about 20.*

Chewy Noels

Set the oven at 350°.

Melt in a pan 9 by 9 inches
  2 tablespoons butter
Beat slightly
  2 eggs
  1 teaspoon vanilla
Mix
  1 cup brown sugar
  5 tablespoons flour
  ⅛ teaspoon baking soda
  ¼ teaspoon salt
  1 cup nut meats, broken in pieces
Add to the eggs. Mix well. Pour into the pan. Bake until firm to the touch (about 25 minutes). Turn out onto wax paper, buttered side up. Dust lightly with

  Confectioners' sugar
Cut in squares or bars. *Makes 25 or more.*

Hazelnut Strips

Beat until stiff
  1 egg white
Beat in gradually
  1 cup confectioners' sugar
  1 cup hazelnuts, ground fine
Pat out on a lightly floured board into an oblong ¼ inch thick.

Beat together
  1 egg yolk
  6 tablespoons confectioners' sugar
  ½ teaspoon vanilla
Spread over the first mixture. Let stand 30 minutes to dry.

Cut in finger-shaped strips with a knife dipped in hot water. Place on a buttered and floured cooky sheet. Let stand 10 minutes.

Bake at 300° until delicately brown (about 15 minutes). Cool and lift from the pan. *Makes 18 or more.*

Florentines

In Austria and Germany there are many variations of this recipe, but this is nearest to the particularly delectable Salzburg version.

Set the oven at 350°.

Mix
  ½ cup heavy cream
  ½ cup sugar
  1 cup almonds or hazelnuts, cut small
  ¼ pound candied orange peel, cut fine
  ¼ cup flour
  Few grains salt
Arrange by teaspoonfuls, 2 inches apart, on a cooky sheet. Flatten with a knife dipped in cold water.

Bake until brown around the edges (about 10 minutes). Cool, flat side up, on a wire cake cooler.

Melt over hot water.
  8-ounce bar semisweet chocolate

Add
   2 tablespoons cream or water
Stir until smooth and spread on the cookies on the flat side. *Makes 24.*

Viennese Crescents

Delicious any time of year, but traditional for Christmas.

Set the oven at 300°.

Cream thoroughly
   1 cup butter
Add
   ¼ cup sugar
   2 cups flour
   1 cup ground almonds (unblanched)
   1 teaspoon vanilla
Mix well. Shape with fingers in crescents about 3 inches by 1 inch and ½ inch thick. Roll in
   Confectioners' sugar
Place on cooky sheets. Bake 35 minutes. Cool. Roll in sugar. *Makes about 36.*

Pecan Delights. Increase sugar to ½ cup and use 2 cups chopped pecans in place of almonds. Add 3 teaspoons water. Shape like dates.

Spitzbuben. Increase sugar to 1 cup. Pat out with hands on floured board. Cover with wax paper and roll ⅛ inch thick. Cut out with a small biscuit cutter. Bake. Put together in pairs with currant jelly.

Nut Balls. Use almonds, hazelnuts, pecans, walnuts or black walnuts. Use 1½ cups flour. Shape in balls the size of large marbles.

Meringues (Kisses)

Egg whites beat best if they are at room temperature, not icy cold. Use eggs at least 3 days old. For very dry meringues, the baking must be so slow that the meringues color only slightly as they bake. Some meringue-type cookies are baked in a hotter oven to make them chewy.

Cover a cooky sheet with paper (not waxed). Set the oven at 250°.

Beat until very stiff and dry
   2 egg whites
Beat in, a spoonful at a time
   6 tablespoons sugar
Continue beating until the mixture holds its shape when you lift a spoonful. Add
   1 teaspoon vanilla
Fold in carefully
   2 tablespoons sugar
Shape on the cooky sheet with a pastry bag and tube or with a spoon.

Bake 50 minutes. Remove from the paper. If the meringues stick, wipe the back of the paper with a damp cloth. *Makes 6 large or 18 small meringues.*

Meringue Shells. Arrange by spoonfuls or shape in 3-inch rings. Bake. Crush the center. Put together in pairs with whipped cream or ice cream. Serve with crushed strawberries, chocolate or other sauce. Filled with ice cream, these are called **Meringues Glacées.**

Nut Meringues. Add ½ cup or more chopped nut meats (almonds, hazelnuts, walnuts, peanuts or hickory nuts). Shape. Sprinkle with nut meats and bake.

Date and Nut Meringues. Fold in ½ cup chopped nut meats and ¼ pound dates, cut fine. Pecans are especially good. Bake 25 minutes at 350°. *Makes 40 small meringues.*

Creole Kisses. Add finely pounded Nut Brittle (p. 14) made with almonds. Shape. Sprinkle with shredded almonds and sift sugar over them. Bake 25 minutes at 300°.

Swiss Bonnets. Set aside about ½ cup of the beaten meringue. To the rest add ¾ cup ground nut meats (half almonds and half filberts are delicious). Shape small meringues. Bake 10 minutes. Top with the rest of the meringue and whole nut meats. Continue baking.

Pecan Kisses

Do not attempt these delectable tidbits on a damp day. They should be very chewy but firm.

Butter and flour two cooky sheets. Set the oven at 325°.

Beat until very stiff
  1 egg white
Add gradually, beating constantly
  1 cup light brown sugar
  ¼ teaspoon salt
  ½ teaspoon vanilla
Fold in
  1 cup pecan meats, chopped fine
Put teaspoonfuls on the cooky sheets. Bake until dry on top (8 to 12 minutes); they will be firmer when cold. *Makes 24.*

Pecan Berkeleys. Use dark brown sugar, 1 teaspoon vanilla and 2 cups unchopped pecan halves. Bake at 300°.

Chocolate Meringue Cookies

Set the oven at 300°.

Melt over hot water
  1 ounce chocolate
Remove from the heat. Stir in
  ⅔ cup confectioners' sugar
  1 egg white
  1 teaspoon vanilla
Mix until smooth. Add until thick enough to roll out
  Confectioners' sugar (about 1 cup)
Sprinkle a board with
  Granulated sugar
Roll the mixture ¼ inch thick. Sprinkle with more granulated sugar. Cut out with a small biscuit cutter.

Bake on a cooky sheet until dry (about 30 minutes). *Makes 18.*

Chocolate Coconut Kisses

Butter cooky sheets lightly. Set the oven at 350°.

Sift together
  1½ cups confectioners' sugar
  1 tablespoon flour
Beat until they stand in soft peaks

  3 egg whites
Beat in the sugar mixture, 2 tablespoonfuls at a time. Add
  1 teaspoon vanilla
Fold in
  ½ cup shredded coconut
  1 package chocolate bits (6 ounces)
Arrange by teaspoonfuls on the cooky sheets.

Bake until dry (12 to 15 minutes). Cool slightly and remove from the pans. *Makes about 50.*

Chocolate Nut Meringues

Butter 2 cooky sheets. Set the oven at 300°.

Melt and set aside to cool slightly
  2 ounces unsweetened chocolate
Blanch and chop
  ⅔ cup almonds
Beat until very stiff
  2 egg whites
Add gradually, beating constantly
  ⅞ cup confectioners' sugar
Carefully fold in the chocolate and ½ cup of the nut meats. Put on the cooky sheets by teaspoonfuls. Sprinkle with the rest of the nut meats.

Bake 40 minutes. *Makes about 40.*

Cinnamon Stars

Set the oven at 300°. Butter 2 cooky sheets lightly.

Beat until stiff
  3 egg whites
Mix
  1 cup granulated sugar
  1 tablespoon flour
  1½ teaspoons cinnamon
  1⅓ cups chopped unblanched almonds
  Grated rind of ½ lemon
Fold into the egg whites. Put a sheet of wax paper on a board. Sprinkle with
  ¼ cup confectioners' sugar sifted with
  ¼ cup flour
Put the dough on it and cover with another sheet of wax paper. Pat and roll out ¼ inch thick. Shape with a star cutter. Put on the cooky sheets.

Bake 20 minutes. Spread with
Confectioners' Frosting (p. 491)
Makes 36.

Viennese Wafers

Butter and flour a cooky sheet. Set the
oven at 350°.

Mix in a bowl
  1 egg white
  ½ teaspoon vanilla
  ½ teaspoon lemon juice
Mix
  ¼ cup confectioners' sugar
  ¼ cup finely chopped almonds or
    filberts
  2 teaspoons flour
Stir into the egg white. Put on the cooky
sheet by small teaspoonfuls.

Bake until dry (about 12 minutes). Frost,
if you like, with
  Confectioners' Frosting (p. 491)
Makes 18.

Applesauce Cookies

Butter cooky sheets. Set the oven at 425°.

Sift together
  2 cups flour
  1 teaspoon baking soda
  ½ teaspoon salt
  1 teaspoon cinnamon
  1 teaspoon nutmeg
  ½ teaspoon powdered cloves
Cream together until light
  ½ cup butter or margarine
  ½ cup brown sugar
  ½ cup white sugar
Stir in
  1 egg
  1 cup smooth applesauce
Add the flour mixture. Add
  1 cup seeded or chopped raisins
  ½ cup chopped nut meats
Arrange by spoonfuls on cooky sheets.

Bake until lightly browned (8 to 10 minutes). *Makes 40 or more.*

Applesauce Bars. Spread in a pan about
9 by 15 inches, lined with foil. Bake at
350° until brown (30 to 40 minutes).
While warm, spread with confectioners'

sugar moistened with hot milk. Cool and
cut in bars.

Mincemeat Cookies

Set the oven at 350°.

Cream
  1 cup shortening
Beat in
  ½ teaspoon vanilla
  1 cup honey or 1½ cups sugar
  3 eggs, well beaten
Sift together and add
  3¼ cups flour
  1 teaspoon salt
  1 teaspoon baking soda
Stir in
  1 cup chopped nut meats
  1 package mincemeat (9 ounces) or
    1½ cups homemade mincemeat,
    drained if necessary
Arrange by teaspoonfuls on buttered
cooky sheets. Bake until light brown
(about 15 minutes). *Makes about 75.*

Date Pinwheels

Cream
  1 cup shortening
Beat in gradually
  2 cups light brown sugar
Stir in
  3 eggs, well beaten
Sift together
  4 cups flour
  ½ teaspoon salt
  ½ teaspoon baking soda
Add to the first mixture. Mix well. Chill.
Divide in two or three parts. Roll in
oblongs ¼ inch thick. Spread with date
filling (below) and roll up. Wrap in wax
paper or foil and chill overnight.

Cut in ½-inch slices and arrange on
cooky sheets.

Bake at 400° until firm (about 10 minutes). *Makes 60 or more.*

Date Pinwheel Filling. Mix 2¼ cups
chopped dates with 1 cup sugar and 1
cup water. Cook 10 minutes or until
thick and add 1 cup chopped nuts.

Wasps' Nests

Traditional Christmas cookies, but wonderful any time of year.

Butter and flour cooky sheets. Set the oven at 300°.

Shred lengthwise
    ½ pound blanched almonds
Cook together until the syrup spins a thread (240°)
    ½ cup sugar
    ¼ cup water
Stir in the almonds.

Grate or chop fine
    1 package semisweet chocolate
      (8 ounces)
Beat until very stiff
    3 egg whites
Add by spoonfuls, beating constantly
    2 cups confectioners' sugar
Add the chocolate and the almond mixture. Put half-teaspoonfuls of the dough on the cooky sheets.

Bake until dry (about 25 minutes). Let stand 10 minutes and remove from the pan. *Makes 100.*

Macaroons

True macaroons are made of egg whites, sugar and almond paste, but the name is often applied to other chewy cookies.

Mix thoroughly with your hands
    ½ pound almond paste (homemade, p. 505, or packaged)
Add, little by little
    1 cup sugar
    3 egg whites, unbeaten
Blend thoroughly and sift in
    ⅓ cup confectioners' sugar
    2 tablespoons pastry or cake flour
    ⅛ teaspoon salt
Cover cooky sheets with paper (not waxed). Put teaspoonfuls of the mixture on the paper and flatten with fingers dipped in cold water or shape with a pastry bag and tube. Cover and let stand 2 hours or more.

Bake 30 minutes at 300°. Put the paper on a damp cloth and remove the macaroons. *Makes about 30.*

To vary, add finely chopped candied cherries to the mixture or decorate tops before baking with raisins, or bits of cherry.

Almond Macaroons. Sprinkle before baking with almonds, blanched and shredded or chopped.

Chocolate Fingers. Shape in fingers. Put together in pairs with Chocolate Filling (p. 492). Dip the ends in sugar syrup, then in chocolate shot.

Crescents

Mix with your hands
    ½ pound almond paste (homemade, p. 505, or packaged)
    ½ cup confectioners' sugar
    1 egg white
Shape in a long roll. Cut in ¾-inch pieces. Roll each piece in
    Chopped blanched almonds
Shape in crescents. Put on a lightly buttered cooky sheet. Let stand 20 minutes. Bake 20 minutes at 300°. Cool. Frost with
    Confectioners' Frosting (p. 491), flavored with lemon juice (enough to make the frosting very tart)
Make the frosting thin enough to spread on the crescents with a pastry brush. *Makes about 30.*

Corn Flake Macaroons

Butter a cooky sheet. Set the oven at 350°.

Beat until stiff
    1 egg white
Stir in
    ½ cup sugar
    ½ cup shredded coconut
    1 cup corn flakes
    ¼ teaspoon almond extract
    ¼ teaspoon vanilla
    Few grains salt
Put on the cooky sheet by teaspoonfuls.

Bake 20 minutes. *Makes 18.*

Chocolate Chip Macaroons. Use only ¼ cup sugar. Instead of coconut, use ⅓ cup chocolate bits or semisweet chocolate cut in small pieces.

Peanut Macaroons

Butter a cooky sheet. Set the oven at 300°.

Prepare
    5 tablespoons chopped skinned peanuts
Beat until stiff
    1 egg white
Add gradually, beating constantly
    ¼ cup sugar
Add the peanuts. Stir in
    1 teaspoon vanilla
Put on the cooky sheet by teaspoonfuls, 1½ inches apart. Garnish each with half a peanut.

Bake until dry (12 to 15 minutes). *Makes 16.*

Prune Macaroons

Butter 2 cooky sheets. Set the oven at 350°.

Mix
    ½ can sweetened condensed milk
    1 cup shredded coconut
    ¼ teaspoon salt
    1 cup dried prunes, cut small
    2 cups corn flakes
    ½ teaspoon vanilla
Shape in small balls with your fingers. Place on the cooky sheets.

Bake 10 minutes. *Makes about 60.*

Peanut Butter Macaroons

Butter a cooky sheet. Set the oven at 375°.

Mix
    1 can sweetened condensed milk
    ½ cup peanut butter
    ½ teaspoon lemon juice
    ¼ teaspoon salt
    1 cup chopped peanuts
    1 teaspoon vanilla
Put on the cooky sheet by teaspoonfuls.

Bake 12 minutes. *Makes about 40.*

To vary. Instead of peanuts, use 2 cups raisins, shredded coconut, chopped dates, bran flakes or corn flakes.

Chocolate Coconut Cookies

Butter a cooky sheet. Set the oven at 350°.

Heat until the chocolate melts
    1 can sweetened condensed milk
    3 ounces unsweetened chocolate
Add
    2 cups shredded coconut
    1 cup pecan meats, in pieces
    1 teaspoon vanilla
    Few grains salt
Put on the cooky sheet by teaspoonfuls.

Bake 10 minutes. *Makes about 40.*

Cinnamon Fingers

Butter a cooky sheet. Set the oven at 400°.

Mix
    1 can sweetened condensed milk
    1 teaspoon cinnamon
    Few grains salt
    ½ teaspoon vanilla
Dip in the mixture
    Sliced bread, cut in fingers
Put on the cooky sheet.

Bake until brown, turning once. Dry on a cake cooler.

Rum Balls

No baking to make these. Store at least a week to develop the best flavor.

Prepare
    2 cups vanilla wafer crumbs, rolled
      fine
Add
    1 cup finely chopped coconut or pecan
      meats
    1 cup confectioners' sugar
    2 tablespoons cocoa
    2 tablespoons white corn syrup
    ⅓ cup rum, brandy, Cointreau or
      whiskey (Bourbon or rye)
Mix well. Shape by teaspoonfuls into firm balls. Roll in
    Confectioners' sugar, instant coffee or
      dry cocoa
Store tightly covered. *Makes about 50.*

Cupcakes

Use any cake or gingerbread recipe. For a small family, you may like to mix a cake batter and bake part in a small loaf tin, the rest in cupcake tins. Cupcakes bake better with slightly less flour, so use 1 tablespoon less to the cup if you are adapting a recipe to bake as cupcakes.

Sprinkle with confectioners' sugar or cover with a frosting (pp. 490ff.). Garnish with chopped nuts, nut meat halves, bits of candied cherry, or chocolate shot.

Filled Cupcakes. Cut thin slices off the tops of plain cupcakes. Scoop out some of the center. Fill with jam, marmalade, preserves, whipped cream, Chocolate Filling (p. 492) or other filling. Replace the tops. Frost as desired.

Boston Cupcakes

Butter 12 cupcake tins. Set the oven at 375°.

Cream together until light and fluffy
   ⅓ cup butter
   1 cup sugar
Stir in
   2 eggs, well beaten
Sift together
   1⅜ cups pastry or cake flour
   2 teaspoons baking powder
   ¼ teaspoon mace
   ¼ teaspoon salt
Add to the first mixture alternately with
   ½ cup milk
Spoon into the pans.

Bake about 20 minutes. *Makes 12.*

Lemon Queens

Butter and flour 18 or more small cupcake tins. Set the oven at 350°.

Cream together
   ¼ cup butter
   ½ cup sugar
Stir in
   Grated rind of ½ lemon
   1 teaspoon lemon juice

   2 egg yolks, beaten until thick
Sift together
   ⅝ cup flour
   ¼ teaspoon salt
   ⅛ teaspoon baking soda
Add to the first mixture and beat well. Fold in
   2 egg whites, beaten stiff
Spoon into the tins, having them two-thirds full.

Bake until the cakes shrink slightly from the pans. *Makes 18 or more.*

Peanut Butter Cupcakes

At their best when freshly baked.

Put paper baking cups in muffin tins (16 or more, according to size). Set the oven at 375°.

Cream together until smooth
   ¼ cup peanut butter
   ¼ cup butter
Beat in
   ¾ cup brown sugar
   1 egg
   ¼ teaspoon salt
   ½ teaspoon vanilla
Sift together
   1 cup pastry flour or ¾ cup all-purpose flour
   1¼ teaspoons baking powder
Add to the first mixture in small amounts, alternating with
   ⅜ cup milk
Fill the paper cups half full.

Bake about 20 minutes. Frost with
   Portsmouth Frosting (p. 491)
Makes 16 or more.

Marguerites

Butter 18 2-inch cupcake tins. Set the oven at 350°.

Mix thoroughly
   2 eggs, slightly beaten
   1 cup light brown sugar
   ½ cup flour
   ¼ teaspoon baking powder
   ¼ teaspoon salt
   1 cup pecan meats, cut small

Fill the tins two-thirds full. Put on each
  Pecan meats
Bake until the cakes shrink slightly from
the pans (8 to 15 minutes). *Makes 18.*

Marguerite Bars. Spread the mixture in
a buttered pan 8 by 8 inches. Bake, cool,
and cut in squares or bars.

Molasses Marguerites

Mix thoroughly
  1 egg
  ⅓ cup butter (softened)
  ⅓ cup extra fine sugar
  ⅓ cup molasses
  ⅞ cup flour
  1 cup pecan meats, cut small
Fill pans. Bake like Marguerites (above).

Lady Fingers

Butter lady finger tins or cover cooky
sheets with paper (not waxed). Set the
oven at 350°.

Beat until in soft peaks
  3 egg whites
Add gradually, beating constantly
  ⅓ cup extra fine sugar
Without washing the beater, beat until
thick and lemon-colored
  2 egg yolks
  ½ teaspoon vanilla
  ⅛ teaspoon salt
Fold in the egg whites until just blended.
Fold in little by little
  ⅓ cup sifted flour
Do not overbeat. Spoon into the tins or
shape with a pastry bag and plain tube
onto the paper. Sprinkle with sugar.

Bake about 12 minutes. Use a long sharp
knife to remove easily from the paper.
Makes about 30.

Sponge Drops. Put teaspoonfuls on the
cooky sheets and bake as above. Put together in pairs with Paris Cream (p. 447)
or whipped cream.

California Tea Cakes. Put homemade
(above) or baker's lady fingers together
sandwich fashion, with a filling of mashed

cream cheese and chopped candied ginger.

Party Cakes

Bake Genoise (p. 474) or any sponge cake
mixture in shallow pans. Cool and cut in
rounds with a small cooky cutter. Cut
each round in three layers.

Put the layers together with thin coatings
of any frosting (Orange Portsmouth and
Chocolate Frosting (p. 491) are excellent)
and spread the frosting around the sides
and on top. Garnish in any of the ways
suggested for cup cakes (p. 454).

Mocha Cakes. *The usual name for these
popular little cakes, even though the
flavor is not coffee.* Put the layers together with Chocolate Butter Frosting
(p. 494). Spread frosting around the sides
and roll in shredded coconut. Put frosting in a pastry bag and, starting at the
center, coil the frosting around to cover
the surface. Garnish the center with a
candied cherry.

Coconut Snowballs

Cut angel food in 3-inch cubes or pull
into irregular pieces. Roll in Seven-
Minute Frosting (p. 493), then in grated
coconut. Place on wax paper to dry.

Almond Cakes

Butter 24 or more small cup cake tins.
Set the oven at 375°.

Cream together until light and fluffy
  ½ cup butter
  ¾ cup sugar
Stir in
  2 eggs, well-beaten
Sift together
  1⅓ cups pastry flour
  2 teaspoons baking powder
  ¼ teaspoon salt
Add to the first mixture alternately with
  ⅓ cup milk
Stir in gently
  1 cup almonds, blanched and cut in
    pieces
Fill the pans two-thirds full.
Bake about 20 minutes. Frost or not.

Petits Fours

Party cakes for special festivities.

Bake Cream Sponge Cake (p. 472), Angel
Cake (p. 475), or Genoise (p. 474) in shallow pans. Cool and cut in strips 1¼
inches wide, then in squares, rectangles
or triangles. Put in rows on a cake cooler
with plenty of space between the rows.

Set over a shallow pan. Heat Petits Fours
Frosting (below) over hot water until
thin enough to pour. If the frosting is
too thick, thin it with water. If it is too
thin, stir in confectioners' sugar.

Pour the frosting over the cakes, moving
steadily to the end of the row and back
again. Lift the cake cooler gently and
move it back and forth to loosen the
dripping frosting. Scrape out the frosting in the pan, reheat and use for the
rest of the cakes.

Let the cakes dry. Lift them with a
spatula and trim the bottom edges with
a sharp knife.

To dip petits fours. Hold each piece of
cake on a fork and dip it in the frosting.
Set on a cake cooler to dry. The difficulty
with this method is that crumbs may fall
into the frosting.

To decorate petits fours. Put on each
frosted cake a nut meat, a bit of candied
fruit or a sprinkle of chocolate shot,
dragées or tiny colored candies. For
more elaborate decorations, see p. 490.

Petits Fours Frosting

Put in a saucepan
  2 cups sugar
  ⅛ teaspoon cream of tartar
  1 cup hot water
Boil to a thin syrup (226°). Cool to
slightly above lukewarm (100°). Add
until just thick enough to coat a spoon
  Confectioners' sugar (1 cup or more)
Test by pouring a little frosting over a
cake.

To color the frosting. For a series of
colors, tint the frosting delicately with
food coloring and frost one row of cakes.
Reheat the frosting and add more coloring for the next row. Continue until all
the cakes are frosted, adding more color
each time. The series may be (1) yellow,
green and brown (with melted chocolate); (2) white, pink, rose and red; or
(3) white, yellow, pale orange and deep
orange. If you are frosting a great many
cakes, it may be easier to divide the
frosting in separate bowls and color each.
Cover the bowls with foil to keep the
frosting moist.

Cakes

Presenting a perfect cake to family or guests is a great satisfaction — and not a difficult task. Some new and simple recipes have been added to Fannie Farmer's treasured heirlooms, many of which have been followed in the same family for over seventy years. You may like to begin your cake-making with one of the easiest — Lightning Cake (p. 470) or Huntington Chocolate Cake (p. 468).

Serving Cake

A few ideas, but browsing in this chapter will suggest many others.

For breakfast. Serve warm and without frosting.

Applesauce Cake (p. 466)
Blueberry Cake (p. 482)
Banana Cake (p. 463)
Dutch Apple Cake (p. 482)
Gingerbread (p. 466)
Shortcake (p. 484; an old New England custom)

With mid-morning or mid-afternoon tea or coffee. The cake should be one that is easy to hold in the fingers, preferably with only a simple icing. An attractive way to present Dundee Cake or Pound Cake is to place the loaf on a small breadboard and cut each slice as you serve your guests.

Dundee Cake (p. 476)
Pound Cake (p. 464)
Quick Tea Cake (p. 462)
Black Walnut Tea Cake (p. 465)
Queen Cake (p. 463)

With frozen desserts. If the ice cream is very rich or is served with a sauce, offer with it a simple sponge cake, a delicate angel food or chiffon cake. With sherbet, the cake may be richer — a layer cake or chocolate or nut cake.

With fruit. Nut cakes are especially delicious.

As dessert. Any layer cake, icebox cake or upside-down cake is appropriate. See also

Cottage puddings (p. 481)
Gingerbread (p. 466) with whipped cream or applesauce
Fresh Coconut Cake (p. 465)
Chocolate Roll (p. 484)
Jelly Roll (p. 483)
Boston Cream Pie (p. 483)
Chocolate Cream Pie (p. 483)
Washington Pie (p. 483)
Vienna Cake (p. 483)
Tortes (p. 485)

For special occasions. *Birthdays:* Make any layer cake or Birthday Fruit Cake (p. 478). To decorate (p. 490). *Holidays:* Fruit Cakes (pp. 475ff.). *Wedding Cake* (p. 480).

Ways to use leftover cake. Cut unfrosted cake in squares, steam over hot water, and serve with whipped cream or any pudding sauce. Or use in:

Tipsy Pudding (p. 362)
English Trifle (p. 363)
Icebox Pudding (p. 387)
Bread puddings (pp. 367ff.). Use

cake crumbs in place of bread crumbs and decrease the sugar. Rum Balls (p. 453). Use cake crumbs as part of the crumbs.

In whipped cream. Fold cubes or crumbs into whipped cream. Serve with crushed fruit or a sauce.

Chocolate Ice Cream Balls. Roll firm scoops of vanilla ice cream in chocolate cake crumbs and set in the freezer until ready to serve.

Ice Cream on Toasted Cake. Toast half-inch slices of any pound cake. Top with ice cream and serve immediately while the cake is still warm.

Ingredients

Have all ingredients at room temperature, not icy cold, for easiest blending. Measure ingredients carefully. Too much shortening, sugar or baking powder may cause the cake to fall, to run over the top of the pan, or to be too crumbly to handle. Too much flour or too little liquid will make it humped and uneven, tough or dry.

Flour. Sift flour before measuring unless the package directs otherwise. Flour may be so packed down that you would have too much if you spooned it out without sifting. Sift onto wax paper to save using an extra bowl. A single-screen sifter is easier to keep clean than one with several screens.

An experienced cake baker will set aside one-quarter of the flour and add only as much of it as is needed when the cake batter is mixed. Reducing the flour makes a cake very delicate.

Cake flour is very fine and light. Pastry flour makes a very tender cake, slightly less dry than one made with cake flour.

All-purpose and bread flours absorb more liquid, so it is often wise to cut down the amount of flour by 2 tablespoons to the cup unless the recipe definitely calls for them.

If you use all-purpose or bread flour, be particularly careful not to overbeat, as that develops the gluten in these hard wheat flours and will make the cake stretchy and tough.

Shortening. For plain cakes, butter or margarine is desirable to give the cake its characteristic flavor. For chocolate or spice cakes use butter or any of the excellent cooking fats or oils. If you use unsalted fat, you may wish to add more salt (1 teaspoon to each cup of fat). If you use oil or a solid fat, use one-eighth less than the amount called for in the recipe, since butter is about seven-eighths fat, and hydrogenated fats have air whipped in to make them easier to cream.

Eggs. Eggs beat to greater volume at room temperature than when cold, but it is easier to separate them when they are cold. If you are using pullet eggs or very large eggs, measure by the cup (p. 7).

Baking powder. Most of the recipes in this book are adapted to all types of baking powder. If a change is needed, a note in the recipe explains.

Flavoring. High-grade extracts are often an economy, because they are more concentrated, so that less is needed.

Successful Cake-Making

A perfect cake is light, fine and even-textured, with a tender, slightly moist surface. The top should be smooth and flat or only slightly rounded. A cake should have a "velvety" crumb when you taste it. Sponge cake should appear slightly "pebbled" on the surface.

Cake pans should be the right size for the amount of batter. If the pan is too large the cake will be dry and crusty. If it is too small, the batter will run over the top as it rises. If you have too much batter for the pan you are using, bake part in cupcake tins.

As a general guide, a recipe containing 2 cups of flour may be baked in a loaf pan 4 by 9 inches, in a square pan 8 or 9 inches square and 2 inches deep, in two 8 or 9 inch layer cake tins or in a 12-section muffin tin.

Preparing the pan. Do not butter pans for sponge or angel cakes. For other cakes, butter the bottom of the pan only. Cakes rise evenly if the sides are not buttered. Use a pastry brush or a crushed piece of wax paper dipped in melted butter. Butter gives a delicious flavor to the crust of the cake and so is recommended, but any good cooking fat will keep the cake from sticking. After spreading the butter, sprinkle lightly with flour, then shake out the extra flour. With a very delicate cake batter, the safest way is to grease the pan, then cover the bottom with a piece of wax paper cut to fit, and then grease again.

Mixing the batter. Inexperienced cooks often overbeat and so break down the air bubbles after they are formed. This makes a cake heavy, dry and uneven. For details about mixing different types, see Butter Cakes (p. 460), Sponge and Angel Food Cakes (p. 472), One-Bowl Cakes (p. 470) and Fruit Cakes (p. 475).

Filling the pan. Spread the batter well into the corners and sides of the pan, with the center slightly lower. Fill pans about two-thirds full to allow for rising.

Baking. Preheat if your oven requires it so that the temperature will be right when the batter is ready. Occasionally ask your utility company to check the oven regulator.

If the oven is too hot, the cake will be too small, cracked and heavy. If it is too

cool, the cake may run over the top of the pan, stick to the pan, or be coarse or soggy. Not enough baking may cause the cake to fall or break as it comes from the pan. Baking too long makes a cake dry and hard.

Set the cake as near the center of the oven as possible so that the heat will circulate evenly. Do not overcrowd the oven and do not bake cake while there is much moisture in the oven — custards baking in a pan of water, for example. After 20 minutes, if the cake is baking unevenly because the oven heats unevenly, turn the pan around.

Baking times given in recipes are approximate, so when the suggested time for baking is nearly over, test the cake by pressing lightly with a fingertip. If the cake is done it will spring back. Or test with a wire cake tester, which will come out clean when the cake is done.

High altitude baking. At 3500 feet or higher, cakes need some modifications to avoid being dry, coarse and crumbly. As the outside air pressure decreases, the amount of leavening within the cake (baking powder or baking soda or both) must also be reduced. Decrease the leavening by one-third at 3500 feet, by one-half at 5000 feet, and by two-thirds above 5000 feet. Beat egg whites less than the recipe suggests — until soft and fluffy but still very moist-looking. Raise the baking temperature by 25°.

For recipes especially adapted to baking at high altitudes, consult state departments of agriculture, which issue booklets of appropriately modified recipes.

Taking the Cake from the Pan

Sponge cake. Invert on a wire cooler. Let stand until cold. Loosen with a spatula or a knife.

Butter cake. Invert on a cake cooler. Let the cake stand until it begins to shrink from the sides of the pan. Loosen with a spatula if necessary, but gently, so that you will not break the tender crust.

Angel food and chiffon cake. Invert and let stand until cold. If your tube pan does not have rests to raise it above the table, set the tube in a milk bottle so that the cake will hang free while it is cooling.

Cutting the Cake

Cut a round cake in narrow or wide pie-shaped wedges.

Cut a loaf cake in squares or slices, or in diamonds or triangles.

Cut fruit cake in small squares or slices, or serve the loaf whole, cutting off pieces as needed.

Separate sponge cake in pieces with two forks or a special sponge cake divider. Do not cut with a knife.

On p. 480 you will find directions for cutting a wedding cake.

Butter Cakes

Cakes made with shortening — butter, margarine, vegetable shortening or oil — are finer-grained than the fluffy sponge-type cakes and so are easier to make into layer cakes and loaf cakes with a topping.

Making Butter Cakes

Set out the ingredients. Prepare the pans and preheat the oven, if required. See p. 459 for details.

Mixing by hand. If you are adding the whites separately, beat them until they stand up in soft peaks, beating in some of the sugar called for in the recipe — 1 tablespoon for each egg white. Set aside while you prepare the rest of the batter. The sugar will keep the beaten egg whites stiff. Without washing the beater, beat the egg yolks until thick and lemon-colored.

Cream the butter until it is very soft and fluffy by rubbing it against the side of the bowl with a blending fork or a wooden mixing spoon. Add the flavoring. Beat in the sugar, a little at a time, and continue beating until the mixture is like whipped cream. Beat in whole eggs or egg yolks. Thorough beating up to this stage makes a fine light cake.

Stir in the flour mixture by thirds, alternating with the milk. Add some of the flour last. Beat only enough to blend well. Fold in the beaten egg whites gently (p. 4) until flecks of white are evenly distributed.

There is a difference in the texture of cake if the eggs are separated or added whole. Adding the beaten whites last makes a light fluffy cake. Adding eggs whole makes a fine-grained cake.

Mixing with an electric beater or mixer. Beat the egg whites first with 1 tablespoon sugar for each white, and set aside. Without washing the beater, work the shortening until soft and creamy (about 1 minute at high speed). Add the flavoring. Beat in the rest of the sugar until light and fluffy. Stop the beater once or twice and scrape down the sides of the bowl with a rubber scraper. Add the egg yolks and beat 1 minute at high speed. Scrape down. Add the flour mixture and the milk by hand (see above) or at very slow speed so that you will not overbeat the batter. Fold in the egg whites with a mixing spoon.

Boston Favorite Cake

The standard butter cake recipe. For a small family, bake in cupcake tins, frost some and use the others for cottage pudding with a vanilla or lemon sauce. If you use all-purpose flour, reduce the amount by 2 tablespoons and be careful not to overbeat.

Butter a pan 9 by 9 by 2 inches or two 8-inch layer pans or 12 muffin tins. Set the oven at 350° for a square pan, 375° for layers or cupcakes.

Sift together
    1¾ cups pastry or cake flour
    ½ teaspoon salt
    2 teaspoons baking powder
Cream thoroughly
    ⅓ cup butter or margarine
Add
    ½ teaspoon vanilla
Beat in gradually
    1 cup sugar
Beat until fluffy. Beat in
    2 egg yolks
Stir in ½ cup of the flour mixture. Stir in
    ¼ cup milk
Add another ½ cup of the flour mixture and
    ¼ cup milk
Add the rest of the flour mixture and beat just enough to blend well.

Beat until they stand up in soft peaks
    2 egg whites
Fold into the batter. Spoon into the pans. Bake square cake 30 to 45 minutes, layers and cupcakes 20 to 30 minutes.

With an electric mixer or beater. Do not separate the eggs. Add to the creamed butter and sugar one at a time, beating well.

Chocolate Chip Cake. Fold in ½ cup chocolate bits or semisweet chocolate, cut in pea-size pieces.

Citron or Currant Cake. Add 1 cup citron, thinly sliced, or 1 cup currants. To add fruit while filling the pan, see Light Fruit Cake (p. 476).

Coconut Layer Cake. Bake in two layer cake pans. Spread Seven-Minute Frosting between the layers and on top. Sprinkle thickly with freshly grated or canned shredded coconut and pat it in gently.

Date and Nut Cake. Reserve ¼ cup of the flour and mix it with ¼ cup each of dates, cut small, and nut meats, broken in pieces. Fold gently into the batter.

Honey Cake. Replace all or part of the sugar with honey. Sift ½ teaspoon ginger and ½ teaspoon cinnamon with the flour.

Marble Cake. Add 1 square unsweetened chocolate, melted, to half the mixture. Fill a loaf pan by spoonfuls, alternating plain and chocolate mixtures.

Priscilla Cake. Increase the sugar to 1⅓ cups and use 3 eggs. This makes a slightly richer cake.

Spanish Cake. Flavor with ½ teaspoon cinnamon or ¼ teaspoon mace instead of vanilla. Bake in a loaf or in layer cake pans. Spread Caramel Frosting (p. 496) between the layers and on top.

Walnut Cake. Add ¾ cup walnut meats, broken in pieces. Increase the baking powder to 2¾ teaspoons. Cover with any white frosting, crease in squares, and put half a walnut meat on each square.

Cream Cake

Set the oven at 325°. Butter two 8-inch layer cake pans or a pan about 7 by 10 inches.

Beat together thoroughly
    2 eggs
    ⅞ cup sugar
    ⅔ cup light cream
    1 teaspoon vanilla
Mix and sift into a bowl
    1⅔ cups pastry or cake flour
    2½ teaspoons baking powder
    ½ teaspoon salt
Stir in the egg mixture. Pour into the pan.

Bake about 30 minutes. Frost as desired.

One-Egg Cake

For a simple loaf cake, cupcakes or Up-side-Down Cake (p. 482).

Set the oven at 350°. Butter a pan 8 by 8 inches or 12 cupcake tins.

Sift together
  1⅓ cups pastry or cake flour
  2 teaspoons baking powder
  ¼ teaspoon salt
Cream until light and fluffy
  ¼ cup butter or margarine
Beat in gradually
  ¾ cup sugar
  ½ teaspoon vanilla
  1 egg, well beaten
Stir in ½ cup of the flour mixture, then
  ¼ cup milk
Stir in another ½ cup of the flour and another
  ¼ cup milk
Add the rest of the flour and spoon into the pan.

Bake about 25 minutes.

Quick Tea or Coffee Cake. Spread in a buttered and floured shallow pan 8 by 8 inches. Sprinkle with sugar or cinnamon sugar (1 teaspoon cinnamon to ¼ cup sugar). Bake. Serve warm.

Seed Cake. Add 1½ teaspoons caraway seeds to Quick Tea Cake batter.

Golden Layer Cake

Easy to make, not too rich, and excellent as a layer cake with any filling or put together with whipped cream.

Butter two 7 or 8 inch layer cake pans. Set the oven at 375°.

Sift together
  1½ cups pastry or cake flour
  3 teaspoons baking powder
  ¼ teaspoon salt
Cream thoroughly
  ¼ cup butter
  ¾ cup sugar
  1 teaspoon vanilla
Beat in, one at a time
  3 egg yolks
Beat until fluffy.

Add alternately with the flour mixture
  ½ cup milk
Spread in pans.

Bake about 20 minutes.

Gold Cake

Particularly good topped with Coffee Frosting (p. 491) and sprinkled with grated coconut.

Butter and flour two pans 8 by 8 by 2 inches. Set the oven at 350°.

Sift together
  1¾ cups pastry or cake flour
  2½ teaspoons baking powder
  ¼ teaspoon salt
Cream thoroughly
  ½ cup butter
Beat in gradually
  1 cup sugar
Continue beating until fluffy.

Beat until lemon-colored
  1 egg
  5 egg yolks (⅓ cup)
  ½ teaspoon vanilla
Stir into the butter and sugar. Stir in the flour mixture alternately with
  ½ cup milk
Beat just enough to blend. Spoon into the pans.

Bake about 45 minutes.

Lord Baltimore Cake. Bake in three buttered and floured 7-inch layer pans. Put together with Lord Baltimore Filling (p. 496).

Velvet Cake

Butter a pan 8 by 10 inches or two 9-inch layer pans. Set the oven at 375° for layer cake pans or 350° for loaf pan.

Separate
  4 eggs
Beat the whites until stiff. Beat in gradually
  ½ cup sugar
Without washing the beater, beat the yolks until thick with
  ½ cup cold water

Cream
  ½ cup butter or margarine
Beat in gradually
  1 cup sugar
Add the beaten yolks.

Sift
  1½ cups pastry or cake flour
  ½ cup cornstarch
  ½ teaspoon salt
  4 teaspoons baking powder
Add to the butter mixture. Beat well and fold in the egg whites. Spread in the pan.

Bake about 40 minutes.

Almond Velvet Cake. Before baking, cover the top with ⅓ cup shredded almonds. Sprinkle with confectioners' sugar.

Princeton Orange Cake. Use orange juice in place of cold water and add the grated rind of 1 orange.

Orange Nut Cake. Spread Princeton Orange Cake batter in a loaf pan and sprinkle with ½ cup chopped walnut meats and ¼ cup confectioners' sugar. Bake and cool. Split in two layers and put together with Orange Filling (p. 496).

Snow Cake (White Cake)

Butter two 8 or 9 inch layer pans. Set the oven at 350°.

Beat until stiff
  3 egg whites
Beat in gradually
  ½ cup sugar
Cream until light and fluffy
  ½ cup butter
Beat in
  ½ cup sugar
  ½ teaspoon vanilla or ¼ teaspoon almond extract
Sift together
  1½ cups pastry or cake flour
  2 teaspoons baking powder
  ¼ teaspoon salt
Add to the butter mixture alternately with
  ½ cup milk

Fold in the beaten egg whites. Spread in the pans.

Bake about 45 minutes. Put together with Prune Almond Frosting (p. 496). Frost the top and sides with Seven-Minute Frosting (p. 493) or White Mountain Cream (p. 495).

White Nut Cake. Add 1 cup nut meats, cut in pieces.

Lady Baltimore Cake. Double the recipe. Bake in three 9-inch tins. Put together with Lady Baltimore Filling (p. 496).

Coffee Caramel Cake. Melt ½ cup sugar in a small heavy pan. Cook slowly until almost black. Add ½ cup hot coffee and stir until dissolved. Cool. Use in place of milk. Before putting the batter in the baking pan, fold in ½ cup sliced nut meats. Black walnuts are particularly good. Frost with Penuche Frosting (p. 493).

Banana Cake

Set the oven at 350°. Butter a 9-inch square pan.

Cream until light and fluffy
  ½ cup butter
Beat in gradually
  1½ cups sugar
Add
  2 eggs, slightly beaten
Beat thoroughly. Add
  1 cup mashed banana
  1 teaspoon vanilla or lemon extract or
    ½ teaspoon of each
Sift together
  2 cups pastry or cake flour
  ½ teaspoon baking soda (1 teaspoon
    if sour milk or cream is used)
  ¼ teaspoon salt
Add the flour mixture to the butter mixture alternately with
  ½ cup milk or cream, sweet or sour
Spoon into the pan.

Bake about 40 minutes. Frost with Cream Cheese Frosting (p. 493), or serve in squares with whipped cream on top.

Banana Coconut Cake. Melt ¼ cup butter, stir in 7 tablespoons brown sugar, 1 cup grated coconut and 1 cup chopped nuts. Spread over the baked cake.

Banana Nut Cake. Add ½ cup chopped nut meats to the mixture. Bake in layer cake tins. Put the layers together with whipped cream. Sprinkle with confectioners' sugar, or put White Mountain Frosting (p. 495) between and on top.

Grandmother's Pound Cake

Use an electric mixer for superior cake. Pound cake improves if stored a day or two. Butter is its characteristic flavor, but you may like to add ½ teaspoon mace, 2 tablespoons brandy or orange juice or 1 tablespoon caraway seeds.

Butter and flour a large loaf pan or two or more small ones. Set the oven at 300°.

Cream until light and fluffy
  1 cup butter
  1⅔ cups sugar
Beat in, one at a time
  5 eggs
When creamy, fold in
  2 cups pastry or cake flour
  ¼ teaspoon salt
Spoon into the pan.

Bake about 1½ hours.

Ginger Pound Cake. Omit the vanilla and add 2 tablespoons yellow ginger to the mixture.

Imperial Cake. Cut ½ pound seeded raisins in pieces and dredge lightly with flour. Break ½ cup walnut meats in pieces. Grate the rind of ½ lemon. Prepare the cake batter and add 2 teaspoons lemon juice. Fold in the raisins, nuts and lemon rind, and bake.

Molasses Pound Cake

Butter and flour a large loaf pan. Set the oven at 350°.

Cream until light and fluffy

  ⅔ cup butter
  ¾ cup sugar
Add
  2 eggs, well beaten
  ⅔ cup milk
  ⅔ cup molasses
Sift together
  2⅛ cups pastry or cake flour
  ¾ teaspoon baking soda
  1 teaspoon cinnamon
  ½ teaspoon allspice
  ¼ teaspoon ground cloves
  ¼ teaspoon mace
Add to the first mixture. Stir in
  ½ cup seeded raisins, cut in pieces and dredged with flour
  ⅓ cup citron, cut in thin strips and dredged with flour
Spoon into the pan.

Bake about 40 minutes.

Queen Cake

Almost as fine-grained as pound cake.

Butter a shallow pan 6 by 10 inches, or three 8 or 9 inch cake pans. Set the oven at 350°.

Sift together
  1⅔ cups pastry or cake flour
  ¼ teaspoon salt
  ¼ teaspoon baking soda
Cream until light and fluffy
  ⅔ cup butter
Beat in the flour mixture. Add
  1½ teaspoons lemon juice
Beat until stiff but not dry
  6 egg whites
Beat in, little by little
  1¼ cups confectioners' sugar
Spoon over the batter. Cut and fold until well blended, but do not beat. Spoon into the pan.

Bake about 50 minutes.

White Fruit Cake. Add ⅔ cup candied cherries, cut in pieces, ⅓ cup almonds, blanched and shredded, ½ cup citron, thinly sliced, and 1 teaspoon almond extract. Bake in a large loaf pan or 2 small ones about 1 hour at 325°.

Fresh Coconut Cake

A large coconut should provide enough liquid. If not, add enough milk to make 1 cup.

Butter two 9-inch layer pans. Set the oven at 375°.

Prepare (p. 13), reserving the coconut milk
  1 cup grated fresh coconut
Separate
  3 eggs
Beat the whites until they stand in soft peaks. Beat in gradually
  ½ cup sugar
Without washing the beater, beat the egg yolks until thick.

Cream
  ¾ cup shortening
  ½ teaspoon vanilla
Beat in gradually
  1 cup sugar
Stir in the egg yolks and ¼ cup of the prepared coconut. Beat well.

Sift together
  2¼ cups pastry flour
  2¼ teaspoons baking powder
  ½ teaspoon salt
Add alternately with 1 cup coconut milk. Fold in the egg whites. Spoon into the pans.

Bake about 25 minutes. Put the layers together with Seven-Minute Frosting (p. 493) and cover the top and sides with the frosting. Sprinkle the top and sides with the rest of the coconut.

Black Walnut Tea Cake

Set the oven at 375°. Butter a shallow pan 9 by 9 inches.

Cream
  ½ cup butter or margarine
Beat in
  ½ cup brown sugar
  ¾ cup white corn syrup
  2 teaspoons vanilla
Add, one at a time, beating thoroughly
  4 eggs
Sift together
  2½ cups pastry or cake flour
  3 teaspoons baking powder
  ¼ teaspoon salt
Add to butter mixture alternately with
  ½ cup milk
Spread in the pan. Sprinkle with
  ½ cup chopped black walnuts
  ½ cup brown sugar
Pat in lightly.

Bake about 20 minutes. Cut in squares. Serve warm with tea or coffee.

Spice Cakes and Gingerbreads

An adaptable group of cakes which can be presented in many ways. Especially appropriate served with tea or coffee or with simple fruit desserts. For a small family, these cakes may be adapted to be served at two meals — part as dessert topped with whipped cream, Gervaise (p. 405) or Lemon Sauce (p. 402), and the rest as cake, frosted or not. See also Gingerbread Upside-Down Cake (p. 482) and the suggestions for serving cake (p. 457).

Spice Cake

Other spice cake recipes are Honey Cake (p. 461), Spanish Cake (p. 461), Ginger Pound Cake and Molasses Pound Cake (p. 464).

Butter and flour two 8- or 9-inch square tins. Set the oven at 375°.

Sift together
  2 cups flour
  1 teaspoon cinnamon
  1 teaspoon powdered cloves
  ½ teaspoon allspice
  ½ teaspoon salt
  1 teaspoon baking soda
  2 teaspoons baking powder
Beat until thick and lemon-colored
  2 eggs
Beat in gradually
  1 cup sugar
  2 tablespoons molasses
Beat well. Add alternately with the flour mixture
  1 cup sour milk or buttermilk
Stir in lightly
  ⅔ cup melted shortening or oil
Spoon into the tins.

Bake about 25 minutes. Frost with Quick Caramel Frosting (p. 493) or Portsmouth Frosting (p. 491).

Harvard Cake. In place of white sugar and molasses, use 2 cups brown sugar.

Applesauce Cake

If you prefer a spicier cake, add 1 teaspoon ginger or ¼ cup finely cut candied ginger.

Set the oven at 350°. Butter and flour a 9-inch pan, or two 8-inch pans if you prefer thin squares of cake.

Mix thoroughly
  1 cup applesauce, sweetened or not
  ⅞ cup brown sugar
  ½ cup melted shortening or salad oil
Sift into a large bowl
  1¾ cups flour
  1 teaspoon baking soda
  ½ teaspoon salt

  1 teaspoon cinnamon
  ½ teaspoon powdered cloves
Add
  ½ cup raisins
  ½ cup nut meats, cut in pieces
Add the applesauce mixture. Blend well and spoon into the pan.

Bake about 40 minutes.

Jam Cake

Butter and flour two 9-inch layer tins. Set the oven at 375°.

Sift together
  2 cups flour
  1 teaspoon allspice
  1 teaspoon cinnamon
  1 teaspoon nutmeg
  1 teaspoon baking soda
  ½ teaspoon salt
Cream until light and fluffy
  ¼ cup butter
  1 cup sugar
Add
  3 eggs, beaten until light
Mix
  1 cup blackberry, raspberry or straw-
    berry jam
  ¼ cup sour milk
Stir into the batter by thirds, alternating with the flour mixture. Spoon into the tins.

Bake about 25 minutes. Frost with Portsmouth Frosting (p. 491).

With sweet milk. Omit the baking soda and add 3 teaspoons baking powder. Use sweet milk in place of sour.

Gingerbread

For a spicier gingerbread, add ½ teaspoon cinnamon and ¼ teaspoon each of powdered cloves and nutmeg.

Butter a shallow pan 8 or 9 inches square or 12 muffin tins. Set the oven at 325° for the square pans, 350° for the muffin tins.

Sift together
  1½ cups flour
  ⅓ cup sugar

2 teaspoons baking powder
1 teaspoon ginger
¼ teaspoon salt
Combine
¼ cup butter
½ cup boiling water
When the butter melts, add
½ cup molasses
Stir into the flour mixture and beat just enough to make a smooth batter. Spread in the pans.

Bake about 35 minutes in the square pan or 15 minutes in the muffin tins.

Sour Cream Gingerbread

Made with butter, this gingerbread stays moist and delicious for days. For a simpler gingerbread, omit the butter.

Butter a shallow pan 8 or 9 inches square. Set the oven at 350°.

Beat
2 eggs
Add
½ cup sour cream
½ cup molasses
½ cup brown sugar
Beat well. Sift together
1½ cups pastry or cake flour
1 teaspoon baking soda
1 teaspoon ginger
¼ teaspoon salt
Stir into the first mixture. Add

½ cup melted butter or margarine
Beat well and pour into the pan.

Bake about 30 minutes.

Soft Molasses Gingerbread

Set the oven at 325°. Butter a pan 8 or 9 inches square.

Sift together
2 cups all-purpose flour
1½ teaspoons baking soda
1½ teaspoons ginger
½ teaspoon salt
Heat together
1 cup molasses
⅓ cup butter or other shortening
Cool. Add
½ cup sour milk or buttermilk
1 egg
Beat thoroughly. Stir into the flour mixture and beat just enough to make a smooth batter. Spoon into the pan.

Bake about 35 minutes.

Applesauce Gingerbread. Add ½ cup cold applesauce with the molasses.

Raisin or Prune Gingerbread. Before stirring in the liquids, add ½ cup raisins or cooked prunes, drained and cut small.

Nut Gingerbread. Before stirring in the liquids, add ½ cup broken nut meats.

Chocolate Cakes

Perhaps the most widely popular cakes, from the simple Huntington Chocolate Cake (p. 468) to Rich Devil's Food (p. 469). See the index for other chocolate cakes, such as Chocolate Sponge Cake (p. 473).

Any chocolate cake recipe is delicious in such desserts as Chocolate Cottage Pudding (p. 481); or baked as cupcakes (p. 454) and frosted or filled; or baked in shallow pans and used in Party Cakes (p. 455) or Hungarian Chocolate Cake (p. 484). For leftover chocolate cake, see Chocolate Ice Cream Balls (p. 458), or use in Chocolate Bread Pudding (p. 368) instead of bread.

Huntington Chocolate Cake

Actually a one-bowl cake (p. 470). Melt the chocolate in a saucepan large enough to use as the bowl for mixing the cake.

Butter a pan 8 by 8 inches. Set the oven at 350°.

Melt over very low heat
 2 ounces chocolate
 ½ cup shortening
Remove from the heat and add
 1 teaspoon vanilla
Sift together
 1 cup pastry flour
 ⅞ cup sugar
 1 teaspoon cream of tartar
 ½ teaspoon baking soda
 ½ teaspoon salt
Add to the chocolate mixture alternately with
 ½ cup milk
Beat in, one at a time
 2 eggs
Beat well. Spread in the pan.

Bake about 30 minutes.

Chocolate Cake

Use water (for an especially tender cake), coffee or sour milk in place of sweet milk. With sour milk, use 1 teaspoon baking soda and no baking powder.

Butter a pan 6 by 9 inches or two 9-inch layer cake pans. Set the oven at 350°.

Cream well
 ½ cup shortening (or use ½ cup oil)
Beat in
 1½ cups sugar
 1 teaspoon vanilla
 2 ounces chocolate, melted over hot
  water
 2 eggs, well beaten
Sift together
 2 cups pastry or cake flour
 2 teaspoons baking powder
 ½ teaspoon salt
Add to the first mixture alternately with
 1 cup milk
Spread in the pan.

Bake about 30 minutes.

Chocolate Pecan Cake. Increase the sugar to 2 cups, the chocolate to 4 ounces, and the milk to 1½ cups. Add 1 cup chopped pecans. Bake in a 10-inch tube pan about 50 minutes. Let stand 24 hours before serving. Serve in wedges topped with whipped cream. Sprinkle with chopped pecans.

Chocolate Potato Cake. Reduce the flour to 1½ cups. Beat ½ cup hot mashed potatoes into the mixture after adding the eggs.

Chocolate Cream Cake. Put layers together with whipped cream. Sprinkle with powdered sugar. Serve with Chocolate Sauce (p. 399).

Chocolate Spice Cake. Sift 1 teaspoon cinnamon and ½ teaspoon powdered cloves with the flour.

Chocolate Fruit Cake. Add to the batter ⅓ cup, each, candied cherries, seeded raisins and walnut meats, cut in pieces. Spoon into a tube pan. Bake 50 minutes.

Chocolate Mocha Cake

Butter a pan 8 by 8 inches. Set the oven at 325°.

Beat until light
 1 egg
Beat in
 1 cup sugar
 ⅓ cup shortening or oil
 1 teaspoon vanilla
Put in a 1-cup measure
 2 ounces chocolate
Fill the cup with
 Hot coffee
Let stand until the chocolate is soft. Pour off the coffee into another cup and add the chocolate to the egg mixture. Sift together
 1⅓ cups flour
 1 teaspoon baking powder
 1 teaspoon baking soda
Add the flour mixture and the coffee alternately to the egg mixture. Spread in the pan.

Bake about 25 minutes. Especially good frosted with one of the variations of Butter Frosting II (p. 493).

Fudge Layer Cake

Butter three layer cake pans. Set the oven at 350°.

Cream until light and fluffy
  ½ cup shortening
  1 cup sugar
  ½ teaspoon vanilla
Cook together until smooth
  4 ounces chocolate
  3 tablespoons boiling water
  ⅓ cup sugar
Beat into the creamed mixture. Add one at a time, beating thoroughly
  3 eggs
Sift together
  1¾ cups flour
  1 teaspoon cream of tartar
  ½ teaspoon baking soda
  ½ teaspoon salt
Add to the first mixture alternately with
  ½ cup milk
Pour into the pans.

Bake about 25 minutes. Put together with Mocha Butter Frosting (p. 494).

Devil's Food

This cake is sometimes called Black Chocolate Cake.

Butter and flour a pan 9 by 12 inches or two pans 9 inches square. Set the oven at 350°.

Melt over very low heat or in a double boiler
  4 ounces chocolate
Add
  ⅔ cup light brown sugar
  1 cup milk
  1 egg yolk, slightly beaten
Stir and cook over hot water until smooth. Set aside to cool.

Beat until stiff
  3 egg whites
Beat in gradually

  ⅓ cup light brown sugar
Cream until light and fluffy
  ⅓ cup shortening
  2 teaspoons vanilla
Add gradually, beating constantly
  ⅔ cup light brown sugar
Stir in
  2 egg yolks, beaten thick
Sift together
  2 cups flour
  ¼ teaspoon salt
  1 teaspoon baking soda
Add to the shortening mixture alternately with
  1½ cups milk
Add the chocolate mixture. Beat well. Fold in the egg whites. Spoon into the pan.

Bake about 35 minutes.

Rich Devil's Food

Butter a pan 9 inches square. Set the oven at 350°.

Cook until thick in a double boiler
  4 tablespoons cocoa
  2½ tablespoons sugar
  2 tablespoons water
Remove from the heat. Stir in
  ½ cup milk
Separate
  2 eggs
Beat the whites until stiff. Beat in gradually
  ½ cup sugar
Cream together until light
  ½ cup shortening
  1 teaspoon vanilla
  ½ cup sugar
Beat in the egg yolks, one at a time. Add the cocoa mixture.

Sift together
  1 cup flour
  ½ teaspoon cream of tartar
  ½ teaspoon salt
  ½ teaspoon baking soda
Beat into the batter. Fold in the egg whites. Spoon into the pan.

Bake about 35 minutes.

Chocolate Buttermilk Cake

No eggs in this cake.

Butter and flour a pan 9 by 12 inches. Set the oven at 375°.

Sift together
  1⅔ cups flour
  1 cup sugar
  ½ cup cocoa
  1 teaspoon baking soda
  ½ teaspoon salt
Beat in
  1 cup buttermilk or sour milk
  ½ cup melted shortening or oil
  1½ teaspoons vanilla
Stir until smooth. Spread in the pan.

Bake about 30 minutes.

Sour Cream Chocolate Cake

A rich cake with a distinctive flavor.

Butter a pan 8 inches square. Set the oven at 350°.

Mix
  1 cup thick sour cream
  1 cup sugar
  1 teaspoon vanilla
  1 tablespoon butter, melted
Sift together and add
  1½ cups cake or pastry flour
  ⅔ cup cocoa
  1 teaspoon baking soda
  ½ teaspoon salt
Beat in, one at a time
  3 eggs
Spread in pan; bake about 25 minutes.

One-Bowl Cakes

The quick-mix method of cake-making is easy, requires but one bowl and takes only a few minutes. The proportion of ingredients is different from that in other recipes, so use only recipes that have been tested for this method. The batter will be smooth and thin.

Lightning Cake (Hot Milk Cake)

Small, delicious and easy. Excellent either frosted or with a special topping as in the recipe for Lazy Daisy Cake.

Set the oven at 375°. Butter a square pan 8 by 8 by 2 inches.

Beat until thick
  2 eggs
  1 teaspoon vanilla
Beat in, a little at a time
  1 cup sugar
Sift together and stir in
  1 cup sifted all-purpose flour
  1 teaspoon baking powder
  ¼ teaspoon salt
Heat until the butter melts
  ½ cup hot milk
  1 tablespoon butter

Stir into the first mixture and beat 1 minute or until smooth. Pour into the pan.

Bake about 25 minutes.

Lazy Daisy Cake. Leave the baked cake in the pan. Mix 3 tablespoons melted butter, 3 tablespoons brown sugar, 2 tablespoons cream and ½ cup chopped nuts or coconut. Spread over the cake. Put under the broiler and cook until the topping is lightly browned. Watch carefully and turn so that the topping browns evenly.

Quick Gold Cake

Set the oven at 350° for tube or layer pan, at 325° for loaf pan. Set out a

10-inch tube pan, two 8-inch layer cake pans or a 9 by 5 inch loaf pan. Do not butter the pans.

Sift together into a mixing bowl
   2¼ cups cake flour
   3 teaspoons baking powder
   1 teaspoon salt
   1¼ cups sugar
Add
   ½ cup salad oil (not olive oil)
   ½ cup milk
Stir until the flour is dampened, then beat 2 minutes. Add
   ½ cup milk
   2 eggs or 5 egg yolks
   1 teaspoon vanilla or 2 teaspoons grated lemon rind
Beat 2 minutes longer. Pour into the pan or pans.

Bake about 55 minutes in a tube or loaf pan, 30 minutes in layer pans.

Quick Fudge Cake

Set the oven at 350°. Butter a pan 12 by 8 by 2 inches.

Place in a mixing bowl
   3 ounces unsweetened chocolate, cut fine
Add
   ¾ cup boiling water
Stir until the chocolate melts. Cool. Sift into the chocolate mixture
   1¾ cups cake flour
   1½ cups sugar
   ¾ teaspoon salt
   ½ teaspoon baking powder
   ¾ teaspoon baking soda
Add
   ½ cup salad oil (not olive oil)
Beat 1 minute by hand or with electric beater at lowest speed. Add
   ⅓ cup sour milk
   1 teaspoon vanilla
   2 eggs

Beat 2 minutes, keeping the sides of the bowl scraped down at all times. Spoon into the pan.

Bake 30 to 40 minutes.

Quick White Cake

Set the oven at 350°. Butter a 10-inch tube pan or two 8-inch layer pans.

Sift into a mixing bowl
   2 cups cake flour
   1 teaspoon salt
   1⅓ cups sugar
Add
   ½ cup salad oil (not olive oil)
   ⅔ cup milk
Stir until the flour is dampened and beat 1 minute. Stir in
   3 teaspoons baking powder
Add
   ⅓ cup milk
   4 egg whites
   1 teaspoon vanilla
Beat 2 minutes. Pour into the pans.

Bake 25 to 40 minutes.

Quick Date Cake

Set the oven at 350°. Butter and flour 12 muffin pans or a 9-inch square cake pan.

Put into a mixing bowl
   ⅓ cup soft butter or margarine
   1 cup brown sugar
   2 eggs
   ½ cup milk
   1¾ cups all-purpose flour
   2 teaspoons baking powder
   ½ teaspoon cinnamon
   ½ teaspoon grated nutmeg
   ½ pound dates, cut in pieces
Beat 3 minutes with a wooden spoon. Pour into the pans.

Bake 30 to 40 minutes.

Sponge and Angel Food Cakes

True sponge cake has no leavening except the air beaten into the eggs. Beating the eggs thoroughly is essential if the cake is to be perfect, but overbeating after the flour is added will spoil the light texture. For further details on beating and folding, see pp. 3–4.

To take sponge cake, angel food and chiffon cake from the pan, pp. 459–460.

True Sponge Cake

The classic recipe — no baking powder.

Set the oven at 325° if you are using a tube pan or other deep pan, 350° for layer or muffin tins.

Separate
  5 eggs
Beat the whites until they stand up in soft peaks. Beat in, a tablespoon at a time
  ¼ cup sugar
Without washing the beater, beat the yolks with
  1 tablespoon lemon juice
until thick and lemon-colored. Beat in gradually
  ¾ cup sugar
Pour over the beaten whites and fold together gently with a spoon or a rubber spatula until well blended.

Sift together
  1 cup flour
  ¼ teaspoon salt
Fold into the egg mixture. Spoon into an unbuttered 9-inch tube pan, two 9-inch layer pans or 12 to 18 muffin tins. Cut through the batter gently several times to break any large air bubbles.

Bake a large cake about 1 hour, layers and small cakes about 30 minutes. (To test, press lightly with a finger. If the cake is done it will spring back.)

Invert on a wire cake cooler. Let stand until cold. Loosen with a spatula and ease the cake out of the pan.

Hot Water Sponge Cake

Baking powder insures the lightness of this cake.

Set the oven at 350°.

Separate
  2 eggs
Sift together
  1 cup pastry or cake flour
  1¼ teaspoons baking powder
  Few grains salt
Beat the whites until they stand up in soft peaks. Beat in gradually
  ¼ cup sugar
Add to the egg yolks
  ¼ cup hot water
  ½ teaspoon vanilla
Beat until thick. Beat in
  ½ cup sugar
Pour the yolks over the whites and cut and fold until well blended. Fold in the flour mixture. Spoon into a small unbuttered tube pan or a lightly buttered 9-inch square pan or 12 cupcake tins.

Bake 20 to 30 minutes. To test, see True Sponge Cake (above).

Cream Sponge Cake

For a layer cake, jelly roll or Vienna Cake. A perfect birthday cake because its light texture goes well with a rich frosting. Excellent for cupcakes, too.

Set the oven at 325° for a tube pan, 350° for layers.

Separate
  4 eggs
Sift
  1 cup pastry or cake flour
  1¼ teaspoons baking powder

¼ teaspoon salt

Beat the egg whites until they stand up in soft peaks. Beat in

¼ cup sugar

Without washing the beater, beat the egg yolks until thick and lemon-colored. Beat in

1 teaspoon vanilla
1½ tablespoons cold water
1½ tablespoons lemon juice
¾ cup sugar

Pour over the whites and fold together until well blended. Fold in the flour mixture. Pour into two 8-inch layer cake pans or an 8-inch tube pan.

Bake 40 to 50 minutes in a tube pan, 25 to 30 in layers. To test, see True Sponge Cake (p. 472).

Mocha Cake. Add to the batter ½ cup walnut meats broken in pieces. Bake in an 8-inch tube pan about 45 minutes. Cool. Split and fill with French Coffee Cream Filling (p. 495). Cover the top with Confectioners' Frosting (p. 491), flavored with instant coffee.

Daffodil Cake (Marble Sponge)

Set the oven at 325°. Set out a large tube pan but do not butter it.

Beat until foamy
1¼ cups egg whites (about 9)
Add
½ teaspoon salt
1 teaspoon cream of tartar

Beat until stiff but not dry. Beat in, a little at a time
1⅛ cups sugar

Divide in half. Fold into one part
½ cup pastry or cake flour, sifted
½ teaspoon vanilla

Fold into the other part
6 egg yolks, well beaten
⅔ cup pastry or cake flour, sifted
½ teaspoon orange or lemon extract
½ teaspoon salt

Put by spoonfuls into the pan, alternating yellow and white.

Bake about 1¼ hours. Turn upside down. Let stand until cold before remov-

ing from the pan. Sprinkle with sifted confectioners' sugar.

Sunshine Cake

Set the oven at 350°. Set out a large tube pan but do not butter it.

Beat until they stand up in soft peaks
10 egg whites
Beat in
½ cup confectioners' sugar
1 teaspoon cream of tartar
Beat until thick
7 egg yolks
Add
1 cup confectioners' sugar
1 teaspoon lemon or almond extract

Beat well. Pour over the whites and fold together gently until well blended. Sift over the egg mixture
1 cup pastry or cake flour
¼ teaspoon salt

Cut and fold together. Pour into the pan.

Bake about 50 minutes. Invert on a wire cooler and let stand until cold.

Chocolate Sponge Cake

Butter a 9-inch tube pan. Set the oven at 350°.

Put in the top of a double boiler
1 bar (6 ounces) sweet baking chocolate
¼ cup water

Set over hot water until the chocolate is melted.

Beat until light and fluffy
4 eggs
Beat in gradually
¾ cup sugar
½ teaspoon vanilla
⅛ teaspoon salt

Add the chocolate mixture. Fold in
½ cup flour, sifted

Spoon into the pan.

Bake about 45 minutes. Frost with Butter Frosting (p. 493).

Genoise

Half the standard French recipe, but enough for a two-layer cake or two dozen petits fours.

Butter two 8-inch layer cake pans or a pan about 10 by 6 inches. Line the bottom of the pans with wax paper and butter again. Set the oven at 350°.

Clarify (p. 8)
　¼ cup butter
Set aside to cool to lukewarm.

Put in a mixing bowl
　3 eggs (at room temperature)
　½ cup fine granulated sugar
　½ teaspoon vanilla
Beat (easiest with an electric beater at high speed) until thick enough to stand in peaks when the beater is lifted out. Using a rubber spatula, fold in gently by spoonfuls
　½ cup sifted cake or pastry flour
Sprinkle the melted butter over the batter. Blend gently. Pour into the pans.

Bake 35 to 40 minutes. Turn out carefully onto a cooling rack. Peel off the paper. Frost or fill and frost with
　Butter Cream (p. 491) or a variation
See also Vienna Cake (p. 483).

Angel Food Cake

Make angel food the day before you plan to serve it. It "ripens" to a finer flavor and texture.

Set the oven at 325°. Dust a 10-inch tube pan with flour but do not butter it.

Beat with a flat wire whisk or a beater until foamy
　1 cup egg whites (8 or more)
　¼ teaspoon salt
Add
　1 teaspoon cream of tartar
Beat until the egg whites stand up in soft peaks. Add
　½ teaspoon almond extract
　1 teaspoon vanilla

Sift together four times
　1¼ cups fine granulated sugar
　1 cup cake flour
Fold carefully into the beaten whites, 2 tablespoons at a time, using a whisk or spatula. Fold gently over and over until the mixture is even. Spoon into the pan.

Bake 50 minutes, then turn off the heat and leave the cake in the oven 10 minutes longer. Turn the pan upside down on a wire rack (p. 459) and let stand until the cake is cold (at least 1 hour).

Cocoa Angel Cake. Substitute ⅓ cup dry cocoa for ¼ cup flour. Sift with the flour. Omit almond extract. Cover the whole cake with a thin layer of whipped cream.

Hot Milk Angel Cake

For the finest flavor, bake the day before serving.

Set the oven at 350°. Set out a small tube pan but do not butter it.

Sift together four times
　1 cup sugar
　1⅓ cups cake flour
　3 teaspoons baking powder
　¼ teaspoon salt
Stir in, little by little
　⅔ cup scalded milk
Add
　1 teaspoon vanilla
Beat until stiff
　2 egg whites
Fold into the batter. Pour into the pan.

Bake about 45 minutes.

Chiffon Cake

Almost as light as angel food.

Set the oven at 325°. Set out a 10-inch tube pan but do not butter it.

Sift into a large mixing bowl
　2¼ cups cake flour
　3 teaspoons baking powder

1½ cups sugar
1 teaspoon salt

Make a well in the center. Pour in
½ cup salad oil (not olive oil)
5 egg yolks
¾ cup cold water
2 teaspoons vanilla

Beat thoroughly until satin-smooth (2 minutes with an electric beater).

Beat until stiff
1 cup egg whites (7 or 8)
½ teaspoon cream of tartar

Pour the first mixture over the egg whites a little at a time, gently folding it in with a spatula or a rubber scraper until evenly blended. Do not beat or stir. Pour into the pan.

Bake 50 minutes. Increase the heat to 350° and bake until the top springs back when you dent it with your finger (about 15 minutes). Take from the oven and turn the pan upside down on a wire rack (p. 459). Let stand until cold. Loosen the cake from the sides of the tin with a spatula.

Chocolate Chiffon Cake. Use only 2 cups flour. Sift with it ¼ cup cocoa.

Lemon or Orange Chiffon Cake. Omit the vanilla. Add 2 teaspoons grated lemon or orange rind.

Spice Chiffon Cake. Use brown sugar in place of white. Add 1 teaspoon cinnamon and ½ teaspoon each of nutmeg, powdered cloves and allspice.

Chiffon Nut Cake. Just before pouring the batter (or any variation) into the pan, add 1 cup nut meats, chopped fine.

Fruit Cakes

See also simple fruit cakes such as Applesauce Cake (p. 466), Spice Cake (p. 466) with added raisins, Raisin Gingerbread (p. 467), Chocolate Fruit Cake (p. 468), White Fruit Cake (p. 464), and Imperial Cake (p. 464), all of which have some fruit in them.

To prepare fruit. Leave currants and seedless raisins whole. Cut seeded raisins in half with wet scissors. Cut cherries in half. Slice candied pineapple, citron and fruit peels thin. Cut dates and nuts in quarters. Fruit prepared for fruit cake is available, especially at holiday time.

To prepare pans. Use deep loaf pans. Butter the pans lightly and line with aluminum foil. Glass or ovenware casseroles, small or large, are attractive, especially if you are planning the fruit cake as a gift. Butter lightly but do not line with foil. After baking, cool, put on covers, and set cakes away to ripen.

To decorate. Spread with a thin layer of almond paste, canned or homemade (p. 505), moistened with egg white. When firm, frost and decorate as you like (pp. 489ff.).

For a more elaborate effect, remove from the oven 15 minutes before baking is completed. Brush with slightly beaten egg white and quickly arrange on the cake a pattern of bits of candied fruit and nuts. Return to the oven to finish baking.

To store. Cool baked cakes 30 minutes. Loosen around the edges with a knife and turn out on cake racks. When entirely cold, wrap in heavy wax paper and tie securely. Store in a crock or tin box with a tight cover. If baked in a casserole, store in the casserole.

Rich fruit cakes improve in flavor if aged at least two weeks before using. If you like, sprinkle stored fruit cakes very lightly with brandy once a week until used. This helps keep the cake moist and improves the flavor.

Light Fruit Cake

The pieces of whole fruit make this a particularly handsome cake — a cake with style as well as delicious flavor.

Set the oven at 250°. Line three large loaf pans or 5 or 6 small ones with aluminum foil.

Cream
  1 cup butter
Beat in
  2 cups white sugar
  1 teaspoon vanilla
Beat until fluffy. Beat in, one at a time
  7 egg yolks
Sift together
  3 cups pastry or 2¾ cups all-purpose flour
  ½ teaspoon salt
  2 teaspoons baking powder
Add to the butter mixture alternately with
  1 cup milk
Fold in
  1 pound white raisins
  1 pound pecan meats
Fold in
  7 egg whites, beaten stiff
Have ready for decorating the layers
  1 pound candied cherries, red and green
  1 pound candied pineapple fingers
  1 pound whole Brazil nut meats
  1 pound pitted dates (place a nut in each, and roll in sugar)
Put a thin layer of the cake batter in each pan. Arrange on the batter whole fruit (using one kind of fruit for each layer). Cover with a layer of batter. Repeat until the fruit is used and put a layer of batter on the top. To make loaves even, work with all the pans at the same time. Fill the pans to ¾ inch from the top.

Bake about 2½ hours.

Dark Fruit Cake

A moist rich cake which improves with age. Make it in two large loaf pans or in several smaller ones. Details on making fruit cake (p. 475).

Cover with boiling water
  1 pound mixed candied fruit, cut small
Let stand 2 hours. Drain.

Mix together and set aside
  1 cup seeded raisins, cut in pieces
  ¾ cup dried currants
  ½ cup candied citron, cut small
  1 jar (4 ounces) candied cherries
  1 cup chopped pecans
Set the oven at 325°. Line the pans with aluminum foil.

Sift together
  2 cups all-purpose flour
  ½ teaspoon baking soda
  1 teaspoon cinnamon
  ½ teaspoon each of allspice and mace
  ¼ teaspoon ground cloves
Beat together
  ½ cup soft shortening or oil
  ¾ cup brown sugar
  ½ teaspoon lemon extract
Stir in
  2 eggs
  ½ cup molasses
  ½ cup milk
Add the flour mixture, fruit and nuts. Mix gently together. Fill the pans.

Bake about 1¼ hours.

Dundee Cake

A famous old recipe. Serve it with tea, coffee or sherry. To serve in the traditional style, put the whole loaf on a plate or cutting board and slice it as you serve it.

Line two or three small loaf pans with aluminum foil. Set the oven at 275°.

Cream until light and fluffy
  ⅞ cup butter
Beat in gradually
  ⅔ cup sugar
Add, one at a time, beating 5 minutes after adding each
  4 eggs
Stir in
  ⅓ cup almonds, blanched and chopped

Sift together
  2½ cups pastry flour or 2¼ cups all-
    purpose flour
  1 teaspoon baking powder
  ½ teaspoon salt
Add to the flour
  1 cup seedless raisins
  1⅓ cups currants or seeded raisins,
    cut in pieces
Mix well and add to the first mixture
with
  ⅓ cup candied orange and lemon
    peel, cut small
  2 tablespoons orange juice
Mix thoroughly. Fill the pans. Cover the
tops with
  Blanched almonds, candied cherries
    and citron
Bake about 1¼ hours. As soon as the
cakes begin to brown, cover them with
a sheet of brown paper.

Pecan Whiskey Cake

Line three loaf pans with aluminum foil.
Set the oven at 250°.

Separate
  6 eggs
Beat the whites until they stand in soft
peaks. Beat in
  1 cup sugar
Without washing the beater, beat the
yolks until thick.

Cream
  ¾ pound butter
Beat in gradually
  1 cup light brown sugar
  1 cup white sugar
Add the egg yolks and beat well.

Mix
  1 cup flour
  2 pounds pecan nut meats
  1 pound light raisins
Sift together
  2 cups flour
  1 teaspoon baking powder
  1 teaspoon nutmeg
Add to the butter mixture. Add
  1 cup Bourbon whiskey

Stir in the floured nuts and raisins. Fold
in the whites. Fill the pans.

Bake about 2 hours.

Nancy's Pecan Cake. *This cake does not
need to ripen, but may be cut successfully the day it is made.* Reduce the nut
meats to ⅔ cup and the raisins to ¼
cup. Use ⅓ the amount of all the other
ingredients.

Election Cake

*An old-fashioned Connecticut specialty.
The leavening is yeast, so allow plenty
of time.*

Put in a bowl
  1 cup warm water (not hot)
Sprinkle over it
  1 package yeast
Add
  1 tablespoon sugar
  1 tablespoon salad oil
  2½ cups flour
Beat thoroughly, cover, and let rise overnight or at least 6 hours.

Butter 3 loaf tins. Cream
  1 cup butter
Cream in
  2 cups dark brown sugar
Add
  4 eggs, well beaten
Stir in
  1 tablespoon grated lemon rind
  1 tablespoon lemon juice
Sift together
  1½ cups flour
  1½ teaspoons baking soda
  ½ teaspoon powdered cloves
  ½ teaspoon mace
  ½ teaspoon nutmeg
  ½ teaspoon salt
Add to the butter mixture. Add
  2 cups seeded raisins
  1 cup whiskey
Stir into the yeast batter and beat to
blend well. Divide the dough in the tins.
Cover and let rise 1 hour.

Bake about 1 hour at 350°.

Birthday Fruit Cake

Butter and flour a large angel cake tin. Set the oven at 300°.

Place in a bowl and mix well
    ½ cup seeded raisins, cut in pieces
    ½ cup walnut meats, cut in pieces
    ⅓ cup currants
    2 tablespoons candied orange peel, cut fine
    ¼ cup flour
Separate
    2 eggs
Beat the whites until stiff. Beat in gradually
    ¼ cup brown sugar
Cream
    ½ cup butter or other shortening
Beat in
    1 cup brown sugar
    1 teaspoon orange extract
    1 teaspoon vanilla
Beat the egg yolks slightly and stir them in.

Sift together
    2 cups flour
    3 teaspoons baking powder
Add to the creamed mixture alternately with
    ⅔ cup milk
Fold in the egg whites. Fill the pan, distributing the floured fruit on the layers as for Light Fruit Cake (above).

Bake about 1¼ hours. Cover with Royal Frosting (p. 492).

Wedding Fruit Cake

The traditional dark rich fruit cake. Serve either this type or Bride's Cake (p. 480), which is a white cake with a fruit cake layer on top, or serve both.

Vary this recipe by adding more fruits, such as 1 pint preserved strawberries or 1 pound candied cherries. Or add 1 pound almonds, blanched and cut fine.

If your oven is too small to bake four large loaves at once, add half the soda to half the batter and bake two loaves. When they are done, add the rest of the soda *to the remaining batter and bake the other two loaves.*

Line 4 large loaf pans with aluminum foil.

Cream until light and fluffy
    1 pound shortening
Beat in, little by little
    1 pound brown sugar
Stir in
    1 cup molasses
    12 egg yolks, well beaten
Sift together
    3 cups all-purpose flour
    4 teaspoons cinnamon
    4 teaspoons allspice
    1½ teaspoons mace
    2 teaspoons nutmeg
Add to the first mixture.

Mix
    ⅓ cup flour
    3 pounds seeded raisins, cut in pieces
    2 pounds sultana raisins
    1½ pounds candied citron, sliced thin and cut in strips
    1 pound dried currants
    ¼ cup chopped preserved lemon rind (½ rind)
    ½ cup chopped preserved orange rind (½ rind)
Add to the batter. Add
    1 cup brandy
    4 ounces chocolate, melted (optional)
Fold in
    12 egg whites, beaten stiff
Just before putting the batter in the pans, add
    ¼ teaspoon baking soda, dissolved in 1 tablespoon hot water
Fill the pans and cover the tops closely with aluminum foil.

Set the oven at 250°. On the oven bottom place several shallow pans filled with hot water to a depth of 1 inch. Set the pans of fruit cake on the shelf above.

Bake 3 hours, remove the pans of water, and remove the aluminum foil from the tops of the cakes. Bake 1½ hours to dry out the cakes.

Cutting
the Wedding Cake

1

Cut the lowest tier
all around,

2

then the middle
tier,

3

then the lowest
tier again,

4

and save the top
for the bride.

Bride's Cake

This recipe serves 30 guests (or more if you cut smaller pieces). For 60 guests, make the recipe twice in two separate batches. Twice the recipe makes a cake with a double 12-inch layer topped by a double 8-inch layer.

Do not overcrowd the oven or the cakes will bake unevenly. Put some of the pans of batter in the refrigerator while the others are baking.

Set the oven at 350°. Butter an 8-inch layer cake pan and a 12-inch round pan.

Sift together
    3⅜ cups cake or pastry flour
    5 teaspoons baking powder
    2¼ cups sugar
    1½ teaspoons salt
Add
    ¾ cup shortening (soft)
    1 cup milk
    1½ teaspoons vanilla
Beat with a large spoon until well mixed (or 2½ minutes at medium speed in an electric mixer). Add
    ½ cup milk
    ¾ cup egg whites (6 or 7), unbeaten
Beat well. Put about one-third of the batter in the 8-inch layer pan, the rest in the 12-inch pan.

Bake the 8-inch layer 30 to 35 minutes, the 12-inch layer 35 to 40 minutes.

Fruit Cake Layer for Bride's Cake

A small rich layer to top the wedding cake.

Line with foil a deep round pan 5 inches in diameter. Butter well. Set the oven at 250°.

Sift together
    ¾ cup flour
    ½ cup sugar
    1 teaspoon baking powder
    ⅛ teaspoon salt

Stir in
    ¼ cup melted shortening
    ¼ cup water
    2 eggs, well beaten
Mix
    ⅓ cup each of white raisins, coconut and chopped toasted almonds
    ¼ cup each of citron, candied orange peel and candied lemon peel, all cut fine
    ¼ cup candied cherries, halved
    ¼ cup flour
Add to the cake batter. Fill the pan. Bake 2½ hours.

Icing for the Wedding Cake

If more convenient, make the icing in smaller batches. Make double this amount for the larger cake.

Cream until light and fluffy
    ½ cup butter or margarine
    ½ cup vegetable shortening
Blend in gradually
    8 cups sifted confectioners' sugar
Beat until smooth. Stir in
    ½ cup cream
    1½ tablespoons vanilla
Mix well.

Spread between the layers and over the top and sides. Decorate with dragées or other ornaments. On the top set silver bells, bride and groom figures, or fresh flowers in a small glass covered with icing.

Cutting the Wedding Cake

Start with the bottom layer, as shown on p. 479. Use a long sharp knife. Dip it frequently in hot water and cut with a sawing motion, not straight down.

As the pieces of cake are cut, arrange them on a large cake tray to be passed to the guests. Sometimes they are packed in tiny boxes for the guests to take home. It is a pleasant custom for the bride to keep the top layer for her first party.

Cottage Pudding and Other Cake Desserts

See also suggestions for serving cake (p. 457), and the recipes for tortes and icebox cakes. For another cake type of dessert, see Lemon Pudding (p. 367).

Cottage Pudding

An adaptable recipe. For a small family bake either in cupcake tins or a small square tin. Use part for cottage pudding and frost the rest for another meal. For a richer dessert, top with whipped cream. One-Egg Cake (p. 462) is excellent for cottage pudding, too.

Set the oven at 400°. Butter a shallow cake pan, 8 by 8 inches, a small angel cake pan or cupcake tins.

Sift together
   1½ cups flour
   2 teaspoons baking powder
   ½ teaspoon salt
   ½ cup sugar
Mix
   1 egg, well beaten
   ½ cup milk
   ½ cup butter, melted
Stir gently into the flour mixture. Pour into the pan.

Bake until brown and crusty (20 to 25 minutes).

Serve warm with
   Vanilla Sauce (p. 402), Creamy Chocolate Sauce (p. 399), Lemon Sauce
   (p. 402), Orange Sauce (p. 404),
   or Melba Sauce (p. 404), or with
   crushed and sweetened strawberries,
   sliced peaches or stewed blueberries
Serves 6.

Chocolate Chip Cottage Pudding. Add 1 package chocolate bits to the batter. Serve with Vanilla Sauce (p. 402) or whipped cream.

Chocolate Cottage Pudding

Delicious either warm or cold.

Bake Chocolate Cake (p. 468) in an angel cake pan. Remove from the pan and cool. Fill the center with sweetened and flavored whipped cream. Pour Thin Chocolate Sauce (p. 399) around the cake. Or bake the cake in a shallow pan, cut in squares, and top with the cream.

Apple Pan Dowdy

Set the oven at 350°. Butter a 1½-quart baking dish.

Put in the baking dish
   3 cups tart apples, peeled and sliced
Sprinkle with
   ½ cup molasses or brown sugar
   ¼ teaspoon nutmeg
   ¼ teaspoon cinnamon
   ¼ teaspoon salt

Bake until the apples are soft.

Meanwhile prepare
   Cottage Pudding batter (above)
Spread it over the apples. Continue baking until the top is brown and crusty (about 25 minutes).

Serve from the dish or turn out with the apples on top. Serve with
   Hard Sauce (p. 402) or whipped cream
Serves 6.

Cherry, Rhubarb or Blueberrry Pan Dowdy. Stew the fruit, sweeten to taste, and pour into the baking dish. Heat, if necessary, and pour the batter over it. Bake as above.

Apple Cobbler

Good with canned fruit, too.

Butter an 8 by 8 inch baking dish or casserole. Set the oven at 425°.

Prepare
  2 cups sliced pared tart apples
Add
  Few grains salt
  Sugar to taste
  1 egg, well beaten, or 1 tablespoon
    quick tapioca or flour
Spread in the baking dish and dot with butter. Spread over the top
  Cottage Pudding (p. 481) or Shortcake
    (p. 484) batter
Bake about 30 minutes. Serve with
  Whipped cream, Vanilla Sauce (p.
    402), or Foamy Sauce (p. 403)
Serves 6.

Berry Cobbler. Use blackberries, loganberries or blueberries.

Cherry Cobbler. Pit the cherries. Cook 5 minutes in just enough water to keep them from burning. Sweeten to taste.

Peach Cobbler. Use peaches. Put in a peach pit or two for extra good flavor.

Dutch Apple Cake

Spread Cottage Pudding (above), Shortcake (p. 484) or Lightning Cake (p. 470) batter ¾ inch thick in a buttered round or oblong pan. Pare 5 tart apples, core, cut in eighths, and press the sharp edges of the apples into the batter in parallel rows. Sprinkle with ½ cup sugar mixed with ½ teaspoon cinnamon, also 2 tablespoons currants or seedless raisins, if liked.

Bake at 350° until apples are tender (about 25 minutes).

Serve with Hard Sauce (p. 402), Soft Custard (p. 362), Lemon Sauce (p. 402) or whipped cream. *Serves 6 to 8.*

Plum, Peach or Apricot Kuchen. Use stoned plums, peaches or apricots in place of apples.

Blueberry Cake. Pour the batter into a pan 8 by 8 inches. Cover with ½ to 1 cup blueberries. Sprinkle with ¼ cup sugar mixed with ½ teaspoon cinnamon, if liked. Bake. Cut in squares. Serve warm.

Upside-Down Cake

Melt in a heavy frying pan or a cake pan
  ¼ cup butter
Add
  1 cup brown sugar
Spread it evenly in the pan. If desired, sprinkle with
  Pecan nut meats
Put in the pan, close together
  Peach halves or drained canned sliced
    pineapple
Sprinkle with lemon juice. Cover with
  Cottage Pudding batter (p. 481)
Bake at 400° until the top is brown and crusty (about 35 minutes). Turn out on a serving dish, fruit side up. Garnish with whipped cream. *Serves 6.*

Coconut Upside-Down Cake

Put in a pan 6 by 10 or 8 by 8 inches
  6 tablespoons butter
  ½ cup brown sugar
  2 tablespoons water
Cook and stir over low heat until melted. Stir in
  1 cup toasted coconut
Pour over the coconut
  Cottage Pudding (p. 481) or One-Egg
    Cake (p. 462) batter
Bake at 350° about 45 minutes. Serve with whipped cream topped with a sprinkling of toasted coconut. *Serves 6.*

Gingerbread Upside-Down Cake

Melt ¼ cup butter in an oblong baking pan or shallow casserole. Add ⅓ cup dark brown sugar and stir until melted. Arrange canned peach or pear halves, cut side down, evenly in the syrup.

Sprinkle with lemon juice. Cover with any Gingerbread (p. 466) batter.

Bake. Loosen the edges and turn out onto a serving plate, fruit side up. Serve with plain or whipped cream. *Serves 6.*

Apple Gingerbread. Peel, core, and quarter tart apples to make 2 cups. Cook 10 minutes in syrup (½ cup sugar boiled with ½ cup water). Use in place of peach or pear halves.

Boston Cream Pie

Traditionally called "pie" but actually a layer cake, not a pie in the usual sense.

Bake in two 7 or 8 inch layer cake tins Boston Favorite Cake (p. 461), One-Egg Cake (p. 462) or Golden Layer Cake (p. 462). Put the layers together with whipped cream, Cream Filling (p. 495) or Rich Cream Filling (p. 495). Sprinkle the top with confectioners' sugar or spread with Chocolate Frosting (p. 492).

Chocolate Cream Pie. Use Chocolate Filling (p. 492) between the layers.

Washington Pie. Use raspberry jam between the layers. Sprinkle the top with confectioners' sugar.

Vienna Cake

Make Cream Sponge Cake (p. 472) or Genoise (p. 474), increasing the egg whites to 6. Spoon into a 9-inch tube pan.

Bake at 325° about 1 hour. Turn upside down on a wire cooler. Cool, remove from the pan, and cut crosswise in four layers of equal thickness.

Make 1½ times the recipe for Butter Cream Filling (p. 495) and flavor one-third of it with 1 ounce chocolate, melted. Put the layers together with plain filling in the center, chocolate filling in the others. Cover the top and sides with plain filling. Sprinkle all the frosted surface with crushed nut brittle (almond or peanut).

Another way to make Vienna Cake is to put Caramel Glaze (p. 491) on the top and have no frosting on the top or sides.

Rum Cake

Cut in serving-size sections a 9-inch Sponge (p. 472) or Angel Cake (p. 475), homemade or not. Press together in the original shape.

Sprinkle with rum, using about ¼ cup, or as much as the cake will absorb. Whip ½ pint cream, sweeten, and flavor as you like or fold into it a jar of Nesselrode sauce. Spread evenly over the top and sides of the cake.

Jelly Roll

Line the bottom of a shallow pan (about 9 by 13 inches) with heavy wax paper. Butter the paper and the sides of the pan.

Cover the bottom of the pan with Hot Water Sponge Cake (p. 472) or half the recipe for Cream Sponge Cake (p. 472). (Use the rest for a few cupcakes if you make the whole amount.) Spread evenly.

Bake at 350° until firm (about 13 minutes). Do not overbake.

Turn out onto a towel sprinkled thickly with confectioners' sugar. Pull off the paper quickly. If the edge is very crusty, cut off thin strips from the edges of the cake so that it will roll without breaking. Use a long, thin sharp knife.

Roll the cake in a towel and let stand a few minutes. Unroll and spread with jam or jelly. Roll up firmly and wrap in wax paper until serving time. Sprinkle the top with confectioners' sugar.

Lemon or Orange Roll. Spread with Lemon or Orange Filling (p. 496).

Ice Cream Roll. Do not unroll until serving time. Spread with a thick layer of vanilla ice cream soft enough to spread but not melted. Roll up. Serve with a sauce or not.

Whipped Cream Roll. Spread with whipped cream sweetened and flavored with vanilla, instant coffee, maple syrup or chocolate. Rum goes well with coffee or chocolate. Mix in chopped nuts if you like.

Angel Food Roll. Make half the recipe for Angel Food (p. 475). Prepare the pan as above. Bake at 325° about 20 minutes. Fill as above.

Chocolate Roll

Butter and flour a jelly roll pan about 10 by 14 inches. Set the oven at 350°.

Separate
    5 eggs
Beat the whites until stiff. Mix and beat in, a little at a time
    1 cup confectioners' sugar
    3 tablespoons cocoa
Without washing the beater, beat the yolks until thick and fold them in. Spread evenly in the pan.
Bake until the cake shrinks from the edges (about 20 minutes). Turn out on a cloth sprinkled with
    Confectioners' sugar
Cut off the edges of the cake if they are crisp. Cover the cake with a slightly dampened cloth. Cool. Spread with
    ½ pint heavy cream, whipped and sweetened, flavored with vanilla or rum
Roll firmly and put on a serving dish with the fold underneath. Sprinkle lightly with
    Confectioners' sugar
Slice and serve with
    Chocolate Sauce (p. 399)
Serves 6 to 8.

Hungarian Chocolate Cake. Cut the cake in four even pieces. Spread three with whipped cream. Stack evenly (no cream on top). Melt 2 ounces unsweetened chocolate in a double boiler, add ½ cup confectioners' sugar and 1 tablespoon hot water. Blend well, add 1 egg, beat until smooth, add 3 tablespoons

butter, and spread over the sides and top of the cake.

Strawberry or Raspberry Shortcake

Old-fashioned shortcake is made with biscuit dough, not cake, and is served with unsweetened heavy cream, not whipped cream. Perfect for a leisurely Sunday breakfast as well as for dessert.

Wash and drain
    1 quart berries
Remove the stems. Set aside a few perfect berries to garnish the cake. Crush the rest slightly and sweeten to taste.

Butter a 9-inch round cake pan. Set the oven at 425°.

Sift together
    2 cups flour
    4 teaspoons tartrate-type baking powder (2 teaspoons "quick-acting" type)
    ½ teaspoon salt
    1 tablespoon sugar
    Few grains nutmeg
With a blending fork or fingers, work in
    ¼ cup butter
Stir in, little by little
    Milk (about ¾ cup)
until the dough holds together but is still soft. Turn out on a floured board and divide in two parts. Pat or roll out into 9-inch rounds. (To make individual shortcakes, cut out rounds with a large biscuit cutter.) Put one round in the pan. Spread lightly with
    2 tablespoons melted butter
Place the other half on top.

Bake 12 minutes. Split the two layers apart carefully with a fork. Spread with
    2 tablespoons butter (or more)
Warm the crushed berries slightly and put between the layers and on top. Garnish with the whole berries. Serve warm with
    Heavy cream
Serves 6.

For richer shortcake. Increase the sugar to ⅓ cup and the butter to ⅓ cup. Add a well-beaten egg before stirring in the milk (about ⅓ cup).

Other fruits for shortcake. Blackberries, warm applesauce, sliced and sugared bananas, warm stewed blueberries, sliced and sweetened peaches or apricots.

Blackberry Rolypoly

Set the oven at 425°. Butter a pan 8 by 12 inches.

Prepare
  Shortcake dough (above)
Roll into an oblong ½ inch thick. Brush with

  2 tablespoons melted butter
Mix
  6 cups blackberries
  1 cup sugar
  ½ teaspoon salt
Sprinkle half the fruit mixture over the dough. Roll up like a jelly roll. Put in the pan with the fold on the bottom. Put the rest of the fruit around the roll.

Bake about 30 minutes. Cut in slices and serve with
  Whipped cream or Lemon Sauce (p. 402)
Serves 6 to 8.

Blueberry Rolypoly. Use blueberries in place of blackberries.

Tortes and Other Rich Cake Desserts

Making Tortes

Austrian cooking is famous for tortes, which are rich, often rather heavy cakes. When you invite guests for dessert, torte and coffee make a perfect combination.

To fill the pans. Use pans with removable rims or spring-form tube pans, so that you can remove the baked torte without breaking it. Butter or oil the pan lightly and sprinkle with flour. Spoon in the batter, spreading it evenly.

To bake. Preheat the oven to 325°. Bake until the torte shrinks from the pan (about 25 minutes for layers, 40 or more for a large cake).

To serve. Cool. Serve with whipped cream, sweetened and flavored, or put layers together with whipped cream and put whipped cream or an icing on the top. Serve in wedges.

Almond or Pecan Torte

Pecans make a moister, richer torte than almonds.

Separate
  4 eggs
Beat the whites until stiff. Beat in
  ¼ cup confectioners' sugar
Set aside. Without washing the beater, beat the yolks until thick and lemon-colored. Beat in
  ¾ cup confectioners' sugar
Add
  ½ cup chopped almonds or pecans
  ⅓ cup grated unsweetened chocolate
  ¾ cup fine cracker crumbs
  1 teaspoon baking powder
Fold in the beaten whites. Spoon into a 9-inch pan and bake (above). Cool. Split carefully into 2 layers. Put together with
  Whipped cream
Serves 6.

Carrot Torte

Large dry carrots are best for this pretty and surprisingly delicious dessert.

Separate
    4 eggs
Beat the whites until stiff. Beat in
    ¼ cup sugar
Set aside. Without washing the beater, beat the yolks until thick and lemon-colored. Beat in
    ¾ cup sugar
Add
    1 cup grated raw carrot
    Grated rind of 1 lemon
    Juice of ½ lemon
    ½ cup flour
    1 teaspoon baking powder
Fold in the beaten whites.

Bake (p. 485) in two 8- or 9-inch layer cake pans. Cool. Put together with
    Whipped cream
Serves 6.

Walnut Torte

Butter and flour two 9-inch layer cake tins. Set the oven at 350°.

Separate
    5 eggs
Beat the whites until stiff. Beat in gradually
    ¼ cup sugar
Set aside. Without washing the beater, beat the yolks until thick and lemon-colored. Beat in
    ¾ cup sugar
Stir in
    2 cups ground walnut meats
    1 cup bread crumbs
    1 teaspoon baking powder
    1 teaspoon vanilla
Fold in the beaten whites. Spread in the tins.

Bake 25 minutes. Cool. Put between the layers
    Nut Filling (below) or whipped cream
Cover with
    Whipped cream
Serves 6 to 8.

Nut Filling. Put in a saucepan 1 cup milk, 1 tablespoon sugar, 1 teaspoon butter, ½ cup chopped nuts, ½ cup bread crumbs. Cook until thick. Cool. Add 1 teaspoon vanilla.

Hazelnut Torte

As an added touch, sprinkle chopped hazelnuts over the frosting or whipped cream when the torte is ready to serve.

Separate
    4 eggs
Beat the whites until stiff. Beat in
    ¼ cup sugar
Without washing the beater, beat the yolks until thick and lemon-colored. Beat in
    ¾ cup sugar
Stir in
    ⅔ cup ground roasted hazelnuts
    2 tablespoons rum
    1¾ cups mashed potatoes, packed
        lightly
    1 tablespoon vanilla
Fold in the beaten whites.

Bake (p. 485) in an 8-inch spring-form pan. This moist mixture may take as long as 1½ hours. *Serves 8.*

Date and Nut Torte

Cut leftover torte in finger-shaped pieces and serve as date and nut bars.

Mix
    1 cup chopped dates
    1 teaspoon baking soda
    1 cup boiling water
Let stand 1 hour.

Set the oven at 325°. Cream
    1 tablespoon butter
Add
    1 cup sugar
    ½ teaspoon salt
    2 eggs, well beaten
    1 cup sifted flour
    1 cup nut meats, broken in pieces
Add the dates. Spread in a buttered pan, about 10 by 14 inches.

Bake 40 minutes. Cool. Cut in squares. Serve with

Whipped cream

Serves 8.

Icebox Cake

Prepare any of the fillings below.

Line a mold or a large bowl with

Strips of Sponge (p. 472), Angel Food (p. 475) or Pound (p. 464) Cake or lady fingers (about 30)

Spoon in the filling. Or put the cake and the filling in the bowl in layers. Chill 12 hours or longer.

Turn out onto a serving dish and cover with

Whipped cream

Serves 6.

Butter Filling. Cream ½ cup unsalted or washed (p. 8) butter. Beat in 1 cup confectioners' sugar until fluffy. Beat in 4 egg yolks, one at a time. Flavor with vanilla or rum and fold in 4 egg whites beaten stiff.

Chocolate Filling. Add to Butter Filling 1 ounce unsweetened chocolate, melted with 1 tablespoon water or coffee and cooled to lukewarm.

Lemon Filling. Add the juice and grated rind of 1 lemon to Butter Filling before folding in the egg whites.

Macaroon Filling. Add ½ cup macaroon crumbs (dried, rolled and sifted) to Butter Filling.

Coffee Icebox Cake. Soak the cake or lady fingers in coffee and cream (2 tablespoons cream to 1 cup coffee). Flavor Butter Filling to taste with instant coffee. For a richer filling, add 1 cup chopped toasted almonds.

Chocolate Icebox Cake

Very rich and delicious. Prepare French Chocolate Mousse (p. 365) this way, too.

Put in a cup

½ cup cold water

1 envelope gelatine (1 tablespoon)

Melt over hot water

2 ounces unsweetened chocolate

¾ cup hot water or coffee

Stir in the soaked gelatine. Separate

3 eggs

Beat the whites until stiff. Beat in, a tablespoon at a time

⅓ cup sugar

Without washing the beater, beat the yolks until thick. Beat in the chocolate mixture. Fold gently into the beaten egg whites. Add

1 small Sponge (p. 472), Angel Food (p. 475) or Pound (p. 464) Cake, cut in ½-inch cubes

Mix gently until well blended. Spoon into a mold.

Chill, turn out on a serving dish and cover with

Whipped cream

Serves 6.

Brazil Nut Cake

Butter a shallow pan about 10 by 14 inches. Set the oven at 350°.

Separate

6 eggs

Beat the whites until they stand in soft peaks. Beat in, gradually

½ cup sugar

Set aside. Without washing the beater, beat the yolks until thick and lemon-colored with

½ cup sugar

¼ teaspoon salt

Fold in the beaten whites and

2 cups ground Brazil nuts

Spread in the pan.

Bake about 30 minutes (see Sponge Cake, p. 472). Cool.

Cut in squares and serve topped with

Whipped cream

Serves 8 or more.

Fudge Pie

Make Brownie mixture (p. 444) but omit the nuts. Spread in a well-buttered and floured 7 or 8 inch pie tin.

Bake 30 minutes at 350°. Cool. Serve in wedges with whipped cream or ice cream.

Nut Roll

Butter a jelly roll pan about 10 by 14 inches. Line with wax paper and butter the paper. Set the oven at 350°.

Separate
　6 eggs
Beat the whites until they stand in soft peaks. Beat in
　¼ cup sugar
Set aside. Without washing the beater, beat the yolks until thick and lemon-colored. Beat in
　½ cup sugar
Mix
　1½ cups chopped pecans or walnuts
　1 teaspoon baking powder
　Few grains salt
Stir into the egg yolk mixture. Fold in the beaten whites. Spread evenly in the pan.

Bake 20 minutes. Cover with a damp towel and chill. Turn out onto a towel and peel off the paper.

Whip
　1½ cups heavy cream
Sweeten to taste. Add
　Vanilla or rum to taste
Spread evenly over the cake. Roll like a jelly roll. Wrap firmly in wax paper and chill. Cut in slices. *Serves 8 or more.*

Frostings and Fillings

Sponge cakes and pound cakes are usually served plain or with only a light sprinkling of confectioners' sugar. Homemade frosting gives a simple "store" cake an appetizing look. For a small family, frost part of a cake and serve the rest as a Cottage Pudding, Boston Cream Pie or Washington Pie.

Types of Frosting

Sweet topping (p. 491) baked or broiled on the cake is the simplest of all.

Confectioners' frostings are easy, too, and the amount can be adapted for smaller or larger cakes.

Cooked frostings made with egg white are a little fussier to make but worth the trouble if you have time.

Fudge-type frostings must be carefully made so that they will not be hard and sugary. A candy thermometer insures success.

Rich butter frostings stay creamy for several days.

Filling Layer Cakes

Cool the cake. Put the bottom layer upside down so that a level surface is uppermost. Spread with a filling (pp. 495–497) or use part of the frosting as filling.

Frosting Cakes

Spread uncooked frosting while the cake is still warm but not hot. Cool the cake before spreading with a cooked frosting. If the frosting is very soft, put it on just before serving the cake.

Have the frosting stiff enough to pile on the cake without sliding off. Try a little on the cake to be sure. If necessary, beat in a little more confectioners' sugar (for uncooked frosting), or put cooked frosting in a double boiler and beat over hot water until thick. If the frosting is too thick, beat in a few drops of hot water.

Spread the frosting over the cake with a spatula or the back of a large spoon. It is prettier if you do not smooth it on too evenly. If you are frosting the sides of the cake, do them first, then put the rest of the frosting on top and swirl it to the edge.

Simple Cake Decorating

Scatter any of the following over the frosting or arrange in a pattern. Pat gently into place.

Nut meats, whole or chopped.
Coconut, preferably fresh grated. Toasted or tinted (p. 13).
Chocolate shot, dragées or tiny colored candies.
Colored sugar.
Candied fruit.

Chocolate Glaze. Melt unsweetened chocolate with butter (1 tablespoon for each ounce). Cool slightly and dribble over white frosting after it has set. To make lines or a criss-cross effect, streak the chocolate with a fork.

Decorating with a Pastry Bag

Practice making designs on wax paper before attempting a fancy cake.

Prepare Royal (p. 492) or Ornamental Frosting (p. 495) or any Butter Frosting (pp. 493–494). Other frostings become hard and dry after standing.

Cake decorating sets include a pastry bag or a metal cylinder with a set of tubes to shape the frosting in various ways.

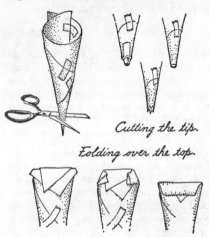

Cutting the tip.

Folding over the top.

To make a paper pastry bag. *If you are using more than one color, make a bag for each.* Fold a sheet of heavy typewriter paper or baker's paper into a tight cornucopia with a sharp point. Fasten firmly with Scotch tape. Pinch the point flat and cut it (1) straight across to make a ribbon design; (2) in two points for leaves; (3) in three points for stars. Or drop fancy metal tubes into the bags.

To fill a pastry bag. Fill not more than one-third full at a time. Bring the top edges together, fold in at the corners, then fold down to the level of the frosting.

To decorate the cake. Put a thin layer of frosting on the cake, let it dry, then cover with a thicker layer. Mark lines on the frosting with a toothpick as a guide to putting on the pattern. Hold the filled pastry bag or cylinder close to the top of the cake. Guide the point with one hand and push the frosting out with the other by folding down the top of the bag or pushing down the cylinder plunger.

Birthday Cakes

Candles are the traditional decoration — and the simplest. There are many pretty holders, or you can concoct your own — of colored paper or frosting. A special cake board — with a row of candle holders around the edge — is attractive. For more elaborate decoration, use a cake decorating set or trim the cake with candy ornaments or with initials or greetings made of candy letters.

For children, frost a simple cake such as Cream Sponge (p. 472). If you have some of the little wooden bird candle holders, you can put a flock of them on the cake with a scattering of tiny candies for them to feed on.

For a merry-go-round cake, dip animal crackers in melted dipping chocolate and press them into the sides of the cake or stand them around the top. Put a gay paper awning above, held aloft by peppermint candy sticks or colored straws.

Broiled Frostings

A simple way to put a delicious topping on a cake without making a frosting separately.

Spread over a warm, freshly baked cake, such as One-Egg Cake (p. 462) or Lightning Cake (p. 470). Set under the broiler for a few minutes until the frosting is delicately brown. Watch carefully and turn so that the topping browns evenly.

Coconut Jelly Frosting. Spread the cake with any tart jelly. Cranberry jelly is especially good. Sprinkle with shredded coconut.

Broiled Coconut Frosting. Mix 1 cup brown sugar, 3 tablespoons cream, 2 tablespoons melted butter and ½ cup shredded coconut.

Lazy Daisy Frosting. Mix 3 tablespoons melted butter, 3 tablespoons brown sugar, 2 tablespoons cream and ½ cup chopped nut meats or shredded coconut.

Butterscotch Nut Frosting

Spread this simple mixture over un-baked plain or spice cake in a shallow pan.

Beat until stiff
    1 egg white
Beat in gradually
    ¾ cup brown sugar
    ⅛ teaspoon salt
Spread on the cake batter. Sprinkle with
    ¼ cup broken nut meats
Bake on the cake.

Coconut Meringue Frosting. Use ½ cup coconut in place of nuts. Use white sugar. Add 1 tablespoon grated orange rind.

Caramel Glaze

For any simple cake.

Cook 1 cup sugar with ½ cup water and ½ teaspoon cream of tartar to 252° (firm ball stage, p. 000). Pour evenly over the baked cake. Crease with an oiled sharp knife to mark the pieces for cutting.

Confectioners' Frosting I

This simple frosting can be delicious if you beat it thoroughly so that it is creamy. A small electric beater helps, but you can use a wooden spoon.

Put ¼ cup boiling water in a small bowl. Stir in confectioners' sugar (sifted, if necessary) until thick enough to spread. Beat thoroughly. Flavor with vanilla or rum, or make one of the variations suggested below.

Lemon or Orange Confectioners' Frosting. Use cool lemon or orange juice in place of water.

Coffee Confectioners' Frosting. Add 1 teaspoon instant coffee and 1 teaspoon butter to the water.

Mocha Frosting. Make Coffee Confectioners' Frosting, adding 2 tablespoons cocoa to the sugar.

Confectioners' Frosting II

Especially successful for cake decorating because the shortening keeps the frosting from becoming dry. Since it is white to start with, it is simple to color it as you like. See also Icing for the Wedding Cake (p. 480).

Cream well
    ½ cup vegetable shortening
    Few grains salt
Beat in
    Confectioners' sugar (about 1½ cups)
Stir in
    2 tablespoons cream or milk
Add more sugar if needed to make the frosting thick enough to spread or put through a pastry bag. Color and flavor as desired.

Portsmouth Frosting

Butter and cream make this frosting especially smooth and delicious.

Melt in a small heavy pan
    ¼ cup butter
Remove from the heat. Add
    ¼ cup cream or milk
Beat in
    Confectioners' sugar
until thick enough to spread. Beat until smooth. Flavor with
    Vanilla or rum
or make one of the variations (p. 492).

Orange Portsmouth Frosting. Use orange juice as the liquid. Stir in an egg yolk for brighter color and smoothness.

Chocolate Portsmouth Frosting. Stir in Dutch cocoa to taste or 1 ounce unsweetened chocolate, melted over low heat.

Royal Frosting

Another basic frosting to vary in any of the ways suggested on page 491.

Put in a large bowl
1 cup confectioners' sugar
¼ teaspoon cream of tartar
⅓ cup boiling water
1 egg white
Beat with a rotary beater or an electric beater at high speed, until the frosting is thick enough to stand in peaks. This will take 8 minutes or more, but it does the frosting no harm to interrupt the beating from time to time.

Chocolate Frosting or Filling

Put in the top of a double boiler
2 ounces unsweetened chocolate
1 tablespoon butter
½ cup milk
Cook until the chocolate melts. Stir well. Let stand until lukewarm. Stir in
2 cups confectioners' sugar
½ teaspoon vanilla
Beat until thick enough to spread.

Creamy Chocolate Frosting

Grate into a saucepan
2 ounces unsweetened chocolate
Add
1 cup sugar
3 tablespoons cornstarch
Mix well. Stir in
1 cup boiling water
Cook and stir until thick and smooth. Add
1 tablespoon butter
1 teaspoon vanilla
Few grains salt
Beat thoroughly.

Fudge Frosting

Mix in a saucepan
2 ounces unsweetened chocolate, cut small
1½ cups sugar
7 tablespoons milk
¼ cup butter
1 tablespoon corn syrup
¼ teaspoon salt
Bring to a rolling boil, stirring constantly. Boil 1 minute. Cool. Add
1 teaspoon vanilla
Beat until thick.

Quick Fudge Frosting I

Melt 1 package (7 or 8 ounces) semisweet chocolate with ½ cup butter. Beat until thick.

With sour cream. Melt the chocolate and stir it into ½ cup thick sour cream.

Quick Fudge Frosting II

Put in a double boiler
2 ounces unsweetened chocolate
1 can sweetened condensed milk
Stir until the chocolate is melted. Add
1 teaspoon vanilla
Few grains salt
Add drop by drop, until the frosting is thin enough to spread
Hot water (about 1 tablespoon)

Vanilla Fudge Frosting

Melt in a pan
1 teaspoon butter
Add
1½ cups sugar
½ cup milk
Few grains salt
Stir and heat to the boiling point. Boil without stirring to the soft ball stage (234°).

Cool and beat until thick enough to spread. Add
½ teaspoon vanilla
If the frosting begins to stiffen too much, heat it over hot water. Spread evenly on

the cake with the back of a spoon. Mark as soon as firm.

Chocolate Fudge Frosting. Add 1½ ounces unsweetened chocolate as soon as the boiling point is reached. Flavor with ⅛ teaspoon cinnamon.

Penuche Frosting

For a richer frosting, use heavy cream in place of milk and butter.

Mix in a saucepan
1 cup brown sugar
½ cup white sugar
Few grains salt
⅓ cup milk
2 tablespoons butter
1 tablespoon corn syrup
Bring slowly to the boiling point, stirring constantly. Boil 1 minute.

Cool to lukewarm. Add
½ teaspoon vanilla
Beat until thick enough to spread.

Sultana Nut Frosting

Cook to the soft ball stage (234°)
2 cups brown sugar
¾ cup heavy cream
Pour onto a marble slab or a large platter. Cool.

Work until creamy with a spatula or a large wooden spoon. Add
¼ cup seedless raisins
¼ cup walnut meats, cut small
Spread on the cake.

Maple Fudge Frosting

Mix in a saucepan
1⅓ cups sugar
⅔ cup grated maple sugar
½ cup butter
⅔ cup cream
Cook (about 13 minutes) to the soft ball stage (234°). Cool.

Beat until thick enough to spread.

Caramel Fudge Frosting. Use brown sugar in place of maple sugar.

Quick Caramel Frosting

Melt in a small pan
½ cup butter
Add
½ cup brown sugar
Cook and stir over low heat until the sugar melts. Add
¼ cup milk
Cool.

Beat in until thick enough to spread
Confectioners' sugar (about 1¾ cups)
1 teaspoon vanilla

Cream Cheese Frosting

Work until soft
4 tablespoons cream cheese
Add
1 egg white, slightly beaten
1½ cups confectioners' sugar
½ teaspoon vanilla
½ teaspoon salt
Beat thoroughly.

Sour Cream Raisin Frosting

So rich that you may prefer to use it only as filling, topping the cake with a simple frosting.

Mix in a double boiler top
1 cup sour cream
1 cup sugar
1 cup seeded raisins
Cook over hot water until thick.

Butter Frosting I

Beat until very creamy
¼ cup butter (unsalted, for the most delicious flavor)
Stir in
1 egg yolk
Beat in, 2 tablespoons at a time
1 cup confectioners' sugar
Beat hard until light and fluffy. Flavor with vanilla or other flavoring.

For a large cake, double the amount of butter and sugar, but use only 1 egg yolk.

Butter Frosting II

Cream together
1/4 cup butter
1/4 cup vegetable shortening
Beat until thick
1 egg yolk
Boil to 240°
1/2 cup sugar
1/4 cup water
Pour slowly over the egg yolk, beating well. Beat in the shortening, bit by bit. Beat well. Flavor to taste.

Chocolate Butter Frosting. Melt 1/2 package (4 ounces) semisweet chocolate over hot water with 1 tablespoon coffee or water. Stir until smooth. Cool to lukewarm. Beat into the frosting.

Coffee Butter Frosting. Cream 1 teaspoon instant coffee with the shortening.

Mocha Rum Butter Frosting. Melt 1 ounce unsweetened chocolate with 1 tablespoon strong coffee or flavor to taste with vanilla. Stir in 1 1/2 tablespoons rum. Cool to lukewarm. Beat into the frosting.

Fluffy Butter Frosting

Cream
1/4 cup butter
Add gradually, beating constantly
1/2 cup confectioners' sugar, sifted
Beat until stiff
2 egg whites
Beat in gradually
1 cup confectioners' sugar, sifted
Combine the mixtures and add enough more sugar to make the frosting thick enough to hold its shape. Vary the flavoring as suggested under Butter Frosting (above).

Seven-Minute Frosting

Most cooks make "boiled" icing this easy way.

In the top of a double boiler mix
3/4 cup sugar
2 tablespoons water

1/8 teaspoon cream of tartar or 1 teaspoon light corn syrup
Few grains salt
1 egg white
Beat 1 minute with a rotary beater (hand or electric type). Set over boiling water and beat until stiff enough to stand up in peaks. With an electric beater, the frosting may be stiff enough in 4 minutes.

Remove from the heat and continue beating until thick enough to spread. Add
1/2 teaspoon vanilla
or make one of the variations listed below.

Caramel Frosting. Use 1/2 cup brown sugar and 1/4 cup white. Add broken walnut meats.

Coconut Frosting. Add 1/4 cup shredded coconut (preferably freshly grated) to the finished frosting. Spread over the cake and sprinkle coconut thickly over the top.

Coffee Frosting. Use 1/2 cup white sugar and 1/4 cup brown. Flavor with instant coffee to taste. Shredded coconut is good with this.

Lemon or Orange Frosting. Use cool lemon or orange juice in place of water. When ready to spread, add 1/2 teaspoon each of grated orange and lemon peel, or 1 teaspoon candied orange peel, cut small.

Marshmallow Frosting. Cut 8 marshmallows in small pieces and add to the finished frosting. Fold over and over until the frosting is stiff enough to hold its shape.

Nut or Fruit Frosting. To the finished frosting, add chopped walnuts, almonds, figs, dates or raisins, separately or in combination.

Peppermint Frosting. Add 1/4 teaspoon oil of peppermint and a few drops of green coloring.

White Mountain Cream

The classic "boiled frosting" at its fluffy best made with 2 egg whites.

Put in a saucepan
  1 cup sugar
  ⅓ cup water
  ⅛ teaspoon cream of tartar
  Few grains salt
Cook until the syrup spins a 6-inch thread (240°). To keep the syrup from crystallizing, cook it slowly and cover for the first 3 minutes.

Beat until stiff
  2 egg whites
Pour the syrup slowly over the egg whites, beating constantly. Beat until thick. Add
  ½ teaspoon vanilla
or make one of the variations suggested under Seven-Minute Frosting (p. 494).

Ornamental Frosting

To use in a pastry bag for elaborate cake decoration.

Put in a saucepan
  2 cups sugar
  ⅛ teaspoon cream of tartar
  1 cup hot water
Boil to 240°. Pour gradually over
  3 egg whites, beaten stiff
Continue beating until firm enough to shape.

Cream Filling
(Crème Patissière)

For layer cakes and cream puffs. Egg yolks make a rich, golden filling, but a whole egg thickens it just as well.

Scald in a double boiler
  1 cup milk
Mix in a bowl
  ½ cup sugar
  3 tablespoons flour or 1 tablespoon cornstarch
  Few grains salt
Stir in the milk. Pour back into the double boiler and cook 15 minutes, stirring until the filling thickens. Add
  2 egg yolks or 1 egg, slightly beaten
Cook and stir 5 minutes longer. Cool.

Flavor with
  Vanilla or other flavoring
Enough for a 2-layer cake or 6 to 8 puffs.

For a richer filling, stir into the hot filling 1 tablespoon butter.

Banana Cream Filling. Add 1 cup mashed banana pulp (forced through strainer) and 2 tablespoons lemon juice.

Caramel Cream Filling. Use ½ cup flour. Add ⅓ cup Caramel Syrup (p. 14).

Chocolate Cream Filling. Increase sugar to 1 cup. Scald milk with 2 ounces unsweetened chocolate. Flavor with vanilla.

Coffee Cream Filling. Flavor to taste with instant coffee.

Macaroon Cream Filling (Frangipan). Add 2 tablespoons butter and 4 tablespoons dried and rolled macaroons. Flavor with lemon extract, rum, sherry or brandy.

Mocha Cream Filling. Flavor Chocolate Cream Filling with instant coffee.

Praline Cream Filling. Add ⅔ cup Praline Powder (p. 14).

Rich Cream Filling. Use only ¾ cup milk. Flavor in any of the ways suggested above. Cool and fold in ¼ cup heavy cream, beaten stiff.

Butter Cream Filling

Mix in a double boiler top
  ⅓ cup sugar
  ⅓ cup flour
Add gradually, stirring constantly
  2 cups milk
Cook until thick over boiling water, stirring constantly (about 15 minutes). Stir in, bit by bit
  1 cup butter
Flavor with
  1 teaspoon vanilla or other flavoring

Honey or Maple Frosting or Filling

Beat until stiff
    1 egg white
Cook to 238°
    ½ cup honey or maple syrup
Pour the honey or syrup slowly over the egg white, beating constantly. Continue beating until thick enough to hold its shape.

Lady Baltimore Filling

Make Seven-Minute Frosting (p. 494). Add to one half the frosting
    ⅓ cup chopped pecan meats
    3 figs, cut in thin strips
    ½ cup seeded raisins, chopped
    ½ teaspoon almond extract
Use as the filling for 1 large white cake. Use the rest of the frosting for the top and sides of the cake.

Lord Baltimore Filling

Make Seven-Minute Frosting (p. 494). Add to one half the frosting
    ½ cup rolled dry macaroons
    ¼ cup chopped pecan meats
    ¼ teaspoon orange extract
    ¼ cup chopped blanched almonds
    12 candied cherries, cut in quarters
    2 teaspoons lemon juice
    3 teaspoons sherry
Use as the filling for 1 large yellow cake. Use the rest of the frosting for the sides and top of the cake.

Prune Almond Filling

Make Seven-Minute Frosting (p. 494). and stir into it ½ cup pitted cooked prunes, cut small, and ⅓ cup chopped blanched almonds.

Lemon Filling

Mix in a small saucepan
    1 cup sugar
    2½ tablespoons flour

Add
    ¼ cup lemon juice
    Grated rind 2 lemons
    1 egg, slightly beaten
    1 teaspoon butter
Cook over low heat to the boiling point, stirring constantly. Cool.

Lemon Coconut Cream

Mix in a double boiler top
    Juice and grated rind of 1 lemon
    1 cup fine sugar
    2 egg yolks, slightly beaten
Cook over boiling water 10 minutes, stirring constantly. Add
    1 cup shredded coconut

Orange Filling

Mix in a double boiler top
    ¾ cup sugar
    ¼ cup flour
    Grated rind of 1 orange
    ⅓ cup orange juice
    1 tablespoon lemon juice
    2 egg yolks or 1 egg, slightly beaten
    Few grains salt
Cook over boiling water 15 minutes, stirring constantly. Cool.

Butterscotch Filling

Mix in a small saucepan
    ½ cup brown sugar
    2 tablespoons butter
Cook 2 minutes or until the syrup is brown. Add
    ½ cup milk
Cook and stir over low heat until well blended.

Mix
    3 tablespoons flour or 1 tablespoon cornstarch
    ½ teaspoon salt
    ½ cup milk
Add to the first mixture. Cook 15 minutes over hot water. Add
    2 eggs, slightly beaten
Cook and stir 2 minutes. Cool. Add
    ¼ teaspoon vanilla

Chocolate Whipped Cream Filling

Melt together
    4 ounces unsweetened chocolate
    2 tablespoons butter
Cool slightly. Add
    ½ pint heavy cream
    2 cups confectioners' sugar
    Few grains salt
Beat until thick and smooth (20 minutes with a hand egg beater, 8 to 10 minutes with an electric beater).

Cocoa Whipped Cream Filling

Mix
    ½ pint heavy cream
    ½ cup confectioners' sugar
    ¼ cup dry cocoa
    Few grains salt
Let stand overnight (or for several hours) in the refrigerator.

Beat until thick. Flavor with
    Vanilla

French Cream Filling

Beat until stiff
    ½ pint heavy cream
Beat in slowly
    ¼ cup confectioners' sugar
Fold in
    1 egg white, beaten stiff

    Few grains salt
    ½ teaspoon vanilla

French Coffee Filling. Add instant coffee to taste.

French Strawberry Filling. Increase the sugar to ⅓ cup. Fold in ½ cup mashed strawberries.

Fruit Cream Filling

If you are not serving the cake immediately, add ½ teaspoon gelatine soaked in 1 tablespoon cold water and dissolved in 1 tablespoon boiling water. This will keep the filling somewhat firm.

Prepare
    ⅓ cup figs, cut small
    ⅓ cup prunes, cut small
    ¼ cup chopped walnut meats
Beat until stiff
    ½ pint heavy cream
Beat in slowly
    ⅓ cup confectioners' sugar
    Few grains salt
    2 teaspoons lemon juice
Fold in the fruit and nuts.

Syracuse Filling. In place of fruit and nuts, add 6 marshmallows, cut small, 4 macaroons, dried and rolled, 9 candied cherries, cut small, and ½ teaspoon vanilla.

Candies and Nuts

Perfect candies and home-salted nuts are toothsome additions to the cook's repertory. Calorie-wise moderns serve rich sweets with coffee as dessert rather than as extra tidbits. Making a batch of candy may be a party in itself, whether it be fudge, molasses taffy or one of the uncooked fruit sweets. Attractively packed nuts and candies are ideal gifts.

Candy Making

Candies cook best in dry cool weather. In warm sticky weather they may be sugary.

The pan should be large enough so that the candy will not boil over. To help prevent crystallizing, stir with a wooden spoon, not a metal one. Cook to the stage recommended in the recipe, testing with a candy thermometer or in cold water.

Testing with a thermometer. Never put a thermometer directly into the boiling syrup. Heat it first in water brought slowly to the boiling point. This will also test the accuracy of the thermometer, which should register 212° (at or near sea level) when the water boils. Then put the thermometer in the candy kettle and cook the candy to the required temperature (slightly lower at very high altitudes). After use, place the thermometer immediately in very hot water and let it cool gradually.

Testing in cold water. Dip about ½ teaspoon of the boiling syrup into a cup of cold water and shape it with your fingers. Use fresh water for each testing. When the candy is nearly ready, take the pan from the heat while you are testing so that cooking will stop. The stages are:

Soft ball (234° to 238°). The ball of candy flattens out somewhat.
Medium soft ball (238° to 240°). The ball of candy just barely holds its shape.
Firm ball (244° to 250°). The ball of candy is firm but not hard.
Hard ball (265°). The ball of candy is very firm and hard.
Hard crack (270° to 310°). The ball of candy is brittle when you tap it against the side of the cup. The syrup separates into threads when poured into the cup.

Chocolate Fudge

Perfect fudge is smooth and creamy. Corn syrup insures this, but you can make good fudge without it. Use a wooden spoon for stirring and beating.

Put in a heavy saucepan
   2 cups sugar
   ¾ cup milk or thin cream
   2 tablespoons light corn syrup
   2 ounces unsweetened chocolate or
   4 tablespoons cocoa
Set over moderate heat. Stir gently until the chocolate melts, afterwards just enough to keep the fudge from burning. Cook to the soft ball stage (234°).

Remove from the heat. Add, without stirring it in

2 tablespoons butter
Let stand until almost cold.

Add
 1 teaspoon vanilla
Beat until the fudge is no longer glossy and is thick and creamy. Pour into a slightly buttered pan about 8 by 14 inches. Mark in squares. *Makes 1½ pounds (about 18 large pieces).*

Chocolate Sour Cream Fudge. Use sour cream in place of milk and butter.

Chocolate Nut Fudge. Before pouring into the pan, add ½ to 1 cup broken nut meats.

Chocolate Marshmallow Fudge. Before pouring into the pan, add 12 marshmallows cut in pieces with wet scissors.

Twenty-Minute Fudge

Mix
 1 egg, well beaten
 3 tablespoons cream
 1 teaspoon vanilla
 ¼ teaspoon salt
 1 pound confectioners' sugar
Melt together
 4 ounces unsweetened chocolate
 1 tablespoon butter
Add to the first mixture. Stir in
 1 cup chopped walnut meats or marshmallows, cut in pieces, or some of each
Spread in a buttered pan 8 by 8 inches. Cut in squares. *Makes 1½ pounds.*

Million-Dollar Fudge

Put in a bowl
 6 ounces semisweet chocolate
 12 ounces German sweet chocolate
 1 cup marshmallow cream
Put in a saucepan
 2 cups sugar
 1 tablespoon butter
 ¾ cup evaporated milk
Set over low heat and bring gradually to

the boiling point. Boil 6 minutes. Pour over the chocolate mixture and add
 ⅛ teaspoon salt
 ½ teaspoon vanilla
Beat until the chocolate melts. Stir in
 1 cup chopped nut meats
Spread in a lightly buttered pan about 8 by 12 inches.

Let stand a few hours before cutting in squares. Store in a tin box. *Makes about 3 pounds.*

Divinity Fudge

Put in a saucepan
 1½ cups light brown sugar
 ½ cup water
 1 teaspoon vinegar
Cook to the firm ball stage (244°). Meanwhile, beat until stiff but not dry
 1 egg white
Pour the syrup slowly over the egg white, beating until creamy. Add
 ½ cup chopped nuts or coconut
 ½ teaspoon vanilla
Drop by teaspoonfuls on wax paper or spread in a buttered pan about 8 by 8 inches and cut in squares. *Makes about 1 pound.*

Opera Fudge

Put in a saucepan
 2 cups sugar
 1 cup heavy cream
 Few grains salt
Cook and stir over moderate heat. When at the boiling point add
 ⅛ teaspoon salt
Continue as for Chocolate Fudge (p. 498). When creamy, cover with a damp cloth and let stand ½ hour. Sprinkle over the fudge
 ½ teaspoon vanilla
Work it into the fudge with your hands. Press the fudge into a shallow pan lined with wax paper. When firm, cut in squares. *Makes about 1 pound.*

For variety, color and flavor differently or add chopped nuts or candied fruit.

Chantilly Cream Squares

Put in a saucepan
   2 cups sugar
   ¾ cup heavy cream
   1 cup milk
   2 tablespoons light corn syrup
   ⅛ teaspoon salt
Cook and stir to 238° (soft ball stage). Add
   1 teaspoon vanilla
Beat until creamy. Add
   1 cup nut meats, broken in pieces
Pour into a buttered pan about 11 by 7 inches. Cut in squares. *Makes about 1½ pounds.*

Peanut Butter Fudge

Put in a saucepan
   2 cups sugar
   ⅛ teaspoon salt
   ¾ cup milk or cream
   2 tablespoons light corn syrup
Cook to the soft ball stage (234°). Cool to lukewarm and add
   4 tablespoons peanut butter
   1 teaspoon vanilla
Beat until creamy. Pour into a lightly buttered pan about 8 by 8 inches. Let stand until firm and cut in squares. *Makes 1 pound.*

Marshmallow Peanut Fudge

Put in a saucepan
   2 cups sugar
   ⅔ cup milk
Cook to the soft ball stage (234°). Add
   1 small jar marshmallow cream
     (about 1 cup)
   1 cup peanut butter
   1 teaspoon vanilla
Mix well and pour into a buttered pan about 9 by 9 inches. Cool and cut in squares. *Makes about 2 pounds.*

Pecan Penuche

Put in a saucepan
   3 cups light brown sugar
   1 cup sour cream
   ¼ cup dark corn syrup

Cook to the soft ball stage (234°). Add
   1 tablespoon butter
   1 teaspoon vanilla
Let stand without stirring until the candy cools to 112°. Add
   1 cup pecan halves
Stir until stiff enough to drop by teaspoonfuls on wax paper. Let stand a few hours before removing from the paper. Store in layers with wax paper between. *Makes about 2 pounds.*

New Orleans Pralines

Scandalously rich and delicious.

Put in a saucepan
   3 cups sugar
   1 cup light cream
   Few grains salt
Cook to 234° (soft ball). When nearly ready, melt in a small heavy pan
   1 cup dark brown sugar
Add to the syrup. Add
   3 cups pecan meats, broken in pieces
Cook 2 minutes. Stir well. Drop by spoonfuls on wax paper or a buttered cooky sheet. *Makes 18.*

Maple Pralines

Pecans, hickory nuts or black walnuts are wonderful in this recipe.

Put in a saucepan
   1⅛ cups confectioners' sugar
   1 cup maple sugar
   ½ cup cream
Boil to the soft ball stage (234°). Let stand until cool.

Beat with a wooden spoon until thick. Add
   2 cups nut meats, broken in pieces
Drop from the tip of a spoon on wax paper or spread in a buttered pan about 9 by 9 inches and cut in squares. *Makes about 1½ pounds.*

Toffee

Put in a heavy saucepan
   2 cups brown sugar

¼ cup butter
1 tablespoon vinegar
2 tablespoons boiling water
Few grains salt
Cook to 290° (hard crack). Pour into a buttered pan about 8 by 14 inches. Cool slightly and mark in squares. *Makes about 1 pound.*

Butterscotch Candy. Add ¼ cup molasses and increase the vinegar to 2 tablespoons. Instead of pouring into a pan to cool, you may prefer to drop by teaspoonfuls on a buttered cooky sheet.

Velvet Molasses Candy

Also called Molasses Taffy.

Put in a heavy pan
½ cup molasses
1½ cups sugar
½ cup water
1½ tablespoons vinegar
Cook, stirring constantly, to the boiling point. Add
¼ teaspoon cream of tartar
Boil to 256°, stirring constantly during the last part of the cooking. When nearly done, add
¼ cup melted butter
⅛ teaspoon baking soda
Pour into a buttered pan. As the candy cools around the sides, fold towards the center. When it is cool enough to handle, butter your hands and pull it, using your fingertips and thumbs, until it is porous and light-colored. Shape into a rope and cut in small pieces with scissors or a sharp knife. Put on wax paper to harden. *Makes about 1 pound.*

To flavor, add to the cooked candy a few drops of oil of peppermint or wintergreen, ½ teaspoon vanilla or lemon extract, or ¼ teaspoon powdered cloves or cinnamon.

Peanut Molasses Candy

Melt in a saucepan
3 tablespoons butter
Add

2 cups molasses
⅔ cup sugar
Boil to 256°. Stir in
2 cups salted peanuts (skinned)
Pour into a buttered pan 10 by 18 inches. Cool slightly and mark in squares. *Makes about 2 pounds.*

Butterscotch Nut Brittle

Butter a pan about 8 by 14 inches.

Sprinkle in the pan
1 cup chopped nut meats
Put in a heavy saucepan
1 cup sugar
¼ cup molasses
½ cup butter
1 tablespoon vinegar
2 tablespoons boiling water
Few grains salt
Cook to 290° (hard crack). Pour over the nuts. Cool slightly and mark in squares. *Makes about 1 pound.*

Peanut Brittle

Spread in a pan
1½ cups shelled and skinned raw peanuts
Sprinkle with
¼ teaspoon salt
Heat 5 minutes in a 350° oven.

Put in a saucepan
1 cup sugar
½ cup corn syrup
½ cup water
Cook, stirring until the syrup begins to boil. Wash down the sides of the pan with a wet pastry brush. Cook to 300° (hard crack stage). Add the nuts and
1½ tablespoons butter
½ teaspoon lemon extract
Pour into a shallow buttered pan. As soon as cool enough to handle, stretch with your fingers to make as thin as possible. Break in irregular pieces. *Makes about 1 pound.*

Nut Brittle. Prepare the same way, using almonds, Brazil nuts or walnuts or a combination of nuts.

Maine Peanut Brittle

Butter a 9 by 9 inch pan. Spread in it
   1 cup chopped roasted peanuts
Put in a small heavy pan
   2 cups sugar
Cook over low heat, stirring constantly,
until the sugar melts into a thin syrup.
Pour it over the nuts. Mark in squares
when nearly cold. *Makes about 1 pound.*

Nut Bars. Make the brittle with Brazil
nuts, walnuts or almonds instead of peanuts.

Charleston Benne Candy. *True benne
is wild sesame.* Put 1 cup sesame seed in
a heavy skillet and stir over moderate
heat until slightly brown. Make the brittle, using the sesame seeds in place of
peanuts.

Almond Butter Crunch

Chop fine
   ½ pound blanched almonds
Spread in a pan and toast lightly in a
350° oven. Put in a saucepan
   1 cup butter
   1 cup sugar
Cook over low heat until the sugar melts.
Add half the nuts. Cook to 310°, stirring
occasionally. Pour into a lightly buttered
pan about 8 by 8 inches. Cool.

Heat over hot water until nearly melted
   1 package semisweet chocolate or
      chocolate bits (about 7 or 8 ounces)
Stir until smooth. Spread half of it over
the cooled nut mixture. Sprinkle with
half the reserved nuts. Cool.

Turn the candy upside down on wax
paper and spread the other side with
melted chocolate and nuts the same way.
Cool.

Break in irregular pieces. *Makes 1¼
pounds.*

Caramels

Put in a heavy saucepan
   1 cup sugar
   ⅔ cup corn syrup

   ½ cup light cream
Stir until the sugar dissolves. Boil, stirring gently, to the soft ball stage (234°).
Add
   ½ cup light cream
Boil as before to 234°. Add another
   ½ cup light cream
Boil again to 234°. Add
   1 teaspoon vanilla
If sugary, add more cream and boil again.
Pour into a lightly buttered pan so that
the mixture is about ¾ inch deep. Let
stand 12 hours.

Cut in squares. Wrap each square in wax
paper. *Makes about 1 pound.*

To vary. Just before pouring into the
pan to cool, add broken nut meats,
shredded coconut or raisins.

Chocolate Caramels. Add 3 ounces
grated unsweetened chocolate with the
last ½ cup of cream.

Mr. B's Caramels

*The carefully developed recipe of a per-
fectionist.*

Set a deep saucepan on the kitchen
scales. Weigh into it
   10 ounces light corn syrup
   4 ounces strained honey
   1 pound sugar
Add
   ¼ teaspoon salt
   1 cup heavy cream
Cook to the firm ball stage (244°), stirring constantly. Remove from the heat.
Add
   1 cup heavy cream
Cook to 236°, stirring constantly. Add
   1 tablespoon butter
Cook to 240°, stirring constantly. Remove from the heat. Add
   1 teaspoon vanilla
Pour into a buttered pan 8 by 8 by 2
inches. Set in a cold place. When firm,
turn out on a board and cut in squares.
Wrap in wax paper. *Makes about 2½
pounds.*

Mr. B.'s Chocolate Caramels. Add 4 ounces unsweetened chocolate to the first mixture. Follow directions as above, but bring to 242° at the final cooking and increase the vanilla to 1½ teaspoons.

After-Dinner Mints

Mix in a saucepan
    2 cups sugar
    ⅔ cup boiling water
    ¼ teaspoon cream of tartar
    1 teaspoon mild vinegar
Boil without stirring to 256° (very firm ball). Pour onto an oiled marble slab or into a shallow pan. Cool, lift (avoiding a stirring motion), and pull, keeping the grain all one way.

During the pulling, sprinkle the candy with a few drops of flavoring, using
    Vanilla, orange extract, lemon extract, oil of peppermint, wintergreen, clove or cinnamon
Add food coloring at the same time, if you like.

When the candy is too stiff to pull, stretch it into a long rope ½ inch thick, and cut into small pieces with scissors. Drop the pieces into a bowl of confectioners' sugar and stir until well coated. When dry, store in a glass jar, cover, and let stand (not refrigerated) at least 4 days before serving.

Old-Fashioned Peppermints

Put in a pan
    1½ cups sugar
    ½ cup boiling water
Stir until the sugar dissolves. Boil to 256° (very firm ball). Add
    6 drops oil of peppermint
Beat until creamy. Drop from the tip of a teaspoon onto wax paper. Reheat the syrup from time to time if it becomes too thick to shape.

Wintergreen Wafers. Flavor with oil of wintergreen instead of peppermint. Tint delicately with food coloring.

Chocolate Cream Peppermints

Put in a bowl
    2 tablespoons light cream, heated
Stir in slowly
    1½ cups confectioners' sugar
    ½ tablespoon melted butter
    3 drops oil of peppermint
Work until creamy, using your hands. Shape in balls and flatten.

Dip (p. 505) in
    Melted coating chocolate

Champion Nougat

Mix in a bowl
    ¼ cup sweetened condensed milk
    1 teaspoon vanilla or brandy
    Few grains salt
    1 tablespoon brown sugar
Stir in
    ¾ cup powdered skim milk
    ¼ cup chopped nut meats
Knead until smooth. Roll between your palms into a rope 1 inch thick. Dust with sugar and cut in 1-inch pieces.

Coffee Nougat. Omit the brown sugar. Add 1 tablespoon instant coffee.

French Nougat

Put in a heavy pan
    1 cup confectioners' sugar
Stir over low heat until melted. Add
    1 cup finely chopped almonds
Pour onto an oiled marble slab or platter. Using a spatula, fold the nougat as it spreads, keeping it constantly in motion. As soon as cool enough to handle, divide in four parts and shape in long rolls about ⅓ inch thick. Keep the rolls moving until they are almost cold.

When they are cold, hold each roll over the sharp edge of a broad-bladed knife and snap in pieces about 1½ inches long. (You will need to have someone hold the knife for you.) If you like, dip the pieces in chocolate (p. 505). *Makes 20 pieces.*

Fondant

The standard base for many candies. To keep fondant creamy, do not stir it after the sugar dissolves, and let it cool before working it.

Put in a smooth, heavy saucepan
  2 cups sugar
  1¼ cups water
Stir over low heat until the sugar dissolves. Add
  ⅛ teaspoon cream of tartar or 2
  tablespoons light corn syrup
Cover and boil 3 minutes. Remove the cover, put in a candy thermometer, and boil to the soft ball stage (238°). During cooking, crystals will form on the sides of the pan. Wipe them off with a wet pastry brush.

Remove from the heat and let stand until all bubbles have disappeared.

Without scraping the pan, pour the fondant onto a marble slab or a large platter which has been wiped with a damp cloth. Cool until just barely warm. Scrape and turn the fondant towards the center with a spatula until it is white and creamy. It will begin to lump at this stage. Knead with your hands until the fondant is perfectly smooth. Add flavoring, if used (below), and knead again. Cover with a cloth wrung out of cold water and let stand ½ hour.

Cut in pieces. Store in a glass jar covered with a wet cloth or a glass cover. Let stand 3 or 4 days before using. *Makes 1 pound.*

Butter Fondant. Add 2 tablespoons butter and ½ teaspoon vanilla. Knead until creamy.

Maple Fondant. Use half maple sugar and half white sugar.

To flavor and color fondant. After the fondant has been kneaded, work in Dutch cocoa, instant coffee, rum, or a few drops of oil of peppermint or wintergreen, in very small portions at a time to be sure of not adding too much. Add vegetable coloring at the same time, using the point of a toothpick so that the color will be delicate. If the fondant is to be used for coating, the flavoring and coloring may be added while the fondant is being melted.

To dip in fondant. Melt fondant over hot water; flavor and color (above). Do not allow fondant to become hot. If too thick, add a few drops of cold water. Drop one center at a time into the melted fondant. Stir with a two-tined fork or a candy dipper until entirely covered, lift up, and put on wax paper. Make a coil over the top of the bonbon with the dipper or fork. Stir the fondant frequently.

Fondant Confections

Bonbons. Roll bits of fondant (any flavor) into 1-inch balls between your palms. Fondant alone is very sweet, so you may prefer to roll it around a nut meat or a piece of candied fruit. Set on wax paper to dry. Roll in chopped nuts, shredded coconut, instant coffee, cocoa or silver shot. Or shape and let stand to become firm (3 hours or longer), then dip in fondant (above) or in chocolate (see Chocolate Creams, below).

Cream Mints. Melt ¾ cup fondant over hot water, flavor with 1 drop oil of peppermint, wintergreen, clove or orange. Color if liked. If desired, add 2 tablespoons chopped nuts. Drop from the tip of a spoon on wax paper. Dry thoroughly.

Fondant-Dipped Nut Meats. Use walnuts, pecans or almonds. Melt fondant over low heat. Dip nut meats in it and put on a cake rack to dry.

Fondant-Stuffed Dates (p. 506).

Chocolate Creams

Dip bonbons (above) or fudge squares in chocolate.

To dip in chocolate. The room temperature should be about 65°. Melt coating chocolate (no other type) over hot, not boiling water. Beat gently until the chocolate feels a little cooler than your hand (80° to 85° on candy thermometer). Dip the centers, one at a time, as described for dipping in fondant (p. 504).

Almond Paste

Canned almond paste is available, but it is simple to make.

Grind three or four times in a meat chopper, using the finest cutter
  1 pound blanched almonds
The nuts should be very finely ground.

Put in a saucepan
  1 pound sugar
  1 cup water
Cook to 240°. Mix with the chopped almonds and add
  ½ cup orange juice
Stir until creamy. Spoon onto a marble slab or a platter dusted with
  Confectioners' sugar
Let stand until cool.

Pack in air-tight containers and store in a cool dry place at least a week before using. *Makes 2 pounds.*

Blender Almond Paste

Put in an electric blender
  ½ cup orange juice
  1 cup blanched almonds
  1 cup sugar
Whirl until the nuts are very fine. Add
  1 cup blanched almonds
Whirl again until very fine. Store, covered, in the refrigerator.

Marzipan

Rose water is the traditional flavoring. Buy it at a drugstore.

Mix thoroughly
  1 cup Almond Paste (above)
  1 cup confectioners' sugar
  Few drops rose water or orange extract

Put on a marble slab or a chilled platter. Knead 20 minutes.

Shape with your fingers into tiny fruits and vegetables. Paint with food coloring or dip in a small bowl of coloring. Tuck in cloves for stems and bits of angelica as leaves. Set on a cake rack to dry. For a Christmas glitter, crystallize (below).

To crystallize. Cook 5 pounds sugar with 2½ cups water to 223°. Do not stir after the sugar is dissolved. Remove from the heat very gently and let stand undisturbed until perfectly cold. Place shaped and painted marzipan in a pan in a single layer. Cover completely with the syrup, pouring it with as little agitation as possible. Let stand at least 8 hours. Drain in a sieve. Dry on a wire rack.

Marzipan Potatoes. Shape. Roll in a mixture of cocoa or instant coffee and confectioners' sugar. Do not crystallize.

Nut Balls

Put in a bowl
  ¼ cup corn syrup
  1 teaspoon vanilla
  ⅛ teaspoon salt
Mix and add
  ½ cup powdered skim milk
  ¼ cup chopped nut meats
Stir with a knife until well blended. Pat into a ball and put on a board sprinkled lightly with sugar. Knead until creamy. Let stand until firm enough to shape in 1-inch balls. Roll in
  Sugar
Makes about ½ pound.

Fruit Balls. Use candied fruit, cut small, in place of nuts.

Peppermint Balls. Flavor with ½ teaspoon peppermint instead of vanilla. Omit the nuts, using an extra ¼ cup powdered milk instead.

Peanut Butter Chewies

Mix in a bowl
    ½ cup crunchy peanut butter
    2 tablespoons honey
    1 teaspoon vanilla
Add
    Few grains salt
    ¾ cup powdered skim milk
Stir with a knife until well blended.
Add
    Confectioners' sugar to taste
Shape in 1-inch balls. Roll in
    Peanuts, chopped fine, or confec-
      tioners' sugar
Makes about ½ pound.

Coconut Cakes

Cook in a double boiler until the mixture clings to a spoon
    2 cups fresh grated coconut
    2 tablespoons corn syrup
    7 tablespoons sugar
Stir in
    1 egg white
Cook until the mixture feels sticky when
you try it between your fingers. Spread
in a wet pan, cover with dampened
paper and chill.

Shape in small balls, first dipping your
hands in cold water.

Heat a cooky sheet slightly, grease with
salad oil, and put the coconut cakes
on it. Bake 20 minutes at 300°. *Makes 20.*

Chocolate Coconut Cakes

Melt over hot water
    2 ounces unsweetened chocolate
Add
    1½ cups sweetened condensed milk
    1 teaspoon baking powder
Mix well. Stir in
    Coconut (about 4 cups, or 3 small
      packages)
until the mixture is firm enough to shape
by teaspoonfuls on a buttered cooky
sheet. Bake at 325° until firm to touch
(10 to 15 minutes). *Makes 36.*

Peach Leather

*A specialty from Charleston, South Caro-
lina.*

Put through a meat chopper twice, using
the finest cutter
    2 pounds dried apricots
    1 pound dried peaches
Sprinkle a board thickly with
    Fine sugar
Put the fruit mixture on it and pat and
roll it until it is ⅛ inch thick. Cut in
strips 1¼ by 2 inches. Roll each strip
into a tight roll.

Store in a tightly closed box. *Makes 3
pounds.*

Carolina Date and Nut Cakes

*Actually a confection, but especially
good served with coffee as a dessert or as
party refreshment.*

Put in a saucepan
    2 cups sugar
    1 cup milk
    1 tablespoon butter
Cook to the soft ball stage (238°). Add
    1 package (8 ounces) pitted dates, cut
      small
    Few grains salt
Stir 10 minutes over low heat. Add
    2 cups chopped nut meats
Cool. Shape in a roll 2 inches thick.
Wrap in foil and chill in the refrigerator.
Cut in ¼-inch slices. *Makes about 2
pounds.*

Stuffed Dates or Prunes

Pit large dates or prunes. If the prunes
are very dry, put them in a strainer and
set over boiling water until they soften.
Cool before stuffing. Stuff with any of the
fillings listed below. Roll in granulated
sugar or shake (4 to 6 at a time) in a
paper bag containing ¼ cup sugar. One
teaspoon cinnamon may be mixed with
the sugar.

    Walnut or pecan meats, broken in
      pieces

Salted almonds
Brazil nut meats
Candied ginger, cut fine
Candied pineapple, cut fine
Fondant (p. 504)
Peanut butter mixed with orange
juice
Marshmallows quartered and dipped
in finely chopped coconut

Fruit Bars

Put through a food chopper
1 cup dried figs
1 cup pitted dates
2 cups walnut meats
Mix well. Press firmly into a buttered
pan about 9 inches square. Cut into
squares or bars, or shape with your fingers in balls. Roll in
Fine sugar
Makes about 1¼ pounds.

To vary, use half walnut meats and half
pecans. Or add the grated rind of 1
orange and 1 tablespoon orange juice,
apricot or peach brandy or rum.

Raisin Roll

Put through a food chopper
1½ cups raisins
½ cup walnut meats
Mix well. Add
Salt to taste
Shape firmly into a roll about 3 inches
thick. Chill and slice.

Makes about ½ pound.

Salted Nuts

*At their best served while still warm.
Reheat if necessary.*

Blanch (p. 13) Brazil nuts and filberts.
Blanch almonds or not, as you prefer.
Shell peanuts and slip off the skins. Shell
pecans and walnuts, keeping the nut
meats unbroken if possible.

Spread in a shallow pan. Dot with 1
tablespoon butter for each cup of nuts
or sprinkle with olive oil. Brown in a
400° oven, stirring every 5 minutes so the
nuts will toast evenly. Do not overcook,
because nuts darken as they cool. Pecans
are ready as soon as the butter sizzles.

Spread on a paper towel to dry. Sprinkle
with salt.

Sautéed Nuts. Cook the nut meats, a few
at a time, in a small frying pan lightly
greased with butter or olive oil. Dry and
salt as above.

Roasted Chestnuts

Using a sharp paring knife, cut a ½-inch
crisscross gash on the flat side of each
nut. Put the nuts in a shallow pan and
add, for each cup of nuts, 1 teaspoon
butter or oil. Bake about 20 minutes in
a 450° oven. Stir the nuts occasionally
so that they will be well coated. *Serve
warm with drinks or as a snack.*

Sherried Walnuts

Mix in a bowl
¾ cup brown sugar
2 tablespoons sherry
1 tablespoon light corn syrup
Add
1½ cups walnut meats
Stir until the nuts are well coated. Roll
in sugar and put on wax paper to dry.

Brazil Nut Chips

Perfect with cocktails.

Cover shelled Brazil nuts with cold
water. Bring slowly to the boiling point.
Simmer 3 minutes, drain, and cool.

Cut in thin lengthwise strips and spread
in a shallow pan. Dot with butter (1
tablespoon for each cup of nuts). Sprinkle with salt.

Bake 15 minutes at 350°, stirring occasionally. Drain on a paper towel.

Spiced Nuts

Have ready
   1 cup nut meats (almonds, pecans,
     walnuts, Brazil nuts)
Mix in a small bowl
   ¼ cup sugar
   1 tablespoon cinnamon
   ⅛ teaspoon ground cloves
   ⅛ teaspoon nutmeg
In another bowl, beat slightly
   1 egg white
Rub the nut meats a few at a time in the
egg white with your fingers to coat them
thoroughly. Drop into the bowl of sugar
and spices and coat each nut completely.
Place on a buttered cooky sheet and bake
30 minutes at 300°.

Sugared Pecans or Almonds

Put in a heavy frying pan
   1 cup sugar
   ½ cup water
Cook 5 minutes. Add
   ½ pound pecan meats or blanched
     almonds
Cook and stir until the syrup begins to
look white and slightly sugared. Add
   1 teaspoon vanilla
   ½ teaspoon cinnamon
Set the pan aside for 10 minutes; then set
it on an asbestos pad over low heat. Stir
constantly until the sugar coating softens
enough to pour. Pour on a cake cooler
with a sheet of wax paper under it. Separate the nuts to dry.

Orange Pecans. Omit the cinnamon.
Cook 2 tablespoons grated orange rind
with the syrup.

Glacéed Nuts

Have ready
   1 pound blanched almonds or pecan or
     walnut meats
Put in a saucepan
   2 cups sugar
   1 cup boiling water
   ⅛ teaspoon cream of tartar
Cook to the boiling point, washing down
the sides of the pan from time to time

with a pastry brush dipped in cold water.
Boil without stirring until the syrup
begins to color (310° on a candy thermometer).

Place the pan in a larger pan of cold
water to stop the boiling instantly, then
remove from the pan of cold water and
set in a pan of hot water.

Take up the nuts, one at a time, on a
skewer and dip in the syrup to coat completely. Drain off the syrup and put the
nuts on wax paper to dry.

Glacéed Fruits

*A clear cool day is essential for success
in making these epicurean tidbits. Serve
them the day they are made. They are
delicious with after-dinner coffee or at
an engagement party or a wedding reception.*

Prepare white grapes, whole strawberries,
sections of mandarins, oranges or kumquats or candied cherries. Take the
grapes separately from the clusters, leaving a short stem on each grape.

Prepare syrup as for Glacéed Nuts
(above). Hold the fruit with pincers
(grapes and berries by the stem) and dip
one piece at a time in the syrup. Dry on
wax paper.

Crystallized Mint Leaves

Wash mint leaves, pat dry, remove from
the stems, and spread on paper towels
until thoroughly dry. Brush each leaf
with egg white beaten until stiff. Dip in
fine sugar flavored with oil of spearmint
or peppermint. Place close together on a
cake rack covered with wax paper. Let
stand in a 250° oven until dry. Repeat
if the leaves are not thoroughly coated.

Candied Orange or
Grapefruit Peel

Cook to the boiling point
   1 cup sugar
   ½ cup water

Add

1 cup prepared peel (below)

Cook slowly until the peel is almost transparent (230° on a candy thermometer). Take up the peel with a skimmer and spread on a plate to cool. Roll in granulated sugar. Spread on wax paper to dry. Store in a glass jar.

To make chewy peel, use only ¼ cup water and add 2 tablespoons corn syrup.

To prepare orange peel. Cut the peel in lengthwise sections. Cover with cold water, bring to the boiling point, and cook slowly until soft (about 15 minutes). Drain. Scrape out the white part with a spoon and cut the peel in thin strips with scissors.

To prepare grapefruit peel. Cut the peel in lengthwise sections. Soak overnight in 1 quart cold water with 1 tablespoon salt. Drain, cover with cold water, bring to the boiling point, and boil 20 minutes. Repeat three times and cook in the last water until tender (about 4 hours). Drain and cut in strips ⅛ inch wide.

Chocolate-Dipped Orange Peel. Dip candied orange peel (unsugared) in melted coating chocolate (p. 505). Dry on wax paper.

Popcorn

Packaged popcorn is especially selected for popping. Buy only what you need at the time, because corn that has been stored too long may be too dry to pop.

Pop only a small amount of corn at a time to allow for expansion (½ cup makes about 1 quart).

Melt a tablespoon of butter or cooking oil in a heavy pan which has a tight cover. Put in the corn, cover, and cook over moderate heat, shaking constantly until the popping stops. Uncover, and remove any hard kernels which did not pop.

Buttered Popcorn. For 1 quart of popped corn, melt 3 tablespoons butter in a large saucepan, add the corn, and stir until the corn is thoroughly coated. Sprinkle with salt.

Sugared Popcorn. For 1 quart of popped corn, melt 2 tablespoons butter in a pan. Add 1½ cups brown sugar and ⅓ cup water. Boil to 238° (soft ball stage). Pour over the corn. Stir until every kernel is well coated.

Popcorn Balls

Put in a large pan

3 quarts popped corn

Put in a saucepan

2 cups sugar

1½ cups water

½ cup white corn syrup

Cook to 260° without stirring. Add

⅛ teaspoon salt

⅓ teaspoon mild vinegar

1 tablespoon vanilla

Boil to 264°.

Pour the syrup slowly over the popcorn and stir with a wooden spoon to coat each kernel. Butter your hands slightly and shape the corn lightly into 3-inch balls. Set on wax paper to harden. Wrap in wax paper.

Molasses Popcorn Balls

Prepare

3 quarts popped corn (above)

Cook to 270° (hard crack stage)

1 cup molasses

1 cup corn syrup

1 teaspoon mild vinegar

Stir in

3 tablespoons butter

½ teaspoon salt

Make into balls (Popcorn Balls, above).

Jellies, Jams and Preserves

Jellies, jams and preserves add a piquant touch to any meal and can make a delicious dessert of a simple cake. They are ideal gifts, attractively wrapped or packed in a basket.

State and government departments of agriculture issue helpful booklets on making jellies and jams, with special attention to ways to use regional fruits.

Fruit Jelly
(general recipe)

Perfect jelly has an appetizing flavor. It is beautifully colored, translucent, and tender enough to cut easily with a spoon, yet firm enough to hold its shape when turned from the glass. The general process is the same for all jellies, so that a separate recipe is not needed for each fruit. Special recipes begin on page 511.

Equipment. Have ready a kettle large enough to hold four times the volume of the juice and sugar, a long-handled spoon, a ladle, and cheesecloth or a jelly bag and stand. A jelly or candy thermometer simplifies jelly-making. Also useful if you are making jelly of fruits which may be low in pectin is a jellmeter for testing the pectin content.

Fruit for jelly should be slightly underripe. Fruits rich in pectin are tart apples, green barberries, tart blackberries, boysenberries, loganberries, crabapples, currants, green gooseberries, Concord grapes, sour guavas, fresh prunes, plums and quinces. Other fruits and dead-ripe fruits need to have commercial pectin added (p. 511) or be combined with pectin-rich fruits.

Prepare the fruit in small amounts to keep its fresh flavor. Two pounds of prepared fruit yield about 2 pints of juice, which, with the sugar, will make about four 6-ounce glasses of jelly. Wash thoroughly, but do not pare any fruit except pineapple, because fruit skin is rich in pectin. Cut large fruit in pieces, small fruit like crabapples in half. Remove the cores from quinces but not from other fruits.

Extract the juice. Put the prepared fruit in a flat-bottomed saucepan. Crush soft fruits, grapes and berries and add only enough water to keep the fruit from burning. Add just enough water to other fruit to be seen through the top layer. Cover and cook slowly until the juice flows freely (3 minutes for berries, 15 minutes or more for hard fruits).

Put through a coarse sieve or a colander. Place a damp jelly bag or several layers of damp cheesecloth over a large enough bowl to hold the strained juice. Pour the juice into the cloth. Unless you have a stand to hold the bag, tie it to a towel rack so that the juice will drip freely into the bowl. For crystal-clear jelly, do not squeeze or press the bag. For a greater yield, squeeze or press the juice through the bag, then strain again without pressing.

To extract the juice in a pressure saucepan, crush the fruit and add ¼ cup water for each 2 pounds. Put on the cover and bring the pressure to 15 pounds. Remove from the heat and let the pressure drop to normal. Strain through a fine sieve. This is the easiest method of all for juicy berries and grapes.

Add the sugar (warmed for a few minutes in a slow oven). Measure no more than 4 cups of juice into a saucepan and boil 5 minutes (20 minutes for quince juice). Add ¾ cup sugar for each cup of juice (the usual proportion; some of the special recipes call for a different amount). To test fruit juice for the precise amount of sugar needed, use a jellmeter or pour 3 tablespoons denatured alcohol into a glass, add 1 tablespoon fruit juice, shake gently and let stand 1 minute. If solid jelly is formed which can be lifted in one piece with a spoon, use 1 cup sugar to each cup of juice in making jelly. If large flakes are formed, use ¾ cup sugar to each cup of juice. If small flakes are formed, boil the juice longer to concentrate the pectin. *Discard the tested jelly.*

Cook to the jelly stage. Boil the fruit juice and sugar rapidly until it jells (220° on the jelly thermometer). Skim the froth from the top of the jelly. (If you are not using a thermometer, begin testing after 5 minutes; take up a spoonful of juice, cool it a moment, then pour it back into the kettle from the side of the spoon; when the jelly is ready, drops of jelly will come together and "sheet" off the spoon.)

Not jellying

Jellying only when two drops form at once

Pour into glasses. Before starting to make jelly or jam, wash the glasses and put them in a kettle of cold water. Heat the water gradually to the boiling point.

Turn off the heat. When the jam or jelly is ready, remove the glasses, drain, and place on a tray covered with a cloth wrung out of hot water. Fill the glasses to within ¼ inch of the rims. Otherwise it may be difficult to remove the paraffin without crushing it into the jelly.

Seal by covering with a thin layer of paraffin (melted in a small saucepan over hot water). Tilt the glass so that the paraffin will touch the edge all around. The jelly should be completely covered, but the layer of paraffin no thicker than ⅛ inch. A thick layer will pull away from the edge. Do not reuse paraffin.

Label the glasses with the variety of jelly or jam and the date it was made.

Store in a cool dark place.

Fruit Jelly
(with added pectin)

Some fruits do not have enough acid or pectin if used alone (see p. 510), but can be made into excellent jelly by combining with other fruits or by adding commercial pectin. Follow the manufacturer's instructions exactly.

Many like to add pectin even when making jelly of fruits naturally rich enough in pectin to jell, because it increases the yield from the fruit and insures jellying. The flavor of jellies made with added pectin is fresh and appetizing but too sweet for some tastes.

Apple Jelly

Wash tart red apples. Three pounds (with added water) yield about 4 cups of juice. Cut out any blemishes and the stem and blossom ends, but do not pare or remove the core. Cut in eighths. Follow the general directions for making jelly (p. 510), adding 4 cups of water for each 3 pounds of apples. Tart apple juice is high in pectin and so can be combined successfully with other juices to make firm jelly.

Blueberry or Raspberry Apple Jelly. Use equal amounts of berry juice and apple juice. Add a tablespoon of lemon juice for each 2 cups of fruit juice.

Crabapple Jelly. Core, stem, and cut in half.

Mint Jelly. Make in small quantities, as the color is apt to fade. Use light-colored apples or crabapples, or pare bright-colored apples before extracting the juice. After cooking the juice and sugar about 5 minutes, add chopped mint leaves and stems (1 cup to 4 cups of juice) or flavor to taste with spearmint extract when the jelly is ready to pour into glasses. Color delicately green with vegetable coloring while the jelly is boiling. Strain.

Rose Geranium Jelly. Place a rose geranium leaf in each glass and fill with apple jelly. When the jelly is almost firm, lift the leaf so that it is suspended in the jelly; then cover with paraffin.

Spiced Apple Jelly. For 3 pounds of apples, prepare a spice bag with 1 teaspoon whole cinnamon, 1 teaspoon whole allspice, and ½ teaspoon whole cloves. Put in the pan with the apples, add ½ cup mild vinegar and 2½ cups water, and extract the juice.

Currant Jelly

Remove leaves but not stems. Extract juice, cooking (p. 510) the fruit very slowly till it is colorless. The juice may jell (p. 511) in 3 minutes.

Currant Raspberry Jelly. Use equal parts raspberry and currant juice.

Gooseberry Jelly. Remove the stem and blossom ends.

Grape Jelly

Wild grapes make a tart jelly that is superb with meats or chicken. Be sure there are plenty of green, unripened grapes among them.

Wash and drain the grapes. Remove about half of the stems. Extract the juice in a pressure cooker, or crush in a flat-bottomed pan and cook slowly about 10 minutes or until the juice flows freely. Add a little water if necessary to keep the grapes from sticking to the pan. Store the strained juice in the refrigerator overnight so that the crystals which sometimes form will settle.

Carefully pour off the juice, discarding the sediment, if any. Continue, following the general directions for making jelly (p. 510).

Spiced Grape Jelly

At its best made with wild grapes. Venison Jelly is its old-fashioned name.

Wash, drain, and remove the stems from
    4 quarts grapes
Crush in a flat-bottomed pan. Add
    1 pint mild cider vinegar
    ¼ cup whole cloves
    ¼ cup stick cinnamon (in pieces)
Cook slowly 15 minutes. Strain or drip through a jelly bag. Boil the juice 20 minutes. Add
    3 pounds sugar
Cook to the jelly stage (p. 511). *Makes about 12 glasses.*

Guava Jelly

Slice. Follow the general directions for making jelly (p. 510), but cook the fruit but cook the fruit 45 minutes or more to extract the juice, or extract it in a pressure cooker. For each 4 cups of guava juice, add the juice of 1 lime.

Quince Jelly

Wash firm ripe quinces and rub off the fuzz. Remove the stems, cores and seeds. Slice. Follow the general directions for making jelly (p. 510), but cook the fruit 45 minutes or more to extract the juice, or extract the juice in a pressure cooker. Equal parts of quince juice and apple juice make excellent jelly.

Paradise Jelly

Cut in pieces, discarding the stem and
blossom ends
  12 tart apples
Wash, discarding bruised ones
  1 pound cranberries
Quarter, core, and chop fine
  6 quinces
Combine the fruits, extract their juice,
and follow the general directions for
making jelly (p. 510), using
  1 cup sugar for each cup juice
Makes about 12 glasses.

Fruit Jam
(general recipe)

*For the finest flavor and color, make jam
in small quantities, preferably only 1
quart of prepared fruit at a time. One
quart makes 2 to 3 pints of jam.*

Prepare the fruit. Wash thoroughly.
Pare pineapples. Peel peaches and apricots. Remove pits, cores and stems. Crush
berries (also see special recipes below)
and other small fruit in the pan. Cut
other fruits in small pieces.

Measure the fruit into a flat-bottomed
pan. Cook until the fruit is tender and
the juice begins to flow, adding just
enough water to keep the fruit from
burning.

Add the sugar (heated in the oven so that
the hot fruit will not be cooled by it),
using 3 cups for each 4 cups of fruit. Stir
over the heat until the sugar dissolves.

Boil rapidly (to preserve color and
flavor) until the syrup is thick and clear
(8 to 20 minutes). Stir as needed to prevent sticking.

If there is a large amount of syrup in
proportion to the fruit, let the jam stand
until it is cool, and stir well to distribute
the bits of fruit evenly before you fill
the jars.

Fill the glasses or jars (p. 511). Jam is
usually stored in screw-top jars without
sealing with paraffin. Label and store.

Fruit Jam
(with added pectin)

Fruit low in natural pectin (fully ripe
fruit) may be used for jam by adding prepared pectin. Follow the manufacturer's
instructions. The yield per pound of
fruit is greater because the juice does not
have to be reduced.

Apricot Pineapple Jam

Cover with cold water
  1 pound dried apricots
Cook until soft. Drain, reserving the
juice. Chop the fruit and add the drained
juice. Add
  1 large can crushed pineapple (with
    its juice)
Measure the fruit and juice, and add
  Heated sugar (⅔ the amount of fruit
    and juice, or less if liked less sweet)
Cook until thick. *Makes 4 pints.*

Cherry Jam

Put in a flat-bottomed saucepan
  ¼ cup water
  4 cups pitted cherries
Bring to the boiling point. Cover and
simmer 15 minutes. Add
  7 cups heated sugar
Bring to the boiling point. Boil rapidly
3 minutes, stirring constantly. Add
  1 bottle commercial pectin
Stir 5 minutes and skim. Add
  ¼ teaspoon almond flavoring
Makes eleven 6-ounce glasses.

Gooseberry Jam

Boil together for 5 minutes
  3 pounds sugar
  2 cups red currant juice
Add
  4 pounds gooseberries
Boil 40 minutes, skimming occasionally.
Set aside 24 hours.

Drain off the syrup. Pack the berries in
jars. Boil the syrup until as thick as
honey and pour it over the berries.
Makes 6 pints.

Black Currant Jam

Wash the currants and remove the stems. Put through a food chopper, then through a coarse sieve. Measure, and add an equal amount of sugar. Bring rapidly to the boiling point, stirring well. Cook 20 minutes.

Raspberry Jam

A jelly thermometer simplifies making this jam. Otherwise it may be over-cooked.

Crush with a masher in a flat-bottomed saucepan
   4 cups raspberries
Cook 15 minutes to reduce the juice. Meanwhile, heat in the oven
   3 cups sugar
Add to the berries and cook to 214°, stirring with a wooden spoon to keep the jam from sticking. Skim off the foam. Spread the jam in a shallow dish and let stand until cool before putting in jars. *Makes about 2 pints.*

Blackberry Jam. You may prefer to remove the seeds by putting the cooked berries through a coarse sieve or food mill before adding the sugar.

Raspberry Currant Jam. Use 3 cups raspberries and 1 cup currants.

Sally's Raspberry or Strawberry Jam

Put in a flat-bottomed saucepan
   1 quart raspberries or strawberries
   (cut large ones in half)
Add
   1 cup sugar
Set over low heat, stir gently, and bring to the boiling point. Boil 3 minutes. Add
   1 cup sugar
Cook as before. Add
   1 cup sugar
Cook as above. Skim off any foam. Taste;

if too sweet, add a little lemon juice. Spread in a shallow dish to cool. If too thin, cook 5 minutes longer and cool. Spoon into jars. *Makes 2 pints.*

Raspberry Currant Preserve

Have ready
   4 quarts raspberries, washed if necessary
Extract the juice (p. 510) from
   3 pounds currants
Add
   3 pounds sugar
Heat to the boiling point and cook slowly 20 minutes.

Add 1 quart of the raspberries. Bring the syrup to the boiling point, skim out the berries and put in jars. Repeat until all the berries are used. Fill the jars with syrup. *Makes about twelve 8-ounce jars.*

Sunshine Strawberries

Wash and hull perfect strawberries. Arrange in layers in a deep kettle with an equal amount of sugar. Let stand ½ hour, then bring to the boiling point and cook 20 minutes. Spread on platters, cover with glass, and set in the sun several days or until the syrup is thick. Stir gently several times each day. Bring indoors after sunset.

Sunshine Cherries. Use sour cherries. Cook until just tender but still firm. Continue as above. Delicious with ice cream.

Strawberry Preserves

Cook together to 238° (soft ball stage)
   3 cups sugar
   1 cup water
Wash, hull, and drain thoroughly
   1 quart strawberries
Add to the syrup, cover, and remove from the heat. Let stand 10 minutes.

Skim if there is any foam on top. Remove the berries and set them aside. Cook the syrup to 238°, add the berries again, and let stand 15 minutes over very low heat.

Skim, remove the berries, and again cook the syrup to 238°. Add the berries once more and cook slowly until the syrup is thick. Let stand 24 hours before filling the jars. *Makes 2 pints.*

Cranberry Conserve

Cranberry Jelly and other cranberry recipes to be used the day they are made (p. 85).

Pick over and wash
  4 cups cranberries
Add
  ⅔ cup cold water
Cook until the skins break. Force through a strainer or a food mill. Add
  ⅔ cup boiling water, apple juice or pineapple juice
  ¼ pound seedless raisins
  1 orange, sliced, seeded, and cut small
  1½ pounds sugar
Bring to the boiling point. Simmer 20 minutes. Add
  ½ pound walnut or filbert meats, cut in pieces
Cool. *Makes about three 6-ounce glasses.*

Cranberry Ginger Conserve. Add ½ cup preserved ginger, cut small.

Grape Conserve

Wash and remove the stems from
  5 pounds Concord grapes
Separate the pulp from the skins. Heat the pulp gently to free the seeds, stirring so that it will not stick. Put through a sieve and discard the seeds.

Cut into thin slivers
  ½ orange, preferably navel
Seed if necessary and add to the grape pulp and skins. Measure. Set out
  Sugar (an equal amount)
Put half the fruit and half the sugar in each of two broad flat saucepans. Cook slowly until the conserve is thick (test by putting a spoonful on a cold plate). Add
  ½ cup walnut meats, in pieces
Makes about ten 6-ounce glasses.

Orange Marmalade

Tart Seville-type oranges make the finest marmalade. Some fruit shops stock them for a short time in late winter. You can sharpen the flavor of common oranges by adding a lemon, sliced very thin.

Select smooth unblemished oranges. Wash thoroughly. Slice as thin as possible and remove the seeds. Measure without draining. To each quart of sliced fruit add 1½ quarts of water and let stand overnight.

Cook slowly until the peel is tender (2 to 2½ hours).

Measure the fruit (undrained) and add two-thirds as much sugar. Cook rapidly to the jelly stage (p. 511) (30 to 60 minutes). *Makes about 5 pints.*

Ginger Marmalade. Add 2½ cups chopped ginger to each quart. For a sweeter marmalade, increase the sugar.

Three-Fruit Marmalade

Select thin-skinned tart fruit.

Scrub thoroughly
  1 grapefruit
  1 orange
  1 lemon
Hold the fruit on a board and slice very thin, saving the juice. Discard all the seeds and the grapefruit core. Measure the fruit and the juice into a large saucepan. Add
  Water (three times the quantity of fruit)
Cover, simmer 2 hours, and let stand overnight.

Measure the fruit (undrained) and add
  Sugar (an equal amount)
  ¼ teaspoon salt
Divide into two or three pans. Cook to the jelly stage (p. 511), stirring frequently. Let stand 1 hour, stirring several times to distribute the peel evenly before putting the marmalade into the glasses. *Makes about twelve 6-ounce glasses.*

Spiced Orange Slices

Delicious with duck.

Cut in ¼-inch slices and seed
    6 large oranges, unpeeled
Put in a saucepan. Cover with water, simmer ½ hour, and drain.

Put in a saucepan
    3½ cups sugar
    1 cup mild vinegar
    1 stick cinnamon
    ½ tablespoon whole cloves
Boil 5 minutes. Add some of the orange slices, having the syrup cover them completely. Cover and cook until the slices are clear (about ½ hour). Remove the slices and cook the remaining ones the same way. Cover with syrup and let stand overnight.

Drain off the syrup and cook until thick. Add the orange slices and heat to the boiling point. *Makes about eight 6-ounce glasses.*

Kumquat Preserves

Put in a saucepan
    2 cups sugar
    1 cup water
Boil 5 minutes. Add
    1 quart fresh kumquats
Cook gently 45 minutes or until tender. *Makes six 6-ounce glasses.*

Peach Conserve

Put in a kettle
    1 quart cold water
    1 pound dried skinned peaches
Let stand overnight. Add
    1 cup seeded raisins, cut in pieces
    Juice 1 lemon
    Juice 1 orange
    1 whole orange (cut in thin slices and
        seeded)
    1 pound sugar
Bring to the boiling point. Boil rapidly until the syrup is thick and the fruit is clear, stirring occasionally to prevent sticking. Add
    ½ pound walnut meats, cut in pieces
Makes about eight 6-ounce jars.

Pear Ginger

Stem and core
    4 pounds pears (underripe)
Cut in small pieces. Add
    4 ounces (1 small jar) crystallized
        ginger
    2 lemons, quartered and seeded
Put through a meat grinder, saving the juice. Put in a heavy saucepan. Add the juice and
    2 pounds sugar
    1 cup water
Cook slowly until thick (about 3 hours). Pears vary in flavor, so after the first hour, taste, and add more lemon juice or more sugar. *Makes eight or more 6-ounce glasses.*

Pear Harlequin

Wipe, stem, and core
    3 pounds pears (underripe)
Cut in small pieces. Add
    1 small can pineapple, crushed or bits
    Juice and grated rind of 1 orange
Measure. For each 4 cups add
    3 cups sugar
Cover and let stand overnight.

Simmer until thick (about 2 hours). Add (cutting the cherries in half)
    1 4-ounce bottle maraschino cherries
Stir well. *Makes eight 6-ounce jars.*

Plum Gumbo

Wipe and remove the pits from
    3 pounds plums
Cut in pieces. Chop
    1 pound seeded raisins
Wipe, seed, and cut in thin slices
    2 oranges
Put the fruit in a deep kettle. Add
    3 pounds sugar
Bring to the boiling point and simmer until as thick as marmalade. *Makes about eight 6-ounce jars.*

Damson Preserves

Wipe damson plums and prick them well with a needle. Weigh. For each pound of fruit, put in a saucepan 1½ cups sugar and ½ cup water. Bring to the boiling point and skim.

Add the plums, a few at a time, so that the fruit will keep its shape during cooking. Cook until soft.

To work faster, divide the syrup in two pans and work with both at once.

Rhubarb Conserve

Wash, peel, and cut in 1-inch pieces
    4 pounds rhubarb
Put in a kettle. Add
    5 pounds sugar
    1 pound seeded raisins
    2 oranges (grated rind and juice)
    1 lemon (grated rind and juice)
Mix well. Cover and let stand ½ hour. Bring to the boiling point and simmer 45 minutes, stirring frequently. *Makes twelve 6-ounce glasses.*

Rhubarb Fig Marmalade

Combine in a large saucepan
    1 pound unpeeled rhubarb (cut fine)
    1 pound sugar
    ¼ pound dried figs, cut small
    Juice ½ lemon
Cover and let stand 24 hours. Cook rapidly to the jelly stage (p. 511). *Makes about six 6-ounce glasses.*

Tomato Marmalade

Cut in pieces
    3 pounds tomatoes
Cut in very thin slices, discarding the seeds
    1 orange
    ½ lemon
Add to the tomatoes. Add
    1½ pounds sugar
Cook slowly 3 hours, stirring to prevent sticking. *Makes six 6-ounce glasses.*

Tomato Conserve. Cook ½ pound seedless raisins with the marmalade. When ready to pour into glasses, stir in ¼ pound chopped walnut meats.

Apple Butter

A general rule. Vary the spices to suit your taste. Make other fruit butters of fresh apricots, peaches, plums, or the pulp left in the jelly bag after making jelly. Crush the fruit and add just enough water (not cider or vinegar) to keep it from sticking.

Cut into pieces (do not peel or core)
    4 pounds tart apples
Cover with
    2 cups cider, mild cider vinegar or
      water
Cook until soft. Put through a sieve. Measure. Add
    ½ cup sugar for each cup of pulp
    Few grains salt
    2 teaspoons cinnamon
    1 teaspoon clove
    ½ teaspoon allspice
    1 lemon (grated rind and juice)
Cover and cook over low heat until the sugar dissolves. Uncover and cook quickly until thick and smooth when you spoon a bit onto a cold plate. Stir with a wooden spoon during the cooking so that the apple butter will not stick and burn. *Makes about ten 6-ounce glasses.*

Quince Honey

When cold, quince honey should be about the color and consistency of honey.

Pare and grate
    3 large quinces (underripe)
Put in a saucepan
    1 cup boiling water
    5 cups sugar
Heat slowly, without boiling, until the sugar melts. Brush down the sides of the pan with a pastry brush dipped in cold water to remove any crystals. Add the quince pulp and cook 15 to 20 minutes. If the quinces are ripe, add, after the first 10 minutes of cooking
    1 teaspoon lemon juice
This helps to prevent sugaring. *Makes about six 6-ounce jars.*

Brandied Peaches

Delicious with lamb or chicken, or as a dessert, with or without ice cream.

Dip perfect peaches quickly in hot water and peel. If the peaches have thin skins, you may prefer not to peel them — rub off the fuzz with a clean cloth and prick each peach twice with a fork.

For each 6 peaches, boil 3 cups water with 2 cups sugar 10 minutes. Cook the peaches in the syrup, a few at a time, until tender when tried with a toothpick (about 5 minutes).

Pack into jars. Add 2 tablespoons brandy to each pint jar and fill the jars with syrup. Store a month before using.

Brandied Cherries. Wash firm cherries. Leave on the short stems and cook as above.

Tutti-Frutti

Essential for success with this Victorian luxury are a big old-fashioned stone jar with a heavy cover and a cool storage place.

Put 1 quart brandy in a large stone crock (at least 2-gallon size). As fruits come into season, put them into the jar (hull strawberries and raspberries; pit cherries; peel, pit and cut apricots and peaches and cut in pieces; cut pineapple in chunks). For each 2 cups of fruit, add 2 cups of sugar.

Put on the cover, tying it on if necessary. Set in a cool place. Stir daily until all the fruit has been added. Cover tightly (or seal in jars if more convenient) and store 3 months before using.

Serve on ice cream or stir into soft ice cream and refreeze.

Pickles and Relishes

Even though excellent pickles are marketed, it is a satisfaction and an economy to prepare a stock of your own making. Pickles are easy to make and variations are innumerable. Develop your own specialties by adding different spices and vegetables to basic recipes.

Ingredients

Vegetables and fruits should be slightly underripe so that the finished pickle will be crisp. Wash or wipe before cutting.

Vinegar should be mild. Read the label — the vinegar should contain no more than 5 per cent acid. White vinegar is often used for light-colored pickles, but it does not have the fruity flavor of cider vinegar.

Salt should be pure, not table salt, so that the liquid will not be cloudy.

Spices should be fresh. To keep pickles from darkening, use whole spices and tie them loosely in a square of muslin. Remove them before packing the pickles in jars.

Sugar. Use granulated white sugar unless the recipe calls for brown sugar.

Pickling Problems

Soft or slippery pickles are spoiled, due to inaccurate measurements or improper storage.

Shriveling comes from using too much vinegar, sugar or salt.

Darkening is caused by the minerals in hard water or by using ground spices. Do not cook pickles in copper or iron, which also causes change in color.

To Pack Pickles

Old-time cooks stored pickles in large jars or crocks in a cool cellar. Nowadays most families find it more convenient to store them in pint or half-pint jars. Prepare jars, fill to overflowing with hot pickles, and cover immediately with tops, unless the recipe gives special directions.

Bread and Butter Pickles

Young cucumbers (6-inch size) and tiny white onions make the best pickle.

Prepare
   6 cups thin-sliced cucumbers
Peel and slice
   1 pound onions
Seed and shred
   1 green pepper
Mix well. Add
   ¼ cup salt
Cover and let stand 3 hours.

Mix (omitting the turmeric if you prefer)
   2 cups brown sugar
   ½ teaspoon turmeric
   ¼ teaspoon ground cloves
   1 tablespoon mustard seed
   ½ teaspoon celery seed (or more)
   2 cups mild cider vinegar
Bring slowly to the boiling point and boil 5 minutes.

Drain the vegetables thoroughly in a colander, rinsing well with cold water. Add them to the hot syrup and heat slowly to just below the boiling point, stirring occasionally. *Makes 4 pints.*

Saccharin Pickles

Particularly useful if you grow your own cucumbers. Add them a few at a time as they develop. If more convenient, pack the cucumbers in jars, fill to overflowing with the pickling syrup, and put on tops at once. If you wish to omit the horse-radish, increase the mustard to ½ cup.

Mix
    1 gallon mild vinegar
    1 teaspoon powdered saccharin
    1 teaspoon powdered alum
    ½ cup salt
    ½ teaspoon powdered cloves
    1 teaspoon powdered allspice
    1 tablespoon powdered cinnamon
    4 tablespoons dry mustard
    1 cup grated horseradish
Pour into a large crock (2 gallons or larger). Add, as they grow to the proper size (1 to 2 inches)
    Cucumbers, scrubbed
Add no more than will be covered by the liquid. Let stand at least two weeks before using.

Cucumber and Onion Pickle

Slice
    12 young cucumbers
    6 onions
Add
    ½ cup salt
Cover with water and let stand 2 hours.

Drain. Add
    2 cups mild cider vinegar
    ½ cup sugar
    2 teaspoons mustard seed
    2 teaspoons celery seed
    2 teaspoons black pepper
    1 teaspoon ginger
    1 teaspoon turmeric
Bring to the boiling point. *Makes 4 pints.*

Olive Oil Pickles

Slice paper-thin
    1 dozen 6-inch cucumbers

Add
    1 quart boiling water
    ½ cup salt
Let stand overnight. Drain thoroughly and pack in clean jars.

Mix
    ½ cup olive oil
    4 ounces white mustard seed
    4 ounces black mustard seed
    3 cups mild vinegar
Pour over the cucumbers. *Makes 3 pints.*

Dill Pickles

Select small slim cucumbers 3 or 4 inches long.

Cover with cold water
    Cucumbers (about 50)
Let stand overnight. Drain and pack in jars.

Put in a saucepan
    1 quart mild vinegar
    ¾ cup salt
    2 quarts water
Bring to the boiling point. Pour over the cucumbers. Add to each jar
    Dill, one or more sprigs
    A clove of garlic (if you like it)
If some of the liquid oozes out during the first week, open the jars and add enough more liquid (mixed in the same proportion) to cover the cucumbers completely. *Makes 6 to 8 quarts.*

Icicle Pickles

Drain and serve well-chilled as a relish or hors d'oeuvre.

Peel and remove the seeds from
    Large cucumbers
Cut in strips ½ inch wide. Cover with
    Ice water
Let stand overnight. Drain and pack upright in sterilized pint jars. For each 3 or 4 jars, boil together for 3 minutes
    3 cups white vinegar
    1 cup water
    3 cups sugar
Add

¼ cup salt
Pour over the cucumbers to fill the jars.
Let stand 6 weeks before using.

Ripe Cucumber Pickles

Pare and remove the seeds from
  4 large ripe cucumbers
Cut into large chunks. Sprinkle with
  Salt
Let stand 3 hours and drain.

Mix in a saucepan
  1½ cups mild vinegar
  1½ cups sugar
  1½ teaspoons mustard seed
  1½ teaspoons celery seed
  ½ teaspoon turmeric
Add the cucumbers. Simmer until the
cucumbers are easily pierced with a fork.
Pack them in jars and cover with syrup.
Makes 2 pints.

Pickled Beets

Cook until tender
  4 bunches young beets
Plunge into cold water and slip off the
skins. Leave tiny beets whole. Slice the
larger ones.

Mix in a saucepan
  1 quart mild vinegar
  1½ cups sugar
  ½ teaspoon allspice berries
  1 stick cinnamon
  1 teaspoon whole cloves
Add the beets. Simmer 15 minutes. Pack
the beets in clean hot jars. Fill the jars
with the hot syrup. Put on the tops.
Process 20 minutes in a boiling water
bath (p. 529).

Pickled Onions

Peel small white onions. Cover with
brine, allowing 1½ cups salt to 2 quarts
boiling water. Let stand 2 days.

Drain and cover with more brine. Let
stand 2 days and again drain.

Make more brine and heat to the boiling

point. Put in the onions and boil 3 minutes. Put the onions in clean hot jars,
mixing in bits of mace, white peppercorns, cloves, bits of bay leaf and slices of
pimiento. Fill the jars to overflowing
with vinegar heated with sugar (1 cup
sugar to 1 gallon vinegar). Put on covers
while hot.

To vary, add, for each gallon of vinegar,
1 ounce gingerroot or ¼ cup freshly
grated horseradish. Other seasonings may
be substituted for the combination suggested above, such as basil, nutmeg,
celery seed, chili peppers, mustard seed,
dill, chervil and rosemary.

Mustard Pickle

Wash and prepare
  1 quart small pickling cucumbers
  1 quart cubed cucumbers (3 large)
  1 quart green tomatoes, cut small
  1 quart button onions, peeled
  4 sweet green peppers, cut fine
  1 large cauliflower, cut in small pieces
Mix
  2 cups salt
  4 quarts water
Pour over the vegetables. Let stand overnight.

Bring to the boiling point and drain in
a colander.

Mix
  1 cup flour
  6 tablespoons dry mustard
  1 tablespoon turmeric
Stir in
  Enough vinegar to make a smooth
    paste
Add
  2 cups sugar
  Mild vinegar (2 quarts in all)
Boil until thick and smooth, stirring constantly. Add the vegetables and cook
until they are just heated through. Overcooking makes them soft instead of crisp.
Pour into jars and put on covers immediately. *Makes 8 pints.*

Red Cabbage Pickle

Mix well and let stand overnight
  2 teaspoons salt
  2 small heads red cabbage, sliced thin
    (about 2 quarts)
Drain. Add
  ¼ teaspoon pepper
  2 tablespoons mustard seed
Mix well.

Mix
  1 quart mild vinegar
  ½ cup sugar
  2 tablespoons mixed pickling spices
    (in a spice bag)
Bring slowly to the boiling point and
pour, boiling hot, over the cabbage.
Makes 3 pints.

Piccalilli

Put through a chopper, using the coarse
knife
  5 green tomatoes
  5 green peppers
  2 sweet red peppers
  5 onions, peeled
  1 small cabbage, quartered
Sprinkle with
  ¼ cup salt
Cover and let stand overnight.

Cover with cold water and drain. Add
  3 cups brown sugar
  1½ teaspoons celery seed
  1 tablespoon mustard seed
  1 tablespoon whole cloves
  2-inch piece of stick cinnamon
  1 tablespoon allspice berries
  2 cups mild cider vinegar
Bring to the boiling point and cook
slowly 15 minutes. *Makes 4 pints.*

Chowchow

*Variations are endless. Change the pro-
portions of vegetables or the seasoning
as you like.*

Cut in small pieces
  1 quart small green tomatoes
  6 small cucumbers
  2 red or green peppers
  1 small head of cauliflower
  1 bunch celery
  1 or 2 cups small onions
  1 quart green beans (whole)
Cover with
  2 quarts boiling water
  ¾ cup salt
Let stand 1 hour. Drain. Rinse with cold
water.

Heat to the boiling point
  2 quarts mild vinegar
  4 tablespoons mustard seed
  1 ounce turmeric
  1 tablespoon allspice
  1 tablespoon pepper
  1 tablespoon ground clove
Add the vegetables. Cook until tender,
stirring frequently. *Makes about 10
pints.*

Celery and Tomato Relish

Put in a saucepan
  2 cups sugar
  2 tablespoons salt
  1 teaspoon dry mustard
  1 teaspoon powdered cloves
  1 teaspoon allspice
  1 teaspoon cinnamon
  1 teaspoon celery seed
Mix thoroughly. Add
  1½ cups mild vinegar
  6 bunches celery, chopped (no leaves)
  15 tomatoes, chopped
  1 red pepper, chopped
Bring to the boiling point and simmer
1½ hours. *Makes about 4 pints.*

Corn Relish

Cut the corn from
  1½ dozen ears corn
Remove and discard the leaves and roots
from
  1 bunch celery
Chop the stalks fine. Put the corn and
celery in a saucepan. Add
  1 quart mild vinegar
  1 small cabbage, chopped
  4 onions, sliced thin
  2 green peppers, chopped

Mix
   2 cups sugar
   1 cup flour
   ½ cup salt
   ½ teaspoon mustard
   ¼ teaspoon cayenne
   ½ teaspoon turmeric (for color)
Add
   1 quart mild vinegar
Add to the vegetables and bring to the
boiling point. Simmer 40 minutes. *Makes
4 to 6 pints.*

Pepper Relish

Remove the seeds from
   24 peppers, green or red, or half of
      each
Peel
   12 onions
Put the vegetables through a chopper;
then put in a saucepan. Cover with
boiling water and drain. Cover with cold
water, bring to the boiling point, and
drain. Add
   1 quart mild vinegar
   2 cups sugar
   3 tablespoons salt
   1 tablespoon mustard or celery seed
Cook 10 minutes. Taste, and add sugar
or salt, if needed. *Makes 6 or 7 pints.*

Pepper Relish with Celery. Chop 6 stalks
of celery and add with the vinegar.

Tomato Relish I

Peel and chop tomatoes to make
   3 pints pulp
Add
   1 cup chopped celery
   4 tablespoons chopped red pepper
   4 tablespoons chopped onion
   4 tablespoons salt
   6 tablespoons sugar
   6 tablespoons mustard seed
   1 tablespoon grated nutmeg
   1 teaspoon cinnamon
   ½ teaspoon ground cloves
   2 cups mild vinegar
Put in a stone jar and cover. Let stand

at least 1 week before using. This uncooked mixture will keep 6 months.
Makes about 4 pints.

Tomato Relish II

Put through a chopper
   3 bunches celery (roots and leaves
      removed)
   4 seeded green peppers
   2 peeled onions
Add
   12 large tomatoes, peeled and cut in
      pieces
   2 tablespoons salt
   2 tablespoons sugar
   3 cups mild vinegar
Simmer until thick (about 1½ hours).
Makes 2 or 3 pints.

Sweet Tomato Relish

Mix
   2 quarts chopped green tomatoes
   2 chopped green peppers
   2 cups chopped onion
   1 pint mild vinegar
   ¼ cup salt
   3 cups sugar
   ½ cup mixed pickling spices (in bag)
Bring to the boiling point and cook
slowly 30 minutes, stirring occasionally.
Remove the spice bag. *Makes 4 pints.*

Green Tomato Relish

Mix
   2 quarts chopped green tomatoes
   ¾ cup salt
Cover, let stand 24 hours, and drain.

Add
   1 teaspoon pepper
   1½ teaspoons mustard
   1½ teaspoons cinnamon
   ½ teaspoon allspice
   1½ teaspoons ground cloves
   ¼ cup white mustard seed
   1 quart mild cider vinegar
   2 red or green peppers, sliced
   1 chopped onion
Bring to the boiling point and cook 15
minutes. *Makes 4 pints.*

Tomato Soy

Mix
    4 quarts peeled and sliced red
        tomatoes
    2 onions, peeled and chopped
    ¼ cup salt
Cover, let stand 24 hours, and drain.

Add
    ¼ cup mixed pickling spices (in bag)
    1 pint mild vinegar
Cook slowly 2 hours. Add
    1 cup sugar
    2 tablespoons white mustard seed
Cook 5 minutes. Remove the spice bag.
Makes 3 pints.

Chili Sauce

*Increase the amount of spices if you like,
but spices darken the sauce.*

Put in a saucepan
    8 cups peeled tomatoes, cut in pieces
        (about 12)
Cook slowly 1 hour.

Put through a chopper
    1 green pepper
    1 onion
Add to the tomatoes. Cook 30 minutes.
Add
    ½ cup sugar
    1 tablespoon salt
    ½ teaspoon pepper
    1 teaspoon cinnamon
    1 teaspoon ground cloves
    ½ teaspoon allspice
    1 teaspoon nutmeg
    1 cup mild vinegar
Boil until thick (about 10 minutes).
Makes 3 pints.

Sweet Chili Sauce. Chop 1 large tart
apple with the pepper and onion. Increase the sugar to 1 cup.

Tomato Catsup

Chop
    10 pounds ripe tomatoes, peeled
    3 onions
    2 sweet red peppers, seeded

Add, if liked
    ½ clove garlic
Cook slowly until soft. Put through a
fine sieve. Simmer until reduced one-
half (about 30 minutes). Add, putting
the whole spices in a spice bag
    ¾ cup brown sugar
    2-inch stick cinnamon
    1 teaspoon peppercorns
    1 teaspoon whole cloves
    1 teaspoon allspice berries
    1 teaspoon celery seed
    1 cup mild vinegar
    1 tablespoon salt
    2 teaspoons paprika
    ¼ teaspoon cayenne
Cook slowly until very thick. Stir frequently. Remove the spice bag. *Makes 3
or 4 pints.*

Grape Catsup

Wash and crush in a saucepan
    5 pounds ripe Concord grapes
Simmer until soft. Press through a sieve
or vegetable mill, discarding skins and
seeds. Add
    3 pounds sugar
    1 pint mild vinegar
    1 tablespoon cinnamon
    1 tablespoon allspice
    1 tablespoon ground cloves
    ½ teaspoon salt
    1 tablespoon pepper
Bring to the boiling point and simmer
until as thick as liked (30 minutes or
more). *Makes about 4 pints.*

To make in electric blender. Put the
stemmed grapes in the blender and whirl
30 seconds. Put through a sieve or vegetable mill to strain out the seeds. Continue as above.

Plum Catsup

Put in a saucepan
    5 pounds plums
    3 tart apples, quartered but not
        peeled or cored
    2 cups mild vinegar

Cook until the fruit is tender. Put through a food mill. Add

4 cups brown sugar
3 tablespoons cinnamon
2 teaspoons powdered cloves
2 teaspoons salt
½ teaspoon mace

Cook until thick. *Makes 5 pints.*

Apple Chutney

Put in a bowl

3 cups chopped green tomatoes

Sprinkle with

2 tablespoons salt

Let stand 12 hours and drain.

Mix

1 quart mild cider vinegar
2 tablespoons salt
1 pound dark brown sugar

Chop

12 tart apples, cored
2 Spanish onions, sliced

Put all the ingredients in a saucepan. Add

1 pound raisins, seedless or sultanas
2 tablespoons ground ginger
⅔ cup finely cut mint leaves

Cook over low heat until the apples and onions are tender (about 30 minutes). Mix

2 tablespoons flour
¼ cup water

Stir it into the chutney. Simmer 5 minutes. *Makes about 4 pints.*

To vary, omit the ground ginger and use instead ½ pound chopped green ginger or 1 jar (6 ounces) preserved ginger, cut small. Use ripe tomatoes instead of green ones. Add 2 ounces chili peppers, if you like.

Peach Chutney

Peel, pit and cut in pieces

Peaches (to make 4 cups)

Put in a heavy saucepan

2 cups mild vinegar
3 cups sugar

Bring to the boiling point. Add the peaches and

½ pound dried currants or raisins
2 cloves garlic, chopped fine
1 small jar candied ginger, chopped fine

Cook 2 hours, stirring occasionally to prevent sticking. *Makes three or four 6-ounce jars.*

Pickled Cherries

Pit firm sour cherries. Cover with mild vinegar. Let stand overnight. Drain and weigh. Put in a stone crock and add an equal weight of sugar. Cover. Stir daily until the sugar is entirely dissolved (7 or 8 days). Store in the crock or pack in jars.

Pickled Fruits

Mix in a saucepan

1 cup mild vinegar
1 cup water
1 cup brown sugar
1 cup white sugar
1 tablespoon cloves
1 stick cinnamon, broken in pieces

Boil 5 minutes. Add the prepared fruit (see below) a little at a time, and simmer until tender. Lift out the fruit with a skimmer and pack into jars. Add hot syrup to within ¼ inch of the top, preparing more syrup if necessary.

Pickled Crabapples. Do not pare. Cut out the blossom end. Prick several times. *10 to 15 make a pint.*

Pickled Kumquats. Cover with salt water (1 tablespoon salt to each quart of water). Let stand 24 hours.

Rinse, cover with water, and boil 30 minutes. Drain, add fresh water, and cook until the kumquats are tender. Cook in the syrup until translucent.

Pickled Peaches. Dip in boiling water, then in cold, and slip off the skins. Cut freestone peaches in half and remove the pits. Leave clingstone peaches whole.

Pickled Pears. Use firm, slightly under-ripe fruit. Pare large fruit, cut in halves or quarters, and remove the cores. Remove the blossom end from Seckel pears, pare or not, and prick well. Use white vinegar to prevent darkening.

Cherry Olives

Piquant with cocktails or salad.

Pack closely in two pint jars
    1 quart sour cherries, washed but not
      stemmed
Add to each jar
    1½ teaspoons salt
    ½ cup mild vinegar
Fill the jars with cold water. Put on the covers and turn upside down. Let stand 2 weeks before using. *Makes 2 pints.*

Sweet Cherry Olives. Add 1½ teaspoons sugar to each jar. Large white cherries are especially delicious this way.

Spiced Currants

Wash and drain
    1½ pounds currants
Remove the stems. Add
    1 pound brown sugar
    ½ cup mild cider vinegar
    ½-inch piece of stick cinnamon or 1
      teaspoon cinnamon
    1 teaspoon powdered cloves
    1 teaspoon allspice (if liked)
Heat to the boiling point. Cook slowly 1 hour. Remove the cinnamon stick if used. *Makes about five 6-ounce glasses.*

Gooseberry Catsup. Use 2 pounds gooseberries in place of currants. Cook about 2 hours.

Gooseberry Relish

Put through a food chopper
    5 cups gooseberries, washed and
      stemmed
    1½ cups seeded raisins
    1 onion, sliced

Add
    1 cup brown sugar
    3 tablespoons dry mustard
    3 tablespoons ginger
    3 tablespoons salt
    ¼ teaspoon cayenne
    1 teaspoon turmeric (omit, if you
      prefer)
    1 quart mild vinegar
Bring slowly to the boiling point and simmer 45 minutes. Strain through a coarse sieve. *Makes about 4 pints.*

Spiced Rhubarb

Mix in a saucepan
    2½ pounds young pink rhubarb, cut
      in 1-inch pieces
    2 pounds sugar
    1 cup mild cider vinegar
    1 teaspoon cinnamon
    ½ teaspoon ground cloves
Bring to the boiling point and simmer until as thick as marmalade. *Makes five or six 6-ounce glasses.*

Watermelon Pickle

Lime water makes crisper pickles than salt water. Buy lime (calcium oxide) at the drugstore.

Cut watermelon rind in 5 or 6 inch pieces. Cover with boiling water. Boil 5 minutes, drain and cool. Cut off the tough green skin and all the pink pulp. Cut the rind in desired shapes. Weigh or measure.

Cover with salt water (½ cup salt to each quart of water) or lime water (2 tablespoons lime to each quart of water). Let stand 6 hours in salt water or 3 in lime water.

Drain, rinse, and cover with fresh water. Simmer until tender. Drain. Add to Pickling Syrup (below). Simmer until the rind is clear and the syrup thick, adding water if necessary. Remove the spice bag. Pack in jars.

Citron Melon Pickle. Peel, cut in half, and remove the seeds. Cut the flesh in cubes. Cook in Pickling Syrup (below) and pack in jars.

Horseradish

Use very sparingly on cold beef or in Horseradish Sauce (p. 96).

Scrape horseradish roots and drop into cold water to prevent discoloration. Drain and put through a food chopper or crush in an electric blender. Fill clean, cold pint jars about two-thirds full. Add 1 teaspoon salt to each jar and fill with white vinegar. Put on the tops.

Pickling Syrup

Put in a deep saucepan
  1 quart mild vinegar
  1 cup water
  2 pounds sugar (or more)
Tie in a piece of cheesecloth
  1 tablespoon whole cloves
  1 stick cinnamon (1 ounce), broken in
    pieces

Add to the syrup. Simmer until the sugar dissolves. *Enough for about 2 pounds (or 1½ to 2 quarts) of fruit.*

For a spicier syrup, add 1 tablespoon allspice berries and/or a piece of ginger-root.

Red Pepper Jelly

This very hot sauce adds zest to cock-tail sauces or sandwich and canapé spreads.

Seed and put through a chopper
  6 large hot red peppers
Cover with cold water, bring to the boiling point, boil 5 minutes, and drain off the water thoroughly. Add
  1 lemon, quartered and seeded
  Mild vinegar (enough to cover)
Cook 30 minutes. Add
  1½ cups sugar
Boil 10 minutes. Remove the lemon. *Makes four 6-ounce jars.*

Canning

Fashions in food preservation are changing rapidly. Markets offer a variety of fresh and frozen fruits and vegetables throughout the year. Modern apartments and houses often lack the cool, dry, dark cupboards needed for keeping home-canned foods in the best condition. Freezing is a simpler and safer process, and more and more families own freezers. Commercially canned foods are often better than homemade, unless you have a garden of your own or are near a source of freshly picked high-quality produce.

Using Canned Foods

Inspect commercial or home-canned foods carefully, and discard if there are indications of spoilage — "off" odor, color or texture, or cloudiness or sediment in the liquid.

Molds are the result of incorrect processing, broken seal or contact of the food with equipment that is not completely sterilized (jars, tops, spoons, cloth, etc.). A light mold on fruits, tomatoes and rhubarb is not thought to affect the rest of the jar, but discard any food with a heavy mold.

Flat-sour may develop in products picked warm and canned on hot muggy days or stored too quickly where air cannot circulate around the jars. It may also result from canning too large a quantity at one time.

Do not throw away the liquid from the jar, since many vitamins are soluble in water. To serve it with the vegetable, pour off the liquid and boil it down until there is very little left, then add the vegetable and heat. If the liquid is not to be served with the vegetables or meat, store it in a jar and use it in soup or gravy.

Preparing Jars for Canning

Large-mouthed jars are easy to fill. Use jars with vacuum-seal metal covers (new covers for each canning) or with rubber rings and (1) solid metal screw tops, (2) glass tops and two bails, or (3) glass tops and screw bands. Use new rubber rings each time.

Inspect the jars carefully and discard any with even a tiny nick. Run your finger around the edge to detect nicks or cracks.

Test rubber-ring jars for leakage by half filling with hot water, sealing and inverting.

Test jar rubbers by folding double and pressing firmly: a good rubber does not crack. Scrub thoroughly and rinse.

Wash the jars thoroughly and rinse. Keep the jars, tops and rubbers in warm water until ready to fill.

Filling Jars

Dip a tested rubber ring in hot water and fit it in place on the jar. (Vacuum-seal jars require no rubber rings.) Set a wide funnel on the jar. Pack to within ½ inch of the top. Pack vegetables loosely, especially corn, peas and shell beans. Press tomatoes down to squeeze out extra juice. Pack fruits as tightly as possible without crushing. If fruit has been pre-cooked, lift it out of the syrup, pack in the jar, and add the liquid to within ½ inch of the top. Tomatoes need only their own juice. Add ½ teaspoon salt for each pint of vegetables. Run a knife down into the jar to release any air bubbles. Wipe off the rim or rubbers.

To close. Dip the cover in hot water and set on the jar. If you are using a vacuum-seal cover, put on the screw band and screw gently but firmly into place, but do not force. Partially seal other jars: (1) Bail type. Put the upper bail in place, but leave the other one loose. (2) Screw top or band. Screw until resistance is felt, then turn back a quarter turn.

Processing Filled Jars

Follow the manufacturer's directions in using a pressure canner.

Put the rack to hold the jars in a boiling water bath canner and fill with enough water so that it will be 1 inch deep above the tops of the jars. If you do not have a special canner, use a large covered kettle and put a rack or a pad of towels or paper in the bottom. If you use a pressure canner for this method, leave the petcock open.

Let the water heat to simmering while you prepare the food and fill the jars. As each jar is filled and closed, lower it carefully into the canner. Allow ½ inch between the jars for good circulation of water.

When most of the jars are in place, increase the heat so that the water will boil quickly.

After all the jars are added, bring the water to a full rolling boil and begin counting the processing time. Keep the water boiling steadily during the whole processing time.

Removing Jars from the Canner

Lift out the jars. Do not disturb the covers or bands on vacuum seal jars. On all jars using rubbers, complete the seal by (1) lowering the other bail or (2) screwing the covers or bands tightly. Set on a wooden rack or a pad of towels or newspapers out of a draft. Do not invert.

After 24 hours, check the seal on all jars (below); then wipe the jars, label, and store in a dark dry place, cool but not freezing.

To check, remove the screwbands or bails and lift by the lid; if the lid is loose, the seal is not firm. Reprocess or use the food immediately. Test vacuum-jars by inverting; if there is leakage, the seal is not tight.

Syrup for Canning and Freezing Fruit

Cook the sugar and water together until the sugar dissolves. Add to the jar *boiling hot*. Syrup is added for flavor and to keep fruit firmer, but fruit will keep perfectly canned in its own juice or in boiling water.

Thin Syrup. Use 1 cup sugar to 3 cups water.

Medium Syrup. Use 1 cup sugar to 2 cups water.

Heavy Syrup. Use 1 cup sugar to 1 cup water.

Canning Fruits and Tomatoes

Select clean, sound, fully ripe fruit. If it is to be canned whole or in halves, it should be uniform in size. Wash it thoroughly and prepare according to the directions below. Prepare only enough for one canner load at a time. Keep the rest in the refrigerator.

To keep apples, apricots and peaches from darkening, drop the pieces as you prepare them into water containing 1 tablespoon each of salt and vinegar to 2 quarts of water.

Pack the prepared fruit into jars, add syrup (above), if used, adjust the lids, and process the required time. For details, see above. Fruit and tomatoes contain enough acid so that they can be processed safely in a boiling water bath canner.

Apples (2½ to 3 pounds for a quart jar). Pare, core, and cut in pieces. Boil 5 minutes in Thin Syrup or water. *Process pints 15 minutes, quarts 20.*

Applesauce. Prepare as usual (p. 347). Heat to simmering and pack into jars within ¼ inch of the top. *Process 10 minutes.*

Apricots (2 or 3 pounds for a quart jar). Cut in half and remove pits. Simmer in syrup until tender. *Process pints 20 minutes, quarts 25.*

Blueberries (about 2 quarts for 3 pint jars). Remove stems. Put the berries in a square of cheesecloth. Gather up the corners to form a bag and dip into a kettle of boiling water. After 15 seconds, remove from the water. If no spots of juice show on the cloth, dip again. Plunge into cold water, drain, and pack tightly into jars. *Process pints 16 minutes.*

Cherries (2 to 2½ pounds for a quart jar if pits are removed). Stem and pit or not. Pack in jars and cover with syrup to within ½ inch of the top. *Process pints 20 minutes, quarts 25.*

Or add ½ cup sugar to each quart of cherries (more for sour cherries) and heat slowly to the boiling point. *Process 10 minutes.*

Peaches (2 to 3 pounds for a quart jar). Dip in boiling water, then in cold, and remove the skins. Cut in half and remove the pits. Slice or not. Heat thoroughly in hot syrup. If the peaches are very juicy, heat with sugar instead of syrup until the sugar dissolves. *Process pints 20 minutes, quarts 25.*

Pears (2 to 3 pounds for a quart jar). Peel and core, cut in half or leave whole with the stems on. Heat thoroughly in hot syrup. *Process pints 20 minutes, quarts 25.*

Pineapple (2 pounds for a quart jar). Cut in ½-inch slices. Pare and cut out the core. Simmer in syrup until tender. *Process 20 minutes.*

Plums (1½ to 2½ pounds for a quart jar). Prick the skins if you are canning plums whole. Cut freestone plums in half and remove the pits. Heat to the boiling point in syrup, or in sugar if the plums are very juicy. *Process pints 20 minutes, quarts 25.*

Raspberries and Blackberries (1½ quarts for a quart jar). Remove caps and stems. Fill jars to within ½ inch of the top. Shake the berries down so that the jar will be full. Cover with boiling syrup to within ½ inch of the top. *Process pints 10 minutes, quarts 15.*

Rhubarb (1½ pounds for a pint jar). Cut in ½-inch pieces. Measure and add ½ cup sugar for each quart. Let stand 30 minutes to draw out the juice and bring to the boiling point. *Process 10 minutes.*

Strawberries do not can successfully. Use them for jam.

Tomatoes (3 pounds for a quart jar; 1 bushel for 18 quarts). Dip in boiling water, then in cold, to loosen the skins. Cut out the stem and the white core, if there is any. Peel and leave whole or cut in pieces. Press firmly into the jars. Add ½ teaspoon salt for each pint. Add no water. *Process pints 35 minutes, quarts 45.*

Or quarter peeled tomatoes, cook in their own juice to the boiling point, and add salt. *Process 10 minutes.*

Canning Fruit Juices

Canned juices are delicious as the basis for fruit drinks or sauces or as the liquid for jellied salads or dessert. Can juices without sugar to make up into fresh jellies during the winter as you need them.

Extract the juice as for jelly (p. 510) and sweeten or not. Fill jars to ¼ inch from the top and adjust the lids. Process 5 minutes in a boiling water bath canner. Tighten the lid, label, and store.

Spiced Blackberry Juice. Crush 2 quarts berries. Add 1 teaspoon each of allspice and whole cloves, 1 stick cinnamon and a whole nutmeg. Add ½ cup water and simmer 30 minutes, or put in a pressure saucepan, bring to 15 pounds pressure, remove from the heat, and let the pressure drop to normal. Strain. Add ½ cup sugar and bring to the boiling point. Put in jars and process. Use to add color and flavor to a summer punch or to hot Mulled Cider (p. 38) for a winter drink. *Makes about 1½ pints.*

Grape Juice. Wash and stem perfect grapes. Extract the juice (p. 510). Strain. Let stand in the refrigerator overnight. Carefully pour off the juice, discarding the dregs. Add ½ cup sugar for each quart of juice and boil 20 minutes.

Raspberry Juice. Crush raspberries and extract the juice (p. 510). Add sugar to taste and bring to the boiling point.

Rhubarb Juice. To extract the juice, see page 36.

Tomato Juice

Wash and drain firm, fresh ripe tomatoes. Cut out the stems, white cores and any soft spots. Cut small and simmer in small quantities until soft enough to put through a sieve or food mill.

Add 1 teaspoon salt for each quart of juice. Reheat at once just to the boiling point. Fill jars to within ¼ inch of the top. *Process pints or quarts 10 minutes in a boiling water bath canner.*

Vary by adding sugar and spices to taste.

Savory Tomato Juice

Delicious for tomato juice cocktail, tomato aspic or soup.

Cut in pieces into a saucepan
  ½ bushel tomatoes
  10 large carrots
  4 large green peppers
  4 large onions
  ½ pound green beans
  3 kohlrabies
  1 bunch celery
  1 bunch parsley
Cook until soft. Rub through a food mill or a colander. Season to taste with
  Salt, pepper and Worcestershire
Fill jars. *Process 5 minutes in a boiling water bath canner. Makes 12 quarts.*

Canning Vegetables

Processing in a pressure canner is the only method approved for canning vegetables. If you use a pressure saucepan, add 20 minutes to the recommended processing time, because a pressure saucepan cools quickly.

Select young tender vegetables of the same size and ripeness. Can as soon as possible after gathering, preferably within 2 hours.

Wash the vegetables thoroughly and prepare as directed below. Prepare only enough for one canner load at a time. Keep the rest in the refrigerator.

Cover with boiling water and boil 5 minutes. Drain and pack in hot jars. Add ½ teaspoon salt for each pint jar. Fill to within ½ inch of the top with boiling water.

Seal and process (p. 529).

Cool, label, and store in a cool, dry, dark place.

The most commonly canned vegetables are listed below. For canning other vegetables, see state or government bulletins or the booklets issued by the manufacturers of canning jars. Broccoli, Brussels sprouts, cabbage, cauliflower, kohlrabi, onions and turnips are apt to discolor when canned.

Asparagus (1½ pounds for a pint jar). Trim off the scales and tough ends. Leave whole or cut in 1-inch pieces. *Process pints 25 minutes, quarts 30.*

Beans, green or wax (¾ pound for a pint jar). Snip off the ends. Leave whole or cut in 1-inch pieces. *Process pints 20 minutes, quarts 25.*

Beans, lima (2 pounds in the shell for a pint jar). Can only young limas. Shell. *Process pints 40 minutes, quarts 50.*

Beets (1 to 1½ pounds for a pint jar). Cut off the tops, leaving 1-inch stems. Cook in boiling water 15 minutes. Dip in cold water and peel. Leave baby beets whole. Slice or dice larger beets. *Process pints 25 minutes, quarts 35.*

Corn (4 to 6 ears for a pint jar). Use only pint jars. Prepare only 2 or 3 dozen ears at a time and work quickly.

Husk, remove silk, and wash. For whole-kernel corn, cut off the kernels but do not scrape the cobs. For cream-style corn, use a corn scraper or cut off only the tips of the kernels and scrape the cob. Cover the soft pulp with boiling water (1 pint to 1 quart of corn) and bring to the boiling point. Pack whole-kernel corn to within 1 inch of the top and fill the jars with boiling water. Pack cream-style corn to within ½ inch of the top. Add ½ teaspoon salt to each jar. *Process whole-kernel corn 55 minutes, cream-style corn 85 minutes.*

Peas (2 pounds in the shell for a pint jar). Shell. Can in pints only. *Process 40 minutes.*

Garden Special

This is a tasty basis for vegetable soup, or to use in a stew or casserole with hamburg or chopped meat combined with cooked rice, spaghetti or potatoes, or as a sauce with fish. See also Jellied Garden Special (p. 283).

Put in a deep kettle
   6 sweet peppers, green or red, cut in
      pieces and seeded
   1 quart diced onions
   1 quart diced celery, coarse stalks and
      leaves included
   1 quart water or tomato juice
Cook 20 minutes. Add
   4 quarts ripe tomatoes, peeled and
      quartered
   3 tablespoons salt
   2 tablespoons sugar
   ½ teaspoon pepper
Bring to a boil and put into hot jars. *Process in boiling water 40 minutes for quarts, 30 minutes for pints. Makes 10 to 12 pints.*

Freezing

Freezing is simpler than canning and preserves color, texture and flavor more successfully. As a result, more and more families own freezers, and even kitchenette cooks are finding many ways to use refrigerator freezer compartments. Freezers save shopping time and money by making it possible to take advantage of special bargains and quantity buying. Another big attraction is that much of the cooking for holiday and company meals can be out of the way days or even weeks in advance.

General Directions

Speed is essential to success in freezing; freeze the food as soon as possible after preparation.

Foods keep best if they are frozen quickly at 0° or below and stored at 0° or below as well. Higher temperatures may cause undesirable changes in flavor, texture and color. The temperature in the freezer compartment of a refrigerator usually fluctuates, since the door is opened and closed frequently. For this reason a freezer compartment is principally useful for storing commercially frozen products and leftovers to be used within a short time.

If you use a community freezer locker, keep the food packed in ice until you take it to be frozen at the locker.

Bulletins from the United States Department of Agriculture as well as state publications and freezer booklets contain many useful suggestions about freezing and recommend local varieties of fruits and vegetables especially suited to freezing.

Follow the manufacturer's directions for your freezer.

If you are freezing a large quantity of food at one time, set the freezer at −10°, so that the temperature will not rise too much when all the food is added. Have all packages touch the freezer walls during freezing, but leave some space around the packages for circulation of air. Foods must freeze quickly, so do not overload the freezer.

Freezer Containers

Proper wrapping prolongs the storage life of hard-to-keep foods. Containers especially made for freezing are moistureproof and vaporproof. Select the size that will contain enough for only one meal for your family, so that you will not have leftovers. Frozen food is never so delicious when reheated and should never be refrozen. Glass jars designed especially for freezing are excellent, especially for cooked foods. Round jars or packages take up more room than square ones.

Allow for expansion of food during freezing. Leave at least ½ inch head space in packages (1 to 1½ inches in glass). Packages which are too full will bulge and may open at the seams.

Label and date each package and use those with the earliest dates first.

Freezing Fruit

Freeze only fully ripe, freshly picked fruits in perfect condition. Berries, peaches and cherries keep their natural goodness especially well. Allow 1½ to 1⅔ cups of prepared fruit for a 1-pint carton.

Prepare the syrup (p. 529) if the fruit requires it, and chill in the refrigerator. (The dry sugar method is particularly successful for soft juicy berries — see under individual fruits below.)

Prepare the fruit for freezing (below).

Pack in containers, using sizes according to your plan for using the fruit — as for sauce, pie filling, ice cream topping, or for making jam or jelly. Add sugar or syrup, if used. Pack fruits mixed with sugar or syrup in leakproof containers. Leave ¾ inch headway, but fill the space with crumpled cellophane or wax paper to keep the fruit covered with syrup so that it will not lose its attractive color.

To keep the fresh color of apricots, cherries, peaches and plums, add to each cup of syrup ¼ teaspoon ascorbic acid crystals dissolved in 2 teaspoons cold water.

Label, giving contents and date.

Freeze at 0° or below. Put the packages into the freezer as soon as they are filled.

Preparing Fruit

Wash quickly but thoroughly. Discard imperfect berries and cut blemishes from large fruit.

Apples, baked. Chill. Pack in containers, separating one from another with cellophane.

Apples for pie. Peel, core, and slice directly into cold water enough apples for 1 pie. Drain, steam 2 minutes, and pack immediately into a plastic bag. To pre-vent darkening, sprinkle with ascorbic acid crystals or sugar (½ cup for 1 pint). Put immediately into the freezer. Repeat until all are used.

Applesauce. Cook as usual (p. 347). Chill.

Apricots. Follow directions for peaches.

Blackberries, boysenberries, dewberries, loganberries. Freeze only fully ripe berries. Discard the stems. *For dessert,* pack in Heavy Syrup (p. 529). *For jam, pie or sauce,* mix 6 cups fruit with 1 cup sugar. Turn the berries over and over until most of the sugar dissolves. Or pack without sugar. *For fruit purée,* crush berries, mix with 1 cup sugar to 8 cups berries, and stir until the sugar dissolves.

Blueberries, elderberries, huckleberries. Discard the stems. *For dessert,* crush slightly, pack in Medium Syrup (p. 529). *For pie, sauce, jelly or jam,* freeze without sugar, or use 1 cup sugar to 6 cups fruit, stirring until the sugar is dissolved.

Cherries, sour. Stem and pit. *For dessert,* cover with Heavy Syrup (p. 529). *For pie and cooked desserts,* use 1 cup sugar to 1 quart cherries, stirring until the sugar is dissolved.

Cherries, sweet. Stem and pit, or leave whole. Work quickly so that the fruit will not darken. Cover with Heavy Syrup (p. 529) to which ascorbic acid crystals have been added (above). A mixture of sour and sweet cherries is delicious.

Cranberries. Stem. Freeze whole without sugar.

Currants. Stem. Freeze whole, without sugar, or use 1 cup sugar to 1 quart currants, stirring until most of the sugar dissolves.

Gooseberries. Snip off both ends. *For pie or preserves,* freeze without sugar. Or crush slightly and mix with 1 cup sugar to 1 quart berries.

Peaches. Select perfect tree-ripened peaches. Keep at room temperature 2 or 3 days after picking. Peel one peach at a time and halve, quarter or slice directly into cartons. Cover completely with Medium or Heavy Syrup (p. 529). Freeze immediately and store at 0° or below, never higher.

Pears. Pears do not freeze well.

Pineapples. Pare and cube. Pack without added sugar, or with 1 part sugar to 4 parts fruit, or cover with Heavy Syrup (p. 529).

Plums, prunes. Cut in half and remove pits. Cover with Heavy Syrup (p. 529), adding ascorbic acid (p. 534).

Raspberries. If dusty, wash quickly in ice water. Discard the stems. Cover with Medium or Heavy Syrup (p. 529). Or carefully mix 1 quart berries with ¾ cup sugar. They may also be picked from the bushes directly into the freezing cartons and frozen without sugar.

Rhubarb. Early spring rhubarb freezes best. Cut into 1-inch lengths and make into sauce. Or pack and cover with Medium or Heavy Syrup (p. 529). Or freeze without cooking or adding sugar.

Strawberries. Wash in ice water and remove caps. Cut in half or slice into containers and cover with cold Medium or Heavy Syrup (p. 529). Or mix berries with sugar (¾ cup to 1 quart berries). Stir to dissolve the sugar.

Fruit Juices

Frozen juices may be the basis for refreshing drinks, jellied salads or desserts, or may be made into jellies at any convenient time. Frozen fruit juices are especially delicious if you serve them while there are still a few ice crystals in them — thaw the sealed container in the refrigerator 6 hours or more. Mix juices well to blend evenly.

Prepare the juice, chill if necessary, and pour quickly into glass jars, leaving 1-inch head space. Seal and freeze.

Orange (Valencias are best), Lemon and Grapefruit Juice. Chill, squeeze by hand with a glass juicer and strain.

Other fruit juices and tomato juice. Extract as described on p. 510. Freeze without processing.

Vegetables

Vegetables are at their best when young and tender — tiny green beans, sweet juicy peas, baby carrots and beets. Vegetables which do not freeze well are those with high water content which are usually served raw, such as lettuce, cucumbers and fresh tomatoes.

The shorter the time from garden to freezer the better. If you cannot freeze vegetables immediately, keep them in the refrigerator until you are ready to prepare them.

Prepare for freezing according to the directions which follow.

Scald to retain fresh color and flavor, to save freezer space, and to reduce the number of bacteria. Scald only small amounts at a time, so that the water will return to the boiling point no more than 1 minute after the vegetable is put into the kettle. The length of time for scalding each vegetable is given below.

Have ready a large kettle of rapidly boiling water. Put the prepared vegetable in a basket or a piece of cheesecloth. Lower into the water, lift up and down so that the vegetable is heated evenly. Scald the required time (see below), counting the time as soon as the vegetable is put into the kettle.

Chill. Remove the scalded vegetable from the kettle and chill immediately under running cold water or in ice water. Drain.

Pack in freezer containers. Press down firmly to force out the air, which tends to dry out the vegetable. Leave a little head space but not too much — packages that are too full tend to bulge, but too much head space may cause the food to dry out. No exact rule can be given for all vegetables — one must learn by experience.

Label, stating the date and the method of preparation, or keep a freezer record giving details, so that you can make changes the next time if you like.

Freeze at 0° or below. Put each package into the freezer as soon as it is filled.

Preparing Vegetables

Wash thoroughly, removing every trace of garden grit or soil. Use a brush on solid vegetables, and wash spinach and other leafy or delicate vegetables in warm sudsy water, with all particles of soap or detergent completely dissolved. Rinse thoroughly in clear water. Cut off coarse stems and outer leaves.

Cut or sort the pieces so that they will be about the same size.

Asparagus. Do not freeze exceptionally thick or thin stalks. Discard tough ends. Remove scales. Cut stalks to fit the package or cut in 1-inch pieces. *Scald 4 minutes.*

Beans, green or wax. Sort, wash, and snip off the stem end. Cut into short lengths or lengthwise, French style. *Scald 2 minutes.*

Beans, lima and other shell beans. Shell and sort, removing those that are too old. *Scald 3 minutes.*

Beans, green soy. *Scald 4 minutes* in the pod. Cool, and remove the beans by squeezing the pods.

Beets. Freeze only young tender beets. *Scald baby beets 2½ minutes,* but cook beets more than 2 inches in diameter until tender. Chill, peel, leave whole (if tiny), slice or cube.

Broccoli. Wash carefully. Let stand ½ hour in salt water. Drain and cut off woody sections. Separate into uniform pieces for packaging. *Scald 3 minutes.*

Brussels sprouts. Let stand ½ hour in salt water. Drain. *Scald 4 minutes.*

Carrots. Scrape young carrots. Leave baby carrots whole. Cut larger ones in pieces. *Scald 3 minutes.*

Cauliflower. Divide into flowerets. *Scald white cauliflower 3 minutes in 1 gallon of boiling water with 2 teaspoons of powdered citric acid added to it. Scald purple cauliflower 3 minutes in plain water.*

Celery. Cut in 1-inch pieces. *Scald 4 minutes.*

Corn on the cob. Husk, wash, and sort in even sizes. *Scald small ears (1¼ inches in diameter) 6 minutes, medium ears 8, and large ears (over 2 inches at the large end) 10 minutes.* Chill, wrap in aluminum foil or put into plastic bags and freeze.

Corn, whole-kernel. *Scald the corn 4 minutes on the cob.* Chill. Cut the whole kernels from the cob, being careful not to include any of the cob.

Corn, cream-style. *Scald the corn 4 minutes on the cob.* Cut off the upper part of the kernels, scraping the cobs with the knife to remove the juice and heart of the kernel. Leave ½ inch head space in the containers.

Eggplant. Peel. Cut in ⅓-inch slices. *Scald 4 minutes in 1 gallon of boiling water to which 2 teaspoons of ascorbic acid have been added.*

Greens (beet and turnip tops, kale, mustard, spinach, Swiss chard). Wash leaves carefully to remove all grit. Discard injured leaves and tough stems. *Scald 2 minutes, using 3 gallons of boiling water for a small amount of vegetable.*

Kohlrabi. Cut off tops and roots. Wash, peel, and dice, or leave whole if small. *Scald 1 minute.*

Mushrooms. Trim and slice. Cook small amounts at a time in butter (about 5 minutes). Cool.

Okra. Leave whole. *Scald small and medium-size pods 3 minutes, large ones 4 to 5 minutes.* Package in amounts needed for soup or to serve as a vegetable.

Parsley. *Scald 15 seconds,* chill, and drain. Put into small envelopes, seal, and freeze. (To use, chop while still frozen.)

Parsnips. Trim, scrape, and slice. *Scald 3 minutes.*

Peas. Shell. *Scald 1 minute.*

Peppers. Cut in halves or slices. Pack in small amounts convenient to use. *Scald 2 minutes.*

Pimientos. Roast 4 minutes in a 400° oven. Rinse in cold water to remove the charred skins.

Potatoes, French-fried. Fry as usual (p. 266). Chill by setting in a pan over ice. To reheat for use, spread in a shallow pan in a 350° oven.

Potatoes, mashed. Raw potatoes soften when frozen, but mashed potatoes freeze well. Cool quickly by setting the cooking pan in ice. When reheating for use, add a topping of crumbs or grated cheese.

Potatoes, sweet. Cook until almost tender. Cool, peel, and cut in halves or slices, or mash. To prevent darkening, mix 2 tablespoons orange or lemon juice with each quart of mashed potatoes. Sliced or whole sweet potatoes may be covered with Heavy Syrup (p. 529).

Pumpkin. Cook until soft, mash, and cool.

Squash, summer, any variety (p. 256). Cut young tender squash in ½-inch slices. *Scald 3 minutes.*

Squash, winter. Cook until soft, mash, and cool. Pack.

Succotash. Prepare whole-kernel corn and lima beans separately. (*See scalding time for corn and beans above.*) Mix and pack.

Meat and Large Game

Young healthy animals furnish the best meat. Have the meat prepared at a frozen food locker plant for storing in a home freezer, or follow the directions in the bulletins issued by the United States Department of Agriculture or by state extension services.

Fat or salty meats do not keep their flavor as well as fresh lean meat. Use sausage and ground meat within 3 months, fresh pork 3 to 6, lamb and veal 6 to 9, and beef 6 to 12.

Age or ripen some meats to improve tenderness and flavor. Store the carcasses at 32° to 38° before cutting in pieces for freezing. This may be done at the freezer plant or in a cool, dark, airy place. Age lean young beef and game 5 days, heavy beef 5 to 10 days, mutton 2 to 3 days. Do not age lamb, veal or pork.

Cured and smoked meats may be stored in the freezer if there is no other convenient storage place. Hams keep in good condition longer in solid pieces than in slices.

Cut in sizes convenient for family meals. Bone to save space in the freezer. If any bones are left in the meat, be sure there are no rough edges which might punch holes in the wrapping. Trim off excess fat.

Package by wrapping snugly (to eliminate air pockets) in heavy aluminum foil or special freezer paper. If more than one piece is put in a package (steaks, chops or ground meat patties), put sheets of cellophane or freezer wrap between them. Seal completely with freezer tape. Stockinette outer covers are not essential for home freezers, where the packages are handled less than in freezer plants.

Label each package, giving contents and date.

Freeze immediately at 0° or below. Space the packages so that air will circulate around them until they are hard-frozen.

Thaw or not before cooking, as convenient. Large cuts of solidly frozen meats cook less evenly than thawed meats, unless they are cooked very slowly. Leave meats in the freezer wrapping while thawing to avoid drying. Thaw in the refrigerator or at room temperature. Thaw sliced meat such as chops and steaks at room temperature for 30 minutes.

Poultry and Game Birds

Freeze the various sizes of chicken and turkey at the time of year when they are most plentiful and therefore at the lowest price (spring for broilers, summer for fryers, fall for larger birds).

Have the birds prepared for freezing at a freezer plant, or follow the directions for slaughtering, cleaning and dressing in the bulletins issued by the United States Department of Agriculture or by the state extension services.

Prepare the birds according to the way you plan to cook them. Cut-up chickens take less freezer space than whole birds. (If the bird is to be roasted whole, remove most of the body fat, wrap the giblets and neck in freezer paper, and place the package inside the bird.)

Do not stuff birds. Split broilers and pack with two pieces of freezer paper between the halves. Chill at least 12 hours before freezing.

Package, freeze, and store like meat (p. 537).

Thaw slowly to keep the flesh moist. Defrost in the refrigerator overnight or at room temperature (2½ hours for broilers and other small birds, 5½ hours for roasters, 8 hours for a 10-pound turkey). To shorten the time, place on the kitchen table in front of an electric fan.

Fish

Fish should be frozen the day it is caught. For complete information, follow the directions in United States Government bulletins.

Prepare fish as if to cook immediately. Cut large fish in fillets or steaks.

Pack fatty fish (bonito, butterfish, herring, mackerel, salmon, shad, tuna and whitefish) immediately and freeze. Put all other fish in salt water (1 cup salt to 1 gallon of water) and let it stand 30 seconds. Drain and wrap in freezer paper.

Use within 3 months for best flavor and texture.

Thaw before cooking only enough to separate the pieces (about 45 minutes at room temperature or 3 to 4 hours in the refrigerator).

Shellfish

To prepare, wash shucked oysters or clams in salt water (1½ tablespoons to 1 quart) and drain. Pick over cooked shrimp, lobster meat or crab meat, removing bits of shell.

Pack in freezer cartons.

Thaw slowly, for the best flavor (6 hours in the refrigerator or 2 hours at room temperature).

Use cooked shellfish within a month — it toughens if stored too long.

Dairy Products

Butter or margarine. Wrap in freezer paper or leave in store wrapper. Unsalted butter keeps longer than salted butter. Thaw in the refrigerator.

Cheese. Freeze in small packages, as cheese that has been frozen dries out rapidly after thawing.

Heavy cream. Freeze whipped or not.

Eggs

Freeze only perfect fresh eggs. Do not freeze cracked eggs. Break the eggs and mix lightly with a fork or pack the whites and yolks separately. Put the amount in each carton which will be needed at one time. Yolks packed alone will coagulate unless mixed with salt (for 6 yolks 1 teaspoon) or sugar, honey or corn syrup (for 6 yolks 2 tablespoons). Whites need nothing added and are as satisfactory for making angel cakes as fresh whites.

Bread, Cake, Cookies and Pastry

Save fuel and time by baking more than enough for one meal and freezing the rest. Baked foods retain their full flavor, color and oven freshness for 4 to 12 months. Fruit cake, mince pies and fruit cookies will keep even longer.

Unbaked doughs and batters lose some of their leavening power after a few weeks. For best results use within 1 month. Cooky and pie doughs keep several months.

Freeze packaged baked goods in their sealed wrappers if you plan to use them within a week. If they are to be kept longer, wrap them again in moisture-proof and vaporproof paper.

Toast sliced frozen bread without thawing. Leave other foods at room temperature for a short time before using.

Bread and rolls made with yeast are more successful if they are baked and cooled before freezing. Baked bread thaws very quickly because it contains very little moisture. Without unwrapping, heat frozen baked rolls in a 400° oven 5 or 10 minutes. Reheating freshens rolls. See also Twice-Baked Rolls (p. 330).

Quick breads which are usually served cold, such as Date and Nut Bread, Honey Bread and Cranberry Bread. Let stand an hour or more at room temperature before serving. Heat gingerbread or cottage pudding if you are serving it with a sauce.

Waffles. Heat frozen waffles in an electric toaster.

Doughnuts. Reheat at 400° just long enough to thaw without drying.

Cakes. Freeze angel, sponge and fruit cakes after baking. Freeze butter cakes either baked or as batter. Cake batter made with egg yolks does not freeze successfully. Bake a cake for freezing in a pan with the bottom lined with greased wax paper or in a foil pan which can be wrapped and stored. Cool the cake thoroughly. Wrap in cellophane, seal, and freeze at 0° or below. When the cake is frozen hard, put it in a box so that it will not be crushed. To freeze cake batter, spoon it into cartons or paper cups and freeze at 0° or below. Thaw before baking until the batter is just soft enough to put into pans. If the batter is thawed too long, the cake will be heavy.

Cookies. Freeze any stiff cooky dough in a roll or shaped into cookies. Defrost a roll only enough to slice into cookies. Bake shaped cookies without defrosting. Bake delicate cookies before freezing and package carefully in a box so that they will not crush.

Cream puffs. Prepare the batter, cool and put in a freezer bag. When ready to use, heat the batter until it is just tepid. Make small puffs for hors d'oeuvres or profiteroles (p. 428).

Fruit pies and mince pies freeze very well. Line aluminum foil freezer pans with pastry, put in the filling, and put on the top crust. Do not cut vents in the top crust. Freeze at 0°. Bake without thawing at 425° until the crust is golden-brown (about 1 hour). Cut the vents in the top crust after the pie has been in the oven about 5 minutes. Deep-dish pies are very successful made with only a top crust.

Pie crust. Roll out in pie-size rounds or in smaller rounds for tarts. Stack with sheets of cellophane between the rounds and pack in boxes. Freeze.

Ice Cream and Sherbet

Freeze only smooth velvety ice cream made in a crank freezer. French-type ice creams (p. 485) freeze well. Pack in freezer cartons and cover snugly with a piece of cellophane cut to fit to help prevent crystals. Close the carton.

Fruit sherbets made with gelatine (p. 488) keep well in a freezer. Commercial ice creams do not keep well more than 2 or 3 weeks in a home freezer.

Sandwiches

Spread both slices of bread with softened (not melted) butter. Fill and freeze. Use fillings made of meat, cheese or fish. Mix peanut butter with just enough jelly, applesauce or honey to spread well. Do not use fillings which contain raw vegetables or any material which would soak into the bread.

For lunchboxes and picnics. Frozen sandwiches thaw completely in about 4 hours and taste fresher (even though made days or weeks before) than sandwiches made the same day which have not been refrigerated. Freeze lunchbox sandwiches individually.

For parties. Wrap rolled, ribbon or checkerboard sandwiches firmly in freezer paper and seal. Arrange canapés and open-faced sandwiches on a tray, cooky sheet or cellophane-covered cardboard. Do not garnish. Wrap in cellophane and heat-seal.

To thaw, remove thin canapés from the freezer 20 minutes before serving time. Thicker sandwiches or ones with shrimp topping will take longer. Thaw rolled, ribbon or checkerboard sandwiches and slice. Garnish the canapés or sandwiches as you like.

Prepared Foods

Many cooked or ready-to-serve foods freeze successfully and are a great convenience in preparing emergency meals. Keep two or three complete meals in your freezer ready for unexpected guests or quick meals. Enjoy the extra carefree hours with your family or guests by preparing and freezing the dinner well in advance.

Freezing cooked foods is not always time-saving. Some foods take less time — and less heat — to prepare fresh than frozen. Best for freezing are seasonal foods, dishes that can be prepared in quantity almost as quickly as in small amounts, and foods that need only slight thawing. Cooked eggs do not freeze well — the whites toughen.

Casserole dishes and stews freeze best if they are made with enough sauce so that the meat balls or pieces of meat, fish or fowl are completely covered during freezing. For a fresh casserole topping when reheating, cover with buttered crumbs (p. 7) or grated cheese and set in a 400° oven to thaw and heat. Do not overcook casseroles when preparing them for freezing.

Cocktail tidbits. Freeze small cheese pastries, cooked shrimp, cocktail sausages or other small hors d'oeuvres. Pack cocktail spreads in small cartons.

Chicken and meat pies. Make individual deep-dish pies with pastry tops. Heat in a 450° oven without thawing.

Desserts. Freeze ice creams, sherbets, cakes, cookies, gingerbread and pies following directions on pp. 539–540. Freeze cut-up fruit for fruit cup (not fresh apples, grapes or nut meats) and serve while still partly frozen. Freeze individual or large puddings and reheat, frozen or thawed, in a steamer or in a pan of hot water in a 400° oven.

Roasts do not freeze as well cooked as raw. The outer slices may have a stale flavor. Roast chickens and turkeys take almost as long to thaw and heat as to roast fresh. Leftover roast meats may be frozen to use cold.

Salads. Do not freeze raw vegetables or salad greens. Aspics and other molded salads freeze especially well. Add the dressing at serving time. Freeze cooked meat and poultry ready to make into salad. Mixed fruit salad is successful, but do not include in the combination fresh apples or grapes or nut meats. Sprinkle fruit with lemon juice to help keep its bright color. Do not thaw salads completely before you serve them.

Sauces. Freeze barbecue and spaghetti sauces in cartons.

Soups. Soups which require long cooking can be made in quantity and frozen for later use. Sieve cooked vegetables to use as the basis for cream soups. To drive out the air, which destroys some food values, pack firmly in cartons. Thaw in a double boiler without stirring before you add the liquid.

Other foods which freeze well are, for example, baked beans, hash, Swiss steak, pot roast, beef bourguignonne, lobster Newburg, veal birds, chicken fricassee, stuffed peppers, meat loaf, scrapple and puréed baby foods.

Leftovers. Chill quickly to prevent spoiling. Remove the bones from leftover meats. Leave in as large pieces as possible. Pack compactly. Reheat leftover gravy, chill, and pack.

Table of Calories

The number of calories given is approximate. For more detailed information consult government bulletins.

Beverages

Coffee, tea, any amount	0
Cocoa made with milk, 1 cup	200
Cider, 1 cup	125
Ginger ale, lemonade, 1 cup	100
Grape juice, 1 cup	170
Tomato juice, 1 cup	50
Beer, 12 ounces	170

Breads and Cereals

Bread, whole-wheat or enriched, 1 slice	65
Muffin; sweet roll	100 to 165
Pancake (4-inch)	60
Waffle	215
Dry cereal, 1 cup	120 to 140
Rice, cooked, ½ cup	50
Wheat germ, 1 tablespoon	15
Oatmeal, cooked, ½ cup	75
Crackers, 2	15
Macaroni, cooked, 1 cup	200

Dairy Foods

Milk, whole, 1 cup	165
Skimmed, buttermilk, 1 cup	85
Dry skimmed, 1 tablespoon	30
Evaporated, unsweetened, 1 tablespoon	25
Condensed, sweetened, 1 tablespoon	75
Cream, light, 1 tablespoon	30
heavy, 1 tablespoon	50
Yogurt, 1 tablespoon	50
Cheese, cottage, 1 cup	170
Cheese, other, 1 ounce	100 to 200

Meats, Poultry, Fish and Eggs

Beef, lamb, veal, lean to medium fat, no bones, cooked, 3 ounces	250
Pork, no bones, cooked, 3 ounces	300
Bacon, 1 slice	50
Frankfurter	125
Meat stew with vegetables, 1 cup	200
Poultry, no bones, cooked, 3 ounces	150
Creamed chicken, ½ cup	200
Fish, lean, cooked, 3 ounces	100
fat, cooked, 3 ounces	175
Shellfish, cooked, shelled, 4 ounces	100
Egg	75

Soups

Consommé, 1 cup	10
Cream soup, 1 cup	200

Salad Dressings, Gravies and Sauces

(1 tablespoon of each)

French dressing	100
Mayonnaise	100
Thin gravy	15
Thickened gravy	25
Cream sauce	25
Cheese sauce	35
Catsup; tomato sauce	25
Hollandaise	90
Butterscotch sauce	100
Chocolate sauce	45
Hard sauce	50

Vegetables

Beans and peas, dried, cooked, ½ cup	150
Celery, ½ cup diced	10
Corn, 1 ear (½ cup)	80
Lettuce, 2 large leaves	5
Lima beans, fresh, cooked, ½ cup	90
Mushrooms, cooked, ½ cup	15
Peas, fresh, ½ cup	50
Pepper, green	15

Potato, sweet, medium size — 165
Potato, white, medium size — 110
Radish — 1
Others, cooked, ½ cup — 30 to 50

Fruits

*(Canned fruits in syrup —
double the calorie count.)*

Apple — 60
Apricots, 3 — 50
Avocado, ¼ — 140
Banana — 90
Berries (except strawberries), 1 cup — 80
Cherries, pitted, 1 cup — 65
Dates, pitted, ½ cup — 250
Fig, dried — 50
Grapefruit, ½ — 75
Orange — 70
Orange juice (½ cup) — 60
Peach — 50
Pear — 100
Pineapple, diced, 1 cup — 75
  canned, with juice, 2 slices — 100
Prunes, unsweetened, 4 — 75
Raisins, dry, 1 tablespoon — 25
Strawberries, 1 cup — 50
Tomato, medium size (½ cup) — 20

Desserts

Cake, angel, 2-inch wedge — 110
  Cupcake, iced, 1 — 160
  Fruit cake, 1 ounce — 105
  Plain cake, 3 by 2½ inches — 180
  Pound cake, 1 ounce — 130
  Sponge cake, 2-inch wedge — 120

Gingerbread, 2-inch cube — 180
Cooky, plain (3-inch) — 110
Doughnut — 135
Custard, ½ cup — 150
Gelatine dessert (plain), ½ cup — 75
Ice cream, ½ cup — 150
Sherbet, ½ cup — 120
Pie, 4-inch wedge of 9-inch pie,
  2-crust — 325
  1 crust — 270

Nuts

Brazil nut — 50
Filberts (hazelnuts), hickory nuts,
  shelled, ¼ cup — 250
Peanuts, almonds, shelled, ¼ cup — 200
Pecans, walnuts, shelled, ¼ cup — 160

Candies

Caramel — 100
Chocolate cream — 40
Fudge, plain, 1-inch cube — 100
Marshmallow (large) — 25
Nut brittle, 3-inch square — 130

Miscellaneous

Brewer's yeast, 1 tablespoon — 20
Butter; margarine, 1 tablespoon — 100
Cooking fats and salad oils,
  1 tablespoon — 115
Chocolate, unsweetened, 1 ounce — 140
Olive — 7
Peanut butter, 1 tablespoon — 90
Sugar, syrups, jam, 1 tablespoon — 90

Index

A

Weights and Measures

In adapting a foreign recipe it may be necessary to experiment a little, since the ingredients may be slightly different from American ones.

A few grains, pinch, dash, etc. (dry) = less than 1/8 teaspoon
A dash (liquid) = a few drops
3 teaspoons = 1 tablespoon
4 tablespoons = 1/4 cup
2 cups = 1 pint
2 pints = 1 quart
4 quarts (liquid) = 1 gallon
8 quarts (dry) = 1 peck
4 pecks (dry) = 1 bushel
1 ounce = 28 grams (about)
1 pound = 454 grams (about)
1 kilogram = $2\frac{1}{10}$ pounds (about)
1 liter = 1 quart (about)
1 jigger = 1½ fluid ounces (3 tablespoons)
1 large jigger = 2 fluid ounces (1/4 cup)

Temperature Definitions

180° ~ Simmering point of water
212° ~ Boiling point of water
234°-240° ~ Soft ball stage for syrups
255° ~ Hard crack stage for syrups
320° ~ Caramel stage for syrups
220° ~ Jellying point for jams
and jellies

At altitudes above 3000 feet, lower air pressure causes differences in the boiling point of water and syrups. Consult government bulletins for details.

Oven Heats

250°, ~ Very slow
300° ~ Slow
325° ~ Moderately slow
350° ~ Moderate
375° ~ Moderately hot
400° ~ Hot
450°-500° ~ Very hot

Occasionally have your oven regulator tested for accuracy.